RACE IN AN ERA OF CHANGE

RACE IN AN ERA OF CHANGE

A READER

Heather Dalmage

PROFESSOR OF SOCIOLOGY AT
ROOSEVELT UNIVERSITY

Barbara Katz Rothman

PROFESSOR OF SOCIOLOGY AND
ANTHROPOLOGY AT BARUCH
COLLEGE, CUNY

NEW YORK   OXFORD

OXFORD UNIVERSITY PRESS

2011

Oxford University Press, Inc., publishes works that further Oxford University's
objective of excellence in research, scholarship, and education.

Oxford   New York
Auckland   Cape Town   Dar es Salaam   Hong Kong   Karachi
Kuala Lumpur   Madrid   Melbourne   Mexico City   Nairobi
New Delhi   Shanghai   Taipei   Toronto

With offices in
Argentina   Austria   Brazil   Chile   Czech Republic   France   Greece
Guatemala   Hungary   Italy   Japan   Poland   Portugal   Singapore
South Korea   Switzerland   Thailand   Turkey   Ukraine   Vietnam

Copyright © 2011 by Oxford University Press, Inc.

Published by Oxford University Press, Inc.
198 Madison Avenue, New York, New York 10016
http://www.oup.com

Oxford is a registered trademark of Oxford University Press.

Library of Congress Cataloging-in-Publication Data

Race in an era of change : a reader / edited by Heather Dalmage, Barbara Katz Rothman. — 1st ed.
      p. cm.
   Includes bibliographical references.
   ISBN: 978-0-19-975210-2 (acid-free paper)
   1. United States—Race relations.   2. United States—Ethnic relations.   3. Ethnicity—United States.
4. Racism—United States.   5. Social change—United States.   6. United States—Social conditions—1945-
I. Dalmage, Heather M., 1965-   II. Rothman, Barbara Katz.
   E184.A1R295 2011
   305.800973—dc22   2010026796

Printing number: 9 8 7 6 5 4 3 2 1

Printed in the United States of America
on acid-free paper.

CONTENTS

v

PART IV **RACIALIZED AND RACIALIZING INSTITUTIONS**

Economy and Work

Housing and Environment

Education

Policing and Prison

A PREFACE FOR THE INSTRUCTOR

We have tried to make this reader user-friendly for you as well as your students. We know from our own teaching experience that local needs and interests vary, and this may be particularly so in the subject area of race. The chapters are placed in an order that we find works with our students.

We begin with a first part that defines the guiding theme of the book, "racial formations," and then in Part II look at the ways that people do "racial thinking." We conclude Part II with an article on Whiteness, a concept that students may find the most foreign and challenging; for that reason, we have included a brief introduction to the concept.

The idea of "assigned and claimed" racial identities, the subject of Part III, may also be challenging, and there, we offer a special introduction to the section. Part IV, which contains the bulk of the readings, is organized by social institution, and Part V concludes the book by looking beyond American shores and borders.

That is how we like to teach this course, but you may well have other ways that work for you. For that reason, we have largely avoided introductions to "Parts" (with the two exceptions noted above), and instead, we introduce each article separately. This should make it easier to use these articles in whatever way works best in your classroom. For example, you might want to pull out all of the articles that focus on one racial identity, such as Native American issues, and assign them together. Or you might want to start with some topic that is currently in the news in your own locality, such as a housing crisis, a health care issue, or a recent environmental event, and move forward through the course from there.

Our introductions to the articles place them briefly in context, and they conclude with questions. These questions are designed to get the student focused as they begin reading. You may also want to use these questions to start classroom discussion.

At the end of each article, we offer a different kind of question, one designed to get students thinking about their personal experiences and to exercise their sociological imaginations as they reflect on race. We have found it productive to ask students to pick a few of these questions (just how many is something only you can decide) and then write about them. Some faculty ask students to share this kind of writing on classroom websites; some prefer to keep it more private: this, too, is your decision.

ACKNOWLEDGMENTS

My colleague, friend, and mentor: Barbara Katz Rothman. Big love.

At Roosevelt University, thanks to my students: Nancy Michaels and Bill Byrnes. I am also thankful for the unending support I receive from Chuck Middleton, Lynn Weiner, and Mike Maly, and to all my students in the various Race courses I've taught over the years.

—*Heather Dalmage*

My colleague, friend, and mentor too, Heather Dalmage. Big love.

—*Barbara Katz Rothman*

We would also like to thank for their time and insight those who reviewed the book in its earliest stages, including Joyce M. Bell, University of Georgia; Maria Chavez, Western Washington University; Thomas D. Hall, DePauw University; and Jennifer Lerner, Northern Virginia Community College.

RACE IN AN ERA OF CHANGE

RACIAL FORMATION THEORY

1.
FROM RACIAL FORMATION IN THE UNITED STATES

MICHAEL OMI AND HOWARD WINANT

Michael Omi and Howard Winant substantially changed the way that American Sociologists think about race by introducing the concept of "racial formation," which they define as "the socio-historical process by which racial categories are created, inhabited, transformed and destroyed." Racial formation depends on competing *racial projects*. These racial projects are both ideological framings, or explanations for why society is racially structured in particular ways, and efforts to reorganize and redistribute resources along racial lines. Racial projects are the link between our cultural images of race and our social structures.

Omi and Winant speak of several competing racial projects, each vying for dominance—the racial project that is believed by the most people with the most power will determine the way race is structured. In America, the dominant project for the last several decades has been the Neoconservative racial project, which claims to be color-blind but uses racially coded words. The Far Right racial project makes claims to white supremacy and the need to protect white privilege. The Far Left racial project claims that the government needs to intervene to ensure the protection of "group-based rights." The number of projects is, of course, unending.

The dominance in contemporary America of the Neoconservative racial project explains so many things that are happening in America today: color-blind racial agendas, the focus on individual choice rather than group rights, even the "tokenism" of far-right individuals of color in high-status positions. As you read this article, think about what other racial projects would look like in contemporary American society.

WHAT IS RACE?

There is a continuous temptation to think of race as an *essence*, as something fixed, concrete, and objective. And there is also an opposite temptation: to imagine race as a mere *illusion*, a purely ideological construct which some ideal non-racist social order would eliminate. It is necessary to challenge both these positions, to disrupt and reframe the rigid and bipolar manner in which they are posed and debated, and to transcend the presumably irreconcilable relationship between them.

The effort must be made to understand race as an unstable and "decentered" complex of social

meanings constantly being transformed by political struggle. With this in mind, let us propose a definition: *race is a concept which signifies and symbolizes social conflicts and interests by referring to different types of human bodies.* Although the concept of race invokes biologically based human characteristics (so-called "phenotypes"), selection of these particular human features for purposes of racial signification is always and necessarily a social and historical process. In contrast to the other major distinction of this type, that of gender, there is no biological basis for distinguishing among human groups along the lines of race.[1] Indeed, the categories employed to

Excerpted from Michael Omi and Howard Winant, *Racial Formation in the United States*: From the 1960s to the 1990s, 2nd ed. New York: Routledge, 1994.

differentiate among human groups along racial lines reveal themselves, upon serious examination, to be at best imprecise, and at worst completely arbitrary.

If the concept of race is so nebulous, can we not dispense with it? Can we not "do without" race, at least in the "enlightened" present? This question has been posed often, and with greater frequency in recent years.[2] An affirmative answer would of course present obvious practical difficulties: it is rather difficult to jettison widely held beliefs, beliefs which moreover are central to everyone's identity and understanding of the social world. So the attempt to banish the concept as an archaism is at best counterintuitive. But a deeper difficulty, we believe, is inherent in the very formulation of this schema, in its way of posing race as a *problem*, a misconception left over from the past, and suitable now only for the dustbin of history.

A more effective starting point is the recognition that despite its uncertainties and contradictions, the concept of race continues to play a fundamental role in structuring and representing the social world. The task for theory is to explain this situation. It is to avoid both the utopian framework which sees race as an illusion we can somehow "get beyond," and also the essentialist formulation which sees race as something objective and fixed, a biological datum.[3] Thus we should think of race as an element of social structure rather than as an irregularity within it; we should see race as a dimension of human representation rather than an illusion. These perspectives inform the theoretical approach we call racial formation.

RACIAL FORMATION

We define *racial formation* as the sociohistorical process by which racial categories are created, inhabited, transformed, and destroyed. Our attempt to elaborate a theory of racial formation will proceed in two steps. First, we argue that racial formation is a process of historically situated *projects* in which human bodies and social structures are represented and organized. Next we link racial formation to the evolution of hegemony, the way in which society is

organized and ruled. Such an approach, we believe, can facilitate understanding of a whole range of contemporary controversies and dilemmas involving race, including the nature of racism, the relationship of race to other forms of differences, inequalities, and oppression such as sexism and nationalism, and the dilemmas of racial identity today.

From a racial formation perspective, race is a matter of both social structure and cultural representation. Too often, the attempt is made to understand race simply or primarily in terms of only one of these two analytical dimensions.[4] For example, efforts to explain racial inequality as a purely social structural phenomenon are unable to account for the origins, patterning, and transformation of racial difference.

Conversely, many examinations of racial differences—understood as a matter of cultural attributes *à la* ethnicity theory, or as a society-wide signification system, *à la* some poststructuralist accounts—cannot comprehend such structural phenomena as racial stratification in the labor market or patterns of residential segregation.

An alternative approach is to think of racial formation processes as occurring through a linkage between structure and representation. Racial *projects* do the ideological "work" of making these links *A racial project is simultaneously an interpretation, representation, or explanation of racial dynamics, and an effort to reorganize and redistribute resources along particular racial lines.* Racial projects connect what race *means* in a particular discursive practice and the ways in which both social structures and everyday experiences are racially *organized*, based upon that meaning. Let us consider this proposition, first in terms of large-scale or macro-level social processes, and then in terms of other dimensions of the racial formation process.

RACIAL FORMATION AS A MACRO-LEVEL SOCIAL PROCESS

To interpret the meaning of race is to frame it social structurally. Consider for example, this statement by Charles Murray on welfare reform:

My proposal for dealing with the racial issue in social welfare is to repeal every bit of legislation and reverse every court decision that in any way requires, recommends, or awards differential treatment according to race, and thereby put us back onto the track that we left in 1965. We may argue about the appropriate limits of government intervention in trying to enforce the ideal, but at least it should be possible to identify the ideal: Race is not a morally admissible reason for treating one person differently from another. Period.[5]

Here there is a partial but significant analysis of the meaning of race: it is not a morally valid basis upon which to treat people "differently from one another." We may notice someone's race, but we cannot act upon that awareness. We must act in a "color-blind" fashion. This analysis of the meaning of race is immediately linked to a specific conception of the role of race in the social structure: it can play no part in government action, save in "the enforcement of the ideal." No state policy can legitimately require, recommend, or award different status according to race. This example can be classified as a particular type of racial project in the present-day U.S.—a "neoconservative" one.

Conversely, *to recognize the racial dimension in social structure is to interpret the meaning of race.* Consider the following statement by the late Supreme Court Justice Thurgood Marshall on minority "set-aside" programs:

> A profound difference separates governmental actions that themselves ate racist, and governmental actions that seek to remedy the effects of prior racism or to prevent neutral government activity from perpetuating the effects of such racism.[6]

Here the focus is on the racial dimensions of *social structure*—in this case of state activity and policy. The argument is that state actions in the past and present have treated people in very different ways according to their race, and thus the government cannot retreat from its policy responsibilities in this area. It cannot suddenly declare itself "color-blind" with out in fact perpetuating the same type of differential, racist treatment.[7] Thus, race continues to signify difference and structure inequality. Here, racialized social structure is immediately linked to an interpretation of the meaning of race. This example too can be classified as a particular type of racial project in the present-day U.S.—a "liberal" one.

To be sure, such political labels as "neoconservative" or "liberal" cannot fully capture the complexity of racial projects, for these are always multiply determined, politically contested, and deeply shaped by their historical context. Thus, encapsulated within the neoconservative example cited here are certain egalitarian commitments which derive from a previous historical context in which they played a very different role, and which are rearticulated in neoconservative racial discourse precisely to oppose a more open-ended, more capacious conception of the meaning of equality. Similarly, in the liberal example, Justice Marshall recognizes that the contemporary state, which was formerly the architect of segregation and the chief enforcer of racial difference, has a tendency to reproduce those patterns of inequality in a new guise. Thus he admonishes it (in dissent, significantly) to fulfill its responsibilities to uphold a robust conception of equality. These particular instances, then, demonstrate how racial projects are always concretely framed, and thus are always contested and unstable. The social structures they uphold or attack, and the representations of race they articulate, are never invented out of the air, but exist in a definite historical context, having descended from previous conflicts. This contestation appears to be permanent in respect to race.

These two examples of contemporary racial projects are drawn from mainstream political debate; they may be characterized as center-right and center-left expressions of contemporary racial politics.[8] We can, however, expand the discussion of racial formation processes far beyond these familiar examples. In fact, we can identify racial projects in at least three other analytical dimensions: first the political spectrum can be broadened to, include radical projects, on both the left and right, as well as along other political axes. Second, analysis of racial projects can take place not only at the macro-level of racial policy-making, state activity, and collective action, but also at the micro-level of everyday experience. Third, the concept of racial projects can be applied across historical time, to identify racial formation dynamics in the past. We shall now offer examples of each of these types of racial projects.

THE POLITICAL SPECTRUM OF RACIAL FORMATION

We have encountered examples of a neoconservative racial project, in which the significance of race is denied, leading to a "color-blind" racial politics and "hands off" policy orientation; and of a "liberal" racial project, in which the significance of race is affirmed, leading to an egalitarian and "activist" state policy. But these by no means exhaust the political possibilities. Other racial projects can be readily identified on the contemporary U.S. scene. For example, "far right" projects, which uphold biologistic and racist views of difference, explicitly argue for white supremacist policies. "New right" projects overtly claim to hold "color-blind" views, but covertly manipulate racial fears in order to achieve political gains.[9] On the left, "radical democratic" projects invoke notions of racial "difference" in combination with egalitarian politics and policy.

Further variations can also be noted. For example, "nationalist" projects, both conservative and radical, stress the incompatibility of racially defined group identity with the legacy of white supremacy, and therefore advocate a social structural solution of separation, either complete or partial.[10] As we saw in Chapter 3, nationalist currents represent a profound legacy of the centuries of racial absolutism that initially defined the meaning of race in the U.S. Nationalist concerns continue to influence racial debate in the form of Afrocentrism and other expressions of identity politics.

Taking the range of politically organized racial projects as a whole, we can "map" the current pattern of racial formation at the level of the public sphere, the "macro-level" in which public debate and mobilization takes place.[11] But important as this is, the terrain on which racial formation occurs is broader yet.

RACIAL FORMATION AS EVERYDAY EXPERIENCE

At the micro-social level, racial projects also link signification and structure, not so much as efforts to shape policy or define large-scale meaning, but as the applications of "common sense". To see racial projects operating at the level of everyday life, we have only to examine the many ways in which, often unconsciously, we "notice" race.

One of the first things we notice about people when we meet them (along with their sex) is their race. We utilize race to provide clues about *who* a person is. This fact is made painfully obvious when we encounter someone whom we cannot conveniently racially categorize—someone who is, for example, racially "mixed" or of an ethnic/racial group we are not familiar with. Such an encounter becomes a source of discomfort and momentarily a crisis of racial meaning.

Our ability to interpret racial meanings depends on preconceived notions of a racialized social structure. Comments such as, "Funny, you don't look black," betray an underlying image of what black should be. We expect people to act out their apparent racial identities; indeed we become disoriented when they do not. The black banker harassed by police while walking in casual clothes through his own well-off neighborhood, the Latino or white kid rapping in perfect Afro patois, the unending *faux pas* committed by whites who assume that the non-whites they encounter are servants or tradespeople, the belief that non-white colleagues are less qualified persons hired to fulfill affirmative action guidelines, indeed the whole gamut of racial stereotypes—that "white men can't jump," that

Asians can't dance, etc., etc.—all testify to the way a racialized social structure shapes racial experience and conditions meaning. Analysis of such stereotypes reveals the always present, already active link between our view of the social structure—its demography, its laws, its customs, its threats—and our conception of what race means.

Conversely, our ongoing interpretation of our experience in racial terms shapes our relations to the institutions and organizations through which we are imbedded in social structure. Thus we expect differences in skin color, or other racially coded characteristics, to explain social differences. Temperament, sexuality, intelligence, athletic ability, aesthetic preferences, and so on are presumed to be fixed and discernible from the palpable mark of race. Such diverse questions as our confidence and trust in others (for example, clerks or salespeople, media figures, neighbors), our sexual preferences and romantic images, our tastes in music, films, dance, or sports, and our very ways of talking, walking, eating, and dreaming become racially coded simply because we live in a society where racial awareness is so pervasive. Thus in ways too comprehensive even to monitor consciously, and despite periodic calls—neoconservative and otherwise—for us to ignore race and adopt "color-blind" racial attitudes, skin color "differences" continue to rationalize distinct treatment of racially identified individuals and groups.

To summarize the argument so far: the theory of racial formation suggests that society is suffused with racial projects, large and small, to which all are subjected. This racial "subjection", is quintessentially ideological. Everybody learns some combination, some version, of the rules of racial classification, and of her own racial identity, often without obvious teaching or conscious inculcation. Thus are we inserted in a comprehensively racialized social structure. Race becomes "common sense"—a way of comprehending, explaining, and acting in the world. A vast web of racial projects mediates between the discursive or representational means in which race is identified and signified on the one hand, and the institutional and organizational forms in which it is routinized and standardized on the other. These projects are the heart of the racial formation process.

Under such circumstances, it is not possible to represent race discursively without simultaneously locating it, explicitly or implicitly, in a social structural (and historical) context. Nor is it possible to organize, maintain, or transform social structures without simultaneously engaging, once more either explicitly or implicitly, in racial signification. Racial formation, therefore, is a kind of synthesis, an outcome, of the interaction of racial projects on a society-wide level. These projects are, of course, vastly different in scope and effect. They include large-scale public action, state activities, and interpretations of racial conditions in artistic, journalistic, or academic fora,[12] as well as the seemingly infinite number of racial judgements and practices we carry out at the level of individual experience.

FROM SCIENCE TO POLITICS

It has taken scholars more than a century to reject biologistic notions of race in favor of an approach which regards race as a *social* concept. This trend has been slow and uneven, and even today remains somewhat embattled, but its overall direction seems clear. At the turn of the century Max Weber discounted biological explanations for racial conflict and instead highlighted the social and political factors which engendered such conflict.[13] W. E. B. Du Bois argued for a sociopolitical definition of race by identifying "the color line" as "the problem of the 20th century."[14] Pioneering cultural anthropologist Franz Boas rejected attempts to link racial identifications and cultural traits, labelling as pseudoscientific any assumption of a continuum of "higher" and "lower" cultural groups.[15] Other early exponents of social, as opposed to biological, views of race included Robert E. Park, founder of the "Chicago school" of sociology, and Alain Leroy Locke, philosopher and theorist of the Harlem Renaissance.[16]

Perhaps more important than these and subsequent intellectual efforts, however, were the political struggles of racially defined groups themselves. Waged all around the globe under a variety of banners such as anticolonialism and civil rights, these battles to challenge various structural and cultural racisms have been a major feature of 20th-century politics. The racial horrors of the 20th century—colonial slaughter and apartheid, the genocide of the holocaust, and the massive bloodlettings required to end these evils—have also indelibly marked the theme of race as a political issue *par excellence*.

As a result of prior efforts and struggles, we have now reached the point of fairly general agreement that race is not a biologically given but rather a socially constructed way of differentiating human beings. While a tremendous achievement, the transcendence of biologistic conceptions of race does not provide any reprieve from the dilemmas of racial injustice and conflict, nor from controversies over the significance of race in the present. Views of race as socially constructed simply recognize the fact that these conflicts and controversies are now more properly framed on the terrain of politics. By privileging politics in the analysis which follows we do not mean to suggest that race has been displaced as a concern of scientific inquiry, or that struggles over cultural representation are no longer important. We do argue, however, that race is now a preeminently political phenomenon.

WHAT IS RACISM?

Since the ambiguous triumph of the civil rights movement in the mid-1960s, clarity about what racism means has been eroding. The concept entered the lexicon of "common sense" only in the 1960s. Before that, although the term had surfaced occasionally,[17] the problem of racial injustice and inequality was generally understood in a more limited fashion, as a matter of prejudiced attitudes or bigotry on the one hand,[18] and discriminatory practices on the other.[19] Solutions, it was believed, would therefore involve the overcoming of such attitudes,

the achievement of tolerance, the acceptance of "brotherhood," etc., and the passage of laws which prohibited discrimination with respect to access to public accommodations, jobs, education, etc. The early civil rights movement explicitly reflected such views. In its espousal of integration and its quest for a "beloved community" it sought to overcome racial prejudice. In its litigation activities and agitation for civil rights legislation it sought to challenge discriminatory practices.

The later 1960s, however, signalled a sharp break with this vision. The emergence of the slogan "black power" (and soon after, of "brown power," "red power," and "yellow power"), the wave of riots that swept the urban ghettos from 1964 to 1968, and the founding of radical movement organizations of nationalist and Marxist orientation, coincided with the recognition that racial inequality and injustice had much deeper roots. They were not simply the product of prejudice, nor was discrimination only a matter of intentionally informed action. Rather, prejudice was an almost unavoidable outcome of patterns of socialization which were "bred in the bone," affecting not only whites but even minorities themselves.[20] Discrimination, far from manifesting itself only (or even principally) through individual actions or conscious policies, was a structural feature of U.S. society, the product of centuries of systematic exclusion, exploitation, and disregard of racially defined minorities.[21] It was this combination of relationships—prejudice, discrimination, and institutional inequality—which defined the concept of racism at the end of the 1960s.

Such a synthesis was better able to confront the political realities of the period. Its emphasis on the structural dimensions of racism allowed it to address the intransigence which racial injustice and inequality continued to exhibit, even after discrimination had supposedly been outlawed[22] and bigoted expression stigmatized. But such an approach also had clear limitations. As Robert Miles has argued, it tended to "inflate" the concept of racism to a point at which it lost precision.[23] If the "institutional" component of racism were so pervasive and deeply rooted, it became difficult to see how the democratization of U.S. society could be achieved, and difficult to explain what progress had been made. The result was a levelling critique which denied any distinction between the Jim Crow era (or even the whole longue durée of racial dictatorship since the conquest) and the present. Similarly, if the prejudice component of racism were so deeply inbred, it became difficult to account for the evident hybridity and interpenetration that characterizes civil society in the U.S., as evidenced by the shaping of popular culture, language, and style, for example. The result of the "inflation" of the concept of racism was thus a deep pessimism about any efforts to overcome racial barriers, in the workplace, the community, or any other sphere of lived experience. An overly comprehensive view of racism, then, potentially served as a self-fulfilling prophecy.

Yet the alternative view—which surfaced with a vengeance in the 1970s—urging a return to the conception of racism held before the movement's "radical turn," was equally inadequate. This was the neoconservative perspective, which deliberately restricted its attention to injury done to the individual as opposed to the group, and to advocacy of a color-blind racial policy.[24] Such an approach reduced race to ethnicity,[25] and almost entirely neglected the continuing organization of social inequality and oppression along racial lines. Worse yet, it tended to rationalize racial injustice as a supposedly natural outcome of group attributes in competition.[26]

The distinct, and contested, meanings of racism which have been advanced over the past three decades have contributed to an overall crisis of meaning for the concept today. Today, the absence of a clear "common sense" understanding of what racism means has become a significant obstacle to efforts aimed at challenging it. Bob Blauner has noted that in classroom discussions of racism, white and non-white students tend to talk past one another. Whites tend to locate racism in color consciousness and find its absence color-blindness.

In so doing, they see the affirmation of difference and racial identity among racially defined minority students as racist. Non-white students, by contrast, see racism as a system of power, and correspondingly argue that blacks, for example, cannot be racist because they lack power. Blauner concludes that there are two "languages" of race, one in which members of racial minorities, especially blacks, see the centrality of race in history and everyday experience, and another in which whites see race as "a peripheral, nonessential reality."[27]

Given this crisis of meaning, and in the absence of any "common sense" understanding, does the concept of racism retain any validity? If so, what view of racism should we adopt? Is a more coherent theoretical approach possible? We believe it is.

We employ racial formation theory to reformulate the concept of racism. Our approach recognizes that racism, like race, has changed over time. It is obvious that the attitudes, practices, and institutions of the epochs of slavery, say, or of Jim Crow, no longer exist today. Employing a similar logic, it is reasonable to question whether concepts of racism which developed in the early days of the post–civil rights era, when the limitations of both moderate reform and militant racial radicalism of various types had not yet been encountered, remain adequate to explain circumstances and conflicts a quarter-century later.

Racial formation theory allows us to differentiate between race and racism. The two concepts should not be used interchangeably. We have argued that race has no fixed meaning, but is constructed and transformed sociohistorically through competing political projects, through the necessary and ineluctable link between the structural and cultural dimensions of race in the U.S. This emphasis on projects allows us to refocus our understanding of racism as well, for racism can now be seen as characterizing some, but not all, racial projects.

A racial project can be defined as *racist* if and only *if it creates or reproduces structures of domination based on essentialist*[28] categories of race. Such a definition recognizes the importance of locating racism within a fluid and contested history of racially based social structures and discourses. Thus there can be no timeless and absolute standard for what constitutes racism, for social structures change and discourses are subject to rearticulation. Our definition therefore focuses instead on the "work" essentialism does for domination, and the "need" domination displays to essentialize the subordinated.

Further, it is important to distinguish racial awareness from racial essentialism. To attribute merits, allocate values or resources to, and/or represent individuals or groups on the basis of racial identity should not be considered racist in and of itself. Such projects may in fact be quite benign.

Consider the following examples: first, the statement, "Many Asian Americans are highly entrepreneurial"; second, the organization of an association of, say, black accountants.

The first racial project, in our view, signifies or represents a racial category ("Asian Americans") and locates that representation within the social structure of the contemporary U.S. (in regard to business, class issues, socialization, etc.). The second racial project is organizational or social structural, and therefore must engage in racial signification. Black accountants, the organizers might maintain, have certain common experiences, can offer each other certain support, etc. Neither of these racial projects is essentialist, and neither can fairly be labelled racist. Of course, racial representations may be biased or misinterpret their subjects, just as racially based organizational efforts may be unfair or unjustifiably exclusive. If such were the case, if for instance in our first example the statement in question were "Asian Americans are naturally entrepreneurial," this would by our criterion be racist. Similarly, if the effort to organize black accountants had as its rationale the raiding of clients from white accountants, it would by our criterion be racist as well.

Similarly, to allocate values or resources—let us say, academic scholarships—on the basis of racial categories is not racist. Scholarships are awarded on a preferential basis to Rotarians, children of insurance company employees, and residents of the Pittsburgh metropolitan area. Why then should they not also be offered, in particular cases, to Chicanos or Native Americans?

In order to identify a social project as racist, one must in our view demonstrate a link between essentialist representations of race and social structures of domination. Such a link might be revealed in efforts to protect dominant interests, framed in racial terms, from democratizing racial initiatives.[29] But it might also consist of efforts simply to reverse the roles of racially dominant and racially subordinate.[30] There is nothing inherently white about racism.[31]

Obviously a key problem with essentialism is its denial, or flattening, of differences within a particular racially defined group. Members of subordinate racial groups, when faced with racist practices such as exclusion or discrimination, are frequently forced to band together in order to defend their interests (if not, in some instances, their very lives). Such "strategic essentialism" should not, however, be simply equated with the essentialism practiced by dominant groups, nor should it prevent the interrogation of internal group differences.[32]

Without question, any abstract concept of racism is severely put to the test by the untidy world of reality. To illustrate our discussion, we analyze the following examples, chosen from current racial issues because of their complexity and the rancorous debates they have engendered:

- Is the allocation of employment opportunities through programs restricted to racially defined minorities, so-called "preferential treatment" or affirmative action policies, racist? Do such policies practice "racism in reverse"? We think not, with certain qualifications. Although such programs necessarily employ racial criteria in assessing eligibility, they do not generally essentialize race, because they seek to overcome specific socially and historically constructed inequalities.[33] Criteria of effectiveness and feasibility, therefore, must be considered in evaluating such programs. They must balance egalitarian and context-specific objectives, such as academic potential or job-related qualifications. It should be acknowledged that such programs often do have deleterious consequences for whites who are not personally the source of the discriminatory practices the programs seek to overcome. In this case, compensatory measures should be enacted to vitiate the charge of "reverse discrimination."[34]

• Is all racism the same, or is there a distinction between white and non-white versions of racism? We have little patience with the argument that racism is solely a white problem, or even a "white disease."[35] The idea that non-whites cannot act in a racist manner, since they do not possess "power," is another variant of this formulation.[36]

For many years now, racism has operated in a more complex fashion than this, sometimes taking such forms as self-hatred or self-aggrandizement at the expense of more vulnerable members of racially subordinate groups.[37] Whites can at times be the victims of racism—by other whites or non-whites—as is the case with anti-Jewish and anti-Arab prejudice. Furthermore, unless one is prepared to argue that there has been no transformation of the U.S. racial order over the years, and that racism consequently has remained unchanged—an essentialist position *par excellence*—it is difficult to contend that racially defined minorities have attained no power or influence, especially in recent years.

Having said this, we still do not consider that all racism is the same. This is because of the crucial importance we place in situating various "racisms" within the dominant hegemonic discourse about race. We have little doubt that the rantings of a Louis Farrakhan or Leonard Jeffries—to pick two currently demonized black ideologues—meet the criteria we have set out for judging a discourse to be racist. But if

we compare Jeffries, for example, with a white racist such as Tom Metzger of the White Aryan Resistance, we find the latter's racial project to be far more menacing than the former's. Metzger's views are far more easily associated with an essentializing (and once very powerful) legacy: that of white supremacy and racial dictatorship in the U.S., and fascism in the world at large. Jeffries's project has far fewer examples with which to associate: no more than some ancient African empires and the (usually far less bigoted) radical phase of the black power movement.[38] Thus black supremacy may be an instance of racism, just as its advocacy may be offensive, but it can hardly constitute the threat that white supremacy has represented in the U.S., nor can it be so easily absorbed and rearticulated in the dominant hegemonic discourse on race as white supremacy can. All racisms, all racist political projects, are not the same.

• Is the redrawing—or gerrymandering—of adjacent electoral districts to incorporate large numbers of racially defined minority voters in one, and largely white voters in the other, racist? Do such policies amount to "segregation" of the electorate? Certainly this alternative is preferable to the pre–Voting Rights Act practice of simply denying racial minorities the franchise. But does it achieve the Act's purpose of fostering electoral equality across and within racial lines? In our view such practices, in which the post–1990 redistricting process engaged rather widely–are vulnerable to charges of essentialism. They often operate through "racial lumping," tend to freeze rather than overcome racial inequalities, and frequently subvert or defuse political processes through which racially defined groups could otherwise negotiate their differences and interests. They worsen rather than ameliorate the denial of effective representation to those whom they could not effectively redistrict—since no redrawing of electoral boundaries is perfect, those who get stuck on the "wrong side" of the line are particularly disempowered. Thus we think such policies merit the designation of "tokenism"—a relatively mild form of racism—which they have received.[39]

Parallel to the debates on the concept of race, recent academic and political controversies about the nature of racism have centered on whether it is primarily an ideological or structural phenomenon. Proponents of the former position argue that racism is first and foremost a matter of beliefs and attitudes, doctrines and discourse, which only then give rise to unequal and unjust practices and structures.[40] Advocates of the latter view see racism as primarily a matter of economic stratification, residential segregation, and other institutionalized forms of inequality which then give rise to ideologies of privilege.[41]

From the standpoint of racial formation, these debates are fundamentally misguided. They frame the problem of racism in a rigid "either-or" manner. We believe it is crucial to disrupt the fixity of these positions by simultaneously arguing that ideological beliefs have structural consequences, and that social structures give rise to beliefs. Racial ideology and social structure, therefore, mutually shape the nature of racism in a complex, dialectical, and overdetermined manner.

Even those racist projects which at first glance appear chiefly ideological turn out upon closer examination to have significant institutional and social structural dimensions. For example, what we have called "far right" projects appear at first glance to be centrally ideological. They are rooted in biologistic doctrine, after all. The same seems to hold for certain conservative black nationalist projects which have deep commitments to biologism.[42] But the unending stream of racist assaults initiated by the far right, the apparently increasing presence of skinheads in high schools, the proliferation of neo-Nazi computer bulletin boards, and the appearance of racist talk shows on cable access channels, all suggest that the organizational

manifestations of the far right racial projects exist and will endure.[43] Perhaps less threatening but still quite worrisome is the diffusion of doctrines of black superiority through some (though by no means all) university-based African American Studies departments and student organizations, surely a serious institutional or structural development.

By contrast, even those racisms which at first glance appear to be chiefly structural upon closer examination reveal a deeply ideological component. For example, since the racial right abandoned its explicit advocacy of segregation, it has not seemed to uphold—in the main—an ideologically racist project, but more primarily a structurally racist one. Yet this very transformation required tremendous efforts of ideological production. It demanded the rearticulation of civil rights doctrines of equality in suitably conservative form, and indeed the defense of continuing large-scale racial inequality as an outcome preferable to (what its advocates have seen as) the threat to democracy that affirmative action, busing, and large-scale "race-specific" social spending would entail.[44] Even more tellingly, this project took shape through a deeply manipulative coding of subtextual appeals to white racism, notably in a series of political campaigns for high office which have occurred over recent decades. The retreat of social policy from any practical commitment to racial justice, and the relentless reproduction and divulgation of this theme at the level of everyday life—where whites are now "fed up" with all the "special treatment" received by non-whites, etc.—constitutes the hegemonic racial project at this time. It therefore exhibits an unabashed structural racism all the more brazen because on the ideological or signification level, it adheres to a principle of "treating everyone alike."

In summary, the racism of today is no longer a virtual monolith, as was the racism of yore. Today, racial hegemony is "messy." The complexity of the present situation is the product of a vast historical legacy of structural inequality and invidious racial representation, which has been confronted during the post–World War II period with an opposition more serious and effective than any it had faced before. As we will survey in the chapters to follow, the result is a deeply ambiguous and contradictory spectrum of racial projects, unremittingly conflictual racial politics, and confused and ambivalent racial identities of all sorts. We begin this discussion by addressing racial politics and the state.

NOTES

1. This is not to suggest that gender is a biological category while race is not. Gender, like race, is a social construct. However, the biological division of humans into sexes—two at least, and possibly intermediate ones as well—is not in dispute. This provides a basis for argument over gender divisions—how "natural," etc.—which does not exist with regard to race. To ground an argument for the "natural" existence of race, one must resort to philosophical anthropology.
2. "The truth is that there are no races, there is nothing in the world that can do all we ask race to do for us....The evil that is done is done by the concept, and by easy—yet impossible—assumptions as to its application." (Kwame Anthony Appiah, *In My Father's House: Africa in the Philosophy of Culture* [New York: Oxford University Press, 1992].) Appiah's eloquent and learned book fails, in our view, to dispense with the race concept, despite its anguished attempt to do so; this indeed is the source of its author's anguish. We agree with him as to the non-objective character of race, but fail to see how this recognition justifies its abandonment. This argument is developed below.
3. We understand essentialism as *belief in real, true human, essences, existing outside or impervious to social and historical context.* We draw this definition, with some small modifications, from Diana Fuss, *Essentially Speaking: Feminism, Nature, & Difference* (New York: Routledge, 1989) p. xi.
4. Michael Omi and Howard Winant, "On the Theoretical Status of the Concept of Race" in Warren Crichlow and Cameron McCarthy, eds., *Race, Identity, and Representation in Education* (New York: Routledge, 1993).
5. Charles Murray, *Losing Ground: American Social Policy*, 1950–1980 (New York: Basic Books, 1984), p. 223.
6. Justice Thurgood Marshall, dissenting in *City of Richmond v. J. A. Croson Co.*, 488 U.S. 469 (1989).
7. See, for example, Derrick Bell, "Remembrances of Racism Past: Getting Past the Civil Rights Decline." in Herbert Hill and James E. Jones, Jr., eds., *Race in America: The Struggle for Equality* (Madison: The University of Wisconsin Press, 1993) pp. 75–76; Gertrude Ezorsky, Racism and Justice: The Case for Affirmative Action (Ithaca: Cornell University Press, 1991) pp. 109–111; David Kairys, *With Liberty and Justice for Some: A Critique of the Conservative Supreme Court* (New York: The New Press, 1993) pp. 138–41.
8. Howard Winant has developed a tentative "map" of the system of racial hegemony in the U.S. circa 1990, which focuses on the spectrum of racial projects running from the political right to the political left. See Winant, "Where Culture Meets Structure: Race in the 1990s," in idem, *Racial Conditions: Politics, Theory, Comparisons* (Minneapolis: University of Minnesota Press, 1994).
9. A familiar example is use of racial "code words." Recall George Bush's manipulations of racial fear in the 1988 "Willie Horton" ads, or Jesse Helms's use of the coded term "quota" in his 1990 campaign against Harvey Gantt.

10. From this perspective, far right racial projects can also be interpreted as "nationalist." See Ronald Walters, "White Racial Nationalism in the United States," *Without Prejudice* Vol. 1, no. 1 (Fall 1987).

11. To be sure, any effort to divide racial formation patterns according to social structural location—"macro" vs. "micro," for example—is necessarily an analytic device. In the concrete, there is no such dividing line. See Winant, "Where Culture Meets Structure."

12. We are not unaware, for example, that publishing this work is in itself a racial project.

13. See Weber, *Economy and Society*, Vol. 1 (Berkeley: University of California Press, 1978), pp. 385–87; Ernst Moritz Manasse, "Max Weber on Race," *Social Research*, Vol. 14 (1947) pp. 191–221.

14. Du Bois, *The Souls of Black Folk* (New York: Penguin, 1989 [1903]), p. 13. Du Bois himself wrestled heavily with the conflict between a fully socio-historical conception of race, and the more essentialized and deterministic vision he encountered as a student in Berlin. In "The Conservation of Races" (1897) we can see his first mature effort to resolve this conflict in a vision which combined racial solidarity and a commitment to social equality. See Du Bois, "The Conservation of Races," in Dan S. Green and Edwin D. Driver, eds., *W. E. B. Du Bois On Sociology and the Black Community* (Chicago: University of Chicago Press, 1978) pp. 238–49; Manning Marable, *W. E. B. Du Bois: Black Radical Democrat* (Boston: Twayne, 1986) pp. 35–38. For a contrary, and we believe incorrect reading, see Appiah, *In My Father's House*, pp. 28–46.

15. A good collection of Boas's work is George W. Stocking, ed., *The Shaping of American Anthropology, 1883–1911: A Franz Boas Reader* (Chicago: University of Chicago Press, 1974).

16. Robert E. Park's *Race and Culture* (Glencoe, IL: Free Press, 1950) can still provide insight; see also Stanford H. Lyman, *Militarism, Imperialism, and Racial Accommodation: An Analysis and Interpretation of the Early Writings of Robert E. Park* (Fayetteville: University of Arkansas Press, 1992); Locke's views are concisely expressed in Alain Leroy Locke, *Race Contacts and Interracial Relations*, ed. Jeffrey C. Stewart (Washington, DC: Howard University Press, 1992), originally a series of lectures given at Howard University.

17. For example, in Magnus Hirschfeld's prescient book, *Racism* (London: Victor Gollancz, 1938).

18. This was the framework, employed in the crucial study of Myrdal and his associates; see Gunnar Myrdal, *An American Dilemma: The Negro Problem and Modern Democracy*, 20th Anniversary Edition (New York: Harper and Row, 1962 [1944]). See also the articles by Thomas F. Pettigrew and George Fredrickson in Pettigrew et al., *Prejudice: Selections from The Harvard Encyclopedia of American Ethnic Groups* (Cambridge, MA: The Belknap Press of Harvard University, 1982).

19. On discrimination, see Frederickson in ibid. In an early essay which explicitly sought to modify the framework of the Myrdal study, Robert K. Merton recognized that prejudice and discrimination need not coincide, and indeed could combine in a variety of ways. See Merton, "Discrimination and the American Creed," in R. M. McIver, ed., *Discrimination and National Welfare* (New York: Harper and Row, 1949).

20. Gordon W. Allport, *The Nature of Prejudice* (Cambridge, MA: Addison-Wesley, 1954) remains a classic work in the field; see also Philomena Essed, *Understanding Everyday Racism: An Interdisciplinary Theory* (Newbury Park, CA: Sage, 1991). A good overview of black attitudes toward black identities is provided in William E. Cross, Jr., *Shades of Black: Diversity in African-American Identity* (Philadelphia: Temple University Press, 1991).

21. Stokely Carmichael and Charles V. Hamilton first popularized the notion of "institutional" forms of discrimination in *Black Power: The Politics of Liberation in America* (New York: Vintage, 1967), although the basic concept certainly predated that work. Indeed, President Lyndon Johnson made a similar argument in his 1965 speech at Howard University:

    But freedom is not enough. You do not wipe away the scars of centuries by saying: Now you are free to go where you want, do as you desire, and choose the leaders you please.

    You do not take a person who, for years, has been hobbled by chains and liberate him (sic), bring him up to the starting line of a race and then say, "You are free to compete with all the others," and still justly believe that you have been completely fair.

    Thus it is not enough just to open the gates of opportunity. All our citizens must have the opportunity to walk through those gates.

    This is the next and more profound stage of the battle for civil rights. We seek not just freedom but opportunity—not just legal equity but human ability—not just equality as a right but equality as a fact and as a result. (Lyndon B. Johnson, "To Fulfill These Rights," reprinted in Lee Rainwater and William L. Yancey, *The Moynihan Report and the Politics of Controversy* [Cambridge, MA: MIT Press, 1967, p. 125].)

    This speech, delivered at Howard University on June 4, 1965, was written in part by Daniel Patrick Moynihan. A more systematic treatment of the institutional racism approach is David T. Wellman, *Portraits of White Racism* (New York: Cambridge University Press, 1977).

22. From the vantage point of the 1990s, it is possible to question whether discrimination was ever effectively outlawed. The federal retreat from the agenda of integration began almost immediately after the passage of civil rights legislation, and has culminated today in a series of Supreme Court decisions making violation of these laws almost impossible to prove. See *Ezorsky, Racism and Justice; Kairys, With Liberty and Justice for Some.* As we write, the Supreme Court has further restricted antidiscrimination laws in the case of *St. Mary's Honor Center v. Hicks.* See Linda Greenhouse, "Justices Increase Workers' Burden in Job-Bias Cases," *The New York Times,* 26 June 1993, p. 1.

23. Robert Miles, *Racism* (New York and London: Routledge, 1989), esp. chap. 2.

24. The *locus classicus* of this position is Nathan Glazer, *Affirmative Discrimination: Ethnic Inequality and Public Policy,* 2nd ed. (New York: Basic Books, 1978); for more recent formulations, see Murray, *Losing Ground;* Arthur M. Schlesinger, *The Disuniting of America: Reflections on a Multicultural Society* (New York: W. W. Norton, 1992).

25. See Chapter 1.

26. Thomas Sowell, for example, has argued that one's "human capital" is to a large extent culturally determined. Therefore the state cannot create a false equality which runs counter to the magnitude and persistence of cultural differences. Such attempts at social engineering are likely to produce negative and unintended results: "If social processes are transmitting real differences—in productivity, reliability, cleanliness, sobriety, peacefulness [!]—then attempts to impose politically a very different set of beliefs will necessarily backfire...." (Thomas Sowell, *The Economics and Politics of Race: An International Perspective* (New York: Quill, 1983) p. 252).

27. Bob Blauner "Racism, Race, and Ethnicity: Some Reflections on the Language of Race" (unpublished manuscript, 1991).

28. Essentialism, it will be recalled, is understood as belief in real, true human essences, existing outside or impervious to social and historical context.

29. An example would be the "singling out" of members of racially defined minority groups for harsh treatment by authorities, as when police harass and beat randomly chosen ghetto youth, a practice they do not pursue with white suburban youth.

30. For example, the biologistic theories found in Michael Anderson Bradley, *The Iceman Inheritance: Prehistoric Sources of Western Man's Racism, Sexism' and Aggression* (Toronto: Dorset, 1978), and in Frances Cress Welsing, *The Isis (Yssis) Papers* (Chicago: Third World Press, 1991).

31. "These remarks should not be interpreted as simply an effort to move the gaze of African-American studies to a different site. I do not want to alter one hierarchy in order to institute another. It is true that I do not want to encourage those totalizing approaches to African-American scholarship which have no drive other than the exchange of dominations—dominant Eurocentric scholarship replaced by dominant Afrocentric scholarship. More interesting is what makes intellectual domination possible; how knowledge is transformed from invasion and conquest to revelation and choice; what ignites and informs the literary imagination, and what forces help establish the parameters of criticism." (Toni Morrison, *Playing in the Dark*, p. 8; emphasis original.)

32. Lisa Lowe states: "The concept of 'strategic essentialism' suggests that it is possible to utilize specific signifiers of ethnic identity, such as Asian American, for the purpose of contesting and disrupting the discourses that exclude Asian Americans, while simultaneously revealing the internal contradictions and slippages of Asian Americans so as to insure that such essentialisms will not be reproduced and proliferated by the very apparatuses we seek to dis-empower." Lisa Lowe, "Heterogeneity, Hybridity, Multiplicity: Marking Asian American Differences," *Diaspora*, Vol. 1, no. 1 (Spring 1991) p. 39.

33. This view supports Supreme Court decisions taken in the late 1960s and early 1970s, for example in *Griggs v. Duke Power*, 401 U.S. 424 (1971). We agree with Kairys that only "… [F]or that brief period in our history, it could accurately be said that governmental discrimination was prohibited by law" (Kairys, *With Liberty and Justice For Some*, p. 144).

34. This analysis draws on Ezorsky, *Racism and Justice*.

35. See for example, Judy H. Katz, *White Awareness: Handbook for Anti-Racism Training* (Norman: University of Oklahoma Press, 1978).

36. The formula "racism equals prejudice plus power" is frequently invoked by our students to argue that only whites can be racist. We have been able ro uncover little written analysis to support this view (apart from Katz, ibid., p. 10), but consider that it is itself an example of the essentializing approach we have identified as central to racism. In the modern world, "power" cannot be reified as a thing which some possess and other's don't, but instead constitutes a relational field. The minority student who boldly asserts in class that minorities cannot be racist is surely not entirely powerless. In all but the most absolutist of regimes, resistance to rule itself implies power.

37. To pick but one example among many: writing before the successes of the civil rights movement, E. Franklin Frazier bitterly castigated the collaboration of black elites with white supremacy. See Frazier, *Black Bourgeoisie: The Rise of a New Middle Class in the United States* (New York: The Free Press, 1957).

38. Interestingly, what they share most centrally seems to be their antisemitism.

39. Having made a similar argument, Lani Guinier, Clinton's nominee to head the Justice Department's Civil Rights Division was savagely attacked and her nomination ultimately

blocked. See Guinier, "The Triumph of Tokenism: The Voting Rights Act and the Theory of Black Electoral Success," *Michigan Law Review* (March 1991).

40. See Miles, *Racism*, p. 77. Much of the current debate over the advisability and legality of banning racist hate speech seems to us to adopt the dubious position that racism is primarily an ideological phenomenon. See Mari J. Matsuda et al., *Words That Wound: Critical Race Theory, Assaultive Speech, and the First Amendment* (Boulder, CO: Westview Press, 1993).

41. Or ideologies which mask privilege by falsely claiming that inequality and injustice have been eliminated. See Wellman, *Portraits of White Racism*.

42. Racial teachings of the Nation of Islam, for example, maintain that whites are the product of a failed experiment by a mad scientist.

43. Elinor Langer, "The American Neo-Nazi Movement Today," *The Nation*, July 16/23, 1990.

44. Such arguments can be found in Nathan Glazer, *Affirmative Discrimination*. Charles Murray, *Losing Ground* and Arthur M. Schlesinger, Jr., *The Disuniting of America*, among others.

JOURNALING QUESTION

The United States now has its first president of African descent. How do you think this will affect the dominant racial projects in America?

2.

THE RACIAL FORMATION OF AMERICAN INDIANS

Negotiating Legitimate Identities within Tribal and Federal Law

EVA MARIE GARROUTTE

Omi and Winant focused on the formation of black and white as racial groups in America, and many people argue that that is the essential race divide in this country. Some think of America as made of "white" and "non-white"; some argue it is better to think of it as "black" and "non-black." But since the beginning of this country, U.S. racial formation has been more complicated than that because of the presence of "native" peoples—those who lived in this land who were neither European settlers nor African slaves. Garroutte explains the unique situation of the Indian peoples whose racial identity is an ongoing subject of legal debate. What are the racial projects that Indian tribes undertake, and how do these differ from those in which U.S. government engages?

Michael Omi and Howard Winant define "racial formation" as the process by which individuals are divided, by historically mutable rules, into racial categories.[1] American Indians differ from other twenty-first-century racial groups in the extent to which their racial formation is governed by law, yet students of race and ethnicity are frequently unfamiliar with the unique processes of racial formation in this group. This article is a simple introduction to some of the legal definitions—both federal and tribal—that regulate American Indian racial formation. It also examines the consequences of the particular processes of racial formation that apply to Indian people. Finally, it considers the questions of who is able to satisfy legal definitions of identity and who is unable to do so and some of the many reasons that the "Indians" and "non-Indians" who emerge from the rigors of the definitional process do not always resemble what one might expect.[2]

TRIBAL LEGAL DEFINITIONS

There are a large number of legal rules defining American Indian identity, and they are formulated and applied by different actors for different purposes. I will begin with the ones that tribes use to determine their citizenship. Many people are surprised to discover that each tribe sets its own legal criteria for citizenship. They imagine that the U.S. government controls such aspects of tribal lives. In reality, tribes typically have the right to create their own legal definitions of identity and to do so in any way they choose. Indeed, this prerogative is commonly viewed legislatively as one of the most fundamental powers of an Indian tribe.[3]

The most common tribal requirement for determining citizenship revolves around "blood quantum" or degree of Indian ancestry. About two-thirds of all federally recognized tribes of the coterminous United States specify a minimum blood quantum

---

Eva Marie Garroutte, "The Racial Formation of American Indians: Negotiating Legitimate Identities within Tribal and Federal Law," *The American Indian Quarterly* 25 2001: 224–39. Notes have been renumbered and edited.

in their legal citizenship criteria, with one-quarter blood degree being the most frequent minimum requirement.[4]

Degree of blood is calculated on the basis of the immediacy of one's genetic relationship to ancestors whose bloodlines were (supposedly) unmixed. The initial calculation often begins with a "base roll," a listing of tribal membership and blood quanta in some particular year.[5] These base rolls make possible very elaborate definitions of identity. They allow one to reckon that the offspring of, say, a full-blood Navajo mother and a white father is one-half Navajo. If that half Navajo child in turn produced progeny with a Hopi person of one-quarter blood degree, those progeny would be judged to be one-quarter Navajo and one-eighth Hopi. Alternatively, they could also be said to have "three-eighths general Indian blood." Certain tribes require not only that citizens possess tribal ancestry but also that this ancestry comes from a particular parent. Thus, the Santa Clara Pueblo (New Mexico) will not enroll children in the tribe without paternal descent, and the Seneca Tribe (New York) requires maternal descent.

Such modern definitions of identity based on blood quantum closely reflect nineteenth- and early-twentieth-century theories of race introduced into indigenous cultures by Euro-Americans. These understood blood as quite literally the vehicle for the transmission of cultural characteristics: "'Half-breeds' by this logic could be expected to behave in 'half-civilized,' i.e., partially assimilated, ways while retaining one half of their traditional culture, accounting for their marginal status in both societies.[6] Given this standard of identification, full bloods tended to be seen as the "really real," the quintessential Indians, while others were (and often continue to be) viewed as Indians in diminishing degrees.[7]

These theories of race articulated closely with political goals characteristic of the dominant American society. The original stated intention of blood quantum distinctions was to determine the point at which the various responsibilities of that dominant society to Indian peoples ended. The ultimate and explicit federal intention was to use the blood quantum standard as a means to liquidate tribal lands and to eliminate government trust responsibility to tribes along with entitlement programs, treaty rights, and reservations.[8] Indians would eventually, through intermarriage combined with the mechanism of blood quantum calculations, become citizens indistinguishable from all other citizens.

A significant number of tribes—almost one-third of those populating the lower forty-eight states—have rejected specific blood quantum requirements for determining tribal citizenship. They often require, instead, that any new enrollee be simply a lineal (direct) descendant of another tribal member. They may also invoke additional or alternative criteria. For instance, the Tohono O'Odham (Arizona) consider residency definitive, automatically admitting to citizenship all children born to parents living on the reservation. The Swinomish (Washington) take careful stock of various indicators of community participation, ignoring blood quantum, while the Lower Sioux Indian Community (Minnesota) requires a vote of the tribal council. In still other tribes, community recognition or parental enrollment may also be a means to or a prerequisite for enrollment, and a few tribes only accept applicants whose parents submit the necessary paperwork within a limited time after their child's birth. Some tribes also require members to fulfill certain minimal duties, such as maintaining annual contact with the tribal council, in order to maintain their citizenship in good standing.[9]

TRIBAL IDENTITY NEGOTIATIONS: CONSEQUENCES

Tribes, in short, possess the power to define their citizenship through self-generated legal definitions, and they do so in many different ways. Legal definitions regulate the right to vote in tribal elections, to hold tribal office, and generally to participate in the political, and sometimes the cultural, life of the tribe. One's ability to satisfy legal definitions of identification may also determine one's right to share in certain tribal revenues (such as income generated by tribally controlled businesses). Perhaps most significantly, it may determine the right to live on a reservation or to inherit land interests thereon.

As this list suggests, failure to negotiate an identity as a "real" Indian within the legal definition of one's tribe can lead to some dire outcomes for individual people. For instance, legal criteria can tear apart families by pushing certain members off the reservation while allowing others to stay. Thus, in 1997 an article in *Indian Country Today* described the following family scenario: "Mr. Montoya has lived at Santa Clara Pueblo, his mother's home, his whole life. He raised his four children at the pueblo, and now has grandchildren there."[10] But Mr. Montoya cannot be enrolled at Santa Clara (New Mexico) because, since 1939, the pueblo has operated by a tribal law that allows for enrollment only on the basis of paternal descent—and his father was not from Santa Clara but, rather, from the nearby Isleta Pueblo. Montoya has inherited rights to his mother's property in Santa Clara, but his ability to enforce those rights remains uncertain.

Families in Montoya's situation sometimes cannot tolerate the tenuousness of their position and choose to abandon the pueblo, their relatives, and their intimate participation in the traditional, tribal culture wherein they were born and raised. But family dissolution "by legal definition" has elsewhere occurred by force. It has occurred to the extent that mixed-race children have been actively expelled from the reservation, even in cases in which the children had been living there under the care of an enrolled relative.

Such an event occurred on the Onondaga Reservation in the recent past. The Onondaga, by a law that reverses the practice of the Santa Clara Pueblo, are matrilineal, enrolling children only if their mothers are tribal citizens. In 1974, the tribal council ordered all noncitizens to leave the reservation or face ejection. This order included even noncitizen spouses, who were mostly women, and the children born to Onondaga men by such women. The Onondaga men could stay—but only if they chose to live apart from their wives and children. The national journal of Native news and issues, *Akwesasne Notes*, reported that the rationale behind the expulsion was that, over a period of years, a large number of non-Indians had moved onto Onondaga land and the council feared that the federal government might consequently dissolve the reservation.[11] Most individuals affected by the ruling left peaceably; others had to be forcibly removed. One family burned down its home before leaving.

Legal definitions, then, allow tribes to determine their citizenship as they choose. This determination allows them to delimit the distribution of certain important resources, such as reservation land, tribal monies, political privileges, and the like. But this is hardly the end of the story of legal definitions of identity.

FEDERAL LEGAL DEFINITIONS

Although tribes possess the right to formulate legal definitions for the purpose of delimiting their citizenship, the federal government has many purposes for which it, too, must distinguish Indians from non-Indians, and it uses its own, separate legal definition for doing so. More precisely, it uses a whole array of legal definitions. Because the U.S. Constitution uses the word Indian in two places but defines it nowhere, Congress has made its own definitions on an ad hoc basis.[12] A 1978 congressional survey discovered no less than thirty-three separate definitions of "Indians" in use in different pieces of federal legislation.[13] These may or may not correspond with those any given tribe uses to determine its citizenship.

Thus, most federal legal definitions of Indian identity specify a particular minimum blood quantum—frequently one-quarter but sometimes one-half—and others do not. Some require or accept tribal citizenship as a criterion of federal identification, and others do not. Some require reservation residency or ownership of land held in trust by the government, and others do not. Many other laws affecting Indians specify no definition of identity, such that the courts must determine to whom the laws apply. Because of the wide variation in federal legal identity definitions, and their frequent departure from the various tribal ones, many individuals who are recognized by their tribes as tribal citizens are nevertheless considered non-Indian for some or all governmental purposes. The converse can be true as well.

There are a variety of contexts in which federal legal definitions of identity become important. The matter of economic resource distribution—involving access to various social services, monetary awards, and opportunities—will probably come immediately to the minds of many readers. The particular legal situation of Indian people and its attendant opportunities and responsibilities are the result of historic negotiations between tribes and the federal government, in which the latter agreed to compensate tribes in various ways for the large amounts of land tribes surrendered, often by force. Benefits available to those who can satisfy federal definitions of Indian identity are administered through a variety of agencies, including the Bureau of Indian Affairs, the Indian Health Service, the Department of Agriculture, the Office of Elementary and Secondary Education, and the Department of Labor, to name a few.[14]

Legal definitions also affect specific economic rights deriving from treaties or agreements that some (not all) tribes made with the federal government. These may include such rights as the use of particular geographic areas for hunting, harvesting, fishing, or trapping, as well as certain water use rights.[15] Those legally defined as Indians are also sometimes exempted from certain requirements related to state licensure and state (but not federal) income and property taxation.[16]

Legal definitions also determine the applicability of a number of protections available to individual Indians from the federal government. Notable among these are an Indian parent's rights under the Indian Child Welfare Act of 1978 (25 U.S.C. 1901 et seq.). Before the passage of this act, as many as 25–35 percent of Indian children in some states were being removed from their homes and placed in the care of non-Indians through such means as adoption and foster care. Many commentators have suggested that a number of Indian families lost their children less because they were genuinely unsuitable parents and more because they refused to abandon traditional cultural values in favor of those enforced by the essentially white, middle-class, social service bureaucracy.[17] For instance, it is a rather common custom in many Indian cultures to share child-rearing responsibilities among various members of the extended family, with the outcome that children do not necessarily live with their biological parents. It has been a common complaint among Indian families that Social Services representatives have automatically assumed, in such cases, that a child suffers parental "neglect" and have used this reasoning as an excuse to initiate foster care placement.

The Indian Child Welfare Act was passed in order to stem the wholesale transfer of children out of their families, tribes, and cultures. It requires that, when Indian children must be removed from their homes, efforts be made to place them with another family member or at least with another Indian family rather than a non-Indian one. The law allows Indian people a means to protect the integrity of their family units and to ensure some cultural continuity for children.

Just as importantly, federally specified legal definitions provide for certain religious freedoms. For one thing, they allow Indian people to seek protection from prosecution for the possession of specific ceremonial objects, otherwise restricted by law. (For instance, many Indian people own eagle feathers that they use in prayer and ceremonies, although non-Indians are not permitted to possess any part of this endangered species. Similarly, Indian members of the Native American Church ingest peyote, legally classified as a hallucinogen, as a sacramental substance in closely controlled worship settings. Non-Indians are forbidden to possess it.) Since the passage of the Native American Graves Protection and Repatriation Act of 1990, federal legal definitions also allow Indian people to claim sacred ceremonial objects, as well as to receive and rebury the remains of their ancestral dead, if these are being held in federally funded museums for display or study (as they very frequently are).

Federal legal definitions of Indian identity can even affect some individuals' ability to pursue their livelihood. A particularly controversial protection that has recently become available to those legally defined as Indians revolves around the Indian Arts and Crafts Act of 1990. Arguments for this legislation started from the recognition that many buyers consider artwork more desirable and valuable if it is created by an Indian person. They proceeded to the observation that a great deal of art was therefore being falsely labeled as Indian-made. The same arguments then concluded that such misrepresentations were seriously reducing the revenues of artists who were, in fact, Indian.[18]

The Indian Arts and Crafts Act forbids any artist who is not a citizen of a federally or state-acknowledged tribe from marketing work as "Indian produced." Penalties for violation of the act include large fines and imprisonment. Certain galleries and organizations have also voluntarily chosen to restrict exhibitions and art commissions to people who can demonstrate that they are Indians by reference to formal, legal criteria.[19]

IDENTITY AND LEGITIMACY

All the legal rights and protections sketched above offer their significant advantages only to those who are able to make claims to Indianness that are formally judged as legitimate within tribal or federal definitions of identity. However, many people cannot manage to pass successfully through one or the other of these definitions. (As noted before, there is no guarantee that those definitions correspond.) By what process is the legitimacy of claims to Indian identity asserted and evaluated within definitions of law? Who is able to negotiate a legal identity, and who is not? How is it that people with seemingly identical characteristics may meet with very different outcomes within the process of racial formation set out in legal definitions? The answers to such questions are frequently quite astonishing.

Let us begin with a consideration of the criterion of blood quantum. Some people of American Indian ancestry find their identity claims challenged because their blood quanta are judged too low, by one standard or another. The question of how much "blood" is "enough" for an individual to call him- or herself Indian is hotly contested in Indian country—and well beyond. As sociologist Eugeen Roosens writes,

> There is…[a] principle about which the whites and the Indians are in agreement…[P]eople with more Indian blood…also have more rights to inherit what their ancestors, the former Indians, have left behind. In addition, full blood Indians are more authentic than half-breeds. By being pure, they have more right to respect. They are, in all aspects of their being, more integral.[20]

Degree of biological ancestry can take on such a tremendous significance in tribal contexts that it literally overwhelms all other considerations of identity (especially when it is constructed as "pure"). As Cherokee legal scholar G. William Rice points out, "Most [people] would recognize the full-blood Indian who was enrolled in a federally recognized tribe as an Indian, even if the individual was adopted at birth by a non-Indian family and had never set foot in Indian country nor met another Indian."[21]

In this, American Indian claims to identity are judged very differently under the law than the claims of other racial groups have been, even into the present day. We see this most clearly if we consider the striking difference in the way that the American popular and legal imaginations work to assign individuals to the racial category of "Indian" as opposed to the racial category "black." As a variety of researchers have observed, social and legal attributions of black identity have often focused on the "one-drop rule" or rule of "hypodescent."[22] . . .

Although people must show only the slightest trace of "black blood" to be forced (with or without their consent) into the category "African American," modern American Indians must formally produce strong evidence of often rather substantial amounts of "Indian blood" to be allowed entry into the corresponding racial category. The regnant racial definitions applied to Indians are simply quite different than those that have applied (and continue to apply) to blacks. Modern Americans, as Native American studies professor Jack Forbes puts the matter, "are always finding 'blacks' (even if they look rather un-African), and . . . are always losing 'Indians.' "[23]

Another group of people who may find the legitimacy of their racial identities challenged or denied comprises individuals of tribally mixed ancestry. This can be true even for those whose total American Indian blood quanta are relatively high. The reader will remember that the majority of tribes make documentation of a minimum blood quantum—often one-fourth degree Indian blood—part of their legal definitions of identity and that the federal government does the same for at least some of its various purposes. In light of this requirement, consider the hypothetical case of a child possessing one-half Indian ancestry and one-half white ancestry, meaning that he or she has one parent who is exclusively white and one parent who is exclusively Indian. This child's identity claim is likely to get a green light from both the federal government and the tribe—so long as his or her Indian ancestry comes from a single tribe. But compare these potential fortunes with those of another child whose half-Indian heritage derives from several different tribes. Let us say that this second child, in addition to his or her one-half

white ancestry, is also one-eighth Sisseton Dakota, one-eighth Cheyenne, one-eighth Assiniboine, and one-eighth Sicangu Lakota. This child is, like the first child, one-half Indian. But each tribe of his or her ancestry requires its citizens to document a one-quarter blood degree, from that tribe only. From the perspective of each individual tribe, this child possesses only one-eighth tribal blood and is therefore ineligible for citizenship. As far as the several tribes are concerned, he or she is simply non-Indian within their legal definitions of identity.

Some people of Indian ancestry fall afoul, in legal definitions of identity, of still another potential snare. This entanglement has to do with one's ability to establish relationship to a historic Indian community in the way that many legal definitions require. As previously noted, individuals seeking tribal or federal identification as Indian must typically establish that one, or more, of their ancestors appears on one of the tribe's base rolls. Unfortunately, many people who clearly conform to any other definition of Indian identity do not have ancestors who appear on the base rolls, for a multitude of reasons. Historians agree that the process by which many tribal rolls were initially compiled was almost unbelievably complicated. In the compilation of some tribal rolls, including the Dawes Rolls (1899–1906), from which all of today's enrolled Oklahoma Cherokees (and various other tribes) must show descent, the process that registrants endured took so long that a significant number of them died before the paperwork was completed. This meant that their descendants would be forever barred from becoming tribal citizens.

Even when applicants did manage to live long enough to complete the entire process of enrollment, they frequently found themselves denied. Dawes commissioners enrolled only a small fraction of all those who applied, and they readily agreed that they had denied many people of indubitably tribal ancestry.[24]

Other Indian people of the period actively resisted their registration on the Dawes Rolls, either individually or collectively. For instance, among Oklahoma Creeks, Cherokees, Chickasaws, and Choctaws in the late nineteenth and early twentieth centuries, conservative traditionalists or "irreconcilables" fought a hard fight against registration with the Dawes Commission. The reason was that the Dawes Roll was the explicit first step in what President Theodore Roosevelt had rapturously declared (in his first annual address to Congress in 1901) would be "a mighty, pulverizing engine to break up the tribal mass."[25] The effort, in a nutshell, was to destroy indigenous cultures by destroying their foundation—their collective ownership of land—and to integrate the Indians thus "liberated" into the dominant American culture. It was to allow for Indians to be remade into individual private owners of small farms who would quickly become independent of government attention and expenditures.

Probably no one could have foreseen all of the specific, catastrophic results that would befall tribes with the destruction of the old, traditional system of land tenure. The irreconcilables, however, at least intuited the outlines of the coming disaster. In the words of historian Angie Debo, they "clung to the old order with the stubbornness of despair."[26] In many tribes opposition to allotment ran high. In some, leaders arose who used all their resources, from cunning to force, to discourage their fellows' enrollment and subsequent allotment.[27]

Government patience with such conservative obduracy soon wore thin, and the more influential and uncooperative leaders and their families were hunted out and forcibly enrolled. (Cherokee leader Redbird Smith consented to his own enrollment only after he was finally jailed for his refusal.) However, others who shared his sentiments did manage to elude capture altogether and were never entered onto the census documents used today as the base rolls for many tribes.

The stories of Redbird Smith, and others like him, are narratives of a determined and principled resistance to a monumental step in the process of the Indians' forced acculturation to the dominant American culture. Yet the descendants of those traditionalists who succeeded in escaping census enumeration find themselves worse off, in the modern legal context, for their forebears' success in the fight to maintain cultural integrity. By the criteria their tribes have now established, they can never become enrolled citizens. This fact frequently affects, in turn, their ability to satisfy federal definitions.[28]

All of the foregoing demonstrates that there are great numbers of peculiarities of exclusion spawned by legal definitions of identity. The reverse side of this observation, however, is that a number of people who may have no ancestral connections to tribes have been and are defined as Indian in the legal sense alone. In some places and times, for instance, non-Indian spouses of Indian people have been allowed to become legal citizens of Indian nations. Among several Oklahoma tribes, certain African American slaves, formerly owned by Indian people, were likewise made, by due legal process following the Civil War, into tribal citizens even in the absence of any Indian ancestry.[29] And, where census registration implied eligibility for distribution of tribal lands, as it did in Oklahoma, it was not uncommon for individuals with no Indian ancestry, but with active homesteading ambitions and perhaps unscrupulous lawyers in tow, to seek to acquire places on the rolls through dishonest means. Thousands of them succeeded.[30] In so doing, they earned for themselves the name of "five-dollar Indians," presumably in reference to the amount required to bribe the census enumerator.

Finally, this discussion of the oddities that legal definitions of identity have created would not be complete without the acknowledgment that it is not only non-Indian people who have made their way onto the tribal census lists and thus "become" Indian, in the legal sense. Nonexistent people sometimes did, as well. An amusing example comes from the 1885 census of the Sicangu Lakota (South Dakota). As historian Thomas Biolsi records, census takers at the Rosebud Agency "recorded some remarkable English translations of Lakota names."[31] Nestled in among the common and dignified appellations—Black Elk, Walking Bull, Dull Knife, and others—are personal names of a more colorful class: Bad Cunt, Dirty Prick, Shit Head. "What happened," Biolsi notes, "is not difficult to unravel: Lakota people were filing past the census enumerator, and then getting back in line—or lending their babies to people in line—to be enumerated a second time using fictitious and rather imaginative names."[32] Because this particular census was being taken for the purpose of distributing rations, the ploy was one aimed at the very practical goal of enhancing survival—but the Lakota apparently felt that even such serious work need not be undertaken without humor.

For the purposes of the present discussion, I should note that at least some of the historic oddities of Indian census rolls have continued to create more of the same—forever. That is, while the nonexistent Indians of Rosebud clearly could not have produced children, the living, breathing, "five-dollar Indians" who bought their way onto the census rolls in Oklahoma and other states certainly could. It is impossible to estimate the number of modern-day descendants of those numerous non-Indian "Indians," but one might suppose that

it could be fairly large. It seems probable that at least some descendants have maintained tribal enrollment and the privileges attendant on a legally legitimated identity, even while many people of actual Indian descent were and are unable to acquire the same.

In conclusion, the example of Indian identity illustrates the complex and often mystifying nature of racial formation processes as they apply to American Indians. "Indianness" emerges out of complex negotiations that occur within the context of specifiable legal definitions of identity. There are many ways to gain and to lose it that may have little to do with the qualities that most people assume to be of central importance in determining racial identity. At the same time, achieving an Indian identity that satisfies various legal criteria (or failing to do so) has serious consequences. The specific elements of the racial formation process for Indian people make Native Americans' experience unique among those of modern-day U.S. racial groups.

ADDED MATERIAL

From *Real Indian: Identity of the Survival of Native American.* (c) 2002 The Regents of the University of California. Used with the permission of University of California Press.

NOTES

1. Michael Omi and Howard Winant, *Racial Formations in the United States: From the 1960s to the 1980s* (London: Routledge, 1986).
2. It should be noted that legal definitions are only one of the several crosscutting and competing definitions that are invoked to define American Indians. I have considered these other definitions at length in Eva Marie Garroutte, *Real Indians: Identity and the Survival of Native America* (Berkeley: University of California Press, 2002).
3. This tribal right was determined in the 1905 court case *Waldron* v. *United States* (143 F. 413, C.C.D.S.D., 1905) and later clarified in a celebrated lawsuit, *Martinez* v. *Santa Clara Pueblo* (540 F.2d 1039, 10th Cir. 1976). However, as with nearly every other rule in Indian country, there are exceptions. A handful of tribes are federally required to hold to specific criteria in defining tribal membership—for instance, by maintaining a specific blood quantum standard for citizenship. In most legal discussions, the right to determine citizenship is closely tied to the concept of tribal sovereignty. See Sharon O'Brien, *American Indian Tribal Governments* (Norman: University of Oklahoma Press, 1989); Charles F. Wilkinson. *American Indians,*

Time,_and the Law: Native Societies in a Modern Constitutional Democracy (New Haven: Yale University Press, 1987).

4. Russell Thornton surveyed 302 of the 317 tribes in the lower forty-eight states that enjoyed federal acknowledgment in 1997. He found that 204 tribes had some minimum blood quantum requirement, while the remaining ninety-eight had none; see Thornton, "Tribal Membership Requirements and the Demography of 'Old' and 'New' Native Americans," *Population Research and Policy Review* 16 (1997): 37.

5. Although a few tribes have no written records of citizenship even today—some of the Pueblos, for instance, depend on their oral traditions—the majority of tribes maintain written membership documents, which are called "tribal rolls"; see Russell Thornton. *American Indian Holocaust and Survival: A Population History* (Norman: University of Oklahoma Press, 1987), 190. The roll chosen as definitive for later citizenship determinations is known as the "base roll." The General Allotment Act of 1887 provided for the creation of some base rolls, but most were compiled in response to the Indian Reorganization Act of 1934. Tribes continued to create membership listings that they use as base rolls after 1934 as well. In some cases, tribes created their base rolls only a few years ago. This is true, for instance, with the Passamoquoddy (Maine), who (having only enjoyed federal acknowledgment as a tribe for two decades) use a 1990 census for their base roll.

6. C. Matthew Snipp, "Who Are American Indians? Some Observations about the Perils and Pitfalls of Data for Race and Ethnicity," *Population Research and Policy Review* 5 (1986): 249.

7. For an excellent discussion of the evolution, over several centuries, of ideas about blood relationship among European and Euro-American peoples and transference of these ideas into American Indian tribal populations, see Melissa L. Myer, "American Indian Blood Quantum Requirements: Blood Is Thicker than Family," in *Over_the Edge: Remapping the American West*, ed. Valerie J. Matsumoto and Blake Allmendiger (Berkeley: University of California Press, 1999).

8. Thomas Biolsi, "The Birth of the Reservation; Making the Modern Individual among the Lakota," *American Ethnologist* 22, no. 1 (February 1995): 28–9; Patricia Limerick, *The Legacy of Conquest: The Unbroken Past of the American West* (New York: W.W. Norton, 1988).

9. To view a variety of tribal constitutions and their citizenship requirements, see http://thorpe.ou.edu/.

10. "Mixed Marriages Present Some Property Problems," *Indian Country Today* (26 May–2 June 1997): D10.

11. Akwesasne Notes 6 (Autumn 1974): 32.

12. The two mentions of "Indians" in the Constitution appear in passages regarding the regulation of commerce and the taking of a federal census. The word tribe also appears once in the Constitution, in the Commerce Clause.

13. Sharon O'Brien, "Tribes and Indians: With Whom Does the United States Maintain a Relationship?" *Notre Dame Law Review* 66 (1991): 1481.

14. These agencies administer resources and programs in areas such as education, health, social services, tribal governance and administration, law enforcement, nutrition, resource management, tribal economic development, employment, and the like. The most recently published source describing various programs and the requirements for participation is Roger Walk, *Federal Assistance to Native Americans: A Report Prepared for the Senate Select Committee on Indian Affairs of the U.S. Senate* (Washington DC: Government Printing Office, 1991).

15. For a discussion of the history of American Indian hunting, fishing, and water rights, see Wilcomb E. Washburn, *Red Man's Land/White Man's Law: A Study of the Past and Present Status of the American Indian* (New York: Charles Scribner's Sons, 1971).

16. Non-Indian students in my classes sometimes tell me that Indians also regularly receive such windfalls as free cars and monthly checks from the government strictly because of their race. It is my sad duty to puncture this fantasy. The common belief that Indians receive "free money" probably stems from the fact that the government holds land in trust for certain tribes. As part of its trust responsibility, it may then lease that land, collect the revenue, and distribute it to the tribal members. Thus, some Indians do receive government checks, but these do not represent some kind of bread from heaven; they are simply the profits derived from lands that the Native Americans own. For details on the special, political-economic relationship of Indians to the federal government in relation to taxation and licensure, see Gary D. Sandefur, "Economic Development and Employment Opportunities for American Indians," in *American Indians: Social Justice and Public Policy, Ethnicity and Public Policy Series,* vol. 9, ed. Donald E. Green and Thomas V. Tonneson (Milwaukee: University of Wisconsin System Institute on Race and Ethnicity, 1991).

17. Suzan Shown Harjo, "The American Indian Experience," in *Family Ethnicity: Strength in Diversity,* ed. Harriet Pipes McAdoo (Newbury Park CA: Sage, 1993); R. B. Jones, "The Indian Child Welfare Act: The Need for a Separate Law," available at http://www.abanet.org/genpractice/compleat/f95child.html, accessed 1995.

18. To be specific, the Commerce Department estimated in 1985 that specious "Indian art" imported from foreign countries created $40–80 million in lost income, or 10–20 percent of annual Indian art sales, for genuine Indian artists every year (H.R. 101–400, 101st Cong., 1st Sess., Congressional Record [1990]: 4–5).

19. An excellent, detailed discussion of this legislation appears in Gail K. Sheffield, *The Arbitrary_Indian: The Indian Arts and Crafts Act of 1990* (Norman: University of Oklahoma Press, 1997), 30–31. The Indian Arts and Crafts Act's specification that there are two types of Indian tribes—the federally acknowledged and the state acknowledged—raises another point significant to the present discussion. Although this article discusses identity definitions as they concern individuals, definitions also concern entire groups. Both federal and state governments formally classify certain groups as "acknowledged" Indian tribes and invest them with specific rights and responsibilities not shared by other groups. While the accompaniments of the extension of state acknowledgment to a tribe are highly variable (and sometimes trivial), the consequences of federal acknowledgment are always profound.

    By acknowledging a group of claimants as an Indian tribe, the federal government extends "government-to-government" relations to it. It legally constitutes that tribal group as a sovereign power and as a "domestic dependent nation," as determined in court cases including *Cherokee Nation* v. *Georgia* (1831) and (even more importantly) *Worcester* v. *Georgia* (1832). These are extremely powerful statutes. In fact, the legal case *Native American Church* v. *Navajo Tribal Council* (1959) made clear that federally acknowledged tribes enjoy a governmental status higher than that of states. For a more detailed discussion of legal cases pertaining to tribal sovereignty, see O'Brien, *American Indian Tribal Governments.*

20. Eugeen E. Roosens, *Creating Ethnicity: The Process of Ethnogenesis* (Newbury Park CA: Sage, 1989), 41–42. Roosens is discussing the situation of Canadian Indians, but the same remarks apply to American Indians.

21. G. William Rice, "There and Back Again—An Indian Hobbit's Holiday: Indians Teaching Indian Law," *New Mexico Law Review* 26, no. 2 (Spring 1996): 176.

22. Naomi Zack, "Mixed Black and White Race and Public Policy," *Hypatia* 10, no. 1 (winter 1995): 120–32.

23. Jack D. Forbes, "The Manipulation of Race, Caste, and Identity: Classifying Afroamericans, Native Americans and Red-Black People," *Journal of Ethnic Studies* 17, no.4 (1990): 24.

24. Kent Carter, "Deciding Who Can Be Cherokee: Enrollment Records of the Dawes Commission," *Chronicles of Oklahoma* 69, no. 2 (summer 1991): 174–205.

25. Theodore Roosevelt, *The Works of Theodore Roosevelt*, vol. 15: State Papers as Governor and President, 1899–1909 (New York: Scribner's Sons, 1926), 129. Contrast Roosevelt's optimism about allotment with the opinion of U.S. Commissioner of Indian Affairs John Collier, who would later call it "the greatest single practical evil" ever perpetrated on American Indians (quoted in Fergus Bordewich, *Killing the White Man's Indian* [New York: Doubleday, 1996], 124).

26. Angie Debo, *And Still the Waters Run: The Betrayal of the Five Civilized Tribes* (Princeton: Princeton University Press, 1972), 53.

27. In Oklahoma, the Creeks were especially resistant. Under the leadership of Chitto Harjo, or "Crazy Snake," their full bloods set up their own government and council in 1901. They also appointed a cadre of law enforcement officers known as "light-horsemen" to deal with tribal citizens who had accepted allotments and to give warning to those who might be considering a similar action. The light-horsemen roamed the countryside, confiscating enrollment papers and sometimes arresting and whipping their possessors. After being arrested by federal, mar-shals and found guilty of such activities, Chitto Harjo and his followers continued to defy allotment through legal means, hiring lawyers and sending lobbyists to Washington. The Oklahoma Cherokees used their own strategies, often under the guidance of traditionalist leader Redbird Smith. When field parties from the Dawes Commission "came to a full blood settlement, they found amusements planned in remote places to call the Indians away. When they tried to secure the names [of Cherokees eligible for allotment] from their neighbors, witnesses were threatened with bodily harm" (Debo, *And Still the Waters Run*, 45). For further discussion of tribal resistance to allotment, see D. S. Otis, *The Dawes Act and the Allotment of Indian Lands* (Norman: University of Oklahoma Press, 1973), 40–46.

28. Modern tribes do realize that some of their proper members are being excluded from legal citizenship, and most have created a mechanism for dealing with this reality. Many tribal constitutions allow for legally "adopting" individuals who do not meet formally specified identity criteria. The adoption provision, sometimes called "selective enrollment," allows for a "safety net" to protect persons judged by some criteria to have a claim on tribal citizen-ship but who, for whatever reason, cannot satisfy the usual requirements. Isleta Pueblo (New Mexico), for example, allows for the adoption of individuals with one-half Indian blood from other tribes besides its own but forbids the adoption of non-Indians, while some tribal constitutions even provide for the adoption of non-Indians (O'Brien, *American Indian Tribal Governments*, 175).

In practice, however, adoptions tend to be rather rare and to be limited to certain categories of people—members' spouses, reservation residents, children who meet a blood quantum requirement but whose parents are not enrolled, and so on. And in most cases adoption is only partial salvation. Adopted individuals may not enjoy full privileges in the tribe, such as voting rights or the ability to pass tribal citizenship to off-spring. Perhaps even more significantly, the federal government refuses to recognize as Indian anyone who cannot demonstrate at least some blood connection to a tribe, for any purposes, even if the tribe agrees to enroll that person; see Stephen L. Pevar, *The Rights of Indians and Tribes: The Basic ACLU Guide to Indian and Tribal Rights*, 2d ed. (Carbondale: Southern Illinois University Press, 1992), 13. See further *U.S.* v. *Rogers* (45 U.S. 566 [1846]) and *State* v. *Attebery* (519 P.2d 53 [Ariz. 1974]). Thus, even with the "safety net" of tribal adoption in place, many people still cannot achieve a legitimated Indian identity within all of the legal definitions that are likely to be important to them.

29. Modern descendants of such individuals—referred to then and now as "freedmen"—often continue to maintain documentation of tribal affiliation. Presently, they do not qualify for social service benefits, mineral rights, and other benefits that sometimes accrue to those who are tribal citizens by blood. Since 1996, two groups of African American freedmen have been engaged in legal struggles with the Seminole Nation (Oklahoma). A central issue has been their right to share in a $56 million settlement that the tribe received in a land claims case. In 2000, the tribe stripped the black Seminoles of their tribal membership. The Department of the Interior, however, declared the action illegal. See Herb Frazier, "Black Seminoles Seek $100m on Retribution from Government," *Charleston Post and Courier*, 3 December 1999: 1; William Glaberson, "Who Is a Seminole, and Who Gets to Decide?" *New York Times*, 29 January 2001: Al, A14.
30. Debo, *And Still the Waters Run*, 38.
31. Biolsi, "The Birth of the Reservation."
32. Biolsi, "The Birth of the Reservation," 28.

JOURNALING QUESTION

Indian identity continues to have a legal component in ways that other racialized identities in the United States do not. How would you feel if you had to legally "prove" your racial identity?

3.
LATINO RACIAL FORMATIONS IN THE UNITED STATES
An Introduction

NICHOLAS DE GENOVA AND ANA Y. RAMOS-ZAYAS

What Omi and Winant did around the formation of black and white in America can be done for every other "racial project" that constructs race groups. One of the more interesting such projects in America today is the construction of a "race group" out of people who are united by language: people who speak Spanish. "Latinos" or "Hispanics" are the largest immigrant group in the United States and, De Genova and Ramos-Zayas argue, have formed into a race group even though the language of "culture" and "ethnicity" is often used.

Can we take what we learn about the Latino Racial Formations and apply it to the question of Asian and Middle Eastern groups? What racial projects are currently forming those disparate peoples, immigrants from different countries, with different religions and different languages, into "racial formations"?

Like much of the Latino Studies scholarship by sociologists, political scientists, and literary or cultural critics, anthropological research on "Latinos" (or "Hispanics") in the United States is often trapped by a tendency to subsume its subject under the conceptual frameworks of "culture" or "ethnicity." Indeed, anthropological research, due to predictable disciplinary inclinations, may be especially susceptible to the appeal of "culture" or "ethnicity" as preferred of analytic categories....Culturalist explanations of intra-Latino "ethnic" identifications tend to presuppose substantive, if not essentialized, commonalities *internal* to groups with origins in Latin America, and thereby also take for granted their a priori status *as groups*. Our perspective on "Latino *racial* formations," in contrast, focuses on the dynamic and relational processes of power inequalities and subordination to a white supremacist state that account for the

eminently historical production of these "groups" as such, and thereby situate them within a wider social field framed by the hegemonic polarity of racialized whiteness and Blackness in the United States. Thus, the "Latino" (or "Hispanic") label tends to be always-already saturated with racialized difference. With these considerations as an organizing theme, this collection of essays investigates both the possibilities for and limits to pan-Latino identity (*Latinidad*) and identification (*Latnismo*) within the broader framework of racialization.

The intrinsic incoherence of social categories such as "Latino" or "Hispanic," combined with their persistent meaningfulness, are telltale indicators of the ongoing reconfiguration of "Latinos" as a racial formation in the United States. It is commonplace among many commentators, not the least of which is the U.S. Bureau of the Census, to assert that Latinos are not a "race" and that Latinos may

Excerpted from Nicholas De Genova and Ana Y. Ramos-Zayas, "Latino Racial Formations in the United States: An Introduction," *The Journal of Latin American Anthropology* 8(2):2–17 Copyright © 2003, American Anthropological Association. References have been edited.

be, variously, white or black, or "some other race" that presumably entails any number of conceivable "interracial" mixtures. Yet these claims inevitably take refuge in rather anachronistic crudely biological notions of "race" and overly simplistic naturalized reifications of "racial" difference understood in terms of phenotype and "color." The legacy of Latin American *criollo* nationalisms that promote ideologies of *mestizaje*, similarly, does not really supply a viable alternative; while they abide by a contrary logic of racialized distinction and meanings, these official endorsements of the racially "mixed" character of their respective "nations" share the same fundamental premises of discrete originary races whose innumerable combinations have yielded identifiable phenotypic categories. As an effect of these conceptual lacunae, many of the prominent contributions to the Latino Studies scholarship opt instead to rely upon the analytic categories of "culture" or "ethnicity" in order to specify and theorize "Latino" identity and community formations, and thus evade the question of "race" and radalization altogether.

Relying upon biological or phenotypic notions of discrete racial categories, the U.S. Census has explicitly reserved the "Hispanic" category as an officially non-"racial" one. By treating "Hispanic" as an "ethnic" designation, Latinos are thereby encouraged to identify "racially" as white, Black, or Native American—in short, as anything but Latino. Nevertheless, this hegemonic "ethnic" distinction instituted by the U.S. state has been particularly instrumental for the allocation of affirmative action entitlements, deliberately constructing "Hispanics" as an effectively homogenized "minority" population analogous to African Americans. Thus, the "Hispanic" status of Latinos is widely treated as a racial condition all the same. Latinos' responses to the "race" question on the Census confirm precisely this fact of their everyday social experiences: while a significant number, confronting the peculiar and narrowly limited options available on the form, readily identify as "white" (even if many may never

do so on virtually any other occasion), what is more revealing is that a comparable number opt instead for the nondescript, "none of the above" category of "Some other race." Consequently, social categories such as "Hispanic" or "Latino" are notorious for the ambiguities and incongruities they entail for efforts in the United States to identify and name diverse groups of people with origins in Latin America. Nonetheless, these labels have become pervasive and increasingly salient, both for hegemonic projects that homogenize these groups as a "minority" population, a political constituency, or a market segment, as well as for efforts that seek to produce community and build strategic coalitions for self-representation.

The process by which particular Latin American groups have come to be homogenized as "Hispanics" (or alternatively, as "Latinos") cannot be divorced from the ways in which such pan-Latino labels were first formulated by the U.S. federal government. The "Hispanic" label was devised by the U.S. state as a deliberate strategy of erasure with regard to the more particular histories of Chicanos and Puerto Ricans, precisely at that historical moment of political crisis characterized by the racial militancy of the 1960s and 1970s (Oboler 1995; cf. Omi and Winant 1986). In 1969 U.S. President Richard Nixon's proclamation of a "National Hispanic Heritage Week" served to conflate the different historical experiences of Mexicans and Puerto Ricans at the precise juncture when Chicanos and Puerto Ricans were each engaged in increasingly militant and often nationalist acts of cultural affirmation *as distinct groups*, with particular histories of subjugation and resistance, and emphasizing their specific (and potentially divergent) political demands (Oboler 1995:81–84).[1] The heightened public awareness in the aftermath of the Civil Rights era—at both local and national levels—of the existence and increasing political assertiveness of historically disenfranchised groups of Latin American descent, was unprecedented in the history of the United States (Oboler 1995:83). At a historical juncture when there were still only very small numbers of other Latino nationalities in the United States, however, the federal government's efforts to submerge the two major Latin American national-origin groups under the unitary and homogenizing "Hispanic" label reveals an insistent effort to undermine the specific demands of Chicanos and Puerto Ricans. Furthermore, the invention of "Hispanic" homogeneity also created an unprecedented opportunity for the numerically small but remarkably influential community of Cuban exiles (who were predominantly from elite or professional middles-class backgrounds, racially white-identified, politically conservative) tO mobilize their newfound "Hispanic" identity as a platform (see Acuña 1996:9; Oboler 1995:82). Thus, against Chicano and Puerto Rican affirmations of indigenous and national identities that embraced Third World anticolonial nationalism, anti-Castro Cubans supplied a vociferous "Hispanic" expression of Cold War–era anticommunism that was resolute in its newfound allegiance to U.S. nationalism and capitalism.

The promotion of a Hispanic "ethnic" identity, moreover, could serve to distract Latin American populations from mobilizing politically–on the basis of "race" or "nation"—within the United States in ways that identified U.S. military interventions and political and economic domination in Latin America and the Caribbean as the colonial or imperialist contexts for the marginalization, inequality, and racial subordination experienced by migrants from Latin American countries and their U.S.-born or raised children. The Hispanic "ethnic" construct was rapidly institutionalized ideologically in homogenized multiculturalist representations, largely produced and disseminated through educational curricula as well as the mass media. These representations reduced Latino "ethnic" identity to a collection of "cultural" elements that sustained essentialist constructions of the presumed values, beliefs, and everyday practices purportedly shared by members of all Latin American nationality groups. Hence, public education institutions

have performed a kind of officially mandated "cultural sensitivity" through the implementation of multiculturalist curricula, often incorporating the recognition of "Hispanic Heritage Month" through celebrations and discussions that focus on "traditional" foods, music, family values, and folkloric displays, while neglecting any meaningful consideration of the social, economic, and historical contexts surrounding the racialization of Latinos as "minorities" in the United States.

The proliferation of mass-mediated marketing images of homogenized "Latinos" or "Hispanics," though not exclusively a top-down process, likewise, has been historically inseparable from the state's historical attempts to homogenize the militant particularisms of Latin American nationality groups during the Civil Rights era. Both the Latino and Hispanic labels, but especially the more aggressively de-politicized Hispanic label, increasingly became hegemonic categories of capital with the construction and cultivation of specialized Spanish-speaking market segments. Commercially-motivated constructions of "the Hispanic audience" for advertising purposes produced a largely undifferentiated or massified notion of Latinos as a discrete and unitary racialized market, notably conflating racial nonwhiteness with a presumed dominance of Spanish language that served as a proxy for "low" socioeconomic status (Rodríguez 1998). By focusing on the Spanish language as a paramount basis of Latinidad, furthermore, "Hispanic marketing" and "Hispanic-driven media" have repackaged Latinos through images that effectively "render them pleasing to corporate clients," fashioning them as "traditional and extremely family-oriented," and by implication, "stubbornly brand-loyal consumer[s]" (Davila 2002:4). This recasting of Latinos as rigidly tradition-bound embodiments of cultural "authenticity" contributes to Hispanic marketing's role in promoting a simplistic, generic, and depoliticized Latinidad that is readily disseminated and eminently marketable (see Davila 2002; Rodríguez 1998).

The homogenized cultural markers and historical experiences of "the Hispanics" which have been largely "invented" and propagated by politicians, uncritical social science, and the mass media and advertising sectors, have certainly inspired some to ambivalently question or frankly repudiate such generic labels as Hispanic or Latino altogether. Others have nonetheless come, to varying extents, to internalize these terms, or at least to strategically appropriate them for various purposes of self-identification and self-organization (Aparicio 1997; Aparicio and Chávez-Silverman 1997; Jones-Correa 1998; Oboler 1995; Padilla 1985). The names of social collectivities, and racialized groups in particular, of course, are sites of struggle between hegemonic labeling and efforts at self-representation. Upon its introduction, in addition to supplanting specific national–colonial heritages, the term "Hispanic" served as a surrogate for such prior administrative–demographic categories as "Spanish-surname" and "Spanish-speaking," both of which had inevitably failed to adequately encompass the anomalies of U.S.-born English-speaking Latinos, Latinos with non-Spanish surnames, or the nonwhite children of "interracial" marriages—all of whom belonged to the fundamentally racialized category for which these other terminological alternatives had been deployed (see Jones-Correa and Leal 1996:217). Although one criticism of the "Hispanic" label is its transparent Eurocentrism and the implication that the people of the Spanish-speaking Americas are fundamentally apprehensible as derivatives of their former colonizer, the term *Latino* (although it arguably allows for the inclusion of Portuguese-speaking Brazilians) is not strictly any less Eurocentric.[2] *Latinoamericano* (rather than *hispanoamericano*) is, however, the far more frequently used term *within* Latin America. It is precisely for these reasons that "Latino" has been the widely preferred category among those who embrace a pan-Latin American identification but reject the "Hispanic" label imposed historically by the U.S. state.

The adoption and internalization of a pan-Latino identity among Latin American nationality groups in the United States are often central to processes of middle-class formation and articulations of upward social mobility aspirations among Latinos (Oboler 1995; cf. Acuña 2000:386–421; Foley 1998). Unlike many working-class people in Suzanne Oboler's research (1995) who frankly rejected the Hispanic label as a strategy to facilitate their subordination, many upwardly aspiring middle-class Latin Americans embraced the more inclusive category as a way to mobilize together and coordinate their efforts in order to achieve the privileges of the white middle class. Various formulations of Latinismo, or the strategic deployment of a Latino or Hispanic identity; in addition to the more parochial maneuvers of privilege and status that may unify middle-class people beyond their nationally-inflected particularities, have also been shown to enable cross-class efforts at political mobilization....

Not only have Latinidad and Latinismo been promoted as bases for oppositional organizing in relation to institutionalized politics, but also as viable strategies in the everyday processes of community formation. In an effort to problematize narrow notions of politics, the analytical concept of "Latino cultural citizenship," initially articulated by Renato Rosaldo (1994; cf. Flores and Benmayor 1997), has emphasized the need to formulate how Latino "cultural" specificity—in its divergence from the normative ideals on which U.S. citizenship and "American" national identity are premised—may be upheld as a vital and enduringly visible dimension of Latinos' struggles for political empowerment and social incorporation. Given that, even as U.S. citizens, Latinos have not reaped the purportedly universal benefits afforded by citizenship, but actually have been rendered suspect as a potential menace to national unity, the claims of cultural citizenship are presented as an alternative medium for Latinos to demand recognition, expand entitlements, and deepen the meanings of social and political membership, without succumbing to assimilation-ist mandates to surrender their specific "cultural" identities. By developing a wide array of distinctive forms of collective assertion and visibility, includ-ing everyday processes of community formation as well as grassroots activism that retain nationally-inflected particularities and simultaneously culti-vate a shared sense of Latinidad, this perspective posits that Latinos are better situated to claim rights in a manner that expands the boundaries of social inclusion and eventually secures political entitle-ments (Rosaldo and Flores 1997). A serious poten-tial shortcoming of this vision is that it ultimately seems to sustain rather than subvert the basic prem-ises by which racialized inequality is organized and managed through the multiculturalist rhetoric of the U.S. state, whereby the effective normaliza-tion and subordination of "difference" is facilitated through its accommodation. Nevertheless, the "cultural citizenship" perspective has important potential advantages for simultaneously addressing the racialized subjugation of both citizen and non-citizen Latinos. It affirms the possibility and neces-sity of political agency that is not confined, to the state's formal constructions of juridical citizenship and rights, and resituates virtually every aspect of Latino community formation within a broadly con-ceived understanding of the political.

The prospect of community formation among distinct national-origin groups on the basis of a shared sense of Latino identity, however, never ceases to be problematic. Struggles over hegemonic labeling and efforts at self-representation are not only oriented "outward" beyond the group's vari-ously conceptualized boundaries, but also simul-taneously operate internally among contending claims among presumed "Latino" subgroups. A politics of inclusion and exclusion, therefore, is at stake in competing productions of who can be, counted as "authentic" or "legitimate" Latinos. As Juan Flores (2000:141–165) argues, the viability of pan-Latino categories of identification hinges on their inclusiveness toward the full range of social

experiences, including the divergence between con-temporary configurations of Latino "immigrant" groups in contradistinction to the "native born." In the context of the "New Nueva York," for instance, the possibility for a tenable Latinismo faces the sig-nificant challenge of extending notions of language and cultural authenticity to include the experience of English-dominant Puerto Ricans, in particu-lar, as well as U.S. Puerto Ricans, more generally, whose social identities have been partly formulated in relation to African Americans as well as other Francophone and Anglophone Caribbean commu-nities, in addition to Puerto Ricans "over there" on the island (Flores 2000:164). The Latino label, therefore, is inevitably configured in diverse ways in relation to the particular Latin American groups who vie with one another in specific locations. Furthermore, one of the central conflicts over the constitution of these locally-inflected notions of Latinidad ultimately involves the racialized stigma of an abject "minority" status that is unevenly dis-tributed among distinct Latino groups.

The boundaries of inclusion and exclusion with the Latino category, then, are remarkably elastic and contested. Indeed, much of the principal ana-lytical theorizing of Latinidad has relied upon a notion of Latino identity as a kind of "instrumental ethnicity," emphasizing the U.S. state's imposition of the Hispanic label and the deliberate subsequent deployment of symbolic markers and "cultural" commonalities for strategic political goals (cf. Jones-Correa 1998)....

If we dispense with any such culturalist essen-tialisms about the "content" within the infinitely manipulable boundaries of Latino "group" iden-tity, then, what indeed is the meaningful basis for such substantive commonalities between and among distinct Latino groups? This, finally, is the organizing question that unifies this collection thematically. Broadly speaking, the basis for such commonalities must be located in an analysis of the shared historicity of peoples throughout Latin America in relation to the colonial and imperialist projects of the U.S. nation-state, in concert with the concomitant historical as well as contemporary racializations of both Latin America, as a whole, and Latinos in the United States (González 2000). Such a perspective has the advantage of situating Latino commonalities within a broader transnational perspective that connects U.S. Latinidad to Latin American history and, more specifically, to the historical specificity of the U.S. nation-state's imperial projects in Latin America that have so commonly produced Latino migrations to the United States. The imperial history of the U.S. nation-states relations with Latin America has always been a preeminently political one, and moreover, an overtly racialized one. Indeed, any adequate theorization of Latino social formations in the United States demands a critical scrutiny of how the homogenizing racialized discourses of U.S. imperialism with respect to Latin America have been implicated in the organizing conceptual frameworks for the incorporation of U.S. Latinos as a generic and unitary "minority" group (Aparido and Chávez-Silverman 1997; Burnett and Marshall 2001; Saldívar 1991, 1997).

NOTES

1. For a Chicano perspective on Nixon's "Hispanic" strategy, see Acuña 2000:389; for a comparative discussion of the discrepant nationalisms of Chicanos and Puerto Ricans, see Klor de Alva 1989.
2. Whereas the notion of *Hispanidad* was actively promoted in the Americas during the 19th century by Liberal Spain (cf. Pike 1971), parallel ideological formulations of *Latinidad* can be similarly traced to Fiance's political ambitions in the Americas during the era of Napoleon III (see Davis 2000:13). In contrast, throughout the era of "Latin" American Independence struggles and thereafter, hemispheric internationalist formulations of Americanismo were explicitly juxtaposed to the Anglo-Saxonist usurpation of "American"-ness by the United States (see De la Campa 1999; Saldívar 1991), ranging from Simón Bolívar's contention in the late 1810's that "Para nosotros la patria es América" (Oboler 1995:181 n. 2; cf. Padilia 1990) to José Martí's formulation in 1891 of Nuestra América (1979; cf. Saldívar 1991), to the revitalization of Martí's hemispheric anti-imperialist vision by the Cuban Revolution of 1959, perhaps most forcefully articulated in the "Second Declaration of Havana" of February 4, 1962 (Casa de las Américas 1979:179–207), and reworked in Ernesto "Che" Guevara's Third Worldist "tricontinentalism" as a reconceptualization of "Nuestra América" as the Latin American "continent" (see Guevara 1987; cf. Fernandez Retamar 1976, 1981, 1989).

REFERENCES CITED

Acuña, Rodolfo 1996 Anything but Mexican: Chicanos in Contemporary Los Angeles. New York: Verso.

———. 2000 Occupied America: A History of Chicanos. 4th edition. New York: Harper and Row.

Aparicio, Frances R. 1996 On Sub-Versive Signifiers: Tropicalizing Language in the United States. *In* Tropicalizations: Transcultural Representations of Latinidad. Frances R. Aparicio and Susana Chávez-Silverman, eds. Pp. 194–212. Hanover, NH: Dartmouth College, University Press of New England.

Aparicio, Frances R., and Susana Chávez-Silverman 1997 Introduction. *In* Tropicalizations: Transcultural Representations of Latinidad. Frances R. Aparicio and Susana Chávez-Silverman, eds. Pp. 1–17. Hanover, NH: Dartmouth College, University Press of New England.

Burnett, Christina Duffy, and Burke Marshall, eds. 2001 Foreign in a Domestic Sense: Puerto Rico, American Expansion, and the Constitution. Durham: Duke University Press.

Casa de las Américas 1979 Three Documents of Our America. Havana: Casa de las Américas.

Dávila, Arlene M. 2001 Latinos, Inc.: The Marketing and Making of a People. Berkeley: University of California Press.

Davis, Mike 2000 Magical Urbanism: Latinos Reinvent the U.S. Big City. New York: Verso.

De la Campa, Román 1999 Latin Americanism. Minneapolis: University of Minnesota Press. Fernández Retamar, Roberto.

———. 1976 Nuestra América y Occidente. Casa de las Américas 98:3–57.

———. 1981 Caliban: Apuntos sobre la cultura en nuestra América. *In* Para el Perfil Definitivo del Hombre. Pp. 219–90. Havana: Editorial Letras Cubanas.

———. 1989 Caliban and Other Essays. Edward Baker, trans. Minneapolis: University of Minnesota Press.

Flores, Juan 2000 From Bomba to Hip-Hop: Puerto Rican Culture and Latino Identity. New York: Columbia University Press.

Flores, William V. and Rina Benmayor, eds. 1997 Latino Cultural Citizenship: Claiming Identity, Space, and Rights. Boston: Beacon Press.

Foley, Neil 1998 Becoming Hispanic: Mexican Americans and the Faustian Pact with Whiteness. *In* Reflexiones 1997: New Directions in Mexican American Studies. Neil Foley, ed. Pp. 53–70. Austin: Center for Mexican Amercan Studies Books, University of Texas at Austin.

González, Juan 2000 Harvest of Empire: A History of Latinos in America. New York: Viking; Penguin.

Guevara, Ernesto Che 1987 Che Guevara and the Cuban Revolution: Writings and Speeches of Ernesto Che Guevara. New York: Pathfinder Press.

Jones-Correa, Michael 1998 Between Two Nations: The Political Predicament of Latinos in New York City. Ithaca: Cornell University Press.

Jones-Correa, Michael, and David L. Leal 1996 Becoming "Hispanic": Secondary Panethnic Identification Among Latin American–Origin Populations in the United States. Hispanic Journal of Behavioral Sciences 18(2):214–254.

Klor de Alva, Jorge 1989 Aztlán, Borinquen and Hispanic Nationalism in the United States. *In* Aztlán: Essays on the Chicano Homeland. Rudolfo Anaya and Francisco Lomelf, eds. Pp. 135–171. Albuquerque: University of New Mexico Press.

Martí, José 1979[1891] Nuestra América. *In* Three Documents of Our America. Havana: Casa de las Americas.

Oboler, Suzanne 1955 Ethnic Labels, Latino Lives: Identity and the Politics of (Re)Presentation in the United States. Minneapolis: University of Minnesota Press.

Omi, Michael, and Howard Winant 1986 Racial Formation in the United States: From the 1960s to the 1980s. New York: Routledge.

Padilla, Felix M. 1985 Latino Ethnic Consciousness: The Case of Mexican Americans and Puerto Ricans in Chicago. Notre Dame: University of Notre Dame Press.

———. 1990 Latin America: The Historical Basis of Latino Unity. Latino Studies Journal 1(1):7–27.

Pike, Frederick B. 1971 Hispanismo, 1898–1936: Spanish Conservatives and Liberals and Their Relations with Spanish America. Notre Dame: University of Notre Dame Press.

Rodríguez, América 1998 Racialization, Language, and Class in the Construction and Sale of the Hispanic Audience. *In* Reflexiones 1997: New Directions in Mexican American Studies. Neil Foley, ed. Pp. 29–52. Austin: Center for Mexican American Studies Books, University of Texas at Austin.

Rosaldo, Renato 1994 Cultural Citizenship and Educational Democracy. Cultural Anthropology 9(3):402–411.

Rosaldo, Renato, and William V. Flores 1997 Cultural Citizenship, Inequality, and Multiculturalism. *In* Latino Cultural Citizenship: Claiming Identity, Space, and Rights. William V. Flores and Rina Benmayor, eds. Pp. 27–38. Boston: Beacon Press.

Saldívar, José David 1991 The Dialectics of Our America: Genealogy, Cultural Critique, and Literary History Durham: Duke University Press.

———. 1997 Border Matters: Remapping American Cultural Studies. Berkeley: University of California Press.

JOURNALING QUESTION

Do you or your family have a language other than English? If you do, what connections do you feel to others who speak that language? How could you organize politically around that connection? If you don't speak another language, how does that shape your friendship networks and understandings of the world?

PART

RACIAL THINKING

Essentialism

4.
SEX AND CONQUEST

Domination and Desire on Ethnosexual Frontiers

JOANE NAGEL

One of the clearest places we see ideas of racial essentialism is in images of sexuality, where racialized others are understood as animals, pure creatures of sex. This imagery is dramatically clear in the history of what were called the "savages," the native people of the Americas. Joane Nagel shows how the sexual conquest of the native people went hand in hand with the conquest of the native land by European explorers. Further, she shows how the "winning of the west" was a racial project that continues in the contemporary imagination, shaping not only ideas about the Indians but ideas about white masculinity as well. Without the history of this racial project, how might contemporary images of masculinity be different?

SEX AND CONQUEST: THE WINNING OF THE U.S. WEST

Early European travelers who followed Columbus and Vespucci wrote home describing native men and women as primitive and promiscuous. In his history of the "white man's Indian," Robert Berkhofer reports that the first English language publication about the new world reflected this view:

> These folke lyven lyke bestes without any reson-ablenes and the wymen be also as common. And the men hath conversacyon with the wymen/ who that they ben or who they fyrst mete/ is she his syster/ his mother/ his daughter/ or any other kyndred. And the wymen be very hoote and dysposed to lecherdnes.[1]

As Berkhofer notes, the new printing press circulated this and similar sensational and graphic reports (this one translated from an early-sixteenth-century Dutch pamphlet) across Europe, and, despite the morally indignant tone of the text, the floodgates opened as Europeans eager to settle this sexually savage, brave New World swarmed across the Atlantic. Certainly these and later lurid accounts of Indian sexual practices and availability held a certain allure to the mostly male European emigrants.

Scholars question the biases and agendas of many European reports about indigenous peoples since they served as justifications for colonial and later American policies of annihilation, "pacification," civilization, and assimilation of Indian

---

Excerpted from Joane Nagel, "Sex and Conquest: Domination and Desire on Ethnosexual Frontiers," in *Race, Ethnicity, and Sexuality: Intimate Intersections, Forbidden Frontiers* (New York: Oxford University Press, 2003), 63–90. Notes have been renumbered and edited.

populations.[2] Given the loaded nature of sexual matters, sexual descriptions had a special capacity to impress readers and to shape powerful and lasting images of native America. These early sexualized depictions of native peoples combined with those of later colonial and American chroniclers to form a general portrait of "Indian life" as morally and culturally inferior to European and American societies, though still of much interest to writers and their readers.

While the motives of the whites may have been transparent, what remains unclear is the meaning of these sexual exchanges to the Arikaras or the Clatsops or the Chinooks or the Pueblos. What were these indigenous people thinking when they crossed sexual boundaries; what were the frames of mind and state of affairs on Indian-white ethnosexual frontiers? Ronda provides a clue to solving the mentalities and motivations of various sides in ethnosexual exchanges on the U.S. frontier. It was not only whites with whom native people sought contact. Ronda comments that York, the enslaved African who accompanied his owner, William Clark, was a central attraction of the Lewis and Clark expedition...York's blackness was viewed by the Arikaras as a sign of special spiritual power... To have sexual contact with York was to get in touch with what seemed awesome spirit forces.[3]

It is important to remember that there are many different frontiers scattered across the time and space being discussed here—different peoples, different eras, different locales, and many different conditions facing native peoples and settler populations. In light of such diversity scholars provide a number of accounts of Indian-white sexual encounters. Ronda offers four reasons why Indians might have been willing to enter into sexual exchanges with white travelers in the early nineteenth century: to trade for European goods (ironware, paint, cloth), to forge commercial links (sealed by sexual relations), to express native hospitality, especially on the plains, and as noted above, to obtain whatever

spiritual power non-Indians might possess.[4] Albert Hurtado confirms these several agendas, but he paints a less sanguine portrait of freely given Indian sexual favors. Once again acknowledging wide variation across indigenous communities, conditions, times, and places, Hurtado points out the relative powerlessness of many native women, and reports that sexual exchanges often were coerced, involving rape, forced prostitution, and slavery.[5] Hurtado and Ronda tell a similar story of sexuality and slavery about one of the best known Indian women in history, Sacagawea:

> Sometime in the fall of 1800, the young Lemhi Shoshoni girl, then perhaps twelve or thirteen years old, was camped at the Three Forks of the Missouri with others from her band...the party at Three Forks was attacked by Hidatsa raiders.... Among the prisoners taken were four boys and several women, including Sacagawea. Sometime between 1800 and 1804, she and one other Shoshoni captive were purchased by Toussaint Charbonneau, a trader.... When Lewis and Clark met Charbonneau at Fort Mandan on November 4, 1804.... Sacagawea was already pregnant.[6]

The fact that Sacagawea, a Shoshone teenager, was purchased and then impregnated by Charbonneau, a French trader, was sanitized in subsequent references to her by Lewis and Clark and others as Charbonneau's "wife." This normalized definition of Sacagawea as a willing wife and mother has become an enduring part of the American national narrative, one that was engraved on a U.S. one dollar coin in 2000.

The relationship between Sacagawea and Charbonneau represents one point of contact in the complicated network of ethnosexual frontiers that crisscrossed what Rebecca Faery refers to as the New World's "cartographies of desire."

> The desire of the colonizers for land was conflated with desire for a Native woman who was a representative or stand-in for the land itself; likewise, the effort to "protect" white women from the presumed desire of dark

men, both Indian and African, was a coded insistence on the rights of the colonists to territory already taken or not yet taken but desired. The history of Anglo-America, then, is a map of confluent desires, sexual and territorial, that over time produced and consolidated the map of America as we know it today.[7]

The rape of Indian women often precipitated Indian-white conflicts, particularly during the Gold Rush, when, according to Hurtado, rapes by whites were widespread and sometimes enacted by federal officials themselves on reservations, where native women were attacked "before the very eyes of their husbands and daughters...and they dare[d] not resent the insult, or even complain of the hideous outrage.[8] This sympathetic portrayal of native victims of white sexual assault appeared in an 1856 San Francisco newspaper, but such sympathy was the exception, rather than the rule.

There were many far more critical reports in American media about native life and sexuality, often popularized in the form of Indian captivity narratives where whites were the targets of Indian aggression.[9] Captivity narratives were among the first popular publications written in the new world. Analysts have divided them into several categories. Richard Van Der Beets and Richard Slotkin both describe early captivity narratives, whether based in fact or not, as religious allegories in which white captives undergo redemptive suffering at the hands of Indians and find a path back to godliness upon their return to Christian civilization.[10] Roy Pearce and Rebecca Faery add to this list a political propaganda form of captivity narrative designed to defame either the French or, mainly, the Indians by dramatizing their excesses of brutality, lust, and savagery. These captivity narratives were put to use "making a history, shaping a nation," and fashioning a "'suitable' national history and identity, one that placed whiteness and masculinity in a superior position to other categories of identity."[11]

A number of analysts identify a third, and probably the most prolific type of captivity narrative—the "penny" or "dime" novel. Like all literature,

fictional captivity narratives reflected the customs and assumptions of the times, and since many readers were interested in the tales told by women captives, scholars have read the narratives as morality plays about the proper and improper place of women in American colonial and national society depending on the era in which the narrative was written and edited. Examples of popular nineteenth-century novels featuring women captives include James Fenimore Cooper's *The Last of the Mohicans*. The familiarity of the title of this 1826 novel to contemporary Americans is evidence of the enduring popularity of tales of early American gender, sexuality, and ethnicity.[12]

THERE'S A METHOD IN THEIR IMAGININGS

Aside from any erotic imaginings [13] aroused by captivity narratives or passions kindled by opportunities for ethnosexual adventures in Indian-white encounters, questions arise: To what uses were put these centuries of sexualized depictions of Indians? What were the social, political, economic, and policy consequences of these many uncomplimentary sexual descriptions of Indians as wanton savages and brutal rapists? How important were depictions of the sexuality of native men and women in defining the boundary between non-Indians and Indians, savage and civilized, noncitizen and citizen?

Certainly the portrayal of Indians as sexually dangerous was a convenient justification for warfare against native societies and for "removing" Indians from areas chosen by whites for settlement. Sherry Smith notes that although no army officer's wife ever was captured by Indians many of those women wrote about the terrors of captivity:

Woe to the hapless party that fell into the devilish hands of a band of Indians!...Babies had their brains dashed out before the eyes of father and mother, powerless to help them. Lucky would the latter have been, had they been treated in the same way; but what she was to endure would have wrung tears from anything but an Indian.[14]

Smith reports, for instance, that Elizabeth Custer, the wife of George Armstrong Custer, "seemed particularly fascinated by the topic" of the fate of white women taken by Indians, and she quotes Mrs. Custer's conclusion that "death would be merciful in comparison."[15] The images and messages constained in comments like these about Indian sexual threats were powerful justifications for eliminating the "Indian problem" by any means necessary.[16]

The sexual observations about native people made by explorers, missionaries, soldiers, traders, settlers, and reformers were not simply prurient preoccupations or voyeuristic reports, though no doubt they served those masters as well. Sexualized depictions of and beliefs about native peoples became part of the imagining of the U.S. West. Real or putative sexual differences between whites and Indians provided a rationale for seizing native resources to "better" manage and use them, and allowed U.S. political and economic interests to paper over their exploitations by launching programs to "improve" Indian individuals and cultures by civilizing and assimilating American Indians.

Reports of Indian depredations and savagery also became a means of jusitifying white misbehavior and atrocities and provided ample opportunities for white self-aggrandizement. Smith reports that frontier soldiers often described Indian men as skilled warriors, in part to explain a defeat or because "a successful campaign against a formidable foe rather than a weak one could enhance a soldier's reputation back home."[17] The defeat of a strong native opponent also would guarantee continued support for a frontier military presence, a military that sometimes kept itself busy in less than glorious pursuits. Military massacres of Indian women and children were defended by demonizing native women, thus these women whom soldiers sometimes sought as sex partners could be refashioned into suitable adversaries by resexing them as men: "[n]ot a gleam of pity entered her feminine breast. She was a cold-blooded, thirsty vulture, only intent upon her prey, as good as the warrior himself.[18]

Another clue to the usefulness of sexualized images of Indians can be found in the labels and meanings assigned to the whites who openly consorted with Indians. From the earliest days of European colonialism well into the nineteenth century, whites who crossed ethnosexual boundaries into Indian country too often or who lingered too long ran the risk of being morally and ethnically redefined. White men who were thought to have too much intimate association with native cultures, and especially with native women, were suspected of disloyalty in native-white conflicts. For instance, one William Baker, a white man who was reported to "Speake much Indian" and to have "turned Indian in nakednes and cutting of haire, and after many whoredomes, is there maried," was believed to have fought alongside the Pequots during the colonial-Pequot war of 1636. The next year authorities used Baker's sexual liaisons against him, and Connecticut officials tried to arrest him "for uncleanness with an Indian squaw, who is now with child by him."[19] Ann Marie Plane describes intimacies between natives and English settlers in colonial New England and catalogs a number of intermarriages and long-term extramarital unions between Christianized Indians and colonists. She notes, however, the tenuous nature of these arrangements, and concludes that native-white conflicts "may have made the official sanctioning of interracial unions virtually unthinkable."[20]

After U.S. independence, white men who consorted with Indian women were seen less as threats to white security than as risks to white morality. Smith comments that "many nineteenth-century men maintained, at least in public statements, that sexual relations with Indian women degraded white men."[21] This was despite widespread sexual contact between native women and male officers and soldiers stationed out west. A good deal of such ethnosexual adventuring no doubt was overlooked, but John D'Emilio and Estelle Freedman report that more enduring Indian-white sexual liaisons, including marriage, were viewed by some whites as a "shame and disgrace to our country."[22] This view was consistent with the negative descriptions of so-called squaw men, white men (often French traders) who lived with Indian women or took Indian wives, and who were sometimes accused by observers of exploiting their relationship with these women's tribes for their own economic gain. For instance, in his 1883 book, *Our Wild Indians*, frontier veteran Colonel Richard Irving Dodge distinguished between pioneering white trappers or traders who married Indian women and the "squaw-men" who "went native," living with their wives' tribes and sending "their squaws to draw rations, buying and selling the same and, even worse, engaging in the clandestine sale of guns and liquor to their native hosts...and [having] no compunction whatever about abandoning their families."[23] The denigration of whites residing on the native side of the Indian-white ethnic boundary reinforced stereotypes of indigenous sexual and social disreputability and made their mistreatment easier to overlook.

By the beginning of the twentieth century, Indians had been confined to reservations, their economies destroyed, and their lands allotted; native children were undergoing forced acculturation in boarding schools with English-only policies, Christian indoctrination, and training in proper [white] moral, gender, and sexual behavior.[24] As the decades progressed, reservation communities were colonized by the creation of federally linked tribal governments, and programs were designed to eliminate reservations altogether by relocating native people into the cities. The goal of late-nineteenth and early-twentieth-century Indian policy was to dismantle the Indian/non-Indian ethnic boundary and absorb natives into the American "mainstream." Real Indians were to be relegated to history, and the imagined Indian was transformed in whites' minds, if not in native realities, from a hypersexualized savage into a tamed domestic put in service to the American national project. America could now use this new, improved, safely resexualized, and thus truly noble savage to refashion its own image of itself.

WHITE SKIN, AND RED MASKS

Gender and sexuality played roles not only in whites' imaginings of Indians, but, in a strange twist of cultural history, Indian sexuality and native masculinity also played a role in whites' imaginings of themselves. There is an other side to sex and conquest that involves not white men and native women or white women and native men; it involves only men—red and white. This installment in the American chronicle of sex and conquest centers the construction of U.S. nationalism and American manhood out of the ruins and stolen remnants of native nations and masculinities.

White men's attraction to native masculine virility has a long history stretching back to the early days of the American Republic and reaching forward into the present. In *Playing Indian*, Philip Deloria documents that throughout U.S. history Americans, mainly white men, have dressed up and acted in ways they imagined to be Indian. He cites, for instance, the 1773 Boston Tea Party, when white colonists donned costumes and makeup to simulate Mohawks;[25] their "Indian" antics were partly to disguise their identities and partly to intimidate their opponents with feigned Iroquois confederacy fierceness. Whites used native symbolism and simulated "Indian" ceremonies to create solidarity and community in men's fraternal organizations and private clubs such as the nineteenth-century. Improved Order of Red Men or the League of the Iroquois,[26] and "the Indian"[27] had a central place in youth organizations designed to build American character and citizenship, such as the Boy Scouts and the Woodcraft Indians.[28] Contemporary Indian play can be witnessed by even the most casual observer today in football stadiums and baseball parks where fans wear "war paint," do "war dances," chant "war songs," and make "Indian" gestures such as "tomahawk chops."[29]

The large-scale appropriation of Indianness, in particular the consumption of Indian virility and potency by mainly white men, began at the turn of the twentieth century when two social trends converged in the United States: the defeat of native nations followed by their internment on reservations and a crisis of confidence in American masculinity as the country moved from an agricultural, rural economy to an urban, industrial society. According to historians, in the late nineteenth century American manhood had lost its moorings.[30] Southern men, despite their tradition of military service and honor, had lost the Civil War to a North whose men they perceived as feminized and weak.[31] Northern white men faced a variety of challenges in the increasingly urban landscapes where they worked and lived: immigrants with their cheap labor and political machines, monopolistic capitalist trusts that controlled wages and prices, boom and bust cycles associated with the unregulated U.S. economy, and women with their demands for political rights and economic opportunities.[32]

Scholars argue that these social, economic, and political changes destabilized American men's sense of independence and efficacy and challenged the historical vision of American strength, adventurousness, and virility.[33] This vision and the challenges it confronted were articulated in 1883 when Frederick Jackson Turner proclaimed the closing of the U.S. frontier and the end of the American frontier spirit. Turner's diagnosis of what was troubling America and his gloomy prognosis about the poor national health of post-frontier America set in motion a search for a tonic to restore American national vision and virility.[34] One place Americans looked, especially American men, for a source of renewal was to the symbol of the frontier—"the Indian," who was now conveniently imprisoned and emasculated on reservations—the better to pose no real threat to the weakened Americans.

Although Indians were thus out of sight (and their total disappearance constantly predicted), they were not out of the minds of Americans. Then as now, the Indian appeared in stories told to a mass public, not only in dime novels and captivity narratives, but also in Wild West shows and early films.[35] Through these endeavors, Americans reinvented and sanitized the Indian to appeal to popular audiences and to serve nostalgic reconstructions of America's frontier days. Whites also used the Indian to reimagine and rebuild American masculinity into an iconic form that has survived into the present.

The contemporary metal of U.S. national manhood was forged out of the collision of native and nonnative masculinities in the country's first major nationalist imperialist project: Manifest Destiny—a vision and set of policies that designed and justified westward expansion as an inalienable right of America and Americans. The westward expansion of the boundaries of the United States at the expense of indigenous individuals and nations is inscribed in American popular culture and popular histories as a series of military events.[36] Colonial images of the Indian warrior in these military encounters were presented first in newspaper accounts, periodicals, and lectures, and later in books, theater, film, and television.[37] Countless scenes in popular media showed brave U.S. frontier soldiers confronting and conquering dangerous but endangered Indian men. The Indians were seen to be clinging to an archaic way of life, making their last desperate, but doomed stand against the superior and inevitable march of civilization across a modernizing western American landscape. The only good Indian was *not* a dead Indian, but rather a subjugated and sanitized Indian—an Indian that could be conquered repeatedly in white men's Indian play.

The Indian wars are not over. Nor has the boundary disappeared between the Indians and non-Indians who populate the Americas of past and present. Romanticized, sexualized natives still inhabit the imaginations of Americans and continue to haunt Americans' images of themselves.

Indians can be found in the same social texts and contexts in which they were captured in the eighteenth and nineteenth centuries, not only on athletic fields or in romantic and adventure fiction, but in anthropology and history…and sociology, in photography, television, and film, in national parks and monuments, in the contemporary men's movement, in countless commercial and cultural spaces such as coffeetable picture books, print and visual vertisements, coins, art, music, holiday pageants and celebrations, and in clubs, websites, societies, and organizations symbolically and institutionally designed to constitute and enact America and Americanness.

I invite readers to take a walk down the book aisle in any American discount store, supermarket, or bookstore and to look at the covers of romance novels. There you will find "the Indian" memorialized in depictions of long-haired, bare-chested muscular dark and handsome men with lovely, lithe some white women swooning in their arms…further stroll down the aisle to the "true story" adventure novels with their powerful, Indianized white (or "half-breed") men confronting the feminized forces of repression and threats to their rugged individualism, manly autonomy, and inalienable right to freedom: the *Rambos* and *Billy Jacks* of contemporary American adventure fiction and film. In both women's romance and men's adventure fiction, the prominence of sexualized, gendered native images embracing the bodies of white women and worn on the faces of white men, show us that the Indian-white ethnosexual frontier remains an open chapter in the ongoing saga of American culture and identity.

CONCLUSION

This chapter has examined the links between sex and conquest, the role of sexuality in the construction of an enduring ethnic boundary between Indians and non-Indians, and how the sexualization of indigenous peoples has shaped the views of Americans and served the interests of colonial and American governments. The American settling of the U.S. West was not only an epic of competitive positioning by colonial powers, conflicts with indigenous peoples, and spreading settler populations across the continent. The "conquest of the West" involved a series of sexualized encounters between Europeans and Indians that reflected a confrontation of sexualities and sexual systems. This clash of sexualities was an important feature in the development of ideologies that defined each group and the construction of ethnic boundaries that divided them. Definitions of sexual morality distinguished "civilized" Europeans and Americans on the one hand from "savage" Indians on the other.

European colonizers and settlers of the New World had both a practical and prurient interest in the native population—as slaves, guides, emissaries, and sexual partners. Euro-American exploitation of the New World's land and inhabitants was a hallmark of the conquest of the Americas. The settlers who followed in the wake of the early adventurers saw the new land and its peoples through the same set of lenses, and they were driven to satisfy the same kinds of desires. The New World was an exotic and erotic landscape, an imaginary land of milk and honey that lingered in the minds of Europeans throughout the period of colonial settlement and into the era of sovereign state formation on both American continents.

In the United States the vision of America as a place to be colonized and conquered became a central theme in national self-imagining and nation building. The early European explorers' image of themselves as morally superior, benevolent, and called upon to civilize as well as consume the New World was inscribed on the American national identity and institutionalized in the American national state. America's expansionist moral mission grew from the seeds planted at the point of European contact, blossomed into late-nineteenth and early-twentieth-century U.S. imperial control of both continents and regions of the Pacific, and matured into an established perennial American power that has thrived in and dominated the global environment. As the United States has matured from a commercial and political upstart into a mature mercantile and military power, the image of "the Indian" endures as a signifier both of American conquest and the indomitable American spirit.

NOTES

1. Robert F. Berkhofer Jr., *The White Man's Indian: Images of the American Indian from Columbus to the Present* (New York: Alfred A. Knopf, 1978), 9–10.
2. See Stodola Derounian-Stodola, Kathryn Zabelle, and James A. Levernier, *The Indian Captivity Narrative, 1550–1900.* (Ner York: Twayne, 1993); Berkhofer, *The White Man's Indian*; Kathleen M. Brown, *Good Wives, Nasty Wenches; and Anxious Patriarchs: Gender, Race, and Power in Colonial Virginia* (Chapel Hill: Published for the Institute of Early American History and Culture by the University of North Carolina Press, 1997); and "Brave New Worlds: Women's and Gender History," *Willam and Mary Quarterly* 50 (1993): 311–28.
3. James Ronda, *Lewis and Clark among the Indians* (Lincoln: University of Nebraska Press, 1984), 64.
4. Ibid., 63; see also Kirsten Fischer, *Suspect Relations: Sex, Race, and Resistance in Colonial North Carolina* (Ithaca: Cornell University Press, 2002), especially chapter 2.
5. Albert Hurtado, "When Strangers Met: Sex and Gender on Three Frontiers," in *Writing the Range: Race, Class, and Culture in the Women's West*, ed. Elizabeth Jameson and Susan Armitage (Norman: University of Oklahoma Press, 1997), 122–42; see also Sylvia Van Kirk, "The Role of Native Women in the Creation of Fur Trade Society in Western Canada, 1670–1830," in *The Women's West*, ed. Susan Armitage and Elizabeth Jameson (Norman: University of Oklahoma Press, 1987), 53–62; Patricia Limerick, *The Legacy of Conquest: The Unbroken Past of the American West* (New York: W.W. Norton & Company, 1987), 50ff; Anne M. Butler, *Daughters of Joy, Sisters of Misery: Prostitutes in the American West, 1865–90* (Urbana: University of Illinois Press, 1987), 9ff.
6. Ronda, *Lewis and Clark among the Indians*, 256.
7. Rebecca Blevins Faery, *Cartographies of Desire: Captivity, Race, and Sex in the Shaping of an American Nation* (Norman: University of Oklahoma Press, 1999).
8. Hurtado, "When Strangers Met," 135.
9. For one of the most complete sets of Indian captivity narratives, see *Garland Library of Narratives of North American Indian Captivities*, vols. 1–111 (New York: Garland Publications, 1977).
10. Richard van der Beets, *Held Captive by Indians: Selected Narratives, 1642–1836* (Knoxville: University of Tennessee Press, 1974); Richard Slotkin, *Regeneration through Violence: The Mythology of the American Frontier, 1600–1860* (Middletown, CT: Wesleyan University Press, 1973).
11. Faery, *Cartographies of Desire*, 15; Roy Harvey Pearce, "The Significance of the Captivity Narrative," *American Literature* 19 (1947): 1–20.
12. Especially since film versions are currently available on videotape and DVD; Renee Berland examines the imagined relationships between white women and native men in two novels, *The Last of the Mohicans* and Lydia Marie Child's *Hobomok*; she argues that Childs's tale of an eroticized, romantic encounter between a young Wampanoag man and Mary Conant, a

young woman settler, depicts white women as active agents, whereas Cooper's women, Alice and Cora Munro, are more passive and more victimized when they become romantically involved with and are assaulted by native men:

> By the end of the book [*The Last of the Mohicans*] Cora is actually dead, and described as the ghostly bride of an Indian, "transplanted … to a place where she would find congenial spirits, and be forever happy." Alice is invisible, borne away within a litter "when low and stifled sobs alone announced [her] presence." *Hobomok*, on the other hand, allows Mary Conant to transcend her spectrality, and leave behind her angelic purity. She marries Hobomok and gives birth to a son. Later, she divorces him, keeping custody of their child and retaining her own wealth. Her own possession of her body is affirmed when she goes on to marry again.

In both novels, native men simultaneously are sources of white fear and objects of white desire, and in both novels the women pay with their lives (at least once) for acting on their ethnosexual desires; Renee L. Berland, *The National Uncanny: Indian Ghosts and American Subjects* (Hanover: Dartmouth College, 2000), 65. Christopher Castiglia contrasts "typical" popular captivity narratives marked by "savage Indian tormentors and women captives who rely for rescue on [white] masculine financial or military agency," with more nontraditional forms in which

> narrative patterns question the structures the stories elsewhere support, signaling discursive conflicts *within* white culture…[where] the captive either fights the Indians in order to avoid capture, or, once captured, uses her own strengths to escape…[or where captives] either refuse to return to Anglo-American culture or make clear that their lives among the Indians were no worse than among whites. (Christopher Castiglia, *Bound and Determined: Captivity, Culture-Crossing, and White Womanhood from Mary Rowlandson to Patty Hearst* [Chicago: University of Chicago Press, 1996], 25).

13. The next two sections of this chapter are based on collaborative work with David Anthony Tyeeme Clark; I wish to thank Tony for introducing me to recent feminist scholarship on the U.S. West and for sharing with me his creative adventurous work recovering native voices and challenging conventional views of "the Indian" in scholarship and in the American imagination; see David Anthony Tyeeme Clark and Joane Nagel, "White Men, Red Masks: Appropriations of 'Indian' Manhood in Imagined Wests," in *Across the Great Divide: Cultures of Manhood in the American West*, ed. Matthew L. Basso, Dee Garceau, and Laura McCall (New York: Routledge, 2000), 109–30.

14. Sherry L. Smith, *The View from Officers' Row: Army Perceptions of Western Indians* (Tueson: University of Arizona Press, 1990), 18.

15. Ibid., see also Shirley A. Leckie, *Elizabeth Bacon Custer and the Making of a Myth* (Norman: University of Oklahoma Press, 1993).

16. See Russell Thornton, *American Indian Holocaust and Survival* (Norman: University of Oklahoma Press, 1987).

17. Smith, *The View from Officers' Row*, 148.

18. Ibid., 68.

19. Ibid.

20. Ann Marie Plane, *Colonial Intimacies: Indian Marriage in Early New England* (Ithaca: Cornell University Press, 2000), 37.

21. Ibid., 70.

22. John D'Emilio and Estelle B. Freedman, *Intimate Matters: A History of Sexuality in America* (New York: Harper and Row, 1988), 88.

23. Quoted by David D. Smits, "'Squaw Men,' 'Half-Breeds,' and Amalgamators: Late Nineteenth-Century Anglo-American Attitudes toward Indian-White Race Mixing," *American Indian Culture and Research Journal* 15 (1991): 29–61, 39; see Richard Irving Dodge, *Our Wild Indians: Thirty-three Years Personal Experience among the Red Men of the Great West* (New York: Archer House; Inc., [1883] 1959).

24. For a discussion of religious schools' efforts to inculcate "proper" sexual and gender demeanor, see Theda Perdue, *Cherokee Women: Gender and Cultural Change, 1700–1835* (Lincoln: University of Nebraska Press, 1998).

25. Philip Joseph Deloria, *Playing Indian* (New Haven: Yale University Press, 1999).

26. See Mark C. Carnes, *Secret Ritual and Manhood in Victorian America* (New Haven: Yale University Press, 1989).

27. The notion of "the Indian" is borrowed from the work of Gerald Vizenor, in particular, *Fugitive Poses: Native American Indian Scenes of Absence and Presence* (Lincoln: University of Nebraska Press, 1998).

28. See Jeffrey P. Hantover, "The Boy Scouts and the Validation of Masculinity," in *Men's Lives*, 74–81. 5th ed., Michael S. Kimmel and Michael A. Messner, (Boston, MA, Allyn and Bacon. 2000).

29. For a discussion of Indian sports mascots, see C. Richard King and Charles F. Springwood, *Team Spirits: The Native American Mascot Controversy* (Lincoln: University of Nebraska Press, 2001) and "Fighting Spirits: The Racial Politics of Sports Mascots," *Journal of Sport and Social Issues* 24 (2000): 282–304.

30. This concern over declining masculinity was shared by Europeans. Lieutenant General Robert Baden-Powell, founder of the Boy Scout Movement in England and author of *Scouting for Boys*, published in 1908, saw scouting as a way to bolster weakening English manhood; see Robert H. MacDonald, *Sons of the Empire: The Frontier and the Boy Scout Movement, 1890–1918* (Toronto: University of Toronto Press, 1993), 18; see also Alan Trachtenberg, *The Incorporation of America: Culture and Society in the Guilded Age* (New York: Hill and Wang, 1982); Michael S. Kimmel, *Manhood in America* (New York: The Free Press, 1996); Joe L. Dubbert, "Progressivism and the Masculinity Crisis," in *The American Man*, ed. Elizabeth H. Pleck and Joseph H. Pleck (Englewood Cliffs, NJ: Prentice-Hall, 1980); Peter G. Filene, *Him/Her/Self: Sex Roles in Modern America* (Baltimore: Johns Hopkins University Press, 1986), 69–93; E. Anthony Rotundo, *American Manhood: Transformations in Masculinity from the Revolution to the Modern Era* (New York: Basic Books, 1993), 185–93.

31. Nina Silber, *The Romance of Reunion: Northerners and the South, 1986–1900* (Chapel Hill: University of North Carolina Press, 1993).

32. For instance, Jeffrey Hantover argues that in the growing white middle class,

    the professionalization and sanctification of motherhood, the smaller family size, the decline in the number of servants who could serve as buffers between mother and son, and the absence of busy fathers from the home made the mother-son relationship appear threatening to proper masculine socialization. ("The Boy Scouts and the Validation of Masculinity," 75).

33. See Gail Bederman, *Manliness and Civilization: A Cultural History of Gender and Race in the United States, 1880–1917* (Chicago: University of Chicago Press, 1995); John Higham, "The

Reorientation of American Culture in the 1890s," in his *Writing American History: Essays on Modern Scholarship* (Bloomington: Indiana University Press, 1978), 78–102; James R. McGovern, "David Graham Phillips and the Virility Impulse of the Progressives," *New England Quarterly* 39 (1966): 334–55.

34. Frederick Jackson Turner, "The Significance of the Frontier in American History," *Annual Report of the American Historical Association for the Year 1893* (Washington, DC: U.S. Government Printing Office, 1894).

35. See Sara J. Blackstone, *Buckskins, Bullets, and Business: A History of Buffalo Bill's Wild West* (New York: Greenwood Press, 1986); Raymond William Stedman, *Shadows of the Indian: Stereotypes in American Culture* (Norman: University of Oklahoma Press, 1982); Berkhofer, *The White Man's Indian*.

36. For an account of the so-called Indian wars as a defensive struggle, see Ward Churchill, "The 'Trial' of Leonard Peltier," preface to Jim Messerscmidt, *The Trial of Leonard Peltier* (Boston: South End Press, 1983).

37. Such images have been seen in Hollywood productions since the earliest days of cinema; for discussions of depictions of the Indian in American popular film, see Peter C. Rollins and John E. O'Connor, eds., *Hollywood's Indian: The Portrayal of the Native American in Film* (Lexington: University Press of Kentucky, 1998); Donald L. Kaufman, "The Indian as Media Hand-Me-Down," in *The Pretend Indians: Images of Native Americans in the Movies*, ed. Gretchen M. Bataille and Charles L.P. Silet (Ames: Iowa State University Press, 1980), 22–34; Alison Griffiths, "Science and Spectacle: Native American Representation in Early Cinema," in *Dressing in Feathers: The Construction of the Indian in American Popular Culture*, ed. S. Elizabeth Bird (Boulder: Westview Press, 1996), 79–95.

JOURNALING QUESTION

Where today do you see representations of white masculinity as conquerors? How has that image changed since the nineteenth century?

5.
THE "BATTY" POLITIC
Toward an Aesthetic of the Black Female Body

JANELL HOBSON

While racial essentialism sometimes focuses on the sexual abandonment and availability of the other, it can also label racialized others as grotesque, beyond the scope of sexual attractiveness. Hobson offers the sad history of the "Hottentot Venus," a young woman exhibited as a "freak" or curiosity, and the lingering consequences of that image in Western imagination. In her complete article, she examines contemporary photography's uses of black bodies; in this excerpt, she focuses on the way a contemporary dance troupe of black women riffs off of this history to create an image of resistance. How do images of race, and raced images of gender, enter into our own minds, shaping our feelings about our own and other(ed) bodies?

INTRODUCTION

When tennis champion Serena Williams, days: before winning the 2002 U. S. Open; appeared on the courts, in a Black spandex suit, media frenzy ensued. Her black female body, adorned in all its "ghetto" glamour—bleached-blonde braids and a tight-fitting, suit that outlined the contours of her posterior, among other things—managed to disrupt (literally and figuratively) the elitist game of tennis. Williams, who defended herself by stating that she wanted to wear something "comfortable" as she moved around the tennis court, was nonetheless attacked in the press for her "tackiness" and "inappropriate" display of sexuality.

This seemingly exaggerated response to William's choice of sportswear reveals an anxiety that is best understood within a larger historical context of attitudes toward the exhibition of the black female body. This history—a history of enslavement, colonial conquest and ethnographic exhibition—variously labeled the black female body "grotesque," "strange," "unfeminine," "lascivious,"

"obscene." This negative attitude toward the black female body targets one aspect of the body in particular: the buttocks. Popular exhibitions in the nineteenth century, for example, displayed a South African woman, known as the "Hottentot Venus," for this "strange" singular attraction. Similarly, the attention to and criticisms of Serena Williams's body, alluded to above, call unabashed attention to her generously-sized backside, thus inviting comments such that sexiness was "lewd" and "obscene."

As this brief discussion of Williams suggests, the meaning assigned to this aspect of the black female body has a long and complex history, a history worthy of further investigation. Subsequently, this essay analyze the prevalent treatment of black female bodies as grotesque figures, due to the problematic fetishism of their rear ends, and consider how an aesthetic based on a black feminist praxis might offer a different way of treating the representation of black female sexuality. In what follows, then, I first revisit the history of the Hottentot Venus, whose

Excerpted from Janell Hobson, "The 'Batty' Politic: Toward an Aesthetic of the Black Female Body," Hypatia 18 2003: 87–105. Notes have been renumbered and edited.

derriere shaped prevalent ideas of black female deviance and hypersexuality. Second, I examine discourses of sexual desire for the black female backside and how this desire frames the body in terms of sexual grotesquerie while reinforcing aesthetic values that exclude black women from categories of beauty. Third, I analyze how a few black feminist artists—namely photographers Carla Williams and Coreen Simpson—struggle to represent black female bodies differently. Finally, I consider the role of dance and performance, through the example of the dance troupe Urban Bush Women, in repositioning the black female body—specifically the "batty," or rear end—as a site of beauty and of resistance.

THE HOTTENTOT VENUS REVISITED

Perhaps no other figure epitomizes the connections between grotesquerie, sexual deviance, and posteriors than the "Hottentot Venus." *Saartjie* Baartman, the first in a line of South African women exhibited, was brought to London in 1810. It is quite possible that other South African women followed in this trajectory, since Hottenntot Venus exhibitions continued well after Baartman's death in 1816 (Gilman 1985, 88; Edwards and Walvin 1983, 181–82). Baartman was put on display, first by Dutch exhibitor Hendrik Cezar, as a mythical and "strange" shaped "Hottentot" a display framed by a history of colonial domination. From the little that we know of her history, Baartman was a Khoisan captive from the colonial Cape of South Africa.[1] She may have been separated from her family—including her parents and husband—during warfare between the Dutch and the indigenous population, and was forced to labor as a servant for a Boer farmer, Peter Cezar: What we do know for sure is that, during her labor at Cezar's firm, Baartman caught the attention of Cezar's brother Hendrik, who entered into a contract with her in which she would share in the profits made on her exhibition in Europe.[2]

The popularity of the Hottentot Venus exhibition gave rise to numerous cartoons featuring Baartman's prominent behind, grossly exaggerated

for comical effect. She was even featured on the five of clubs in a special deck of playing cards in 1811(Willis and Williams 2002, 62). The lesson that audiences in London and Paris learned from attending these shows was not only that Baartman's body was "ugly" and "freakish" but that this "ugliness" was considered "beautiful" in Africa. This is emphasized in the broadsides and advertisements of the show, which described Baartman as a "most correct and perfect specimen of her race" (Lindfors 1985, 133; Strother 1999, 25). The appellation "Hottentot" also invoked in the minds of her audience travelogues of this period, which described in mythic tales "strange" encounters with these most mysterious of Africans—the "Hottentots." In her study of iconography of Hottentots (the ethnic group Khioikhoi), Z. S. Strother (1999) suggests that this group, first encountered by Dutch settlers, spoke a complicated language with "clicks" and practiced such "abhorrent" customs (according to Dutch standards) as oiling their skins with animal fat, which served as a sun block in the hot climate. In fact, the word "Hottentot" means "to stammer," again suggesting that the Dutch—unable to grasp the complex sounds in this foreign language—made the assumption that there *was* no language and, hence, no means of culture and civilization. As Strother explains, "It is first and foremost because they were presumed to lack true human language that the Hottentot was assigned the role of a creature bridging human and animal realms" (1994, 4). This cultural misunderstanding—motivated by cultural arrogance—constructs an ideology of racial "difference" essentially inspired by a sense of racial "superiority."

Such "differences" between African and European men might suggest that the latter group would "obviously" not find Baartman an appealing figure. As Robert Chambers records in his 1864 history of Baartman's exhibition: "With an intensely *ugly* figure, distorted beyond all European notions of beauty, she was said to…possess the kind of shape which is most admired among her countrymen, the Hottentots" (Edwards and Walvin 1983, 172). In other words, only men of African descent— specifically the group known as "Hottentots" who were already perceived as existing on the "lowest rung" of humanity (Pieterse 1992,41)—could find the figure of a "Hottentot" woman attractive. Yet, for all the refinement and civilization of European men, Baartman's exhibition was so popular that satirists often called into question the fascination that European men *did* have for this African woman on display, as in one French cartoon, titled *The Curious in Ecstasy.*

This fascination was the subject of a French vaudeville play *The Hottentot Venus, or Hatred of Frenchwomen,*[3] performed at the Theater of Vaudeville in Paris on November 29,1814, the same year Baartman debuted in that city. This play mocked French male attraction to Baartman and advocated the "superior" value of French women. It even accused those who "preferred" savage women of lacking patriotism and national fervor. That the play centered on the efforts of an aristocratic woman, Amelia, to "save" her betrothed cousin, Adolph, from the clutches of a "savage Hottentot," indeed to bring him back to his senses, highlights the deep anxieties inherent in the public display of a foreign black woman—even through the guise of humor. The play further implies that any desire for a "Hottentot Venus" was truly "hatred of French women." Because the desire of one supposedly meant hatred of the other, the French popular press, like the vaudeville play, kept reassuring themselves that the "monstrous" form of Baartman provided such a contrast to the "pretty faces" of the women their own country (Strorher 1999, 31). Note the absence here of white women's bodies—and possibly an absence of sexuality—through emphasis on their facial features.

Such prurient interest and comic dismissal of any possibility of Baartman's sex appeal found a powerful ally in science, which dehumanized her further through the scientific inquiry into her human status and, subsequently, the nature of her genitalia.[4] Napoleon's Surgeon General, George Cuvier, one of the most celebrated naturalists of his time, set about the acquisition, upon Baartman's death, of her cadaver to examine the "racial" features of her body. He subsequently molded a cast of her body and dissected her genitalia, on which he based a two-page description of their characteristics, comparing them to those of primates, which he included in an academic report presented to the scientific academy in France in 1817.[5] Cuvier also preserved Baartman's genitalia in a jar of formaldehyde fluid, which was exhibited, along with her skeleton and brain, at the Muséeacutede I'Homme in paris as late as the early 1980s. Not only did this treatment of Baartman's private parts usher in pseudo race science—which attempts to locate racial characteristics within the biological body—but it also shaped the ways in which black female bodies are viewed, with emphasis on the rear end as a signifier of deviant sexuality. As a result, such associations of the black female rear end with hypersexuality and animalistic characteristics emerge not just in pseudoscientific studies of human anatomy but also in popular culture.

While Baartman's genitalia—on exhibit at a natural history museum—shaped discourses on race science, the Hottentot Venus show continued, as previously mentioned. One such Venus entertained guests at a Parisian ball given by a Duchess du Barry in 1829 (Gilman 1985, 88). Still another appeared at a fair in Hide Park on the Coronation Day of Queen Victoria in 1838. As an observer, T. E. Crispe, recalls in his "reminiscences": "From a Hottentot point of view the beauty of the dusky goddess consisted in an abnormal development, and a strength which enabled her to carry a drayman round the arena without inconvenience. On this *steed* [italics added] of Africa, I, a featherweight, was placed a straddle, and holding to a girdle round her waist—the almost sole article of her apparel—I plied a toy whip on the flanks of my beautiful jade, who, screaming with laughter, raced me round the circle (Edward and Walvin 1983,182)." This disturbing and probably fabricated scene of a white Englishman "riding" the backside of a rude South African woman (and this time, the Hottentot Venus "delights" in this performance as a "steed"—unlike the often sullen Baartman who was described as resentful of her treatment on exhibition) carries with it all the sexual connotations of bestiality and female submission. This is also a powerful drama-tization of Western imperialism at the dawn of the Victorian era.

THE "BATTY" AS SITE OF RESISTANCE

The title of this essay is an obvious pun on the phrase, "body politic," yet the choice of "batty," the Jamaican vernacular term for the rear end, requires explanation. The "batty," in Jamaican culture and to a larger extent in West Indian culture, is taken rather seriously and given certain reverence in dis-courses of beauty and sexual desire. Whether in working-class Jamaican dancehall settings or in car-nival street scenes in Trinidad and the Caribbean Diaspora of Brooklyn, Toronto, or London, black female batties are let loose and uninhibited in glo-rious celebrations of flesh and sexual energy. Even though such displays have historically been char-acterized as "riotous and disorderly" (Barnes 1997, 290), such movements of the batty, in the contexts of dancehall and carnival, invite a public discourse that challenges colonial constructs of "decency" and "white supremacy." Hence, "batty" implies for me a more liberatory and unashamed view of the body.

The batty can thus function as a site of resis-tance, rather than reinforcing shame and self-deprecating humor. This is captured, for example, in the Jamaican legend of Nanny of the Maroons. The legend is as follows. A fugitive slave in the eighteenth century who forged her own commu-nity in the Jamaican rainforests with other fugi-tives known as maroons is credited with defeating English armies by catching their bullets in her but-tocks and hurling back their ammunition.[6] In this myth, Nanny's batty, much like those of our con-temporary Jamaican dancehall "queens." suggests

possibilities for the black female body as a site for decolonization. She also serves as a powerful con-trast to the enslaved black woman, whose exploited sexuality fueled the economies of slavery and colo-nialism through forced reproduction and labor, and to the Hottentot Venus, whose powerful batty was diminished by freak show display and scientific dissection.

The dance troupe Urban Bush Women is one contemporary example continuing in the path of resistance. Perhaps drawing on such histories, this troupe provides an important discourse on the "batty" that attempts to develop an aesthetic of the black female body, as well as to establish this part of the anatomy as a site of resistance, through their 1995 dance piece, *Batty Moves*. Choreographed by the group's founder, Jawole Willa Jo Zollar, this per-formance captures the sensibilities of a ballet and modern-dance trained performer who "got tired of tucking and holding and apologizing" for the movements of her buttocks in these Western-based dance forms (Asantewaa 1998). As such, the perfor-mance constantly fluctuates between the gestures of ballet—such as pliés and arabesques, which require the strict, rigid, and disciplined nonmovement of the derrière—and the butt-accentuated moves in Afro-based and Caribbean dances.

Batty Moves begins with a line of dancers, dressed in form-fitting leotards, positioning their backs to the audience. As a result, they find them-selves in the position of "object," in the stance of a Hottentot Venus on exhibit. However, this his-torical body undergoes transformation as each dancer moves and poses in ways that suggest that their batties will no longer function as fetishes but as expressive extensions of their mobile, energetic bodies. Indeed, this point of transformation occurs when one dancer, reflecting on this performance, decided, upon hearing an audience member "gasp" at the sight/site of her body: "I'm going to shove it in your face, so you can just take it!"[7]

This resolve of the dancer reflects her need to resist this disapproval of her rear end, to in fact, "shove it" all the more, as a defiant gesture that dares to claim the black female batty as visible, pronounced, sexy, *and* beautiful. This resistance is not just an individual protest. Rather, she expresses defiance of a historical tradition that degrades black women's bodies. One by one, each dancer performs and defines for herself, through spoken-word language and dance moves, the body beautiful, finally culminating in a group dance—rigorously thrusting their behinds toward the audience throughout the entire performance—that reclaims the powers of the batty in communal affirmation. Borrowing Jamaican slang for the title of this piece, Urban Bush Women not only celebrate the sexual provocations of black women's rear-end-shaking dances in Jamaican dancehall settings but also create an African diasporic discourse in which black women, across the Atlantic divides, can begin a cultural exchange in which their behinds figure prominently in the arenas of hip-hop, reggae, soca, and, calypso. While these male-centered music forms objectify black women's backsides, often in extreme, misogynistic language, black women—through their dance moves—nonetheless negotiate dance spaces to assert their sexuality. In response to Urban Bush Women's performance of *Batty Moves*, dance critic Eva Yaa Asantewaa (1998) notes, "They took back, from men on the street and society in general, the power to name, direct, praise, or critique their buttocks" (Upbeat Program).

Across the diaspora, black women often begin in girlhood to center their sexuality by performing with their backsides. Whether in the

African-American ring game, "Little Sally Walker," where young girls are encouraged to "shake it to the east, shake it to the west," or in the similar Afro-Caribbean "Brown Girl in the Ring," who is urged to "show me your motion," these circles of black girls provide a female-centered space for affirmation and pleasure in their bodies, even as these scripts prepare them later for the male gaze. As adult women, this display becomes not only more sexualized but racialized as well, as black women find their bodies subject to misinterpretation and mislabeling by the dominant culture. Not only that, but these bodies no longer respond to self-motivated desires and expressions but to the requests of others—whether to black male desires in such hip-hop shouts as "shake what your Mama gave ya" and such soca-calypso demands as "wine yuh waist," or to other black women's policing call to "tuck it in."

We may need to recreate that circle of women—first enacted in childhood—who reaffirm that our bodies are fine, normal, capable, and beautiful. We may also need to enlarge that circle to include men, who can challenge their own objectifying gazes, and non-blacks, who can overcome the equation of blackness with deviance. Most of all, black women, who have been unmirrored for so long, must confront the prevailing imagery of grotesque derrières and black female hypersexuality to distinguish the myths and lies from our own truths and the ways in which we wish to represent ourselves. Only then will we be able to follow the lead of Serena Williams, proudly displaying our behinds while continuing our winning streak.

NOTES

I am grateful to Rosemarie Garland Thomson and Kimberly Wallace-Sanders, major influences on my work on the Hottentot Venus. I am also grateful to Carla Williams, who provided much-needed information on the illustrations included here, both in correspondence with me and her book, coauthored with Deborah Willis, *The Black Female Body: A Photogenic History* (2002).

1. Saartjire Baartman's ethnic origin is disputed George Cuvier (1817), who dissected Baartman's cadaver, described her as belonging to the "Bushman race," known as San. Z. S. Strother (1999) believes that the term "Hottentots," referred to in European travel narratives describes the

Khoikhoi tribe. Biographical accounts of Baartman are provided by Gilman (1985), T. Dencan Sharpley-Whiting (1999), and the 1998 film *The Life and Times of Sara Baartman*, directed by Zola Mascko.

2. For details, on legal records pertaining to Baartman, see Edwards and Walvin (1983, 171–82).

3. A translation of this play—originally titled *La Venus Hottento: ou la haine aux francaises*—is included in the Appendix of Sharpley-Whiting's *Black Venus* (1999). In addition, the second chapter in this book provides a close reading of this play.

4. Having become obsessed with the question of whether or not a "hottentot apron," which indicated an over-development of the vaginal lips, existed among Khoikhoi and San females—as was rumored by early European travelers in regions of South African—French natural scientists endeavored to prove that such existence illustrated inherent biological differences between Africans and Europeans.

5. This report is included in the *Notes of Museum d'Histoire Naturelle* (1817).

6. A historical account of Nanny of the Maroons in Jamaica is included in *Spirits of the Passage* (1997), edited by Madeleine Burnside and Rosemarie Robotham; also Jamaican author Michelle Cliff includes this local legend in her novels. See, for example, *Abeng* (1984) and *Free Enterprise* (1993).

7. The interview of this dancer is included in the video *Women's Work* (1996).

REFERENCES

Asantewaa, Eva Yaa. 1998. Upbeat program shakes its batty: Urban Bush Women, Aaron Davis Hall, NYC. Retrieved 19 October 2002 from the World Wide Web: http://www.danceonline.com/rev/bush.html.

Barnes, Natasha. 1997. Face of the nation: Race, nationalisms, and identities in Jamaican beauty pageants, in *Daughters of Caliban: Caribbean women in the twentieth century*, ed. Counsuelo Lopez Springfield. Bloomington: Indiana University Press.

Burnside, Madeleine, and Rosemarie Robotham 1997. Spirits of the Passage: *The Transatlantic slave trade in the seventeenth Century*. New York: Simon and Schuster.

Carroll, Noel. 2000. Ethnicity, race, and monstrosity: the rhetorics of horror and humor. In *Beauty matters*, ed. Peggy-Zeglin-Brand. Bloomington: Indiana University Press.

Cliff, Michelle. 1984. *Abeng*. New York: Dutton.

———. 1993 *Free Enterprise*. New York: Dutton.

Cuvier, George. I817. Extrait d'observations; faites sur le cadavre d'une femme connue a Paris et a Londres sous.le nom de Venus Hottentote. Notes of museum *d'Histoire naturelle* Paris.

Edwards, Paul, and James Walvin. 1983. *Black personalities in the era of the slave trade*. Baton Rouge: Louisiana State University Press.

Gilman, Sander. 1985. *Difference and pathology*. Ithaca: Cornell University Press.

The life and times of Sara Baartman. 1998. Dir. Zola Maseko. First Run/Icarus Films. Videocassette.

Lindfors, Bernth. 1985. Courting the Hottentot Venus. *Africa* 40 (I): 133–48.

Pieterse, Jan Nederveen. 1992. *White on black: Images of Africa and blacks in Western popular culture*. New Haven: Yale University Press.

Sharpley-Whiting. T. Dencan. 1999. *Black Venus: Sexualized savages, primal fears, and primitive narratives in French*. Durham, N.C.: Duke University Press.

Strother, Z. S. 1999. Display of the body Hottentot. In *Africans on stage*, ed. Bernth Lindfors, 1–61. Bloomington: Indiana University Press.

Willis, Deborah, and Carla Williams. 2002. *The black female body: A photographic history. Philadelphia*: Temple University Press.

Women's work. 1996. Dirs. Jawole Willa Jo Zollar, Marianne .Henderson, and Bruce. Berryhill. Virginia Museum of Fine Arts. Videocassette.

JOURNALING QUESTION

Look at some photographs of black women in popular magazines, and compare them to photographs of white women. What differences do you see in the ways that black and white women are presented?

6.

FROM *THE BOOK OF LIFE*

A Personal Guide to Race, Normality, and the Implications of the Genome Project

BARBARA KATZ ROTHMAN

Images of the body—savages noble or not, dancing bodies celebrating the body or genitalia on display in museums—are an older way of essentializing race. The newer imagery locates difference not in skin or in body shape, but in the DNA, the "genetic make-up" of people—and of peoples, groups of people conceptualized as "races." In this section, Barbara Katz Rothman looks at the work of the Human Genome Project itself as a race project, re-forming race images even as it declares that race does not exist. How has the Human Genome Project worked to reify the idea of race at the same time that it declares all humans are 99.9% the same genetically?

RATES AND RACES

I've found my sociological training, my sociological imagination, surprisingly useful and appropriate in studying genetics. That probably sounds contradictory—most of what we read and hear about genetics counterposes it to sociology as different ways of understanding. Things are either nature (genetics) or nurture (sociology). Why do little boys play with trucks? Something on the Y chromosome? Or something on the TV?

So certainly there are oppositions between the two ways of thinking. But there is something profound that resonates between sociology and genetics. Both make sense at the level of the population in ways that they will never make sense at the level of the individual.

The first sociological study was Emile Durkheim's analysis of suicide. Just over a century ago, Durkheim compared suicide rates between different groups to understand the phenomenon of suicide and to understand something about the way the groups were organized. From where we are

now, all of us at least somewhat sociologically literate, that seems reasonable. But just think about it: he was trying to explain something that was so intimate, so personal, so deeply individual, by comparing social groups. It was a magnificent intellectual breakthrough.

If Finns have higher suicide rates than Italians, what can that tell you? It cannot tell you anything about why any given Finn kills himself. No one, I should think, kills himself *because* he is Finnish. And it can't tell you which Finn is going to kill himself and which not. But it does tell you that the annual rate of suicide among Finns and among Italians is surprisingly, remarkably stable, year in and year out. The *rate* is a characteristic of the population. No matter how high the suicide rate is, it is still the case that hardly anyone kills himself The chances of any given person killing himself go from really remote to really very remote as you compare one society to another. At the level of the individual, knowing the suicide rate for the population is fairly useless: it doesn't allow prediction and it doesn't aid

Excerpted from Barbara Katz Rothman, "Rates and Races" and, "The Human Genome Diversity Project" *The Book of Life: A Personal Guide to Race, Normality, and the Implications of the Genome Project*, (Boston: Beacon Press, 2001), 86–107.

explanation. At the level of the whole, at the level of the population, though, it does both of those. Studying suicide rates can enable you to predict the rate of any given country for the coming year, and to predict whether that rate will go up or down within that country given certain social changes.

If you are interested in the varieties of human experience, you can learn most of what is interesting within any given society. You can find Italian suicides and Finns who overcame every conceivable adversity without thoughts of suicide. The interesting, extraordinary and complex differences between individuals exist within the population. But if you want to study the population, if you want to study Finnish or Italian society, you won't get there by reading suicide notes. You'd do better to look at the rates of suicide—and of births, marriages, crimes, drug use, alcohol use, literacy, etc.

So it is with genetics. There are differences between populations and there are differences among individuals. As I discussed earlier, most of the range of human variation can be found between individuals within any given population. And what does distinguish populations is mostly useless at the individual level for prediction or for explanation.

Variation in blood groups, for example, exists in pretty much all populations. If you want to do a transfusion, you have to type for A, B and O, and will find people of each type all over the planet. And yet population differences do exist. Given the earlier association of race with blood, an enormous amount of research went into distinguishing populations by blood-group frequencies, with early claims to distinguish "European" blood. It played out in a more complex way. Differences can be found in ABO frequencies between populations, but one is hard pressed to find meaning there. As Jonathan Marks points out, "A large sample of Germans, for example, turns out to have virtually the same allele percentages (A = 29, B = 11, O = 60) as a large sample of New Guineans (A=29, B=10, O=60). A study of Estonians in eastern Europe

(A = 26, B = 17, O = 57) finds them nearly identical to Japanese in eastern Asia (A = 28, B = 17, O = 55).

The ABO frequencies are a characteristic of the population. If there is a disaster in Estonia and you are in charge of bringing in blood supplies for transfusion, knowing the distribution of ABO among Estonians is valuable information. If you are a doctor faced with a bleeding Estonian, the information on distribution rates is useless. And if you are a researcher with a vial of blood, knowing its type won't tell you if it is Estonian or not. Rates, whether of suicide or of blood groups, are characteristics of populations, not individuals.

That has two consequences, at two levels. One is that you cannot learn about individuals from groups, or about groups from individuals. They are separate levels of analysis. As a sociologist, I've learned to think about prediction at the level of the whole, and sometimes at the level of segments of the whole—but I've also learned *not* to try to make predictions at the level of the individual. I think in terms of rates. So I can think about the relationship between, say, social class and health, and know that the higher people are in the socioeconomic system, the greater the chance of their being healthy and of having healthy children. And at the same time, it doesn't surprise me one bit when a wealthy person dies young, when a rich and powerful person loses a child to disease, or when a poor, uneducated person lives to a hundred having raised ten healthy children and scores of healthy grandchildren and great-grandchildren. I don't think of any of that as contradicting what I know about the relationship between class and health, because what I know is about relationships, correlations, rates, and not individual causality.

That is why it makes sense to me that Estonians and Japanese have relatively high rates of type B blood, and it also makes sense to me that the vast majority of Estonians and Japanese do not have type B blood. The rate is high relative to other rates; the individual instance is low.

One of the more satisfying ways we think about social class in sociology is in Max Weber's terms: as "life chances." Anything can happen to anybody, but your chances of certain kinds of things happening vary with your class position. The poorest kid in the most miserable neighborhood with uneducated, unemployed parents can grow up to win the Nobel Prize in physics, and the richest kid from the wealthiest suburb can end up sleeping in doorways. But that doesn't take away from the fact that the first kid's chances of success are different from the second kid's, just as a Japanese kid has (slightly) greater chances of type B blood than does a German kid. That sociological perspective is useful for reading genetics. When I read, for example, that Ashkenazi Jews have a higher rate of a gene associated with breast cancer, I read that as a sociologist: I note the association, and I note the implications for life chances, and I also note the limits of that for individual prediction.

The second set of consequences of understanding rates as characteristics of populations is that you can, usefully, study populations *as* populations. They can't be reduced to the level of the individual, but populations *can* be studied at their own level. What can we learn when we study population genetics, rates of genetic distributions within populations?

When we talk about groups of people and their genes, what immediately comes to the (American) mind is *race*. As race moved inward, from the body to the blood to the gene, genetic differences became the measure of race. But race, biologists and anthropologists tell us, has no meaning; it doesn't exist scientifically, objectively.

Race has shaped the lives of people on earth in every possible way. An enormous number of people have suffered, died, because of race. How could race be so perfectly obvious to see, so enormously powerful in its consequences, and yet not exist? What could it possibly mean to say that something *that* real isn't real?

Race implies discontinuities in the differences among people around the world, and race also implies some essential differences. To sort people by race is to use one category and assume others, to mark race by one trait and then expect to see other traits sorted along with it: to start with skin color and find IQ; to start with hair type and go to rhythm. No single trait means race: they have to cluster into categories by which people can be distinguished, or what have you?

Jonathan Marks, whose work in this area I've become so fond of, gives a good example to explain some of this. If you had a big pile of blocks of different sizes and asked a child to sort them into "large" and "small," the child could do it. If a number of children attempted that task, there would be complete agreement about some, maybe most of the blocks—the largest and the smallest. "The fact that the blocks can be sorted into the categories given, however, does not imply that there are two kinds of blocks in the universe, large and small—and that the child has uncovered a transcendent pattern in the sizing of the blocks. It simply means that if categories are given, they can be imposed upon the blocks."

Sure we can sort people by, say, skin color, and get considerable agreement, at least at the extremes, about which people go into which group. But skin color, like block size, is a single trait. What if some of the blocks were plastic, some wood and some metal? The child could sort by that and get a completely different arrangement of blocks. And if some of the blocks had grooved edges and some smooth? The child could sort by that too, with yet another arrangement. And if the blocks were painted red, yellow and blue? You could sort blocks any way you want to, but if the color, size, grooves and material are not systematically related to each other (if not all grooved blocks are larger than smooth blocks, or all yellow blocks metal) then you're going to end up with entirely different piles depending on what you sorted for.

People can be sorted by color. But they can also be sorted by any number of other characteristics. The presence of a skin fold on the eye. The presence of loops, whorls or arches in their fingerprints. The presence of specific genes, like the sickle-cell gene. The ability to digest lactose. Each sorting will give you different "race" groups, just like each sorting of the blocks will give you different piles. And no amount of sorting will tell you about the essential types of blocks, or people, in the world.

When you sort people by skin color you get some people from India sorted with some people from Africa—the way my Dutch neighbors saw it. Sort by eye fold, and one group of Africans goes in the same race as the Asians, and the rest of Africans go with the Europeans. Sort by fingerprint type and most Europeans and most Africans go in one group, with Khoisans and some central Europeans in another and Mongolians and Australian aborigines in a third race. Sort by sickle-cell trait and Nelson Mandela's people, the Xhosas, get classified with the Swedes while most African groups get classified with the Greeks. Sort by lactose tolerance and northern and central Europeans go with Arabians and the west African Fulani, while most of the rest of the African groups go with the east Asians, American Indians and southern Europeans. Sort by ABO blood groups and the Germans go with the New Guineans and the Estonians with the Japanese.

Do you think you've actually discovered some important characteristic of the Estonians now that you know that? Is there some indication that perhaps, had that fact been known, Estonians would have been in camps with Japanese during World War II and the Germans would have declared the New Guineans of Aryan blood?

Skin color and various cranial measurements were abysmal failures in classifying people into demarcated racial groupings. Blood typing raised hopes that science could get to the bottom of it, could accurately sort people by an objective criterion. But that didn't work either, with each new factor in blood typing serving only to further muddy what distinctions could be made.

With molecular genetics, and its ability to see differences not in the body or in the blood, but inside the cell, new hopes were raised—here we could locate race, locate the fundamental groupings of people. And here too confusion reigns as the genes that mark "race" twinkle on and off all over the world.

There aren't any markers that set people apart into race groups. There are any number of characteristics that can be used to sort people, that can be imposed, like "large" and "small" on the blocks, but none that emerges as an inherent difference. There is too much genetic variation within populations, and too little between them, for "race" to make sense. Race can and will continue to be imposed on human groupings, but the clusterings that exist do not display any discontinuity that makes a boundary or boundaries discernable. Those boundaries will always be in the eye of the beholder.

Does that mean that we can't learn anything about humans from the ways that genes do cluster in populations? Of course not: the first thing we learned is that there aren't any races. The various groupings of people both separated out too recently in human evolution and have had too much continued interbreeding to sort out into distinct groups. We vary all right, but not in massive, structured, systematic ways.

The other thing we may hope to learn is something about our history. Individual genes carry no history: they are present in one allele or another, with no narrative about how they got there. You can't read history from a single genome. You don't really need genomes to understand that. Think about a "mixed-race" child, say one who is "half" of African descent and "half" of Asian descent. That child has two grandparents of African descent and two grandparents of Asian descent. Looking at the child, you cannot tell which grandparent mated with which: did an African couple produce one of the child's parents and an Asian couple the other?

Or did two Afro-Asian couples produce two Afro-Asian parents who produced that child?

Can clusters of genomes, patterns of genetic distributions, tell us something more about history, more about how they got that way? If two groups share some characteristic, some gene, with each other and with no one else, we can ask how that came to be. Like looking at the Afro-Asian child, we can read a number of possible stories from that. An attempt to read those stories, to gather a narrative of human travel through the planet from our genetic clusters, has been attempted. That is the goal, or one of the goals, of the the Human Genome Diversity Project.

THE HUMAN GENOME DIVERSITY PROJECT

The Human Genome Diversity Project presents itself as an attempt to read human evolutionary history from our DNA. The plan is to get DNA samples from 25 individuals from each of several hundred groups of indigenous peoples around the earth, and from that try to tell how we became who and what and where we are.

The Human Genome Diversity Project is founded on the idea that there *are* genetic "isolates," groups of people who are mixing genes only with each other and not with the rest of the world. The project operationalizes the concept of isolation by setting the date at around 1500, and saying aboriginal populations are those that were "in place" before then. It's an interesting model of the world. First we split off and wandered the planet, then we settled in place for a long, long time of isolation, and then Columbus arrived and things got mixed up. But as Jonathan Marks points out, "prior to Columbus there was Prince Henry the Navigator; prior to Prince Henry there was Marco Polo; prior to Marco Polo there were the Crusades; prior to the Crusades there were the Mongols and Huns; prior to the Mongols and Huns there were the Romans; prior to the Romans there was Alexander the Great. And those are just the European highlights."

We use the model of the Polynesians setting off in canoes and landing on isolated islands, like the Maori in New Zealand—as if the movement of people was a one-time dispersal outward to isolated posts. But if you take a good look at a globe, we don't actually have the separate continents they taught us to name in elementary school. You can pretty much walk the whole planet, and there's no reason not to criss-cross, retrace steps, wander around. The one thing we do know about people is that when populations of them interact, crossing each other's paths, little mixed babies are a sure product. So static isolation is probably not a good model for what happened to us as a species.

Maybe the problem is that the founders of the project were geneticists, rather than anthropologists, and missed everything that anthropologists have been saying in the second half of this century. In an earlier and more naive time, anthropologists went off and studied "tribes." In what was called the classic ethnographic period, from 1910 to 1960, the anthropologists typically went in for a year or so, checked out the kinship system as described, got the origin tales of the community, and observed their customs and practices. They worked with one or just a few informants and learned history. The history they learned was, it now seems obvious, just one history of that community, just one story. The actual messiness of life got overlooked: the ways that differences within the community played out; the ways that people from outside of the community married or bred in and people from inside married or bred outside; and the ways that origin tales had, as they always have, a political as well as a theological tale to tell. Most origin tales say, we were always here; we were the first people here; we are the true people of this land. More sophisticated contemporary field work has shown enormous amounts of diversity and "gene flow" between tribal societies once thought to be isolated.

If there aren't isolated aboriginal peoples, then sampling from them makes no sense: we're back to the disproved logic of race, in which you first divide the population into race groups, and then compare across race to discover racial difference. The Human Genome Diversity Project supporters vehemently decry the concept of race: they are interested in small populations, demes or clines or ethnos as they are variously called. But call it anything you want: if they are not intrinsically different and if they are not isolated, then you cannot learn history by looking at them now.

All of which is not to deny the obvious, the thing we come back to over and over again: people do tend to look like the people they live among. At the Stanford conference, Jonathan Marks argued that if what they are really interested in is the diversity in the population as it has spread itself around the planet, then put a big grid across the globe, and take samples from each box. It is a much safer way of getting that information, a way that doesn't risk endlessly recreating race categories even as we try to argue against them.

Communities, peoples, tribes, societies, groups of any sort, construct themselves *socially*. Reading membership from DNA reads against the text, substitutes "objective" or scientific information for the ways communities construct themselves. Consider this: genetically, I'd be just as related to some Cossack that might have raped my great-great-grandmother as to the woman herself. African Americans in the United States can trace their ancestry as much to any I given owner who brutalized a young woman slave as to that young woman slave. As communities of people we have carefully crafted stories, histories of who we are, of what we choose to pass on and what we choose to let wash over us. These stories are not our ignorance speaking: they are our collective wisdom.

I have a small woven straw basket on my desk. It's a beautiful miniature of a rice-winnowing basket made by a Gullah woman living near Charleston, South Carolina. Africans who knew rice-growing techniques were captured from the area around Sierra Leone and brought as slaves to the geographically similar region near Charleston. Bits of language, fragments of songs, rice-cultivation techniques and these basket-making skills have survived in this community of slave descendants. A contemporary baskets-weaver in Sierra Leone can recognize as one of her people's baskets a basket woven by an African American woman many generations removed from Africa.

You can read history in a basket, and you can read history in a cell. The relatedness of the two basket weavers might show up in their DNA as well, bits passed down generation to generation. Language and skills carry history; DNA carries history.

Could DNA be just one more way to read history? If it were, it could be relatively harmless, and kind of interesting. But we know, from our history, that when we face alternative tales—one told in our grandmothers' songs and stories, and one told in the language of science, that science takes on the authoritative voice, and becomes the *real* story, and the other becomes an "old wives' tale."

Genetic thinking places "authenticity," *real* membership in a community, in the cells of the individuals, not in the fabric of the people. Genetic thinking takes power away from people to tell their own history, and gives power to people with the technology to scientifically read that history. Science and technology, we like to think, are themselves morally and politically neutral, and we only have to worry about them if they are in the "wrong hands." Maybe so—certainly science and technology in the wrong hands are very much worth worrying about, and nowhere is that more true than in the sphere of race. But are there right hands? Or doesn't the very existence of "isolates of historic interest" being studied to the tune of 25 to 35 million dollars suggest that questions of "race," of "identity," of "descent" can never be understood without the power relationships that created them?

Genetics didn't create racism. Genetics, not just as a science or set of technologies or practices, but genetics as a way of thinking about the world, maintains and supports racist thinking just as much as it has the potential to undercut and counter racist thinking. There is this endless interplay between an ideology, a way of thinking, and the science that is being developed. Scientific discoveries come out of ways of thinking, and scientific advances capture the imagination, give us ways of thinking. There isn't some pure science going on out there somewhere, producing facts which then get used to produce the way we understand the world.

Ours is a world in which some people are resources for other people. The same power relationships that "discovered" the dark continent and the new world, that brought back spices and gold and people, now brings back samples of plant and human genetic diversity. And—still—puts them up for sale. In a racist society, in a world in which race is a system of power and oppression, genetic thinking is going to be used to support that oppression. How much our science of genetics will support or will undercut racism won't depend on the "facts" genetics has to offer: it will depend on the world in which those facts are offered.

JOURNALING QUESTION

It now is possible to have your DNA tested and compared with the DNA of people all over the world, to see which groups are most closely related to you. Why would you want—or NOT want—to do this for yourself?

A VOICE FROM THE PAST
Race and Progress

FRANZ BOAS

Our first *Voice from the Past* is from Franz Boas. A German American anthropologist, Boas was one of the earliest critics of essentialist thinking, and this piece is drawn from his Presidential Address to the American Association for the Advancement of Science in 1931. Other than the archaic use of the term *Negro*, would you have to do much editing to present this argument today?

Permit me to call your attention to the scientific aspects of a problem that has been for a long time agitating our country and which, on account of its social and economic implications, has given rise to strong emotional reactions and has led to varied types of legislation. I refer to the problems due to the intermingling of racial types.

If we wish to reach a reasonable attitude, it is necessary to separate clearly the biological and psychological aspects from the social and economic

Excerpted from Frank Boas, "Race and Progress," in *Race, Language, and Culture* (New York: Macmillan, 1940), 3–17.

implications of this problem. Furthermore, the social motivation of what is happening must be looked at not from the narrow point of view of our present conditions but from a wider angle.

The facts with which we are dealing are diverse. The plantation system of the South brought to our shores a large Negro population. Considerable mixture between White masters and slave women occurred during the period of slavery, so that the number of pure Negroes was dwindling continually and the colored population gradually became lighter. A certain amount of intermingling between White and Indian took place, but in the United States and Canada this has never occurred to such a degree that it became an important social phenomenon. In Mexico and many parts of Central and South America it is the most typical case of race contact and race mixture. With the development of immigration the people of eastern and southern Europe were attracted to our country and form now an important part of our population. They differ in type somewhat among themselves, although the racial contrasts are much less than those between Indians or Negroes and Whites. Through Mexican and West Indian immigration another group has come into our country, partly of South European, partly of mixed Negro and mixed Indian descent. To all these must be added the East Asiatic groups, Chinese, Japanese and Filipinos, who play a particularly important role on the Pacific Coast.

The first point in regard to which we need clarification refers to the significance of the term race. In common parlance when we speak of a race we mean a group of people that have certain bodily and perhaps also mental characteristics in common. The Whites, with their light skin, straight or wavy hair and high nose, are a race set off clearly from the Negroes with their dark skin, frizzly hair and flat nose. In regard to these traits the two races are fundamentally distinct. Not quite so definite is the distinction between East Asiatics and European types, because transitional forms do occur among normal White individuals, such as flat faces, straight

black hair and eye forms resembling the East Asiatic types; and conversely European-like traits are found among East Asiatics. For Negro and White we may speak of hereditary racial traits so far as these radically distinct features are concerned. For Whites and East Asiatics the difference is not quite so absolute, because a few individuals may be found in each race for whom the racial traits do not hold good, so that in a strict sense we cannot speak of absolutely valid hereditary racial traits.

On the whole it is much easier to find decided differences between races in bodily form than in function. It cannot be claimed that the body in all races functions in an identical way, but that kind of overlapping which we observed in form is even more pronounced in function. It is quite impossible to say that, because some physical function, let us say the heart beat, has a certain measure, the individual must be White or Negro—for the same rates are found in both races. A certain basal metabolism does not show that a person is a Japanese or a White, although the averages of all the individuals in the races compared may exhibit differences. Furthermore, the particular function is so markedly modified by the demands made upon the organism that these will make the reactions of the racial groups living under the same conditions markedly alike. Every organ is capable of adjustment to a fairly wide range of conditions, and thus the conditions will determine to a great extent the kind of reaction.

I believe the present state of our knowledge justifies us in saying that, while individuals differ, biological differences between races are small. There is no reason to believe that one race is by nature so much more intelligent, endowed with great will power, or emotionally more stable than another, that the difference would materially influence its culture. Nor is there any good reason to believe that the differences between races are so great that the descendants of mixed marriages would be inferior to their parents. Biologically there is no good reason to object to fairly close inbreeding in healthy groups, nor to intermingling of the principal races.

I have considered so far only the biological side of the problem. In actual life we have to reckon with social settings which have a very real existence, no matter how erroneous the opinions on which they are founded. Among us race antagonism is a fact, and we should try to understand its psychological significance. For this purpose we have to consider the behavior not only of man, but also of animals. Many animals live in societies. It may be a shoal of fish which any individuals of the same species may join, or a swarm of mosquitoes. No social tie is apparent in these groups, but there are others which we may call closed societies that do not permit any outsider to join their group. Packs of dogs and well-organized herds of higher mammals, ants and bees are examples of this kind. In all these groups there is a considerable degree of social solidarity which is expressed particularly by antagonism against any outside group. The troops of monkeys that live in a given territory will not allow another troop to come and join them. The members of a closed animal society are mutually tolerant or even helpful. They repel all outside intruders.

Conditions in primitive society are quite similar. Strict social obligations exist between the members of a tribe, but all outsiders are enemies. Primitive ethics demand self-sacrifice in the group to which the individual belongs, deadly enmity against every outsider. A closed society does not exist without antagonisms against others. Although the degree of antagonism against outsiders has decreased, closed societies continue to exist in our own civilization. The nobility formed a closed society until very recent times. Patricians and plebeians in Rome, Greeks and barbarians, the gangs of our streets, Mohammedan and infidel, and our modern nations are in this sense closed societies that cannot exist without antagonisms. The principles that hold societies together vary enormously, but common to all of them are social obligations within the group, antagonisms against other parallel groups.

Race consciousness and race antipathy differ in one respect from the social groups here enumerated. While in all other human societies there is no external characteristic that helps to assign an individual to his group, here his very appearance singles him out. If the belief should prevail, as it once did, that all red-haired individuals have an undesirable character, they would at once be segregated and no red-haired individual could escape from his class no matter what his personal characteristics might be. The Negro, the East Asiatic or Malay who may at once be recognized by his bodily build is automatically placed in his class and not one of them can escape being excluded from a foreign closed group. The same happens when a group is characterized by dress imposed by circumstances, by choice, or because a dominant group prescribe for them a distinguishing symbol—like the garb of the medieval Jews or the stripes of the convict—so that each individual no matter what his own character may be, is at once assigned to his group and treated accordingly. If racial antipathy were based on innate human traits this would be expressed in interracial sexual aversion. The free intermingling of slave owners with their female slaves and the resulting striking decrease in the number of full-blood Negroes, the progressive development of a half-blood Indian population and the readiness of intermarriage with Indians when economic advantages may be gained by such means, show clearly that there is no biological foundation for race feeling. There is no doubt that the strangeness of an alien racial type does play an important rôle, for the ideal of beauty of the White who grows up in a purely White society is different from that of a Negro. This again is analogous to the feeling of aloofness among groups that are characterized by different dress, different mannerisms of expression of emotion, or by the ideal of bodily strength as against that of refinement of form. The student of race relations must answer the question whether in societies in which different racial types form a socially homogeneous group, a marked race consciousness develops. This question cannot be answered categorically, although interracial conditions in Brazil and the disregard of racial affiliation in the relation between Mohammedans and infidels show that race consciousness may be quite insignificant.

When social divisions follow racial lines, as they do among ourselves, the degree of difference between racial forms is an important element in establishing racial groupings and in creating racial conflicts.

The actual relation is not different from that developing in other cases in which social cleavage develops. In times of intense religious feeling denominational conflicts, in times of war national conflicts take the same course. The individual is merged in his group and not rated according to his personal value.

However, nature is such that constantly new groups are formed in which each individual subordinates himself to the group. He expresses his feeling of solidarity by an idealization of his group and by an emotional desire for its perpetuation. When the groups are denominational, there is strong antagonism against marriages outside of the group. The group must be kept pure, although denomination and descent are in no way related. If the social groups are racial groups we encounter in the same way the desire for racial endogamy in order to maintain racial purity.

On this subject I take issue with Sir Arthur Keith, [who] is reported to have said that "race antipathy and race prejudice nature has implanted in you for her own end—the improvement of mankind through racial differentiation." I challenge him to prove that race antipathy is "implanted by nature" and not the effect of social causes which are active in every closed social group, no matter whether it is racially heterogeneous or homogeneous. The complete lack of sexual antipathy, the weakening of race consciousness in communities in which children grow up as an almost homogeneous group; the occurrence of equally strong antipathies between denominational groups, or between social strata—as witnessed by the Roman patricians and plebeians, the Spartan Lacedaemonians and Helots, the Egyptian castes and some of the Indian castes—all these show that antipathies are social phenomena. If you will, you may call them "implanted by nature," but only in so far as man is a being living in closed social groups, leaving it entirely indetermined what these social groups may be.

No matter how weak the case for racial purity may be, we understand its social appeal in our society. While the biological reasons that are adduced may not be relevant, a stratification of society in social groups that are racial in character will always lead to racial discrimination. As in all other sharp social groupings the individual is not judged as an individual but as a member of his class. We may be reasonably certain that whenever members of different races form a single social group with strong bonds, racial prejudice and racial antagonisms will come to lose their importance. They may even disappear entirely. As long as we insist on a stratification in racial layers, we shall pay the penalty in the form of interracial struggle. Will it be better for us to continue as we have been doing, or shall we try to recognize the conditions that lead to the fundamental antagonisms that trouble us?

The Social Construction of Race

7.

"I DID NOT GET THAT JOB BECAUSE OF A BLACK MAN..."

The Story Lines and Testimonies of Color-Blind Racism

EDUARDO BONILLA-SILVA, AMANDA LEWIS, AND DAVID G. EMBRICK

Story telling is how we make sense of the world and the things that happen to us. Some stories make us feel better or are told to make other people feel better. One of the stories white people can tell themselves now is that they personally are not racists. As this article shows, they tell this story in a number of ways—by comparing themselves to others, by distancing themselves from America's racist history, and by claiming an anti-white racism exists. These stories are told by people who may truly be progressive, decent people trying to navigate a racial divide they themselves did not make. Nonetheless, how do these stories reinforce that race line?

Storytelling is central to communication. According to Barthes (1977:79), "Narrative is present in every age, in every place, in every society; it begins with the very history of mankind and there nowhere is nor has been a people without a narrative." To a large degree, communication is about telling stories. We tell stories to our spouses, children, friends, and coworkers. Through stories we present and represent ourselves to the world. In short, we tell stories and these stories, in turn, make us (Somers, 1994).

In this article we examine the dominant *racial stories* of the post–civil rights era. Because all stories are told within particular ideological formations, it is important to highlight their relationship to

ideologies. We define *racial ideology* as the *broad racial frameworks, or "grids," that racial groups use to make sense of the world, to decide what is right or wrong, true or false, important or unimportant*. And given that all societies are structured in dominance, the frameworks of the rulers (whether men, the bourgeoisie, or whites) are more likely to crystallize as "common sense" (van Dijk, 1999). Eduardo Bonilla-Silva (2003a,b) has operationalized the notion of racial ideology as an interpretive repertoire consisting of frames, style, and racial stories.[1] One sign that an ideology has gained dominance is that its central logic has come to be perceived as "common sense," so that actors in different positions and in different contexts deploy similar kinds of narratives to

Excerpted from Eduardo Bonilla-Silva, Amanda Lewis, and David G. Embrick, "'I Did Not Get that Job Because of a Black Man': The Story Lines and Testimonies of Color-Blind Racism," *Sociological Forum* 19 (2009): 555–810. References and notes have been renumbered and edited.

explain social reality. Such racial stories can then be understood as part of the contemporary, dominant racial ideology as it is manifested in everyday life (Lewis, 2003).

...We define story lines as the *socially shared tales that incorporate a common scheme and wording*. These racial story lines resemble legends or fables because, unlike testimonies (see below), they are most often based on impersonal, generic arguments with little narrative content—they are readily available, ideological, "of course" narratives that actors draw on in explaining personal or collective social realities. In story lines, characters are likely to be underdeveloped and are usually social types (e.g., the "black man" in statements such as "My best friend lost a job to a black man" or the "welfare queen" in "Poor black women are welfare queens").[2] "The ideological nature of such story lines is revealed by the similar schemata and wording used in their telling (e.g., "the *past is the past*"), and by their use in a range of locations by a wide variety of actors for similar ends.

We proceed as follows. First, we describe the theory and the racial context behind our analysis. Then we describe the data and methods for this study. Next we analyze the dominant story lines of color-blind racism.[3] Then, for comparative purposes, we briefly discuss how these stories affect white racial progressives and blacks. We conclude with a discussion of the ideological role of racial stories.

THEORY AND RACIAL CONTEXT FOR THE ANALYSIS OF RACIAL STORIES

Although racism often involves prejudice, antipathy, and irrationality, most researchers now concede that it has a material and, therefore, rational foundation (Bonilla-Silva, 1997; Feagin, 2000; Fredrickson, 2002). Racism springs not from the hearts of "racists," but from the fact that dominant actors in a racialized social system receive benefits at all levels (political, economic, social, and even psychological), whereas subordinate actors do not (Bonilla-Silva, 1997). Racial outcomes then are not the product of individual "racists" but of the crystallization of racial domination into a *racial structure*: a network of racialized practices and relations that shapes the life chances of the various races at all levels. Hence, domination in hegemonic racial orders such as ours is produced by the collective normal actions of *all* actors rather than by the behavior of a few "racists" (on hegemonic domination, see Omi and Winant, 1994).

The implications of this understanding of racism for our analysis are that the frameworks, affective dispositions (which range from sympathy to apathy and animosity), and stories that actors use or exhibit tend to correspond to their systemic location—actors at the top of a racial order tend to display views, attitudes, and stories that help maintain their privilege, whereas actors at the bottom are more likely to exhibit oppositional views, attitudes, and counternarratives.

But racialized social systems are not fixed, and neither are the ideologies that accompany them. For instance, the racial structure of the United States underwent a tremendous transformation in the 1960s and 1970s (Bloom, 1987). Demographic (urbanization of blacks), political (development of minority organizations), and economic factors (industrialization) in combination with organized (civil rights movement) and "spontaneous" challenges (race riots) to the Jim Crow order led to the development of what various authors label the "new racism" (Brooks, 1990; Smith, 1995). According to Bonilla-Silva and Lewis (1999:56), the elements that make up this new racial structure are "(1) the increasingly covert nature of racial discourse and practices; (2) the avoidance of racial terminology and the ever growing claim by whites that they experience 'reverse racism'; the elaboration of a racial agenda over political matters that eschews direct racial references; (4) the invisibility of most mechanisms to reproduce racial inequality; and finally, (5) the rearticulation of a number of racial practices characteristic of the Jim Crow period of race relations."

...With the emergence of a new normative climate on racial matters, old-fashioned racial views substantially receded (Schuman, 1997). Hence today few whites subscribe to the classical ideas of Jim Crowism, and the vast majority agrees with the principles of racial equality and equal opportunity (Schuman, 1997). However, except for a small and decreasing number of scholars (Lipset, 1996; Sniderman and Carmines, 1997), most analysts argue that these changes do not signify the "end of racism" (D'Souza, 1995). Instead, the new consensus among survey researchers is that racial prejudice has gone underground or is expressed in a "subtle" (Pettigrew and Martin, 1987) "modern" (McConahay, 1986), or "symbolic" way (Kinder and Sanders, 1996) or as "laissez-faire racism" (Bobo et al., 1997). Kinder and Sanders' (1996:106) capture the essence of the new prejudice in the following passage:

> A new form of prejudice has come to prominence, one that is preoccupied with matters of moral character, informed by the virtues associated with the traditions of individualism. At its center are the contentions that blacks do not try hard enough to overcome the difficulties they face and that they take what they have not earned. Today, we say, prejudice is expressed in the language of American individualism.

Elsewhere Bonilla-Silva (2003a) has labeled the racial ideology that glues the post–civil rights racial structure as "color-blind racism" (Bonilla-Silva, 2003a). He contends that the main frames of this ideology are the denial of the centrality of discrimination ("Discrimination ended in the sixties!"), the abstract extension of liberal principles to racial matters ("I am all for equal opportunity; that's why I oppose affirmative action"), the naturalization of racial matters ("Residential segregation is natural..."), and the cultural explanation of minorities' standing ("Mexicans are poorer because they lack the motivation to succeed"). But ideologies are not just about ideas (see above). To have salience and currency, ideologies must produce narratives that explain the world in ways that make sense to people, that convey its major frames; these stories are then the conveyor belts that transport the new racial frames.

...The subtle, "now you see it, now you don't" character of contemporary racial practices is matched by the apparent nonracialism of color-blind racism. And, as we will try to demonstrate, racial stories fit color-blind racism, as they do not rely on traditional racist discourse to support the racial status quo.

DATA AND METHODS

The data for the analysis comes from two projects on racial attitudes: the 1997 Survey of College Students Social Attitudes and the 1998 Detroit Area Study (DAS)....

Since our goal is to examine the dominant racial stories, we rely almost exclusively on the interview data. The stories we draw upon emerged mostly spontaneously in discussions on race-related issues such as affirmative action, residential and school segregation, interracial friendship, and interracial marriage. Respondents inserted them to reinforce points, underscore the salience of an issue, or as digressions in the middle of racially sensitive discussions.

The interviews for these two studies were race-matched, followed a structured interview protocol, were conducted in respondents' homes or in neutral sites, and lasted between 45 minutes and 2 hours. After the interviews were completed, project assistants transcribed the recorded material verbatim (i.e., included nonlexicals, pauses, etc.). However, to improve the readability of the quotations, we have edited them in this paper. When all the material was transcribed, one of the authors read all the interviews to extract common themes and patterns. At that stage, the same author and project assistants performed a basic content analysis to locate all the instances where respondents inserted these racial stories.

Although all samples have limitations (ours, for example, are not "natural" samples of "speech acts" and do not include as many blacks as we would have liked), ours have advantages over most of those used by qualitative researchers on racial matters. First, our samples are systematic (randomly selected subjects from those who participated in surveys). Second, one of the survey samples has a bias toward racial tolerance (the students' sample), but the other is a random sample. Third, the age, gender, and regional representation in these samples allow us to be confident that the findings are not peculiar to one subpopulation. Lastly, our subsamples for the interviews (representing 10% of students in the survey and 21% of the DAS respondents) as well as the 134 total respondents interviewed are large by qualitative standards. Therefore, we believe that the data for this study allows us to gain insight into the kind of dominant stories that whites deploy while talking about racial matters.[4]

THE STORY LINES OF COLOR-BLIND RACISM

If racial stories were immutable, they would not be useful tools to defend the racial order (Jackman, 1994). Thus, racial stories are intricately connected to specific historical moments and hence change accordingly (Hall, 1990; Omi and Winant, 1994). For example, during the Jim Crow era, the myth of the black rapist became a powerful story line that could be invoked to keep blacks, particularly black men, "in their place" (Clinton, 1982; Hill-Collins, 1990). Today new story lines have emerged to keep blacks in their new (but still subordinate) place (Crenshaw, 1997). The most common story lines we identified were "The past is the past"; "I did not own slaves"; "If (other ethnic groups such as Italians or Jews) made it, how come blacks have not?" and "I did not get a (job or promotion) because of a black man." Although some of these story lines are inter-related (e.g., "The past is the past" and "I didn't own any slaves" appeared often together), we discuss each one separately.

"THE PAST IS THE PAST"

The core of this story line is the idea that we must put our racist past behind us and that affirmative action programs do exactly the opposite by keeping the racial flame alive. Moreover, as the story line goes, these policies are particularly problematic because they attempt to address a past harm done against minorities by harming whites today. This story line was used by more than 50% of college students (21/41) and by most DAS respondents, usually in discussions of race-targeted programs for blacks. A perfect example of how respondents used this story line is provided by Emily, a student at South University (SU), who told the story line in an exchange with the interviewer over the meaning of affirmative action.

> I have, I just have a problem with the discrimination, you're gonna discriminate against a group and what happened in the past is horrible and it should never happen again, but I also think that to move forward you have to let go of the past and let go of what happened um, you know? And it should really start equaling out 'cause I feel that some of, some of it will go too far and it's swing the other way. One group is going to be discriminated against, I don't, I don't believe in that. I don't think one group should have an advantage over another regardless of what happened in the past.

Clear in Emily's logic is the idea that "two wrongs don't make a right." Thus, to compensate blacks for a history of white advantage or black oppresion would involve unjustified, unfair advantage today. Note this view does not involve a denial of past injustice. Instead, it regards the past as unrelated or irrelevant to current realities. Hence, programs designed to redress the "horrible" past are constructed as "reverse discrimination."

Almost all DAS respondents resorted to a version of this story line to express their displeasure with programs they believe benefit blacks solely because of their race. However, these older respondents were more likely to use the story line while venting lots of anger. John II, for instance, a retired architect and homebuilder in his late sixties, used a version of the story line in his response to the question on reparations.

> Not a nickel, not a nickel! I think that's ridiculous. I think that's a great way to go for the black vote. But I think that's a ridiculous assumption, because those that say we should pay them because they were slaves back in the past and yet, how often do you hear about the people who were whites that were slaves and the white that were, ah? Boy, we should get reparations, the Irish should get reparations from the English...

John's statement suggests not only that it is "ridiculous" to give blacks even "a nickel" in compensation for a history of slavery, but that blacks have no special claim with regard to poor treatment ("the Irish should get reparations from the English").

But what is ideological about this story? Is it not true that "the past is the past"? First, whether whites inserted this story line or not, most interpreted the past as slavery even when in some questions we left it open (e.g., questions regarding the "history of oppression") or specified that we were referring to "slavery *and* Jim Crow." Since Jim Crow died slowly in the country (and lasted well into the 1960s to 1970s), the reference to a remote past ignores the relatively recent overt forms of racial oppression that have impeded black progress. Second, such stories effectively "erase" the limiting effects of historic discrimination on the ability of minorities' and blacks' to accumulate wealth at the same rate as whites. According to Oliver and Shapiro (1995), the "accumulation of disadvantages" has "sedimented" blacks economically so that even if all forms of economic discrimination that blacks face ended today, they would not catch up with whites for several 100 years. Third, the "reverse discrimination" element in this story line is central to whites as a rationale for their opposition to all race-based compensatory programs. This story line then does not reflect whites' ignorance of racial history and racial facts. More than anything else, it provides a positive and even moral standpoint for them to explain why certain social programs are unnecessary and problematic.

"I DIDN'T OWN ANY SLAVES"

This story line appeared often in conjunction with the story line of "The past is the past," although it was deployed somewhat less frequently—it was used by about a quarter of the college students (9/41) and a third of DAS respondents. As with the previous story line, this one usually appeared in discussions of affirmative action (see Wellman, 1997). The core of this story line is the notion that present generations are not responsible for the ills of slavery. For instance, Lynn, a Midwest University (MU) student, used this story line to explain her opposition to the idea of a hypothetical company hiring a black rather than a white job applicant because the company had discriminated against blacks in the past.

> I think I would, I would, I'd disagree, I think. I mean, yeah, I think I'd disagree because, I mean, even though it's kinda what affirmative action— well, it's not really, because I don't think like my generation should have to be punished real harshly for the things that our ancestors did...

The story line allowed Lynn to state safely (albeit quite hesitantly) her concerns about affirmative action, even though she had stated before that she supported the program. Again we can see the ideological connection between racial story lines when Lynn responds to evidence of past discrimination manifested in a company's current racial profile (described as 97% white) by suggesting she should not be punished for the actions of her ancestors—essentially saying, "The past is the past." Even though the question here does not refer to slavery but suggests concrete evidence for discriminatory practices by the company in the not-too-distant past, the story line provides a readily available justification for lack of action.

Some DAS respondents deployed this story line to answer a question on whether the government should spend money on blacks' behalf to compensate for past discrimination. For example, Dina, an employment manager for an advertising agency in her early thirties, said,

> No, and I have to say that I'm pretty supportive of anything to help people, but I don't know why that slavery thing has a—I've got a chip on my shoulder about that. It's like it happened so long ago, and you've got these sixteen-year-old kids saying "Well, I deserve [reparations] because my great, great, granddaddy was a slave," Well, you know what, it doesn't affect you. Me, as [a] white person, I had nothing to do with slavery. You, as a black person, you never experienced it. It was so long ago I just don't see how that pertains to what's happening to the race today, so that's one thing that I'm just like "God, shut up!"

As exemplified in Dina's statement, this story line involves more than a denial of personal responsibility for historical discrimination. The claim is in fact much broader: that historical discrimination does not disadvantage blacks today. Therefore, this story conveys the notion that the current social order is race-neutral and based on individual merit and effort....

"IF JEWS, ITALIANS, AND IRISH HAVE MADE IT, HOW COME BLACKS HAVE NOT?"

Another popular story line of the post–civil rights era is "If Jews, Italians, and Irish (or other ethnic groups) have made it, how come blacks have not?" This story is used to suggest that because other groups who experienced discrimination are doing well today, the predicament of blacks' must be their own doing. Although fewer respondents explicitly deployed this story in the interviews, a significant percentage agreed with a survey question on this matter (60% of DAS respondents and 35% of college students). An example of how whites used this story is provided by Kim, a student at SU, who used it to explain why she does not favor government intervention on minorities behalf.

> No. I think that a lot of bad things happened to a lot of people, but you can't sit there and dwell on that. I mean, like the Jewish people, look what happened to them. Do you hear them sitting around complaining about, it and attributing anything bad that happens to them? I've never heard anyone say, "Oh, it's because I'm Jewish." And I know it's a little different because a black, I mean, you can't really, a lot of—you can't really tell on the outside a lot of times, but they don't wallow in what happened to them a long time ago. It was a horrible thing I admit, but I think that you need to move on and try to put that behind you.

Here, this story line is used to question blacks' claims to harm. It also presents a moral racial tale: the way to deal with hard times is to work hard and not to "wallow" in what happened "a long time ago" which, according to the story, is presumably what other racial and ethnic groups have done to move up in this country.

An example of how DAS respondents used this story line comes from Henrietta, a transvestite schoolteacher in his fifties, who inserted the story to answer a question on compensatory government spending on blacks' behalf.

> As a person who was once reversed discriminated against, I would have to say no. Because the government does not need programs if they, if people would be motivated to bring themselves out of the poverty level. Ah... when we talk about certain programs, when the Irish came over, when the Italians, the Polish, and the East European Jews, they all were immigrants who lived in terrible conditions, who worked in terrible conditions too. But they had one thing in common; they all knew that education was the way out of that poverty. And they did it. I'm not saying the blacks were brought over here maybe not willingly, but if they realize education's the key, that's it. And that's based on individuality.

What is ideological about this story? Have not Jews, Irish, and other ethnic groups moved up and even assimilated in America? The problem is that this story line equates the experiences of immigrant groups with those of involuntary "immigrants" (enslaved Africans, etc.). But as Stephen Steinberg pointed out some time ago, most immigrant groups were able to get a foothold in certain economic niches or used resources such as an education or small amounts of capital to achieve social mobility. "In contrast, racial minorities were for the most part relegated to the preindustrial sectors of the national economy and, until the flow of immigration was cut off by the First World War, were denied access to the industrial jobs that lured tens of millions of immigrants. All groups started at the bottom, but as Blauner points out, "the bottom" has by no means been the same for all groups" (Steinberg, 1989:101). Thus, the comparison in this story line is not appropriate, as the historical experiences and opportunities of the groups in question are vastly different.

"I DID NOT GET A JOB (OR A PROMOTION OR WAS ADMITTED TO A COLLEGE) BECAUSE OF A BLACK MAN"

The core of this story is the idea that less qualified minorities (mostly referring to blacks, although occasionally to women) are getting into college or taking jobs that more qualified whites deserve. However, as we will illustrate, this story does not involve concrete experience or knowledge and requires little evidence; the mere presence of a minority person in a particular setting allows whites to ignore the possibility that they are not qualified for a job, a promotion, or admission to a college (for a similar point, see Goldfield, 1997 and Bobo and Suh, 2000). And this story line, although narrated as personal experience, is quite often about distantly removed friends, friends of friends, or neighbors and lacks the spontaneity and vividness of a testimony.

This story line was most often used in discussions about affirmative action or race-based policies. Almost a quarter of the students (10/41) and more than a third of DAS respondents used the story line, "I did not get that job because of a black man." For instance, Bob, a student at SU, opposed providing unique opportunities to minorities to be admitted into Universities:

> I had a friend, he wasn't—I don't like him that much, I think it's my brother's friend, a good friend of my brother's, who didn't get into law school here, and he knows for a fact that other students less qualified than him *did*. And that really—and he was considering a lawsuit against the school. But for some reason, he didn't. He had better grades, better LSAT, better everything, and he....Other people got in up above him, I don't care who it is, if it's Eskimo, or Australian, or what it is, you should have the best person there.

This is a classic example of this story line. Bob's brother has a friend who knows "for a fact" that less qualified minority applicants were admitted into a law school instead of him. For Bob, this is a matter of principle: "the best person (should be) there" whether "it's Eskimo, or Australian."

Darren, a bus driver in his late forties (and other DAS respondents like him), vented lots of animosity toward blacks in his answer to a question on affirmative action. In this context, he inserted the story line to affirm his belief that he had been the victim of reverse discrimination.[5]

> No, other than I have applied at jobs and been turned down because I was white. *Now, I have nothing* against the black person [if he] was qualified better than I was. But when the guy comes into the interview, and I'm off on the side and I can hear them talking, and he can't even speak English, he doesn't know how to read a map, and they're gonna make him a bus driver and hire him over me. I've been doing bus driving off and on since 1973, and I know the guy well enough that [I know] he's a lousy driver. I know why he got the job, and I don't think that's fair.

Although Darren's story seems like a testimony, it has the scheme of this story line. He believes he was passed over for a job by a bus company (presumably the one he currently works for) because he is white. His facts come from what he overheard from an interview with a black applicant. Darren does not provide data on his driving record or the record of the black bus driver.

Complex processes involving multiple applicants are simplified in such stories so that two individuals abstracted from their social context are depicted as going head-to-head in a competition of merit (Wise, 2004). Accordring to the story, race triumphs over merit, and a specific black candidate is imagined as the beneficiary who displaced a specific, deserving white candidate. Collectively this story line is important because it makes the case that whites are the real victims of racial discrimination (Feagin and Vera, 1995; Fine and Weis, 1998) and supports the argument that color-blind decisionmaking is the only fair way to proceed.

COUNTERNARRATIVES: EXAMPLES OF WHITE RACIAL PROGRESSIVES AND BLACKS

Are all whites immersed in color-blind racism? Do they all buy into the racial stories we documented here? Do blacks rely on this ideology and its stories, too? Analysis of the interviews revealed that although most whites are "color-blind," 15% of the college students and 12% of the DAS respondents were "racial progressives" who were significantly less likely to invoke these stories.[6] The analysis also revealed that color-blind racism and its stories had a relatively small impact on blacks (but see below). Instead, white racial progressives and blacks were more likely to provide arguments and narratives *against* the dominant frames and racial stories of color-blind racism.

For example, Beth, a student at WU, said in reference to a white male who opposed affirmative action, "Being a white male I guess you don't realize [sic]… [shit] unless it's shoved in your face." She also told the following story about her interaction with this student:

I said, "Well, if you think it's a quota system, well you're wrong" and that maybe it's hard to see what these people go through all their life and, I mean—Me too, being female, what you go through, just the slight discrimination here and there, this like common slur, you don't understand that. You just think it's a harmless joke, but it's not. It builds up. He was just not getting it.

Beth understood that discrimination affects the life chances of minorities and even expressed support for programs that compensate minorities for past discrimination because, she said, "It's hard to start when you have hit rock bottom, it's hard to climb back up."

Judy, a college professor of nursing in her forties, realized discrimination is still important and described various examples of the old and new styles of discrimination. For example, she said that a black man told her that he was not served at a local hospital because he was black. She also mentioned that many blacks are used as guinea pigs because they are black and poor. Finally, she said that a black woman told her that when she shops in the suburbs, "she notices that people won't give her change in her hand" because they are "fearful of her, and that bugs her to death." Judy, like many racial progressives, used her experience as a woman to understand blacks' plight.[7] For instance, while explaining how the few blacks that move up in society "feel always on display," she connected it to her experiences as a woman:

It's kind of like women, you know, have to be that much better just because of various conditions and practices that occur. So in that way I can understand it, because it's difficult being a woman in this society. It is planned, it's organized by men. It's set up for them, and we've had to struggle to become equal. It's just that way for people of color.

Last is Kay, an MU student, who said that her parents were displeased that she had a black boyfriend: "Not between us, but my parents at first didn't approve of it really. Like my parents always told me that I could be friends with black people, but I couldn't date them. But after a while, they just learned that they were gonna have to accept it." Kay's story does not fit the testimonies discussed above that we classified as dealing with someone close who is racist. For example, she did not use this story to exonerate herself or her parents from the influence of racism ("they just learned they were gonna have to accept it").

An example of the counterarguments provided by blacks comes from Edward, an unemployed man in his fifties, who said the following about affirmative action:

> I'd say that I would have to be for affirmative action simply because you still have ignorant people. Some of these ignorant people are in control and have a little more power than I'd like to think they should have... to prevent other people from having opportunities [so] that ... they can't have growth and development. Affirmative Action is a means and [a] method. Then it's like a key when you got a locked door. You've got to have it.

When asked, "What would you say to those who say affirmative action is unfair to whites?" he responded: "I tell them that "What do you call fair?" If you got everything, it's kind of like saying you are upset because you got ice cream and you don't have a cone. Then put it in a bowl, you already got everything. Don't worry about it."

Blacks also believed that discrimination is an important reason for their present status and provided oppositional testimonies as evidence. For example, Tyrone, an unemployed man in his forties, gave the following testimony in his answer to a question on discrimination:

> I think sometimes you do 'Cause I used to work in Sterling Heights [a neighborhood in Detroit], I used to be out there waiting on the bus, somebody would drive by and call me a "black ass nigger" at least three times out of the week and I'm just trying to work and come home.

However, color-blind racism would not be a *dominant* racial ideology if it had not affected at some level even those who oppose it. For an ideology to become dominant, whether based on class, gender, or race, it must have some salience for those on all rungs of the social ladder; it must muddle in some fashion the ideological waters of the dominated and constrain their resistance (van Dijk, 1999). Thus it was not surprising to find that even white racial progressives and blacks were affected by the dominant racial stories.

One example of this phenomenon is provided by Carla, a black woman in her forties who works as an executive secretary. Although the vast majority of blacks supported affirmative action and reparations, she answered the question on reparations as did most whites.

> That became [a] topic in school. I don't remember what I said, but right now I feel that was so long ago that the people who are here now didn't have anything to do with it. So I don't feel it would, I mean, you can say you're sorry but it's not going to take back what happened. Therefore, I don't think it's necessary.

DISCUSSION

In this article we have examined the dominant racial stories of the post–civil rights era. These stories "make" whites, but also help them navigate the turbulent waters of public discussions on race. However, before accepting the accuracy of our analysis of whites' contemporary race-talk, we must address a few plausible alternative explanations.

The first one is the always present possibility of researcher bias. Did we get the answers we got because we framed questions in a particular way? We believe this is unlikely, since the original purpose of these two studies was to assess if whites' racial attitudes were different in interviews than in surveys (Bonilla-Silva and Forman, 2000) rather than to examine whites' racial stories. Therefore, the questions we asked in the interviews were based on the same issues and questions we included in the survey, and the bulk of the questions in the survey were exactly the same questions that other survey researchers have used in the past.[8] The racial stories we found among these respondents were thus not the products of a fishing expedition for "racists" or of tendentious questions intended to make our respondents answer in a particular way.

Second, some analysts disagree about our interpretation of the ideological function of these stories.[9] However, such disagreement does not challenge our claim about the salience of these stories in whites' contemporary imaginary. The fact that the racial stories we identified occurred so regularly in our diverse sample suggests that such stories are being repeated throughout society. Such widespread repetition is unlikely unless those who tell them believe that they reflect some truth about the way the social world works. The fact that old and young alike, working-class and middle-class, and male and female respondents all told these stories and told them so similarly is evidence that they are *collective* narratives.

Third, some analysts may believe that our goal is to label all whites racist. We went to great lengths to show that although most whites accept these stories as the "truth" about racial matters in America, a segment of the white community (and most blacks) do not accept these stories and have developed incipient counternarratives. Theoretically and substantively speaking, as we have argued in previous work (Bonilla-Silva, 1997, 2001, 2003a), the issue is not one of "good" versus "bad" or "educated" versus "ignorant' whites, but one of documenting the growth of a new racial logic that helps preserve racial inequality. Therefore, our data and analysis suggest not that there are more (or less) "racists" or more or less "racism" than in the past, but that a set of racial stories has emerged and is being deployed by whites from a wide range of social backgrounds and from a variety of geographic locations.

Finally, some may argue that we are presenting white respondents in a monolithic fashion. To this potential charge we say that our respondents, like all humans, exhibit contradictions. Thus, some of the respondents who told the dominant racial stories also had progressive views on specific issues (for example, they supported school integration or busing, or approved of interracial marriage). Similarly, although racial progressives and blacks exhibited radically different views from the majority of whites, a few used some of the dominant racial stories. This fact should not surprise students of racial attitudes in the United States (e.g., Schuman, 1997) who have documented the ambivalent views of whites on racial matters, or students of ideology in general, who have pointed out the contested and always unfinished nature of ideology (Billig et al., 1988). Yet, contradictions in attitudes, ideological positions, as well as behavior do not detract from the fact that all actors end up stating and taking positions on social issues (in our case, racial issues). And these contradictions allow us too, as analysts and policymakers, to think about ways to devise political arguments, policies, and politics for effecting social change.

CONCLUSION

The four story lines we analyzed in this article are powerful tools that help most whites maintain a color-blind sense of self and, at the same time, to reinforce views that help reproduce the current racial order. For example, if whites oppose affirmative action or reparations, they can use the "The past of the past" or "I did not own any slaves" story line to bolster the apparent reasonableness of their argument. If the issue involves accounting for blacks' secondary status in this country, whites can use the story line "If (other ethnic groups such as Italians or Jews) made it, how come blacks have not?" Finally, because the story line "I did not get a (job or promotion) because of a black man" seems personal—even though the facts in such stories tend to be second-hand and remoter—it can offer powerful support to those opposing government programs for minorities.

These story lines also allow many whites to vent deep-seated feelings about racial matters (on racism and emotions, see Feagin, 2000). In case after case, whites evinced anger about what they interpret as blacks' whining ("I didn't own any slaves, and I do not understand why they keep asking for things when slavery ended 200 hundred *goddamned* years ago!") or about not getting into certain jobs or universities ("A friend of mine was not admitted into SU Law School, but many *unqualified* blacks students were, and that's *wrong*"). The story lines then serve whites as legitimate conduits for expressing animosity and resentment toward minorities. Together, these story lines offer a specific interpretation of contemporary racial matters that favors whites and the current racial order: "The past is the past, we never benefited from the past, everyone had it bad and, in fact, and we are the real victims of discrimination today" (Doane, 1997; Gallagher, 1995).

These racial stories are "ideological" because they are part of the post–civil rights color-blind "common sense." They represent the world in an "of course" manner—as if these stories are self-evident. Although such stories, as we have noted, are thin on hard data, misrepresent the importance of discrimination (both old and new), and can be classified as the "sincere fictions" of whites (Feagin and Vera, 1995), they are not experienced as such by whites. Instead, these stories are *real* in the imaginary of whites who subscribe to the dominant racial ideology and shape how they come to understand their lives as well as those of blacks. They are factual to them because both storytellers and (white) listeners share a representational community. Hence, the telling and retelling of these stories, strengthens their understanding about how and why the world is the way it is.[10]

Racial narratives, however, potentially do far more than help whites to understand the world in particular ways: they also justify current racial inequality. For example, when trying to explain why blacks are at the bottom of society, these stories are used to suggest that people's station in life depends on ability and hard work, which explains blacks' status as a result of their own shortcomings (Hoschchild, 1995; Wetherell and Potter, 1992). These racial narratives not only attempt to explain larger racial realities but also have the capacity to shape everyday behavior and interactions. For example, recent work on the behavior of whites toward students of color on college campuses (who often are imagined to be the recipients of unfair advantage) demonstrates the pernicious impact of such stories (Feagin et al., 1996; Lewis et al., 2000; Solorzano et al., 2000).

It is the job of social analysts and activists alike to break the conventionality and commonsense character of these stories. We have provided evidence for a way out of the ideological web of color-blind racism and of these stories through our examples of the way white racial progressives and most blacks are challenging these racial narratives. As discussed here, many of these "ideological dissidents" (van Dijk, 1999) and "race traitors" have even developed oppositional narratives (albeit less coherent than the dominant racial narratives). Thus, our tasks are to recognize the origins and strategic functions of these racial stories and help popularize counternarratives (Delgado, 1999) so we can challenge their role in the maintenance of contemporary "white supremacy" (Mills, 1997).

NOTES

1. We borrow the idea of ideology as an "interpretive repertoire" from Wetherell and Potter (1992).
2. In this paper we address the *dominant* story lines of the post–civil rights era. Therefore, the four story lines we highlight do not exhaust all the stories in the field as there may be secondary stories or stories that are corollaries to the dominant ones.
3. We are aware that other authors have developed somewhat similar arguments on post–civil rights racial discourse (e.g., Bobo's "laissez-faire racism," Jackman's "muted hostility," Kinder

and Sanders "symbolic racism," etc.). However, we use the term color-blind racism because it fits better how whites talk about race in the post–civil rights era. More important, this concept is anchored in different theoretical and methodological traditions. Rather than basing this perspective on whites' "attitudes," we argue this viewpoint represents a new ideological cat formation and use textual (rather than survey) data to document it (see Bonilla-Silva, 2003b).

4. No one has *systematic* data on private, nonnormative interactions on race among whites or nonwhites. The available (unsystematic) data suggest that whites' private race-talk is much more racial in tone and content (see Graham, 1995 and, particularly, Myers, 2003).

5. Despite the regularity with which this story line is deployed, the number of actual cases filed by whites as "reverse discrimination" before EEOC is quite small, and the great majority of them are dismissed as bogus (Wicker, 1996).

6. We classified as racial progressives respondents who supported affirmative action, interracial marriage, and recognized the significance of discrimination in the United States. When respondents exhibited reservations on one of these issues, we searched for other elements disclosed in the interview to help us classify these respondents (e.g., whether they had meaningful relationships with minorities or the degree of racial progressiveness on other race-related issues discussed in the interviews).

7. "Our analysis revealed that white racial progressives were significantly more likely to be working-class women. For a discussion, see Bonilla-Silva (2003b:chap. 6).

8. The instruments for the 1998 DAS survey are available from the Detroit Area Study at the University of Michigan. The instruments for the other survey can be obtained from Eduardo Bonilla-Silva.

9. Charles Murray (1984), Hermstein and Murray (1994), D'Souza (1995) and others have concluded that whites' "common sense" on minorities (the idea that minorities are lazy, not too smart, see racism in everything, etc.) is fundamentally right. Liberal social analysts have read whites' contemporary views as expressions of racial ambivalence (Schuman, 1997).

10. We are trying to convey here the positive role of ideology. As Althusser suggested long time ago, the content of an ideology may be false (misrepresent real social relations), but that ideology shapes the actions and behavior of people and is thus real, because ideology "interpellates" individuals as subjects (in our case, as "racial subjects") from the day they are born (Althusser, 1977. On the notion of "racial subjects," see Goldberg, 1993).

REFERENCES

Althusser, Louis 1977 Posiciones (1964–1975). Mexico City, Mexico: Grijalbo.

Barthes, Roland 1977 Introduction to the Structural Analysis of Narratives London: Fontana.

Billig, Michael, Condor, S., and Edwards, D. 1988 Ideological Dilemmas: A Social Psychology of Everyday Thinking. London: Sage.

Bloom, Jack M. 1987 Class, Race, and the Civil Rights Movement. Bloomington: Indiana University Press.

Bobo, Lawrence, Jamews R. Kluegel, and Ryan Smith 1997 "Laissez-faire racism: The crystallization of a kinder, gentler, antiblack ideology." In Steven A. Tuch and Jack Martin (eds.), Racial Attitudes in the 1990s: Continuity and Change: 15–42. Westport, CT: Praeger.

Bobo, Lawrence, and Susan Suh 2000 "Surveying racial discrimination: Analyses from a multiethnic labor market." In Lawrence Bobo, Melvin L. Oliver, James H. Johnson, and Abel Valenzuela, Jr. (eds.), Prismatic Metropolis: Inequality in Los Angeles: 523–560. New York: Sage.

Bonilla-Silva, Eduardo 1997 "Rethinking racism: Toward a structural interpretation." American Sociological Review 62(3):465–480.

Bonilla-Silva, Eduardo 2001 White Supremacy and Racism in the Post–Civil Rights Era. Boulder, CO: Lynne Rienner.

Bonilla-Silva, Eduardo 2003a "Racial attitudes or racial ideology? An alternative paradigm for examining actors' racial views." Journal of Political Ideologies 8(1):63–82.

Bonilla-Silva, Eduardo 2003b Racism Without Racists: Color-Blind Racism and the Persistence of Racial Inequality in the United States. Lanham, MD: Rowman and Littlefield.

Bonilla-Silva, Eduardo, and Tyrone A. Forman 2000 "I' not a racist, but . . . : Mapping white college students' racial ideology in the USA." Discourse and Society.

Bonilla-Silva, Eduardo, and Amanda E. Lewis 1999 "The now racism: Racial structure in the United States, 1960s–l990s." In Paul Wong (ed.), Race, Ethnicity, and Nationality in the USA: Toward the Twenty-First Century: 55–101. Boulder, CO: Westview.

Clinton, Catherine 1982 The Plantation Mistress. New York: Pantheon Books.

Crenshaw, Kimberlé W. 1997 "Color-blind dreams and racial nightmares: Reconfiguring racism in the post–civil rights era." In T. Morrison and C.B. Lacour (eds.), Birth of a Nation'hood. New York: Pantheon Books.

Delgado, Richard 1999 When Equality Ends: Stories About Race and Resistance. Boulder, CO: Westview.

Doane, Ashley 1997 "While identity and race relations in the 1990s." In Gregg Lee Carter (ed.), Perspectives on Current Social Problems: 157–170. Boston: Allyn and Bacon.

D'Souza, Dinesh 1995 The End of Racism: Principles for a Multiracial Society. New York: Free.

Feagin, Joe R. 2000 Racist America. New York: Routledge.

Feagin, Joe R., and Herman Vera 1995 White Racism: The Basics. New York: Routledge.

Feagin, Joe R., Herman Vera, and Nikitah imani 1996 The Agony of Education: Black Students at White Colleges and Universites. New York: Routledge.

Fine, Michelle, and Lois Weis 1998 The Unknown City. Boston: Beacon.

Fredrickson, George 2002 Racism: A Short History. Princeton, NJ: Princeton University Press.

Gallagher, Charles 1995 "White Reconstruction in the University." Socialist Review 94(1/2): 165–187.

Goldberg, David 1993 Racist Culture: Philosophy and the Politics of Meaning. London: Blackwell.

Goldfield, Michael 1997 The Color of Politics. New York: New York Press.

Graham, Lawrence Otis, 1995, Member of the club: reflections on life in a racially polarized world. New York: Harper Collins Publishers.

Hall, Stuart 1990 "The whites of their eyes: Racist ideologies and the media." In Manuel Alvarado and John Thompson (eds.), The Media Reader: 110–125. London: British Film Institute.

Herrnestein, Richard J., and Charles A. Murray 1994 The Bell Curve. New York: Free Press.

Hill-Collins, Patricia 1990 Black Feminist Thought. Boston: Unwin Hyman.

Hochschild, Jennifer L. 1995 Facing Up to the American Dream. Princeton, NJ: Princeton University Press.

Jackman, Mary R. 1994 The Velvet Glove. Berkeley and Los Angeles: University of California Press.

Kinder, David R., and Lynn M. Sanders 1996 Divided by Color: Racial Politics and Democratic Ideals. Chicago: University of Chicago Press.

Lewis, Amanda 2003 "Everyday race-making: Navigating racial boundaries in schools." American Behavioral Scientist 47(3):283–305.

Lewis, Amanda, Mark Chesler, and Tyrone Forman 2000 "The impact of color-blind ideologies on students of color: Intergroup relations at a predominantly white university" Journal of Negro Education 69(1/2):74–91.

Lipset, Seymour 1996 American Exceptionalism. New York: W.W. Norton.

McConahay, John B. 1986 "Modern racism, ambivalence, and the modern racism scale." In John F. Dovidio and Samuel L. Gaertner (eds.), Prejudice, Discrimination and Racism: 91–126. New York: Academic.

Murray, Charles A. 1984 Losing Ground. New York: Basic Books.

Myers, Kristen. 2003 "White Fright: Reproducing White Supremacy Through Casual Discourse." In, White Out: The Continuing Significance of Racism, Woody Doane and Eduardo Bonilla-Silva, eds. New York: Routledge.

Omi, Michael, and Howard Winant 1994 Racial Formation in the United States. New York: Routledge.

Schuman, Howard 1997 Racial Attitudes in America: Tends and Interpretations. Cambridge, MA: Harvard University Press.

Shapiro, Thomas, Melvin L. Oliver 1995 Black Wealth,/White Wealth: A New Perspective on Racial Inequality (with Melvin L. Oliver). New York: Routledge.

Sniderman, Paul, and Edward G. Carmines 1997 Reaching Beyond Race. Cambridge, MA: Harvard University Press.

Solorzano, Daniel, Miguel Ceja, and Tara Yosso 2000 "Critical race theory, racial microaggressions and campus racial climate." Journal of Negro Education 69(1/2):60–73.

Somers, Margaret 1994 "The narrative constitution of identity: A relational and network approach." Theory and Society 23:605–649.

Steinberg, Stephen 1989 The Ethnic Myth. Boston: Beacon.

van Dijk, Teun 1999 Ideology: A Multidisciplinary Approach. London: Sage.

Wellman, David 1997 "Minstrel shows, affirmative action talk, and angry white men: Marking racial otherness in the 1990s." In Ruth Frankenberg (ed.), Displacing Whiteness: Essays in Social and Cultural Criticism: 311–331. Durham and London: Duke University Press.

Wetherell, Margaret, and Jonathan Potter 1992 Mapping the Language of Racism: Discourse and the Legitimation of Exploitation. New York: Columbia University Press.

Wicker, Tom 1996 Tragic Failure: Racial Integration in America. New York: William Morrow.

Wise, Tim 2004 "White wine: Reflections on the brain-rotting properties of privilege." Znet Magazine. April 20. Available at http://zmag.org/weluser.htm.

JOURNALING QUESTION

When someone doesn't get a job, or doesn't get into a school that he or she really wanted, friends may encourage that person not to "take it personally." Have you ever heard anyone using the "a black man got the job" argument to comfort a white person?

8.

THE BEAUTY QUEUE

Advantages of Lighter Skin

MARGARET L. HUNTER

In the United States, color, more than any other physical characteristic, signifies race. But "color" is also an attribute of individuals—human skin tone varies both within and across "race" categories. For women, appearance has been made especially important, and skin tone is an important part of appearance. So this way of thinking about race has real consequences in the lives of individual women, as Margaret Hunter shows in her interviews with African American and Mexican American women. In both of these cultural groups, a woman's skin tone affects her place in the social hierarchy or in what Hunter calls the "beauty queue." What meanings do "people of color" give to variations in color?

We always laughed in my dorm that the first month of school really light-skinned girls got dates. Then the brown-skinned girls started getting dates. And finally by Christmas when all these relationships were breaking up maybe the darker-skinned girls would get a date.[1]

Pearl Marsh, a darker-skinned woman, told this story to sociologist Maxine Leeds Craig for her study on black women and the politics of beauty. Marsh's description of black women rank ordered by skin color is not an anomaly. The high status of light-skinned women in the dating and marriage market is an endemic feature in both the African American and Mexican American communities. Marsh describes what I call a "beauty queue." The beauty queue is a rank ordering of women from lightest to darkest where the lightest get the most perks and rewards, dates for example, and the darkest women get the least. This chapter outlines the enormous and oppressive role of beauty in women's lives and explores the advantages that light skin brings its wearers.

"Because beauty is asymmetrically assigned to the feminine role, women are defined as much by their looks as by their deeds," writes Rita Freedman, author of *Beauty Bound*.[2] In other words, in a sexist society women's bodies indicate their worth, more often than their minds or actions. Because "beauty" is a cultural construction, it is informed by other kinds of societal status characteristics, most significantly race. This helps explain why in the United States, where white racism still operates, light skin is often associated with beauty. Beauty also acts as a status characteristic that affects women's ability to get jobs or choose a spouse.[3] With these ideas in mind, this chapter explores how cultural assumptions about beauty and skin color affect the lives of Mexican American and African American women in their own voices.

This is the first qualitative and comparative examination of the attitudes of African American and Mexican American women regarding skin tone issues in everyday life.[4] Conversations with the women interviewees suggest that skin color stratification has both similar and different meanings in the African American and Mexican American communities.[5] The women I spoke with revealed

---

Excerpted from Margaret L. Hunter, "The Beauty Queue: Advantages of Light Skin, " in Race, Gender, and the Politics of Skin Tone (New York: Routledge, 2005), 69–92. Notes have been renumbered and edited.

an intense concern about light skin color as a status characteristic. Light skin was seen as a device for approval in families, as well as a near pre-requisite for the designation "beautiful." It was also a focal point of jealousies between female friends and family members. Despite the claim by women of both groups that light skin was considered more beautiful by society than dark, significant differences remain in just how these skin color politics played out in each community.

Notions of beauty are so closely related to color that the terms "light-skinned" and "pretty" were nearly synonymous. This conflation of concepts was particularly true among Mexican American women because in Spanish *güera* means both "light" and "pretty." The English equivalent would be "fair" which also means "light" or "white-skinned" and "pretty." The famous quote from the story *Snow White* serves as a great reminder of this double meaning, when the evil stepmother asks the mirror, "Who is the fairest of them all?" The mirror replies, "Snow White." She is after all, young and beautiful, and as her name implies, undoubtedly white.

I use the metaphor of a queue in this discussion of beauty, and color for three reasons. First, the concept of a queue shows that women are rank ordered by men and by one another, according to their beauty quotient (totality of physical traits) and consequently, according to their skin color. Second, the concept shows how all women are evaluated by their physical appearances to the point that beauty has become a form of social capital for women. Beauty works as capital in the sense that the more of it one has, the more able one will be to marry a high-status husband, and the more able one will be to increase her own income and education. Third, I use the metaphor of the queue because it invokes the image of women waiting in line for male partners. Much of the interaction among women over skin color and beauty is centered on the perceived competition for male partners. In the following analysis I show how beauty works as an ideology and how the beauty queue,

and each person's place in it, is implicitly understood by all women.

A significant number of interviewees admitted at some time in their lives wanting to have lighter skin, lighter eyes, or longer hair. Both African American and Mexican American interviewees believed that light-skinned women were attractive and many African American, but fewer Mexican American women found light-skinned men of their groups to be attractive. Skin color, eye color, and hairstyles that most approximated whites were highly revered and often sought after through colored contacts, hair straightening, and hair coloring by women of both ethnic groups. However, intertwined with the high value on a white bodily aesthetic, was a simultaneous distrust and resentment of women who did possess these white-like traits. This was particularly true for African American women. Mexican American women were more likely to report feeling jealous or resentful of lighter-skinned family members, especially sisters or female cousins. I begin my discussion with the African American interviews, then I will discuss the Mexican American women's interviews, and I end this chapter with a comparison of their experiences and a discussion of forms of reflection and resistance.

AFRICAN AMERICAN WOMEN AND COLOR

Among the African American participants, the most frequent and consistent characterization was that of the "light-skinned, stuck-up, snobby, pretty, black girl." This stereotype came up in almost every interview with an African American, whether dark or light-skinned. Many dark-skinned women discussed this characterization as a truth, or as previously believing in its reality when they were young; and most light-skinned black women discussed battling regularly with this. In general, both lighter-skinned and darker-skinned women agreed that as a rule, light-skinned women were considered by men to be more attractive than dark-skinned women. This belief left many darker-skinned women feeling hostile and resentful toward the lighter women.

Belinda, who is a dark-skinned African American woman said,

> In terms of female-female relationships, I think color affects how we treat each other. Like if you're lighter and I think you're better, and I think the guys want you, then I won't treat you nicely. I'll take every opportunity to ignore you, or not tell you something, or keep you out of my little group of friends, because really I feel threatened, so I want to punish you because you have it better than me.

Belinda is strikingly honest in revealing that she feels threatened by lighter-skinned women and their attractiveness to black men. She also admits that sometimes she feels lighter women are "better" than she is. Her way of coping with the unfair value placed on light skin is to outcast lighter women from her own circle of friends. Belinda clearly sees her hostile actions toward lighter women as "punishment" for having privileges that she does not. Her experience is not unique. Lighter-skinned women often reported feeling socially ostracized and resented by darker-skinned African American women. Belinda's hostile feelings are a compelling example of the pain that can be caused by the emphasis on skin color in the African American community.

I asked Kitara, another dark-skinned black woman I interviewed, to describe how color affected her as a young girl.

> Both my parents are dark-skinned black, too, and they wanted me to have the whole black pride thing.... We never considered skin bleaching or anything like that. We just dealt with it... It hurts when you're younger because you are the butt of jokes. For the longest time you feel like you are just so ugly. I was dark-skinned, tall, and skinny, and that was a bad combination. I was really quiet, I would relax around my friends, but I was quiet.

Kitara's story is particularly compelling because it shows that even well meaning parents, who want you to "have the whole black pride thing" cannot protect their children from the strong cultural messages that denigrate black skin. Kitara implies that she experienced frequent anxiety over the teasing she encountered when she says, "I would relax around my friends." One can imagine a child who is often embattled with other kids over skin color, and can only let her guard down among friends and family.

Throughout the interviews with African American women, the theme of competition for male partners was constant. The demographic reality of the African American community today exacerbates the perception (and reality) of competition for scarce male partners because of the unbalanced sex ratio of African Americans. Because of the large numbers of African American men currently incarcerated, underemployed, and unemployed, many African American women feel a market scarcity of "marriageable" men.[6] This scarcity leads to increased tension and competition among African American women for the limited number of potential male partners, thus increasing animosity over issues of beauty and skin color.

Karla, a light-skinned black woman, told me about her anxieties about skin color issues before she went to college.

> Before I came to [this university] I had this nightmare that I had two black roommates and I just walked in and they were like "Yaarrrgh!" [*said in a hostile voice*]. It was horrible. I mean I have nightmares about this stuff. I don't feel like I'm racist, it just makes me feel really sad. There is one black girl on my floor in the dorms and we're kind of buddying up and it makes me feel really good.

Karla's story is emblematic of the longing for female friendship and connection that is so often stymied by tension from skin color differences. Light-skinned Karla had so much fear of rejection from dark-skinned women that she had nightmares about it. But beneath those anxieties was a real yearning to connect with other black women that she says "makes me feel really good."

This tension among African American women was not only felt by darker-skinned women, but also by lighter-skinned women. Aisha is a mixed-race (black and white) woman, and identified as African American. She expressed regret and frustration as she described a history of conflict between herself and darker-skinned black women.

> I can only say that I've had problems growing up, as far as my race, with full black females and for the simple fact that… I'm sure everyone that has talked to you has said this, but, they just look at you and say, "Oh, you just think you are so cute just because you're mixed and you got good hair." I remember when I was in high school it was my freshman year. There was this guy, he was black, but you know he just didn't interest me. He asked me for my number and I was like, "No, that's okay." I just wasn't interested. Well, these girls must have been friends of his or something, and two or three of them got pissed off because I didn't want to talk to him and they said, "Oh, you just think you're too good and you can't talk to him because you just think you're too cute." And that pissed me off. Even to this day I am still uncomfortable to walk into a room with a bunch of full black girls because I feel like they just look at me up and down and think, "Oh, you just think that you are so cute." I have always thought that it was envy in a way, not because I am the better of anyone, not at all, but I think even they feel that lighter is better. Maybe because they've been told for so long that dark is not pretty and dark is bad.

Aisha, like many of the other women I interviewed, invoked the image of the light-skinned girl who thinks she is "too cute," although she does so in order to challenge it. Aisha makes a compelling observation when she says that she thinks even the darker-skinned girls think lighter is better. She touches on the serious damage internalized racism can do to individuals, as well as to communities. Interestingly, Aisha describes her struggles with other black girls as not only about color, but also racial identity. Despite the fact that she identifies as African American, even though she is mixed, she describes the struggle over color not with "darker-skinned girls," but with "full black girls." For Aisha, and other mixed-race African

American women I interviewed, skin color was closely tied to racial identity and resentment toward lighter-skinned girls was synonymous with resentment toward mixed-race girls. Aisha describes being harassed by darker-skinned/ "full black" girls in high school and characterized herself as a "victim" of their teasing. Several of the light-skinned African American women reported being "victimized" in various ways by darker-skinned African American women. This included being socially sanctioned, being harassed, ostracized, and in one extreme case even included threats of violence. Their alleged "victimization" is a surprising inversion of the larger system of colorism that victimizes darker-skinned people in many ways. This is an important point discursively as well. Clearly, darker-skinned women are at a disadvantage in terms of social status. Yet, it is lighter-skinned women who consistently, throughout each interview, characterized themselves as victims of dark-skinned women.

Delilah is a black woman with a medium brown complexion and very long, curly black hair. Though she does have friendships with other African American women, she reports much tension over "the hair issue" and recounts the following story about the first elementary school she attended.

> The school in that area was majority Filipino and African American, no white people. I went there for a month and then my mother took me out of that school because… girls tried to cut my hair off, they said black girls aren't supposed to have long hair. Black girls hated me. Girls would say, "Oh, you stole my boyfriend." And I said, "I don't even know your boyfriend." They kept saying things like, "I'm gonna beat your ass with a baseball bat…" They chased me down. The school couldn't do anything about it until one of the girls did something to me. And my mom said, "I'm not going to wait for one of these girls to kill her," so I transferred and I went to a school about 30 minutes away.

Delilah's experience is an extreme example of jealousy and distrust among African American girls. Long hair is highly sought after in the black community and is typically associated with whites. The booming hair care industry that includes wigs, weaves, and braids is evidence of the pursuit of long hair.[7] It is rare to find a young black girl who is not "trying to grow her hair out." In fact, many girls and women wear their hair in braids or use hair extensions, not for the Afrocentric look it creates, but sometimes for the opposite reason, to allow their hair to grow out while it is braided. Belinda told me about recently putting her hair in braids.

> Yeah, I got braids to give my hair a break from the chemicals and let it get healthier, so it could grow. But then, that's the whole thing about growing your hair long. Everybody's talking about growing their hair. Everybody wants long pretty hair.

Long hair, often called "good hair" is an important corollary to light skin for high status and beauty in the African American community.[8] In fact, the "good hair/bad hair" issue is so prevalent in the black community, several authors have written children's books to try to destigmatize kinky or nappy hair.[9]

Aisha believed that color was such a significant issue in the African American community because it was a vehicle through which women competed for male partners. She was one of the few respondents who characterized the quest for beauty and status among women as a diversion from larger and more problematic gender relations between women and men in the African American community.

> I think among black women more than any other group of women there is the most competition. I think they are so much in competition with each other that girls who are friends really don't trust their own friends. They still talk shit about their own friends. That's what I've never liked because I'm not that way. I think it's a terrible way to be. If we are going to be in conflict about anything it should be the men and the differences we have with them and how they try to oppress us from a gender perspective. I think it's so ugly really, and that's one of the best words I could use. It's just plain ugly to be in so much competition over men.

Aisha describes the "ugliness" of competition for men as harmful to black women's friendships, and a distraction from problems between men and women. Aisha and Regina both shared with me their concern about the situation among black women, but Aisha's thinking on the topic went even further because she suggests that distrust over color leaves other important community problems unaddressed. In fact, Aisha lays the foundation for the argument that I am trying to build, that competition among women over skin color is a diversion from larger oppressive systems such as racism and sexism. She describes the internalized racism among many African Americans that results in the lack of trust or intimacy in some African American women's relationships.

MEXICAN AMERICAN WOMEN AND COLOR

Attitudes toward skin color and beauty were similar in many ways between African American and Mexican American women. Participants from both groups thought that, as a rule, in order to be considered pretty one had to have light skin. Mexican Americans, as well as African Americans shared painful experiences of being the "dark" one in the family, or of feeling less favored than lighter-skinned family members. Of course, dark skin means different things in each community. Among the African Americans I spoke with, dark skin was not necessarily an important class distinction. Skin color was more of a racial marker; revealing a mixed-race background through light skin, for instance, earned high community status. However, in the Mexican American community, being dark-skinned was linked to being Indian and that contained a whole host of meanings about color, class, modernization, and intelligence. The dark-skinned Mexican American participants described trying to avoid being seen as *India*, and Mexican American participants of all colors reported being familiar with negative stereotypes about Indians in Mexico.

Although the trend to assign negative racial meanings to darker-skinned people is similar, the

Mexican American interviewees did not report the high levels of distrust and animosity among Mexican American women that black women reported in their community. The Mexican American interviewees frequently referred to the term *la güera* which is similar in meaning to "fair" in English; both mean "light" and "pretty" simultaneously. Some of the interviewees considered themselves to be *las güeras*, and others grew up as *las prietas*, "the dark ones."

Barbara is a light-skinned Mexican American woman. I asked her to describe what "looking Indian" meant.

> To look Indian means to look dark, to have slanted eyes, high cheekbones. Especially dark, especially dark. That's what gets pointed out. That's how I always grew up with it. They're always the ones with the nicknames. My brother was the really dark one in my family and he was called the *prieto* which means the dark one. I think it's paternalistic. I think it has negative historical roots, but I think it changes to make it affectionate. You know, *"un negrita"* and stuff like that. In Mexico it s *mi morena*, but I think that that's the way darker-skinned Chicanos are looked upon, to be more Indian. Which is the way that Mexico looks at Indians, to be not as modern, not as sophisticated. It's just not as pretty, or not as... white. Not as attractive.

Barbara points out an ongoing tension in Mexican American culture: the negative and yet affectionate terms such as *"mi negrita," "mi prieto"* and *"mi morena."* She describes them as paternalistic because they make people appear child-like by often using "mi" meaning "my." This may imply ownership, superiority, or affection. These terms are reminiscent of negative and paternalistic terms that African Americans were called during slavery like "little darkies" or "pickaninnies." Barbara, like...Aisha has reflected on this topic enough to have ambivalence about what previously seemed liked harmless nicknames. It is also important to note the strong racial language Barbara invoked about looking Indian. The discourses of modernity and civilization are still present when describing Mexican Indians and are therefore still symbolized when evaluating dark skin color, because it is associated with Indians.

Even young children learn early lessons about skin color and status. Alicia works at an elementary school and describes a conversation between two children there.

> I work as a TA at an elementary school and this little girl started saying, "Teacher! Teacher!" She was really mad and she said, "Jose called me an *India*!" And I looked at her and thought, why does she think that is so bad? She was really upset about it like he called her a bad name. And these were two Latino children. And being called *"India,"* that really struck her like, "That was so evil why did you call me that?" I noticed that.

Even Alicia was surprised by the young children's sharp adherence to racial hierarchies. Both children in the interaction knew that to be considered *India* was degrading. And the girl's appeal to Alicia as an authority figure shows that the girl expected Alicia to also appreciate the gravity of the epithet. Some might want to chalk this incident up to child's play. And though teasing is a part of all children's experience, racial epithets are not and many adults who received those insults as children still harbor the wounds. This teasing does not end in elementary school. I asked Isabel, a dark-skinned Mexican American woman, if skin color ever came up in her high school experience.

> Yeah, I had a friend who looked white, but she spoke Spanish because she was Mexican. She was very popular because she was so light.... A lot of the darker girls were not [popular]. It was a good thing to be light. And a lot of the kids would make fun of me because I would get dark. So they would call me "nigger." And I would take it like, "Yeah, so?" I could care less. What was I going to do? I couldn't do anything about that.

Isabel reveals many meanings of skin color in her comments, most notably the tension between

Blacks and Chicanos in Los Angeles as exemplified in calling dark-skinned Mexican Americans "niggers." Although for most Mexican Americans, dark skin is closely associated with indigenous identity, for others, it is also associated with blackness. For Mexican Americans and other people of color who internalize white racist norms, blackness is something to avoid just as much as Indianness.

Alicia, a darker-skinned Mexican American woman, told me about her own experiences with the quest for physical beauty and how her friends and family encouraged her to look lighter, or at least to avoid looking any darker. It was clear to her that having darker skin was to be avoided through use of makeup, clothes, or hair coloring. It was not overtly associated with attractiveness to men, but was definitely a status issue.

> I'll dye my hair and my mom will say, "Don't dye it that color it "makes you look darker." More value is placed on being light. The girls they make comments like, "Oh, did you see her? She's so pretty. Her eyes, they're so light." The hair color is brought up a lot. "Oh, try this color, it will make you look lighter." Even with lighter skin, my friend dyed her hair jet black and everybody was like, "Yeah, that looks good, it makes you look lighter. I like that."

Alicia expressed her feelings about this topic with exasperation. She seemed to feel that people were overly concerned with color and that there was no such thing as being too light, as evidenced by the fact that even light-skinned people were trying to look lighter. Alicia told this story with some feelings of shame about her appearance, but she clearly had moved in her thinking over the years. She told the story in the past tense and described it as outrageous and unfair, showing that although she experienced colorism, she did not buy into it.

Patricia Zavella's research supports Alicia's contention of color consciousness in the Mexican American community. Zavella writes, "Although some change is occurring regarding the preferred body image, our society still values women who are white—and blond in particular—and who have

European features."[10] Zavella goes on to argue that, "Individuals within Chicano communities may reflect this devaluation, or even internalize it, so that physical features are often noted and evaluated: Skin color in particular is commented on, with *las güeras* (light-skinned ones) being appreciated and *las prietas* (dark-skinned ones) being admonished and devalued."[11] The value of light skin is so enmeshed in Mexican American cultural values that many people do not even realize the pain they cause others by making evaluative comments about skin color.

Alicia was very similar to other women in the study in her reaction to color issues: She was frustrated and hurt by the devaluation of dark skin, but she did not have a sense of why color was so important in our society or how this hierarchy was started. This disjuncture between colorism and beauty standards demonstrates that most women do not have a rubric for understanding skin color politics that includes racism. Issues of beauty and color were often described by people as silly, or petty, but not usually as a part of a larger system of racism. Beauty has become such a powerful economic force in this country that it is seen as independent of other forces of oppression, such as racism and sexism. Making the connection between these concepts is crucial in order to expose the subtle ways that racism and sexism persist in the lives of women of color.

Another Mexican American interviewee, Elena, said that she believed that values of color were so ingrained in Mexican American consciousness, they were often hard to detect. She describes how colorism is almost an unconscious process.

> I don't think that people mean to say that lighter people are pretty, but I know that in general when someone comments on someone being really pretty, it's generally a light person. But I notice when someone's talking about a girl who's pretty, or even a guy who's good looking, they're usually light.

Elena describes how attractiveness is typically noticed only in people who are light-skinned. In this way, she says, people are not overtly saying that only light-skinned women are attractive, but the message is still the same. The cumulative effect of naming beauty only in light-skinned people still communicates that dark skin is undesirable. The corollary to this phenomenon is qualifying beauty in dark-skinned women. For instance, the saying, "She's dark, but she's pretty" is a common one in both the Mexican American and African American communities. It shows that darkness is not normally associated with beauty, but in this exceptional case, the woman in question is dark, *but* pretty—she is able to transcend her skin color. The exception proves the rule.

Many Mexican American respondents described their families in terms of who was lightest and who was darkest and how their skin tones affected their experiences both inside and outside of the family. These descriptions often included family nicknames regarding color or more simply *la güera* and *el prieto*. This practice points to the importance of skin color as an identifier in many Mexican American families.

> The one person we do tease in the family about color is my Uncle Art. He is very light. His whole family is light with blonde hair and light eyes. So it's always kind of a joke. And he developed a country accent because he used to hang out with a lot of white kids in Florida. They would say to him, "Oh, you're the light sheep of the family!" I guess my grandma, when he was born, she thought they switched babies on her because he was so light. She cried about it and everything.
>
> They used to call my aunt, who is dark, "la negra." But they call me "the white one." That's me. I don't know if that's a positive thing or a negative thing.
>
> Yeah, they used to call me "morena" or "prieta" because I was the darkest one of the family. And my other sister, they used to call her "guera" which means light one.

All of these examples from the interviews with Mexican Americans show the important role that skin color plays in family dynamics. In some families, skin color related nicknames were used in playful, more benign ways, and in others they were painful barbs that reinforced status differences among the members. Skin color, related nicknames were commonly reported among almost all of the Mexican American women I spoke with and most women agreed that after the gender, skin color was one of the first traits of newborn babies commented upon in their families.

INTERNALIZING RACISM AND SEXISM

The beauty queue is alive and well in the Mexican American and African American communities. Light-skinned women are privileged in many areas of life, including being defined as the most beautiful, by being at the front of the queue. However, there are also costs for those at the front of the queue—resentment and distrust from darker-skinned women, and possibly fewer opportunities for female friendship. The damage done to female friendships, by the presence of and adherence to the beauty queue, seems to be much more devastating in the African American community than in the Mexican American community. This may be due in part to competition over a perceived scarcity of men. Ironically, even when women are able to see the harm of the beauty queue and of color hierarchy, they often still adhere to it by wishing they were lighter, or had longer hair.

This is an example of how hegemony works. The subjugated people rule themselves according to the laws of the powerful. Whites need no longer police the boundaries of race and status, because people of color have internalized their racial hierarchies. Kitara, a dark-skinned black woman, describes being teased about her dark complexion as a young girl.

> When I was a lot younger you have the jokes, the monkey jokes…I went to a black school and most of us were dark-skinned black, but it was still there. Nobody wanted to be all the way black. They tried to be, "You know I'm Indian" or something…. It wasn't cool to be all the way black.

Kitara's painful story illustrates how African American people have internalized the racist beliefs of whites (monkey jokes) and inflicted them upon one another. According to Kitara, black children try to avoid the stigma of blackness by claiming some type of mixed race heritage ("You know I'm Indian"). In this case, whites need not even be present (an all black school) for racism and colorism to flourish. The hegemony of beauty and color works the same way. Many people of color have internalized racial hierarchies to such an extent that some women claw each other to get to the front of the beauty queue and conform to white standards of beauty. This is a tightly woven matrix of racism and sexism. Several of the women I interviewed commented on the ephemeral nature of colorism. They described it as everywhere, and yet hard to identify or point out.

> Even though I say I haven't seen it blatantly out there, it is still there. I don't know how, but subtly. It just seems like there is this thing where light-skinned girls are prettier and have nicer hair. I can't understand where it came from, but I feel like it's always there.

> I really don't see it as that big of a deal around the color issue, even though I know that it is a deal. I think it is a factor, but it's kind of like underground. No one really speaks about it very much, but it is there, kind of like racism to some extent. Like a lot of white people really don't want to talk about racism although it really exists, and they try to overlook it. Maybe it's to some extent like that.

Both of these quotations describe the way that colorism has seeped into everyday culture so that it is hard to clearly identify, even though everyone sees it. Many of the women I interviewed expressed similar seemingly contradictory sentiments. Color is not a significant issue because no one really talks about it, while at the same time saying that color remains an extremely divisive issue. This is part of the challenge of critically discussing colorism and racism.

It is important to remember who benefits from the ideology of beauty and the beauty queue. Ultimately, both of these constructs serve to maintain sexism and racism because they objectify and commodify women and they value whiteness over brownness and blackness. The power of these systems has seeped into the cultures and consciousness of people of color, encouraging them to value whiteness and to strive toward it.

The majority of the women I interviewed painfully discussed their relationships with other women and their own feelings of inadequacy stemming from their color. They either felt that they were considered ugly because they were too dark, or they felt that they lacked substantial relationships with other women because they were too light and no one trusted them. Other women felt they were constantly being compared to lighter more beautiful women, even by their own friends and family. The most distressing commonality among the interviewees is that almost all of their pain resulting from colorism came from the words and deeds of members of their own ethnic groups. Pamela, a dark-skinned African American woman, said,

> To tell you the truth, I didn't have many black friends in high school because in high school I was teased [about my color]. So I just stuck with the people who didn't really care about my skin color and that was everyone but black people.

And Elena, a lighter-skinned Mexican American, said,

> I faced what I would consider discrimination from my own people I have also faced it from other people, but the bulk of it has been from my own community.

Both light-skinned and dark-skinned women described feeling let down by members of their own ethnic groups when they had painful experiences over skin color. Although African Americans and Mexican Americans have done their part in maintaining colorism and allowing it to enter their relationships with one another, white racism remains the root of this system.

Despite the grim situation of internalized racism in both the African American and Mexican American communities, progress has been made.

Almost without exception, the great majority of the women I interviewed expressed some amount of pride in their ethnic identity. Further, many of the interviewees were engaging in reflection about how color and race have affected their own lives and what they have done to perpetuate, or work against the hierarchies. These are examples of the critical work all people must do in order to see racism and sexism more clearly which will guide them ultimately, to be able to change society.

NOTES

1. Quote from an interview with Pearl Marsh in Maxine Leeds Craig, *Ain't I A Beauty Queen?*
2. Freedman, *Beauty Bound*, 1.
3. Glen Elder, "Appearance and Education in Marriage Mobility," *American Sociological Review* 34 (1969): 519–33. Elaine Hatfield and Susan Sprecher, *Mirror, Mirror: The Importance of Looks in Everyday Life* (Albany: State University of New York Press, 1986). Webster and Driskell, "Beauty as Status."
4. Chapters five and six are based on data from twenty-six qualitative interviews with African American and Mexican American women. The interviews all took place in 1998 on the campus of a large, West Coast university. Students in several large classes were asked if they would like to participate in a study on skin tone. This method yielded interviews with sixteen African American women and ten Mexican American women of various skin colors (see Appendix A). As other studies of colorism have, I used a color palette as a method of assessing lightness or darkness. For each participant, lightness and darkness were assessed in relation to the members of her own ethnic group. This meant that the light-skinned African Americans were generally darker than the light-skinned Mexican Americans.
5. My interview style was influenced by the feminist research methodology literature. See Marjorie DeVault, "Talking and Listening from Women's Standpoint: Feminist Strategies for Interviewing and Analysis," Social Problems 37, no. 1 (1990): 96–116. Mary Margaret Fonow and Judith A. Cook, eds., Beyond Methodology: Feminist Scholarship as Lived Research (Bloomington: Indiana University Press, 1991). Maria Mies, "Towards a Methodology for Feminist Research" in *Theories of Women's Studies*, eds. G. Bowles and R. Klein (New York: Routledge, 1983). Liz Stanley and Sue Wise, *Breaking Out: Feminist Consciousness and Feminist Research* (New York: Routledge, 1983). Catherine Kohler Riessman, "When Gender is Not Enough: Women Interviewing Women," *Gender and Society*, 1, no. 2 (1987): 172–207. Ann Oakley, "Interviewing Women: A Contradiction in Terms" in *Doing Feminist Research*, ed. Helen Roberts (New York: Routledge, 1981). Feminist research methods that focus on interaction and liberation have been developed in response to more traditional, and often male-centered, research methods. Oakley argues that feminist interviewing need not be limited to asked and answered questions, but should include a more interactive dialogue. Not only does this create a more personable and inter-subjective experience for the interviewer and interviewee, but it also yields better, or even more accurate data. Treating the participant as an expert on her own experiences with valuable insights to share also reduces the objectification of the participant and constructs an interview setting that can be, at least ideally, transformative and liberating for both the interviewer and the interviewee.
6. M. Belinda Tucker and Claudia Mitchell-Kernan, "Psychological Well-Being and Perceived Marital Opportunity Among Single African American, Latina, and White Women," *Journal of Comparative Family Studies* 29, no. 1 (1998): 57–72.

7. Ayana D. Byrd and Lori L. Tharps, *Hair Story: Untangling the Roots of Black Hair in America* (New York: St. Martin's Griffin, 2001).
8. Noliwe M. Rooks, *Hair Raising: Beauty, Culture, and African American Women* (New Brunswick: Rutgers University Press, 1996). See also Kia Lilly Caldwell, "Look at Her Hair": The Body Politics of Black Womanhood in Brazil," *Transforming Anthropology* 11, no. 2 (2003): 18–29.
9. See Carolivia Herron, *Nappy Hair* (New York: Dragonfly Books, 1998). bell hooks, *Happy to Be Nappy* (New York: Hyperion Press, 1999).
10. Zavella, "Reflections on Diversity Among Chicanas," 190.
11. Zavella, "Reflections on Diversity Among Chicanas," 190.

JOURNALING QUESTION

Go to a store or a website that advertises products for women of color. What do you learn about desirable skin tones?

9.

DISCOVERING RACIAL BORDERS

HEATHER M. DALMAGE

When a social category is constructed, special attention is paid to the "borders," the places where categories might overlap. It is there that distinctions are drawn. And when the categories are "types" of people, maintaining these borders requires controlling people, an activity Heather Dalmage calls "borderism." How do the forms of borderism she describes—border patrolling, rebound racism, and intensified racism, all of which are directed at people who cross the color line in their family lives—maintain the construction of race categories in America?

…Multiracial family members spend a great deal of time talking, thinking, and theorizing about race. They must. As visible indicators that the color line has been breached, they become lightning rods for racial thoughts, actions, and discussions. At one extreme, they stand as symbolic proof that race no longer matters in society. Some believe that Gunnar Myrdal was right: given enough time, all groups can be absorbed into mainstream culture.[1] The unspoken text is "if blacks and whites are intermarrying, then race must not matter as much anymore." At the other extreme, multiracial family members represent decline, sin, and tragedy. We threaten "the assumption of stable, pure, racial identities," the existence of an essentialist color line.[2]

Unlike multiracial and transracially adopted people who grow up across the color line, interracially married people often grow up in single-race families and communities, learn about themselves and the world through a single-race lens, and later make the decision to cross the color line. Their decision-making processes and the reactions of others show that the color line is internalized and central to human thought, action, and larger social institutions. As these individuals confront the expressed curiosity and hostility of others, they begin to question earlier understandings of race. They begin to think about and "do" race differently. Because multiracial family members visibly challenge race in the United States, their own racial identities and politics cannot be taken for granted.

Throughout history, individuals invested in maintaining the color line have patrolled the line on both sides, albeit for different and often opposing reasons. Whites patrol to protect privilege, blacks as they struggle for liberation. Borders created to protect resources such as goods and power are kept in place by laws, language, cultural norms, images, and individual actions as well as by interlocking with other borders. Many borders exist, and each has a unique history laden with power struggles. Think about some of them: national, religious, political, sexual, gender, racial. People are raised to understand their world through borders. They are taught from an early age to know where borders exist and the consequences for attempting to cross them. For instance, a boy is chastised for wanting to wear a dress or play with dolls while a girl is chastised for wanting to play football. We learn to look for specific indicators, we learn the

Excerpted from Heather M. Dalmage, "Discovering Racial Borders," in *Tripping on the Color Line: Black-White Multiracial Families in a Racially Divided World* (Now Brunswick, NJ: Rutgers University Press, 2000), 33–70. Notes have been renumbered and edited.

boundaries, in the process of categorizing. Later we learn about the power associated with the categories. The greater the power imbalance, the greater the consequences. According to Constance Perin, "boundaries are the main characteristic of any category, and universally they are freighted with significance…boundaries are sources of power… without boundaries, categories have no force."[3] As when touching a hot stove, we learn where the boundaries are and avoid getting too close. We curtail our behaviors, thoughts, and desires so as not to get burned. By doing and seeing what is considered racially appropriate, we reinforce the strength of the categories and build borders.

Borders give each person a sense of ourselves in the world; they help us know where we fit, what our status is, and who our people are. They teach us what is significant in society. When borders are crossed, essentialist explanations are threatened. The borders maintain the shape of the category and are meant to stop one category from leaking into the next. Grace Elizabeth Hale notes, "The act of trying to clarify the boundary between white and black reveal[s] the fluidity of the color line."[4] When borders are crossed, essentialist explanations are threatened. Ultimately, borders maintain the color line and the strength of race by making race appear natural.

BORDERISM

To live near the color line, in the space Gloria Anzaldúa calls the borderlands, means to contend constantly with what I call borderism.[5] Borderism is a unique form of discrimination faced by those who cross the color line, do not stick with their own, or attempt to claim membership (or are placed by others) in more than one racial group. Like racism, borderism is central to American society. It is a product of a racist system yet comes from both sides. The manner in which people react to individuals who cross the color line highlights the investment, the sense of solidarity, and perhaps the comfort these observers have with existing categories. Perhaps

most important, the reaction shows the wide acceptance of racial essentialism as the explanation for the color line. When the color line is crossed, the idea of immutable, biologically based racial categories is threatened. The individual who has crossed the line must be explained away or punished so that essentialist categories can remain in place. Ironically, if race were natural and essential, individuals would not have to engage in borderism. The act of borderism is one of the many ways in which individuals construct or "do" race.

Multiracial family members contend with borderism in many aspects of life. It is both part of the workings of larger institutions and the outcome of individual actions. When families are unable to find accepting places of worship and comfortable neighborhoods, they contend with examples of institutional borderism. A nefarious individual is not responsible for creating these situations. Rather, this borderism has developed in the context of a deeply racist and segregated society. Some borderism, however, does play out on an individual level and is meant to be hurtful. A family disowns a child for not sticking with his own. Peers tell a multiracial child that she is not black enough. An interracial couple is physically accosted in the street. Such borderism may stem from hostility, hatred, or feelings of betrayal and is grounded in ideas about how people ought to act. But it may also reveal concern. For example, before returning to graduate school I was working for a corporation that sent me to the Baltimore–Washington, D.C., area for a summer. It was a racially tense season. The Klan was active, hanging notices all over one town declaring it a "nigger-free zone." In another town white men killed a black man because he was walking with a white woman in a white neighborhood. When my husband, Philip, came to visit, we were cautious. One weekend went without incident until I dropped him off at the train station. We were talking when an elderly black woman walked up to Philip and scolded, "Get away from her; she's going to get you killed. You need to stick with your own." I believe she meant to be helpful to Philip. After all, another black man had just been killed. Nonetheless, these moments can be paralyzing. In such situations there is no way for me to say, "Please, my skin color belies my politics. I am likewise outraged and live with the fear of violence." For me to speak at these moments is to belittle the history of racial oppression and the fact that I do represent, in my physical being, the object and the symbol that has been used to justify so much oppression. Protecting white women's bodies has long been the justification for abusing and lynching thousands of black men and women.[6]

All members of multiracial families face borderism, although as individuals we face specific forms of discrimination based on our race physical features, gender, and other socially significant markers. Borderism consists of three interacting components: *border patrolling*, discrimination that comes from both sides; *rebound racism*, faced by interracially married whites and white-looking members of multiracial families; and *intensified racism*, faced by interracially married blacks.[7] Each form is directed specifically at people who cross the color line. Although I address each as a discrete experience, in reality they are inextricably linked and are always grounded in a larger racist system. As a primary means of re-creating, reproducing, and clarifying the color line, borderism shows how individuals and institutions continue to create race.

BORDER PATROLLING

The belief that people ought to stick with their own is the driving force behind efforts to force individuals to follow prescribed racial rules. Border patrollers often think (without much critical analysis) that they can easily differentiate between insiders and outsiders. Once the patroller has determined a person's appropriate category, he or she will attempt to coerce that person into following the category's racial scripts. In *Race, Nation, Class: Ambiguous Identities*, Etienne Balibar and Immanuel Wallerstein observe that "people shoot each other every day over the question of labels. And yet, the very people who do so tend to deny that the issue is complex or puzzling or indeed anything but self-evident."[8] Border patrollers tend to take race and racial categories for granted. Whether grounding themselves in essentialist thinking or hoping to strengthen socially constructed racial categories, they believe they have the right and the need to patrol. Some people, especially whites, do not recognize the centrality and problems of the color line, as evinced in color-blind claims that "there is only one race: the human race" or "race doesn't really matter any more." Such thinking dismisses the terror and power of race in society. These individuals may patrol without being aware of doing so. In contrast, blacks generally see patrolling the border as both problematic and necessary.

While border patrolling from either side may be scary, hurtful, or annoying, we must recognize that blacks and whites are situated differently. The color line was imposed by whites, who now have institutional means for maintaining their power; in contrast, blacks must consciously and actively struggle for liberation. Repeatedly, people in multiracial families have told me, "The one thing that David Duke and Louis Farrakhan agree on is that we should not exist." What is not analyzed are the different historical legacies that bring both men to the same conclusion. The only form of borderism in which blacks engage is border patrolling, although they can act on prejudicial feelings and discriminate. After centuries of systemic control, only whites can be racist. As Joe Feagin and Hernán Vera explain, "black racism would require not only a widely accepted racist ideology directed at whites, but also the power to systematically exclude whites from opportunities and rewards in major economic, cultural, and political institutions."[9] White and black border patrollers may both dislike interracial couples and multiracial families, but their dislike comes from different historical and social perspectives. Moreover, border patrolling tends to take place intraracially: whites patrol whites, and blacks patrol black and multiracial people.

White Border Patrolling

Despite the institutional mechanisms in place to safeguard whiteness, many whites feel both the right and the obligation to act out against interracial couples. If a white person wants to maintain a sense of racial superiority, then he or she must attempt to locate motives and explain the actions of the white partner in the interracial couple. A white person who crosses the color line threatens the assumption that racial superiority is essential to whites. The interracially involved white person is thus often recategorized as inherently flawed—as "polluted."[10] In this way, racist and essentialist thinking remains unchallenged.

Frequently white families disown a relative who marries a person of color, but several people have told me that their families accepted them again once their children were born. The need to disown demonstrates the desire to maintain the facade of a pure white family.[11] By the time children are born, however, extended family members have had time to shift their racial thinking. Some grant acceptance by making an exception to the "rule," others by claiming to be color blind. Neither form of racial thinking, however, challenges the color line or white supremacy. In fact, both can be painful for the multiracial family members, who may face unending racist compliments such as "I'll always think of you as white."

The strength of racist images is manifested in the comments directed at women who are assumed to be good, upstanding white women. June, a businesswoman who is raising two biracial sons in suburban New Jersey, commented, "I think America still hates [white] women who sleep with black men. And when they see you with these children, they want to believe you adopted them, which is usually the first question people will ask: 'Did you adopt them?' I always just say, 'No, I slept with a black man.'"

June's comments highlight a few issues. First, she does not specify who constitutes "America." Whites may hate these women because they threaten the color line that maintains white privilege and power. At the same time, blacks may hate them because they threaten the unity of African Americans. Second, several white women talked to me about the frequency of the adoption question—one more attempt to explain their behavior. If women who appear to be good turn out to be polluted, white border patrollers become nervous. Their inability to tell "us" from "them" calls into question their own racial identity. The more the border patroller clings to an identity of racial superiority, the more he or she looks for ways to explain away these aberrant white women. Third, like June, many interracially married white women resist allowing whites to recategorize them in an attempt to regain or maintain a sense of superiority. "No, I used the good-old fashioned method" is a common retort to such questioners.

The stereotype of black male sexuality converges with the myth of the chaste and virtuous good white woman, making white female–black male relationships the ones most patrolled by whites.[12] White men contend with a different type of border patrolling in a society that privileges both whiteness and maleness. Historically, white men who interracially marry were reported to come from lower economic classes and were at times designated as crazy.[13] Today the more common image that white interracially married men face is of being in the relationship solely for sex. These men may be seen as committing an individual transgression but are not held responsible for protecting whiteness. In her study of white supremacist publications, Abby Ferber found that "while relationships between white women and black men are condemned, and described as repulsive, relationships between white men and black women were common and remain beyond condemnation."[14] The lack of imagery about white male–black female relations reflects a history of silence among whites concerning their complicity in the rape of black women. Moreover, in a society in which whiteness (and maleness) represents power, privilege, and unearned advantage, many white men view their privilege in the world as normal. They risk "outing" these taken-for-granted privileges when they talk about race.[15]

The white men with whom I spoke were split about the importance of—even the existence of-border patrolling. Unlike black men, black women, and white women, they did not consistently talk about the effects of racialized images. When I asked, "As an interracially married white man, how do you think others view you?" responses were split: half the men spoke of border patrollers; the other half denied the importance of race in their lives and society. The first few times I heard white men deny or disregard the importance of racism and border patrolling, I was surprised. It took me some time and several more interviews to make sense of this.

Joe, the first interracially married white man I interviewed, lived in a predominantly white, upper-class community about an hour from New York City. With his infant daughter on his lap and a tape recorder on the table, he began to unfold the details of his life. I asked how he thinks others view him. He responded, "I can't worry about what other people think. For a long time my wife worried, but once she got over that, we had a big wedding.... It took a lot to convince her that's how we should think about it, and I think she's more comfortable with that." He said that they do not have problems as an interracial couple, that everything is smooth. We were chatting after the interview when his wife walked into the room. She began to cite several problems they had faced because of their interracial relationship. When she referred to each incident, he nodded in agreement.

Several, months later I interviewed Raymond, a white interracially married man living on Chicago's north side. Drinking coffee in a local cafe, he discussed the meaning of race in his life. When I asked him about how others view him, he replied staunchly, "I don't know, and I don't care. I never thought about it. I don't think about it. What do they think when they see my wife and me together? Pardon my language, but I don't give a shit what

they think; I just don't give a shit. I go for months, and that never occupies my mind."

These men may be proving masculinity through a show of strength, rugged individualism, and disinterest and thus verbally disregard border patrolling and racial images. Each, however, repeatedly claimed that race does not matter. Instead, they believed the focus "should be on ethnic backgrounds" or on the fact that "we are all Americans." Men who did not want to recognize racial images tended not to recognize the privilege associated with whiteness, drawing instead on notions of meritocracy. Whether or not they recognized differences, they did not recognize power. Nevertheless, they used their power as white males to create a racial discussion with which they felt comfortable. For instance, Joe's comfort came from not having to hear any racially derogatory comments: "If somebody would make a derogatory comment, I would just say, 'My wife is black.' Usually I wouldn't even have to say, 'I don't want to hear comments like that'—they would just stop." Whiteness is about privilege and power. It is a privilege to be able to set the parameters of racial discussions and expect that others will comply. Moreover, the power of these professional white men overrides the power that white border patrollers may have to influence them.

Privileges granted to people with white skin have been institutionalized and made largely invisible to the beneficiaries. With overwhelming power in society, why do individual whites insist on border patrolling? As economic insecurity heightens and demographics show that whites are losing numerical majority status, the desire to scapegoat people of color, especially the poor, also heightens. As whites lose their economic footing, they claim white skin as a liability. Far from recognizing whiteness as privilege, they become conscious of whiteness only when defining themselves as innocent victims of "unjust" laws, including affirmative action.[16] In their insecurity they cling to images that promote feelings of superiority. This, of course, requires a racial hierarchy and a firm essentialist color line. Border patrolling helps to maintain the myth of purity and thus a color line created to ensure that whites maintain privileges and power.

Black Border Patrolling

Some blacks in interracial relationships discover, for the first time, a lack of acceptance from black communities. Others experienced border patrolling before their marriage, perhaps because of hobbies and interests, class, politics, educational goals, skin tone, vernacular, or friendship networks. Patrolling takes on new proportions, however, when they go the "other way" and marry a white person. While all relationships with individuals not seen as black are looked down on, relationships with whites represent the gravest transgression. Interracially married black women and men often believe they are viewed as having lost their identity and culture—that they risk being seen as "no longer really black." Before their interracial marriage, most called black communities their home, the place from which they gained a sense of humanity, where they gained cultural and personal affirmation. During their interracial relationship many discovered black border patrolling. Cathy Cohen suggests that "those failing to meet indigenous standards of blackness find their life chances threatened not only by dominant institutions or groups, but also by their lack of access to indigenous resources and support."[17] Interracially involved blacks needed to carefully weigh their decision to cross the color line.

Blacks interracial relationships defend themselves against accusations of weakness, neurosis, and betrayal. In *Black Skin, White Masks*, Frantz Fanon writes about black men in interracial relationships: "I marry white culture, white beauty, white whiteness. When my restless hands caress those white breasts, they grasp white civilization and dignity and make them mine."[18] In his psychoanalytic interpretation of the effects of colonization and racism, Fanon suggests that many black men who intermarry suffer from neurosis created in a world in which black men are not valued and thus do not value themselves. They think that a relationship with a white woman will validate them—that is, whiten them. Of black women, Fanon writes, "It is because the Negress feels inferior that she aspires to win admittance into the white world."[19] Without acknowledging the pain caused by border patrolling and the desire many interracially married blacks have to maintain strong ties with other blacks, Fanon labels black men and black women in interracial relationships as pathological and neurotic.

More recently, Paul Rosenblatt and his colleagues conducted a study of forty-two multiracial couples in the Minneapolis–St. Paul area. They conclude that many African Americans feel that "it is inappropriate to choose as a partner somebody from the group that has been oppressing African Americans."[20] Many black border patrollers have an overriding concern about loyalty to the race. If an individual is not being loyal, then he or she is explained away as weak, acting in ways that are complicit with the oppression of other black Americans. In "Essentialism and the Complexities of Racial Identity," Michael Eric Dyson suggests, "Loyalty to race has been historically construed as primary and unquestioning allegiance to the racial quest for freedom and the refusal to betray that quest to personal benefit or the diverting pursuit of lesser goals. Those who detour from the prescribed path are labeled 'sellouts,' 'weak,' 'traitors,' or 'Uncle Toms.'"[21] Thus, black men and women face differing social realities and forms of patrolling.

Black women and men may both feel a sense of rejection when they see an interracial couple, but for each that sense of rejection comes from a different place. In a society in which women's worth is judged largely by beauty—more specifically, Eurocentric standards of beauty—black women are presumed to be the farthest removed from such a standard. Men's worth is judged largely by their educational and occupational status, two primary areas in which black men are undermined in a racist system. Black men with few educational and job opportunities lack status in the marriage market. Thus, when black men see a black woman with a white man, they may be reminded of the numerous ways in which the white-supremacist system has denied them opportunities. The privilege and power granted to whites, particularly to white males, is paraded in front of them; and they see the black women in these relationships as complicit with the oppressor.

Border patrolling plays a central role in life decisions and the reproduction of the color line. As decisions are made to enter and remain in an interracial relationship, the color line is challenged and racial identities shift. Many blacks spoke of the growth they experienced because of their interracial relationship and border patrolling. Parsia, [a successful business woman and a black interracially married mother living in Connecticut] explains, "I used to be real concerned about how I would be perceived and that as an interracially married female I would be taken less seriously in terms of my dedication to African American causes. I'm not nearly as concerned anymore. I would hold my record up to most of those in single-race relationships, and I would say, 'Okay, let's go toe to toe, and you tell me who's making the biggest difference,' and so I don't worry about it anymore." Identities, once grounded in the presumed acceptance of other black Americans, have become more reflective. Acceptance can no longer be assumed. Definitions of what it means to be black are reworked. Likewise, because of border patrolling, many whites in interracial relationships began to acknowledge that race matters. Whiteness becomes visible in their claims to racial identity.

REBOUND RACISM

When whites enter an interracial relationship they experience racism, albeit indirectly. In these cases racism is directed at the black partner but also affects the white partner. Talking specifically about white women, Ruth Frankenberg defines such *rebound racism* as "a force that owes its existence and direction to an earlier aim and impact, yet retains enough force to wound.... While it is hard to measure pain, it is safe to say both that the racism that rebounds on white women has spent some of its force in the original impact it made on their nonwhite partners and that white women nonetheless feel its impact."[22] The effect can be financial, emotional, or physical. While the white partner is not the intended victim, she or he is in a relationship with someone who is. For example, if the black partner does not get a fair raise, this affects the financial well-being of the white partner. If the black partner is given unfair traffic tickets or treated badly at work, this spills over into the family. The white partner with emotional, financial, and familial ties to the black partner gains a sense of the pain and disadvantage doled out to people of color in a system of whiteness.

Candace, like the other interracially married whites with whom I spoke, found that when she is alone, away from her family, whites treat her "perfectly all right." When she is with her family, however, "it's a whole different thing." The *whole different thing* is border patrolling and rebound racism and includes hostile stares and rude treatment in stores and restaurants. June discovered rebound racism while trying to catch a cab with her husband:

> The worst thing is getting a cab in New York City; that is the worst feeling I have ever had with my husband. It was having to get a cab on my own; and then when he would come up, they would drive away. Oh, that to me is the worst because then I could almost feel his pain and feel how awful it must be to deal with this in every aspect of your life, every day. It was so humiliating and so demeaning. I hate those cab drivers. They would pull up; and as soon as he came up, they would drive right away. I mean just leave you standing there with your hand stretched out.

June's pain was directly related to what was happening to her black partner. Because of this and other experiences of rebound racism, she can no longer take race for granted. It now becomes associated with humiliation and hatefulness; a color-blind perspective is no longer possible or desirable. For June the color line is not a distant separation of whites and blacks but a means for protecting white supremacy.

Several years ago my husband and I were driving from Chicago to visit his family. We knew that New Jersey's highway patrol had a reputation for hassling African Americans. We also knew that we would not get to New Jersey until about midnight. We stopped for gas at a busy highway station before we crossed the state line. It is important to go to roadside gas stations because you don't want to get off the main highway when traveling alone together as an interracial couple—especially at night. It was Philip's turn to drive. Much to my chagrin, he was maintaining a steady fifty-five miles per hour. I was unsuccessfully nudging him to speed it up so we could get to his parents' at a reasonable hour when the flashing lights appeared from behind. A young white male police officer pulled us over. Without giving a reason, even when we asked, he demanded our registration, proof of insurance, and both of our licenses. He then put my husband in his car and told me to stay put. After what seemed like an eternity, the officer came to my window and asked me a series of questions: "How long have you two known each other? What is your line of work? What does he do? How long has he been in law school? Where are you going? What are his parents' names? What are your sisters' names? How long have you been in graduate school? What are you studying?" I wanted to say, "Racist cops," but I did my best to answer his questions politely, all the time mindful that he still had Philip in his cruiser. Apparently our answers satisfied the cop because he let Philip return to the car and, without explanation, handed us our licenses and registration, telling us to have a nice night. I don't know how, in the dark of night, he could have seen us in the car. Perhaps he intended to harass a black man and, when he found me there, thought he had hit a jackpot—you know, the old "this must be a kidnapping" or "this white woman must be a prostitute." Perhaps he was able to see us and thought he had found himself a real live interracial Bonnie and Clyde cruising along the Jersey interstate in a Hyundai Excel.

In this instance I experienced rebound racism. I doubt I would have been pulled over if I were by myself or with another white person. While I was not driving that time, I have been on other occasions. I was pulled over once with Philip in the car and given a ticket. I was pulled over several times while alone, and each time received a warning and was let off without ticket. Here, not receiving tickets is a factor of white privilege; receiving a ticket with my husband is a factor of rebound racism and possibly border patrolling.

For many whites, rebound racism makes them more aware of white privilege. Candace told me:

> I have grown tremendously through this relationship. I understand the privilege of skin color. I might have known what that concept was if I would have read it in a book but not the reality of understanding that in life. If I was in an all-white marriage, I think I would have taken an awful lot for granted, and I wouldn't be as sensitive to many things. I often think, "How could I have missed that before?" and because it's suddenly placed in front of you, you're more sensitive.

Many interracially married whites no longer feel they are connected to or benefit from a larger system of whiteness. In *The Color of Water: A Black Man's Tribute to His White Mother*, James McBride writes of his mother's refusal to "acknowledge her whiteness," instead claiming that she was light-skinned. McBride "initially accepted [this claim] as fact but at some point later decided it was not true."[23] Without the opportunity to hear from his mother, we can only speculate why she claimed to be black, when, as her son documents, so many others saw her as a white woman. Maybe she did not want her children to live with the discomfort of being mixed in a single-race world. If she claimed to be black (and could convince others), then her children would be black without question. As a low-income mother of twelve black children, she may have identified most closely with political and social issues important to many African Americans. Perhaps she saw blackness as a privilege. Identities are, after all, shaped by our daily experiences. Maria P. P. Root writes that "the love a child receives, and the faces that reflect who they are, are likely to be some shade of brown. The children will likely internalize an identification with those from whom they come."[24] Isn't it possible that adults may do the same?[25]

INTENSIFIED RACISM

While the white partner experiences rebound racism, the black partner often faces escalated forms of racism because of the interracial relationship. In this case, racism normally directed at blacks is intensified because they have dared to cross the color line through marriage or partnership. Such was the case of the black man killed in suburban Baltimore because he walked with his white girlfriend in a white neighborhood. Black males most often spoke of intensified racism. This is nothing new. During Reconstruction white southerners were manic in their attempts to stop miscegenation and protect white womanhood. Racial hygienic platforms were central to this goal. The system of whiteness was formed in large part through the rape and exploitation of black women and the simultaneous lynching of black men for supposed crimes against white women. Julien, a black interracially married father of five living in a western suburb of Chicago, spoke of the intensified racism he experienced. During our first interview he mentioned that his children had been to his workplace but that his wife never had. The children look very much like their mother except they have caramel-colored skin and curly hair. Given Julien's brown skin and hair texture, most blacks would suspect that his children are multiracial. Many whites, however, are not raised to think about skin color using terms such as *honey, cinnamon, brown,* or *caramel.* They are not part of the language that whites

incorporate into their racial thinking. An individual is either white or black. Thus, Julien felt safe bringing his children to his workplace but not his wife. I asked him to explain why. "I have no way to prove this" he said, "but if they were to find out I was interracially married, I would have been fired because there were some incidents where black guys were going out with white girls and actually brought them to work. I just learned from that experience not to bring her; they got fired. The black guys who were dealing with white girls; they trumped up charges and fired them. She's never been to my work, and she never will." At work, he allows his white bosses to assume his wife is black. Julien is describing a racist system in which, for blacks, crossing the color line can be life-threatening either directly or through denial of the means necessary to survive.

CONCLUSION

Unlike transracially adopted and multiracial people who are raised across the color line, people in interracial relationships discover borderism when they decide to cross the line. This unique form *of* discrimination, grounded in a racist and segregated society, is always at work even when multiracial family members are not present. Yet by examining the experiences of multiracial family members, we can see the myriad ways in which the color line is both reproduced and resisted. Because interracially married people are often raised in single-race worlds, they have internalized borderism. Thus, part of the decision to become involved interracially includes the need to overcome internalized borderist thoughts. Most of them begin questioning color-blind and essentialist perspectives and learn to understand race as more fluid and complex. Skin color and physical features become just one set of criteria used to think about community and belonging. Many of the people I interviewed referred to this growth process (although not all interracially married people accept the invitation to rethink race).

In a society that often rejects people who cross the color line, individuals involved in such relationships have much to consider before making a permanent commitment. Given the significance of race in our society, a basic choice that all couples contend with is whether or not to stay together in the face of borderism. A few individuals claimed that there was no decision; they fell in love, and that was it. For most others, however, a life across the color line and facing borderism did not look all that inviting and in fact was enough to cause some to terminate their relationships.[26] While the number of people involved in interracial relationships are not known, we do know that in 1995 the census bureau estimated that there were only 246,000 black-white interracial marriages in the United States.[27] This is quite a small percentage considering that in the same year there were more than 50 million total marriages.[28] Borderism and its various components are strong and painful enough to keep black-white interracial marriages the least common marriage pattern for both blacks and whites.

NOTES

1. Gunnar Myrdal, *An American Dilemma: The Negro Problem and Modern Democracy*, 20th anniversary ed. (New York: Harper and Row, 1965 [1944]).
2. Abby Ferber, *White Man Falling: Race, Gender and White Supremacy* (Lanham, Md.: Rowman and Littlefield, 1998), 101.
3. Constance Perin, *Everything in Its Place: Social Order and Land Use in America* (Princeton, N. J.: Princeton University Press, 1977), 110–111.
4. Grace Elizabeth Hale, *Making Whiteness: The Culture of Segregation in the South, 1890–1940 (New York: Vintage, 1998), 219.*
5. Anzaldúa, *Borderlands/La Frontera.*
6. Hale, *Making Whiteness.*
7. Ruth Frankenberg, *White Women's Race Matters: The Social Construction of Whiteness* (Minneapolis: University of Minnesota, 1993).
8. Etienne Balibar and Immanuel Wallerstein, *Race, Nation, Class: Ambiguous Identities* (New York: Verso, 1991), 71.
9. Joe Feagin and Hernán Vera, *White Racism* (New York: Routledge, 1995), ix–x.
10. Ferber, *White Man Falling*, 100.
11. Naomi Zack, *Race and Mixed Race* (Philadelphia: Temple University Press, 1994).
12. Ferber, *White Man Falling.*
13. *Zack, Race and Mixed Race;* Joel Williamson, *New People: Miscegenation and Mulattoes in the United States (*New York: New York University Press, *1984);* Spikard, *Mixed Blood.*
14. Ferber, *White Man Falling, 103.*
15. Kate Davy, "Outing Whiteness." *Theatre* 47, 2 (1995); 189–205.
16. Charles Gallagher, "White Reconstruction in the University," *Socialist Review 24,* 1 and 2 (1995): 165–188.
17. Cathy J. Cohen, "Contested Membership: Black Gay Identities and the Politics of AIDS," in Queer *Theory/Sociology,* ed. Steven Seidman (Cambridge, Mass.: Blackwell, 1996), 365.
18. Frantz Fanon, *Black Skins, White Masks* (New York: Grove), 83.
19. Ibid., 60.
20. Paul C. Rosenblatt, Terri A. Karis, and Riehard D. Powell, *Multiracial Couples: Black and White Voices* (Thousand Oaks, Calif.: Sage, 1995), 155.
21. Dyson, "Essentialism," 222.

22. Frankenberg, *White Women*, 112.

23. James McBride, *The Color of Water: A Black Man's Tribute to His White Mother* (New York: Riverhead, 1996), 16.

24. Maria P. P. Root, "The Multiracial Contribution to the Browning of America," in *American Mixed Race: The Culture of Microdiversity*, ed. Naomi Zack (Lanham, Md.: Rowman and Littlefield, 1995), 234.

25. Jane Lazarre thinks of herself as a person of color, and Maureen Reddy writes of "masquerading as white in public." See Lazarre, *Beyond the Whiteness of Whiteness: Memoir of a White Mother of Black Sons* (Durham, N. C.: Duke University Press, 1996); and Reddy, *Crossing the Color Line: Race, Parenting, and Culture* (New Brunswick, N.J.: Rutgers University Press, 1994), 22.

26. Although many people break up permanently, I interviewed individuals who eventually made the decision to commit to an interracial marriage.

27. Claudcttc Bennett, "Interracial Children: Implications for a Multiracial Category" (paper presented at the annual meeting of the American Sociological Association, Washington, D.C., 1995).

28. Rosenblatt et al., *Multiracial Couples*, 5.

JOURNALING QUESTION

What examples of borderism have you seen, either in your own life or in movies or television?

A VOICE FROM THE PAST

The Conservation of Races

W.E.B. DU BOIS

W.E.B. Du Bois was an African American sociologist and author of, among other works, the classic book *The Souls of Black Folk*. This piece, drawn from the papers of the American Negro Academy and published in 1897, was one of the first to question scientific notions of race. At a moment in time when he could speak of separate schools and cars, wage discrimination, and even lynch laws as "pressing but smaller questions," Du Bois was making the argument that a "Negro identity" could exist within an "American identity." This issue of a "two-ness," or a "double consciousness," was one of Du Bois key contributions to our understanding of race in America. Does that concept work for other racial identities as well?

Excerpted from W.E.B. Du Bois, "The Conversation of Races," in Occasional Papers No. 2 (The American Negro Academy. 1897/2003 [electronic version]).

The American Negro has always felt an intense personal interest in discussions as to the origins and destinies of races: primarily because back of most discussions of race with which he is familiar, have lurked certain assumptions as to his natural abilities, as to his political, intellectual and moral status, which he felt were wrong. He has, consequently, been led to deprecate and minimize race distinctions, to believe intensely that out of one blood God created all nations, and to speak of human brotherhood as though it were the possibility of an already dawning to-morrow.

Nevertheless, in our calmer moments we must acknowledge that human beings are divided into races; that in this country the two most extreme types of the world's races have met, and the resulting problem as to the future relations of these types is not only of intense and living interest to us, but forms an epoch in the history of mankind.

It is necessary, therefore, in planning our movements, in guiding our future development, that at times we rise above the pressing, but smaller questions of separate schools and cars, wage-discrimination and lynch law, to survey the whole questions of race in human philosophy and to lay, on a basis of broad knowledge and careful insight, those large lines of policy and higher ideals which may form our guiding lines and boundaries in the practical difficulties of every day. For it is certain that all human striving must recognize the hard limits of natural law, and that any striving, no matter how intense and earnest, which is against the constitution of the world, is vain. The question, then, which we must seriously consider is this: What is the real meaning of Race; what has, in the past, been the law of race development, and what lessons has the past history of race development to teach the rising Negro people?

When we thus come to inquire into the essential difference of races we find it hard to come at once to any definite conclusion. Many criteria of race differences have in the past been proposed, as color, hair, cranial measurements and language. And manifestly, in each of these respects, human beings differ widely. They vary in color, for instance, from the marble-like pallor of the Scandinavian to the rich, dark brown of the Zulu, passing by the creamy Slav, the yellow Chinese, the light brown Sicilian and the brown Egyptian. Men vary, too, in the texture of hair from the obstinately straight hair of the Chinese to the obstinately tufted and frizzled hair of the Bushman. In measurement of heads, again, men vary; from the broad-headed Tartar to the medium-headed European and the narrow-headed Hottentot; or, again in language, from the highly-inflected Roman tongue to the monosyllabic Chinese. All these physical characteristics are patent enough, and if they agreed with each other it would be very easy to classify mankind. Unfortunately for scientists, however, these criteria of race are most exasperatingly intermingled. Color does not agree with texture of hair, for many of the dark races have straight hair; nor does color agree with the breadth of the head, for the yellow Tartar has a broader head than the German; nor, again, has the science of language as yet succeeded in clearing up the relative authority of these various and contradictory criteria. The final word of science, so far, is that we have at least two, perhaps three, great families of human beings—the whites and Negroes, possibly the yellow race. That other races have arisen from the intermingling of the blood of these two. This broad division of the world's races which men like Huxley and Raetzel have introduced as more nearly true than the old five-race scheme of Blumenbach, is nothing more than an acknowledgment that, so far as purely physical characteristics are concerned, the differences between men do not explain all the differences of their history. It declares, as Darwin himself said, that great as is the physical unlikeness of the various races of men their likenesses are greater, and upon this rests the whole scientific doctrine of Human Brotherhood.

Although the wonderful developments of human history teach that the grosser physical differences of color, hair and bone go but a short way toward explaining the different roles which groups of men have played in Human Progress, yet there are differences—subtle, delicate and elusive, though they may be—which have silently but definitely separated men into group. While these subtle forces have generally followed the natural cleavage of common blood, descent and physical peculiarities, they have at other times swept across and ignored these. At all times, however, they have divided human beings into races, which, while they perhaps transcend scientific definition, nevertheless, are clearly defined to the eye of the Historian and Sociologist.

The question now is: What is the real distinction between these nations? Is it the physical differences of blood, color and cranial measurements? Certainly we must all acknowledge that physical differences play a great part, and that, with wide exceptions and qualifications, these eight great races of today follow the cleavage of physical race distinctions; the English and Teuton represent the white variety of mankind; the Mongolian, the yellow; the Negroes, the black. Between these are many crosses and mixtures, where Mongolian and Teuton have blended into the Slav, and other mixtures have produced the Romance nations and the Semites. But while race differences have followed mainly physical race lines, yet no mere physical distinctions would really define or explain the deeper differences—the cohesiveness and continuity of these groups. The deeper differences are spiritual, psychical, differences—undoubtedly based on the physical, but infinitely transcending them. The forces that bind together the Teuton nations are, then, first, their race identity and common blood; secondly, and more important, a common history, common laws and religion, similar habits of thought and a conscious striving together for certain ideals of life. The whole process which has brought about these race differentiations has been a growth, and the great characteristic of this growth has been the differentiation of spiritual and mental differences between great races of mankind and the integration of physical differences.

If we carefully consider what race prejudice really is, we find it, historically, to be nothing but the friction between different groups of people; it is the difference in aim, in feeling, in ideals of two different races; if, now, this difference exists touching territory, laws, language, or even religion, it is manifest that these people cannot live in the same territory without fatal collision; but if, on the other hand, there is substantial agreement in laws, language and religion; if there is a satisfactory adjustment of economic life, then there is no reason why, in the same country and on the same street, two or three great national ideals might not thrive and develop, that men of different races might not strive together for their race ideals as well, perhaps even better, than in isolation. Here, it seems to me, is the reading of the riddle that puzzles so many of us. We are Americans, not only by birth and by citizenship, but by our political ideals, our language, our religion. Farther than that, our Americanism does not go. At that point, we are Negroes, members of a vast historic race that from the very dawn of creation has slept, but half awakening in the dark forests of its African fatherland. We are the first fruits of this new nation, the harbinger of that black tomorrow which is yet destined to soften the whiteness of the Teutonic today. We are that people whose subtle sense of song has given America its only American music, its only American fairy tales, its only touch of pathos and humor amid its mad money-getting plutocracy. As such, it is our duty to conserve our physical powers, our intellectual endowments, our spiritual ideals; as a race we must strive by race organization, by race solidarity, by race unity to the realization of that broader humanity which freely recognizes differences in men, but sternly deprecates inequality in their opportunities of development.

Outing Whiteness

A SPECIAL INTRODUCTION BY THE EDITORS

People who are identified as "white" in America often think of race—if they think of race at all—as something that other people have. They will sometimes say they're "just white" dismissing race as meaningless for their own identity. A white person, when arranging a meeting over the phone with a stranger, will say something like "I'm tall with curly brown hair," or I'll be wearing a red jacket," but will rarely say "I'm white and tall, with curly brown hair."

Even though white people don't think about their own place in the race distribution in America, that racial position affects their lives in big and little ways every day. One thought experiment that might help white people to see that is to include (or maybe just think it in your own head) "white and" in every descriptive thing you say for a day or even a week. "She's white and majoring in Accounting," or "She's white and taking up weight lifting," or "He's white and not doing well in my history class," or "She's white and coming home late tonight." Would saying "black" change the tone of these descriptions at all?

10.

THE FUTURE OF WHITENESS

A Map of the "Third Wave"

FRANCE WINDDANCE TWINE AND CHARLES GALLAGHER

Social movements do not proceed in an orderly and incremental fashion, with each year showing steady progress from the year before. "Waves" make a good metaphor for social movements because they surge forward and then fall back. But the metaphor fails when we think over the long term: Unlike the tides of the seas, social movements can and do create real change, truly move things along, and do not return to their previous position. As things change, as movement actually does occur and progress is made, one can reflect back more thoughtfully on the limitations of the accomplishments of each prior wave. Thus, there are waves of intellectual growth as well as waves of social change. If this wave of anti-racism and the accompanying wave of whiteness studies are successful, do you think that racism will indeed be just an archaic word children look up in the dictionary? Or what do you think the fourth wave will look like?

Excerpted from France Winddance Twine and Charles Gallagher, "The Future of Whiteness: A Map of the 'Third Wave,'" *Ethnic and Racial Studies*, 31 (2008): 4–24. References have been edited.

Much of the recent research on whiteness explores the ideological practices that render white privilege invisible (Lipsitz 1998; Twine 1996, 2004; Frankenberg 2001; Gallagher 2003b; Ansell 2006), the ways in which whiteness is increasingly a contested category (Bhattacharyya, Gabriel and Small 2002; Doane 2003; Andersen 2003), how race politics transform whiteness into a "victimized" marked identity (Wellman 1993; Yancey 2003; Gallagher 2004) and the power relations that allow whiteness to be positioned as a benign cultural signifier (Dyer 1997; Bonnett 2000). Third wave analysis takes as its starting the understanding that whiteness is not now, nor has it ever been, a static, uniform category of social identification (Saxton 1990; Jacobson 1998; Roediger 2005). In this way third wave whiteness avoids the tendency towards essentializing accounts of whiteness by locating race as one of many social relations that shape individual and group identity. A third wave perspective sees whiteness as a multiplicity of identities that are historically grounded, class specific, politically manipulated and gendered social locations that inhabit local custom and national sentiments within the contcxt of the new "global village."

This exceptional third wave of intellectual inquiry into whiteness is now examined in virtually every branch of the social sciences. Social geographers map how residential proximity of whites to racialized minority groups shape racial attitudes and group affiliations (Durrheim 2005; Forrest and Dunn 2006; Kincheloe 2006). Postcolonial scholars examine how accounts of nationalism and whiteness become synonymous with citizenship and which groups are granted "legitimate" access to state resources (Nayak 2002; Garner 2006; Twine 2004). Given the mobilization of far right movements throughout Europe and the United States this line of research is a needed examination of how whiteness and nationalism are used to portray racial minorities as perpetual foreigners, potential terrorists or permanent cultural outsiders (Chan 2006; Juge and Perez 2006; Lamont 2000; Potter and Phillips

2006). Education scholars chronicle how whiteness is learned, internalized, privileged, institutionally reproduced and performed in educational settings (Perry 2002; Gallagher 2003; Lewis 2003; Choulcs 2006). Feminist scholars address how whiteness and gender shape racialized identities and how identity construction and patriarchy are linked to racism, nation and class location (Twine 1996, 1999a, 1999b, 2004; Frankenberg 1993, 2001; Walker 2005).

This diverse scholarship is linked by a common denominator—an examination of how power and oppression are articulated, redefined and reasserted through various political discourses and cultural practices that privilege whiteness even when the prerogatives of the dominant group are contested. Although the symbolic and material value of whiteness is in flux, one can locate whites who belong to economically deprived communities throughout the world. However, the concentration of wealth, power and privilege for the latter groups is, as Howard Winant argues "outliers in the planetary correlation of darkness and poverty" (Winant 2001, p. 305). While whiteness often is synonymous with regimes of terror, genocide and white supremacy, a third wave perspective on whiteness rejects the implicit assumption that whiteness is *only* an unconditional, universal and equally experienced location of privilege and power....

Reflecting on the relational nature of white privilege, Ruth Frankenberg observes that "whiteness as a site of privilege is not absolute but rather crosscut by a range of other axes of relative advantage and subordination; these do not erase or render irrelevant race privilege, but rather inflect or modify it" (Frankenberg 2001, p. 76). Poor whites living in the southern part of the United States, London or Africa typically do experience white skin privilege relative to racially subordinated groups. However, whites living in exclusive, all-white gated enclaves throughout the world experience and live whiteness in vastly different ways than poor and socially marginalized white populations. Third wave whiteness makes these contradictions explicit by acknowledging the relational, contextual and situational ways in which white privilege can be at the same time a taken-for-granted entitlement, a desired social status, a perceived source of victimization and a tenuous situational identity. It is these white inflections, the nuanced and locally specific ways in which whiteness as a form of power is defined, deployed, performed, policed and reinvented that is the central focus of third wave whiteness.

FIRST WAVE WHITENESS

The critical treatment of whiteness owes its greatest intellectual debt to the work of W.E.B. Du Bois. Three observations that Du Bois made about race and whiteness provide the theoretical foundation for critical white studies. In *Black Reconstruction in America 1860–1880* (1935) Du Bois argued that white laborers in the United States came to embrace the racial identity of the dominant group, rather than adopt an identity framed around a class solidarity with recently freed slaves, because white workers received a "public and psychological wage" by joining or at least queuing themselves up for admission into the white race. Membership in the dominant group provided laborers on the margins of whiteness an extensive and heady mix of social and material privileges. On the material level white laborers could monopolize economic, social and state resources. At the social psychological level all white workers, but particularly those white workers on the economic or social margins, were provided with an inexhaustible "wage" in the form of social status, symbolic capital and deference from blacks that embracing white supremacy provided. By adopting the racist beliefs and practices of the dominant group, laborers from southern and eastern Europe were able to eventually shed the stigma of occupying a middling racial identity between whites and blacks. The material rewards of whiteness were substantial for immigrant laborers. Whiteness granted workers racially exclusive footing on the first rung of America's expanding industrial mobility ladder, provided an inherited racialized social status to future generations who would come

to see themselves as unambiguously white and created the ability to accumulate and transfer intergenerational wealth (Shapiro 2004).

In *The Philadelphia Negro* (1970 [1899]) Du Bois provides a scathing critique of "color prejudice" that he chronicled in his groundbreaking study of Philadelphia's Seventh Ward. The ideological import, cultural meaning and how the relative invisibility of whiteness by whites maintains white supremacy was observed by Du Bois over one hundred years ago. The larger problem combating the issue of racial prejudice, Du Bois argued, was that "most white people are unconscious of any such powerful and vindictive feeling; they regard color prejudice as the easily explicable feeling that intimate social intercourse with a lower race is not only undesirable but impractical if our present standards of culture are to be maintained" (1970 [1899], p. 322). Du Bois explains that for whites color prejudice "is not today responsible for all or perhaps the greatest part of the Negro problems; or of the disabilities under which the race labors…they cannot see how such a feeling has much influence on the real situation or alters the social condition of the mass of Negroes" (ibid.). What follows in the next thirty-five pages in *The Philadelphia Negro* is Du Bois chronicling the ways white supremacy results in discrimination, institutional racism, prejudice and the material deprivation of blacks, a situation a majority of whites are "unconscious" of, or do not care to "see." This blind spot to racial inequality remains in large part unchanged. In the United States a majority of whites (71 percent) believe blacks have "more" or "about the same opportunities" as whites (Kaiser 2001) even though every quality of life indicator tells a story of continued and in many cases growing racial inequality.

White supremacy, in concert with early modern capitalism, cemented in place a two-tiered, mutually reinforcing system of material and psychological oppression that is painfully evident throughout the globe. Unlike the rather obvious patterns of discrimination and legally sanctioned state sponsored terror that characterized much of U.S. history, contemporary discursive accounts of race and whiteness serve to make the material benefits of whiteness appear normal, natural and unremarkable. Third wave whiteness is an attempt to make the privileges associated with whiteness "consious" by illustrating how white advantage are maintained through various ideological narratives. These accounts include how color blindness as a political ideology is increasingly used to negate institutional racism or state reforms (Twine 1997; Bonilla-Silva 2003; Gallagher 2003; Lewis 2004; Ansell 2006), the use of cultural deficit arguments to explain away racial inequality and demonize racial minorities (Bobo 2001; Bobo and Smith 1998) and how appeals to nationalism are employed to mask the extent to which racism motivates reactionary politics (Lamont 2000). These accounts of inequality also serve to deflect attention away from the critiques of white racial dominance and towards other ostensibly non-racial social concerns like immigration, class inequality, post 9/11 geopolitics and cultural nationalism.

Du Bois details, and critical white studies expounds upon, how whiteness operates as the normative cultural center that is for many whites an invisible identity, Du Bois understood that whiteness is not monolithic nor is it a uniform category of social identification. As Du Bois phrased it in *The Souls of Black Folks* whites in the South were not of a "solid" or uniform opinion concerning racial matters. He explains that "Today even the attitude of the Southern whites towards blacks is not, as so many assume, in all cases the same" (1982 [1903], p. 92). While acknowledging that racial prejudice, institutional racism and white supremacy are core features of U.S. society, Du Bois nonetheless discerned that there was no single white experience concerning race that all whites universally shared. Du Bois's framing of whiteness as a host of competing, situational, mutating and at time warring ethnic identities is a point of inquiry of third wave whiteness.

Finally, Du Bois's observation that "the problem of the twentieth century is the "color line" has been used as prophetic judgement of the struggles the United States would be forced to confront. However the rest of this oft-quoted line demonstrates Du Bois's keen understanding that white supremacy's hegemony was global in scope. The entire line in the opening second chapter of *Souls* reads "The problem of the twentieth century in the problem of the color-line—the relation of the darker to the lighter races of men in Asia and Africa, in America and in the islands of the sea" (1982 [1903], p. 54).

Whiteness as a form of privilege and power "travels" from western countries to colonies throughout the world. As whiteness travels the globe it reinvents itself locally upon arrival. As Raka Shome points out "whether it was the physical travel of white bodies colonizing 'other worlds' or today's neocolonial travel of white cultural products—media, music, television products, academic texts, and Anglo fashion" (1999, p. 108) white hegemony continues to shape the color line. A recent study found that 40 percent of women in Hong Kong, Malaysia, the Philippines, South Korea and Taiwan routinely use whitening creams to both enhance their social status and increase the odds they will be able to "marry up" socioeconomically (Fuller 2006). Bleaching salons and "Fair and Lovely" lightening soaps are part of the $250 million dollar" fairness-cosmetics market" in India (Perry 2005). After controlling for all the relevant variables (English proficiency, education, work experience) researchers in the United States found that immigrants with lighter skin earned up to 15 percent more compared to immigrants with darker skin (*New York Times*, 28 January 2007, p. 19). Not only does whiteness travel the globe but it also reinvents within locally upon arrival.

SECOND WAVE WHITENESS: BLACK THEORISTS, FEMINIST THEORISTS AND CRITICAL LEGAL THEORISTS

Second wave whiteness includes a host of critical race scholars, many of them U.S. blacks who continued on in the Du Boisian tradition of challenging and making white supremacy and institutional racism visible. The seminal works of E. Franklin Frazier, St. Clair Drake, Horace Cayton, James Baldwin and Ralph Ellison (to name just a few) presented unflinching empirical accounts of racism and its root causes. These scholars were the Cassandras of their time, providing detailed, accurate accounts of racial inequality that would went unheeded, disregarded or ignored.

Throughout much of the twentieth-century mainstream, white social scientists did not focus on the institutions that created, reproduced and normalized white supremacy. The focus that guided whites in the academy primarily concerned itself with the pathology of racist individuals rather than the structural forces that produced racist social systems. The question that guided a majority of race research after the Second World War in the United States was framed by Gunnar Myrdal's *An American Dilemma: The Negro Problem and Modern Democracy* (1944). As Myrdal saw it, the dilemma the United States found itself in was the need to reconcile the deeply held belief of equal opportunity for all and profound racism that structured every facet of American society. It was Myrdal's contention that:

> even a poor and uneducated white person in some isolated and backward rural region in the Deep South, who is violently prejudiced against the Negro and intent upon depriving him of civil rights and human independence, has also a whole compartment of in his valuation sphere housing the entire American Creed of liberty, equality, justice and fair opportunity for everybody.
>
> (Myrdal 1944, p. xlviii)

The cognitive dissonance was defined as the tension guilt-wracked whites experienced trying to negotiate the ideal of equal opportunity and the Jim Crow racism in which they were embedded. America's racial dilemma was not the depths of which white supremacy organized every social, economic and cultural aspect of society; nor was it the material or symbolic rewards racism delivered to whites. The problem occurring to Myrdal was to be found

in "what goes on in the minds of white Americans" (1944, p. li). As a matter of sociological research the material and psychological advantages normalized through white supremacy that Du Bois outlined were rejected in favor of an approach that focused on the individual afflictions of the "white mind," rather then the structures that reproduce racism and inequality from one generation to the next.

Toni Morrison, a Pulitzer Prize winning novelist and U.S. black literary theorist, helped usher in scholarship that would shift attention away from psychologistic accounts of racial inequality to ones that examined the discursive practices that render whiteness invisible. In *Playing in the Dark* (1992), a critical interpretation of U.S. fiction, Morrison reveals how whiteness operates as a cultural referent and normative identity through literacy tropes that frame all races but whiteness as marked categories. Through this act of racial negation immigrant populations could both come to understand their own "Americanness as an opposition to the resident black population" (Morrison 1992, p. 47) and frame American as a racial signifier that would come to "mean" only white.

Critical legal theory has also made significant contributions to second wave whiteness by linking how legal institutions define who is white and consequently which groups are entitled to the material and social advantages whiteness confers (Delgado and Stefancic 1996). Using Du Bois's notion that whiteness operates as a "wage" Cheryl Harris (1993), a U.S. black legal theorist, argues that being defined by the courts as white granted rights to groups who were then able to lay claim to the resources (land, jobs, contracts, schools) that only whites could enjoy. She argues that whiteness, like land or buildings, operates as a form of "property" one that needs to be policed, guarded and regulated. Ian Haney Lopez (1996) examines how the law came to define non-white and white status and the implications this definition had for citizenship. Being unfit for naturalization became synonymous with being non-white which also became shorthand for "degeneracy of intellect morals, self restraint" while being white signified "moral maturity self-assurance, personal independence and political sophistication" (Lopez 1996, p. 16). The state did of course maintain white privilege in these court cases, but Lopez argues the parameters of whiteness were altered through this process and the nation itself was permanently remade as racially categories were redefined. This nation building through racial exclusion for some and inclusion for others has been the focus of similar works done on Brazil and South Africa (Twine 1997; Marx 1998).

How racial minorities have been written out of history, the lack of attention to the way immigrants on the racial margins were whitened and the means by which culture and ideology work to constantly recloak whiteness as a normative identity have been a central focus of white studies' second wave. Historians such as David Roediger (1991, 2005), Theodore Allen (1994) and Matthew Jacobson (1998) have retold the story of race and ethnic identity in the United States by examining how changes in American labor practices, the racial ambiguity of European immigrants and the tangible rewards groups received for aligning themselves with the dominant group all conspired to reframe race, rework whiteness and maintain white supremacy.

THIRD WAVE WHITENESS

…This "wave" can be distinguished from earlier waves in several ways. First, third wave whiteness employs a range of *innovative and renovative* research methodologies including the use of Internet sites (Back 2002), racial consciousness biographies (Twine 1999a, 1999b, 2004; McKinney 2005; Knowles 2006; McDermott 2006), music and photo-elicitation interviews (Twine and Steinbugler 2006). The increasing use of what Twine terms "racial consciousness biographies" has enabled sociologists, particularly ethnographers, to carefully explore how whites produce, translate, and negotiate whiteness in their everyday private and public lives. This

wave of research builds upon earlier work in critical race studies by scholars who have examined how people learn race and racism (Van Ausdale and Feagin 2002). One example of this type of innovative use of racial biographies is the work of Karyn McKinney (2004) who collected racial biographies of two hundred university students in two regions in the Unites States….

Second, the third wave of whiteness studies is characterized, by an interest in the cultural practices and discursive strategies employed by whites as they struggle to recuperate, reconstitute and restore white identities and the supremacy of whiteness in post-apartheid, post-industrial, post-imperial, post–Civil Rights. Troy Duster (1997) uses the term "neo-apartheid" to describe these contexts. This reconstitution of white identities, recuperation of white privilege, and less often resistance to racism, has been a central focus of third wave whiteness studies (Gallagher 1997, 2006; Nayak 2002; Weis 2004; Knowles 2006). Some of this work owes a significant debt to feminist scholarship on race, intimacy and the gendered labor of carework that women in heterosexual families are required to provide (Weis 2004; Byrne 2006). This research examines the quotidian production of white identities "on the ground" as people move across public, private, urban, rural spaces….

Third, whiteness studies scholars, based in the United States, are also shifting their analytical lens away from European immigrants and their descendants towards an analysis of white identity formations among immigrant and post-migration communities whose national origins are in the Caribbean, Latin America, Mexico and other nations outside of Europe….Since 1965 the vast majority of immigrants to the United States are coming from Mexico, the Caribbean, Central and South America and only a minority from Europe. In the United States, the addition of the "Hispanic" category to the 1970 census and the subsequent classification of individuals with Spanish surnames as "Hispanic" or Latino has generated new identities and political constituencies at the federal and national level. This community has diverse origins and, rather than being a monolithic group, is fractured not only along lines of class, education and region but between those who self-identify as "white" and those who embrace a "brown" black or multiracial identity. Sociological analyses of the recruitment of ethnic minorities to "whiteness" and the strategic deployment of whiteness by groups currently at its margins are needed to better understand the production of whiteness and the achievement of "white" identities by members of ethnic minorities. The complicated meaning of whiteness and white identities to the Hispanic/Latino populations, has been undertheorized by whiteness studies scholars, particularly as it intersects with age, class, skin color, tenure and region in the United States.

In "White Americans, the new minority?: Nonblacks and the ever-expanding boundaries of whiteness," Jonathan Warren and France Winddance Twine (1997) argued that the white category has expanded in the United States to include groups previously excluded and that it will continue to expand, with blacks continuing symbolically and politically to represent the most significant racially defining other at the national level. Thus, there exists a space for non-black immigrants and their children to position themselves as "white." The evidence that whiteness is continuing to expand in the United States, and that it continues to incorporate ethnics of multiracial, Asian, Mexicans and other Latinos of non-European heritage, is evident among some segments of the U.S. born Asian American population. For Asian Americans whose parents were born in the United States, particularly where one parent is white, the assertion that Asians will remain or be viewed as "forever foreign" (Zhou 2004) does not necessarily reflect the ways in which the white race has historically incorporated groups who have been on the racial margins. A 2000 National Health Interview Survey (Lee 2001) of multiracial offspring found that among those who self-identify as being both Asian and white, close to half of the respondents marked white as their "main race" in follow-up interviews. In interracial relationships where the father was white about two-thirds of multiracial Japanese and Chinese families defined their offspring as white. These families are more likely to live in white suburbs (Farley 1999) and tend to have attitudes on race relations, and more specifically negative attitudes concerning blacks, that are similar to whites (Herring and Amissah 1997). Light skinned, middle-class Latinos, many who self-define as white already, are marrying non-Hispanic whites. It is likely the children of these unions will self-identify and be viewed as members of the white race. The "racial redistricting" (Gallagher 2004) or redrawing of the color line that is taking place in the U.S. points to an expansion of the white population over the next fifty years.

CONCLUSION

In a trenchant analysis of the "properties of whiteness," Troy Duster uses the metaphor of water to describe how white privilege operates. In his words:

> While water is a fluid state, at a certain contingent moment, under thirty-two degrees, it is transformed into a solid state—ice. This is an easy binary formulation. But things get more complicated, because when H_2O, at still another moment boils, it begins to vaporize or evaporate.... Race, like H_2O, can take many forms, but unlike H_2O it can transform itself in a nano-second. It takes time for ice to boil and for vapor to condense and freeze but race can be, simultaneously, Janus-faced and multifac(et)ed— and also produce a singularly dominant social hierarchy. Indeed, if we make the fundamental mistake of reifying any one of those states as more real than another, we will lose basic insights into the nature and character of racial stratification in America. So it depends on when a picture is taken in this sequence and on who takes the picture as to whether race is best understood as fluid or solid or vapor—or has

evaluated into a temporarily locatable nonexistence, a color-blind fragment in time and space.

(Duster 2001, pp. 114–15)

Duster reminds us that "whiteness is deeply embedded in the routine structures of economic and political life. From ordinary service at Denny's Restaurants, to far greater access to bank loans to simple *police-event-free* driving—all these things have come unreflectively with the territory of being white" (2001, p. 114)....Our theoretical aim is to map out new empirical approaches to the analyses of whiteness and white identity formations, in an effort to dismantle racial hierarchies so that someday we live in a racially just world in which children will no longer understand the meaning of the term "racism" or white supremacy. These will be archaic terms they will look up in dictionaries.

REFERENCES

Allen, Theodore W. 1994 *The Invention of the White Race*. vol. 1: *Racial Oppression and Social Control*, London: Verso.

Andersen, Margaret L. 2003 "Whitewashing race: a critical perspective on whiteness," in Ashley Doane and Eduardo Bonilla-Silva (eds), *White Out: The Continuing Significance of Racism*, New York: Routledge, pp. 21–34.

Ansell, Amy 2006 "Casting a blind eye: the ironic consequences of color-blindness in South Africa and the United States," *Critical Sociology*, vol. 32, no. 2–3, pp. 333–56.

Back, Les 2002 "Aryans reading Adorno: cyber-culture and twenty-first century racism," *Ethnic and Racial Studies*, vol. 25, no. 4, pp. 628–51. Special issue on "Beyond Difference" edited by Claire Alexander.

Bhattacharyya, Gargi, Gabriel, John and Small, Stephen 2002 *Race and Power: Global Racism in the Twenty-first Century*, London: Routledge.

Bobo, Lawrence 2001 "Racial altitudes and relations at the close of the twentieth century," in Neil Smelser, W.J. Wilson and F. Mitchell (eds), *America Becoming: Racial Trends and Their Consequences*. Washington DC: National Academy Press, pp. 262–99.

Bobo, Lawrence and Smith, Ryan 1998 "From Jim Crow racism to laissez-faire racism: the transformation of racial attitudes," in Wendy Katlin (ed.), *Beyond Pluralism: The Conception of Groups and Group Identities in America*, Chicago, IL: University of Illinois Press, pp. 198–212.

Bonilla-Silva, Eduardo 2003 *Racism Without Racist: Color-Blind Racism and the Persistence of Racial Inequality in the United States*, New York: Roman and Littlefield.

Bonnett, Alastair 2000 *Anti-Racism*, London: Routledge.

Byrne, Bridget 2006 *White Lives: The Interplay of "Race," Class and Gender in Everyday Life*, London and New York: Routledge.

Chan, Suzanna 2006 "'Kiss my royal Irish ass.' Contesting identity: visual culture, gender, whiteness and diaspona," *Journal of Gender Studies*, vol. 15, no. 1, pp. 1–17.

Choules, Kathryn 2006 "Globally privileged citizenship," *Race Ethnicity and Education*, vol. 9, no. 3, pp. 275–93.

Delgado, Richard and Stefancic, Jean 1996 *Critical White Studies: Looking Behind the Mirror*, Philadelphia, PA: Temple University Press.

Doane, Ashley W. JR 2003 "Rethinking Whiteness Studies," in Ashley 'Woody' Doane and Eduardo Bonilla-Silva (eds). *White Out: The Continuing Significance of Racism*, New York: Routledge.

Du Bois, W.E.B. 1935 *Black Reconstruction in American. 1860–1880*, New York: Harcourt, Brace.

———.1969 *The Souls of Black Folk*, New York: Signet Classic.

———. 1970 *The Philadelphia Negro: A Social Study*, 3rd edition [1st edn, New York: Schocken Books].

Durrheim, Kevin 2005 "Socio-spatial practice and racial representations in a changing South Africa," *South African Journal of Psychology*, vol. 35, pp. 444–459.

Duster, Troy 1997 "Individual Fairness, Group Preferences, and the California Strategy," *Representations*, no. 55, pp. 41–58.

———. 2001 "The 'morphing' of properties of whiteness," in Birgit Brander Rasmussen, Eric Klinenberg, Irene Nexica and Matt Wray (eds), *The Making and Unmaking of Whiteness*, Durham, NC and London: Duke University Press, pp. 113–37.

Dyer, Richard 1997 *White*, London: Routledge.

Farley, Reynolds 1999 "Racial issues: recent trends in residential patterns and intermarriage," in Neil Smelser and Jeffrey Alexander (eds), *Diversity and Its Discontents: Cultural Conflict and Common Ground in Contemporary Society*, Princeton, NJ: Princeton University Press, pp. 112–29.

Forrest, James and Dunn, Kevin 2006, "Racism and intolerance in Eastern Australia: a geographic perspective," *Australian Geographer*, vol. 37, no. 2, pp. 167–86.

Frankenberg, Ruth 1993 *White Women, Race Matters: The Social Construction of Whiteness*, Minneapolis, MN: University or Minnesota Press.

———. 2001 "The mirage of an unmarked whiteness," in Birgit Brander Rasmussen, Eric Klinenberg, Irene J. Nexica and Matt Wray (eds), *The Making and Unmaking of Whiteness*, Durham, NC: Duke University Press, pp. 72–96.

Fuller, Thomas 2006 May 14 "A Vision of Pale Beauty Carries Risk for Asia's Women," New York Times Online, http://www.nytimes.com/2006/05/14/world/asia/14thailand.html.

Gallagher, Charles 1997 "White Racial Formation: Into the 21st Century," in Richard Delgodo and Jean Stefancic (eds), *Critical White Studies: Looking Behind the Mirror*, Philadelphia, PA: Temple University Press, 1997, 6–11.

Gallagher, Charles A. 2003a "Playing the while ethnic card: using ethnic identity to deny contemporary racism," in Ashley 'Woody' Doane and Eduardo Bonilla-Silva (eds), *White Out: The Continuing Significance of Racism*, New York: Routledge, pp. 145–58.

———. 2003b "Color-blind privilege: the social and political functions of erasing the color line in post race America," *Race, Gender & Class*, vol. 10, no. 4, pp. 22–37.

———. 2004 "Racial redistricting: expanding the boundaries of whiteness," in Heather M. Dalmage (ed.), *The Politics of Multiracialism: Challenging Racial Thinking*, Albany, NY: State University Press of New York, pp. 59–76.

Gallagher, Charles 2006 "Color Blindness: An Obstacle to Racial Justice?" in David Brunsma (eds) *Mixed Messages: Multiracial Identities in the "Color-blind Era*," Boulder, CO: Lynne Rienner Publishes.

Garner, Steve 2006 "The uses of whiteness: what sociologists working on Europe can draw from US research on whiteness," *Sociology*, vol. 40, no. 2, pp. 257–75.

Haney Lopez, Ian 1996 *White By Law: The Legal Construction of Race*, New York: New York University Press.

Harris, Cheryl 1993 "Whiteness as property," Harvard Law Review, vol. 106, no. 8, pp. 1709–91.

Herring, Cedric and Amissah, Charles 1997 "Advance and retreat: racially based attitudes and public policy," in Steven A. Tuch and Jack Martin (eds), *Racial Attitudes: Continuity and Change*, Westport, CT: Praeger, pp. 131–46.

Jacobson, Matthew Frye 1998 *Whiteness of a Different Color: European Immigrants and the Alchemy of Race*, Cambridge, MA: Harvard University Press.

Juge, Tony S. and Perez, Michael P. 2006 "The modern colonial politics of citizenship and whiteness in France," *Social Identities*, vol. 12, no. 2, pp. 187–212.

Kaiser Family Foundation 2001 *Race and Ethnicity in 2001: Attitudes, Perceptions and Experiences*, Washington D.C.: Kaiser Family Foundation.

Kincheloe, Joe L. 2006 "The southern place and racial politics: southernification, romanticization and the recovery of white supremacy," *Souls*, vol. 8, no. 1, pp. 27–46.

Knowles, Caroline and photographs by Douglas Harper 2006 "Seeing Race Through the Lens," *Ethnic and Racial Studies*, vol. 29, no. 3, pp. 512–29.

Lamont, Michele 2000 *The Dignity of Working Men: Morality and the Boundaries of Race, Class, and Immigration*, New York: Russell Sage Foundation.

Lee, Sharon 2001 *Using New Racial Categories in the 2000 Census*, Baltimore, MD: Annie E. Casey Foundation, pp. 1–38.

Lewis, Amanda E. 2003 *Race in the Schoolyard: Negotiating the Color Line in Classrooms and Communities*, New Brunswick, NC: Rutgers University Press.

———. 2004 '"What Groups?' Studying whites and whiteness in the era of color-Blindness," *Sociological Theory*, vol. 22, no. 4, pp. 623–46.

Lipsitz, George 1998 *The Possessive Investment in Whiteness: How White People Profit From Identity Politics*, Philadelphia, PA: Temple University Press.

Marx, Anthony 1998 *Making Race and Nation: A Comparison of South Africa, the United States and Brazil*, Cambridge: Cambridge University Press.

Mcdermott, Monica 2006 *Working-Class White: The Making and Unmaking of Race Relations*, Berkeley, CA/Los Angeles, CA/London: University of California Press.

Mckinney, Karyn 2005 *Being White: Stories of Race and Racism*, New York and London: Routledge.

Morrison, Toni 1992 *Playing in the Dark: Whiteness and the Literary Imagination*, Cambridge, MA: Harvard University Press.

Myrdal, Gunnar 1944 *An American Dilemma*, New York: Harper and Brothers.

Nayak, Anoop 2002 '"In the whitest England': new subject positions for the white youth in the post-imperial moment," in Cynthia Levine-Rasky (ed.), *Working Through Whiteness: International Perspectives*, Albany, NY: State University Press of New York, pp. 241–68.

Perry, Alex 2005 November 28 "Could you Please Make Me a Shade Lighter," Time Magazine On-Line, http://www.time.com/time/magazine/article/0,9171,1134744,00.html.

Perry, Pamela 2002 *Shades of White: White Kids and Racial Identities in High School*, Durham, NC: Duke University Press.

Potter, Robert B. and Phillips, Joan 2006 "Both black and symbolically white: the 'Bajan-Brit' return migrant as post-colonial hybrid," *Ethnic and Racial Studies*, vol. 29, no. 5, pp. 901–27.

Roediger, David R. 1991 *The Wages of Whiteness*, New York and London: Verso.

———. 2005 *Working Toward Whiteness: How America's Immigrants Become White*, New York: Basic Books.

Saxton, Alexander 1990 *The Rise and Fall of the White Republic: Class Politics and Mass Culture in Nineteenth-Century America*, New York: Verso.

Shapiro, Thomas 2004 *The Hidden Cost of Being African American: How Wealth Perpetuates Inequality*, Oxford: Oxford University Press.

Shome, Raka 1999 "Whiteness and the politics of location: postcolonial reflections," in Thomas K. Nakayama and Judith N. Martin (eds), *Whiteness: The Communication of Social Identity*, Thousand Oaks, CA: Sage, pp. 107–28.

Twine, France Winddance 1996 "Brown skinned white girls: class, culture and the construction of white identity in suburban communities," *Gender, Place and Culture*, vol. 3, no. 2, pp. 205–24.

——— . 1997 *Racism in a Racial Democracy: The Maintenance of White Supremacy in Brazil*, New Brunswick, NJ: Rutgers University Press.

——— . 1999a "Bearing blackness in Britain: the meaning of racial difference for while mothers of African-descent children," in *Social Identities: Journal of Race, Nation and Culture*, vol. 5, no. 2, pp. 185–210.

——— . 1999b "Transracial mothering and anti-racism: the case of white mothers of 'black' children in Britain," *Feminist Studies*, vol. 25 (Autumn), pp. 729–46.

——— . 2004 "A white side of black Britain: the concept of racial literacy," *Ethnic and Racial Studies*, vol. 27, no. 6, pp. 878–907.

Twine, France Winddance and Steinbugler, Amy 2006 "The gap between 'whites' and 'Whiteness' interracial intimacy and racial literacy," *The Du Bois Review: Social Science Research on Race*, vol. 3. no. 2. pp. 341–63.

Van Ausdale, Debra and Feagin Joe 2002 *The First R: How Children Learn Race and Racism*, Lanham, Maryland: Rowman and Littlefield.

Walker, Liz 2005 "The color white: racial and gendered closure in the South African medical profession," Ethnic and Racial Studies, vol. 28, no. 2, pp. 348–75.

Warren, Jonathan and Twine, France Winddance 1997 "White Americans, the new minority?: Non-blacks and the ever-expanding boundaries of whiteness," *Journal of Black Studies*, vol. 26, no. 2, pp. 200–18.

Weis, Lois 2004 *Class Reunion: The Remaking of the American White Working Class*, New York and London: Routledge.

Wellman, David T. 1993 *Portraits of White Racism*, New York, NY: Cambridge University Press.

Howard Winant 2001 *The World Is A Ghetto: Race and Democracy since World War II*, New York: Basic Books.

Yancey, George 2003 *Who Is White?: Latinos, Asians, and the New Black/Nonblack Divide*, Boulder, CO: Lynne Rienner.

Zhou, Min 2004 "Are Asians becoming 'white?,'" *Contexts* vol. 3, no. 1, pp. 29–37.

JOURNALING QUESTION

"Waves" of whiteness studies are academic, scholarly occurrences. Has the idea of "whiteness studies" reached the families and friends in your life? What do people you know think of when you say "whiteness studies"?

11.
THE "MORPHING" PROPERTIES OF WHITENESS

TROY DUSTER

"Morphing" means changing, transforming. Americans rarely think of race as something that morphs. Yet a quick glance at our own history shows lots of groups that are now called "white ethnics" were once considered non-white. Thse groups include Jews, Italians, Irish, Armenians, just to name a few. Troy Duster talks about not only the historic morphing of whiteness, as the meaning of the categories change across time, but also the instantaneous morphing that occurs in a single encounter. Race may suddenly insert itself into an interaction, as it does in his personal stories in this reading, and everything seems to shift. That ability to "suddenly appear" means, of course, that race is ever-present. So much of our American history is based on race that it cannot be erased or denied of a moment. How can we reconcile the desire we may have to ignore and go past race on an individual level, in our interactions with classmates, teachers, coworkers, and friends, with that historical legacy?

In discussions of race and the recent rediscovery of the American preoccupation with whiteness, it is possible to isolate two overarching but sharply conflicting frameworks that run at cross-purposes. On the one hand, there are those who portray race and whiteness as fluid, continually reflecting emergent and contingent features of social life, emphasizing the relational and ever-changing character of race. On the other hand, it is not difficult to identify historians, writers, and social analysts who have emphasized the deeply embedded, structural, hard, enduring, solid-state features of race and racism, sustained throughout three centuries even as they have acknowledged the occasional shifting boundaries of who gets included in the category "white."

RACE AS ARBITRARY AND WHIMSICAL VERSUS RACE AS STRUCTURAL AND ENDURING

If we take even a casual excursion through the last few centuries of racial classification, there is overwhelming evidence on the side of those who have argued that race is arbitrary, shifting, and often *biologically* and *sociologically* inconsistent, contradictory, and simple-minded. The rule that one drop of black blood makes one black is the easy mark along a full continuum of mind-boggling, ludicrous taxonomies.[1] "Passing" and incoherent "miscegenation laws" and slave-owner/slave offspring do more than simply dot the landscape with the minefields of this topic. This continuum extends well into the present period, in which we find more and more people asserting a mixed-race identity. Since the classification of race is arbitrary and often whimsical (for example, one drop of blood), accepting the idea that race is something identifiable with fixed borders that could be crossed and thus "mixed"— while others are "not mixed"—is supplanting one multitiered fiction with another. At the biochemical level of blood types and hematology, at the neurological level of neurotransmission patterns, at the level of cell function—at all these levels, we are all

Excerpted from Troy Duster, "The 'Morphing' Properties of Whiteness," in *The Making and Unmaking of Whiteness*, eds. Birgit Brander Rasmussen, Eric Klinenberg, Irene J. Nexica, and Matt Wray (Durham, NC: Duke University Press, 2001), 113–37. Notes have been renumbered and edited.

"mixed" by any taxonomy or measure of allele frequency of large population groups.[2] It would seem that we must "score one" for the side that sees the superficiality and artificiality of race.

OTHER VOICES

Yet there is another set of very compelling voices…emphasizing how race, or in this case whiteness and its attendant privilege, is deeply embedded in the routine structures of economic and political life. From ordinary service at Denny's Restaurants, to far greater access to bank loans to simple peaceful, *police-event–free* driving—all these things have come unreflectively with the territory of being white.[3] One does not give up racial privilege, neither in the United States nor in South Africa, by simply denying that it exists. Whites who have come to a point where they acknowledge their racial privilege are in a difficult circumstance morally because they cannot just shed that privilege with a simple assertation of denial.

So who is right? One side sees race as ever-changing. The other side sees enduring race privilege. Oddly both sides are correct. Or, at least, both sides have an important handle on an elementary truth about race. But *empirically*, one could easily ask, if these two positions are poles apart, how can both be correct about race? How can race be both structural and embedded yet superficial, arbitrary, and whimsical—shifting with times and circumstances?

The best way to communicate how this is possible is to employ an analogy—to *water* or, more precisely, H_2O. While water is a fluid state, at certain contingent moments, under thirty-two degrees, it is transformed into a solid state—ice. This is an easy binary formulation. But things get more complicated, because when H_2O, at still another contingent moment boils, it begins to vaporize or evaporate. And now the coup de grace of the analogy of H_2O to race: H_2O in its vapor state can condense, come back and transform into water, and then freeze and hit you in its solid state as an ice block; what you thought had evaporated into the thin air can return in a form that is

decidedly and consequentially real. In short, H_2O is to serve now as more than just my analogy to race—and, in this context, whiteness. Race, like H_2O, can take many forms, but unlike H_2O it can transform itself in a nanosecond. It takes time for ice to boil or for vapor to condense and freeze, but race can be *simultaneously* Janus-faced and multifac(et)ed—and also produce a singularly dominant social hierarchy. Indeed, if we make the fundamental mistake of reifying any one of those states as more real than another, we will lose basic insights into the nature and character of racial stratification in America. So it depends on when a picture is taken in this sequence and on who takes the picture as to whether race is best understood as fluid or solid or vapor—or has evaporated into a temporally locatable nonexistence, a color-blind fragment in time and space.

IF WE ARE ALL ONE RACE, HOW COULD THERE BE "WHITENESS" IN ITS SOLID STATE?

A consortium of leading scientists across the disciplines from biology to physical anthropology issued a "Revised UNESCO Statement on Race" in 1995. This is a definitive declaration that summarizes eleven central issues and concludes that in terms of "scientific" discourse there is no such thing as a "race" that has any scientific utility, at least in the biological sciences: "[T]he same scientific groups that developed the biological concept over the last century have now concluded that its use for characterizing human populations is so flawed that it is no longer a scientifically valid concept. In fact, the statement makes clear that the biological concept of race as applied to humans has no legitimate place in biological science.[4] By the mid-1970s, it had become abundantly clear that there is more genetic variation within the most current common socially used categories of race than between these categories.[5] The consensus is newly formed. For example, in the early part of this century, scientists in several countries tried to link up a study of the major blood groups in the ABO system to racial and ethnic groups.[6] Since researchers knew that blood type B was more common in certain ethnic and racial groups—which they believed to be more inclined to criminality and mental illness—this was often a thinly disguised form of racism.[7] They kept running up against a brick wall.

It is not difficult to understand why they persisted. Humans are symbol-bearing creatures who give meaning to their experiences and to their symbolic worlds. The UNESCO statement of the 1990s is ultimately about the problem of the difference between first-order constructs in science and second-order constructs. Some fifty years ago, Felix Kaufmann made a crucial distinction that throws some light on the controversy.[8] Kaufmann was not addressing whether or not there could be a science of race. Rather, he noted that there are different kinds of issues, methodologies, and theories that are generated by what could be called first-order constructs in the physical and natural sciences versus second-order constructs. For the physical and natural sciences, the naming of objects for investigation and inquiry, for conceptualizing and finding empirical regularities, is in the hands of the scientists and their scientific peers. Thus, for example, the nomenclature for quarks or neurons, genes or chromosomes, nitrogen or sulfides, and so on all reside with the scientist qua scientist in his/her role as the creator of first-order constructs.

This is quite different from the task of the observer, analyst, or scientist of human social behavior Humans live in a pre-interpreted social world: they grow up, from infancy, in a world that has preassigned categories and names for those categories, which were in turn provided by fellow commonsense actors, not by "scientists." Persons live in the world that is pre-interpreted for them, and their continual task is to try to navigate, negotiate, and make sense of that world. The task of the social scientist is therefore quite distinct from that of the natural scientist. While the latter can rely on first-order constructs, the former must construct a set of categories based on the preinterpreted world

of commonsense actors. The central problem is that "race" is now, and has been since 1735, both a first- and second-order construct. This was the year that Linnaeus published *Systema Naturae*, in which he revealed a four-part classification scheme of the human races that has residues still today.

We now turn to the matter of whether race can be studied scientifically. If we mean by that, is there a consensus among the natural scientists about race as a first-order construct, then the answer since about 1970 is categorically no. The UNESCO statement summarizes why this is so at every level that is significant to the biological functioning of the organism, with two exceptions. We have already noted that scientific research on first-order constructs about race as a biological category in science in the last four decades has revealed over and over again that there is greater genetic heterogeneity within rather than between major racial groupings. One of the two exceptions has to do with the fact that the gene frequencies, as demonstrated in the use of specific polymorphic markers, occur more frequently in certain populations than in others.[9] But this distribution of allele frequencies, though occasionally overlapping with racial groupings, is definitely not only a racially defined issue. For example, northern Europeans have greater concentrations of cystic fibrosis than southern Europeans, and both are categorized as "Caucasians." Moreover, southern Europeans have higher rates of beta-thalassemia than northern Europeans—but, even more to the point, sickle-cell anemia is found in greater concentration in Orchomenus, Greece, than among African Americans.[10] While clinical geneticists are quite familiar with these wide patterns of variations between and among persons who appear phenotypically to be of a certain "race," when an African American with cystic fibrosis shows up at a cystic fibrosis clinic, there is as much consternation about this person's possibly being in the wrong place. When a white person with sickle-cell anemia appears in a sickle-cell clinic, there is often explicit speculation that this person is "passing" and is *really* black.[11]

Thus, the "commonsense" question of whether someone is black or white or Asian is frequently difficult to pin down at the margins—but residents of the United States have been acting as if this were self—evident. The allocation of such resources as loans to build houses has been based on such casual visual cues as whether one "appears to be" white or black. Over time, with the patterned distribution of loans, the racialized shape of suburbs and inner cities began to look "quite real"—solidifying into a solid state of racial boundary maintenance—all the while a kind of second-order construct.

RACE, LAW, AND SECOND-ORDER CONSTRUCTS

Three acts were passed by the U.S. Congress in 1934–35 that would seal the accumulation of wealth into white households for the next half-century. There is some new scholarship emerging reexamining the role of race in explaining U.S. domestic policy for the last half-century.[12]

The new work is fascinating in that it points out the systematic, integrated character of policies of the federal government that will surprise most Americans who grew up reading high school civics books that trumpeted the race-neutral character of Franklin Roosevelt's New Deal government policies. For example, Jill Quadagno notes that while there is some truth to the claim that the New Deal was designed to provide a "floor of protection for the industrial working class," it was the brokered compromises over the New Deal that simultaneously "reinforced racial segregation through social welfare programs, labor policy, and housing policy." How, and why?

In 1935 Roosevelt had put together a fragile coalition of northern industrial workers and southern whites still engaged in a primarily agrarian economic order. Blacks were a vital part of that agrarian system, but they could not vote in the South. Thus Roosevelt did not need to even try to court what was not there: the black southern vote. During this period, more than three-quarters of the black population still lived in the South. Most of them sharecropped and were tied to the plantation economy at poverty-level wages. Those who were not sharecroppers were engaged in day labor—with most of these employed at $2.00 per 100 pounds of cotton. This translated to $2.00 per day for a strong worker.[13]

Black women worked as maids, making $2.00 per week on average. White southerners in control of key positions in Congress explicitly voiced fears that any federal programs that would put money directly into the pockets of blades would undermine the very infrastructure of this plantation economy. As chairs of the powerful committees of the House and Senate, they blocked any attempt to change the agrarian system that indentured black sharecroppers. Because of this opposition, which is documented in memoranda between Congress and the White House, Roosevelt compromised, and agricultural workers and servants were excluded from the Social Security Act of 1935. The exclusion of agricultural workers and house servants appears in retrospect to have been race-neutral. At the time, however, *the key actors said they would block all Social Security legislation: if it included blacks.*

Similarly, the Wagner Act of 1935, labeled in some circles as the Magna Carta of labor, was on closer inspection the Magna Carta of white labor.[14] The original version, which permitted the organization of industrial labor and legalized collective bargaining, *prohibited racial discrimination.* But the American Federation of Labor and the same constellation of white southerners who controlled the key committees of Congress fought it, and the final version permitted racial exclusion. Because the racial exclusion language was applied to closed shops, blacks were blocked by law from challenging the barriers to entry into the newly protected labor unions and securing the right to collective bargaining.[15]

Finally, in 1937 Congress passed the National Housing Act, which sealed the fate of America's cities, creating the social policy and economic basis for sustained and exacerbated racial segregation.

While many commentators have blamed "white flight" for the creation of ghettos and barrios, it was actually this heavily coded racial policy of the federal government of the United States that created white enclaves in the suburbs. In 1939 the Federal Housing Authority's *Underwriting Manual* guidelines for granting housing loans explicitly used race as the single most important criterion. The following passage is from Section 937 of the FHA manual that covered the period in question: "If a neighborhood is to retain stability, it is necessary that properties shall be continued to be occupied by the same social and *racial* classes."[16]

On this basis, for the next thirty years, whites were able to get housing loans at 3 to 5 percent, while blacks were routinely denied such loans. For example, of 350,000 new homes built in northern California between 1946 and 1960 with FHA support, *fewer than 100 went to blacks.* That same pattern holds for the whole state, and for the nation as well. Between 1935 and 1950, eleven million homes were built in the United States with federal assistance, and Charles Abrams has documented well his assertion that "discrimination against Negroes was a condition of federal assistance." The official code of ethics of the National Association of Real Estate Boards not only barred its members from selling houses across the racial divide but put teeth behind its code. In a 1943 brochure titled *Fundamentals of Real Estate Practice*, the association outlined grounds for expulsion of realtors who violated race-based sales and then went on to state explicitly what constituted problematic behavior:

> The prospective buyer might be a bootlegger who would cause considerable annoyance to his neighbors, a madame who had a number of Call Girls on her string, a gangster, who wants a screen for his activities by living in a better neighborhood, a colored man of means who was giving his children a college education and thought they were entitled to live among whites....No matter what the motive or character of the would-be purchaser, if the deal would instigate a form of blight, then certainly

the well-meaning broker must work against its consummation.

The urban redevelopment programs sponsored by the federal government under the National Housing Act of 1949 also served to undermine the financial solidity of the black community. The alignment of corridors in the major cities was chosen so that the freeways almost universally cut through core areas of black settlements, while connecting the white suburbs to the central business districts of the cities. As a direct result of these programs, many urban black areas lost their neighborhood shopping districts of successful small businesses. This was soon followed by empirically demonstrable race-conscious systematic mortgage "redlining," which had a downward-spiraling effect on the economic vitality of scores of black communities.[17]

It should now be clear that the assertion of a fact—that median family net worth of individuals in the United States who are socially designed as "white" is $43,279, while the median family net worth of individuals in the United States who are socially designated as "black" is $4,169—is a matter that can be determined to be true or false by the systematic collection of empirical data, and either replicated or refuted. In other words, it can be investigated scientifically, without reference to blood groups, the relationship between genotype and phenotype, or the likelihood that one group is more at risk for cystic fibrosis while the other is more at risk for sickle-cell anemia.

To definitively assert that at the blood group level, or at the level of the modulatory environment for neurotransmission in the brain, there are no real racial differences (read biological) is to reify a particular version of the biological sciences as *science*. This would ignore the capacity of scientific inquiry to apprehend die social reality of the ten-to-one economic advantage of coming from a white household in America versus coming from a black household. Although loan allocations based on crude phenotypical versions of racial differences are second-order constructs, the ten-to-one ratio by "race" noted above is subject to scientific investigation as well. It can be challenged or proven false or replicated over and over again. Nonetheless, patterned social behavior associated with "race" leads to a confusion about the role of genetics and the way in which the analyst peers through the prism of heritability at the direction of the causal arrow. Richard Herrnstein and Charles Murray, James Wilson and Richard Henrnstein, Arthur Jensen, and a wide band of other claimants with no training in genetics make the commonsense mistake of treating race as a biological construct, then reading back through social patterns (scoring on a test; rate of incarceration) to make inferences about the biological underpinnings of social patterns.[18] For example, Herrnstein and Murray posit the dominance of genetics in explaining IQ, concluding that "the genetic component of IQ" is 60 percent. Then, taking IQ as the independent variable, the authors extend this analysis to the genetic explanation of social achievement or failure, so that unemployment, crime, and social standing are "explained" by IQ.[19] Despite a heavy reliance on the genetic explanation of intelligence as measured by test scores, the basic data from the molecular genetics revolution of the last three decades are completely absent.

Herrnstein and Murray posit that genetics plays an important, even dominant role in IQ, proposing that it is a whopping 60 percent of g, a statistical measure assumed to be related to "general intelligence." Neither Herrnstein (a psychologist) nor Murray (a political scientist) demonstrates sufficient knowledge of contemporary developments in the human biosciences to be aware of a fundamental problem in attributing g to genetics. Even single-gene determined phenotypical expressions such as Huntington's disease, beta-thalassemia, and sickle-cell anemia exhibit a wide range of clinical manifestations. For multifactorial conditions—of which, incontestably we must include the evolving thought processes of the brain—the interaction between nutrition, cellular development, and neurological sequencing has been firmly established.

Developments of the last decade reveal a remarkable feedback loop between the brain and the "experience" of an environment. We now can demonstrate that a single neuron displays a variety of activity patterns and will switch between them, depending on the modulatory environment.[20] Anyone aware of current developments in cognitive science knows that a one-way deterministic notion of the firing of the neurotransmitters and subsequent behavior is a deeply reductionist fallacy. Thus to assign to "genetics" a ballpark figure of any kind, without regard to these well-known interaction effects, is to display a profound ignorance of the last three decades of developments in molecular biology and the neurosciences, most especially since Herrnstein and Murray posit genetics (60 percent) as the most powerful explanatory variable.

The inverse of the attempt to get at a biological construct of race is the assertion, by those committed to a class analysis, that class rather than race is ultimately the master stratifying practice in technologically advanced industrial and postindustrial societies. But that is also open to empirical investigation. Both the biological construct and the class construct are attempts at first-order conceptions, and, as such, they appear on the surface to be more scientific. Yet, there is a fundamental error in the logic of inquiry here. As we have seen, when those who make bank loan decisions do so with their own sets of symbolic strategies—*and those practices are routinized*—the stratified outcomes are a compelling site for *scientific* investigation.

The debate about whether race or class is "more real" as a stratifying practice can be better understood by reexamining how the issue is framed. What is it about class that makes it more real than race—save for the empirical fact that more people employ it (or do not) as a way of sorting social, political, and economic relations? The power of apartheid in South Africa and Jim Crow in the United States demonstrates that such facts are as much located in the practices of actors as in the "objective" relations of workers to capital. The answer is that, objectively speaking, class relations are governed by just such an attempt at a first-order construct: the connections to the workplace. But during apartheid (and even after, there is evidence to believe), whites have had greater access to scarce resources than blacks. This is an "objective" reality of a stratifying practice, no less because it is a second-order construct employed by those acting in the world. Rather, during apartheid, it was even definitively a pattern with notable and obvious replicability (i.e., as a stratifying practice).

The trouble with expertise about race is that once we write books and articles about it, we capture some part of it for a particular understanding. We then become committed to that singular version of it, and often become defensive and aggressive in our defense of our "turf" of a particular rendering.[21] But if scholars and researchers have trouble, lay persons have at least as hard a time holding simultaneously conflicting imagery about the multiple realities of race in America. And so I am going to tell a story about my own youth, when I came to understand the contingent character of race and whiteness and how people can make strategic use of it.

RACE IN ITS FLUID STATE:
A PERSONAL TALE

"When I attended college many years ago at Northwestern University, I was one of six black undergraduates on a campus of over seven thousand students. Northwestern is just outside Chicago, something of the midwestern equivalent of Stanford in that it draws heavily from the upper middle-class of the Chicago region. And so it follows that it would be very unlikely that my particular phenotype would be expressed at Northwestern.

While I was there, I came to know Jack Doyle, a fellow student who was from an Irish working-class background. Gruff in manner and tough in appearance, Doyle was also something of a stand-out in that world. He and I became close friends, and we have sustained that friendship long beyond our collegiate careers. After our college days, and

over the years, we would often get together whenever I returned to Chicago. A dozen or so years later, after I got my Ph.D. and was teaching at Berkeley, I returned to Chicago, visiting my mother for a week. One evening, I gave Jack a call, and he came over on this particular hot August night to join me for a beer. Around eleven o'clock at in the night, my mother came home from a neighborhood meeting and said she forgot to get food for the next day's breakfast. She asked if I would drive her around to the store on Sixty-third, just off Cottage Grove. So I said, "Of course," and we got in the car and drove around to the store. Jack Doyle joined us, so there we were—the three of us. We parked on Sixty-third Street, and, while Jack and I sat in the car, my mother went in to the store to get the groceries. I noticed that police cars occasionally would circle, but that was nothing new to me.

After about the third or fourth time around, however, three big, tough-looking, white police officers jumped out, one with gun drawn, and said to us, "Get out of that car." So we got out. They bent us over the hood of the car and frisked us, and then they said to me, "What are you doing here?" But before I could answer, they turned to my friend, "And what are *you* doing here?" Remember, this is an all-black area of Chicago.

And he said, "I've come to visit my friend." One of the police officers said, "Your friend from where?" "Northwestern," I replied. He said, "Northwestern? You're college boys?" Then with sardonic disbelief dripping from the question, he asked, "Okay, college boys—what did you study?" We told them. We were not very convincing because one of them said, quite agitatedly, "I asked you, 'What are you doing here on a Saturday night parked in front of a grocery store?'"Sometimes the truth will not set you free. I told the truth: "I'm waiting for my mother." That's when I saw his billy club. He lifted it slowly, deliberately, and I had the experience of all of this happening as if in slow-motion—as in a baseball pitcher's exaggerated wind-up before the delivery. And all the while he was saying, "You're a real wise ass—" Then, all of a sudden, the voice from the heavens parts, the thick hot August night air. It is my mother's voice booming with authority: "Officer, what's going on here?"

In that one moment, perhaps even a nanosecond, I understood the fluid and contingent and Janus-faced character of race. I saw it happen with my own eyes. With his arm in midair, this tough white cop turned officer-of-the-law and literally turned and tipped his hat to my mother and said, "Madam, we're here to serve and protect you." Yes. A remarkable capacity for transmogrification or, perhaps better, *morphing*. He went from solid state to fluid state. He transformed himself from "an occupying force of domination" into someone there "to protect a woman citizen" from a suspicious character—from the sort of person like me who waits out in front of grocery stores casing the joint"' midnight." Back in the 1960s there were two competing versions of the police. One version said, *"The police are a force to serve and protect you."* Bumper stickers with that slogan were pasted on cars all over the country. Contrarily, there was another set of bumper stickers, disproportionately seen in the black communities of the nation, which read, *"The police are an occupation force."* In America, depending more on your race than anything else, you will routinely see this issue of police "occupation" or "service" through one lens or the other.

The concept of race has that complexity. Writers Noel Ignatiev, John Garvey, and David Roediger have discussed "the abolition of whiteness".[22] That is not a bad idea, depending on context and historical circumstances. However, it might not be a good idea either. That is, what would you say if suddenly after forty-eight to fifty years of apartheid, in which whites had begun to collect and accumulate lots of wealth—land—they suddenly turned around and said, "Let's abolish whiteness—now we're all individuals. Apartheid is over, so we'll all start from scratch. Let's have no group designation by color."

To many, this sounds like hollow rhetoric, more like the ideology of privilege in behalf of the accumulation of more privilege of those who take the position that one cannot simply decontextualize or ahistoricize the notion of race.

In the United States significant wage and salary differences between the races persist, with blacks earning anywhere from about two-thirds to three-quarters of what whites obtain in wages and salaries.[23] Since this gap has narrowed somewhat over the last three decades, analysts who wish to portray the situation as one of a slow improvement inevitably focus on these figures. *However, focusing merely on wages and salary differences obscures a critical measure of wealth: net worth.* Wages and salaries are dependent on employment, and in the current economic situation of the United States there is far less job security than in previous periods. A combination of massive downsizing and layoffs, along with seasonal and part-time employment, characterizes much of the contemporary work setting. Different spheres of work are more likely to employ whites than blacks. For example, blacks are more likely to be employed in the public sector, the focus of systemic and often effective attacks by conservatives for the last decade and a half. All of this means that wages and salaries are not the most secure measures by which to assess the likelihood of sustained socioeconomic improvement and long-term wealth.

At the end of the more than 2,000 years of the official caste system of India, caste law was struck down in the late 1940s, and "all of a sudden" all Indians had equal "formal" legal status. And, of course, what happened was predictable: those groups that had accumulated privilege based on the accumulation of all those years would turn around and say, "We're only individuals." Such a framing of the problem is transparently in the service of the perpetuation of privilege and power. The deck, in short, is stacked when, after systematic accumulation of wealth based on group membership, laws are suddenly passed that have the surface appearance of applying to all. It brings to life Anatole France's famous line, "The law, in its majestic neutrality, forbids both rich and poor from sleeping under bridges at night, begging and stealing bread."

In a society that is racially stratified, the claim that individualistic universalism is the best way to end race or racism—that we should all become color-blind—is itself a not so subtle denial that race has produced deeply consequential structural privilege. But, of course, all whites are not equally privileged. Many do not experience material privilege, and they certainly do not feel it.

RACE IN ITS SOLID STATE

Why study whiteness at this historical moment? What has happened in the last twenty, thirty years in America to generate a remarkable surge of interest in this topic? Several developments help explain it, but one important element is a demographic shift in the urban landscape.

In the last twenty-five years, cities in the United States have undergone the greatest racial transformation of their entire history. In the 1970s almost every major metropolitan area—certainly the top twelves—were primarily white ("Anglo" by those classifications). By 1990, however, the census revealed that of those top twelve, ten now had majority "minority" populations. Indeed, in some jurisdictions, most notably Los Angeles, the ratio had gone from 75 percent white to about 37 percent white. In New York City we witnessed a similar kind of transformation, and that shift was occurring all over the country.

During this period, the white population—especially in urban America—began to experience its "whiteness." It began to feel marked by "race," and, once marked, there's something to observe, to study, and to account for. The need to deny "white flight to the suburbs" and the need to simultaneously deny the accumulation of wealth are reminiscent of the way elites of India and whites in postapartheid South Africa now face their worlds "as individuals." Yet most white Americans find it very hard to swallow that one should even mention these three

countries in the same breath. Indeed, they are often offended.

In *Black Wealth, White Wealth*, Melvin L. Oliver and Thomas M. Shapiro show that net worth either entitles or precludes one from getting a loan to buy a home. The median net worth across the racial divides has been relatively stable over time. As noted earlier, the median net worth of white families in America is $43,279. For African Americans, median net worth is $4,169. To put it another way, whites in the United States have ten times the median wealth of African Americans. The metaphorical fluidness of race becomes a kind of frozen brick of ice when we understand and acknowledge that net worth is the primary measure of access to bank loans—whether for purchasing a house, starting up a business, purchasing a car, or getting the means to go to college or medical or law school. From this perspective, the bland figure of "net worth" has deeply structural consequences.

CONCLUSION

Some of our best research is being done, I think, by writers attentive to the borderlands, addressing and analyzing the contingent, fluid character of whiteness: *how the nature and shape of "whiteness" can change nature and shape (morph!) and yet remain structurally privileged.* Here, the cultural studies critique is most powerful and most able to inform us about what I call the "fluid and evaporating state" of race.[24] But we should not be fooled into the belief that fluidity substitutes for structure. This is simply a matter of when you take the picture. Recall that vapor can condense; and once back in a fluid state, it can freeze. So it is a fundamental mistake to think that, because we have seen this evaporating condition with our own eyes, it is gone forever and chat the use of race will no longer be a powerful stratifying practice in America.

For all the brimming insights of cultural studies around race, a strong caveat is in order. There is a tendency to see *only fluidity* or at least to so emphasize fluidity that one lacks the capacity to see enduring structure. Well, my story about Jack Doyle and the Chicago police says that under certain conditions, things can change dramatically, in the moment, if only momentarily.

I want to end with another story. I was reminded of it by David Roediger, who has written that blacks have been studying whites for a long time and thus have a particular set of insights about "whiteness" that the current vogue of new studies would do well to mine. Indeed, African Americans have been engaged in white studies for at least three centuries. It is a necessity, if one is without formal power, to be attentive and especially alert to power relationships.

I have been a member of the National Advisory Commission for the Human Genome Project's ethical-legal-social issues program. Consequently, I had the occasion to attend meetings at Cold Springs Harbor, New York. As at Northwestern University many years ago, I am often one of a very few African Americans present in a scholarly setting.

The site is in a somewhat remote location a long distance from New York City—and there is no easy public transportation. One deplanes at JFK Airport, and typically one takes a waiting limousine. I get off the plane, go out to the curb, and find this big, stylish limousine indeed waiting for me. The driver is working-class white male by appearance. He greets me with a kind of heartiness and takes my bags, says, "Cold Spring Harbor, sir?" I say, "Yes," and hop in.

But we can't quite get out onto the main exit because of all the traffic, and the person who is sort of directing traffic and guiding things is not very official-looking. He is wearing street clothes and about thirty-five-years-old. This is an African American male, and his gestures and his movements are, to put it mildly, unorthodox. He gives the strong impression that he is self-appointed to this task. The driver of the limousine is waiting patiently to be told when it is okay to move. (To give the story the proper frame, I would say that this particular person directing traffic was being quite creative and sometimes not very responsible.)

On two occasions, he appears to wave my driver on, then quickly changes his mind and says, "Oops!" Finally, he definitively tells my driver, "Pull out right now!" Then another car seems to come from out of nowhere and nearly bends our fender, and my driver says, "Dumb nigger!"

There are about twelve seconds of silence. I do not break it. Finally, he says, "I'm sorry. I'm terribly sorry," and begins to mumble something, I say, "I understand." And for a moment his shoulders seem to relax, and then I say, "I understand how you must feel in this situation." The rest of the ride was in total silence. Ice. What had evaporated and transformed into choreographed class relations had recondensed into race relations.

NOTES

1. The pencil-test is only the latest methodology for precision that I discovered recently on a trip to South Africa. During the apartheid era, only "coloreds" "could work in Capetown. So whether one was classified as black or colored had important consequences for one's livelihood. Thus, some "blacks" would apply to have their status changed from black to colored. The apartheid regime devised a pencil test to make the classification definitive. Applicants were told to place a pencil in their hair. If, when they were told to "shake their head," the pencil fell out, they were classified as "colored"—but they remained black if the pencil was not easily dislodged by a shaking motion.

2. Alleles are different versions of one gene. For example, while the "generic gene" will instruct the proteins and cells to make an eye, a particular allele variation may produce a blue or brown or grayish-green eye. The same for epicanthic fold (or lack of it) over the eye, hair texture, skin

color, and a wide band of human physiognomy. When researchers try to make guesses about which group a person belongs to, they look at variation at several different spots, usually six or seven. What is being assessed is the frequency of genetic variation at a particular spot in the DNA in each population. They are not necessarily looking at genes—they may instead be looking at genetic variation in noncoding DNA. Occasionally, these researchers find a locus where one of the populations being observed and measured has, let's call them for example, alleles H, I, and J and another population has alleles H, I, and K. We know that there are alleles that are found primarily among subpopulations of North American Indians. When comparing a group of North American Indians with a group of Finnish people, one might find a single allele that was present in some Indians but in no Finns (or it's at such a low frequency in the Finns that it is rarely if ever, seen). However, it is important to note and reiterate again and again that this does not mean that all North American Indians, even in this subpopulation, will have that allele. See Stephen Molnar, *Human Variation: Races, Types, and Ethnic Groups*, 3d ed. (Englewood Cliffs, N.J.: Prentice Hall, 1992).

3. The perils of "driving while black" have made it into the houses of several state legislatures already. In California, the state assembly considered such a bill in 1998. At the federal level, in March 1999 Attorney General Janet Reno called for an investigation of "profiling" possible suspects by using race.

4. See S. H. Katz, "Is Race a Legitimate Concept for Science?" in *The AAPA Revised Statement on Race: A Brief Analysis and Commentary* (Philadelphia: University of Pennsylvania, 1995).

5. In addition to Molnar, *Human Variation*, see Anthony P. Polednak, *Racial and Ethnic Differences in Disease* (New York: Oxford University Press, 1969); A. H. Bittles and D. F. Roberts, eds., *Minority Populations: Genetics, Demography and Health* (London: Macmillan, 1992); Malcolm Chapman, ed., *Social and Biological Aspects of Ethnicity* (New York: Oxford University Press, 1993); and Pat Shipman, *The Evolution of Racism: Human Differences and the Use and Abuse of Science* (New York: Simon and Schuster, 1994).

6. For the discussion in this paragraph and for the references to the German literature that are cited below, I am indebted to William H. Schneider, a historian at the University of Indiana.

7. For examples, see Max Gundel, "Einige Beobachtungen bei der Rassenbiologischen Durchforschung Schleswig-Holsteins," *Klinische Wochen schrift* 5 (1926): 1186, and G. A. Schusterov, "Isohaemoagglutinierende Eigenschaften des Menschlichen Blutes nach den Ergebnissen einer Untersuchung an Straflingen des Reformatoriums (Arbeitshauses) zu Omsk," *Moskovskii Meditsinksii Jurnal* 1 (1927):1–6

8. First published in 1944, Felix Kaufmann's *Methodology of the Social Sciences* (New York: Humanities Press, 1958) was one of the key works that was later developed into a more systematic rendition of the problem of first and second order constructs by Alfred Schutz, "Common Sense and Scientific Interpretation of Human Action," in Maurice Natanson, ed., *Collected Papers I: The Problem of Social Reality* (The Hague: Martinus Nijhoff, 1973), 3–47.

9. Molnar, *Human Variation*, 72–79.

10. Troy Duster, *Backdoor to Eugenics* (New York: Routledge, 1990), 89–92.

11. See Melbourne Tapper, *In the Blood: Sickle Cell Anemia and the Politics of Race* (Philadelphia: University of Pennsylvania Press, 1999).

12. I refer primarily to Jill Quadagno, *The Color of Welfare* (New York: Oxford University Press, 1994); Douglas Massey and Nancy Denton, *American Apartheid: Segregation and the Making of the Underclass* (Cambridge, Mass.: Harvard University Press, 1993); and Kenneth O'Reilly, *Nixon's Piano: Presidents and Racial Politics from Washington to Clinton* (New York: Free Press,

1995). There were, of course, earlier analysts who described parts of the picture. For example, Charles Abrams, writing in the 1950s and 1960s, had documented how the Federal Housing Authority's policies were explicitly racist. See his essay "The Housing Problem and the Negro" in *The Negro American*, ed. T. Parsons and K. Clark (Boston: Houghton Mifflin, 1966), 512–24.

13. Quadagno, *Color of Welfare*, 21.

14. The CIO was far more receptive to blacks than the AFL, but complete racial exclusionary practices in many CIO locals continued well into the 1970s.

15. Quadagno, *Color of Welfare*, 23.

16. Quoted in Abrams, "The Housing Problem and the Negro," 523.

17. Literally, those authorized to make loans at banks would draw on a map a red line around a black community, and no one inside that red line could get a loan. Until 1949 the FHA also encouraged the use of restrictive covenants banning African Americans from given neighborhoods and refused to insure mortgages in integrated neighborhoods. Thanks to the FHA, no bank would insure loans in the ghetto, and few African Americans could live outside it. See Quadagno, *Color of Welfare* 24–25, and Massey and Denton, *American Apartheid*.

18. See Richard J. Herrnstein and Charles Murray, *The Bell Curve: Intelligence and Class Structure in American Life* (New York: Free Press, 1994); James Q. Wilson and Richard Herrnstein, *Crime and Human Nature* (New York: Simon and Schuster, 1985); and Arthur R. Jensen, "How Much Can We Boost IQ and Scholastic Achievement?" *Harvard Educational Review* (winter 1969): 1–123.

19. Herrnstein and Murray, *Bell Curve*, 105.

20. Ronald M. Harris-Warrick and Eve Marder, "Modulation of Neural Networks for Behavior," *Annual review of Neuroscience* 14 (1991): 41.

21. Many of my colleagues will recognize the phenomenon that I am describing. Over coffee, over dinner, we will hear a textured version of the complexity of what we know about race. But the very next day, from the public stage, we hear (and speak of) a more singular and unidimensional charaterization of scholarly work and empirical results of research.

22. Noel Ignatiev and John Garvey, eds., *Race Traitor* (New York: Routledge, 1996), and David R. Roediger, *Towards the Abolition of Whiteness: Essays on Race, Politics, and Working Class History* (New York: Verso, 1994).

23. Melvin L. Oliver and Thomas M. Shapiro, *Black Wealth/White Wealthy A New Perspective on Racial Inequality* (New York: Routledge, 1995).

24. See George Lipsitz, *The Possessive Investment in Whiteness: How White People Profit from Identity Politics* (Philadelphia: Temple University Press, 1998).

JOURNALING QUESTION

Imagine you were Troy Duster and the cab driver said what he did. How would you have responded? What is it like to know things like that will be said around you at some point?

12.
PROBLEMATIC WHITE IDENTITIES AND A SEARCH FOR RACIAL JUSTICE

JENNIFER L. EICHSTEDT

Unlike most Americans, people who are activists for racial justice *do* think of themselves as white, and *do* include "white" as part of their self-description. Jennifer Eichstedt interviewed people who were activists, who had gone beyond a vague commitment to racial justice, and who were active in organized groups that do antiracism work. They each had learned to think of themselves as white, and what whiteness means in their lives, through their relationships with people of color. And unlike most white Americans, who view racism as a way of thinking, these white activists saw racism as a system of power. If racism is just prejudice, then all we have to do to end it is change our thinking. If you go and read a bunch of children's books, or watch some children's television, you can see that project in action: often now there are black characters, and Asian and Latino characters, randomly inserted, as neighbors, doctors, teachers. If racism is a system of power, what is the work that white antiracism activists have to do?

"White supremacy is alive and active and I am implicated in it whether I want to be or not—this skin color gives me unearned benefits. At the same time I think I can act in ways to fight racism, I can refuse to be complicit—at least to some degree." (White lesbian and racial justice activist, 1997)

White antiracism activists in the United States are uneasy. Given the current understandings of race and struggles for racial justice, this unease makes sense; whiteness and antiracism sometimes are spoken of, or written about, as if they were antithetical. When racism is understood to be so profitable to whites, what right do any whites have to claim they oppose racism?

According to interviews with and texts written by white antiracism activists and activists of color in the United States, whites who want to be accepted as committed racial justice activists in the post–civil rights/black power era must claim their white identity. That is, they must move beyond saying they are "merely individuals," with no racial location. Instead, they must acknowledge that they are "white"—a social status granted to many people of European ancestry with a particular set of phenotype characteristics—such as light skin, straight (enough) hair, and narrow (enough) nose and lips.[1] Those defined as white also must acknowledge the unearned benefits they receive from the institutionalized racial system. Given this context, much contemporary antiracism[2] work, particularly that conducted by white racial justice activists, is aimed at increasing whites' self-awareness around race and racial privilege (Katz, 1978; Kivel, 1996; McIntosh, 1988; Pharr, 1996). While these seem like admirable goals, there are those who critique the efficacy of these practices. For instance, Bonnett (1997) notes that such antiracism work often rests on very essentialized notions of "whiteness." He points out that often times the terms "white" or "whiteness" are used without ever being

Excerpted from Jennifer L. Eichstedt, "Problematic White Identities and a Search for Racial Justice," *Sociological Forum* 16 (2001): 445–70. References and notes have been renumbered and edited.

defined. This assumption that "we all know what white is" is problematic, he asserts, because it reifies whiteness and negates the extent to which whiteness is multidimensional and contested. Blauner (1995) argues that the definition and discourse of racism that rose to the fore in the black power era stressed racism as a white problem and weakened the potential for antiracism coalitions. He asserts "The discourse of racism predisposes white people to view themselves in terms of a 'deficit model,' one that focuses on human failings rather than on more positive potentials for growth and change" (1995). Blauner suggests that this discourse on white racism is counterproductive because it constructs an *essential, deficient,* whiteness—hardly an identity that anyone would want to embrace. Winant makes a similar point when he argues that much contemporary discourse of whiteness ignores that whiteness itself is always contested and "in formation" (1994, 1998). We also err, he asserts, if we claim that only whites have power and therefore racism is something that only whites have the power to commit (1998). So, these theorists argue that while white racial justice activists work to destabilize systems of racial inequality, they also reify one of the main nodes of racist/racialized dualistic thinking—the node of a homogenous, monolithic, and all-powerful whiteness.

In this paper I argue that the self-defined white antiracism activists that I interviewed do not reify an essentialist construction of whiteness, but in fact work to deconstruct a singular, monolithic whiteness. These white activists engage in definitional work around whiteness and racism that both locates them as people who receive benefits based on their whiteness and creates room for their activism. That is, these activists, while cognizant of essentialized notions of whiteness that operate in the larger discursive space, are not immobilized by them. I demonstrate how the definitional work undertaken by these activists often works to deconstruct essentialist constructions of whiteness and assert contextual, power-cognizant, activist definitions in their

place (Bailey, 1998; Frankenberg, 1993). By essentialist I refer to "a belief in the real true essence of things [and]... invariable and fixed properties" (Fuss, 1989: xi.) In other words, essentialism posits, in this case, that different groups have innate, immutable characteristics that are rooted in their race. Of course, the content of essentialist beliefs is flexible—essentialist beliefs can either posit the object/essence under question as negative, positive, or somewhere in between. In relation to issues of whiteness, essentialism runs the full gamut of possibilities. For instance, some essentialist notions of whiteness assert that whiteness is invariably good, positive, pure, wholesome, and civilized. Such a construction operates in much white-supremacist literature (Daniels, 1997); conversely, its only presence in the narratives I analyze here is as a definition to argue against. At another point of the essentialist spectrum is a vision of whiteness that posits it as invariably shallow, negative, and racist. The activists that I interviewed, while aware of, and informed by, these essentialized notions of whiteness, do not hold to them. Instead, they assert that whites are racist by virtue of historical circumstance and institutionalized racism (Bonilla-Silva, 1996; Carmichael and Hamilton, 1967), not by virtue of biology or racial essence. While not essentialist, this understanding of whiteness does provide the activists I interviewed with a negative understanding of a major part of their identities that they must consciously work to move past. This juggling act is the hallmark of their efforts to manage a problematic white identity.

I argue that while deconstructing whiteness and white privilege would likely facilitate mobilization of whites to antiracism activism, such a presentation is not easily developed given the contemporary language available for discussing race and identity. Particularly debilitating are Western thought patterns that envision qualities in oppositional pairs: good/bad, white/black, right/wrong, day/night. This oppositional, essentialist thinking is foundational in the development of theories of identity.

While some racial justice activists in the nineteenth century worked to develop more complex understandings of the self (Frederick Douglas, Sojourner Truth, the Grimke sisters, and others) it has only been relatively recently that nonessentialist constructions of race and identity have been theorized in academia (Hail, 1990, 1991; Spivak, 1989). While it has become more common for scholars influenced by postcolonial theory to write about identities as fractured, multiple, and shifting, it is still relatively uncommon for members of dominant groups who want to align themselves with the struggles of oppressed people to convincingly use this language to speak of their own positions. This difficulty arises from a number of sources. First, as I explore in more depth later, for whites to minimize the importance of whiteness to their identity and life experiences is often seen as an attempt to sidestep responsibility for ending racial oppression. Second, the distinction between an essentialist view of whiteness as negative and a more nuanced understanding of whites as historically and contemporarily privileged is hampered not only by a general power-evasive ideology (Frankenberg, 1993), but by a more specific public discourse of whites as victims (Giroux, 1998; Lipsitz, 1998). This victim discourse increases resistance to critical assessments of whiteness and stunts our ability to publicly tease out the differences between negative essentialist notions and nonessentialist configurations of whiteness that require power-cognizance. Contemporary public discourse about racial identities and racial justice is also hindered by the lack of language that captures both the structural and agentic aspects of racial identity. Balancing these two aspects of racial power and identity is no easy task but is a must for white antiracism activists. These activists deal with this dilemma primarily through holding understandings of whites as racist and notions of white identities as multiple and flexible in their minds simultaneously and living with the conflict that this produces. That those interviewed for this work are as astute as they are in their nonacademic deconstruction of whiteness is a testament to the power of reflective activism. However, such a balancing act surely has consequences for further mobilization of whites.

METHODOLOGY

My claims and suggestions are based on exploratory research and interviews with sixteen white antiracism activists.[3] I focus on activists who identify themselves as white, and/or who claim a white identity because they are recipients of white skin privilege even though they may "technically" be of mixed ancestry....

Interviewees ranged in age from 24 years to 52 years old. All but four attended college and five grew up working class or economically poor. Interviewees were interviewed with assurances of confidentiality. Interviews were conducted from a standardized interview schedule, though the format was relatively dialogic (Frankenberg, 1993). By dialogic I mean that interviewees were free to ask me questions and to talk about issues that they felt were relevant—even if I had not asked them a related question. During the interviews, which lasted an average of 3 h, I asked participants a number of questions beginning with those that explored their life histories. We also discussed when their awareness of race/difference developed, significant events in their development of an critical race awareness, when they started having a conception of themselves *as white*, their definitions of racism, what paths led them to engage in their antiracism activism, and if antiracism work has shifted their perception of themselves. In some ways questions about identity were the most difficult questions for participants to answer. For some participants the topic of identity was something that they generally do not directly address, even though they are constantly struggling to understand their own. Finally, I engaged in these interviews as a white antiracism activist scholar; that is I identified myself as someone who participates in social activism and views my own research and activism as directly linked.

…Before exploring the activists' constructions of identity, however, I provide an overview of the identity context in which constructions of white identity are debated.

WHITE IDENTITIES

White identities, like identities of racialized minorities, are collective social identities (Doane, 1997; Roediger, 1991). That is, white identities are made salient through in-group processes such as boundary maintenance, identity delineation, and group definition—i.e., through defining who is white and who is not. Blee (1991), Roediger (1991), Rogin (1995), Saxton (1990), and Ware (1992) have successfully explored the historical grounding of this process and some of the groundwork for what has come to be defined as "critical white studies." These authors demonstrate how various white ethnic groups, and white women, were included within (or excluded from) the white fold—a white fold that was simultaneously defining itself as the norm. Whites came to see themselves as racially neutral—it was others who "had race," they were simply "human."

The efforts of white Americans to see themselves as racially neutral, though still common, have been consistently complicated and challenged—particularly by those who are positioned on the racial outside. The dilemma of seeing oneself as racially neutral, while benefiting so dramatically from institutionalized systems of racial oppression, has been noted by activists as well as social theorists (Baldwin, 1965, 1995; Du Bois, 1965 [1903]; hooks, 1989; Myrdal, 1944; Roediger, 1991; Saxton, 1990). These challenges to the construction and meaning of whiteness dramatically escalated with the racial justice movements of the last 40 years. These movements (Civil Rights, Black Power, American Indian, Chicano) challenged the organization of racial privilege in this country and moved politics based around identity into the public consciousness. This consciousness raising was not aimed solely at the politically inactive white populace, but also at whites engaged in progressive or leftist politics as well. White progressives were asked to reconceptualize their often-paternalistic stances toward communities of color. Each of these interventions into political "business as usual" called attention to whiteness as a racial category and whites as recipients of unearned privilege. Whiteness became marked and publicly identified in radical writings by U.S. scholars/activists (Breitman, 1966; Carmichael and Hamilton, 1967; Malcolm X, 1963) and within postcolonial discourses generated abroad (Fanon, 1967; Memmi, 1965). This meant that, at least within progressive circles, whiteness could no longer be considered the empty racial norm against which others were judged. Instead it became a racial category linked in many radical and postcolonial discourses with domination, power, and prejudice (Blauner, 1995; Winant, 1998).

One of the activist constructions of white identity that was burned into the minds of many white Americans, and was occasionally referenced by my participants, was Malcolm X's assertion that whites were "blue eyed devils" (Malcolm X, 1963). Whites in these essentialist accounts are constitutionally selfish and oppressive. However, if we take the assertions of Spivak (1989) and Hall (1990, 1991) seriously, then all identities are multiple, fragmented, and socially constructed. If this is the case then white identities—in fact all dominant group identities—are multifaceted and capable of being transformed. Given this possibility it is important to ask how white identities have shifted in response to various challenges from peoples of color.

WHITE RESPONSES AND CONSTRUCTION OF SELF

The responses of whites to the disruption of whiteness were varied. For instance, the most common white, middle (and upper) class approach to dealing with whiteness resounds in the claims of those whites who assert that whiteness was/is unimportant in their lives (Frankenberg, 1993; Gallagher, 1997). One of the effects of the invisibility/denial of whiteness, especially when coupled with a well-intentioned, middle-class, liberal desire to "get beyond race," is to assert the desirability of color blindness (Williams, 1995).

Other whites have asserted a defensive whiteness (see Wellman, 1997; Giroux, 1998). This recent and relatively common move posits whites, particularly white men, as beleaguered and under siege (Daniels, 1997; Feagin and Vera, 1995; Gallagher, 1997). Of course, the most virulent strains of this refrain come from white–supremacist movements that posit a pure essentialist whiteness that is morally and physically superior to racialized others (Daniels, 1997). It is not, however, only white supremacist groups that are presenting a defensive whiteness. A sense that whites are disadvantaged relative to racial minorities can be found among a wide range of persons (see Feagin and Vera, 1995; Rubin, 1994 for further elaboration). Another response among whites that is important to consider in relation to white antiracism are attempts to distance oneself from being white by highlighting other parts of one's identity.

BUT I'M NOT *REALLY* WHITE . . .

Since the late 1960s (Alba, 1990) there has been a rise in the proportion of white U.S. citizens claiming a white ethnicity. In addition to specifying one's European ancestry, and reclaiming lost family traditions, this shift can also be understood as a way to distance oneself from claims made by people of color about some imagined "standard white American," and from political assertions that whites have "unearned" privilege or are responsible for the disadvantaged position of minorities.

An example of how claiming ethnic identity (or another identity that crosscuts whiteness) might allow whites to sidestep white identity—and by association white responsibility or "white guilt"—comes from Kivel 's *Uprooting Racism: How White People can Work for Racial Justice* (1996). Kivel describes an antiracism training that he was coleading with an African—American colleague. At one point during the training the leaders asked people

of color and whites to work in separate caucuses—at this moment all the white people in the workshop "disappeared"—or more specifically, they attempted to distance themselves from the white part of their identity. One participant said that he wasn't white—he was Italian; another white man said that "you have to be straight to have white privilege," and another said that because he was working class he had it just as hard as any person of color. When his colleague turned to Kivel and asked where all the white people had gone, Kivel responded "Don't ask me, I'm not white, I'm Jewish" (Kivel 1996, 10). Whites in this group, attempted to distance themselves from the unpalatable "guilt" of whiteness by claiming an additionally disadvantaged status. In this case, whites attempted to highlight where they are members of *oppressed groups* in order to deflect the fact that they also receive some benefits as members of the dominant racial group. This is a common rhetorical move among many self-defined white liberals and progressives as they attempt to grapple with a problematic and distressing white identity.

MANAGING A PROBLEMATIC IDENTITY

THE BEGINNING: CLAIMING AN OPPRESSOR STATUS

As noted earlier, most researchers in the area of critical white studies (Dyer, 1997; Frankenberg, 1993; Roediger, 1991; Wellman, 1993; Winant, 1998) would suggest that whiteness operates as an unmarked, and unremarked upon, center in most whites' lives, and in most white institutions. The white activists I interviewed, and the texts I read, suggested that white antiracism activists differ significantly from this norm. What was most common among the people I interviewed, and the texts I explored, was for white activists to acknowledge their white identity, to "admit" that they are racist and receive unearned benefits, and to claim that they can, and should, work to eliminate racism. These activists believed that one of the first steps to becoming an activist was to "own" their whiteness and to articulate a very specific definition of racism.

Naming Selves As White

Everyone who was interviewed was able to discuss what being white meant to them with little prompting. White identity was, for these activists, clearly salient. When asked to describe who they were, or how they would introduce themselves in a letter, they all said, "I'm a white" (Lesbian/Bi/Gay, Jewish, Disabled, Working Class woman/man and so on). "White" was always an explicit identity marker, and as will be apparent from later comments, whiteness was seen as an identity that was central to the activists' sense of self.

Most of the interviewee's narratives demonstrated that activists came to an awareness of their whiteness as adults or late teens. They grew up in families and neighborhoods where whiteness was the unmarked norm. Instead it was their Jewishness, their gender, their religion (Catholic), their body size, or their sexuality that marked their individual or group distinctiveness. The only person for whom this wasn't true was the one white respondent who grew up in a black community. In this case, the activist grew up aware of her whiteness since it was the most noticeable difference from her friends and neighbors. The marking effect that growing up in a black neighborhood had on the development of an (antiracism) white identity is also conveyed in David Wellman's personal narrative of coming to an awareness of race and racism in Thompson and Tyagi's *Names We Call Home* (1996). While the rest of the respondents in the study grew up in all white, segregated neighborhoods where whiteness was taken for granted they all had developed the ability to reconstruct their own personal history of whiteness and to discuss the benefits it confers.

In almost every case, these white respondents were brought to awareness of their whiteness and its social significance through interaction with people of color. Respondents spoke of childhood

and adolescent friends, or, for a few, experiences in college that challenged them to consider the racial order in which they lived. These interactions with people of color were crucial for their developing an understanding of themselves as white. In their words, these friendships were important because they learned "different interpretations of the world." They heard "descriptions of racism that countered what I [they] heard from whites who denied that racism exists." And perhaps most importantly, they had friends whom, in the words of one woman, "called me on my shit and started really challenging me when I said ignorant things".... Learning about life on the (racial) margins from people of color is a theme that was very strong among the activists I interviewed. One woman explained her process of coming to consciousness about her whiteness by describing a period in college where she started intensively reading works by women of color and came to an awareness of race and racism. However she says that at this time race was still about"... those Others who are so 'different' and not about our [white] selves." This racial imagining was disrupted by an interaction she had in a workshop she was attending.

> It wasn't until I was in a seminar/workshop with this man [of color] who I've become very close with and there were like seven or eight white women in this workshop and he asked us this question that changed my life, that I've never been the same since. He asked us "What do you love about the race that you are?" [My question: *Could you answer it?*] No! I felt tremendously guilty and went into this despair. It was all this gross stuff that didn't have anything to do with a healthy consciousness of race, about what being white was about, and I just wanted to be disconnected from myself as white. And so, [I] realized I had not done my work, I was not conscious of my race. And what a privilege that was to not be conscious of my race from the moment I walked out my door and to not feel it.

For her, as for others, a person of color called the fact and meaning of whiteness into sharp relief but it took her a long time to piece together what being white meant to her. However, at that moment she experienced one of the hallmarks of white antiracism narratives: she noted what a "privilege that was to not be conscious of my race from the moment I walked out my door...." At that moment she could not come to a "healthy consciousness of race;" instead, her whiteness was a source of pain. She could find nothing to love about being white. This response makes a lot of sense in relation to the general status of white identity development in the United States—a process that assumes a moral validity for whites and the actions that "whites" throughout history have taken. When white North Americans come to terms with their whiteness, as Alcoff notes, it "exacts a price" (1998: 3). She goes on to say (7):

> This "feeling white," when coupled with repudiation of white privilege, can disable a positive self-image as well as a felt connection to community and history, and generally can distort identity formation.

When other interviewees were asked to describe what being white meant, their assessments were also generally negative. One white woman said, "Being white means being attached to this whole history of racial oppression and exploitation." Another said that having a white identity can be "a source of shame if you are thinking about issues of justice." Others also noted that it carried with it a history of "shame," "abuse," and "oppression."

While virtually all the interviewees described negative attributes of whiteness most of those I interviewed said that their sense of who they were in relation to whiteness has shifted over time. For instance, activists talked about how they began their work with a sense of naivete and a sense that as white people they really *were* morally inferior to people of color. For example, one white woman said:

> You know, going into antiracism work I put people of color on a pedestal. It took me a long time to realize that, like, people are assholes, people are wonderful, anybody can be anything... and I think that a lot of

white folks who go into antiracism work do go into it naively, or idealistically. There's lots of things that happen in the public realm that gets labeled racist, and I think that in the past I would have jumped on that bandwagon and now I don't think I would. I think, I feel I am more of a critical thinker, where before I was really afraid, I was really paralyzed. Now I'm not afraid to say that this is wrong.

What she notes here is a shift in her understanding of herself as a white person involved in antiracism work. She shifts from seeing herself as unworthy/unable to make judgements in relation to race, *as a white person*, to a deconstructed sense of identity that disconnects race, behavior, and one's ability to engage in a critical analysis. However, like others, she notes that when she began her antiracism work she "really wanted approval, to be told I'm a good white person by people of color." However, she goes on to say that, while "in the past I struggled with that... now I try and have integrity. I go into a lot of situations where I have to earn people's respect, but I don't worry about it now. I'm not there to prove anything." Other activists also spoke of realizing that they were trying to get people of color to give them approval and that this came out of a negative sense of whiteness. It is through the antiracism work itself that activists have come to develop a sense of their own integrity and to resist discourses of whiteness that essentialize it as inherently bad or morally inferior. Another activist said,

> I used to be really worried about what every person of color would think of me, or my analysis of something. Now I realize that I might have an analysis [about a racial issue] that a person of color disagrees with and I don't automatically think—oh, they must be right. Maybe I'm right! So, I can weigh these things out now and not just romanticize people of color and their positions.

Clearly, a definition of racism that puts it solely as the province of whites exacerbates the tendency to see people of color as always correct and white people, and their analysis of racial issues, as suspect. In relation to this definition of racism, Blauner (1995), Winant (1998), and I would agree. However, it is important to note that these activists were able to work beyond this negative self-assessment by deconstructing whiteness. Regardless of whether they get beyond this negativity, however, it does seem, as Blauner (1995) fears, that this negative construction of whiteness is bound up with the particular definition of racism developed during the 1960s,[4] a definition fully endorsed by the white activists whom I interviewed.

Definitions of Racism

All but one of the activists clearly identified racism as a system of power in which whites were unduly advantaged or privileged. This definition of racism clearly diverges with popular white conceptions of racial inequality. Each semester I conduct a survey with my incoming students (90% of whom are white) and find that students consistently define racism as some variation of prejudice. These definitions employed by incoming college students are in line with those noted by others conducting research in the field (Doane, 1997; Frankenberg, 1993; Gallagher, 1997) and suggest that the general white population equates racism with prejudice and tends to exclude considerations of history or power. Conversely, those white activists I interviewed strongly argued that racism must be understood as a system where negative prejudice toward people of color, and/or positive prejudice toward whites, is coupled with power. Power here is defined as the ability to see one's views or actions enacted in the world, regardless of the wishes of others.

> The following quotation is representative of the activists' position: [Racism is] institutional and personal oppression of people based on their race to the empowerment and benefit of white people and the disenfranchisement of people of color in the United States and throughout the Western Hemisphere.

Another woman said that it is "institutionalized and internalized" oppression of people of color. A third said, "racism is prejudice plus power. It's the power used to keep whites in control of people of color." Each of these definitions mirrors or parallels the definition that was presented in the 1960s by Carmichael and others. Racism, in this model, is something carried out against people of color. In this construction, people of color are the victims and whites are the oppressors. Interestingly, almost all of the interviewees moved from a definition of racism to talking about how it differed from other things, such as prejudice or bigotry.

The following remark is representative of the activists' position: "Given the history of white exploitation and oppression of peoples of color at the hands white people and its impact in the modern world, it is impossible for a person of color to be a racist." However, while almost all of the participants believed that people of color can't be "racist," they all agree that it is possible for people of color to be prejudiced and/or bigoted; attributes they identified as "wrong" though "understandable."

Further, most of the participants (14/16) spoke explicitly of racism as a "system," in fact some of them (4/16) suggested that the word racism shouldn't even really be used to apply to an individual as in "you are a racist." Instead, they argued one should talk about whether someone's actions "furthered, or bolstered a racist system." These activists argued that thinking about racism solely as a system was useful because it got them out of the dilemma of explaining to white people why their prejudiced views toward blacks were any worse than an African–American's negative views about them. Instead, one could talk about how their prejudiced behavior linked up with an institutionalized system of advantage and disadvantage that was already in place.

The point is that the very language and definitions that these activists employ fully implicate them as beneficiaries of unearned benefits in a system of racism, or white supremacy. Whites, in their definition, are the only ones capable of "racism." The problem with this definition is, as Winant (1998) points out, that people of color are posited as having *no* power. The equation becomes: Whites are all-powerful/people of color are powerless. This is clearly a problematic stance and one that contradicts the idea that the equation "racism = white racism" is *empowering* for people of color. While these activists may be trying to use such constructions strategically (Spivak, 1989) it is difficult to assess this as a positive strategy since it reifies power relationships and denies the process of racial formation. The one positive aspect of this, however, may be the impact that "owning racism" has for these activists. When activists embrace this equation they feel it is impossible to side step the responsibility they have to dismantle racism. This point was made even clearer as participants responded to questions regarding *their own* relationship to a racial system of oppression.

Relationship of Self to Racism

When asked to discuss how they understood their own relationship to racism, every respondent implicated him or herself in racial oppression and said it was impossible to extricate themselves from racism. The following statements are illustrative of this stance.

A white woman who teaches antiracism workshops and engages in other forms of activism said:

> Given where we are in this culture right now I believe that all while people are racist because we benefit from a system of injustice. And that doesn't mean we all have malicious attitudes, it's not just about attitudes. It's because I unwillingly benefit from my color every single day, and in ways that I'm sometimes aware of and sometimes I can't even see, because they just get opened to me.

Another white woman activist responded by saying:

> I am a white woman who certainly benefits from my race. And I think that in terms of class I've more or less been able to move into a comfortable [status], um, that's not guaranteed, especially given the work I do [working with homeless women]... and that I

am you know, a white person with a lot of understandings about race who's done a lot of work to undo, you know, to dismantle racism.

Another respondent, a white gay man, said that when he works with others (both whites and people of color) on issues of racial justice he always says "Before I say a word about racism, you need to know that I'm a racist. I was raised in a racist culture and the racist system works for me because I'm a white man." Such assertions for him are not only assertions of identity but are also understood as politically and strategically important. As this white man goes on to say,

> ...if I'm not willing to start there at that point, I won't have the trust of people of color. Part of my contribution is being aware that I got the comforts I have because of 'blood money'....I also say this because other white people need to know that I don't think I'm better than them...

This theme of white people acknowledging white privilege and their location in a racist system is strongly articulated in much white antiracism literature (e.g., Kivel, 1996; McIntosh, 1988). Whites, according to this view, must recognize their positions as whites, as whites in a racist system, and ultimately as racist whites. That is they must embrace the oppressor label at the same time that they challenge oppressor identity and behavior. To do otherwise, to attempt to disassociate from the racialized group in which one located, is generally seen as impossible or politically inappropriate.

This then is one of the boundary markers that white antiracist activists use to distinguish themselves from other whites, including those whites who say they want to be seen as "antiracist" but who "don't meet the criteria because they can't acknowledge their own privilege." As one woman activist said—"I try not to be judgmental, cause, you know, it's really not my place. But if someone can't really talk about white privilege or their own white privilege, then I think they really have a lot more work to do." This speaks to the difference between being "antiracist" and "nonracist"—a status that these activists don't believe white people can occupy given our racist system. This sort of statement lands activists right back in the middle of positing what seems to be a static and monolithic construction of racist white identity. However, activists consistently denied that whites are incapable of change in an inherent way—instead they argue that the effects of growing up in a racist system embed racist thought and behavioral patterns deep inside whites. Since this appeared to be a pivotal issue, I explored how white activists understood their own location in relation to systems of oppression and did not become immobilized by guilt or a sense of despair.

(MORE EXPLICIT) EFFORTS AT DECONSTRUCTING WHITENESS

There are several ways that whites involved in anti-racism activism try to work through the tension of seeing themselves as racist and finding ways to see themselves as valuable human beings who have something to contribute in the fight for racial justice. One of them is quite basic; these activists came to see racism as a dire problem facing *all people* and not just racial minorities. To quote one activist, "if we don't solve [racism] we are all doomed." Another activist used the relatively common metaphor of a sinking ship, she said "If there is a huge gaping hole in the ship we're all on, the people in the lower decks might drown first but eventually we're all going down." Another said that she came to see "antiracism work as essential for my own survival." In essence, each person I interviewed described coming to see racial politics as central to their own survival and that of their society. They had, to some degree, shed the commonplace white presumption that race is about some racialized Other to whom they are not connected. Instead, they see themselves as racialized, as advantaged by the racial system, and they are convinced that this system will lead to further social decay/destruction.

The significance of this understanding is that they have changed their conception of group position (Blumer, 1958). Their group ceases to be solely defined as other whites, or even other women (writ large), or other (presumably white) gays/lesbians. Their sense of group position moves to take in a much larger sense of community that contradicts white separatism and stresses some common experience that is drastically affected by racism. This, of course, is a thin line to traverse. White activists must be careful in this context not to assert that their experience is the same as peoples of color, but rather to note that we all "are traveling on the same ball through space."

While these activists use this sense of sharing a similar fate as one way of mitigating the troubling fact of whiteness, it is not the only way activists try to balance holding an awareness of themselves as racist *and* constructing a more positive, hopeful outlook about whiteness. To do this they use antiessentialist discourses to argue that no racial identity is "locked in place." For instance, one white woman said, "white folks can change; it just takes our whole lives to really get all this stuff out." In addition to noting that white folks, as one Jewish white activist said with a smile, "aren't genetically prone to racism," many participants stressed that they, and other whites, learned racial oppression and silence from parents and the dominant culture. By asserting that racist behaviors and attitudes are learned, activists hold out the possibility of future generations of whites living in a nonracist world. However, because it is imperative for whites engaged in this work to not appear to be sidestepping the importance of the white privilege that they do receive, these activists are leery of getting too far into what one interviewee called "fantasies of white absolution." Instead whites involved in this work try to destabilize a sense of monolithic whiteness through a variety of methods.

Crosscut Nature of Oppression

Perhaps the most common method for countering a monolithic sense of whiteness/power is for activists to discuss whiteness as crosscut by other axes of oppression. For instance, white activists discussed how useful it is when doing antiracism trainings (which they often hoped would serve as recruitment sites for other activists) to lay out a model of privilege and power that demonstrates that no one is ever completely an oppressor or completely oppressed. That is, whites may be members of the dominant racial group; however, they may also belong to a group that is subordinate in other realms—such as class, gender, or sexual orientation. They hope that this sense of complexity makes it easier for whites to avoid wallowing in guilt or being immobilized when dealing with their location as white people. At the same time, these activists walk a tight rope of not using this complexity to "get off the hook" of complicity in a system of racism. One example of this complexity is the case of white Jewish antiracism activists. One woman's comments are representative of those made by all of the Jewish women. She said:

> Being Jewish and while puts me in an interesting position. As a Jew my inclusion as a while person can always be taken away. I think that my awareness of that makes me more empathetic to the struggles of people of color. On the other hand, I don't have tolerance for Jews who try to deny that they get white privilege because of anti-Semitism. When I walk down the street—people see me first as white and that gets me things. That keeps me from getting pulled over by the cops, and harassed in stores, and stuff like that. But at the same time my Jewishness and experience of oppression on that basis is real. I just think it is illegitimate for me to try to deny my white privilege on that basis, you know?

…People spoke of being gay/lesbian, working class/poor, Jewish, ostracized as Communists, and survivors of incest and sexual assault. They identified these experiences as important in enabling them to make intellectual and emotional connections about other systems of oppression.

In her work Thompson (1996:105) says:

> For white people, making positive changes in racial identity often hinges upon identifying how being

an "outsider" in life—a woman, a Jew, a lesbian, disabled,—and being an "insider"—a white person, a man, a Christian—both shapes people's lives.

One of the white women in my study makes the same point when she asserts:

> I definitely feel that as a while woman I've benefited from racism and gained a lot of privilege from our society. But I also feel that because of my culture, and being Jewish, that I feel like I grew up with a consciousness of oppression that helped me to be aware of racism.

Another woman in my study spoke of a time when she, her brother and her mother received welfare, shopped at Goodwill, and experienced economic deprivation. During this time they became linked with a family that had a substantial amount of money. She says of this time:

> I think it was my own class position … [we] were really treated [by this other family] as second class citizens; they had all this money, they had really nice clothes… and it really caused me a great deal of pain. I really felt like an outsider, I really was treated many times, I felt like my status was that of servant. So that, I think that's how my consciousness of race, which really came about in college, was grounded in that experience of being an outsider. So I could empathize, and understand, and I cared about racism.

Finally, the gay white men I have interviewed also noted the ways their analysis of gay oppression led them to consider racial oppression as a parallel and/or crosscutting system of oppression. One of the men, a white gay Christian minister in the South, said that a black woman who was leading an antioppression workshop in Ohio facilitated his understanding of the links between his own rage and the anger of people of color over racism. She helped him to see that, in his words

> Up 'til I said I was gay, as a white man, I could get what I wanted, but once I came out other while men have been trying to take that away. Only because

I have this difference from the "norm" that I'm starting to see all the other links as well... I was angry because the privilege I had assumed to be my right was threatened... it helped me to see how other people are threatened with extermination and it's never been assumed they have a right to anything...

What is striking in these accounts is that it's not just having the approximating experience that is important, rather it's the development of an analysis that names and critiques the links of oppression in a "white, patriarchal, economically unjust system." The activists I spoke with all talked about the importance of these experiences not only for their own development as antiracism activists but also as an effective organizing tool with other whites. That is, they believed that helping whites get in touch with oppression in other aspects of their lives, or understanding what they "lose" by defining themselves as white, was useful in getting other whites to understand racial oppression.

Two final methods for balancing an understanding of themselves as racist and working as an antiracism activist are (1) for activists to link themselves to a history of white antiracism activism, and (2) being involved in concrete actions to challenge racism. That is, activists stressed the importance of "walking the talk" and being held accountable for their actions. When possible, these activists emphasized the choices they had made on personal and professional level to enact a racially just world. For instance, activists discussed jobs they had left because of racism, public stands they had taken, alliances—particularly with people of color—that they had entered into to fight racism. Each of the participants also spoke of working directly with other whites as an integral part of their antiracism work. They asserted the importance of this work with other whites because they all felt it was an arena in which they could make a difference, and because working with other white antiracism activists provided them with a sense of community and support.

CONCLUSION

In summation, managing a problematic identity presents a particular crisis for dominant group members who work in racial justice movements. While all movements must construct an identity around with which participants may identify and around which they may rally, white antiracism activists must undermine white identity and white supremacy while they simultaneously must embrace their identification of themselves as white and unduly privileged. To some extent this resonates with the dilemma noted by Gamson (1995) found in movements based on identity—movement members must construct an identifiable identity from which to act, but the movement's rhetoric emphasizes the socially constructed nature of identities and thereby works to deconstruct the very identities that activists use to argue for civil rights. Another way of saying this is to say that the very activism employed by the movements destroys the standpoint on which they stand. For white antiracism activists the dilemma is a bit different. They *want* to deconstruct the essentialism of racisms—including the solidification and reification of a static white identity. However, they insist on retaining the rhetorical and analytical piece that recognizes that dominant group members are not in an equivalent place as subordinate group members. They hold on to what may seem to be a static definition of white power to call attention to the degree to which they, as dominant group members, benefit from racism and to point out how insane the system must be if they, *regular white folks*, want to tear it down. Simply said, they work to deconstruct whiteness as a system of meanings and power distributions; however, they are constantly working against other whites' tendencies to deconstruct whiteness as ultimate goal, but they hold onto whiteness not to give them a place from which to act, but as a social location of responsibility. This is an important dynamic to pay attention to among activists who come from a variety of dominant groups since the participation of dominant group members will be necessary for the

success of most social justice work. It is also important to map out other ways that activists, from both
dominant and subordinate groups, develop their
identities and strategies. By tracking deconstruc-
tionist tactics we may be better prepared to construct a world that is socially just.

NOTES

1. This phrase suggests the relational nature of whiteness. It is also meant to signal that the designation of while was something that some European groups such as Irish, Italians, and Jewish
immigrants, had to "earn" since their racial status was contested by those who already considered themselves "white."

2. I use the term "antiracism" versus "anliracist" to signal that the project is not about individual
racists, but about racism as a system of power. I do not use the term "nonracist" since activists
assert that it is impossible for whites to be nonracist when they grow up in a racist system.

3. This work is part of a larger project that explores multiracial and monoracial activist groups
that advocate for racial justice. While this paper focuses solely on white activists it is clear that
these white activists and the groups to which they belong exist in continual dialogue with
activists of color. The fact that I do not explore the attitudes and actions of activists of color in
this paper is not meant to diminish their importance, leadership, and centrality in racial justice movements in any way.

4. This definition is that racism is a combination of prejudice and power, and that since only
whites have institutional power, only whites can be racist.

REFERENCES

Alba, Richard 1990 Ethnic Identity: Transformation of White America. New Haven, CT: Yale
University Press.

Alcoff, Linda 1998 "What should while people do?" Hypatia 13(3)Summer 6–26.

Bailey, Alison 1998 "Locating traitorous identities: Toward a view of privilege-cognizant white
character." Hypatia 13(3): 27–42.

Baldwin, James 1965 Going to Meet the Man. New York: Laurel.

———. 1995 Fire Next Time. New York: Modern Library.

Blauner, Bob 1995 "White radicals, while liberals and while people: Rebuilding the anti-racism coalition." In Benjamin, Bowser (ed.), Racism and Anti-Racism in World Perspective.
Thousand Oaks, CA: Sage.

Blee, Katherine 1991 Women of the Klan: Racism and Gender in the 1920's. Berkeley: University
of California Press.

Blumer, Herbert 1958 "Race as a sense of group position." Pacific Sociological Review1
(Spring): 3–6.

Bonilla-Silva, Eduardo 1996 "Rethinking racism: Toward a structural interpretation." American
Sociological Review 62(3): 465.

Bonnett, Alastair 1997 "Antiracism and the critique of 'white' identities." New Communities
22(1): 97–110.

Breitman, George (ed.) 1966 Malcolm X Speaks: Selected Speeches and Statements. New York:
Grove Press.

Carmichael, Stokely and Charles V. Hamilton 1967 Black Power: The Politics of Liberation in
America. New York: Random House.

Daniels, Jesse 1997 While Lies. New York: Routledge.

Doane, Ashley 1997 "Dominant group ethnic identity in the United States: The role of 'hidden' ethnicity in intergroup relations." The Sociological Quarterly 38(3): 375–397.

Du Bois, W.E.B. 1989 [1903] The Souls of Black Folk. New York: Penguin Books.

———. 1965 [1935] Black Reconstruction. New York: Russell & Russell.

Dyer, Richard 1997 White. New York: Routledge.

Fannon, Frantz 1967 Black Skin, White Masks. New York: Grove Press.

Feagin, Joe R. and Hernan Vera 1995 While Racism: The Basics. New York: Routledge.

Frankenberg, Ruth 1993 White Women: Race Matters. Minneapolis: University of Minnesota Press.

Fuss, Diane 1989 Essentially Speaking: Feminism, Nature and Difference. New York: Routledge.

Gallagher, Charles 1997 "White racial formation." In Richard Delgado and Jean Stefanic (eds.), Critical White Studies: Looking Behind the Mirror. Philadelphia: Temple University Press.

Gamson, Joshua 1995 "Must identity movements self-destruct? A queer dilemma." Social Problems, 42(3): 390–107.

Giroux, Henry 1998 "Rewriting the discourse of racial identity: Towards a pedagogy and politics of whiteness." Harvard Educational Review 67(2): 285–320.

Hall, Stuart 1990 "Cultural identity and diaspora." In J. Rutherford (ed.), Identity, Culture, and Difference. London: Lawrence & Wishart.

———. 1991 "Old & New Identities." In Anthony King (ed.), Culture, Globalization, and the World System. Binghamton, New York: SUNY.

hooks, bell 1989 Talking Back: Thinking Feminist, Thinking Black. Boston, MA: South End Press.

Katz, Judy H. 1978 White Awareness: Handbook for Antiracism Training. Norman, OK: University of Oklahoma Press.

Kivel, Paul 1996 Uprooting Racism: How White People Can Work for Racial Justice. Philadelphia, PA: New Society.

Lipsitz, George 1998 The Possessive Investment in Whiteness: How Whites Benefit from Identity Politics. Philadelphia: Temple University Press.

Malcolm X. 1963 Fire and the Fury: Grass Roots Speeches by Malcolm X. Paul Winley Records.

McIntosh, Peggy 1988 "White privilege and male privilege: A personal account of coming to see correspondences. . . . " In Margaret Anderson and Patricia Hill Collins (eds.), Race, Class and Gender. California: Wadsworth.

Memmi, Albert The Colonizer and the Colonized. Boston: Beacon Press.

Myrdal, Gunnar 1944 American Dilemma: The Negro Problem and Modern Democracy with Richard Sterner and Arnold Rose. New York: Harper and Brothers.

Pharr, Suzanne 1996 In the Time of the Right: Reflections on Liberation. Berkeley, CA: Chardon Press.

Roediger, David R. 1991 The Wages of Whiteness: Race and the Making of the American Working Class. New York: Verso.

Rogin, Michael 1995 Black Skin, White Noise: Jewish Immigrants in the Hollywood Melting Pot. Berkeley, CA: University of California Press.

Rubin, Lillian 1994 Families on the Fault Line: America's Working Class Speaks About the Family the Economy, Race and Ethnicity. New York: Harper Collins.

Saxton, Alexander 1990 The Rise and the Fall of the White Republic: Class Politics and Mass Culture in Nineteenth-century America. New York: Verso.

Spivak, Gayatri C. 1989 "In a word: Interview." Differences 1: 124–155.

Thompson, Becky and Sangeeta Tyagi 1996 Names We Call Home: Autobiography on Racial Identity. Routledge: New York.

Ware, Vron 1992 Beyond the Pale: While Women, Racism and History. London: Verso.

Wellman, David T. 1993 Portraits of White Racism, 2nd edn. New York: Cambridge University Press.

———. 1997 "Minstrel shows, affirmative action talk, and angry white men: Marking racial otherness in the 1990s." In Ruth Frankenberg (ed.). Displacing Whiteness: Essays in Social and Cultural Criticism: 311–331. Durham: Duke University Press.

Williams, Patricia 1995 Seeing a Color-Blind Future: Paradox of Race (Reith Lectures, 1997). New York: Noonday Press.

Winant, Howard 1994 Racial Conditions. Minneapolis: University of Minnesota Press.

———. 1998 "Racism today: Continuity and change in the Post-Civil Rights Era." Ethnic and Racial Studies 24(4): 755–766.

JOURNALING QUESTION

How is race presented in "mainstream" children's television? What is the racial project, to use Omni and Winant's phrase, that well-meaning, mostly white television producers are engaged in?

A VOICE FROM THE PAST

The Color Line

FREDERICK DOUGLASS

Frederick Douglass was born into slavery, escaped to the North, and became one of the most important figures in African American history. He was a noted abolitionist, and his 1845 autobiography was a key document in the movement to free the slaves. The phrase "the color line" is most often attributed to Du Bois, but here Douglass uses it some twenty years before. In this piece, he is questioning white people, "calling them" on their racism, and ends by speaking of the great men (alas! a product of the times, no women!) he has met who are "too great to be small," people who have risen above race prejudice. Finally, consider his image of the executive mansion in light of today's inhabitants.

Excerpted from Frederick Douglass, "The Color Line," (1881) Electronic Text Center, University of Virginia Library.

Few evils are less accessible to the force of reason, or more tenacious of life and power, than a long-standing prejudice. It is a moral disorder, which creates the conditions necessary to its own existence, and fortifies itself by refusing all contradiction. It paints a hateful picture according to its own diseased imagination, and distorts the features of the fancied original to suit the portrait. As those who believe in the visibility of ghosts can easily see them, so it is always easy to see repulsive qualities in those we despise and hate.

Of all the races and varieties of men which have suffered from this feeling, the colored people of this country have endured most. They can resort to no disguises which will enable them to escape its deadly aim. They carry in front the evidence which marks them for persecution. They stand at the extreme point of difference from the Caucasian race, and their African origin can be instantly recognized, though they may be several removes from the typical African race. They may remonstrate like Shylock—"Hath not a Jew eyes? hath not a Jew hands, organs, dimensions, senses, affections, passions? fed with the same food, hurt with the same weapons, subject to the same diseases, healed by the same means, warmed and cooled by the same summer and winter, as a Christian is?"—but such eloquence is unavailing. They are negroes—and that is enough, in the eye of this unreasoning prejudice, to justify indignity and violence. In nearly every department of American life they are confronted by this insidious influence. It fills the air. It meets them at the workshop and factory, when they apply for work. It meets them at the church, at the hotel, at the ballot-box, and worst of all, it meets them in the jury-box. Without crime or offense against law or gospel, the colored man is the Jean Valjean of American society. He has escaped from the galleys, and hence all presumptions are against him. The workshop denies him work, and the inn denies him shelter; the ballot-box a fair vote, and the jury-box a fair trial. He has ceased to be the slave of society. He may not now be bought and sold like a beast in the market, but he is the trammeled victim of a prejudice, well calculated to repress his manly ambition, paralyze his energies, and make him a dejected and spiritless man, if not a sullen enemy to society, fit to prey upon life and property and to make trouble generally.

When this evil spirit is judge, jury, and prosecutor, nothing less than overwhelming evidence is sufficient to overcome the force of unfavorable presumptions.

Everything against the person with the hated color is promptly taken for granted; while everything in his favor is received with suspicion and doubt.

…It is claimed that this…prejudice…is a natural, instinctive, and invincible attribute of the white race, and one that cannot be eradicated; that even evolution itself cannot carry us beyond or above it. Alas for this poor suffering world (for four-fifths of mankind are colored), if this claim be true! In that case men are forever doomed to injustice, oppression, hate, and strife; and the religious sentiment of the world, with its grand idea of human brotherhood, its "peace on earth and good-will to men," and its golden rule, must be voted a dream, a delusion, and a snare.

But is this color prejudice the natural and inevitable thing it claims to be? If it is so, then it is utterly idle to write against it, preach, pray, or legislate against it, or pass constitutional amendments against it. Nature will have her course, and one might as well preach and pray to a horse against running, to a fish against swimming, or to a bird against flying. Fortunately, however, there is good ground for calling in question this high pretension of a vulgar and wicked prepossession.

If I could talk with all my white fellow-countrymen on this subject, I would say to them, in the language of Scripture: "Come and let us reason together." Now, without being too elementary and formal, it may be stated here that there are at least seven points which candid men will be likely to admit, but which, if admitted, will prove fatal to the popular thought and practice of the times.

First. If what we call prejudice against color be natural, i.e., a part of human nature itself, it follows that it must be co-extensive with human nature, and will and must manifest itself whenever and wherever the two races are brought into contact. It would not vary with either latitude, longitude, or altitude; but like fire and gunpowder, whenever brought together, there would be an explosion of contempt, aversion, and hatred.

Secondly. If it can be shown that there is anywhere on the globe any considerable country where the contact of the African and Caucasian is not distinguished by this explosion of race-wrath, there is reason to doubt that the prejudice is an ineradicable part of human nature.

Thirdly. If this so-called natural, instinctive prejudice can be satisfactorily accounted for by facts and considerations wholly apart from the color features of the respective races, thus placing it among the things subject to human volition and control, we may venture to deny the claim set up for it in the name of human nature.

Fourthly. If any considerable number of white people have overcome this prejudice in themselves, have cast it out as an unworthy sentiment, and have survived the operation, the fact shows that this prejudice is not at any rate a vital part of human nature, and may be eliminated from the race without harm.

Fifthly. If this prejudice shall, after all, prove to be, in its essence and in its natural manifestation, simply a prejudice against condition, and not against race or color, and that it disappears when this or that condition is absent, then the argument drawn from the nature of the Caucasian race falls to the ground.

Sixthly. If prejudice of race and color is only natural in the sense that ignorance, superstition, bigotry, and vice are natural, then it has no better defense than they, and should be despised and put away from human relations as an enemy to the peace, good order, and happiness of human society.

Seventhly. If, still further, this averson*[1] to the negro arises out of the fact that he is as we see him, poor, spiritless, ignorant, and degraded, then whatever is humane, noble, and superior, in the mind of the superior and more fortunate race, will desire that all arbitrary barriers against his manhood, intelligence, and elevation shall be removed, and a fair chance in the race of life be given him.

The first of these propositions does not require discussion. It commends itself to the understanding at once. Natural qualities are common and universal, and do not change essentially on the mountain or in the valley. I come therefore to the second point—the existence of countries where this malignant prejudice, as we know it in America, does not prevail; where character, not color, is the passport to consideration; where the right of the black man to be a man, and a man among men, is not questioned; where he may, without offense, even presume to be a gentleman. That there are such countries in the world there is ample evidence. Intelligent and observing travelers, having no theory to support, men whose testimony would be received without question in respect of any other matter, and should not be questioned in this, tell us that they find no color prejudice in Europe, except among Americans who reside there. In England and on the Continent, the colored man is no more an object of hate than any other person. He mingles with the multitude unquestioned, without offense given or received. During the two years which the writer spent abroad, though he was much in society, and was sometimes in the company of lords and ladies, he does not remember one word, look, or gesture that indicated the slightest aversion to him on account of color. His experience was not in this respect exceptional or singular. Messrs. Remond, Ward, Garnet, Brown, Pennington, Crummell, and Bruce, all of them colored, and some of them black, bear the same testimony. If what these gentleman say (and it can be corroborated by a thousand witnesses) is true there is no prejudice against color in England, save as it is carried there by Americans—carried there as a moral disease from an infected country. It is American, not European; local, not general; limited, not universal, and must be ascribed to artificial conditions, and not to any fixed and universal law of nature.

The third point is: Can this prejudice against color, as it is called, be accounted for by circumstances outside and independent of race or color? If it can be thus explained, an incubus may be removed from the breasts of both the white and the black people of this country, as well as from that large intermediate population which has sprung up between these alleged irreconcilable extremes. It will help us to see that it is not necessary that the Ethiopian shall change his skin, nor needful that the white man shall change the essential elements of his nature, in order that mutual respect and consideration may exist between the two races.

Now it is easy to explain the conditions outside of race or color from which may spring feelings akin to those which we call prejudice. A man without the ability or the disposition to pay a just debt does not feel at ease in the presence of his creditor. He does not want to meet him on the street, or in the market-place. Such meeting makes him uncomfortable. He would rather find fault with the bill than pay the debt, and the creditor himself will soon develop in the eyes of the debtor qualities not altogether to his taste.

Some one has well said, we may easily forgive those who injure us, but it is hard to forgive those whom we injure. The greatest injury this side of death, which one human being can inflict on another, is to enslave him, to blot out his personality, degrade his manhood, and sink him to the condition of a beast of burden; and just this has been done here during more than two centuries. No other people under heaven, of whatever type or endowments, could have been so enslaved without falling into contempt and scorn on the part of those enslaving them. Their slavery would itself stamp them with odious features, and give their oppressors arguments in favor of oppression. Besides the long years of wrong and injury inflicted upon the colored race in this country, and the effect of these wrongs upon that race, morally, intellectually, and physically, corrupting their morals, darkening their minds, and twisting their bodies and limbs out of all approach to symmetry, there has been a mountain of gold—uncounted millions of dollars—cresting upon them with crushing weight. During all the years of their bondage, the slave master had a direct interest in discrediting the personality of those he held as property. Every man who had a thousand dollars so invested had a thousand reasons for painting the black man as fit only for slavery. Having made him the companion of horses and mules, he naturally sought to justify himself by assuming that the negro was not much better than a mule. The holders of twenty hundred million dollars' worth of property in human chattels procured the means of influencing press, pulpit, and politician, and through these instrumentalities they belittled our virtues and magnified our vices, and have made us odious in the eyes of the world. Slavery had the power at one time to make and unmake Presidents, to construe the law, dictate the policy, set the fashion in national manners and customs, interpret the Bible, and control the church; and, naturally enough, the old masters set themselves up as much too high as they set the manhood of the negro too low. Out of the depths of slavery has come this prejudice and this color line. It is broad enough and black enough to explain all the malign influences which assail the newly emancipated millions today. In reply to this argument it will perhaps be said that the negro has no slavery now to contend with, and that having been free during the last sixteen years, he ought by this time to have contradicted the degrading qualities which slavery formerly ascribed to him. All very true as to the letter, but utterly false as to the spirit. Slavery is indeed gone, but its shadow still lingers over the country and poisons more or less the moral atmosphere of all sections of the republic. The money motive for assailing the negro which slavery represented is indeed absent, but love of power and dominion, strengthened by two centuries of irresponsible power, still remains.

Having now shown how slavery created and sustained this prejudice against race and color, and the powerful motive for its creation, the other four points made against it need not be discussed in detail and at length, but may only be referred to in a general way.

If what is called the instinctive aversion of the white race for the colored, when analyzed, is seen to be the same as that which men feel or have felt toward other objects wholly apart from color; if it should be the same as that sometimes exhibited by the haughty and rich to the humble and poor, the same as the Brahmin feels toward the lower caste, the same as the Norman felt toward the Saxon, the same as that cherished by the Turk against Christians, the same as Christians have felt toward the Jews, the same as that which murders a Christian in Wallachia, calls him a "dog" in Constantinople, oppresses and persecutes a Jew in Berlin, hunts down a socialist in St. Petersburg, drives a Hebrew from hotel at Saratoga, that scorns the Irishman in London, the same as Catholics once felt for Protestants, the same as that which insults, abuses, and kills the Chinaman on the Pacific slopes—then may we well enough affirm that this prejudice really has nothing whatever to do with race or color, and that it has its motive and mainspring in some other source with which the mere facts of color and race have nothing to do.

After all, some very well informed and very well meaning people will read what I have now said, and what seems to me so just and reasonable, and will still insist that the color of the negro has something to do with the feeling entertained toward him; that the white man naturally shudders at the thought of contact with one who is black—that the impulse is one which he can neither resist nor control. Let us see if this conclusion is a sound one. An argument is unsound when it

proves too little or too much, or when it proves nothing. If color is an offense, it is so, entirely apart from the manhood it envelops. There must be something in color of itself to kindle rage and inflame hate, and render the white man generally uncomfortable. If the white man were really so constituted that color were, in itself, a torment to him, this grand old earth of ours would be no place for him. Colored objects confront him here at every point of the compass. If he should shrink and shudder every time he sees anything dark, he would have little time for anything else. He would require a colorless world to live in—a world where flowers, fields, and floods should all be of snowy whiteness; where rivers, lakes, and oceans should all be white; where all the men, and women, and children should be white; where all the fish of the sea, all the birds of the air, all the "cattle upon a thousand hills," should be white; where the heavens above and the earth beneath should be white, and where day and night should not be divided by light and darkness, but the world should be one eternal scene of light. In such a white world, the entrance of a black man would be hailed with joy by the inhabitants. Anybody or anything would be welcome that would break the oppressive and tormenting monotony of the all-prevailing white.

In the abstract, there is no prejudice against color. No man shrinks from another because he is clothed in a suit of black, nor offended with his boots because they are black. We are told by those who have resided there that a white man in Africa comes to think that ebony is about the proper color for man. Good old Thomas Whitson—a noble old Quaker—a man of rather odd appearances—used to say that even he would be handsome if he could change public opinion.

Aside from the curious contrast to himself, the white child feels nothing on the first sight of a colored man. Curiosity is the only feeling. The office of color in the color line is a very plain and subordinate one. It simply advertises the objects of oppression, insult, and persecution. It is not the maddening liquor, but the black letters on the sign telling the world where it may be had. It is not the hated Quaker, but the broad brim and the plain coat. It is not the hateful Cain, but the mark by which he is known. The color is innocent enough, but things with which it is coupled make it hated. Slavery, ignorance, stupidity, servility, poverty, dependence, are undesirable conditions. When these shall cease to be coupled with color, there will be no color line drawn. It may help in this direction to observe a few of the inconsistencies of the color-line feeling, for it is neither uniform in its operations nor consistent in its principles. Its contradictions in the latter respect would be amusing if the feeling itself were not so deserving of unqualified abhorrence. Our Californian brothers, of Hibernian descent, hate the Chinaman, and kill him, and when asked why they do so, their answer is that a Chinaman is so industrious he will do all the work, and can live by wages upon which other people would starve. When the same people and others are asked why they hate the colored people, the answer is that they are indolent and wasteful, and cannot take care of themselves. Statesmen of the South will tell you that the negro is too ignorant and stupid properly to exercise the elective franchise, and yet his greatest offense is that he acts with the only party intelligent enough in the eyes of the nation to legislate for the country. In one breath they tell us that the negro is so weak in intellect, and so destitute of manhood, that he is but the echo of designing white men, and yet in another they will virtually tell you that the negro is so clear in his moral perceptions, so firm in purpose, so steadfast in his convictions, that he cannot be persuaded by arguments or intimidated by threats, and that nothing but the shot-gun can restrain him from voting for the men and measures he approves. They shrink back in horror from contact with the negro as a man and a gentleman, but like him very well as a barber, waiter, coachman, or cook. As a slave, he could ride anywhere, side by side with his white master, but as a freeman, he must be thrust into the smoking-car. As a slave, he could go into the first cabin; as a freeman, he was not allowed abaft the wheel. Formerly it was said he was incapable of learning, and at the same time it was a crime against the State for any man to teach him to read. Today he is said to be originally and permanently inferior to the white race, and yet wild apprehensions are expressed lest six millions of this inferior race will somehow or other manage to rule over thirty-five millions of the superior race. If inconsistency can prove the hollowness of anything, certainly the emptiness of this pretense that color has any terrors is easily shown. The trouble is that most men, and especially mean men, want to have something under them. The rich man would have the poor man, the white would have the black, the Irish would have the negro, and the negro must have a dog, if he can get nothing higher in the scale of intelligence to dominate. This feeling is one of the vanities which enlightenment will dispel. A good but simpler-minded Abolitionist said to me that he was not ashamed to walk with me down Broadway arm-in-arm, in open daylight, and evidently thought he was saying something that must be very pleasing to my self-importance, but it occurred to me, at the moment, this man does not dream of any reason why I might be ashamed to walk arm-in-arm with him through Broadway in open daylight. Riding in a stage-coach from Concord, New Hampshire, to Vergennes, Vermont, many years ago, I found myself on very pleasant terms with all the passengers through the night, but the morning light came to me as it comes to the stars; I was as Dr. Beecher says he was at the first fire he witnessed, when a bucket of cold water was poured down his back—"the fire was not put out, but he was." The fact is, the higher the colored man rises in the scale of society, the less prejudice does he meet.

NOTE

1. The writer has met and mingled freely with the leading great men of his time—home and abroad, in public halls and private houses, on the platform and at the fireside—and can remember no instance when among such men has he been made to feel himself an object of aversion. Men who are really great are too great to be small. This was gloriously true of the late Abraham Lincoln, William H. Seward, Salmon P. Chase, Henry Wilson, John P. Hale, Lewis Tappan, Edmund Quincy, Joshua R. Giddings, Gerrit Smith, and Charles Sumner, and many others among the dead. Good taste will not permit me now to speak of the living, except to say that the number of those who rise superior to prejudice is great and increasing. Let those who wish to see what is to be the future of America, as relates to races and race relations, attend, as I have attended, during the administration of President Hayes, the grand diplomatic receptions at the executive mansion, and see there, as I have seen, in its splendid east room, the wealth, culture, refinement, and beauty of the nation assembled, and with it the eminent representatives of other nations—he swarthy Turk with his "fez," the Englishman shining with gold, the German, the Frenchman, the Spaniard, the Japanese, the Chinaman, the Caucasian, the Mongolian, the Sandwich Islander, and the negro—all moving about freely, each respecting the rights and dignity of the other, and neither receiving nor giving offense.

    > "Then let us pray that come it may,
    > As come it will for a' that,
    > That sense and worth, o'er a' the earth,
    > May bear the gree, and a' that;
    > "That man to man, the world o'er,
    > Shall brothers be, for a' that."

PART

RACIAL IDENTITIES

A Special Introduction
by the Editors

America is a land of countless identities. Well over a hundred languages are spoken in the schools of our larger cities. Immigrants have arrived here and continue to come from every continent and almost every nation on earth.

So one story of "identities" in America is almost generic: people come, seeking asylum, money, opportunities, hope. And they discover American–each discovers their own America. They find a land often less welcoming, less open than they had hoped for, but they make it work. Children of immigrants, themselves often unwilling immigrants, grow up bilingual, bicultural, navigating between the world of their families and the new world. Schoolyard taunts happen; foreign lunches are made fun of and abandoned; old ways are traded in for the American. Some groups lose identity within a few generations, their "ethnicity" becoming a matter of choice, perhaps a marketing opportunity (Celtic fairs, old-country decorations, language courses to relearn the grandparents tongue, "authentic" restaurants or frozen dinners "just like Mama made"). For groups whose ethnicity has been and remains racially marked, becoming American is a process of becoming hyphenated American, how to be American while always and forever marked as "foreign."

The exceptions to this story are African Americans, who came to this land in chains, and Native Americans, who were here before it was America. They too, however, must live within the land that America has become and find their own ways of negotiating this often unwelcoming land.

In the readings that follow, just a tiny scattering of racial identities are represented. As you read each one, think about just how "representative" it really is. Does the experience of any one or two Asian or Latin American or Caribbean or European groups really tell us what each of the dozens of specific nationalities living in the United States has experienced? Is there a way of talking about immigrants that expresses the experiences of people who fly back and forth to a nearby homeland and those who made an arduous trek across a continent? Of people who came with professional degrees from their homeland that went unrecognized in the United States those who are not literate in their native language? Of people whose immigration was legal and even encouraged, and those who smuggle themselves here in storage containers or sneak across borders with armed guards firing at them?

Think about what in these stories is an essential, inherent part of having a racially marked identity in the United States and what is the product of specific historical and political circumstances and moments.

13.

(UN)NECESSARY TOUGHNESS?

Those "Loud Black Girls" and Those "Quiet Asian Boys"

JOY L. LEI

Many autobiographical tales of identity take school, and particularly high school, as a key moment, a formative moment. Selves are formed along with the racial formations that occur in schools, as children become young adults and take their place in a social world separate from that of their parents. What most high school students seem to want is to be "like everybody else," like the mainstream kids, like the most popular kids—and those all seem to be very much the same from the vantage point of an "outsider." Joy Lei contrasts these two specific racialized gendered groups, black females and southeast Asian American males, and in so doing shows us how "normal, ordinary" is constructed in terms of race and of gender. Does this same process of identity construction continue in basically the same ways in college, or have people learned how to cope with these racial formations and "moved on" in terms of their own identity?

Recent research on race and student identity in U.S. schools has revealed a complicated relationship between identities at the interpersonal level and discourses of knowledge at a structural level (e.g., Davidson 1996; Ferguson 2000; Fordham 1996; Lee 1996). It is within this relationship that the symbolic realm (in which histories, experiences, and people are represented) and material realities collide, interact, and coexist. It is also within this relationship that identities are created, imposed, appropriated, resisted, and embraced.

In the dominant U.S. racial discourse, which has evolved from a history of Eurocentric representations, people of color have been cast in monolithic characterizations that homogenize diverse populations into subordinate racial groups. This discursive system perpetuates the positioning of people of color as the Other, and the white, European American culture as the mainstream and the norm. These regulative representations serve as effective

tools for maintaining the power and status of the dominant group (Hall 1997; Lee 1996; Prager 1982). Locked within confining stereotypes, many individuals of color, the model minorities, the noble savages, the black athletes and musicians, struggle between fulfilling roles that bring them "success" and rejecting them as oppressive mechanisms, finding it difficult to see other alternatives.

In this article, I examine the process of identity construction and its relationship to discursive and representational acts in producing students as academic and social beings. This analysis is part of a two-year ethnographic study I conducted at a public comprehensive high school I call Hope High. I focus on two student population—black females and Southeast Asian American males—and discuss: (1) the ways their racialized and gendered identities were constructed both for them and by them; (2) how others treated these students and made sense of their behavior based on the dominant

---

Excerpted from Joy L. Lei, "(Un)Necessary Toughness?: Those 'Loud Black Girls' and Those 'Quiet Asian Boys'" *Anthropology & Education Quarterly* 34 (2003): 158–81. References have been edited.

discursive and representational systems of racialized and gendered normality; and (3) how the students, in constructing their own identity, responded with strategic acts, resistance, conformity, and disruption to the regulatory systems.

I concentrate on black females and Southeast Asian American males for two reasons. First, patterns emerged from my research that pointed to specific and prevailing representations of these two student groups in ways that did not occur for other groups. This suggested that it was important to pursue an in-depth examination of these representations and their implications for the two student populations as well as for race relations and academic achievement at Hope High. Second, in mainstream culture, the images of black males and Asian/Asian American females have dominated the representation of blacks and Asian Americans respectively, so that there have been more popularized images of black males and Asian/Asian American females than there have been of black females and Asian American males. These stereotypical representations have hypermasculinized black males (e.g., as super athletes and physically aggressive) and hyperfeminized Asian/Asian American females (e.g., as docile and physically petite), overwhelming and shaping the representation of black females and Asian American males. My focus on these two student populations thus offers a relatively rare analysis of black females and Asian American males in the educational literature. I also examine the interplay between the representations of the two student groups, which is even less common in the existing literature.

(UN)NECESSARY TOUGHNESS AT HOPE HIGH

Hope High School was situated in the medium-sized, midwestern city of Jackson.[1] Jackson was similar to many cosmopolitan cities in that there was stark residential segregation by race and socioeconomic status, and significant academic and economic gaps between the white population and the populations of color (black/African Americans, Southeast Asian Americans, and Latino[a]s).

Since 1990, the student population at Hope High has shifted from being predominantly white to being increasingly diverse racially and ethnically, although it remained majority white. The change in the student demographics was attributed to transfer students from nearby large cities (bringing more black students), an influx of Southeast Asian refugees,[2] and a steadily increasing Mexican and Latin American migrant population. At the beginning of the 1997–98 school year, of the 1,776 students at Hope High, 68.4 percent were white, 18.5 percent were black, 8.5 percent were Asian American, 4.3 percent were Hispanic, and 0.5 percent were American Indian.[3] The wide socioeconomic differences in the surrounding community were reflected in the student population. Hope High students ranged from living in affluent, middle and working-class neighborhoods to living in subsidized housing and group homes. Twenty-five percent of the students were eligible for free or reduced-cost lunches.

Data collection for my research began in November 1997 and ended in July 1999. My key informants included 65 students, 6 principals, 23 teachers, and 10 staff members (including counselors for minority students, resource specialists, family–school liaisons, a social worker, a support staff, and a security officer). I approached the individuals in my study with broad questions regarding the significance of race, their racial and ethnic identity, and race relations at Hope High.

Two of the patterns that emerged from the data point to the complex nature of identity construction and the effects of these constructions on students as academic and social beings. The patterns revealed specific and dramatic representations of two student populations. The black female students (commonly referred to as "black girls") were portrayed as loud and tough, and the Southeast Asian American male students (commonly referred to as "Asian boys") were characterized as quiet and clannish.

The interplay of the two representations became apparent as I heard over and over again references to a physical fight, which occurred in the academic year before I began my study, that started between a black female student and a Hmong male student and escalated into a larger fight between black male and female students and Southeast Asian American male students.

THOSE "LOUD BLACK GIRLS"

LOUDNESS AS A STEREOTYPE: LOOK WHO'S YELLING

Whereas most of the people I interviewed acknowledged individual differences, there was a prevailing image of the black girls at Hope High as "loud" and "visible." The following description of black female students by Ms. Corwin (white, Jewish American female; English-as-a-second-language [ESL] teacher)[4] exemplified the typical descriptions offered by teachers, administrators and students:

> I think that they're viewed as loud…large and loud…I think the perception comes from, behavior in the hall. They are…*so* visible, by their behavior that it's easy to generalize from a few kids to the group. And, it is true that there are a lot of very, very loud African American girls. But, obviously, they're not, all. They are noticeable.

In addition to the image of being "large and loud," the black female students were also characterized as aggressive and having a lot of "attitude."

For example, teachers and students described (and I observed numerous times) how some black female students would stand as a group in the hallway between and sometimes during classes, talking to each other loudly and blocking the hallway. Students and teachers found it difficult and frustrating to walk past the black female students. Julie (Cambodian female; junior) described an incident she observed the day of our interview:

> It was like, this white dude was just walking, right, and then these two black girls they were just talking

and, everybody just passed them because they were like in the center of the hallway and then just one dude,…just walking, like normal, like anybody else. And the girl saw him and he like walked past her, and she got so mad, so she like, grabbed him behind the shirt saying, "You shouldn't be walking in front of me, and thinking you are all [higher]" or something like that. She started snapping at him! I was like whoa! I was just walking on the other side, right? And I was like, he didn't do nothing! I don't know why she did that.

In this example, the "loud black girl" disrupted the racialized gender norm in confronting and "snapping" at a white male student and, in a sense, acquired a sense of power in this specific situation. However, as Julie's comments revealed, this disruption was not understood as a challenge to the subordination of black females as racialized, gendered Other. Instead, as Butler states, "Inasmuch as 'identity' is assured through the stabilizing concepts of sex, gender, and sexuality, the very notion of 'the person' is called into question by the cultural emergence of those 'incoherent' or 'discontinuous' gendered beings who appear to be persons but who fail to conform to the gendered norms of intelligibility by which persons are defined" (1990:17).

This stylization of the black female student was a reiteration of sociohistorical representations of black women. As Jewell (1993) argues, the mass media has systematically portrayed cultural images of African American females based on myths and stereotypes that evolved during slavery, in which African American women represent the antithesis of white American conception of beauty, femininity, and womanhood. These cultural images (e.g., as mammy or Sapphire) have justified the limited access that African American females have to societal resources and institutions. "As such, some argue that the media's efforts to masculinize African American women, assigning them physical attributes and emotional qualities traditionally attributed to males (who possess power and wealth) is directly related to the extent that African American women represent a threat to those in power" (Jewell 1993:36). Jewell notes that this threat to male prerogative is "a function of the African American women's refusal to accept gender roles constructed by men in power and the related positions of subordination to which women, in general, have been consigned" (1993:36). Within this sociohistorical context, the construction of the black female students' loudness as negative at Hope High was a reiteration of a history of regulative norms that repudiate African American females as racialized gendered Other.

LOUDNESS AS A STRATEGY

Ariel (African/black female; senior), who was very well known by the administrators, teachers, and students at Hope High for being loud, offered a thoughtful and complex explanation for being loud.

JOY LEI: Was it hard to make friends when, you first came or did you already know people at Hope High?

ARIEL: I knew most people at Hope High but it was easy for myself to make friends 'cuz I would just, "Hi," speak to them and, "What's your name?" ask them. 'Cuz I was always loud so, everybody like, "Okay, who is that girl making all that noise?"

JL: Well you know actually that is one thing that I have heard like, not just you, but I get a general description of the black girls at Hope High as being loud....Do you hear that?

A: Yeah, you do. Because, I don't know, the black girls that I hang around with they just outspoken, it's no reason to be,...I mean, make friends, be yourself, you gotta have fun and it's stereotyped that way in school because people try to make school fun when it's not, so therefore you gotta be loud and get attention from other people. In order to make it fun. And basically it comes from a lot of, you know African American females.

JL: Why?

A: I don't know....Some do it to make boys like them. I do it 'cuz it just me that's what I grew up from, this is how I'm *raised*, you know, loud, my mom's loud.

Ariel talked about being loud as being outspoken, a way of having fun, making friends, getting attention, and "being yourself." She also recognized being loud as a trait shared by her mother and other African American females. It is crucial to develop a complex understanding of loudness as an act of resistance among some African American females. As Fordham suggests that, "those loud Black girls" is a metaphor of African-American women's existence, their collective denial of, and resistance to, their socially proclaimed powerlessness, or 'nothingness'" (1993:25).

A few faculty members seemed to recognize that the behavior and attitudes attributed to black female gender performativity were more complicated than just the black females being obnoxious and "bad students." Mr. Allen (white male; English teacher), for example, found the attitudes of those "loud black girls" to be extremely frustrating:

> There's, also a group [of black female students] that I think tries to achieve success by working their personal perceptions of what it means to be African American. As far as lot of attitude, willingness to scrap with anybody, not necessarily physically fight but "I don't take no shit from nobody,"...that that's the way they're *supposed* to be.

Yet, at the same time, Mr. Allen saw this attitude as a survival strategy and defense mechanism:

> I think a lot of it has to do with their social backgrounds...if you're coming from [a place] where, some basic sort of survival things are the ability to not let anybody give you any grief. And a lot of times that tends to get in the way of more substantial, standardized forms of success.... On the other hand, I think a lot of times African American adolescent girls have a better self-image than a lot of

people give them credit for. Which I think sometimes people get the wrong idea, about what that's all about. They think they're cockier or obnoxious or whatever, when really that's not what's being played. It's almost a defense mechanism.

Mr. Allen recognized the positive self-image reflected in the black girls' "attitude," but had difficulty reconciling it with the negative impact the same attitude can have on how the black females were constructed against "the more substantial, standardized forms of success."

ACADEMIC AND SOCIAL EFFECTS OF BEING LOUD

For some of the teachers at Hope High, the "loud black girls" posed a threat to those in power and the male prerogative, not only symbolically but also in a literal sense. For example, I observed white male teachers walk away from loud black female students in the hallway during class time rather than approach them. Students witnessed this avoidance behavior by the teachers as well, which served to reinforce the image of the black girls as an aggressive threat. One student, Mei Mei (Chinese Vietnamese female; junior), saw the teachers' avoidance of the black female students as an indication of fear:

> You can feel like the teacher doesn't want them to get away with it but then the teacher…is sometimes afraid. Especially if they turn it into a racial issue. And they'll bring it up all the time. So the teacher won't do anything about it.

When I mentioned the hallway interactions to faculty members, their responses supported Mei Mei's observation that there was a fear that the black girls would get louder and more aggressive, thus escalating the situation, and also a fear that the black girls would accuse them of being racist.

During my interview with Chance (black female; senior), who was considered loud and tough by teachers and administrators, she described how teachers took her behavior, which she perceived to be traits of a leader, as threatening their authority and competing for control of the classroom:

> Like, kids are just, "Chance." I'm like man, sometimes I try to be quiet, and they're like, "What's wrong, you're not talking today?" And like I don't do it on purpose, but man teachers be getting all mad and stuff. Like, "She comes and just takes total control over my class." And I'll be like, [I] don't do it on purpose.

Charice went on to describe the ritual of being sent to the principal's office by teachers, whether it was her fault or not, and her active resistance to it, which, in the end, almost always put her at the principal's office. Davidson describes this authoritative control of the teachers to remove the students as a form of *disciplinary technology* (defined as isolating, ordering, and systematic practices) and points out the "disciplinary system that gives unlimited authority to send students from the classroom to in-school suspension marks students as total subordinates and teaches that good students discern and conform to adult rules, arbitrary or not" (1996:4–5). Within this matrix of structuring social and institutional practices, "loud black girls" are marked as "bad students," both to complete the production and to reinforce the normalcy of "good students" in contrast to the Otherness of "bad students." As Fordham concludes, "'those loud Black girls' are doomed not necessarily because they cannot handle the academy's subject matter, but because they resist 'active participation in [their] own exclusion'" (1993:10).

The representation of "those loud black girls" may have derived from actual actions of the black female students; however, the constitutive meanings enacted and attached to the representation served to materialize and sustain a white hegemonic masculinity that shaped the regulative system of racialized gender normality. These meaning effects were generalized to all black female students, which made becoming a "good student" for them impossible, or with costs. Lisette, a high-achieving black senior, discussed how the representation affected their relationship with teachers and other black female students:

> I think that the teachers and students also see the black girls in the negative stereotypes. Because there are a lot of girls here that…portray themselves as that negative, loud-talking, pregnant. And just not keeping themselves well groomed. I think they [teachers and students] tend to see that negative view more than they see the positive. And it's really…very unfair to like people like myself and my friends that aren't like that at all…. There are wars between the black girls too. I mean, they've always called me "stuck up" and until like, this year when they got to know me,…but because I'm not loud, and like I do my hair all the time, most of the time [laughs]. Like, I mean I dress nice and I have on proper fitting bras and everything. I'm not, wearing things…that aren't like appropriate. And I think that's what comes across to the teachers and most of the students…it's what they focus on. Because they see…me, they see my friends, and they see that we're not all like that, but they…tend to focus in on them.

The conflict within Lisette—internalizing the negative stereotype and wanting to distance herself from it but also wanting to challenge it—was exacerbated by the tensions she felt from other black female students and the focus she believed teachers and other students put on the "loud black girls," filtering out contradictions to the dominant image.

Lisette's narrative is filled with stylization of the body, each act reiterating an image of a repudiated Other within academic and social relations. That is, the performative effects of the "loud black girls" necessitated the repetitive citation of "negative, loud-talking, pregnant" (along with the implied lack of moral ethics) and inappropriate dress.

In addition to academic consequences, the representation of "those loud black girls" had social consequences as well. Attractiveness and heterosexual desirability were attributed positively to black males but negatively to black females at Hope High. Although one of the reasons Ariel offered for why

some of the black girls were loud was "to make boys like them," some of the black males suggested that the loudness and "attitude" of black females were reasons for not dating them. For example, Dom, who was a popular black basketball player, spoke about some of the black females within the context of him dating white females:

> It's not because I like somebody because they white, it's just, that was the person I like, this person came and talked to me, and then when I try to talk, you all wanted to like, act crazy and stuff and, you hear people before they coming and stuff…when you hear somebody's voice from around the corner and you don't see them for like thirty seconds later you're like, why would I want to talk to somebody who I hear from the other end of the school, always getting into trouble and stuff like that?

Dom's comments, as well as Lisette's, reflect the ways that white black females are often contrasted in mainstream society. As Fordham points out, white womanhood is often defined as a cultural universal; "In striking contrast, black womanhood is often presented as the antithesis of white woman's lives, the slur or 'the nothingness'… that men and other women use to perpetuate and control the image of the 'good girl' and by extension the good woman" (1993:4). Earl (black/white male; senior) offered this opinion on black female students at Hope High:

> Most of the black girls here are not very attractive, and that's what me and my friends have conceded but, 1 mean, I'm not to say all black women are ugly because, there are, undoubtedly many, many, many beautiful black women but at Hope High School in our little society no there's not! I mean, and there's lots of good looking white girls but there's more whites so that's to be expected.

The oppositional performativity of black and white femininity and womanhood served to uphold the production of the "good girl" and the "good woman" and to render black female students as unattractive within the racist, sexist, and heterosexist discourses of high school dating culture.

REGULATING LOUDNESS

Earlier, I discussed, through Charice's example, how disciplinary technology worked to define what is "normal" in relation to the meaning of "good student," by producing and repudiating the "bad student," that is, the "loud black girls." Davidson (1996) describes another institutional practice—*serious speech acts*—that serves a similar function. Serious speech acts are truth claims asserted by an expert in an area. In schools, "because students may view certain adults (e.g., guidance counselors, teachers, etc.) as privileged authorities with specific knowledge about higher education, life chances, and so on, their assertions may be viewed as serious speech acts—knowledge to be studied, repeated, and passed on to friends" (1996:5). At Hope High, black female students were disciplined for their behaviors by the negative meanings attached to their loudness and visibility. These regulatory practices governed their racialized gendered identity and their self-identity construction.

ARIEL: And when I was just *loud*. . . . I have had teachers or Mr. Dixon [the principal] talk to me saying that, sometimes being loud is OK and sometimes it's not, there's a time and a place for it. So I had to kind of mature over the years, and kind of know that, it looks stupid. 'Cuz, *now* I look at them it's like they just so dang ol' loud. And I don't know the reason for it but it just don't look right, it's not cute. It's like you trying to draw attention and, I'd be loud and I'm having fun or when I'm like *really* talking to somebody or I'm just having fun. But. . . just to do it. . . there's no sense, it's ignorant.

JOY LEI: [W]hen you think about it, when is there a right place for and when is there a wrong place for it?

A: Um, especially in school? If, they saying it's the wrong place for it by the fact we [black people] *are* being stereotyped each moment on whatever we do. And that's one of the biggest things and, I look at it now and say yeah, and when

is the right place, well. . . if you out with your friends depends on where you are, then okay, be yourself. But, it might be certain people walking through the building, anybody that'll be. . . looking up to you. And then you not setting up a good role model.

According to Davidson, "A network of serious speech acts may come to constitute a discursive system; that is, a system that works to control both what is said and how others are conceptualized" (1996:5). For Hope High, numerous in-school and out-of-school speech acts produced a schoolwide and societal discursive system to disavow "those loud black girls" as desirable academic and social beings.

As a result, Ariel learned to manage her "selves" at school by becoming quieter and "calming down" so that she was given respect and people would speak to her. However, she had mixed feelings toward how she learned to "code switch" her loudness:

Yeah, so it's like I really have kept it on down. And even I have had students come up to me and they're like, "You are so much quieter now." And I laugh at it because I'd be like, dang, she's right, you know? It's kinda funny but then, again it's not funny, it's sad. But. . . at least I've made myself a little bit more positive in that perspective? Rather than, "Oh that just that loud, black girl," "that's just that loud girl." And I go well, you did calm *down* so they give me more respect, they speak to me. I wouldn't really wanna talk or hang around anybody that's real loud. That's kinda embarrassing.

Within the regulatory system at Hope High and in the larger U.S. society, "loud black girls" were/are disciplined to contain and manage themselves so as not to threaten white supremacy and dominant masculinity. However, as Jewell argues, "The paradox is that as long as African American women must assume responsibilities for themselves and their families, due to a social and economic system that limits opportunities for African American males and females, they will continue to possess the qualities that threaten patriarchy" (1993:65). Jewell points out that if those in power want African American women to reject the threatening characteristics they possess, then those in power must eliminate the need for such qualities. To do so, however, "would mean that those who are socially and economically privileged would no longer...maintain their advantaged status by limiting the opportunities of others, including African American women" (1993:65). In this sense, the very image of "those loud black girls," which was/is reiterated to maintain the regulative ideals of raced and gendered norms, may be the one most powerful challenge to those ideals.

THOSE QUIET ASIAN BOYS

QUIETNESS AS A STEREOTYPE: LOOK WHO'S (NOT) TALKING

The Southeast Asian American male students at Hope High were almost all from a refugee background. Most were born in Laos, Cambodia, and refugee camps in Thailand, and the majority were Hmong, with a much smaller number of Cambodian, Lao, and an even smaller number of Vietnamese, Thai, and ethnic Chinese students. Also, a significant number of the Southeast Asian American male students were in ESL classes. Whereas the loudness and visibility of the black female students rendered them as the Other, it was the quietness and inconspicuousness of the Southeast Asian American male students that constructed them as the Other. Ms. Day gave the following description:

> Well the Southeast Asian males I've had in class are generally very quiet people. Now whether or not they're like that when they get home, I don't know...When I see some of them in the hallway with their friends...they don't seem quiet at all because they're together. But when they're in a classroom where they are in the minority, I see, *generally*, pretty quiet people. *Although*, you always sort of wonder what's stirring underneath, because sometimes, you pass a kid his paper, and he'll have something written across his knuckles. Or

something where you're sort of wondering, what in the world is this kid up to when he leaves the classroom? You know, it makes you very curious about what else is going on his life, is he, in...I hate the word "gang," it's just, a *silly* name but, in some kind of a group, that identifies themselves a certain way and that acts tougher and...it's a little bit of a mystery what they're like when they leave because...the Asian students won't come up, and just talk to me, like a lot of other students will. Like kids will come, just that, for the heck of it, stop in to say "hi," and say, "I'm doing this and this and this this weekend." I don't think I've ever had an Asian student do that. *Unless* it's an Asian student that has a family that's been *very*..."Americanized." You know, whereas [the "Americanized" Asian students] don't even associate really with, any other Asian kids....It seems like they're very rarely treated as one of the guys.

Several attributes in Ms. Day's narrative are worth noting: the Southeast Asian American males' quietness and lack of talk, their "curious" and "mysterious" behavior outside the classrooms, their possible association with gangs or groups that "act tough," their Asian/foreign-ness, and their marginal masculinity.

The Southeast Asian American male students' quietness seemed both understandable and unsettling for the non-Asian students and teachers. It was understandable because the Southeast Asian American males may have felt uncomfortable speaking in class due to their limited English proficiency or because they were shy. For example, Alisa (Cuban/white female; freshman) described what she observed of one Southeast Asian American male student in her class:

> I have a friend, who's my history class and, he's really shy. And, then when my teacher talks to him his face gets all red because he gets nervous. And then, he goes and hangs with his friends then he acts just fine. But when he's around other kids, he doesn't feel right. It's probably because, he like, knows different language and a different way.

For some students, the quietness of the Southeast Asian American male students made them unnoticeable, almost invisible. Ariel, for example, stated:

> I don't pay no attention to the Asian boys, I really don't. But I do pay attention to the Asian girls, you know? 'Cuz they do *show* themselves more or they talk more, you just *see* them more.... I guess [Asianboys] just been stereotyped in different ways since they...seem like they look at it as they don't count.

At the same time, the quietness of the Southeast Asian American male students was unsettling because they offered little to no information about themselves. It was a "mystery" to Ms. Day what they were like outside her classroom. She linked the quietness to Asian culture by juxtaposing it with the behavior of "Americanized" Asian students. Mr. Bailey (black male; grade-level principal) was also perplexed by the quietness of the Southeast Asian American males and rationalized their behavior as being "torn" between the "old country" and being "Americanized":

> But it's really hard to figure out Asian males. Asian females a little bit easier, they'll talk openly a little bit more. They probably be, two of the groups that don't bare any of their real feelings.... By *far* they've got to be the most *complex* group within the school. Because of the fact that the language, [and they're] *torn* between whether or not they gonna adhere to the customs from the old country. Or, they wanna do things, become more Americanized.

These performative speech acts set up "Asian-ness," specifically Southeast Asian-ness, as diametrically opposed to "American-ness," thus reiterating the normative assumption of Asian as foreign and "not-American." This oppositional dichotomy constituted the Southeast Asian American males' characteristics and behavior as either "Asian" or trying to "become more Americanized," which precluded more complicated and multilayered understandings of their identity construction.

The Southeast Asian American male students' quietness and "clannish" behavior were largely a response to and defense against the nativism and racism they faced in school. As Ms. Day and Alisa noted, and as I observed, the Southeast Asian American students in general and the Southeast Asian American males students with limited English proficiency in particular, presented themselves in public spaces at school differently than when they were with each other in ESL classrooms or at the "Asian tables" in the cafeteria.

SMALLNESS AS A STEREOTYPE: BODY POLITICS

Another iteration of the racialized gender performativity of the Southeast Asian American male students was one based on their physique. At Hope High, the average height of most of the Southeast Asian American male students was around five feet two or three inches and they were usually slender in build. (There was, of course, a range and there were a few obvious exceptions.) It is important to note that this average physique of the Southeast Asian American male students is the "masculine norm" in Laos, Cambodia, and the refugee camps in Thailand. However, transplanted to the United States, where hegemonic masculinity (Connell 1996) is based on the normative ideal of the white, European American, abled, and athletic male body, which demands a higher height (the average being around five feet eleven inches) and stockier build, the average physique of the Southeast Asian American male students was constituted as small and weak. The marginalization of Southeast Asian American masculinity was hinted at in Ms. Day's comments about the exclusion of Southeast Asian American male students from "typical" boys' activities in the classroom. Also, some of the Southeast Asian American female students described them as "puny" and "less attractive." When I asked some of the Southeast Asian American male students whether they thought the perceptions toward their physical size affected their experiences at Hope High, responses were mixed.

DAVUTH: I think it [the perception of Asian guys as smaller and shorter] affects like how we get along with people. Because, I'm always hearing about "Awh man! the girls like," "Awh man they getting *tall* man," all this stuff you know they like the tall guys? Us Asian dudes are like, "Man we're all like short and everything!" They're like, "Man I want to be tall!" and all this stuff. I think that's why.

JOY LEI: So like, what do you do?

D: I don't do nothing I'm tall enough. I think…they just want to be taller because they don't want to feel so short and look like…. Everybody comes up to them, "How old are you?" 'Cuz, they look all short. "How old are you?" and…they're like, "I'm seventeen." They're like, "You don't look seventeen, you look like you're like twelve" or something.

Whereas Davuth recognized the collective representation of the Southeast Asian American male students as small and perceived it as having supplemental effects (such as female students' attraction toward them and being mistaken as children rather than as young adults), Andy maintained that Southeast Asian American males did not see themselves as short. Below are excerpts from my notes of our interview:

> Andy says…even though they're short, they don't consider themselves short. This country [United States] has better food so they grow much more. The Americans are a couple of steps ahead of us but there's no difference. In fact, Andy smiles and says, in Thailand, they're usually scared of the shorter guys because they're quicker.

> I ask if that's a reason why Asian guys are usually in groups. Andy says no, that it's because they're friends. But he does agree that non-Asians may think that Asians are easier to beat up because they're bigger than Asians but that's not always true. Asians usually aren't alone.

Although Andy saw a logical explanation for the difference in physical size between Southeast

Asian males and "Americans" and denied, at first, that Southeast Asian American male students walked around in groups due to their physique, his comments, when taken together, revealed a multilayered narrative that wove together the various dimensions of the Southeast Asian American male identity. That is, they were Southeast Asian males, with the "appropriate" and "normal" physique; they were racial minorities in the U.S. context that constructed them as foreign-Other; and they were produced as a racialized, gendered Other within the regulative ideal of white hegemonic masculinity.

Some staff and faculty noted the majority of Southeast Asian American males did not participate in school sports, which is a criterion for hegemonic masculinity in the United States. Mr. Sparks (white male; coach and physical education teacher) thought it might have to do with their smaller physical stature. He listed some school sports, such as wrestling and tennis, which did not require a larger and taller build and in which he thought Asian American males could do well. Yet, I knew that a number of Southeast Asian American male students went regularly to the gym during lunch and played basketball, and that there was a Hmong soccer league in the local community that competed with other Hmong soccer teams across the state. When I asked some of the Southeast Asian American male students why they did not participate in school sports and extracurricular activities, they cited parental constraints on their participation in any nonacademic school activities and family and employment obligations. They also pointed to racial tension with black students as a reason why they were not more involved in school sports. In this case, the regulative practice of hegemonic masculinity, which led to reiterations of the Southeast Asian American male body as lacking, prevented the faculty and staff from considering other social and racial factors that served to alienate the Southeast Asian American male students from extracurricular activities such as school sports.

The representation of Southeast Asian American males as small and weak translated into perceptions of them as "emasculated" (Eng 2001; Kumashiro 1999; Ling 1997) and easy targets for verbal and physical attack. When I asked Destiny (Hmong female; senior) why she thought there were tensions between the Asian students and the black students, she discussed the issue of control and its association with physical size:

> Maybe it's 'cuz, the control, like we were talking about before…. Like my husband said right? They were here [at Hope High a few years ago as students], him and…all his Asian friends,…They're like, five-seven, five-eight, they were all taller, bigger, than the ones here [laughs], and…they're all seniors, there's like probably 10 of them. They had the control because, they're all together and that made the difference. Now if s like, all the Asian guys leaving, some of them are gone, dropped out, the ones that are here are like, little, small, short. They can't do anything. So I guess, like the black people probably looks down on them like, now you get control a little.

The performative effect of the racialized gendered construction of the Southeast Asian American male students as Other was repeated and internalized both outside of and within the Southeast Asian American communities. In Destiny's eyes, the Southeast Asian American male students at Hope High were "little, small, short," whereas the same Southeast Asian American males would be seen as of average height in Southeast Asia. Both Destiny's and Davuth's comments about Southeast Asian American male students' physical size reflected the stylization of the body in relation to power, control, and desirability.

WHY SO TOUGH? REDEFINING MASCULINITY

Ironically, a third representation of the Southeast Asian American males that Ms. Day alluded to was that they were in gangs of some sort, or in a group that "acts tougher." Gangs are generally linked to violence, crime, and academic failure, and gang members are often seen as threatening. Whether the

Southeast Asian American male students were in gangs or not, Ms. Day's speculation implied a need of the students to be in a group that "acts tough." In fact, the themes of Southeast Asian American male students defending themselves, watching out for each other's back, acting "tough" or "hard," and being in groups were consistent in my interviews with Southeast Asian American female and male students.

Although the gang image seems in conflict with the quiet and invisible representation, it is not unusual that there are two opposing representations of a subordinated group, with one "good" image and one "bad" image. Elsewhere I discussed two dominant representations of Asian Americans as the model minority and as the perpetual foreigner (Lei 1998). Although the two representations are contradictory to each other, they play off of one another to shape the positioning and experiences of Asian Americans in the U.S. racial order. Asian Americans are the model minority, the foreigner or both, depending on what the context needs us to be. That is, the powerful function of representations is their readiness to be used in the manner that will maintain the ideology that created them. At Hope High, the model minority representation was imposed on the quiet Southeast Asian American students who came to school everyday (whether they were succeeding academically or not), and the production of the gang representation, which served to define the "bad Asian," was imposed on Southeast Asian American students (mostly the males but a few females) who were often seen in groups together and who did not always come to school.

The Southeast Asian American males' sense of a need to protect themselves from the threat of physical and verbal harassment, particularly from black students, became a part of their daily life at Hope High after the fight between the black female student and the Hmong male student escalated into more fights and increased the negative tensions between the black students and the Asian American students. Davuth described what the school environment was like for him immediately after the fights between black and Southeast Asian American students.

JOY LEI: So around that time did you feel kind of unsafe coming to school?

DAVUTH: Yeah. Everybody's all, I know I did.

JL: Did people harass you more?

D: No, not that much. But, more than usual. But, they just call and then, you walk past they start talking about you. And then you hear about it and you just want to say something back and then, and then it kept going on for a while. And they kept on saying that thing and I started getting mad and started saying something stuff back at lunch time.... 'Cuz you know how Asian guys just sit at one table? And then, some black girls do like, throwing food at us. And then we got mad and...one of our Asian guys stood up and started yelling at her and...swearing at her...and they kept swearing back and forth...then the other guys got mad and started throwing food.

Symon (Hmong male; junior), talked about his take on the prevailing image of Southeast Asian American males in groups:

> Walking in a group, it's not that they're not going to moss with you, it's just that, you are more comfortable. I mean, if you're by yourself in a group of kids that is different, they *all* stare at you. Which would be like looking down and say, "Please don't say anything to me."...But if you're in a group, and they got a group, they just look at you and they look away. So then you're just like, you can go on what you're doing.

Symon's response suggested that being in a group was more to discourage being messed with so that he could feel more comfortable. Other Southeast Asian American males confirmed that most of them were in groups but not in gangs. They told me that most of the students who were actually in gangs had left or never really went to school anyway.

Mr. Thao, a Hmong intern in the counseling department, shared with me what was discussed in relation to this issue in a support group he organized for Southeast Asian American freshman males who were identified as "at risk" of not being promoted to their sophomore year:

> One of the sections I explore...with the group is how the different size between all the students, and...one of the point that they emphasize is that, because they small, a lot of time they have to be in a certain group...to have somebody back them up. You know even though they small but they have the brain and...they have a heart too, so they have to fight back no matter how small they are.... A lot of kids, they believe that the more people they have in a group, they have more power. *That's* how violence gets started. And it's like, they have more support from their friends too...just by joining a certain group.

By being in a group, the Southeast Asian American males created a dense barrier that protected them from potential harassment. The same barrier, however, served to maintain a lack of communication and understanding between the Southeast Asian American male students and the rest of the school.

(RE)CLAIMING MASCULINITY

A few of the staff and faculty noted changes in some of the Southeast Asian American male students, which was often explained as the effects of "Americanization." It is interesting that the behaviors labeled "Americanized" were the same behaviors that were characterized as "deviant": for example, wearing baggy pants and other types of clothing that were described as an urban hip-hop style, fighting, skipping, gang activity, low academic achievement, and dropping out of school. Besides the urban hip-hop clothing, some of the Southeast Asian American males also adopted gestures and ways of speaking and walking that were stereotypically depicted as "ghetto" and "acting black." Some of the Southeast Asian American males were into breakdancing and a few drove very pumped up sports cars and sport utility vehicles. This adoption of presumed markers of masculinity and African American culture could be seen as acculturation. I would argue that these behaviors also reflected performative acts of achieving "toughness" to counteract the construction of them as masculine Other. By choosing to adopt markers associated with black masculinity, which has been stereotyped as hypermasculine and a threat to white male prerogative (Ferguson 2000), the Southeast Asian American male students gained a tougher image. However, this tougher image also materialized them as deviant academic and social beings.

As "newcomers" to preestablished gender and racial hierarchies in the United States, the Southeast Asian American males' choices to be silent and invisible, to acculturate and adopt certain styles and behaviors, to physically resist the harassment they faced, were all acts of resistance to the negative production of them as abject beings. Mr. Thao poignantly explained this to me in his interview.

> I think that the Asian kids, they try and establish their identity?...A sense of who they are. And I...by doing that, they have to fight, if that's what it takes for them to do?

However, within the context of schooling that reflects discursive systems that regulate racialized and gendered normality, many of the ways that the Southeast Asian American males chose to fight back led to further marginalization from school and academic achievement.

CONCLUSION

In this article, I presented ways that racialized gender performativity was enacted through complex and multilayered processes of negotiation, accommodation, and resistance by the black female and Southeast Asian American male students at Hope High. A major purpose of this article is to challenge and reformulate the current materialization of the "loud black girls" and the "quiet Asian boys."

A risk of this task, however, is furthering the harmful reiterations simply by writing about and discussing them. Recognizing this risk, I want to emphasize that we must be critical of any production of subordinate and marginalized populations as deviant, foreign, or racialized gendered Other, and understand processes of identity construction as laden with the effects of regulative norms and power dynamics.

As Davidson (1996) suggests, power should not be conceptualized as a system of domination that leaves no room for resistance, but rather as practices and discourse that define normality in advance. "Because schools participate in negotiating the meanings students attach to identity, the ways in which teachers and schools handle power and convey ethnically and racially meanings become relevant to the conceptualization of students' behaviors" (Davidson 1996:5).

I have pointed to ways that disciplinary technologies and serious speech acts at Hope High constituted racialized gendered Others, and instituted normative notions of the "good student," the "good/desirable girl/woman," and the "good/desirable boy/man" based on the privileging of white hegemonic masculinity. I have also described how students and teachers regularly resisted and disrupted these regulatory practices, revealing the instabilities of these norms. Butler argues that we need "to consider this threat and disruption not as a permanent contestation of social norms condemned to the pathos of perpetual failure, but rather as a critical resource in the struggle to rearticulate the very terms of symbolic legitimacy and intelligibility" (1993:3).

The ways in which those in authoritative and powerful positions formulate and react to the behavior and bodies of the students have consequences for students' identity construction and academic achievement. Through those in power and through institutional and cultural practices, schools need to recognize that stylization of bodies based on regulative norms such as "race," "sex," "gender," and "sexuality" are not natural but artificially imposed.

How do we privilege certain identifications and foreclose or disavow others so that a student's success is based more on the materialization of his or her body than his or her humanness? By becoming conscious of how schooling participates in the performative effects of regulative regimes, we can, as Butler (1993) urges us to, spawn rearticulations that question the hegemonic force of the very regulatory law that repeatedly imposes on us limited definitions of who we are, who we are not, and who we can become.

NOTES

I deeply appreciate the constructive and insightful comments I received from the anonymous reviewers and *AEQ*'s editor, Dr. Teresa McCarty. I also want to thank *AEQ*'s editorial assistant, Margaret Mortensen Vaughan, for her patience and supportive guidance, as well as her meticulous editing.

1. Pseudonyms for individuals, the school, and the city are used in this article to preserve confidentiality. I created the pseudonyms for the school and the city, whereas the informants created their own pseudonyms.
2. For a sociohistorical chronicle of the origins and refugee experience of Hmong, Lao, and Cambodian populations, refer to recent publications on Southeast Asian refugees (e.g., Chan 1994; Faderman 1998; Hones and Cha 1999; Walker-Moffat 1995).
3. These racial categories were the ones used by the school district.
4. The racial and ethnic descriptors attached to the informants were used by them during our interview(s).

REFERENCES

Butler, Judith 1990 Gender Trouble: Feminism and the Subversion of identity. New York: Routledge. 1993 Bodies that Matter On the Discursive Limits of "Sex." New York: Routledge.

Chan, Sucheng, ed. 1994 Hmong Means Free: Life in Laos and America. Philadelphia: Temple University Press.

Connell, Robert W. 1996 Teaching the Boys: New Research on Masculinity and Gender Strategies for Schools. Teachers College Record 98(2):206–235.

Davidson, Ann Locke 1996 Making and Molding Identity in Schools: Student Narratives on Race, Gender, and Academic Achievement. Albany: SUNY Press.

Eng, David L. 2001 Racial Castration: Managing Masculinity in Asian America. Durham, NC: Duke University Press.

Faderman, Lillian, with Ghia Xiong 1998 I Begin My Life All Over: The Hmong and the American Immigrant experience. Boston: Beacon Press.

Ferguson, Ann Arnett 2000 Bad Boys: Public Schools in the Making of Black Masculinity. Ann Arbor: University of Michigan Press.

Fordham, Signithia 1993 "Those Loud Black Girls": (Black) Women, Silence, and Gender 'Passing' in the Academy. Anthropology and Education Quarterly 24(1):3–32.
—— 1996 Blacked Out: Dilemmas of Race, Identity, and Success at Capital High. Chicago: University of Chicago Press.

Hall, Stuart 1997 Cultural Identity and Diaspora. *In* Identity and Difference. Kathryn Woodward, ed. Pp. 51–59. London: SAGE.

Hones, Donald F., and Cher Shou Cha 1999 Educating New Americans: Immigrant Lives and Learning. Mahwah, NJ: Lawrence Erlbaum Associates.

Jewell, K. Sue 1993 From Mammy to Miss America and Beyond: Cultural Images and the Shaping of U.S. Social Policy. London: Routledge.

Kumashiro, Kevin K. 1999 Supplementing Normalcy and Otherness: Queer Asian American Men Reflect on Stereotypes, Identity, and Oppression. Qualitative Studies in Education 12(5):491–508.

Lee, Stacey J. 1996 Unraveling the Model Minority Stereotype: Listening to the Voices of Asian American Youth. New York: Teachers College Press.

Lei Joy L. 1998 (Op)Posing Representations: Disentangling the Model Minority and the Foreigner. Paper presented at the American Educational Research Association's Annual Meeting in San Diego, April 13–17, 1998.

Ling, Jinqi 1997 Identity Crisis and Gender Politics: Reappropriating Asian American Masculinity. In An Interethnic Companion to Asian American Literature. King Kok Cheung, ed. Pp. 312–337. Cambridge: Cambridge University Press.

Prager, Jeffrey 1982 American Racial Ideology as Collective Representation. Ethnic and Racial Studies 5(l):99–119.

Walker-Moffat, Wendy 1995 The Other Side of the Asian American Success Story. San Francisco: Jossey-Bass

JOURNALING QUESTION

At your college, is there a "normal, ordinary" kind of student to contrast with particular racialized gendered categories of students? Which kinds of students are in these categories?

14.

ISLAMOPHOBIA AND THE "PRIVILEGING" OF ARAB AMERICAN WOMEN

NADA ELIA

Anti-Islamic, anti-Arabic sentiment in the United States predates September 11, 2001, though the bombing of the World Trade Center obviously intensified things enormously. That anti-Islamic feeling has meant very different things for men and for women, however. Islamic and Arab men have been viewed as the enemy, the terrorists, the threat. But what about Islamic and Arab women? Nada Elia shows that the treatment of these women as "victims" of their men is part of that racism, not an exception to it. Women are associated with "culture," dance and food and the lovely customs; men are associated with the politics and the power. How does this gendering of stereotypes strengthen racist ideologies and practices? Which other racial/ethnic groups have had similar gendered treatment in America? Which other racial/ethnic groups have not?

In the present climate of virulent Islamophobia, mainstream American culture seems to favor Muslim women who, unlike their brothers, husbands, fathers, or sons, are not seen as a menace to American society, but rather as powerless victims of their own religion. The impulse to save Muslim women from their male kin pervades various social and political movements in the United States, proving to be a common denominator between ideologies as seemingly disparate as Christian fundamentalism and liberal feminism. Even in the twenty-first century, Western feminism retains its highly exploitative approach to other women: "the much touted openness of academic feminists to 'Third World' women is predicated upon these women's indigenization—that is upon their trivialization as native speakers whose role is to provide the occasional piece of up-to-date information, but more importantly to entertain, in one way or another, audiences hungry for tales about women" (Lazreg 2000, 34–5).

The "othering" and rejection of Arabs and Arab Americans is as old as this country,[1] as is the erroneous homogenization of all Arab Americans as Muslims. Despite consistent attempts to separate church from state—attempts that are now fast being openly eroded by a president who claims that his policy and vision are informed by his frequent communications with God [*Frontline* n.d.)—United States policy and overall culture have been steeped in religion, from the country's Puritan origins to the Christian Zionist worldview currently embraced by the plutocracy. It is no mere coincidence that the nation's first motto, *E Pluribus Unum*, was replaced in 1956 with the more representative "In God We Trust." After all, the embrace of plurality had to stop somewhere, and the lines have historically been drawn most clearly with regards to religion. The confluence of church and state, with the presidential worldview today embracing Christianity and Zionism, is a lethal mix for Arabs and Arab Americans, who are perceived as the quintessential

Nada Elia, "Islamophobia and the "Privileging" of Arab American Women," *NWSA Journal* 18 (2006): 155–61.

enemy. And as Americans speak today of "the clash of civilizations," the foremost "us and them" binary that comes to their minds is not East and West, North and South, capitalism and communism, rich and poor, but Christianity and Islam (Huntington 1993). *Reel Bad Arabs: How Hollywood Vilifies a People* (Shaheen 2001) offers a thorough analysis of the negative depiction of Arabs in the American film industry, from its early years until 2000. As it predates 9/11, this rejection cannot be attributed to the trauma of the terrorist attacks, and is quite clearly based in religious intolerance, the assumption that Arabs are irrevocably "other" because they are Muslim, aliens in this Judeo-Christian culture.

Rejection takes on both overt and covert forms. The overt ones need no elaboration. One of the more insidious covert forms of rejection has been the systematic erasure of Arab Americans from the "American" consciousness. Arab Americans are officially erased from American political discourse and representation; they do not exist as a recognized minority group. Until September 11, 2001, Muslim and Arab Americans were also erased from American popular culture. They were completely absent from "progressive" discourse. From the PBS children's television program *Sesame Street*, to the groundbreaking feminist anthology *This Bridge Called My Back: Writings by Radical Women of Color* (Moraga and Anzaldúa 1983), the discourse of multiculturalism, which claims to represent the wide array of diversity in the United States, excluded Arab Americans.[2] In the nonprogressive media, whenever Muslims were represented, they invariably appeared in the role of villains—and always as foreigners—Arabs, not Arab Americans. This unique "distancing" is best understood when one thinks of other religious minorities in the United States who, while recognized as "minorities," are not necessarily perceived as "foreigners."

The September 11, 2001, terrorist attacks on the symbols of United States world hegemony catapulted Arab and Muslim Americans into the floodlights,

their presence magnified by the unique brand of American paranoia ("they hate us because they hate freedom"), and aggravated by legalized racial profiling. Vilified in the popular media, the government, and academia, Arab Americans are subjected to a multi-pronged campaign of hatred, generally laced with the accusation, that, as Muslims, they are always-already hostile to "democracy," which is proudly represented in the West by the United States, and in the Arab world by Israel, "the region's only democracy." More seriously, the racial profiling of "men with Middle Eastern features" is not only legal today, it is fully embraced by many Americans, as an "acceptable price to pay for security." "Middle Eastern features" are conflated, in the eyes of these same Americans, with Muslim dress. In the immediate aftermath of 9/11, thousands of Arab American men were rounded up, arrested, deported, or otherwise disappeared. Ironically, the women gradually became more visible, as mainstream American culture sought to "liberate" them from their oppressors.

It must be emphasized that a desire to improve women's circumstances, here or abroad, has never characterized the Bush administration, and is in fact at odds with its Christian fundamentalist ideology. Nevertheless, "women's liberation" proved a convenient excuse to attack countries with which the United States was already intent on going to war. At the same time, the centuries-old Western fascination with the veil, now readily visible on American streets, behind the steering wheels of American SUVs, in American malls, and in American college classrooms, was jolted into renewed life, even as Judeo-Christian hatred of Muslim culture was revived. These Muslim women's oppressors were invariably perceived to be their male relatives, rather than the racist, exclusionary, and often violent dominant American discourse.

The failure to identify racism and religious intolerance as a major social wrong in the United States—despite the country's very long history of institutionalized discrimination grounded in these oppressive systems—closely parallels main-stream Western feminism's failure to identify many Arab women's oppressors in their home countries. For these women are veiled, and isn't the veil the region's greatest evil? Thus, many "progressive femi-nists" fail to acknowledge that Palestinian wom-en's freedom of movement, their freedom to vote, to obtain an education and access to health care, and the basic right to have a roof over their heads in their own historic homeland, is denied them not by Arab men, but by the brutal Israeli occupier, very generously backed by American tax dollars. Similarly, most Americans are reluctant to acknowl-edge that Iraqi women's circumstances, once among the most enviable in the Arab world, deteriorated very significantly when the United Nations imposed economic sanctions on Iraq, leading to extreme poverty among the civilians, while Saddam and his cronies lived in obscene luxury. While the dicta-tor was, at best, an "equal opportunity oppressor," female literacy in Iraq under Saddam was the high-est in the region, and Iraqi women were among the most educated and professional in the Arab world. Additionally, one could argue that the Arab regimes most oppressive of women, such as in Kuwait and Saudi Arabia, would not stay in power were it not for their close ties with the American government. And while Arab men must certainly be held account-able for their treatment of Arab women, one must also keep in mind that Arab women are ultimately victimized by the United States and Israel that have very real adverse effects on their everyday lives, and that "Arab women's liberation" (from Arab patriar-chy) would be moot in the political context of an ongoing brutal occupation or tyranny kept in place by the West.

The silencing of Arab and Arab American men—through ostracization, intimidation, impris-onment, or deportation—has led to Arab American women becoming more vocal. Suddenly, we are in demand, as our male partners are disappeared. We are asked to speak at political gatherings, at

Women's Month events, and in academic settings, when "the Middle East" is discussed. Without our men, we have become exotic once again, "desirable" for all the wrong reasons. Muslim Arab American women must then engage with the double stan-dards that view their husbands, brothers, fathers, and sons, as terrorists who must be indefinitely imprisoned, kept at bay, deported or otherwise eliminated from the American scene, while it views Arab American women as potentially productive, "assimilated," "free" American women who would take their children (No boys? What is the cut-off age for "innocence"?) to soccer games, serve on school PTA boards, and occasionally present their "cul-ture" (food and music, and belly dancing, of course, but no political history) to the broader American community, at school or even church events.

The "privileging" of Muslim and Arab American women over their male compatriots is apparent in numerous forums, revealing a pattern of viewing the women as harmless and redeemable, the men as perennial enemies, never to be trusted. Thus the recent cluster of Arab Fulbright scholars to the United States is overwhelmingly female. And Arab as well as Arab American literature available in the United States is predominantly by women writers because publishers deem that what women have to offer the American readership is more inter-esting than what men may have to say. One need only recall how Columbia professor of compara-tive literature Edward Said was told that Arabic is a "controversial language," when he suggested to a New York publisher promoting "third world lit-erature" that Egyptian novelist Naguib Mahfouz's books be translated into English (Said 2001). This was in 1980, at the time when novels by Mahfouz's compatriot, the feminist Nawal Saadawi—who also wrote in Arabics—were lining the shelves of American bookstores. In her case, the language was not considered "controversial" probably because some of the topics she discussed, clitoridectomy and Arab women's sexuality, were too titillating to pass. Today there is a disproportionate ratio of Arab women to men writers available in libraries and bookstores, and assigned in various book groups and course syllabi.

And while the West favors Arab women writers over their male compatriots, even among female authors, those denouncing Islam are favored over those denouncing the occupation of their country by Israeli or American troops. Thus Muna Hamzeh, author of the deeply touching *Refugees in Our Own Land*, where she narrates her experience in a Palestinian refugee camp, is ignored by most American reviewers, critics, and scholars, despite the fact that her memoir compares, in its existential angst, its fear, its despair and pain, to some of the best narratives in that genre. Similarly, Liana Badr, an extremely talented Palestinian novelist (who is also Education Minister in occupied Palestine), is shunned in this country. Randa Ghazy, an Italian of Egyptian origin, has been panned in the United States, even as her novel, *Dreaming of Palestine* (2003), continues to reap praise in Europe, having been translated into six languages. Much less qualified writers get rave reviews in the American press, so long as they deal with that favorite American topic: Muslim women's oppressed sexuality.[3]

Even as Arab American women become more vocal, they are not necessarily advancing a mainstream "feminist" agenda—i.e., one focusing almost exclusively on women's gender oppression. Instead, Arab and Arab American women are engaging in what is, at best, a "reactive" agenda, foregrounding Arab and Arab American men's oppression, their deportation, their detention, the increasing harassment these men face as they, but not their male kin, are welcome into ever wider circles of good-intentioned "hosts." They find themselves, in the opening decades of the twenty-first century, following centuries of Arab presence in the United States, still explaining the most basic aspects of their culture, still refuting egregious stereotypes,

still on the defensive. In 1982, Egyptian-born Leila Ahmed wrote: "If one is of Arabic or Islamic background in America, one is almost compelled to take that stand. And what compels one is…that Americans 'know,' and know without even having to think about it, that [Muslims] are backward, uncivilized peoples totally incapable of rational conduct" (1982, 521), Sadly, there has been little progress since.

One can argue that social acceptance, even at the cost of being exoticized, is better than demonization and detention. One can add that being sought out at public events is preferable to being denied permission to speak. Nevertheless, Arab and Arab American women's causes are not being served by the combination of racism and sexism that allows them a forum of expression. These related systems of discrimination and oppression cannot benefit the disenfranchised. The reality is that the majority of Arab and Arab American women today take the opportunity to speak as an opportunity to denounce mass arrests and detentions of Arab men, and other wrongs faced by the entire community. Critical issues affecting women, issues such as domestic violence in a diaspora context, single parenting away from an extended family, or the increasingly hostile health care system, and the rapidly disappearing social welfare, are pushed to the back burner as women worry about the whereabouts of their brothers, sons, fathers, and husbands.

Two centuries ago, European colonialism, epitomized by France's claim that it was engaging in a "mission civilisatrice," brought about a consolidation of traditional patriarchal values among the colonized Arabs, who were determined not to lose their cultural heritage, and held on, as best they could, to their precolonial ways. In the twenty-first century, the United States is creating an equally counterproductive current. Today, Arabs, Arab Americans, and "people with Middle Eastern features" everywhere are struggling to merely survive the United States' aggressive drive to "bring democracy to the Middle East." In the meantime, Arab and Arab American experiences are converging in novel ways as Western weapons of mass destruction devastate the Arab world, and while Islamophobia thrives in the United States, wreaking havoc in Arab American communities.

NOTES

1. Arabs have been present in the United States from its earliest days, having first crossed the Atlantic as members of the Spanish colonial fleet. With the exception of the Puritans, who willingly crossed the Atlantic, most colonial endeavors depended on the expatriation of "undesirables": criminals, prostitutes, and members of the religious and ethnic minorities.

2. The belated inclusion of Arab Americans in multicultural discourse is reflected, for example, in the PBS show *Postcards from Buster*, which started airing in 2004, and featured a whole episode on a Christian Arab American family living in Brooklyn. While the program must be credited for its positive depiction of an Arab American family, it could be argued that, by not representing Muslims, it is continuing the erasure of this religion as part of the American landscape. Multicultural anthologies published after September 2001 also tend to include at least one Arab American voice, most often a woman's.

3. Norma Khouri's *Forbidden Love* (published in the United States as *Honor Lost: Love and Death in Modern Day Jordan*) is supposed to be a "real life memoir" about honor killings in Jordan. When Jordanians read it, they immediately noticed major inconsistencies in the text. After they documented some 70 fabricated "facts," the book was eventually withdrawn by its publishers, who declared it a hoax. Another equally unconvincing supposedly autobiographical book, *The Almond*, by the pseudonymous Nedjma (whom Arab critics suspect is not even Arab herself) has been reviewed favorably by the *New York Times* (Harrison 2005). The book's subtitle is: *A Muslim Woman's Sexual Awakening*.

REFERENCES

Ahmed, Leila. 1982. "Western Ethnocentrism and Perceptions of the Harem." *Feminist Studies* 8(3):521–34.

Frontline, n.d. "Frontline: The Jesus Factor," a PBS series available at: http://www.pbs.org/wgbh/pages/frontline/shows/jesus.

Ghazy, Randa. 2003. *Dreaming of Palestine*. New York: George Braziller.

Hamzeh, Muna. 2001. *Refugees in Our Own Land*. London: Pluto Press.

Harrison, Sophie. 2005. "The Almond and Embroideries: Dreams of Trespass." *New York Times*, 12 June. Retrieved from http://www.nytimes.com/2005/06/12/books/review/12HARRIS O.html?ex=1149739200&en=e48886dbb7483dff&ei=5070.

Huntington, Samuel. 1993. "The Clash of Civilizations." *Foreign Affairs* 72(3):22–8.

Khouri, Norma. 2003. *Honor Lost: Love and Death in Modern Day Jordan*. New York: Bantam.

Lazreg, Marnia. 2000. "The Triumphant Discourse of Global Feminism" In *Going Global: The Transnational Reception of Third World Women Writers*, eds. Amal Amireh and Lisa Suhair Majaj, 29–38. New York: Garland.

Moraga, Cherríe, and Gloria Anzaldúa, eds. 1983. *This Bridge Called My Back: Writings by Radical Women of Color*. New York: Kitchen Table/Women of Color Press.

"Nedjma" (pseudonmyn). 2005. *The Almond: A Muslim Woman's Sexual Awakening*. New York: Grove Press.

Said, Edward. 2001. "Naguib Mahfouz and the Cruelty of Memory." Retrieved from www.coun-
    terpunch.org/mahfouz.html.
Shaheen, Jack. 2001. *Reel Bad Arabs: How Hollywood Vilifies a People.* Northampton, MA: Interlink.

JOURNALING QUESTION

In what ways have you seen Islamic women presented as victims of their men and their culture? Think about newspapers as well as movies and fiction.

15.
CHECKING THE BOX
The Label of "Model Minority"

NINA ASHER

The idea of a "model minority," an immigrant group that follows all the rules of upward mobility in America and so "makes it," serves many functions. Certainly, it offers praise to the particular model. But perhaps more importantly, it sends a message to those groups that have not make it that their failure is their own fault: the system is permeable, people can move up, and if you have not, then do not blame racism or poverty but your own cultural failings. In a context in which anti-black racism is so totally different than anti-Asian, in which the stereotypes and the institutional discriminations are not comparable, it is clearly not a "fair" comparison. Most of the literature in sociology addresses this question of how "model minority" ideas are used in this way against other groups, particularly African Americans. Nina Asher offers us a different view: what it is like to BE a member of the model minority.

Umm yeah, my parents expect me to do very well in school. They don't mind if I do badly in one subject...minor subject like shop or drafting but I should be doing well in stuff like math and sciences .... But, just get good grades and do well because we are smart people, we are Indians, and we should do well.[1]

Anita,[2] an eleventh-grader in a
New York City high school

Umm, like, we've like, now there are a lot of Indian gangs too. Like Malayalee Hit Squad, Punjabi By Nature, Madina. Things like that.

Nitin, a twelfth-grader in a
New York City high school

LABELING: A WAY OF LIFE

The need to identify, classify, categorize—in other words, create order in one's world—is, very likely, a universal human trait. Labeling is one way of achieving this sense of order: it allows us to create common parameters in order to make recognizable what is around us and find shared bases for our judgments. Labels inform us and carry a wealth of connotative knowledge—in a word or two (for instance, an "Ivy League" education as opposed to just any higher education) they convey critical information which contributes to our sense-making and decision-making within our larger social context.

The democratic desire to ensure that a free society has an informed citizenry is, perhaps, one reason why we rely on labeling as we do—often, even in the most mundane; quotidian aspects of our lives. For instance, it was here in the United States that I first bought individually labeled pieces of fruit—"Chiquita" bananas, "Dole" pineapples, "Sunkist" oranges and so on. Over the years, I have not been able to overcome my bafflement at this practice of labeling each piece of fruit. (Besides, I find that when I am peeling off the label, I have

Excerpted from Nina Asher, "Checking the Box: The Label of "Model Minority," in *Labeling: Pedagogy and Politics*, ed. Glenn N. Hudak and Paul Kihn (New York: Routledge, 2001), 75–91. Notes and references have been edited.

to be extra careful not to damage the fruit.) I have never understood how this practice benefits society and its members, and am troubled by the utter normalcy of such labeling. Labeling, it appears, is so much a part of life that we scarcely notice how all-pervasive it is, much less question its apparent usefulness, purpose, and effects on the social and individual psyche.

The meanings and (ab) uses of labels such as "mentally retarded," "learning disabled," and "dyslexic" have been much debated in education, particularly in the areas of special education and bilingual education. The exclusionary politics and problematic nature of such widely used labels are generally recognized and hotly contested (see, for instance, Brantlinger 1997). By contrast, labels which appear benevolent, positive, and affirming can be seductive even for those labeled, and thus present subtler challenges—for instance, the label of "model minority," under which Asian American students have been popularly packaged, is generally perceived as good, attractive, worth having. This apparently positive representation effectively overshadows more problematic considerations such as "who has the power to define whom and when and how" (McCarthy and Crichlow 1993: xvi).

In this essay I discuss the epistemological and sociopolitical implications of labeling, focusing in particular on the construct of Asian American students as a "model minority" and the role of this perception in the development of their identities. I argue that the model minority construct is hegemonic (Lee 1996) and succeeds in co-opting those thus labeled. I analyze the narratives of South Asian American high school students in an attempt to understand the process by which this label becomes reified and how this contributes to the oversight of the contradictions and complexities of their lives. I focus here on identifying those forces operating in the lives of these young Asian Americans which shape their academic and career choices. To that end, I consider the influences and interaction of such broad social forces as the desire

for middle-class status and the need for financial security, as well as realities specific to the home and school contexts of particular students.

EPISTEMOLOGICAL IMPLICATIONS OF LABELS: INSCRIBING THE "OTHER"

Just as unconsciously as we use (or get used to) labels, we come to see these signifiers as "true" in and of themselves. Labels get reified, become ways of knowing. They serve as identifiers that help us to know and situate ourselves in relation to others (and vice versa) in the larger social context. Labels become boxes, representing categories and criteria that we can check off to define ourselves and others. Thus they allow us to inscribe an 'other' (Fine 1994).

Labels, then, are a convenience. They offer us a framework which lets us believe that we can know or understand, with a degree of confidence, an individual who appears to be different from us. They allow us to arrive at conclusions about someone on the basis of their race, culture, appearance or name, without having to process any information specific to them. The individual or institution being categorized—"person of color," "immigrant," "urban school"—can automatically be assumed to possess certain characteristics generic to that group, *sans* variation. In other words, labels "pre-package" the individual for us and justify any assumptions we might make about them. They frame and limit our vision, saving us from having to see the complexity of and rethink the "other."

Under the label of "model minority" Asian Americans are "known" to be "better educated, to be earning as much as any group, to be well assimilated, and to manifest low rates of social deviance" (Chun 1995: 95). Further, the media have portrayed this population as having succeeded, despite past discrimination, in becoming "a hardworking, uncomplaining minority deserving to serve as a model for other minoritie" (ibid. 96). Asian American students are defined as hardworking "whiz kids," Excelling at math and science, high achievers overall in terms of academic performance, and, unlike other students of color, not educationally disadvantaged (Lee 1996; Nakanishi 1995). This popular inscription of Asian Americans as a monolithic model minority ignores the diverse ethnicities, histories, socioeconomic realities and academic concerns of this population.

Recent writings on the education of Asian Americans note the need to document the diversity within this population (Goodwin et al. 1996; Nakanishi 1995; Pang 1995). Issues such as the educational achievement levels of Asian Americans (see Nakanishi 1995), their representation in teaching and teacher education (see Goodwin et al. 1996 and Preissle 1997), and the inclusion of the voices and concerns of Asian American students (see Lee 1996) are some of the areas in which researchers are unearthing diverse and, at times, troubling realities. However, even as such findings emerge, the notion persists within the larger social context that Asian Americans are, uniformly, a "model minority."

Lee, referring to the "absent voice (s) of Asian America," notes that Asian Americans have been "simultaneously ignored and exalted in the U.S. imagination," and are typically left out of the discourse on diversity:

> perhaps the most insidious reason given for excluding Asian voices from the discourse on race is the stereotype that Asians do not have any problems (i.e., they are model minorities). In the minds of most Americans, minorities like African Americans, Latinos, and Native Americans are minorities precisely because they experience disproportionate levels of poverty and educational underachievement. The model minority stereotype suggests that Asian Americans are "outwhiting white" and have overcome discrimination to be more successful than whites...when Asians are included in the discourse on race it is usually to talk about their "success." Asian Americans are described as hardworking entrepreneurs who are doing well economically (e.g., Korean merchants), and they are described as hardworking

> students who excel in math and science (e.g., Asian American whiz kids). While Asian Americans are stereotyped as model minorities, other racial minorities are stereotyped in overtly negative ways.

> (Lee 1996: 5)

This "insidiousness" of the "model minority" label is a seductive force which can lure those labeled into contributing to its reification, because, after all, which one of us would not want to know ourselves as "successful" and be recognized, particularly by those wielding power, as such? It is also seductive because it allows the "labelers" to recognize themselves as willing to acknowledge, able to accept, indeed open to the success of a "minority" population. Questions as to who is labeling whom and to what end can then be ignored. And this insidiousness is dangerous—it makes those who come under the label complicit in the oversight of their own struggles, allowing these to remain unaddressed. It is also dangerous because it serves to pit one minority community against others, thereby allowing those in power to "divide and rule." Ultimately, then, the seductive nature of this label is dangerous because it first puts into circulation the notion that Asian Americans are "the model minority," and then *invites them to realize it—making them known for and, in fact, identified only by their achievements.*

CONSTRUCTING THE ASIAN AMERICAN SELF AS AN ACADEMIC AND PROFESSIONAL SUCCESS STORY

Common to the stories of all ten participants in my study was the expectation from those at home and at school that they would excel academically, make "good grades," and work towards getting into a "good college." All the participants expected to earn at least one degree and to work at jobs which ensured their financial security. In the paragraphs that follow I share the voices of these South Asian American high school students as they discussed: their experience and negotiation of the external and internal pressures they encountered in the course of learning to excel at academics; the long-range planning and preparation, particularly within the home context, for financially viable careers; and their experiences as Asian Americans within the school context.

People at home consistently expected excellent grades and usually encouraged (sometimes to the point of insistence) the participants to prepare for professional occupations, often in science-related fields. For instance, as Sharmila put it:

> [My parents] want what's best for me, like most parents do. But I think they expect, like, a lot more than most parents....Y'know, I'll come home and say, "Oh, I got a ninety-six on my test," and, I don't know if they are joking or they're serious, but they'll say, "Where'd the other four points go?"

In contrast, the school context generally allowed them a greater degree of flexibility and was more supportive of any diversity in academic and career interests on their part. For example, according to Nitin the teachers and guidance counselors at school encouraged students to explore different options in terms of the curricular offerings:

> Yeah. Like that's why they've different types classes required, so if you are interested in some other things, then you can always try everything out. And then pick, like, you know, decide what you like...what you want to do.

Another student, Poonam, talked about people at school recognizing effort on the part of students, "[People at school] say that if you are working very hard at an AP class and you are getting a B plus that's very good, cuz they rarely give out As in AP class." However, despite the greater openness within the school context, overall these young South Asian Americans experienced pressure in terms of working hard to meet the high standards expected by those at home and at school.

At the same time, they talked about their attempts to rationalize this pressure to excel by either questioning or dismissing their experience,

or recognizing their internalization of it in terms of working hard to achieve. This was illustrated by the following exchange with Vijay:

VIJAY: [My parents] want me to perform at my highest level. Make very good grades. I mean they don't necessarily say anything to pressure me, but...I know they expect me to do very well.

NA: Right. So you don't feel any obvious, stated pressure?

VIJAY: Well, it's weird, I suppose. Because I am saying that they don't put the pressure on me and yet I feel it, so then I guess they do. I know that if I did not do well academically they would not like it, and so, I guess, I put the pressure on myself.

NA: Well, how d'you mean?

VIJAY: I mean I know that they expect that I will make very good grades, even if they don't say it in as many words. And so, then I don't want to disappoint them, so I make myself work harder. So, I feel the pressure, their expectation, and try to meet it. I know that as long as I try to do my best, they won't have a major fit.

In addition, these students were aware that they were constructed as high achievers both within and without the home, particularly because they are Asians—witness Anita's words at the beginning of this essay. Thus, their very Asianness was seen as sufficient reason by those at home and at school to expect academic excellence. As Anita elaborated:

> Like, especially Asian—Indians, Chinese everybody—they expect to do well. Because that is our persona....And we expect ourselves to do well....But a lot of others, like the Black people and White people and the Spanish, they either wanta do well, or they don't....And that's accepted.

It appears then that this expectation to excel academically is embodied in Asian American students and recognized as their particular identity, distinguishing them from students of other racial backgrounds....

A rather obvious factor within the larger social context which influences this expectation of success at school is the desire to ensure future economic and professional success. To that end, the people at home typically expected these students to "take relevant courses" which would help them prepare for college and to follow appropriate career paths such as medicine or business which would guarantee financial success. For instance, Poonam's parents expected her to take classes that "challenge [her] a lot," and her father wished for her to "take lots of science classes and do well at them" so that she could "be a doctor." Poonam was aware that her parents were motivated by their concern for her future happiness:

[My parents] want the best for me. And they see that—you see—that some of the most prosperous people in this country are doctors and, like, I know a lot of them, a lot of kids in this school, their parents are doctors and so they see that doctors have a good income. So they figure that if I am a doctor, I'll make money and I won't be needing anything, I won't be lacking anything in my life.

Messages regarding the need to focus on future economic success were systematically delivered to these young Asian Americans in various ways, and reflected long-range planning on the part of their parents. For instance, these students received specific suggestions and detailed directions from their parents—their fathers in most cases—with regard to planning for future academic and professional pursuits. According to Poonam,

Yeah [my parents] want very good grades. Like they want A plus for everything. If not A plus then A. But my average is about an A minus and I am happy with it because I am working hard and I know I am doing well. But my dad's very strict with this, he thinks I might not get into a good program—he wants me to get into a...six- or seven-year program at some college, so I don't have to do eight years for med. school.

One of the thrusts regarding career choice was the push from home for science-related fields, particularly medicine, over humanities and the social sciences. For instance, Mohan traced the evolution of his career plans, beginning with his wanting to be a cop when he was a kid:

I switched to veterinary medicine, which I really like a lot. And then I switched to animal behaviorology, and then to psychology. But, er, then, er, I guess I matured. [My parents'] expectations to go to medicine, you know, sort of, came down to me. So, I switched. I don't know if it's to satisfy them, but I still want to experience psycho[logy], behaviorology—that's why I am thinking psychiatrist.

Here, although Mohan abandoned the idea of veterinary work, he struggled to marry his own interests and those of his parents. And Mary's mother, although proud of her daughter's talent in art, relegated it to the margin as "only a side hobby," not to be confused with serious professional pursuits. Similarly, when Poonam had expressed interest in psychiatry, her father informed her that "psychiatrists are crazy, crazier than their patients." And with regard to a career as a journalist or a writer— "Something different," according to Poonam—her father said such activities were meant for one's "spare time." Poonam was given the choice of becoming: a doctor or a lawyer, and came to know herself as a future doctor. She said: "I accept it. It's a set thing. Part of being an Indian family—you have to, like, accept certain things, So, like, that's one of the things I have accepted"

The above segments from the participants' stories reveal how they encountered messages, particularly from those at home, to excel academically and succeed financially. It can be argued that the parents of these students, as immigrants to the United States, had to work to establish themselves, and therefore desired financial security and middle-class status for their children. However, this material or socioeconomic desire, understandable though it may be, serves to eliminate a range of career options and interests, including the profession of teaching, thus, unwittingly, reifying the model minority stereotype.

Parental expectations and preferences, then, shaped by socioeconomic forces, and considerations, serve to guide these students down "safe," "respectable," and tried-and-true career paths and to prevent their own personal explorations and expressions of difference. Cultural factors also contribute to the students' compliance—sooner or later, and to varying degrees—with parental wishes. Ironically, while the model minority label highlights the "end result"—the Asian American whiz kid—what gets lost are the negotiations these young Asian Americans engage in, their efforts to resist being railroaded into careers which may not appeal to them, and the gradual process by which they end up accepting or at least falling in with parental wishes.

Further, the fact that Asians in America are generally perceived as compliant, hardworking, and successful contributes to, the image of them as a desirable minority which can be incorporated into existing socioeconomic structures without the risk of repercussions. Such apparently benign characterizations become part of the self-knowledge of Asian Americans and, in effect, ensure that they do live by the label in order to continue being accepted within the mainstream context. Thus, Asian Americans internalize the oppressor (Freire 1982; hooks 1990) and remain on the margins in a number of fields such as "social sciences, humanities, and arts, whose primary vehicle for professional activities is either linguistic communication or interpersonal contacts" (Chun 1995: 105). Therefore, in terms of "story," "representation" and "voice," Asian American narratives are generally absent in the very arenas which offer opportunities to focus on these issues.

The profession of teaching provides a clear example. Although the field of education could serve as a site of self-representation, such intersecting socioeconomic forces as financial security and prestige operate to draw Asian Americans away from teaching, co-opting them in their own marginalization. For instance, according to Sanjoy it was because of "the money issue" that his parents were not supportive of his interest in becoming a teacher. Anita had a similar story. Her parents, she said, had no arguments with her choosing accounting as a career: "They don't care what I do, as long as I am happy." However, practically in the same breath she continued:

> But I'd always wanted to be a teacher, but, my mother is like, "No!"…because they don't think it's a high…high enough paying job. They think if i want to be a college professor it is fine—that pays well. But kindergarten…I want to teach, like, children, but they don't like that because it's not like high, like, well paying enough.

As young Asian Americans, Mohan, Mary, Poonam, Sanjoy, and Anita internalized messages from home and learned to stay on the straight and narrow path in terms of their academic and career choices. Their stories reveal the parental and familial expectations conveyed to them both verbally and non-verbally from their earliest days, and their resultant efforts to resist these expectations and to negotiate alternatives even as they found themselves giving in. As these Asian American high school students yielded to parental wishes, they ended up rethinking themselves, modifying their hopes and dreams. They came to know themselves as future doctors and business-people rather than as psychiatrists, social workers, teachers, writers, and artists. They ended up fitting into the frame of the "successful" model minority, thereby unwittingly contributing to their own marginalization and the reification of the construct.

By contrast, the school context generally offered these students greater flexibility and choice regarding their academic and career options, and encouraged their involvement in extra-curricular activities. In particular the messages from their teachers and guidance counselors at school differed from those they got from parents, in that they allowed for a "greater degree of openness." In Nitin's words, the approach of people at school was "Just do as much as you can. Participate as much as you can. Experience as much as you can. Try different things." And according to Mary, in terms of how best to prepare for one's career, her teachers and guidance counselors encouraged students to be well rounded by diversifying their experiences and exploring their options:

> So, they're trying to let you see what, what that environment looks like and see if your perspective changes. I mean because, like, again, every experience changes you and you might decide, "Wow! I really don't like that." So, I think that's what your teachers and guidance counselors try to encourage. That you actually go, and, like, look at what they do, and then think for yourself whether that's something that you would want.

However, this greater openness within the school context was partially offset for these young Asian Americans by other expectations based on popular images and constructions of Asians in America. As the following conversation with Vijay illustrates, the school context also conveyed messages which prescribed and limited their options:

VIJAY: You know, one thing is that people expect that if you are Asian you'll be a doctor. They'll say, "Oh, you're Asian, so you'll want to be a doctor." And you do see a lot of Asian doctors around.

NA: Right.... Expectation.... And what about things like prestige, respectability, only option for men—do these come into the minds of school people?

VIJAY: Even this thing about Asian doctors, it is particularly expected of Asian males. If you are an Asian male you are going to be a doctor. It is connected with making enough money, security.

NA: OK. Asian males in particular.

VIJAY: There are so many Asian doctors around— mostly men, and so many Asian students opt for medicine…

NA: So you are thinking of Asian males in medicine, hah?

VIJAY: It's a fact but also it is an invented fact or truth.

NA: How d'you mean?

VIJAY: I mean people say that there are lots of Asian doctors and that Asians mostly go for medicine, but that's an invented fact, kind of, because it's not true that only Asians are doctors. They just notice them. There are other [non-Asian] doctors around but somehow they don't get noticed as much as the Asians.

According to Vijay's analysis above, it appears that students of Asian descent—particularly males—were automatically expected to opt for the medical field and were highlighted as such, although there were students of other racial backgrounds who also went to medical school. The contradictions and dynamic tensions in deconstructing such perceived social realities are evident in the above dialectic as Vijay moves from describing the presence of "many Asian doctors" as "a fact" to "an invented fact." Such stereotypical representations of Asian American students serve automatically not only to direct them towards certain career paths, but also to eliminate other options for them, thus belying the apparent openness within the school context.

A related image the participants frequently confronted within the school context was that students of Asian descent are "smart" academically competent. Despite the "greater degree of openness"—the encouragement to explore their options and diversify their interests—within the school context, as Asian Americans these students were expected by their teachers to earn consistently high grades. Mohan, the exception with a "B" average, was aware that his teachers wished for him to emulate his

South Asian American peers and improve his academic performance:

> [My teachers] tell me that I am really smart, but, er, I mean, I'll admit it, I am sort of lazy....I'm not laaazy, I'm not, like, spoilt or anything. I just don't find myself motivated. So, for them, they expect out of me, not to work harder, but to keep me awake....And most of the students you find here, the South Asian [American] kids, they're getting As, I'm sure. But most of them are like, er, their parents are really strict. My parents are too. I just don't find myself motivated.

Mohan's stated "laziness" and "lack of motivation" can be interpreted as expressions of resistance which allow a departure from the frame of being a "model" Asian American student. Ironically, this very resistance, and Mohan's stated exceptionality, served to underscore the "norm" of South Asian American and other Asian American students excelling academically—once again reifying the model minority stereotype.

Sharmila, the participant who distanced herself the most from sources of Indian identification, observed how students of Indian descent are generally perceived as "quiet" at school. In fact, her words reveal her own complicity with this notion:

> Like, I think some people have a certain view, they have, like, a pre-set notion of what, like, an Indian person, like, an Indian student, or child, or whatever would be like. They usually tend to be more quiet and whatever, like, and very smart and whatever. And sometimes, like, I don't know, like, most of the Indian students in this school they are, like, quiet, and, like, you know, most of them are very smart kids. So, I think, you know, that that makes the thing believable....Like, I know myself, I'm not quiet and, like, I've been friends with a lot of people in my grade since fifth grade, so I don't think they see me as any different from themselves.

The external and internal perception of "Indian" students generally being "quiet" and "very smart" can be examined in relation to the "greater degree

of openness" at school in terms of the options that these students were, in fact, able to explore and develop. Such characterizations, along with popular notions—within and outside the school context—of Asian American students as future doctors, served to reify the model minority construct, thereby creating a subtext which contradicted the apparent openness of the school context.

Once again, both Mohan and Sharmila, like Vijay, point to the tension between fact and perception, which, to cite Sharmila's astute observation, "makes the thing believable." Such is the insidiousness of the label. Further, the school context can be understood as the site at which representations from the larger social context translate into the particular expectations that Asian American students encounter. These representations seem to be further reified as they intersect with the expectations from home which the students attempt so hard to meet. Through a different lens, the Asian American student embodies a contested site where expectations from parents and school, social fact and perception, and the student's own participation in and resistance to being boxed in criss-cross one another, creating a paradoxical pattern of validation and contestation, making it difficult to peel off the label.

DISCUSSION

Given the unrelenting push for academic achievement and the career-driven messages from home, it is not surprising that Asian American students learn to work hard, strive for excellence and identify themselves as "smart." As the messages from home and school reinforce each other, these young South Asian Americans internalize them to make their way along traditionally "safe" career paths and are seen as success stories, thereby reifying the model minority construct. However, despite this obvious "success" they are in fact multiply marginalized by the label: their status as a model minority is defined by those within the dominant context; the focus on academic success and financially viable careers ignores the fact that their representation in the social sciences and humanities is curtailed; their struggles to represent themselves and realize their interests remain submerged; and they are sectioned off from students from other minority communities.

The internalized desire to ensure financial security, social respectability and acceptability as part of the middle class drives these students to comply with parental expectations and pursue science- and business-related academic and career paths instead of developing their particular talents and doing "something different" as Poonam would say. This echoes Lee's (1996) conclusions that issues of social class and perception of future opportunities are significant variables in the identity formation of Asian American students, influencing their perception of their positionality in society. Even as these students critique popular constructions of Asian Americans they contribute to their realization, recognizing such traits as "being quiet," "being smart" and "achieving high grades" as characteristic of and integral to the persona of Asian American students. Thus they participate in their own labeling and marginalization.

In order to deconstruct the label of "model minority" and bring to light the diverse educational realities of Asian Americans, educational researchers need to continue documenting the stories of Asian American students and sharing them within the field of education—in the curriculum of the school as well as in teacher education (Goodwin et al. 1997). Further, the lived realities of Asian American students need to be shared beyond the educational context so that they are no longer depicted as an uncomplaining and problem free minority community in the public imagination. And, finally, if we are to arrest further reification of the model minority stereotype, we need to inform and engage in dialogue with the parents and communities of these students (as well as other minority students) regarding their lives at school and the range of academic and career options available to them. If we make it more possible for Asian American students to depart from traditionally "safe" academic and career paths, they will be able to participate more fully in their educational and social contexts and move beyond the confines of the box marked "model minority," into new spaces of re-presentation.

NOTES

1. These two opening quotes are segments of raw data from the study on which this essay draws.
2. Pseudonyms have been used for all the participants and are matched for regional and religious background.

REFERENCES

Brantlinger, E. (1997) "Using Ideology: Cases of Nonrecognition of the Politics of Research and Practice in Special Education," *Review of Educational Research,* 67(4): 425–59.

Chun, K. (1995) "The Myth of Asian American Success and Its Educational Ramifications" in D. T. Nakanishi and T. Y. Nishida (eds) *The Asian American Educational Experience: A Source Book for Teachers and Students* (95–112), New York: Routledge.

Fine, M. (1994) "Working the Hyphens: Reinventing Self and Other in Qualitative Research" in N. K. Denzin and Y. S. Lincoln (eds) *Handbook of Qualitative Research* (70–82), Thousand Oaks, CA: Sage.

Freire, P. (1982) *Pedagogy of the Oppressed*, New York: Continuum.

Goodwin, A. L., Genishi, C. S., Woo, K. A. and Asher, N. (1996) *Growing up Asian in America: The Role of Social Context and Education in Shaping Racial and Personal Identity*, paper presented at the annual meeting of the American Educational Research Association, April 1996, New York.

Hooks, B. (1990) *Yearning: Race, gender, and cultural politics*, Boston, South End.

Lee, S.J. (1996) *Unraveling the "Model Minority" Stereotype: Listening to Asian American Youth*, New York: Teachers College Press.

McCarthy, C. and Crichlow, W. (1993) "Introduction: Theories of Identity Theories of Representation, Theories of Race" in C. McCarthy and W. Crichlow (eds) *Race, Identity and Representation in Education* (xiii–xxix), New York: Routledge

Nakanishi, D. T. (1995) "Growth and Diversity: The Education of Asian/Pacific American" in D. T. Nakanishi and T. Y. Nishida (eds) *The Asian American Educational Experience: A Source Book for Teachers and Students* (xi–xx), New York: Routledge.

Pang, V. O. (1995) "Asian American Children: A Diverse Population" in D. T. Nakanishi and T. Y. Nishida (eds) *The Asian American Educational Experience: A Source Book for Teachers and Students*. (167–79), New York: Routledge.

Rong, X. L. and Preissle, J. (1997) "The Continuing Decline of Asian American Teachers," *American Educational Research Journal*, 34(2), 267–93.

JOURNALING QUESTION

Look at three college websites that advertise to prospective students. Are Asians represented? If so, how?

16.

IDENTITY CRISIS

Indian Identity in a Changing World

PATTY TALAHONGVA

Native Americans, or Indians, occupy a unique place in the United States. Rather than being "immigrants," as other racially coded ethnic groups are, they are indigenous. Immigrants left their home nation to come as individuals or families to the United States; Indians stayed in their nation, and that nation is located within U.S. territory. As citizens of their own nations (or tribes, as we call them), they have particular and specific rights in the United States. But to get those rights recognized, a person has to prove that he or she is, indeed, Indian. The use of the old language of "blood" shows that this is a long-standing problem: even today, people are called "full-blooded Hopi," or "one-eighth Navaho," and so on—a language we never use now with any other race/ethnic group. Native Americans, like all other Americans, are likely to be descended from a variety of different nationalities. Some people have Irish, English, Polish, and Italian great-grandparents; some have Navajo, Hopi, French, and Oneida great-grandparents. How does their special status of Indians determine which group they choose as their primary identity?

At what age does anyone come to the realization of self in terms of ethnicity? For Gary Tahmahkera, his earliest childhood memories are of times spent with his Comanche grandparents and learning the culture and the language. But Tahmahkera is also half-white. "I think all through early school days I was made aware I was Indian by my last name," he recalls. "Generally, the dominant society made it clear you weren't one of them; you were a savage."

Looking back now, he can laugh at his way of coping with being biracial and accepting his two identities. "I really knew I was Indian when I watched *Billy Jack*!," he jokes, referring to the half-Indian and half-white movie character. Tahmahkera grew up knowing he was a Comanche Indian and that he was enrolled in his tribe.

Matt Kelley is Chippewa. "In one sense I wear my Indian identity on my sleeve because of my hair," he says of his shoulder-length hair, which he wears in a ponytail. "I don't go out of my way to tell people I'm Indian, though, unless they ask or it's relevant, or they're Native, too." Kelley didn't realize until he was a teenager that he had a Native heritage, and he's not enrolled in his tribe.

For every single person who walks this earth, the question Who am I?" remains basic and yet complex. For the indigenous peoples of the United States, this question digs deeper into historical trauma of the past and the economic status of the present. There is no single right answer, and likewise there is no single wrong answer. Rather, the definition of being Native American or American Indian really depends on whom you ask. But make no mistake: There is no issue of greater complexity and importance before Native peoples today than the question of who is an Indian and how that is determined.

Patty Talahongva, "Identity Crisis: Indian Identity in a Changing Word," *Native Peoples* (September/October 2005): 58–62.

TRIBAL ENROLLMENT AND BLOOD QUANTUM

Webster defines American Indian as "A member of the aboriginal peoples of the Western Hemisphere except usually the Eskimos; an American Indian of North America and especially the U.S."

If only it were really that simple. Instead, American Indians are the only ethnic group in the U.S. who must prove their heritage in official government documents if they wish to partake of the benefits offered in treaties made with the government. American Indian tribes who have federal recognition status are granted a government-to-government relationship with the U.S. federal government. That covered status ultimately leads to quasi self-government of tribes over their people, their citizens or members.

The Bureau of Indian Affairs is charged with the oversight of tribes as well as the federal recognition process. There are more than 562 federally recognized tribes in the U.S. with 1.7 million citizens, according to the BIA. And there are hundreds more groups seeking that status. The federal recognition process can take decades. One criterion for getting federal recognition is the tribe's enrollment process.

Each tribal nation is free to set its own enrollment requirements. The nation's largest tribe, the Cherokee, has two main bands. The Cherokee Nation of Oklahoma doesn't require a blood quantum (a percentage of one's physical heritage that can be proven by written records to be derived from a specific tribe) but does insist that people desiring to be enrolled can prove their descendancy from Cherokees. However, the Eastern Band of Cherokee, based in North Carolina, requires its members to prove their ancestors were on the 1924 Baker Roll, as well as have 1/16th degree of Eastern Cherokee blood. For the Chippewa-Cree of Montana, you have to be one-quarter blood quantum and prove your descendancy from the original 29 family members.

Some critics say this method is nothing short of a pedigree similar to that of prize dogs or horses. Still, each tribe must have its own answer to the question "Who is an Indian?" For the Navajo, the second-largest tribe in the U.S., the answer is one-quarter Navajo blood. Anything less and the person is not allowed entry to the tribe.

For Natives who are enrolled, there's good-natured joking among them about who's a "card-carrying Indian" and who isn't.

ONE TRIBE'S FIGHT FOR FEDERAL RECOGNITION

Federally recognized tribes receive government funds that are used to run tribal departments. They also are exempt from state and local jurisdictions, including nor having to pay taxes to those entities.

THE STAKES RISE

Indian gaming has changed the face of some tribes who are talking a second look at their enrollment process, especially if they hand out gaming revenue per-capita payments to members.

Tahmahkera is married into the Salt River Pima-Maricopa Indian Community in Arizona. He and his wife Roelene have seven children together. When their eldest son was born, they looked at his tribal enrollment from an economic viewpoint. At the time, Salt River didn't have a casino on its radar. What his son's enrollment boiled down to was educational benefits. His wife's tribe offered more financial aid than his Comanche tribe, so the decision was made to enroll the children at Salt River, where the family resides. But Tahmahkera says they also looked at it from a traditional viewpoint. The Comanche often adopted captives or other people who came upon their band and lived with them.

"It's not how you're enrolled, or where, it's how you're raised," Tahmahkera says. "Because our children are of two tribes, we're raising them with the knowledge of both tribes. That's where the grandparents' influence comes in. They're the ones teaching the language, traditions and history from each tribe." And now that his wife's tribe has a casino and pays our per capita, the children are benefiting even more by being enrolled at Salt River.

However, the tribe is currently asking its members if they should make the enrollment process stricter for the future. They are concerned about too many people trying to get enrolled just for the casino benefits.

SELF-IDENTIFICATION GOOD ENOUGH FOR SOME

But even the lure of these fringe benefits isn't enough for some American Indians. There are many who refuse to enroll in their tribes. Some don't fancy the idea of being a "government-approved" Indian, while others don't have enough blood to meet their tribe's enrollment criteria. Still other people may be "full-blood Indian" but a mixture of several tribes. For instance, their parents may each have two or three tribal affiliations, but the children don't have enough blood from any one single source to enroll in any of their tribal affiliations.

As for Kelley, who's not enrolled in his tribe, he represents another group of American Indians: those who weren't raised in their cultural traditions and discovered their heritage later in life.

"I grew up in and around Davenport, Iowa. I was raised essentially as a white guy." Kelley says, "I view myself as a mixed blood. I didn't find out about this until my grandfather died when I was a teenager. He and the rest of that side of the family had kept it a secret only talked about in whispers and oblique references." But once he learned of his cultural ties to the Bad River Band of Lake Superior Chippewa, Kelley embraced his identity.

"Indian is a sense of identity, but one which has to be backed up by a generic component," he says. "There is no 'way' to be Indian, to act Indian, or think Indian. You are or you aren't; you identify with the traditions of your ancestors or you don't. You can run from it or embrace it, but if it's your heritage, you're Indian."

Kelley is light skinned, and he's used to the baffled reaction people have about his heritage.

"It doesn't bother me. I know that with light skin, green eyes and brown hair I'll always get lot of the 'That's funny, you don't look Indian' reactions. Some people are really focused on tribal enrollment or membership, a view I respect but believe is too rigid. I'm comfortable enough with myself and my background that I don't need validation from everyone I meet; I am who I am."

Pamala Silas, a Menominee tribal member, notes, "I was fostered out as a child, and being enrolled saved my life." Despite her birth mother's troubled life, Silas says she's thankful her mother had the wherewithal to enroll her children. It prevented her abusive foster parents from adopting her.

"Enrollment is not just a personal identity issue; it comes with rights and responsibilities," she says. Gaming, according to Silas, is just another option for tribes if they wish to pursue that right. She rattles off the list of rights granted to enrolled tribal members, which include medical assistance and educational benefits but also traditional fishing and hunting rights.

"I've never lived permanently on my reservation, but I have a birthright," she says. "And do you know how pertinent that is to a girl who's been raised in foster care: That's just priceless." She wonders what would have happened if her mother hadn't enrolled her. "I wouldn't even know what tribe I came from or how to spell it! I am who I am because of being a member of the Menominee Tribe of Wisconsin."

However, when it came to her two children, she had to enroll them in her father's tribe because they didn't meet the blood quantum of the Menominee. They are Oneida, Today her children are learning the traditions of the Oneida and Silas is learning as well. She lost out on that heritage while growing up in Chicago.

As for Kelley, he has two daughters and is trying his best to raise them with some knowledge about their Chippewa heritage. "That's tough, particularly because I wasn't raised with knowledge of, or connection to, my heritage, as well as the fact we don't live in an area with a particularly large or cohesive Indian community. I tell them about it at every opportunity; I read to them, I encourage them to ask questions, and we attend powwows and other cultural events together," Kelley explains.

He's not alone. According to the latest census figures, of the more than half of the country's population who identified themselves as being Native American, most said they lived in urban areas and not on reservations. So, Indian identity questions could be changing even more for future generations who aren't familiar with traditional homelands, whether that's on a reservation or allotment lands. And with that detachment from the land comes some detachment from traditional ceremonies—and even more challenges to the question "Who is Indian?"

As American Indians move into the 21st century, the questions surrounding Indian identity and how it is determined are sure to grow even more complex. Few issue pose greater challenges to tribal governments and their members, and how they respond to this issue will certainly shape the future course of Indian life.

JOURNALING QUESTION

If your family comes from more than one ethnic background, how do you decide how to self-identify? Does it vary depending on the circumstances?

17.

NUEVA YORK—DIASPORA CITY

U.S. Latinos Between and Beyond

JUAN FLORES

South and Central America, like Europe or Asia or Africa, is far from homogeneous. French and German are not "roughly the same," are not interchangeable groups. Most Americans, understand the long and troubling history between these two European countries, would see that as self evident. Yet most Americans are comfortable grouping extremely varied nations into pan-continental groups when that continent is not Europe. The experiences of a Mexican in Texas, a Puerto Rican in New York, a Peruvian in Ohio, are enormously varied. Juan Flores calls our attention to the ways the media constructs all the varied Latin American groups as "non-black" and makes up the "new face" of a changing America. How is the experience of individuals, who define their ethnicity and their cultural heritage in far more specific terms, shaped by this idea of a "browning" of America?

Back in 1999, *New York* magazine was renamed *Nueva York*, at least for the week of September 6. The Spanish word on the issue was an eye-catcher for readers of the popular weekly, and attested to the currency of things, and words, "Latin" among the contemporary public in the United States. The theme of *Nueva York*, after all, was "The Latin Explosion," those words emblazoned in bold yellow and white lettering across the half-exposed mid-section of Jennifer Lopez.

Since the publication of *Nueva York*, Latino fever has been gripping U.S. popular culture at a pitch unprecedented in the protracted history of that continental seduction. Hardly a week passes without still another media special, and hardly an area of entertainment and public life—sports, music, movies and television, advertising, fashion, food—is by now untouched by an emphatic Hispanic presence. Visibility is of course not new to the "Latin look" in American pop culture—think of Carmen Miranda, Ricardo Montalbán or Desi Arnaz—nor is the Latin "flavor," the *salsa y sabor*, a new ingredient in the proverbial melting pot, be it musical, sexual or culinary. But those passing crazes and that subliminal sense of otherness have become in the present generation a veritable saturation of the pop public sphere, the "Latin" way attaining to a ubiquity and prominence that has converted it into an active shaper of contemporary tastes and trends.

Visibility, though, can do as much to obscure as to illuminate, particularly when it remains so preponderantly concentrated in the image making of the commercial culture. In the case of U.S. Latinos, celebrity status and ceremonial fanfare is clearly one of those mirages, effectively serving to camouflage the structured inequality and domination which accounts for their diasporic reality in the first place, and deflecting public attention from the decidedly unceremonious and unenviable social status of the majority of Latino peoples. The spectacular success stories of the few serve only to mask the ongoing reality of racism, economic

Juan Flores, "Nueva York—Diaspora City: U.S. Latinos Between and Beyond," NACLA Report on the Americas 35, 6 (2002), 46–49.

misery and political disenfranchisement endured by most Latinos, who moved northward from their homelands only because of persistent inequalities at global and regional levels.

But the Latino avalanche has given birth to the "sleeping giant," a demographic and cultural monster whose immense commercial and electoral potential has only begun to be tapped and who, if roused, could well upset some of the delicate balances necessary to the prolongation of the "American Century." Typically, awe and fascination mingle with a sense of foreboding, an alarmism over the imminent threat Latinos are perceived to present to the presumed unity of American culture and to an unhampered control over the country's destiny. An integral component of this nervous prognosis, repeated with mantra-like predictability when public discussion turns to the "browning of America," is the identification of Latinos as the country's "fastest growing minority," the group whose numbers are on pace to exceed that of African-Americans as early as the end of the first decade of this new millennium. The fear of an "aliennation"—the title of a xenophobic book on immigration—veils but thinly an even deeper phobia, the fear of a non-white majority. And this without mention of the next sleeping giant: The "brown peril" is soon to be eclipsed by another "yellow peril," as Asian-Americans are poised to outnumber both blacks and Hispanics by mid-century.

Such calculations, however, beg more questions that they answer when it comes to assessing the cultural and political relations that prevail in contemporary society. Most obviously, they take for granted the sociological equivalence of the various "minority" groups, in this case Latinos and African-Americans, as though a diverse set of immigrant and colonially conquered populations occupy the same historical position, and constitute the same kind of collective association, as a group unified, within the United States, on the basis of their common African ancestry and history of enslavement. Of course African-Americans, like all other groups,

have long differed along class, gender, color, regional and other lines, but the seams in the Latino patchwork stand out as soon as we go beyond the media hype and wishful census counts and undertake comparative analysis of any rigor. Even the obvious commonalities like language and religion, for example, turn out to be deceptive at best in light of the millions of U.S. Latinos who are neither primarily Spanish-speaking nor of the Catholic faith. But beyond that, it is certainly a spurious sociological exercise to conjoin in one unit of discourse Puerto Ricans and Mexican Americans on the one hand, whose position in U.S. society is fully conditioned by legacies of conquest and colonization, with, on the other hand, immigrant and exile nationalities of relatively recent arrival from varied national homelands in Latin America. Differences along the lines of economic class and educational and entrepeneurial capital are striking, as are those having to do with issues of race and national cultures.

These marked differences are one reason why Dominican writer Junot Díaz is skeptical about any and all ethnic generalizations, stating about "Latinos" that "I'd rather have us start out as fractured so we don't commit the bullshit and erasures that trying to live under the banner of sameness entails."[1] The most obvious of these erasures for Díaz, aside from the internal differentiation among the varied "Latino" groups, is the reality of racisms—being called a "spic" and reacting to that denigrating denomination. "And rare is the Latino kid who hasn't been called a spic." Discrimination in educational opportunities and in the criminal justice system, for example, is what unites Latinos beyond the multiple cultural variations, along with the strategies developed to confront these social inequalities. "This is a nightmarish place," Díaz concludes, "for people of color."

What is seldom mentioned in the celebrations of Latino identity is the most consequential of the "erasures" involved in pan-ethnic naming—the relation of Latinos to blackness, and to African-Americans in particular. While the Latino concept does generally indicate otherness, "people of color" and non-white, the history of social categorization has selectively equivocated on the issue, and many media representations allow for, or foster, a sense of compatibility with whiteness; the Latino face shown for broad public consumption, whether it is Daisy Fuentes, Keith Hernandez or Chita Rivera, tends to be decidedly from the lighter end of the spectrum. The unspoken agenda of the new Latino visibility, and of the imminent surpassing of African-Americans as the largest minority, is the ascendancy of a non-black minority. To mollify the fears of an invasion from south of the border is the consolation that at least their presence does not involve dealing with more souls of more black folk.

Yet social experience tells us otherwise. The rampant "racial profiling" and waves of police brutality are directed against both African-American and Latino victims, with no color distinctions of this kind playing a role. For the fact is that in many inner-city situations there is no such difference and it is not possible to "tell them apart." What the hegemonic, consumer version of Latino ethnicity obscures is that many Latinos are black, especially according to the codes operative in the United States. And what is more, while this version tends to racialize Latinos toward whiteness, much in tune with the racist baggage of Latin American and Caribbean home cultures, on the streets and in the dominant social institutions "brown" is close enough to black to be suspect.

In Nueva York in particular, where the prevalent Latino presence and sensibility remains Caribbean, this counter-position to blackness is often disconcerting at best, and among many Puerto Rican and Dominican youth the response has been to reaffirm a sense of belonging to an African diaspora. Indeed, in the case of Puerto Ricans this perspective entails not only an emphasis on Afro-Boricua heritages but, because of the decades-long experience of close interaction with African-Americans in New York, an identification and solidarity with American blacks perhaps unmatched by any other group in

the history of the "nation of immigrants." Cultural expression in all areas—from language and music to literature and the visual arts—typically illustrate fusions and crossovers, mutual fascinations and emulations, that have resulted in much of what we identify, for example, in the field of popular music, as jazz, rock and roll and hip-hop. Collectively, and as a reflex of broader social experiences, this demographic reality and this conjoined cultural history put the lie to any wedge driven between Latino and black life and representation.

This Latino "double consciousness" among Puerto Ricans and other Caribbeans goes back generations, in intellectual life to the contributions of Puerto Rican collector and bibliophile Arturo Alfonso Schomburg during the Harlem Renaissance, in music history at least to the 1940s with the beginnings of Latin jazz, and in literature to the writings of Jesús Colón in the 1950s and Piri Thomas in his 1967 novel, *Down These Mean Streets*. In our own times, Latino youth find themselves in tight league with young African-Americans in forging the constantly shifting currents of hip-hop and other expressive styles. In a frequently cited poem, "Niggers-Reecan Blues," the young Nuyorican writer Willie Per domo addresses once again the interracial dilemmas first articulated by Piri Thomas 30 years earlier, and concludes with the dramatic lines[2]:

> *I'm a Spic!*
> *I'm a Nigger!*
> *Spic! Spic! No different than a Nigger!*
> *Neglected, rejected, oppressed and depressed*
> *From banana boats to tenements*
> *Street gangs to regiments....*
> *Spic! Spic! I ain't nooooo different than a Nigger.*

In a similar vein, the spoken word artist "Mariposa" (María Fernández) objects to being called a "Latina writer," as present-day literary marketing would group her, reminding her audience that "I myself feel more in common with my sistahs [African-American women writers] than with, say,

Chicana poets like Sandra Cisneros or Lorna Dee Cervantes."

Yet Mariposa does not consider this intense affiliation with African-Americans to stand in any conflict with her Puerto Rican background. On the contrary, in her signature poem, "Ode to the DiaspoRican," she signals her *"pelo vivo"* (wild hair) and her *"manos trigueñas"* (dark hands) as evidence of her national identity, and rails against those who would deny it:

> *Some people say that I am not the real thing*
> *Boricua, that is*
> *cuz I wasn't born on the enchanted island*
> *cuz I was born on the mainland...*
> *cuz my playground was a concrete jungle*
> *cuz my Río Grande de Loiza was the Bronx River*
> *cuz my Fajardo was City Island*
> *my Luquillo, Orchard Beach*
> *and summer nights were filled with city noises*
> *instead of coquís*
> *and Puerto Rico was just some paradise that we only*
> *saw in picture*
> *What does it mean to live in between...*

Mariposa thus gives voice to the sentiments of many young Puerto Ricans, and of many Latinos in general, in their defiance of a territorially and socially confined understanding of cultural belonging. Place of birth and immediate lived experience are not wholly definitive of cultural identification, which in this view has more to do with political and social experience, and with personally chosen ascription. *"No nací en Puerto Rico,"* she exclaims in the poem's refrain, *"Puerto Rico nació en mi."*

As these instances show, present-day social identities press simultaneously in varied directions, linking individuals and groups along lines that would appear mutually exclusive according to their representation in commercially and ideologically oriented media. *Nueva York, New York* magazine's momentary interlude as a Latino-focused publication, dwarfs the cultural horizons of Latino experience by postulating its categorical differentiation

from blackness, and also by disengaging Latino culture in the United States from its moorings in Latin American and Caribbean realities. Not only are the featured Latino celebrities treated as interchangeable in their collective background, but in the entire issue no mention is made of Mexico, Puerto Rico, Cuba, the Dominican Republic or Colombia except as potential extensions of the U.S. market. What is more, there is no discussion of the massive migrations from those home countries, nor of the historical relations with the United States which have generated modern migratory movements, as the transnational origin and setting for the very presence and position of Latinos in U.S. society.

Today's global conditions impel us beyond these tidy, nationally constricted views of cultural identity which might well be referred to as "consumer ethnicities," The Latino community is if anything a process rather than a circumscribed social entity, and its formation entails complex and often converging interactions with other, purportedly "non-Latino" groups such as African-Americans and American Indians. But the idea of the pan-Latino necessarily implies the trans-Latino, the engagement of U.S.-based Latinos in the composition of cultural and political diasporas of regional and global proportions. The interdependence of old and new "homes," the constant bearing of U.S. policies and practices on the life circumstances in Latin America and the Caribbean, propel more and more Latinos across the hemispheric divide, and resonate loudly in the everyday lives of all Latinos. But beyond those direct geopolitical ties, awakened cultural heritages and congruencies also engage Latinos in more abstract but no less pronounced diasporic affiliations, notably transnational indigenous and "Black Atlantic" trajectories of identity formation.[3]

The "new Nueva York" is rich with these innovative cultural possibilities, and as the newfound home of so many people from so many Latin American countries it now serves as a seminal ground for the rethinking and reimagining of America. One hundred years after the prophetic ruminations of José Martí about the contours of *"nuestra América"* we are now in a position to conceptualize *"América"* itself in its world context, and the multiple lines of an "American" identity as coordinates of radical transnational remappings. The "Latin explosion" receiving so much coverage in the United States today, the hyperboles and hypes generated by *"la vida loca,"* is but one index of a pervasive change in human affairs, leaving all of us asking, with Mariposa, "what does it mean to live in between?"

NOTES

1. "Voices of Change," *New York Magazine*, September 6, 1999, p. 29.
2. Willie Perdomo, Where a Nickel Costs a Dime (New York: W.W. Norton, 1996), pp. 19–21.
3. See Paul Gilroy, The Black Atlantic: modernity and Double Consciousness (Cambridge: Harvard University Press, 1993).

JOURNALING QUESTION

How do the images of Latino Americans that you see in the mass media compare and contrast to the images of African Americans?

18.
THE SOCIAL CONSTRUCTION OF RACE IN TWO IMMIGRANT ERAS

NANCY FONER

They say that those who do not read history are doomed to repeat it. Sometimes reading is not enough: knowing our history is necessary, but not sufficient, to shape our future. Nancy Foner, after comparing how Jews and Italians "became white" with the current experiences of Latino, Caribbean, and Asian immigrants, asks us to think about the future. She offers a number of scenarios, ways that race might continue to function in the United States of the future. One obvious question to ask yourself, as she asks, is "Will the descendants of today's immigrants become white?" But we ask you to also ask yourself if there are good reasons why you, personally, would prefer one of the scenarios she offers for yourself and the children you may someday have? And as you discuss this with your classmates, is there an imaginable future that would be in the interest of *all* your children?

The racial difference between today's non-white immigrant New Yorkers and their white European predecessors seems like a basic—and obvious—fact. Yet much is not obvious about racial matters then and now. At the turn of the twentieth century, when nearly all New York City residents were of European descent, recently arrived Jewish and Italian immigrants were seen as racially distinct from and inferior to those of Anglo-Saxon or Nordic stock. Today, although immigrants from Latin America, Asia, and the Caribbean are often referred to as nonwhite or people of color, these blanket terms oversimplify the nature and impact of race among them.

WHEN JEWS AND ITALIANS WERE INFERIOR RACES

It may have become a cliché in academic circles to speak of race as a social construction, but even when racial categories are acknowledged as social constructions that vary across time and place

they have often been used, as Victoria Hattam has recently put it, in transhistorical terms.[1] Many accounts in the scholarly as well as popular literature speak of "nonwhite" immigrants today in contrast to "white" immigrants in the past as if the term white meant the same thing as it does now. It does not. Race today is basically a color word, but it was not that way in New York a hundred years ago. Then, Jewish and Italian immigrants in New York were seen as racially different from—and inferior to—people with origins in northern and western Europe. They were believed to have distinct biological features, mental abilities, and innate character traits. They looked different to most New Yorkers and were thought to have physical features that set them apart—facial features often noted, for example, in the case of Jews, and "swarthy" skin, in the case of Italians. These stereotypes were used to describe a significant proportion of New Yorkers at the time.... In 1910, Russian and Italian immigrants were almost a fifth of the city's population;

Excerpted from Nancy Foner, "The Social Construction of Race in Two Immigrant Eras," in *In New Land: A Comparative View of Immigration* (New York: New York University Press, 2005), 11–42. Notes have been renumbered and edited.

by 1920, with their children, Italian Americans numbered over 800,000 and the Jewish population had soared to over 1.6 million, or, together, about 43 percent of the city's population.

Did this mean that Jews and Italians were not considered "white"?…Some scholars, like Karen Brodkin, argue that Jews a hundred years ago were not considered fully white; David Roediger and James Barrett suggest the term "inbetween people" as a way to describe Jews' and Italians' ambiguous racial status—seen as above African and Asian Americans yet below "white" people; Matthew Jacobson refers to "probationary whites"; and Michael Topp now adds "inconclusively white.[2] Others emphasize that southern and eastern European arrivals were, to use Thomas Guglielmo's phrase, white on arrival—that they suffered from their racial undesirability but also, simultaneously, benefited from their privileged color status as whites. In line with this approach would be a decision to speak of inferior races of whites and hierarchic gradations of white people.[3] As one historian puts it in his critique of whiteness studies, Americans have had many ways of looking down on people without questioning their whiteness.[4] Clearly we need fine-grained historical research that explores what terms were employed to describe racial differences among Jews and Italians in New York a century ago and the contexts in which they were used, what "white" actually meant then, and the role of considerations other than race—most significantly, religion—in stigmatizing Jews and Italians as inferior and legitimizing discrimination against them.[5]

There may be debate about eastern and southern Europeans' color status—whether, as Guglielmo puts it, they were racial outsiders and color insiders—but it is clear that race in early twentieth-century New York was not the kind of color-coded concept that it is today. And historians would agree that when it came to southern and eastern Europeans, characteristics other than colors—believed to be innate and unchangeable—were involved in defining them as separate races. American scholarship,

as Matthew Frye Jacobson, writes, "has generally conflated race and color, and so has transported a late twentieth century understanding of 'difference' into a period…[when] one might be both white *and* racially distinct from other whites.[6]

From the start, Jews and Italians were recognized as whites in terms of legal and political rights. They were allowed to naturalize as U.S. citizens at a time when American naturalization laws only gave "free white persons" or "persons of African nativity or African descent" the right to naturalize, and when the courts repeatedly denied Asian immigrants access to American citizenship because they were not, in Ian Haney Lopez's phrase, "white by law."[7] In fact, Guglielmo points out that, at the turn of the twentieth century, the naturalization application asked immigrants to provide both their race and color and expected different answers for each; Italians were often listed as southern or northern Italians—for race—and white for color.[8] Jews and Italians were allowed to vote in states that restricted the suffrage to whites, and miscegenation laws were never enforced to prevent their marriages to other Europeans.[9]

Yet if Italians and Jews were white, at the same time they were also, as Jacobson aptly puts it, viewed as "racially distinct from other whites." Whereas today, in Jacobson's words, "we see only subtly varying shades of a mostly undifferentiated whiteness," a hundred years ago Americans saw "Celtic, Hebrew, Anglo-Saxon or Mediterranean physiognomies." Jews and Italians, in Cornell and Hartmann's formulation, were caught in categories constructed by others, although the emphasis needs to be put on the constraints owing to the *way* the categories were constructed by others. Most Jewish New Yorkers, after all, chose to identify as Jewish (and had done so in Europe as well); most Italian immigrants eventually came to see themselves as Italian in America even if town and regional loyalties remained supreme.[10] The problem was being racialized as Italians and Jews—seen as inherently inferior on account of their Italianness or Jewishness and caught in the negative images and connotations associated with these categories.

Far from being on the fringe, full-blown theories about the racial inferiority of eastern Europeans and southern Italians were well within the mainstream of the scientific community at the turn of the twentieth century. Openly propounded by respected scholars, such views were also propagated and given the stamp of approval by public intellectuals and opinion leaders and the press.

The most influential of the books proclaiming a scientific racism was *The Passing of the Great Race*, written by Madison Grant, a patrician New Yorker and founder of the New York Zoological Society. The book set forth the notion that people of inferior breeding from southern and eastern Europe were overrunning the country, intermarrying, and diminishing the quality of the nation's superior Nordic stock—and sweeping America toward a "racial abyss."[11] This theme was picked up by figures of the stature of soon-to-be president Calvin Coolidge, who wrote in a popular magazine in 1921 that "America must be kept American. Biological laws show…that Nordics deteriorate when mixed with other races.[12]

Articles in the press and popular magazines echoed racial views of this kind. Articles with titles like "Are the Jews an Inferior Race?" (1912) and "Will the Jews Ever Lose Their Racial Identity?" (1911) appeared in the most frequently read periodicals. The "marks of their race," said *Harper's* of Lower East Side Jews, "appear in the formation of the jaw and mouth and in the general facial aspect."[13] Jewish racial features, the *New York Sun* (1893) argued, made them unassimilable: "Other races of men lose their identity by migration and by intermarrying with different peoples, with the result that their peculiar characteristics and physiognomies are lost in the mess…

Jews were thought to have visible physical characteristics that marked them off and made them "look Jewish.[14] …

In everyday life, there was a racial vocabulary to describe—and abuse—the new immigrants, and the language of color was sometimes involved. Italians were often described as "swarthy," and a common epithet for them, guinea, connected them to Africa…As late as the 1930s, an American history textbook asked whether it would be possible to absorb the "millions of olive-skinned Italians and swarthy black-haired Slavs and dark-eyed Hebrews into the body of the American people."[15] Trying to capture the way others saw her Italian-born grandmother in the 1930s and 1940s, Louise DeSalvo says she was viewed as a darker shade of white— "Dark White."[16]

Not only was it acceptable to speak about the inferiority of Jews and Italians in newspapers, magazines, and public forums, but also discrimination against them was open and, by and large, legal. Elite summer resorts made no bones about shutting out Jews. In the 1880s, many in upstate New York set up placards: "No Jews or Dogs Admitted Here." When a 1913 New York State law forbade places of public accommodation from advertising their unwillingness to admit anyone because of race, creed, or color, more subtle means were employed. When resorts and private clubs announced that they served "restricted clientele," it was understood that Jews were not allowed.

"Restrictive covenants," clauses in real estate titles that limited the sale or transfer of property to members of certain groups, kept Jews out of some of New York City's most desirable suburban neighborhoods. Toward the end of the 1920s, apartment-house owners in Jackson Heights, Queens advertised that their buildings were "restricted" and prohibited Catholics, Jews, and dogs. A legal battle over the exclusion ensued, but the court upheld the rights of the property owners to choose their own tenants. It was not until a 1948 Supreme Court case outlawed restrictive covenants that such agreements became unenforceable in the courts of law.[17]

There were various forms of open discrimination in employment, too. At the end of the nineteenth century, for example, pay rates for common laboring jobs could vary by racial group….

Also in the post–World War I years, many colleges, universities, and medical schools adopted quota systems that set limits on Jewish admission. Although in 1922 President Lowell of Harvard University openly recommended limiting the number of Jewish students, the allotments there, as elsewhere, were covert, and institutions developed discreet ways to achieve their objectives....It was not until 1946 that New York's City Council passed a resolution threatening the tax-exempt status of nonsectarian colleges and universities that used racial or religious criteria in selecting students; in 1948, New York State (soon followed by New Jersey and Massachusetts) forbade discrimination on grounds of religion and race in higher education.[18]

RACE AND THE NEWEST NEW YORKERS

Today, there are a new set of racial issues on the table in New York. In a time when race is largely coded as color, the issue is not the ambiguity of the term "white" but the complexities underlying the terms "non-white" and "people of color." In the wake of the huge immigration of the past few decades, a new racial/ethnic hierarchy is evolving in New York City—in broad strokes, white/black/Hispanic/Asian, although in reality it is much more complex than this. The black-white dichotomy, which dominated New York race relations for so much of the twentieth century—owing to the mass inflow of African Americans from the South between World War I and the 1960s—remains central, but it is proving inadequate in light of the growing number of not-black and not-white Asians and Hispanics.

BLACK IMMIGRANTS

As people of African descent, West Indian and African immigrants are clearly on the black side of the racial divide. And they are a growing proportion of New York's black population. By 2000, more than a quarter of New York City's non-Hispanic black population was foreign-born. After a decade of heavy in-migration, there were nearly 70,000

Africans (born in a sub-Saharan African country) in New York City or 3.4 percent of the black population; Afro-Caribbeans (people of Afro-Caribbean ancestry) numbered about 524,000 or a quarter of the black population.[19] Because West Indians are the much larger group—and because, by now, there is a fairly extensive literature on their reactions to New York's racial order—the focus here is on them.[20] The term West Indian refers here to people of African descent from the English-speaking Caribbean, although what I say about race also pertains to immigrants from Haiti, who are also considered black. I do not include the growing number of Trinidadian and Guyanese immigrants of East Indian descent, whose ancestors were brought to the Caribbean as indentured laborers to replace slaves after emancipation. East Indians, as they are called in the Caribbean, are a separate, and fascinating, case, since they typically attempt to establish an Asian identity in New York as a way to avoid being labeled "black."

West Indians of African descent cannot avoid this designation. No matter how light their skin tones, immigrants (like the native-born) with known African ancestry continue to be delineated as black. Although legally in retreat, the peculiarly American "one-drop rule" that defined as black a person with as little as a single drop of black blood has had an enduring legacy. West Indians are increasingly visible in New York now that they are an ever-growing proportion of black New York, but they still often find themselves lumped with African Americans. Even when other New Yorkers recognize Caribbean immigrants as West Indian, as foreign, or, as many whites say, "from the islands," West Indians are seen as an ethnic group within the larger black population. Their racial status, in other words, is always salient.

Being viewed as black, and being identified with black Americans, has enormous consequences for their lives....

At one extreme, blatant interpersonal racism—physical attacks or threats, denials of housing or employment specifically for racial reasons, and harassment by the police—is unfortunately still with us. Less dramatic, but still painful, West Indians tell of an accumulation of racial slurs, insults, and slights, and of their sense that whites do not want to associate with them. Young black men, whom many whites see as potentially dangerous, have an especially hard time. It is not unusual for white women to cross the street or clutch their handbags when they see a young black man approach—and they do not stop to wonder whether the man is West Indian or African American. West Indian teenagers describe being followed in stores because they are suspected of shoplifting and having whites recoil from them in fear on the street, in the subway, and in parks. "Because when you go to the stores…people follow you around; you go on the bus and people hold their pocket books," one fourteen-year-old West Indian girl explained. "They don't discriminate against you because you're West Indian. They are discriminating against you because you're black."[21] Mary Waters notes that the teenage boys (from West Indian families) in her study reported far more racial harassment from whites and the police than did the girls, and they also felt less at ease when they left their all-black neighborhoods.[22]

Race is a primary factor in determining where West Indians live. Choice plays a role: like other newcomers, West Indians gravitate to areas with kinfolk and friends, where they find comfort and security in an environment of familiar institutions. Yet racial discrimination and prejudice put severe constraints in their way. West Indians are as segregated from whites as American black…. Real estate agents often steer West Indians to black neighborhoods or withhold information on housing availability elsewhere, and West Indians themselves often prefer communities where they can avoid racism and rejection. "Some neighborhoods," observed one West Indian New Yorker, "are not yet ready for black people. And I don't want to be a hero."[23] Those who have braved open hostility and branched out from

West Indian areas in Brooklyn and Queens to adjacent white communities find that their new neighborhoods become increasingly black. Antiblack prejudice tends to fuel a process of racial turnover as whites begin to leave and no new whites move in; at the same time, the growing number of black families makes the neighborhood seem more welcoming to West Indians (and native blacks) looking for homes. The result is a pattern of segregation in which West Indian residential enclaves are located in largely black areas of the city and the suburbs. Calculations of segregation indices based on 2000 census data indicate that Afro-Caribbean neighborhoods overlap substantially with those of African Americans in the New York metropolitan area, although interestingly Afro-Caribbeans are highly segregated from Africans.[24]

West Indians' lack of access to white neighborhoods—and the inevitable turnover that occurs when middle-class "pioneers" move into "white communities—confines the majority to areas with inferior schools, high crime rates, and poor government services and limits their informal contacts with white Americans. Outside of work (and sometimes at work as well), most West Indians find themselves moving in all-black social worlds. This is fortified, it should be noted, by patterns of marriage, which are another indication of continuing racial prejudice and the distinctive social distance separating whites and blacks in America. Census figures show that white Americans who intermarry are far more likely to wed an Asian or Hispanic than a black person—whether West Indian or African American.[25]

The sting of racial prejudice in New York is especially painful because West Indians come from societies with different racial hierarchies and conceptions of race…. African ancestry carries far more serious consequences in the United States than it does in their home societies, where people of African ancestry are the overwhelming majority (the exceptions are Trinidad and Guyana, with their enormous East Indian populations), where there are hardly any whites or Europeans, and where social class, occupation, wealth, ancestry, and education outweigh skin color in defining social status. A person with dark skin who is highly educated, wealthy, and holds a prestigious occupation is recognized for these characteristics—and is not stigmatized on the basis of his or her skin color. Indeed, one of the most profound adjustments to America is coming to terms with the fact that their skin color has such negative impact on their daily lives and aspirations.[26]

HISPANIC NEWCOMERS

Where Hispanic immigrants fit in is much more complicated. The very category Hispanic is open to contention—some who are labeled this way prefer to be called Latino, and others argue that the category is a statistical fiction that bears little relation to reality. The census treats Hispanic as an ethnic category, since it asks people who say they have Hispanic origins to indicate their race as well. But read nearly any New York newspaper or hear people talk on the street, and it becomes clear that Hispanic stands for something more than ethnicity. There has been a gradual racialization of Hispanics—a belief that physical characteristics, particularly skin color, are involved. Indeed, by treating Hispanics as a group equivalent to blacks in antidiscrimination and affirmative action policies, the federal government has contributed to raising Hispanic to the status of a racial category—what some journalists call a racialized demographic race.[27]

Forty years ago, New Yorkers spoke of Puerto Ricans as one of the city's two minority groups (the other was blacks), but today, in public discourse, the term Hispanic is commonly used. This is not just because the term is a fairly recent creation, coined by U.S. census takers as a way to count the Latin American population. The ethnic composition of New York City's Spanish-speaking population has undergone a sea change. Puerto Ricans first started arriving in large numbers after World War II, the migration peaking in the 1940s and 1950s; since

1970, more Puerto Ricans have left than entered the city. Moreover, the number of Dominicans, Mexicans, Colombians, Ecuadorians, and other Latin Americans in New York continues to rise so that by 2000, Puerto Ricans were only a little more than a third of the city's Hispanic population, down from 61 percent in 1980.[28] (Altogether in 2000, Hispanics were 27 percent of New York City's population.) In public discourse, Hispanics are generally thought of as belonging to a "brown" or "mixed race," but they include people of remarkable racial diversity, ranging from phenotypically white Hispanics who claim strong European heritage to those with dark skin and visible African ancestry.

The label "Hispanic" carries a stigma in New York, often conjuring up images of people who are brown- or tan-skinned, foreign in speech and manner, and unable or unwilling to adapt to U.S. laws, culture, and norms of hygiene.[29] . . .

If Hispanics are increasingly thought of as a race in popular discourse do they identify themselves this way? Immigrants with origins in Latin America and the Spanish-speaking Caribbean, after all, prefer to be known by their group of national origin, not as Hispanic or Latinos; although they share linguistic and cultural roots, they do not comprise a single coherent community, and are divided by, among other factors class, color, and generation.[30] Many second- or third-generation Latinos do not even speak Spanish. The category Hispanic can be seen, in many ways, as being imposed from above by dominant groups. Yet by treating Latinos/Hispanics as a single group, José Itzigsohn argues, the census and government agencies allocating resources, charities and nonprofit groups, and the media and their marketing techniques have combined to foster a sense of panethnic Hispanic/Latino identity. Indeed, Itzigsohn contends that the Latino or Latina label has a racial meaning, designating a racial position different from white and black. At the same time, he also notes that Hispanics adopt and use this label to construct their own personal and collective identities and projects, particularly when there is a common political advantage to cooperation. Panethnicity, in Itzigsohn's words, becomes part of the language of self-identification used by Latinos and Latinas and can be invoked or put aside in different moments for different purposes.[31]

Ongoing cross-national exchanges and interactions in daily life can also promote a sense of Hispanic or Latino identity. This is what Milagros Ricourt and Ruby Danta say has happened in the multiethnic Queens neighborhood of Corona they studied, where no single national group predominates in the Latino population and immigrants of diverse Latin American origins regularly interact in their daily lives on the streets and in apartments, houses, stores, workplaces, and churches. Shared language is a powerful unifier that makes communication and shared experiences possible. National identities remain primary, but a new overarching Hispanic or Latino identity has also emerged among Spanish-speaking immigrants from the Caribbean and South and Central America that can be mobilized by Latino panethnic leaders and organizations.[32]

If daily interaction, political mobilization, and cultural and linguistic commonalities can foster a sense of panethnic identity, another factor behind the desire to identify as Hispanic or Latino is the wish to avoid association with blackness and to be positioned in the racial classification system as non-black.[33] This denial of blackness may help explain why so many Hispanic New Yorkers—nearly half of the people in the New York metropolitan area who checked off Hispanic on the 2000 census—identified, in the race question, as "some other race."[34]

And this leads to the question of color. On one end, are white Hispanics of European ancestry who, if self-identification is anything to go by, are a substantial number. In the 1990 census, a quarter of New York City's Dominicans and over half of the Colombians and Cubans described themselves as white.[35] In 2000, in the wider metropolitan area, about two-fifths of those who checked off Hispanic in the census identified as white.[36] White Hispanics

often cannot escape the stigma associated with the Hispanic label. The remark by one Puerto Rican New Yorker, recorded in Oscar Lewis's *La Vida*, would doubtless strike a familiar chord with many new arrivals. "I'm so white," the respondent said, "that they've even taken me for a Jew, but when they see my Spanish name, they back right off."[37] According to sociologist Clara Rodriguez, regardless of color, knowledge of a person's "Hispanicity" often leads them to be thought of as "other," and "even an accent is heard when it was not before."[38]

Yet there are obvious advantages to being white. One study found that Dominicans who are perceived as white have lower poverty levels than, and enjoy advantages in the labor market over, their darker-skinned compatriots. "When I got my job in the laundry," said one extremely fair-skinned Dominican, "the owners said that even though I spoke Spanish, they would hire me because they didn't want any Blacks working for them."[39] An analysis of residential patterns based on 2000 census data found that Hispanics in the United States who described themselves as white were less residentially segregated from non-Hispanic whites than other Hispanics.[40] Presumably, many of the Hispanics who marry non-Hispanic whites—nationwide, in 1990, nearly half of the white men who intermarried wed Hispanics—are white or very light-skinned.[41]

Dominicans with African features and dark skin find it especially unsettling to be confused with African Americans since they come from a society where the category black is reserved for the highly disdained Haitians and where to be partly white (the case for most Dominicans) is to be nonblack. In the Dominican Republic, Dominicans of mixed phenotype tend to discount their African heritage and say they are "indios," seeing themselves as descendants of the Spanish and indigenous populations.[42] Dark-skinned immigrants from other Latin American countries experience a similar clash of racial orders in New York. Although each country in Latin America has evolved its own racial context because of its unique history, race is generally thought of as a continnum from black to white, with a large number of terms to describe those in-between. Moreover, income and education can have a lightening effect so that a "person who is called *negro* or *prieto* when he is poor and uneducated will almost always be described by some more flattering term, such as *trigueno*, if he rises in status."[43]

Where does this leave the many Hispanic immigrants in New York, whose skin color and other physical features do not qualify them as white but who tend not to be considered black either? In many ways, very much in the middle. These are the people New Yorkers usually have in mind when they use or hear the term Hispanic. On occasion, "not white, not black" Hispanic immigrants may find that they are taken for "light skinned blacks." But on the whole they have avoided the presumptions of inferiority associated with Africa and slavery and have been able to put a visible distance between themselves and black Americans.

Class distinctions add further complexity to the way Hispanic immigrants are seen. Whereas West Indians find that race remains a barrier whatever their class status, for white or light-skinned Hispanics, income, education, and occupation enhance and solidify the advantages they already enjoy. White or light-skinned Hispanic New Yorkers who enter the upper reaches of the middle class, become fluent English speakers, and adopt Anglo-American ways are able to move fairly easily in a native non-Hispanic white social world, and my own observations suggest that such people are increasingly accepted as "white."[44] Less happily, lower-class status reinforces and intensifies racial prejudice against mixed race and black Hispanic immigrants. Outside of New York City, in suburban areas, Hispanic immigrants from poor backgrounds who hold menial jobs—and who out of necessity often live in overcrowded quarters—have often found themselves the victims of animosity from white residents, who see the newcomers as eroding the quality of suburban life. In 2000, two

Mexican day laborers were beaten, nearly to death, in Suffolk County; in 2003, in another racially motivated incident, several white teenagers were charged with firebombing a Mexican family's home in Farmingville.[45]

ASIANS: THE ELASTICITY OF RACE

Asians have undergone a contemporary metamorphosis. The very term Asian is a new one in popular discourse, increasingly used since the post-1965 influx of immigrants from different Asian countries and now that the Chinese are less than half of the city's Asian population. (In 2000, the Chinese were just over 40 percent of the Asian total, followed by Indians, 23 percent, Koreans, 10 percent, and Filipinos, 7 percent.[46] In that year, Asians represented 11 percent of the city's population, up from about 2 percent in 1970). Once looked down on as the yellow peril, East Asians are now touted as the "model minority"—or as one sociologist has put it, "the best of the 'other' [than black or white] category."[47]

In the past, Asian groups were subject to blatant exclusion and discrimination on racial grounds. Until the recent immigration, Asian in New York meant Chinese. Not black, and not white, they were often portrayed as "slanty-eyed" and belonging to the "yellow race," One reason that Chinese immigrants huddled together in Chinatown was fear of racism in the world outside.

Racial prejudice against Asians was enshrined in restrictive immigration and naturalization laws. The Chinese Exclusion Act of 1882 singled out the Chinese as the first and only group to be excluded from the United States on the basis of race, ethnicity, or nationality, and by 1917, Congress had banned the immigration of most other Asians as well.[48] For much of the nation's history, Asian immigrants were denied the right to become citizens...

On the West Coast, where anti-Asian sentiments were particularly virulent, several states adopted laws prohibiting intermarriage between Asians and whites. A 1913 California law, targeting Japanese farmers, barred Asian immigrants from owning land. When a California court held, in 1885, that the public schools had to admit Chinese children, the state legislature passed a bill allowing school districts to set up separate schools for "Mongolians."[49] Most devastating of all, during World War II more than one hundred thousand Japanese Americans who lived on the Pacific Coast were forcibly evacuated and moved to internment camps.

Today, over fifty years later, it is hard to imagine that Asians, as "aliens ineligible for citizenship," used to be cast, as Yen Le Espiritu puts it, as "almost blacks but not blacks." Now the model minority stereotype renders them "almost whites but not whites."[50] New York's Asians rank just below non-Hispanic whites in the city's ethnoracial hierarchy—and they generally meet with greater acceptance from middle-class white New Yorkers than other racial minorities.

As compared to blacks and Hispanics, Asians are the least residentially segregated from non-Hispanic whites in the New York metropolitan area. Especially striking is the growing number of affluent suburban communities, like Scarsdale, where small numbers of Asians live in the midst of large white majorities.[51] Nationwide, there is a high rate of intermarriage between the children of Asian immigrants and non-Hispanic whites.[52] Moreover, a growing number of affluent white families in New York have adopted Asian children. By 1997, about eighteen hundred families belonged to the Greater New York chapter of Families with Children from China; by one account, there were, in that year, atleast one thousand adopted Chinese orphan girls under the age of five in the New York area.[53]

What accounts for the greater acceptance and changed perceptions of Asians today? Partly it is the class composition of the recent Asian immigration and the successes of their children. A large number of the new arrivals from Korea, the Philippines, Taiwan, Hong Kong, Japan, and India come with college degrees, ready to compete for middle-class careers, able to afford homes in middle-class areas,

and intent that their children advance through education. Many of their children have done extraordinarily well. National figures show that native-born Asians are substantially more likely to complete college than whites and other groups.[54] In New York, Asian students are overrepresented at the top of the academic ladder. They make up about half of the student body at Stuyvesant High School, the city's most selective public high school, where entrance is based on notoriously difficult exams.

Views of Asian immigrants' home countries have changed—and this is another factor behind the new racial perceptions. In the past; Americans saw Asia as a backward region. Now, Japan is a modern advanced nation and a world economic power; Singapore, Taiwan, South Korea, and Hong Kong emerged in the postwar period as important modern economies; and China is a major player in world politics and markets.

Asians may now seem *almost* white to some New Yorkers, but, as some have put it, yellow is not white.[55] Asians are still viewed as racially distinct, marked off by physical features and, even when born in the United States, often assumed to be newcomers or, in Mia Tuan's phrase, thought of as "forever foreigners."[56] In terms of skin color, Koreans, Japanese, Chinese "tend to register rather mildly on screens of 'white' American color sensitivity,"[57] The darker skin color of many Indian immigrants puts them at risk of being mistaken for African American, and they emphasixe their ethnic identity and distinctive history, customs, and culture as a way to avoid such mistakes.[58]

Asians still confront prejudice and discrimination. Indeed, a number of Asian-American scholars note that a downside of the model minority stereotype is that it diverts attention away from the existence of continued racism against Asians.[59] There are reports of racial slurs and insults—Korean immigrants, for example, being faced with "go back to China" or "no chinks allowed."[60]...

On occasion, Asians have been victims of racial attacks, and South Asians have been particularly vulnerable.... In the wake of the September 11th attack on the World Trade Center in 2001, South Asian Muslims (and Sikhs mistaken for Muslims) have faced a backlash....The development of a broader Asian identity movement also owes much to discriminatory practices in the United States—as Espiritu puts it, "to the racialization of Asian national groups by dominant groups as well as...responses to these constructions by Asian Americans themselves."[61] White Americans are often insensitive to ethnic differences among Asian populations. Virtually all of the second-generation Chinese and Korean Americans in Nazli Kibria's recent study had, at one time or another, been called *chink* or *Jap*: "By their very nature as racial slurs, these names are...generalized Asian designations; they are used against all Asians, regardless of ethnicity, as expressions of hostility, and those who use them are for the most part unconcerned about making distinctions between Asians."[62] The census classifies Asians as one of the six major racial categories; the media constantly refer to "Asians" often oblivious to nationality distinctions. Moreover, Asian Americans, like Hispanics, are treated as a homogeneous group administratively in distributing economic and political resources, thereby imposing a pan-Asian structure on persons and communities dependent on government support.[63] Indeed, Asian Americans are most likely to come together in situations where cooperation offers the ability to exert political influence to the common advantage.[64]

Unlike Hispanics, no common home-country language provides a basis for unity and communication among Asian Americans, and the cultural practices (including religion) of different national (and subnational) Asian groups are widely divergent. Indeed, research shows that ethnonational identities continue among second-generation Asian Americans. As Nazli Kibria argues, Chinese and Korean American, as well as many other Asian-origin, communities are institutionally and culturally dense, with "a rich and well-defined cultural tradition, in which members feel and experience a deep and extensive sense of belonging and support, as well as distinction and pride."[65] In contrast, a pan-Asian American ethnicity is "thin—something that organizes their existence in only sparse ways.[66]

WILL THE DESCENDANTS OF TODAY'S IMMIGRANTS BECOME WHITE?

And so we come to the future which, paradoxically, requires us, once again, to look back to the past. At the heart of any discussion of immigration and race in America is how today's Latino, Caribbean, and Asian immigration will affect the future of the color line. The notion that dark skin color will impede the progress of the current second and third generation rests on the assumption that today's racial views will continue to be dominant. This may not be the case. If the historical literature teaches us anything, it is that racial categories are highly changeable—and there has been a radical change in the meaning of race in the last hundred years. It is a measure of how dramatic the transformation has been that most Americans have forgotten that Jews and Italians were ever seen as separate races and an inferior kind of European. How did Jews and Italians become racial insiders and unambiguously "white"? Will any of the new groups repeat this pattern? Or will entirely new racial categories and divisions emerge in the wake of the recent immigration?

It may well be misleading to speak of Jews and Italians becoming white or of the whitening process since Jews and Italians were at the outset, in many contexts, recognized as white. But they did, eventually, become part of an all-encompassing white community; they were increasingly referred to (and thought of themselves) as white; and they were no longer viewed as races in the popular mind. It is in this sense that in *From Ellis Island to JFK* I wrote of Jews and Italians becoming "full-fledged whites," "unquestionably," or "fully" white, although perhaps it is preferable to speak, in more general terms, of racialization processes by which groups once disparaged as racial outsiders have become part of the racial majority. Whatever one calls the process, the insights of whiteness studies have helped focus our attention on it, understand it, and capture the dynamics involved A full history of how Jews and Italians, each in their own way, came to be thought of, and to see themselves, as members of a unified white race remains to be written, yet it is possible to sketch out the underlying factors involved.

One was the economic successes of Jews and Italians and their increased intermingling with other European groups. With postwar prosperity, as well as generous GI housing and educational benefits, the children, and later grandchildren, of turn-of-the-century Jewish and Italian arrivals did well. As members of the groups climbed the socioeconomic ladder and mixed residentially with people of northern and western European descent, "their perceived distinctiveness from the majority faded.... Intermarriage both marked the shift and accelerated it."[67]

Obviously, climbing the socioeconomic ladder and adopting the dominant society's ways were not enough to guarantee racial inclusion into the white mainstream. Other immigrant groups in this same period—the Chinese or Japanese, for example—who also became economically successful and assimilated to American ways remained outside the pale of whiteness. Jews and Italians, as I have emphasized, shared a safe haven of legal whiteness with other European groups from the very beginning—and they were not subject to the same kind of systematic, legal, and official discrimination that faced black and Asian immigrants. That the law declared southern and eastern Europeans white—and fit for naturalizations—was a powerful symbolic argument in their favor. Indeed, in early twentieth-century America, politicians often tailored their thinking about the desirability of new European immigrants in the context of campaigns in which the foreign vote counted.[68]

Italians and Jews may have ranked lower than northern and western Europeans but, in the racial continuum of the time, they were a step above Asians who, in turn, were relatively more desirable than blacks.[69] African Americans, it is well to recall, had only just been released from slavery when the last great immigration wave began—and not until the civil rights revolution of the 1960s would the structures of segregation in the American South begin to be dismantled. The racial notions underlying the response of whites toward blacks, as Stanley Lieberson has written, were both deeper and more pervasive than toward European immigrants, wherever they came from. Despite notions of the inherent inferiority of Jews and Italians, it was believed they could become acceptable by abandoning their strange cultures and becoming more "American."[70]

What, then, can we learn from the dynamics of the changing construction of race in the past? If the transformation of Jews and Italians into members of an all-encompassing white community had a lot to do with their starting-off points, their economic achievements, and their attempts to distance themselves from African Americans, will these factors play a role in the future? Of course, some of today's immigrants, like Russians, Poles, and other Europeans, are already recognized as white. But what about those who are now labeled nonwhite?[71] any of the immigrant groups currently thought of as not-white but not black come to be seen as white? Or is it misleading to pose the question this way? Just as "white" meant something different a hundred years ago than it does today, so, too, the very category white may become outmoded in the future as new ways of thinking about racial and ethnic differences, and new racial divisions, emerge. Whereas in the past, Jews and Italians were transformed from races into white ethnics without undergoing any physical change, today, when the language of color is so prominent in racial discourse, intermarriage and the blurring of physical differences among mixed-race offspring are often predicted to be the key agents of change.

Already, the centrality of the black-white divide, which dominated New York race relations for much of the twentieth century, is being challenged and changed by the growing number of Asians and Hispanics who do not fit clearly into either category. Indeed, given high Hispanic birthrates and the prospect of continued Asian and Hispanic immigration, the proportion of Asian and Hispanic New Yorkers will surely rise. High rates of intermarriage—and the growing number of multiracial offspring—are also an indication that we are moving toward a new kind of racial order. Intermarriage, as Joel Perlmann and Mary Waters observe, both reflects the lowering of racial divides that have already occurred and indicates that those divides will decline still further—as a result of intermarriage itself. Second-generation Hispanics and Asians commonly marry people in other ethnoracial groups, most often whites.[72] According to Zhenchao Qian's analysis of 1990 census data, nearly two-thirds of young U.S.-born Asians married non-Asians, the great majority of them whites; and nearly 40 percent of their Latino counterparts married non-Latinos, again the majority of them white.[73] Looking ahead, it is possible that the fourth or fifth generation descendants of the Hispanic and Asian immigrants of our time will be almost all of mixed origin, and almost all will also be the descendants of non-Asians and non-Hispanics.[74]

One scenario for the future suggests that there will be a shift in the way people are assigned to—and in the very meaning of—the category white. In this scenario, the lighter of the multiracials will join whites of European ancestry and light-skinned Hispanics to constitute an expanded white group. The white category, in other words, will be widened to include some new strands, perhaps even successful Asians as well. Of interest in this regard is the large number of immigrants who chose "white" as their racial identity in the 2000 census. Of the 28 million foreign-born counted, two-thirds said they were white, a significant increase over 1990, when half the foreign-born population checked white as their race. "White," suggest Kenneth Prewitt, will perhaps become the catch-all category for the most

new immigrants and their children, who may treat it as a synonym for opportunity and inclusion as it was for the southern and eastern European's a century ago.[75]

In another scenario, the category white will cease to be salient, and the current white-nonwhite division will give way to a new black-nonblack dichotomy. In this scenario, a white-Asian-Hispanic melting pot will be offset by a minority consisting of those with African ancestry—African Americans, Afro-Caribbeans, and African immigrants, and Hispanics of visible African ancestry. There have been speculations that the black category itself could expand, as the most unsuccessful portions of some immigrant groups (presumably darker in skin color) assimilate into the black population.[76]

A shift to a black-nonblack—or as Michael Lind has put it, a black beige—racial order is a troubling forecast, for it sees the boundary dividing blacks from other Americans as the most intractable in the nation, and blacks being consigned, once again, to racial exclusion.[77] It is based, unfortunately, on some hard realities. Although black-white intermarriages in the United States rose from a reported 65,000 in 1970 to 328,000 in 1995, the intermarriage rate is dramatically lower than for Hispanics and Asians.[78] Residential segregation patterns show a similar trend: people of African ancestry, native and immigrant alike, continue to be highly segregated from the white majority—much more so than Asians and lighter-skinned Latinos.[79] Just as the salience of the "Negro question" helped Jews and Italians fuse with Anglo-Americans into a unified white race, so today's immigrants often make efforts to distance themselves from African Americans as a way to gain acceptance and assert claims to equality with whites. Moreover, as I have emphasized, Asians and most Hispanics start out in an in-between status, neither black nor white. As such, they could easily become part of a new nonblack or beige majority.

If the nonblack-black scenario is a worrisome prospect for blacks, yet another forecast sees black-white relations evolving in a different way. In this scenario, increasing intermarriage and intermingling will reduce the salience of current racial and ethnic boundaries, including the black-white divide. "In a society characterized by increasing rates of movement, mixing, and intermarriage, and by growing numbers of persons who assert their multiplicity," write Cornell and Hartmann, "boundaries become less obvious, less potent, and far more difficult to maintain."[80]

One argument is that rates of intermarriage between blacks and whites, though low, are rising and many children of these marriages are demanding social recognition of their mixed ancestry. A hundred years from now, Stanley Crouch predicts, "Americans...will find themselves surrounded in every direction by people who are part Asian, part African part European, part Indian....The sweep of body types, combinations of facial features, hair textures, eye colors, and what are now unexpected skin tones will be far more common."[81] If many Asians and Hispanics are brought into the racial majority, this expansion could "dissolve the transparency of racial distinctions and thus impact upon the distinctions that set African Americans racially apart."[82]

In the aftermath of the civil rights revolution, there has been a remarkable growth in the black middle class as well as an expansion of black college enrollment. The more whites mix with blacks at work, on campus, and other social settings, the more their assumptions about the social meanings attached to skin color are apt to erode. This is especially likely in the upper-middle class, where class may end up trumping race as common school ties, elite occupational status, and various social connections and interests begin to blur ethnic and racial boundaries.

Already, as Gerald Jaynes notes, middle-class blacks often can avoid stigmatization by whites in everyday interactions by making their class position clear. He predicts that as the number of poor Asians and Latinos grows, the tradition of "confounding poverty and dependency with being African American" will die. At the same time, the growing presence of middle-class and elite minorities of color will render "African American and black too imprecise to be sustained as synonyms for 'underclass.'"[83]

Pressure for change may also come from the new multiple race option on the census. Although this option was not heavily used in 2000—only 2.4 percent of the people counted reported themselves as being of two or more races—this is likely to change. By expanding the racial classification system, the multiple race option may call into question the idea of a fixed number of discrete categories. Another possibility is an increase in the number of hyphenated groups that try to step outside the racial taxonomy altogether; "This strategy echoes how American Jews positioned themselves early in the twentieth century, when they resisted being racialized as nonwhite but also refused to become 'Anglo' and thereby lose their cultural identity.[84]

Perhaps, as Alba and Nee suggest, America might evolve in the direction of Latin American racial systems in which race/ethnicity "will lose some of its clear-cut categorical character; it will become more like a spectrum on which an individual's location will be determined by a number of social and physical characteristics and may shift from one social setting to another." Even if this happens, however, Alba and Nee argue that such a development would not eliminate a racial and ethnic stratification system, and placement in it would matter for the life chances of individuals.[85] In countries like Brazil, as David Hollinger points out, physical mixing of blacks and whites has "failed to achieve social justice and to eliminate a color hierarchy." Nor are racial inequalities the only kind of inequalities. As he notes, the "diminution of racism could, leave many members of historically disadvantaged ethno-racial groups in deeply unequal relations to whites simply by virtue of class position. Even the end of racism...would not necessarily ensure a society of equals."[86]

Just how the future will unfold, and which scenario will triumph, is hard to say. These scenarios are, after all, just that—possibilities that allow us to see some of the variables that might shape what happens in the years ahead. Indeed, it may well be that something altogether different will come to pass, involving an amalgam of some of the forecasts outlined above. The process of change is likely to be gradual, though it is bound to involve struggles and divisions, as some groups attempt to alter or widen existing racial categories while others resist. It seems a safe bet, however, that the racial order will look very different in thirty or forty years from the way it does now and that the changes will have enormous implications for the children of today's immigrants as well as for the immigrants of tomorrow. A hundred years ago, New Yorkers would never have imagined that Jews and Italians would be thought of, in racial terms, the same way as old-stock, White-Anglo-Saxon Protestants. As unforeseen economic, demographic, and political changes take place in the years to come, there will, no doubt, be equally astonishing surprises that lie ahead.

NOTES

1. Hattam 2001: 63.
2. Brodkin 1998; Barrett and Roediger 1997; Jacobson 1998; Topp 2003.
3. Guglielmo 2003; Gratton 2002.
4. Kolchin 2002: 165.
5. Arnesen 2001; Brody 2001; E. Foner 2001.
6. Guglielmo 2003: 93; Jacobson 1998: 6.
7. Lopez 1996.
8. Guglielmo 2003: 174.
9. E. Foner 2001.
10. On the development of a national Italian identity among Italians in the United States, see Guglielmo 2003 and Luconi 2001.
11. Grant 1916. *The Passing of the Great Race* appeared in 1916, but achieved peak popularity in the 1920s.
12. Quoted in Lind 1995: 108.
13. *New York; A Collection from Harper's Magazine* 1991: 304.
14. See Jacobson 1998: 171–199.
15. Barker, Dodd, and Commager, cited in Fitzgerald 1979: 79–80.
16. DeSalvo 2003: 28.
17. Dinnerstein 1994: 93; see also Daniels 1997: 104–105.
18. Ibid.: 86, 159.
19. Logan and Mollenkopf 2003. In these figures, Afro-Caribbeans refer to those with ancestry in predominantly black, non-Spanish-speaking nations such as Jamaica and Haiti.
20. See, for example, the full-length studies by Kasinitz (1992), Vickerman (1999), and Waters (1999a), as well as the chapters in Foner 2001e.
21. Bashi Bobb and Clarke 2001: 226.
22. Waters 2001.
23. Quoted in Waldman 1998.
24. Logan and Deane 2003; see also Crowder and Tedrow 2001.
25. Harrison and Bennett 1995; Bean and Stevens 2003.
26. Vickerman 2001a: 207, 210. See also the chapters in Foner 2001e.

27. Gonzales and Rodriguez 2003.
28. Dominicans are the second-largest Hispanic group, representing 27 per-cent of the city's Hispanic population, followed by South Americans (16 percent) and Mexicans (9 percent) (Logan and Mollenkopf 2003).
29. Cf. Fox 1996: 33.
30. Massey 1993.
31. Itzigsohn 2004; Foner and Fredrickson 2004. On the cole of New York's Hispanic marketing industry in the creation of panethnic categories and images of and for Latinos see Davila 2001. There are varying definitions of panethnicity. George Fredrickson defines panethnicity as what happens when previously discrete ethnic groups seek to join together in reaction to the dominant group's tendency to homogenize them for the purpose of discriminating against them (Foner and Fredrickson 2004). David Lopez and Yen Le Espiritu define panethnicity as "the development of bridging organizations and solidarities among subgroups of ethnic collectivities that are often seen as homogeneous by outsiders" (1997: 195).
32. Ricourt and Danta 2003.
33. Itzigsohn 2004.
34. Logan 2003.
35. Grasmuck and Pessar 1996: 284.
36. Logan 2003.
37. Quoted in Rodriguez 1994: 136.
38. Rodriguez 2000: 20.
39. Pessar 1995a: 42–43; Grasmuck and Pessar 1996.
40. Logan 2003.
41. Harrison and Bennett 1995: 165.
42. Grasmuck and Pessar 1996: 289–290; Pessar 1995b: 43.
43. Fox 1996: 24; Rodriguez 1996. See also Rodriguez 2000, ch. 6.
44. Andrew Hacker (2003) has recently made the same point.
45. Smith 2003.
46. Logan and Mollenkopf 2003. These figures refer to ancestry or origin.
47. Tuan 1998: 9.
48. For a detailed account of the history of legal restrictions on the Chinese, see Lee 2.003.
49. Wollenberg 1995.
50. Espiritu 1997: 109.
51. Alba et al. 1995.
52. In the late 1990s, more than a quarter of married Asians, including the native- and foreign-born, had a non-Asian spouse, typically someone white (Bean and Stevens 2003: 238–239).
53. Scott 1997; see also Sanjek 1994.
54. Harrison and Bennett 1995: 174. The odds of interracial marriage with whites sharply increases for Asian Americans with college and postgraduate educational attainment (Alba and Nee 2003: 265).
55. Tuan 1998: 164.
56. Tuan 1998.
57. Harold Isaacs, quoted in Mazumdar 1989: 34. In terms of color prejudice, "'brown,' even a non-American born as in Indonesians and Filipinos—is a good deal less mild; but it is 'black'—wherever it comes from—that sets the racial-color counters clicking the most

violently. The Indian, shading along a wide spectrum from fair to brown to black, arouses these reactions in varying measures."

58. See Lessinger 1995.
59. Other damaging consequences that have been mentioned are that it leads people to ignore the pressing needs of the significant number of poorer, less successful Asian immigrants; it may result in undue pressure on young Asians to do well in school and their careers; and it may be used to discredit blacks and His panics by implying that if only they worked and studied hard, they, too, would be as successful as Asians (see Kwong 1987; Takaki 1993; and U.S. Commission on Civil Rights 1992).
60. Dublin 1996: 146.
61. Espiritu 2004.
62. Kibria 1002: 72.
63. Espiritu 2004.
64. Foner and Ftedrickson 2004.
65. Kibria 2002: 199–200.
66. Ibid.: 199.
67. Alba and Nee 1997: 846.
68. Barrett and Roediger 1997: II.
69. Lieberson 1980: 30.
70. Ibid.: 34–35.
71. The very term nonwhite, as Roediger (2002: 17) points out, exemplifies the tendency in contemporary America "to place whites at the normative center of everything and to marginalize everyone else."
72. Perlmann and Waters 2004. Their analysis of the historical experience of Italian immigrants shows that after the birth cohort of 1906–10 (women who turned twenty on the eve of the Depression), outmarriage for second generation Italian women increased markedly, so that for the cohort of women who reached twenty during World War II, outmarriage stood at 41 percent.
73. Cited in Alba 1999: 18. See also Qian, Blair and Ruf (2001). According to an analysis of Current Population Survey data for 1995 to 2001, almost one-third of all married third-generation Asians and Latinos arc married to white (Bean and Stevens 2003:236).
74. This is what Joel Perlmann and Mary Waters (2.004) refer to as a "very strong hypothesis."
75. Prewitt 2004: 157. In 2000, almost half of the nation's Hispanics identified themselves as "white" on the census, a slight decline from 1990 when the percentage was 54 percent (Logan 2003).
76. For racial forecasts for the future see Alba 1999; Alba and Nee 2003; Bean and Stevens 2003; Gans 1999; Lind 1998; Perlmann and Waldiqger 1997; Saniek 1994.
77. Lind 1998.
78. Yetman 1999: 253. Black-white marriages were still against the law in every state but one south of the Mason-Dixon line as late as 1967, when a Supreme Court decision ended legal restrictions on marriage against any and all color lines (Hollinger 2003: 1365).
79. See Alba and Denton (2004), who note the sharp distinction between the typical residential situation of Latinos and Asians and that of African. Americans, who arc more likely to reside in areas where their own group is in the majority and white neighbors are infrequent. Despite continued large-scale in migration in the 1980s and 1990s, Asians and Hispanics remain

only moderately segregated from non-Hispanic whites. Black immigrants (including Latinos who self-describe as black) tend to be more segregated from whites, and channeled into or near black neighborhoods. An analysis of the segregation of black populations that looked at national metropolitan area averages found that the segregation of African Americans, Afro-Caribbeans, and the African-born from whites declined slightly between 1990 and 2000, but continued to be strikingly high (Logan and Deane 2003).

80. Cornell and Hartmann 1998: 244.
81. Crouch 1996: 170.
82. Alba 1999: 20.
83. Jaynes 2004: 115.
84. Prewitt 2004: 152, 157; sec also Hattam 2004.
85. Alba and Nee 2003: 290–291.
86. Hollinger 2003: 1389.

REFERENCES

Alba, Richard. 1999. "Immigration and the American Realities of Assimilation and Multiculturalism." *Sociological Forum* 14: 3–25.

Alba, Richard, and Nancy Demon. 2004. "The Old and New Landscapes of Diversity: Residential Patterns of Immigrant Minorities." *In Not Just Black and White: Historical and Contemporary Perspectives on Immigration, Race and Ethnicity in the United States,* edited by Nancy Foner and George Fredrickson New York: Russell Sage Foundation.

Alba, Richard, Nancy Denton, Shu-yin Leung, and John R. Logan. 1995 "Neighborhood Change under Conditions of Mass Immigration: The New York City Region, 1970–1990." *International Migration Review* 29: 625–656.

Alba, Richard, and Vicror Nee. 1997. "Rethinking Assimilation Theory for a New Era of Immigration." *International Migration Review 31: 816–874.*

———. 2003. *Remaking the American Mainstream.* Cambridge: Harvard University Press.

Arnesen, Eric, 2001. "Whiteness and the Historians' Imagination." International Labor and Working-Class History 60: 3–32.

Barrett, James, and David Roediger. 1997. "In between Peoples: Race Nationality and the 'New Immigrant' Working-Class." *Journal of American Ethnic History* 16: 432–445.

Bashi Bobb, Vilna, and Averil Clarke. 2001 "Experiencing Success: Structuring the Perception of Opportunities for West Indians." *In Islands in the City: West Indian Migration to New York,* edited by Nancy Foner. Berkeley: University of California Press.

Bean, Frank D., and Gillian Stevens. 2003. *America's Newcomers and the Dynamics of Diversity.* New York: Russell Sage Foundation.

Brodkin. Karen. 1998. *How Jews Became White Folks, and What That Says About Race in America.* New Brunswick, N.J.: Rutgers University Press.

Brody, David. 2001. "Charismatic History: Pros and Cons." *International Labor and Working-Class History* 60: 43–47.

Cornell, Stephen, and Doughlas Hartmann. 1998. *Ethnicity and Race* Thousand Oaks, Calif.: Pine Forge Press.

Crouch, Stanley. 1996. "Race is Over." *New York Times Magazine,* September 26, 170–171.

Crowder, Kyle, and Lucky Tedrow. 2001. "West Indians and the Residential Landscape of New York." *In Islands in the City,* edited by Nancy Foner. Berkeley: University of California Press.

DeSalvo, Louise. 2003. "Color: White/Complexion: Dark." *In Are Italians White? How Race Is Made in America*, edited by Jennifer Guglielmo and Salvatorc Salerno. New York: Routledge.

Dinnerstein, Leonard. 1994. *Antisemitism in America*. New York: Oxford University Press.

Dublin, Thomas (ed.). 1996. *Becoming American, Becoming Ethnic: College Students Explore Their. Roots.* Philadelphia: Temple University Press.

Espiritu, Yen Le. 1997. *Asian American Women and Men.* Thousand Oak Calif.: Sage Publications.

Fitzgerald, Frances. 1979. *America Revised.* New York: Vintage.

Foner, Eric. 2001. "Response to Eric Arnesen." *International Labor and Working-Class History* 60: 57–60.

Foner Nancy, (ed.). 2001e. *Islands in the City: West Indian Migration to New York.* Berkeley: University of California Press.

Fox, Geoffrey. 1996. *Hispanic Nation* New York: Birch Lane Press.

Gans, Herbert. 1999. "The Possibility of a New Racial Hierarchy in the Twenty-First Century United States." *In The Cultural Territories of Race: Black and White Boundaries*, edited by Michele Lamont. Chicago: University of Chicago Press.

Gonzalez, Patrisia, and Roberto Rodriguez. 2003. "The Unintended Census Race." *Hispanic Vista. com*, July 25.

Grant, Madison. 1916. *The Passing of the Great Race.* New York: Scribner's.

Grasmuck, Sherri, and Patricia Pessar. .1996. "Dominicans in the United States: First and Second Generation Settlement." In *Origins and Destinies*, edited by Silvia Pedraza and Ruben Rumbaut. Belmont, Calif.: Wadsworth.

Gratton, Brian. 2002. "Race, the Children of Immigrants, and Social Science Theory." *Journal of American Ethnic History* 21: 74–84.

Guglielmo, Thomas. 2003. *White on Arrival: Italians, Race, Color, and Power in Chicago, 1890–1945.* New York: Oxford University Press.

Hacker, Andrew. 2003. "Saved?" *The New York Review of Books*, August 14: 22–24.

Harrison, Roderick, and Claudette Bennett. 1995. "Racial and Ethnic Diversity." *In State of the Union*: *Volume Two, Social Trends*, edited by Reynold: Farley. New York: Russell Sage Foundation.

Hattam, Victoria C. 2001. "Whiteness: Theorizing Race, Eliding Ethnicity." *International Labor and Working-Class History* 60: 61–68.

Hollinger, David. 2003. "Amalgamation and Hypodescent: The Question of Ethnoracial Mixture in the History of the United States," *American Historical Review.*108: 1363–1390.

Itzigsohn, Jose. 2004. "The Formation of Latino and Latina Panethnic Identities." *In Not Just Black and White: Historical and Comtemporary Prespectives on Immigration, Race, and Ethnicity in the United States*, edited by Nancy Foner and George Fredrickson. New York: Russell Safe Foundation.

Jacobson, Matthew. 1998. *Whiteness of a Different Color: European Immigrants and the Alchemy of Race.* Cambridge: Harvard University Press.

Jaynes, Gerald, 2004. "Immigration and the Social Construction of Otherness: Underclass Stigma and Intergroup Relations." *In Not Just Black and White: Historical and Contemporary Perspectives on Immigration, Race and Ethnicity in the United States*, edited by Nancy Foner and George Fredrickson. New York: Russell Sage Foundation.

Kibria, Nazli. 2002. *Becoming Asian American: Second-Generation Chinese and Korean American Identities.* Baltimore: Johns Hopkins University Press.

Kolchin, Peter. 2002. "Whiteness Studies: The New History of Race in America." *Journal of American* History 89: 154–173.

Kwong, Peter. 1987. *The New Chinatown*. New York: Hill and Wang.

Lee, Erika. 2003. *At America's Gates*. Chapel Hill: University of North Carolina Press.

Lessinger, Johanna. 1995. *From the Ganges to the Hudson*. Boston: Allyn And Bacon.

Lieberson, Stanley. 1980. *A Piece of the Pie: Blacks and White Immigrants since 1880*. Berkeley: University of California Press.

Lind, Michael. 1995. "American by Invitation." *New Yorker*, April 24, 107–113.

———.1998. "The Beige and the Black." *New York Times Magazine*, August 16, 38–39.

Logan, John R. 1997. "The Ethnic Neighborhood, 1920–1970." Working Paper no. 112. New York: Russell Sage Foundation.

———. 2003. "How Race Counts for Hispanic Americans." Report of the Lewis Mumford Center, State University of New York at Albany.

Logan, John R., and Glenn Deane. 2003. "Black Diversity in Metropolitan America." Report of the Lewis Mumford Center, State University of New York at Albany.

Logan, John, and John Mollenkopf. 2003. "People and Politics in America's Big Cities: The Challenges to Urban Democracy." Paper presented at the conference on The Immigrant Metropolis: The Dynamics of Intergenerational Mobility in Los Angeles and New York, Russell Sage Foundation.

Lopez, Ian Haney. 1996. *White by law: The Legal Construction of Race*. New York: New York University Press.

Luconi, Stefano. 2001. *From Paesani to White Ethnics: The Italian Experience in Philadelphia*. Albany: State University of New York Press.

Massey, Douglas S. 1993. "Latinos, Poverty, and the Underclass: A New Agenda for Research." *Hispanic Journal of Behavioral Sciences* 15: 449–475.

Mazumdar, Sucheta. 1989. "Race and Racism: South Asians in the United States." *In Frontiers of Asian American Studies*, edited by Gail Nomura, Russell Endo, Stephen Sumida, and Russell Leong. Pullman: Washington State University Press.

New York: A Collection front Harper's Magazine. 1991. New York; Gallery Books.

Perlmann, Joel, and Roger Waldinger. 1997. "Second Generation Decline? Children of Immigrants, Past and Present: A Reconsideration." *International Migration Review* 32: 893–923.

Perlmann, Joel and Mary C. Waters. 2004. "Intermarriage Then and Now; Race, Generation and the Changing Meaning of Marriage." *In Not Just Black and White: Historical and Contemporary perspectives on Immigration, Race, and Ethnicity in the United States*, edited by Nancy Foner and George Fredrickson. New York: Russell Sage Foundation.

Pessar, Patricia. 1995a. *A Visa for a Dream*. Boston: Allyn and Bacon.

Prewitt, Kenneth. 2004. "The Census Counts, the Census Classifies." *In Not Just Black and White: Historical and Contemporary Perspectives on Immigration Race, and Ethnicity in the United States*, edited by Nancy Foner and George Fredrickson. New York: Russell Sage Foundation.

Qian, Zhenchao, Sampson Lee Blair, and Stacey Ruf. 2001. "Asian American. Interracial and Interethnic Marriages: Differences by Education and Nativity." *International Migration Review* 35: 557–586.

Ricourt, Milagros, and Ruby Danta. 2003. *Hispanas de Queens: Latino Panethnicity* in a *New York City Neighborhood*. Ithaca: Cornell University Press.

Rodriguez, Clara. 1994. "Challenging Racial Hegemony: Puerto Ricans in the United States." *In Race*, edited by Steven Gregory and Roger Sanjck. New J Brunswick, N.J.: Rutgers University Press.

———. 1996. "Racial Themes in the Literature: Puerto Ricans and Other Latinos." *In latinos in New York*, edited by Gabriel Haslip-Viera and Sherrie Baver. Notre Dame: University of Notre Dame Press.

———. 2000. *Changing Race: Latinos, the Census, and the History of Ethnicity in the United States.* New York: New York University Press.

Roediger, David. 2002. *Colored White: Transcending the Racial Past.* Berkeley: University of California Press.

Sanjek, Roger. 1994. "Intermarriage and the Future of Races in the United States." *In Race*, edited by Steven Gregory and Roger Sanjek. New Brunswick, N.J.: Rutgers University Press.

Scott, Janny. 1997. "Orphan Girls of China at Home in New York." *New York Times.* August 19.

Smith, Robert C. 2003. "Diasporic Memberships in Historical Perspective: Comparative Insights from the Mexican and Italian Cases." *International Migration Review* 37: 724–759.

Tataki, Ronald. 1993. *A Different Mirror.* Boston: Little, Brown.

Tuan, Mia. 1998. *Forever Foreigners or Honorary Whites?* New Brunswick, N.J.: Rutgers University Press.

U.S. Commission on Civil Rights. 1992. *Civil Rights Issues Facing Asian Americans in the 1990s.* Washington, D.C.: U.S. Commission Civil Rights.

Vickerman, Milton. 1999. *Crosscurrents: West Indian Immigrants and Race.* New York; Oxford University Press.

———. 2001a. "Jamaicans: Balancing Race and Ethnicity." *In New Immigrants New York*, edited by Nancy Foner. Rev. ed. New York: Columbia University Press.

Waldman, Amy. 1998. "Old Places, New Faces: In Southern Brooklyn, Coexistence But Not Quite Community." *New York Times* (City Section), April 12.

Waters, Mary C. 1999a. *Black Identities: West Indian Immigrant Dreams and American Realities.* Cambridge: Harvard University Press.

———. 2001. "Growing Up West Indian and African American: Gender and Class Differences in the Second Generation." *In Islands in the City: West Indian Migration to New York*, edited by Nancy Foner. Berkeley: University of California Press.

Wollenberg, Charles. 1995. "'Yellow Peril' in the Schools." *In The Asian American Educational Experience*, edited by Don Nakanishi and Tina Yamano Nishida. New York: Routledge.

Yetman, Norman. 1999. "Patterns of Ethnic Integration in America." *In Majority and Minority: The Dynamics of Race and Ethnicity in America*, edited by Norman Yetman. Boston: Allyn and Bacon.

JOURNALING QUESTION

Do you think the children of adopted Chinese girls will be white, or will a racialized identity remain? What about their grandchildren?

RACIALIZED AND RACIALIZING INSTITUTIONS

Economy and Work

19.

ECONOMIC IMPERATIVES AND RACE RELATIONS

The Rise and Fall of the American Apartheid System

SHERRY CABLE AND TAMARA L. MIX

It may sound strange to speak of an American "apartheid" system—after all, it's been a long time since racial segregation and discrimination were outlawed in the United States. But in this paper, Sherry Cable and Tamara L. Mix show that from the Civil War to the present day, black Americans in both the North and the South have been segregated into lower-paying occupations. In times of economic growth, they claim, black Americans can prosper, but when times are rough, black workers suffer more. In the 1970s, even as affirmative action programs were ending, the loss of skilled industrial jobs in the United States stabilized the earnings gap between black and white men—the black men earn only 75% of what the white men do. Is it inevitable, in a capitalist system, that some group will be exploited in the interests of other groups, or is economic and occupational justice possible?

...We argue that, because the industrial revolution arrived on U.S. shores after the Civil War, economic imperatives shaped the labor pool in a way that produced occupational segregation by race that subsequently spread to other social institutions. Our analysis of the historical connections between economic imperatives and race relations is derived from numerous written sources. Our contribution lies less in the discovery of new data than in our deployment of a wide variety of secondary sources to weave a logical argument and shed light on contemporary racial differentials in lifechances. We first analyze the connection between U.S. efforts to achieve global economic dominance and the construction and operation of the American apartheid system. We then examine the phase of unchallenged U.S. economic dominance concomitant with the dismantling of the apartheid system that was followed by the fading of U.S. dominance and White backlash against Black economic and political gains....

U.S. ASCENT TO GLOBAL DOMINANCE: THE CREATION AND MAINTENANCE OF THE AMERICAN APARTHEID SYSTEM

Between 1877 and 1918, the U.S. economy shifted from an agricultural to an industrial base. Elites' desire to contend for global economic dominance motivated the state to adopt actions that

---

Excerpted from Sherry Cable and Tamara L. Mix, "Economic Imperatives and Race Relations: The Rise and Fall of the American Apartheid Systems," *Journal of Black Studies*, 34, 2(2003), 183–203. References have been edited.

accommodated the economic imperatives of an industrial "wannabe" to expand production and compete with global powers. In this section, we describe the context of the emergence of occupational segregation, Northern and Southern forms of occupational segregation, and the spread of segregation to other institutions—political, residential, and educational—that forged a legal policy of racial apartheid that underlay the U.S. ascent to global economic dominance by 1945.

THE CONTEXT

The requisites for expanded production after the Civil War were a greatly enlarged industrial labor pool for Northern factories and a vast supply of Southern agricultural workers to replace the newly freed slaves. The state supported Northern industrialization through policies that augmented corporate privileges and increased the flow of immigrants. The state accommodated Southern labor needs through its nonenforcement of the civil rights amendments to the Constitution. These state actions in support of economic expansion created an atmosphere that was tolerant of racial and ethnic discrimination.

The state supported industrialism by extending to corporations legal rights that guaranteed the economic and political dominance of corporate elites. Public opposition to price and production control by corporate cartels pressured Congress in 1890 to pass the Sherman Antitrust Act. But the act was essentially nullified in an immediate series of U.S. Supreme Court decisions that progressively narrowed the interpretation of the 14th Amendment and perverted the amendment's intention from the protection of Black rights to the protection of corporate rights. Corporate attorneys argued that the amendment entitled corporations to the same status and rights as individuals and that corporate money was therefore protected by the due process clause of the amendment. McAdam (1982) finds that, between 1868 and 1911, 576 of the 604 U.S. Supreme Court decisions involving the 14th Amendment dealt with corporate rights rather than

Black rights. Of the 28 cases involving Black rights, rights were denied in 22. Thus, instead of serving as the constitutional foundation for the protection of Black rights, the 14th Amendment was distorted to consolidate corporate power and aid in the U.S. bid for global economic dominance.

With the infrastructure of a small industrial base already in place, the North was poised for rapid industrialization, but a large labor pool was required to keep wages down and profits soaring. The state responded with flexible immigration policies, through which the flow of immigration could be regulated to meet corporate requirements. A rapid influx of immigrants to the North quickly swelled workers' ranks: European immigration peaked between 1880 and 1917, when about 25 million non-Protestant, lower class, White ethnics arrived from southern and eastern European nations such as Italy, Russia, Poland, and the Austro-Hungarian Empire (Marger, 1991). The White ethnics expanded the labor pool, sharpened job competition, and depressed wages. Workers channeled their economic frustrations into conflict among themselves that heightened racist ideologies and that frequently erupted along racial and ethnic lines (Zinn, 1995).

State actions accommodated Northern and Southern labor needs by further weakening the foundation of Black rights. Legal challenges based on racial equity collapsed as U.S. Supreme Court rulings in support of racial segregation signaled the state's refusal to enforce post–Civil War amendments. In 1883, the Court declared that the Civil Rights Act of 1875 was unconstitutional. The 1896 *Plessy v. Ferguson* decision upheld a Louisiana statute mandating racially segregated railroad cars, ruling that the provision of separate facilities for Blacks and Whites was not a violation of constitutional rights. This decision established the "separate but equal" doctrine and constitutionally encouraged the passage of a comprehensive series of local statutes enforcing racial segregation throughout the South. Tagged as Jim Crow laws from the plantation song refrain "jump, Jim Crow," the statutes eroded Black rights and legally sanctioned widespread segregation.

OCCUPATIONAL SEGREGATION

The powerful combination of corporate economic and political dominance, intense and conflict-laden job competition, and federal tolerance of Jim Crow laws produced a legal and social environment in which occupational segregation by race was routinely accepted. Occupational segregation took different regional forms.

Northern Segregated Labor Unions

The occupational segregation of Northern Blacks was effected through the segregation of industrial labor unions. Corporate and political elites' common goal to make the nation a global economic power drove them to exploit workers through low wages, long work days, and dangerous working conditions. Industrial workers resisted by forming a labor movement and mounted a series of nationwide strikes that peaked in 1886, when 500,000 workers engaged in 1,400 strikes (Zinn, 1995). Corporate elites hired Pinkerton and other private police operatives to quell the rebellions, but the strikes nevertheless achieved some advances for White workers in wages and working conditions.

Black industrial workers did not benefit from corporate concessions to strikers because they were systematically excluded from the emerging labor movement. White ethnics were gradually assimilated into the dominant culture and institutions, but Blacks were not. Instead, they became a more focused target for White workers' competition-intensified racial animosities. White workers' marked racism was exacerbated by the corporate strategy to divide workers by using Blacks as strikebreakers. Early labor movement leaders recognized the greater pressure that could be applied on corporate interests by a racially united workforce, but their efforts failed to overcome workers' racism and integrate labor.

The failure of initial efforts to unite Black and White workers imprinted the labor movement with racism, establishing a norm that increased the likelihood that subsequent union-building would succumb to rank-and-file racism. The rigid segregation of labor unions produced occupational segregation and "created a privileged group of White workers at the expense of Black workers" (Foner, 1974, p. ix) that reinforced corporate labor control strategies and diluted labor union efforts to organize effectively in the major industries.

The Southern Cotton Tenancy System

Occupational segregation in the South was manifested in the cotton tenancy system. While the rest of the nation industrialized and either revolutionized agricultural methods or abandoned farming, the South remained "relentlessly rural, relentlessly agricultural, relentlessly cottonized, and relentlessly unmechanized" (Schwartz, 1976, p. 4). When federal troops were withdrawn at the end of Reconstruction, Southern large landowners' positions improved, but they confronted the problem of forming a labor pool without slavery that was large and cheap enough to farm their land profitably. The remedy was the cotton tenancy system, described in detail by Schwartz (1976).

The cotton tenancy system fostered the occupational segregation of Southern Blacks under conditions of extreme poverty. Both White and Black tenant farmers were injured by the system, but Black farmers were disproportionately harmed. Reconstruction had provided Blacks neither land nor money as compensation for enslavement. Thus, they began tenant farming at a distinct disadvantage from their White counterparts. With little incentive to move North because the unions excluded them, vast numbers of Southern Blacks were forced to rent farms and borrow heavily. As a consequence, Black farmers "sunk quickest and became trapped first" in the cotton tenancy system (Schwartz, 1976, p. 10).

THE SPREAD OF OCCUPATIONAL SEGREGATION TO OTHER INSTITUTIONS

Because of the overlap of social institutions, occupational segregation in the North and South infected other institutions and combined to forge a legal policy of racial separation. We focus particularly on the political, residential, and educational institutions.

Northern and Southern occupational control of Blacks was augmented by devastating constraints on Blacks' electoral leverage. For several generations after Reconstruction ended, the Democratic Party dominated in the South and the Republican Party elsewhere (McAdam, 1982; Schattschneider, 1960). As a consequence, competitive party politics dramatically diminished; with few exceptions, political contests were so uneven that "voters had no significant choices" (Schattschneider, 1960, p. 85). In the North, the total Black population was too small to warrant consideration by the dominant Republicans, leaving Northern Blacks' political leverage negligible (McAdam, 1982). In the South, where a far larger proportion of the electorate was Black, outright disfranchisement nullified numerical superiority. Beginning in 1890 Mississippi, a series of statutes passed by Southern states and municipalities revoked Blacks' right to vote, employing a variety of measures such as poll taxes, residency requirements, literacy tests, and property ownership (Marger, 1991). The statutes produced nearly total Black disfranchisement in the South by the early 20th century and rendered Blacks with no political leverage against a Democratic Party dedicated to White supremacy. Without political power, Blacks had no legitimate avenue to oppose occupational segregation and its effects multiplied geometrically.

Occupational segregation led directly to residential segregation. Without reliable transportation, both Black and White Northern industrial workers tended to live close to their job sites in densely populated tenements. Because of racist ideologies, workers settled into racial and ethnic enclaves. Over time, most White ethnics were assimilated, achieving higher occupational positions that allowed them to move into higher status neighborhoods where they interacted with White Anglos. Blacks were not assimilated and remained segregated in deteriorating urban neighborhoods. In the rural South, Black tenant farmers were geographically dispersed in tightly segregated settlements. Residential segregation assured that the regular social interaction between Blacks and Whites that might have mitigated racist ideologies was severely curtailed and animosities maintained.

Educational segregation was a product of both residential segregation and Congressional mandate. Residential segregation assured educational segregation because schools were typically organized as neighborhood schools, leaving them separated by race, class, and ethnicity. The 1917 Smith-Hughes Act was intended to foster industrialization and increase U.S. competitiveness in world markets by providing federal support for primary and secondary vocational education (Rushing-Edwards, 1998). Advocating a class-based curriculum that differentiated vocational from academic training, the act endorsed race-based vocational education for agricultural, domestic, and low-skilled industrial workers (Spring, 1986). Educational segregation took slightly different regional forms.

In the North, corporate and state elites identified the non-Anglicized immigrant as the most serious impediment to U.S. economic dominance. Perceiving public education as the remedy, they urged educators to improve schools in ways that would make the American worker more productive and the nation more competitive in the global economic race. Educational leaders and school boards, made up primarily of professionals and business elites, adopted the factory model of production to organize schools (Spring, 1986). Blacks and immigrants received strikingly inferior educations to those of the rich, as their educations prepared them for positions as factory workers and domestics.

The South consistently lagged behind the rest of the nation in establishing tax-supported public schooling. Southern states in 1890 had the highest illiteracy rates and the lowest educational levels in the country (Rushing-Edwards, 1998). Black leaders promoted public schools as the path for advancing their position in society (Rushing-Edwards, 1998). But large landowners saw little benefit in public education and were committed, instead, to maintaining a cheap labor pool to support the largely agricultural economy (Wright, 1986). They were joined in opposition to public education by many poor Whites, who feared job competition with educated Black workers (Anderson, 1988; Wright, 1986). As a result, public schools were developed in the South that most suited the economic needs of the large landowners.

The consequence of public schools structured to fit economic imperatives was minimal education for Blacks (Ayers, 1992; Link, 1988). Northern schools focused on the integration of European immigrants and Black migrants into an industrial workforce, whereas Southern schools supported Black agricultural and domestic education. Education legitimated occupational segregation and reproduced the stratification system.

Permeating, reinforcing, and justifying the structures of racial segregation was a hegemonic cultural ideology that devalued all non-Anglos but particularly Blacks. Racist ideologies legitimating the denial of Black rights on the grounds of inferiority were supported, justified, and given scientific validity through Social Darwinism. Schools, churches, and the popular literature taught that individual achievement was due to racial traits, a sign of White Anglos' innate superiority. The racist rhetoric popularized by nativist movements made a patronizing, moral obligation of the imposition of Anglo culture on non-Anglos and the continued subordination of Blacks.

APARTHEID AND ECONOMIC DOMINANCE

Widespread segregation in the North and South by 1918 produced a new form of legalized Black enslavement, the American apartheid system. The characteristic structural overlap of social institutions carried occupational segregation, driven by the needs of economic expansion and legitimated by a hegemonic culture that endorsed racist ideologies, into other institutional realms and paved the way for a wider, deeper racial segregation. With disfranchisement nearly eradicating Black economic and political rights, statutes and customs in the North and South restricted Blacks in all areas of social life. Black Americans were routinely denied the vote, due process, and upward mobility; they were sequestered in inferior neighborhoods, schools, and public facilities. The racial stratification system qualifies as an apartheid system because it was an extreme form of legal, political-economic, race-based stratification in which the non-White minority was by law spatially and socially separated and kept from equal opportunities in occupation, political participation, and education.

As surely as the antebellum Southern plantation economy had been founded on slavery, so the U.S. ascent to global economic dominance was founded on the American apartheid system. State and corporate elites maintained the apartheid system to assure the occupational segregation that produced the large competitive labor pools that fueled rapid economic expansion. State intervention increased in economic and social policies to the point that a symbiotic relationship emerged between corporations and the state (Kolko, 1967).

World War I stimulated demands for war materials, requiring increased laborers in steelmaking, meatpacking, auto manufacturing, munitions, shipyards, mines, and transportation. The demand for a larger labor force coincided with an intense labor shortage, due to males' induction into the armed services and new restrictions on European immigration generated by widespread nativist sentiments. The labor shortage appeared to be a boon to Southern Blacks because it created new employment opportunities (Foner, 1974; Leiman, 1993). Hundreds of thousands of Southern Black workers migrated to the North between 1915 and 1918. But corporations and unions arrived at unwritten agreements that confined Blacks to low-level and menial occupations (Foner, 1974). At war's end, White soldiers returned and generated severe competition for even menial jobs that resulted in Whites' intimidation of Blacks. Massive numbers of Blacks were discharged and replaced by White workers. An industrial working class arose with the emergence of effective labor unions, but racial antipathy kept the unions segregated.

The October 1929 stock market crash precipitated a severe global economic crisis. Although the Great Depression bore some similarities to other economic downturns, it was unprecedented in its length and in the level of poverty it brought. The state significantly increased its active role in economic policy; government controls became more direct. The depression was a disaster for all workers—unemployment rose from 3 million to between 15 and 17 million (Foner, 1974, p. 189). But it devastated Black families more than Whites because they lived closer to the margins of survival. In 1929, about one fifth of all Black industrial workers were unemployed, based on the principle of last-hired, first-fired (Foner, 1974). During the 1930s, from one third to one half of the Black labor force was unemployed—more than 50% higher than that for native Whites (Leiman, 1993) and significantly higher than for foreign-born Whites (Foner, 1974). Blacks lost jobs in the industrial, agricultural, and service sectors. In the North, White workers displaced Blacks even in common labors—building roads, digging ditches, and repairing railroad tracks. In the South where 68% of Blacks resided in rural areas and were employed in cotton farming, cotton crop production dropped substantially and cotton's dominant role in the Southern economy ended (McAdam, 1982). The absence of agricultural jobs drove Blacks to urban areas and northward (Foner, 1974). At lowered wages, Whites took over service jobs from Black waiters, hotel workers, elevator operators, and in nearly all areas. When Blacks did not peacefully surrender their jobs, vigilante groups were frequently organized to intimidate them (Foner, 1974, p. 189). In some sections of the country, 80% of the Black population was on public assistance (Pinkney, 2000). Under the American apartheid system, Black families felt the effects of the depression first and bore its heaviest burdens.

Roosevelt's New Deal policies for ending the depression had two primary purposes: the reorganization of capitalism to stabilize the boom-and-bust business cycle, and the provision of enough unemployment aid to reduce the appeal of radical groups. Foner (1974) argues that the New Deal generally acquiesced to racebased wage differences that divided the working class and hurt all workers by diminishing the chances of Black and White workers uniting in protest. But Pinkney (2000) asserts that, despite drawbacks, the policies offered Blacks benefits such as appointment to agency positions, increased unemployment benefits, and a more favorable political climate for the pursuit of Black civil rights. Whatever the costs and benefits of the New Deal for Black workers, occupational segregation was unabated, economic recovery came at the disproportionate expense of Blacks, and the apartheid system was maintained.

Discrimination in education continued between the world wars. Public education policy was vitally shaped in the first half of the century by industrial philanthropist families such as the Rockefellers and the Rosenwalds, who formed a network of institutional elites with interlocking directorates. The Rockefeller family's General Education Board, established in 1903, eventually acquired significant control of national educational philanthropy (Rushing-Edwards, 1998) and assured White control of Black institutions by routinely supporting White supremacy, separate and unequal funding for primary and secondary education, industrial education for Northern Blacks, and farming and home economics education for Southern Blacks.

The U.S. entrance into World War II and the consequent demand for the production of war materials generated in a wave of widespread prosperity that the nation rode to postwar global economic dominance. Southern Blacks moved North to work in war industries. Although Blacks serving in the military were rigidly segregated, discrimination in war industries abated when the threat of a massive march by Blacks in Washington, D.C., pressured Roosevelt to issue an executive order barring racial discrimination in industries with government contracts. The United States's military leadership role in World War II and the postwar transition from war production to peacetime production readied the nation's economic take-off and its replacement of Great Britain as the number one economic power in the world. This pinnacle was achieved because of the American apartheid system, which assured conflict among laborers and buried Blacks at the bottom of a hierarchy that was perpetually reproduced through political and educational institutions.

ECONOMIC DOMINANCE, ECONOMIC DECLINE: FROM LIBERATION BACK TO SEGREGATION

We have argued that economic imperatives led to occupational segregation and the construction of the American apartheid system. In this section, we briefly track changes in economic imperatives from 1945 to the present to examine their continuing effects on race relations and the fate of the apartheid system.

ECONOMIC DOMINANCE AND THE FALL OF APARTHEID

In the postwar period, the United States experienced unparalleled economic prosperity and achieved world economic dominance. Between 1945 and 1970, global redistribution of the production of goods and services promoted U.S. economic development: U.S. workers produced most of the manufactured goods and U.S. farms produced most of the food consumed in the United States, Western Europe, and Japan (Schaeffer, 2003, p. 20). State intervention in the economy expanded further to promote and maintain continuing economic

growth, facilitating capital accumulation via policies favorable to business. The multinational corporation arose in a "most forceful convergence of state and corporation" (Marger, 1987, p. 118).

The explosion in U.S. production and wealth that occurred between 1945 and 1970 altered the stratification system. Economic prosperity fostered the emergence of an urban middle class of White business and professional families. Expanded production significantly increased the demand for labor. As a consequence, the wages and working conditions of most industrial laborers were considerably improved (Rothman, 1999). Although labor unions continued racist practices and policies (Foner, 1974), jobs were so plentiful that large numbers of Black workers were able to enter more skilled industrial jobs and technical careers. A substantial Black middle class emerged for the first time in U.S. history. As wages rose and economic growth continued to expand, the apartheid system fell. Its demise, like its creation, was closely linked to global economic processes. Two forces combined to bring down the American apartheid system: internal pressures from Black activists and external pressures from U.S. trade partners.

Effectively blocked from conventional political participation, Blacks had consistently struggled against the apartheid system through social movement activities (Jalata, 2002). Perhaps the most prolonged and ultimately successful movement began in the early 20th century and bore fruit in the postwar era. This critical effort focused on educational segregation. Many Black leaders rejected Booker T. Washington's assimilationist plan for Blacks' gradual acquisition of citizenship rights as they proved their worth to Whites through vocational industrial education. W.E.B. Du Bois and others emphasized education that promoted political action and, in 1909, they founded the National Association for the Advancement of Colored People (NAACP), calling for desegregation, access to equal educational opportunities, the right to vote, and the enforcement of the 14th and 15th Amendments (Pinkney, 2000).

The NAACP began an aggressive, long-term strategy of legal challenges to educational segregation.

Beside the internal pressures from Black resistance, external criticisms from other nations influenced state actions on the apartheid system. In the postwar era of global anticommunism and the decolonization of non-White nations, the American apartheid system became an obstacle to U.S. efforts to promote democracy over communism (Horne, 1996; Lyman, 1991; McAdam, 1982; Rushing-Edwards, 1998; Skrentny, 1998). Western European trading partners and allies, Soviet detractors, and newly decolonized Third World governments pressured the United States to eradicate White supremacy at home to fortify and legitimate its foreign policy efforts and maintain its world leadership role. U.S. leaders responded. Truman in 1946 created the first national committee on civil rights and, in 1948, issued an executive order that banned racial segregation and discrimination in the military. The U.S. Supreme Court began in 1946 to issue rulings against segregation in various venues.

External criticisms of U.S. racism in 1954 converged with the NAACP's legal strategy of challenging segregated schools to generate the beginning of the end of the American apartheid system. In *Brown v. Board of Education of Topeka* (1954), the Supreme Court ruled that racial segregation in public schools was inherently unequal and a violation of the 14th Amendment. The *Brown* decision forcefully struck down the "separate but equal doctrine" and established the legal basis for two decades of Black insurgency aimed at shattering the apartheid system. McAdam (1982) identifies specific periods of subsequent Black insurgency. *Brown* inspired the first period, from 1955 to 1960, in which insurgency characterized by petitions, sit-ins, and the bus boycott was led by Black churches, historically Black colleges, and Southern local NAACP branches. The peak of Black insurgency from 1961 to 1965 featured the founding of dozens of Black liberation movement organizations; massive demonstrations; countless sit-ins at all-White lunch counters, barbershops, laundromats, and train stations; voter registration drives; economic boycotts; and court actions. Congress passed the Civil Rights Act in 1964 and the Voting Rights Act in 1965. Black insurgency then declined between 1966 and 1970, after successfully unraveling the American apartheid system of de jure discrimination. Thus, economic imperatives significantly contributed to both the construction of the apartheid system and its demise.

ECONOMIC DECLINE: WHITE BACKLASH AND DE FACTO OCCUPATIONAL SEGREGATION

In 1971, just as Blacks began to experience more parity in occupational and educational opportunities and to anticipate greater equality in all societal sectors, the United States posted a modest trade deficit. The deficit was the first since 1893, but it signaled the loss of a significant share of U.S. manufacturing and a trend toward the globalization of production (Schaeffer, 2003). Between 1970 and 1979, U.S. global economic dominance waned as Western European and Japanese corporations doubled their share of world manufacturing (Schaeffer, 2003). The deindustrialization of the 1970s was followed in the 1980s and 1990s by changes in U.S. monetary and trade policies that encouraged U.S. corporations to reorganize production. Reorganization was accomplished in manufacturing and service industries by merging with other firms, deploying technologies that automated less skilled work, and laying off workers (Rothman, 1999; Schaeffer, 2003). Consequently, U.S. industries regained markets in the 1990s, when Japanese and Western European economies slumped.

Deindustrialization significantly reduced the proportion of manufacturing jobs. The corporate downsizing that accompanied reorganization further reduced jobs and lowered wages. A major consequence of deindustrialization and downsizing was the channeling of the labor force into high-skill and low-skill employment (Rothman, 1999; Schaeffer, 2003). New, high-skill jobs with above-average wages were created, but they were typically organized around specialized expertise, such as computers, and required a minimum of a college education. Low-skill jobs—cashiers, janitors, retail salespersons, waiters—brought low wages and few benefits. A hole appeared in the traditional occupational structure with the disappearance of a stable sector of the economy that had previously provided skilled jobs (Rothman, 1999).

These economic shifts after 1970 intensified job competition and brought an abrupt return to race-based, occupational segregation—a de facto occupational segregation. Progress halted in the reduction of the earnings gap between White men and Black men, stagnating at about 75% since the 1980s (Bennett, 1995). In the dichotomization of the occupational structure, Black workers were disproportionately left in low-skill jobs and reduced to part-time work (Rothman, 1999). The new occupations requiring college training did not benefit working-class Black workers who were unable to attain such training.

The occupational segregation of Blacks again promoted segregation in other social spheres. By the late 1970s, inflamed racial sentiments erupted in a White backlash against Black economic and political gains. Whites protested affirmative action programs with claims of "reverse discrimination." The seminal legal case is the *Regents of the University of California v. Allan Bakke* (1978), in which a White applicant denied admission to medical school sued the school for giving preferential treatment to minorities. The U.S. Supreme Court ruled in 1977 that the university's admissions program violated Title VII of the Civil Rights Act of 1964.

That and subsequent similar rulings legitimated the view of many Whites that racial parity had been achieved and that further attempts would discriminate against Whites. With *Bakke* as legal precedent, many quota systems, affirmative action programs, and busing-for-school-segregation were subsequently abandoned across the country. Black workers were once again relegated to low-paid and dead-end jobs, segregated in dangerous neighborhoods with poor public services, and forced to send their children to understaffed, underequipped schools. With fewer opportunities for upward mobility, greater numbers of families fell into an underclass disproportionately made up of Blacks (Massey, 1990).

REFLECTIONS

Economic imperatives drive the structure of the labor market in capitalist societies. Many analysts have asserted the relationship between economic trends and race relations. A few have empirically documented the relationship for specific time periods. Our contribution in this article is the presentation of a panoramic sweep of U.S. history that indicates the continual penetration of economic imperatives into other social institutions. A competitive labor market is necessary to keep wages down and profits up. Someone must be at the bottom of the labor heap and dark skin is an easily identifiable mark: Skin color matters. Occupational segregation pierces and shapes social institutions to segregate Black Americans at the bottom of all social hierarchies.

U.S. economic dominance established the conditions under which apartheid was dismantled. But, just when Black liberation seemed most promising, economic decline brought a return to racial business-as-usual. Success and failure were achieved at nearly the same historical instant. High expectations were met with closed doors; efforts at upward mobility were met with hate crimes, racial profiling, and the grotesque and lethal mutilation of an ordinary Black family man in Jasper, Texas. Are we entering another cycle of Black enslavement and resistance? If so, the cycle is unlikely to be stopped again by forces accompanying economic dominance—global economic processes are unlikely in the near future to result in one nation's dominance. One might reasonably wonder if the greatest current threat to U.S. security is the continuing exploitation of Black Americans for the sake of economic growth.

REFERENCES

Anderson, J. D. (1988). *The education of Blacks in the South, 1860–1935.* Chapel Hill: University of North Carolina Press.

Ayers, E. L. (1992). *The promise of the New South,* New York: Oxford.

Bennett, C. (1995). *The Black population in the United States* (Current Population Reports, Series, pp. 20–480). Washington, DC: Government Printing Office.

Brown v. Board of Education of Topeka, U.S. Supreme Court, 347 U.S. 483 (1954).

Foner, P. S. (1974). *Organized labor and the Black worker, 1619–1973.* New York: Praeger.

Horne, G. (1996). Race for the globe: U.S. foreign policy and racial interests. In B. P. Bowser & R. G. Hunt (Eds.), *Impacts of racism on White Americans* (pp. 88–112). Thousand Oaks, CA: Sage.

Jalata, A. (2002). Revisiting the Black struggle: Lessons for the 21st century. *Journal of Black Studies, 33,* 86–116.

Kolko, G. (1967). *The triumph of conservatism: A reinterpretation of American history.* New York: Free Press.

Leiman, M. M. (1993). *The political economy of racism: A history.* London: Pluto Press.

Link, W. A. (1988). Privies, Progressivism, and public schools: Health reform and education in the rural South, 1909–1920. *Journal of Southern History, 54,* 4.

Lyman, S. M. (1991). The race question and liberalism: Casuistries in American constitutional law. *International Journal of Politics, Culture, and Society, 5*(2), 183–247.

Marger, M. N. (1987). *Elites and masses.* Belmont, CA: Wadsworth.

Marger, M. N. (1991). *Race and ethnic relations: American and global perspectives.* Belmont, CA: Wadsworth.

Massey, D. S. (1990). American apartheid: Segregation and the making of the underclass. *American Journal of Sociology, 2,* 329–357.

McAdam, D. (1982). *Political process and the development of Black insurgency, 1930–1970.* Chicago: University of Chicago Press.

Pinkney, A. (2000). *Black Americans.* Upper Saddle River, NJ: Prentice Hall.

Plessy v. Ferguson, U.S. Supreme Court, 163 U.S. 537 (1896).

Regents of the University of California v. Allan Bakke, U.S. Supreme Court, 438 U.S. 265 (1978).

Rothman, R. A. (1999). *Inequality and stratification: Race, class, and gender.* Upper Saddle River, NJ: Prentice Hall.

Rushing-Edwards, W. (1998). *Mediated inequality: The role of governmental, business, and scientific elites in public education.* Unpublished doctoral dissertation, Department of Sociology, University of Tennessee–Knoxville.

Schaeffer, R. K. (2003). *Understanding globalization: The social consequences of political, economic, and environmental change.* New York: Rowman & Littlefield.

Schattschneider, E. E. (1960). *The semisovereign people.* Hinsdale, IL: Dryden Press.

Schwartz, M. (1976). *Radical protest and social structure: The Southern Farmers' Alliance and cotton tenancy, 1880–1890.* Chicago: University of Chicago Press.

Skrentny, J. D. (1998). The effect of the cold war on African-American civil rights: America and the world audience, 1945–1968. *Theory and Society, 27,* 237–285.

Spring, J. (1986). *Education and the rise of the corporate state: The American school.* New York: Longman.

Wright, G. (1986). *Old South New South: Revolutions in the Southern economy since the Civil War.* New York: Basic Books.

Zinn, H. (1995). *A people's history of the United States: 1492–present.* New York: HarperCollins.

JOURNALING QUESTION

In your own experience, what job categories are most often occupied by black men? By black women?

20.

ARE EMILY AND GREG MORE EMPLOYABLE THAN LAKISHA AND JAMAL?

A Field Experiment on Labor Market Discrimination

MARIANNE BERTRAND AND SENDHIL MULLAINATHAN

It is one thing to think about racism as a vague, general force in society. It is another to think about how it actually works in the lives of individuals. When someone applies for a job, there are any number of reasons why that person might, or might not, get it, and it is hard to evaluate the role that racism might play. Marianne Bertrand and Sendhil Mullainathan used an experimental technique to isolate this role. Their data show that regardless of the quality of the resume, names that sound African American do less well. If parents dropped "ethnic sounding" names of all types, or if employers were required to review applications with the names blanked out, would that lessen racial discrimination in employment?

Every measure of economic success reveals significant racial inequality in the U.S. labor market. Compared to Whites, African-Americans are twice as likely to be unemployed and earn nearly 25 percent less when they are employed (Council of Economic Advisers, 1998). This inequality has sparked a debate as to whether employers treat members of different races differentially. When faced with observably similar African-American and White applicants, do they favor the White one? Some argue yes, citing either employer prejudice or employer perception that race signals lower productivity. Others argue that differential treatment by race is a relic of the past, eliminated by some combination of employer enlightenment, affirmative action programs and the profit-maximization motive. In fact, many in this latter camp even feel that stringent enforcement of affirmative action programs has produced an environment of reverse discrimination. They would argue that faced with identical candidates, employers might favor the Africans-American one.[1] Data limitations make it difficult to empirically test these views. Since researchers possess far less data than employers do, White and African-American workers that appear similar to researchers may look very different to employers. So any racial difference in labor market outcomes could just as easily be attributed to differences that are observable to employers but unobservable to researchers.

To circumvent this difficulty, we conduct a field experiment that builds on the correspondence testing methodology that has been primarily used in the past to study minority outcomes in the United Kingdom.[2] We send resumes in response to help-wanted ads in Chicago and Boston newspapers and measure callback for interview for each sent resume. We experimentally manipulate perception of race via the name of the fictitious job applicant. We randomly assign very White-sounding names

Excerpted from Marianne Bertrand and Sendhil Mullainathan, "Are Emily and Greg Move Employable Than Lakisha and Jamal? A Field Experiment on Labor Market Discrimination," *The American Economic Review* 99 (2004): 991–1011. Notes and references have been edited.

(such as Emily Walsh or Greg Baker) to half the resumes and very African-American-sounding names (such as Lakisha Washington or Jamal Jones) to the other half. Because we are also interested in how credentials affect the racial gap in callback, we experimentally vary the quality of the resumes used in response to a given ad. Higher-quality applicants have on average a little more labor market experience and fewer holes in their employment history; they are also more likely to have an e-mail address, have completed some certification degree, possess foreign language skills, or have been awarded some honors.[3] In practice, we typically send four resumes in response to each ad: two higher-quality and two lower-quality ones. We randomly assign to one of the higher- and one of the lower-quality resumes an African-American-sounding name. In total, we respond to over 1,300 employment ads in the sales, administrative support, clerical, and customer services job categories and send nearly 5,000 resumes. The ads we respond to cover a large spectrum of job quality, from cashier work at retail establishments and clerical work in a mail room, to office and sales management positions.

We find large racial differences in callback rates.[4] Applicants with White names need to send about 10 resumes to get one callback whereas applicants with African-American names need to send about 15 resumes. This 50-percent gap in callback is statistically significant. A White name yields as many more callbacks as an additional eight years of experience on a resume. Since applicants' names are randomly assigned, this gap can only be attributed to the name manipulation.

Race also affects the reward to having a better resume. Whites with higher-quality resumes receive nearly 30-percent more callbacks than Whites with lower-quality resumes. On the other hand, having a higher-quality resume has a smaller effect for African-Americans. In other words, the gap between Whites and African-Americans widens with resume quality. While one may have expected improved credentials to alleviate employers' fear that African-American applicants are deficient in some unobservable skills, this is not the case in our data.[5]

The experiment also reveals several other aspects of the differential treatment by race. First, since we randomly assign applicants' postal addresses to the resumes, we can study the effect of neighborhood of residence on the likelihood of callback. We find that living in a wealthier (or more educated or Whiter) neighborhood increases callback rates. But, interestingly, African-Americans are not helped more than Whites by living in a "better" neighborhood. Second, the racial gap we measure in different industries does not appear correlated to Census-based measures of the racial gap in wages. The same is true for the racial gap we measure in different occupations. In fact, we find that the racial gaps in callback are statistically indistinguishable across all the occupation and industry categories covered in the experiment. Federal contractors, who are thought to be more severely constrained by affirmative action laws, do not treat the African-American resumes more preferentially; neither do larger employers or employers who explicitly state that they are "Equal Opportunity Employers." In Chicago, we find a slightly smaller racial gap when employers are located in more African-American neighborhoods.

CONCLUSION

This paper suggests that African-Americans face differential treatment when searching for jobs and this may still be a factor in why they do poorly in the labor market. Job applicants with African-American names get far fewer callbacks for each resume they send out. Equally importantly, applicants with African-American names find it hard to overcome this hurdle in callbacks by improving their observable skills or credentials.

Taken at face value, our results on differential returns to skill have possibly important policy implications. They suggest that training programs alone may not be enough to alleviate the racial gap in labor market outcomes. For training to work, some general-equilibrium force outside the context of our experiment would have to be at play. In fact, if African-Americans recognize how employers reward their skills, they may rationally be less willing than Whites to even participate in these programs.

NOTES

1. This camp often explains the poor performance of African-Americans in terms of supply factors. If African-Americans lack many basic skills entering the labor market, then they will perform worse, even with parity or favoritism in hiring.
2. See Roger Jowell and Patricia Prescott-Clarke (1970), Jim Hubbuck and Simon Carter (1980), Colin Brown and Pat Gay (1985), and Peter A. Riach and Judith Rich (1991). One caveat is that some of these studies fail to fully match skills between minority and nonminority resumes. For example some impose differential education background by racial origin. Doris Weichselbaumer (2003, 2004) studies the impact of sex-stereotypes and sexual orientation. Richard E. Nisbett and Dov Cohen (1996) perform a related field experiment to study how employers' response to a criminal past varies between the North and the South in the United States.
3. In creating the higher-quality resumes, we deliberately make small changes in credentials so as to minimize the risk of overqualification.
4. For ease of exposition, we refer to the effects uncovered in this experiment as racial differences. Technically, however, these effects are about the racial soundingness of names....
5. These results contrast with the view, mostly based on nonexperimental evidence, that African-Americans receive higher returns to skills. For example, estimating earnings regressions on several decades of Census data, James J. Heckman et al. (2001) show that African-Americans experience higher returns to a high school degree than Whites do.

REFERENCES

Brown, Colin and Gay, Pat. *Racial discrimination 17 years after the act*. London: Policy Studies Institute, 1985.

Council of Economic Advisers. *Changing America: Indicators of social and economic well-being by race and Hispanic origin*. September 1998, http://w3.access.gpo.gov/eop/ca/pdfs/ca.pdf.

Heckman, James J. and Siegelman, Peter. "The Urban Institute Audit Studies: Their Methods and Findings," in Michael Fix and Raymond J. Struyk, eds., *Clear and convincing evidence: Measurement of discrimination in America*. Lanham, MD: Urban Institute Press, 1992, pp. 187–258.

Hubbuck, Jim and Carter, Simon. *Half a chance? A report on job discrimination against young blacks in Nottingham*. London: Commission for Racial Equality, 1980.

Jowell, Roger and Prescott-Clark, Patricia. "Racial Discrimination and White-Collar Workers in Britain." *Race*, November 1970, 11(4), pp. 397–417.

Nisbett, Richard E. and Cohen, Dov. *The culture of honor: The psychology of violence in the South*. Boulder, CO: Westview Press, 1996.

Riach, Peter A. and Rich, Judity. "Testing for Racial Discrimination in the Labour Market." *Cambridge Journal of Economics*, September 1991, *15*(3), pp. 239–56.

Weichselbaumer, Doris. "Sexual Orientation Discrimination in Hiring." Labour Economics, December 2003, *10*(6), pp. 629–42.

———. "Is it Sex or Personality? The Impact of Sex-Stereotypes on Discrimination in Applicant Selection." *Eastern Economic Journal*, Spring 2004, 30(2), pp. 159–86.

JOURNALING QUESTION

How do you think parents should go about choosing names for their children?

Housing and Environment

21.

EXPLOITING RACE AND SPACE

Concentrated Subprime Lending as Housing Discrimination

BENJAMIN HOWELL

In earlier years, people of color, and particularly black Americans, could not get mortgages at all. "Red lines" were drawn around black neighborhoods, and mortgages were not available within them. More recently, mortgage brokers were actively offering high-interest ("subprime") loans to people in black neighborhoods. Some of these mortgages went to people who would not qualify for a "prime loan" (a loan with lower interest rates), but many of these subprime loans were targeted to people who would qualify for better rates. And this targeted approach followed the old redlining practice.

With extraordinarily, exploitatively high-interest rates, the dream of owning a home becomes the nightmare of losing it. Foreclosure rates rose dramatically in the United States during 2008—people lost their homes to the mortgage lenders, leading to the dramatic stock market events of later that year. Were black people disproportionately being steered to high-interest subprime mortgages? As with other forms of discrimination, this "reverse redlining" can be hard to prove, but Benjamin Howell presents data showing that this is precisely what was happening.

Think about other kinds of aggressive selling that occurs in black neighborhoods specifically and in poor ethnic neighborhoods more generally. Does this concept of exploitation as a form of racial discrimination apply to other situations as well?

PROLOGUE

"Helen Latimore, a black woman, brought a suit charging racial discrimination in real estate lending by Citibank."[1] So begins an opinion affirming summary judgment against Latimore, a South Chicago homeowner denied a $51,000 home equity loan because Citibank appraisers valued her home at $45,000.[2] The bank refused to accept a recent appraisal valuing the house at $82,000 because the comparable sales on which it was based were taken from properties more than six blocks away.[3] In concluding that no reasonable jury could find that the bank denied Latimore the loan because of her race, the court noted, almost as an aside, that Latimore eventually found a smaller loan at a higher interest rate.

Excerpted from Benjamin Howell, "Exploiting Race and Space: Concentrated Subprime Lending as Housing Discrimination," *California Law Review* 94 (2004): 101–48. Notes have been renumbered and edited.

Clyde Hargraves, reverend of the Little Ark Baptist Church in a predominantly black section of the District of Columbia, received an unsolicited telephone call from a mortgage broker who said he had heard of the church's financial trouble.[4] The church was $70,000 in debt. Reverend Hargraves, convinced by the broker that the church would have difficulty securing a smaller loan, pledged the church property to secure a $160,000 loan, which, as he discovered only at the closing, included a $26,000 origination fee and a 25% interest rate for the first four year.[5] When he tried to reach the broker to complain about the fee, the broker's phone had been disconnectect.[6] After two years of struggling to make the payments the Little Ark Church declared bankruptcy; the mortgage broker foreclosed on the property and sold it for more than $200,000 profit.[7] The broker, Capital City Mortgage, directed its marketing almost exclusively toward borrowers in black neighborhoods: 94% of its loans in the District were tied to properties in majority black census tracts.[8]

INTRODUCTION

At an inner-city intersection, where globalized capital and free-market finance meet America's shameful history of racial segregation and subordination, a new and insidious form of racial discrimination lurks. Where lending discrimination once took a binary form—bigoted loan officers rejecting loan applicants because of their skin color—the new model of discrimination is exploitation. Unscrupulous lenders now prey on a history of racial redlining[9] by aggressively marketing overpriced loan products with onerous terms in the same neighborhoods where mainstream lenders once refused to lend.[10]

Subprime lending, the extension of loans to those with less-than-perfect credit at higher rates, has developed almost overnight into a multibillion dollar industry. As the California Supreme Court recently recognized, by bringing access to capital to borrowers who do not meet the "prime" market's creditworthiness standards, subprime lending may have "enabled an entire class of individuals

with impaired credit to enter the housing market or access the equity in their homes."[11] However, the rise in subprime lending has also opened the door to "predatory lenders," who resort to high-pressure sales tactics, half-truths, and outright fraud to convince borrowers to take out subprime loans with excessive fees and exorbitant interest rates.[12] One economic model estimates that homeowners lose $9 billion in home equity to predatory lenders annually.[13] Policy makers face the difficult task of determining when a lender's destructive profit-maximizing practices cross the line of legality.[14]

The most disturbing aspect of the rapid rise of subprime and predatory lending is its significant racial and geographic concentration. A report by the United States Treasury and the Department of Housing and Urban Development (HUD) found that black borrowers were five times more likely to take out a subprime home equity loan than white borrowers[15]—a trend that persists at higher income levels.[16] Moreover, a Federal Reserve Board governor noted that as many as half of subprime borrowers have credit scores that would qualify them for a prime loan.[17] Together, these statistics suggest that black borrowers consistently overpay for home finance.

Subprime lending is geographically concentrated in the same minority neighborhoods once denied access to banks and excluded from federal homeownership programs because of their racial composition. Although geographic discrimination alone is not actionable under the Fair Housing Act (FHA or Title VIII),[18] if a lender exploits historic racial segregation by marketing higher-priced loans to minority neighborhoods to profit from borrowers' lack of other options, such profiteering may constitute actionable housing discrimination.

THE HISTORY OF AMERICA'S RACIAL GEOGRAPHY

Empirical research establishes that subprime mortgage lending is severely concentrated in particular geographic areas[19] and amongst certain racial groups.[20] This concentration is the direct result of historic racial discrimination by both private and state actors. Despite the passage of the FHA in 1968, the United States remains nearly as segregated as it was in the 1960s.[21] Indeed, "among all areas of civil rights taken up during the 1960s, neighborhood segregation proved to be the most emotional and resistant to change"[22] and today America's racial geography remains largely as it was in the 1940s.[23] Furthermore, geographic income segregation is increasing,[24] as is the racial wealth gap.[25] Given this stark physical and economic segregation, if subprime lending is concentrated on the race axis, concentration along the geographical axis logically follows, and vice versa.

As financial transactions tied to real property, residential mortgages are inextricably linked to the political and racial geography of the United States and the country's history of state-sanctioned racial segregation. Today credit and banking markets remain highly segmented across racial and geographical boundaries.[26] Because, as one study has shown, lender characteristics may be a better predictor of whether a borrower will receive a subprime loan than are borrower characteristics,[27] disparities in the geographic distribution of prime lenders will affect the concentration of subprime lending more than the financial profiles of prospective borrowers in those areas. Moreover, the concentration of subprime lending is self-reinforcing: as the effects of high-interest rates and onerous loan terms further impair the creditworthiness of borrowers and increase neighborhood foreclosure rates, the spiral of neighborhood disinvestment intensifies and the demand for subprime loans increases.[28]

REDLINING IN THE BANKING INDUSTRY

Lack of access to traditional sources of home purchase finance played an integral role in the maintenance of de facto racial segregation in the early twentieth century.[29] "Redlining" is the "practice of denying the extension of credit to specific geographic areas due to the income, race, or ethnicity of its residents."[30] In the first half of the twentieth century, mainstream banks largely redlined black neighborhoods.[31] Denied access to mainstream lenders, blacks were forced to borrow from black-owned financial institutions or informal lenders who charged above-market rates.[32]

The term "redlining" comes from the color-coded maps that the Home Owners Loan Corporation (HOLC), a federally operated lender that offered low-interest loans during the Great Depression, used to determine the areas in which it would lend.[33] The HOLC coded as red the lowest-quality, highest-risk neighborhoods and largely refused to lend in such areas.[34] Black areas were consistently coded red.[35] Commentators have noted that the HOLC's color-coded maps "lent the power, prestige and support of the federal government to the systematic practice of racial discrimination in housing."[36]

Scholars disagree about the extent to which the HOLC maps led to redlining by private lenders.[37] However, even those who question such a causal relationship admit that private lenders in redlined black neighborhoods charged higher interest rates.[38] Regardless of the extent of the federal government's role in "initiat[ing] and institutionalizing" redlining,[39] white borrowers' access to residential mortgage loans during the 1930s and 1940s was far superior to black borrowers' access.

Federal Adoption of Real Estate Appraisal Methods: The Reinforcement of Segregation

In the 1930s, the federal government relied on the quasi-scientific urban sociology espoused by proponents of formalized real estate appraisal to create a standardized scale of real estate value that was essential to the Federal Housing Administration's mortgage insurance program.[40] Just as HOLC maps helped institutionalize redlining during the Great Depression,[41] the work of Federal Housing Administration appraisers (or "valuators")[42] channeled mortgage insurance to white, suburban areas and away from black, inner-city neighborhoods.[43]

The Federal Housing Administration used its Underwriting Manual to determine which residential mortgages to insure.[44] The Manual "laid the ground work for today's appraisal theory and practices."[45] The Manual generalized that "the central downtown core of the city…can usually be outlined and considered…ineligible" for mortgage insurance.[46] This exclusion of downtown areas had significant racial and class implications.[47] However, early FHA Manuals reveal an even more pronounced racial bias. In prescribing a formula for the rating of a property's location, the 1936 Manual gave 20% weight to a neighborhood's "Protection from Adverse Influences."[48] Chief among such "adverse influences" was the potential for a change in the "racial occupancy" of the neighborhood.[49] The 1936 Manual required appraisers to give higher values to neighborhoods that had protection from the "infiltration of…inharmonious racial groups.[50] Such protections included zoning ordinances,[51] deed restrictions,[52] and even physical barriers to "infiltration" such as "hills and ravines" and "high speed traffic arter[ies]."[53]

The preference for insulated white neighborhoods was so pronounced that, in the Administration's eyes, "properties owned by blacks did not even warrant a rating, because there was nothing to rate them against."[54] By exhibiting a bias against the central city and racially integrated neighborhoods, and by steering homeownership assistance efforts to white suburban communities,"[55] the Federal Housing Administration ensured the self-fulfilling prophecies of its own biased measures of value.

The appraiser's functional need for discrete areas from which to draw comparables resulted in the overlaying of an invisible grid of value-laden boundaries onto the physical landscape of urban America.[56] This invisible grid is self-reinforcing, supporting a real estate valuation system that has increasingly driven land-use policy toward conformance with the principle that like uses should be clustered and unlike uses should be excluded.[57]

Within this paradigm of privileged and unprivileged uses, racial value judgments were abstracted into a purportedly objective system of real estate appraisal that, in fact, embodies "a certain set of values that tend to advantage one group of people over another."[58]

THE FAIR HOUSING ACT

In 1968, just six days after the assassination of Martin Luther King, Jr., and less than two months after the presidentially appointed Kerner Commission concluded, "[o]ur Nation is moving toward two societies, one black, one whiter—separate and unequal,"[59] President Johnson signed the FHA[60] into law. The legislation sought to eliminate the effects of state-sanctioned racial segregation and "provide, within constitutional limitations, for fair housing throughout the United States."[61] Senator Mondale, author of much of the FHA, stated that the law was designed to achieve "truly integrated and balanced living patterns."[62] With such clear congressional intent, courts have consistently interpreted the statute expansively.[63] Courts have attributed to Congress an intent to "alter the whole character of the housing market.[64] In addition, the FHA's principal purpose has been described as promoting "open, integrated residential housing patterns.[65] The FHA has been used not only to challenge, ex post, individual instances of housing discrimination, but also to ensure that proposed housing practices or policies affirmatively advance the goal of integrated housing.[66]

The FHA's Prohibitions

Under Section 804 of the FHA, it is unlawful:

(a) To refuse to sell or rent after the making of a bona fide offer, or to refuse to negotiate for the sale or rental of, or otherwise make unavailable or deny, a dwelling to any person because of race, color, religion, sex, familial status, or national origin.

(b) To discriminate against any person in the terms, conditions, or privileges of sale or rental of a dwelling, or in the provision of services or facilities in connection therewith, because of race, color, religion, sex, familial status, or national origin.[67]

Section 805 of the FHA applies only to banks or other firms "whose business consists in whole or in part in the making of commercial real estate loans."[68] It is illegal for such actors to "deny a loan or other financial assistance" for the purpose of "purchasing, constructing, improving, repairing, or maintaining a dwelling" on the basis of the protected categories of race, color, religion, sex or national origin.[69] Section 805 specifically addresses "the amount, interest rate, duration, or other terms or conditions" of home loans or financial assistance.[70] Therefore, charging higher interest rates on the basis of race exposes a lender to liability under the FHA. Although these sections apply to distinct aspects of fair housing provision, courts interpret the discrimination element in each section similarly. Specifically, the courts have broadly interpreted the phrase "otherwise make unavailable or deny."[71]...expansive interpretation of the FHA supports the development of fair housing doctrine suited to address the new exploitation paradigm of housing discrimination.

SUBPRIME LENDING IN THE 1990S: CAPITAL MARKETS, THE INNER CITY AND MARKET FAILURE

Residential real estate lending exploded throughout the 1990s,[72] and the percentage of the overall market constituted by subprime real estate loans grew at an even greater rate.[73] In 2001 the *Wall Street Journal* reported a tripling in the number of outstanding subprime mortgage loans since 1995,[74] and HUD has estimated that lenders originated $160 billion worth of subprime loans in 1999, compared to $35 billion in 1994.[75] This explosive growth can be attributed to deep structural changes in mortgage markets in the past quarter-century, including increases in available capital made possible by securitization, the increase in risk-based pricing

facilitated by technological advances, and a steady trend in banking industry deregulation. Although the structural shifts responsible for the growth of subprime lending have increased access to residential lending capital, such shifts have also led to the concentration of subprime loans in formerly redlined inner-city neighborhoods.

STRUCTURAL SHIFTS IN THE MORTGAGE LENDING INDUSTRY

Securitization

Perhaps the most significant structural change in mortgage markets in the past twenty years is the linkage of global capital and residential real estate loans. This linkage was made possible by securitization—the pooling of loans to form securities which are subsequently sold into a secondary market.[76] Securitization dramatically increased the amount of capital available to mortgage lenders and was the most significant cause of subprime lending's rapid growth.[77]

The sale of mortgages into a secondary mortgage market maximizes the amount of available residential lending capital by permitting lenders to use the proceeds from such sales to make additional loans. The federal government first created a secondary market for mortgages in the 1930s to combat the Depression-era shortage of residential loan funds.[78] In the 1970s, Government Sponsored Entities (GSEs) Fannie Mae and Freddie Mac created and sold securities backed by federally insured home loans to further increase the aggregate available residential lending capital.[79] Securitization in the private sector became possible in the 1980s when ratings agencies began to rate privately issued mortgage-backed securities, giving investors confidence in securities not backed by the federal government.[80] From 1984 to 1998, the percentage of outstanding securitized residential loans grew from 23% to 52% of all outstanding residential loans.[81] Through private securitization the residential mortgage market, along with credit markets more generally, became integrated with the capital markets of Wall Street.[82]

New Players: Mortgage Brokers and Other Non-Deposit Lenders

Traditionally, subprime lending was dominated by specialized consumer-finance companies that specialized in lending to those with impaired credit.[83] Through the 1990s, however, big subprime players were increasingly swept up by even bigger mainstream banks.[84] The most high profile of such deals was Citigroup's acquisition of subprime giant The Associates in 2000.[85] Although they profited from the subprime sector, mainstream banks largely maintained separation between their subprime and prime divisions.[86]

Securitization also made possible the increased market share of nondeposit institutions, namely mortgage brokers, who typically originate loans on behalf of wholesale lenders which in turn sell the mortgages into the secondary market.[87] The transition of mortgage origination from federally insured deposit institutions, which hold mortgages in their own asset portfolios, to mortgage brokers and wholesale lenders, which sell the loans into the secondary market, has rearranged incentives in the industry.[88] Mortgage brokers have less incentive to offer fairly priced loans because they do not directly bear the risk of default.[89] Rather, mortgage brokers, who originated close to 60% of mortgage loans in 2002, are motivated to maximize their commissions by originating the largest loan possible.[90]

Further, yield-spread premiums, one of the primary forms of mortgage broker compensation,[91] reward mortgage brokers for steering borrowers to overpriced loans.[92] Yield-spread premiums are payments from wholesale lenders to mortgage brokers amounting to a percentage of the difference between the interest rate of the newly originated loan and the lender's published par rate.[93] Such payments give mortgage brokers an incentive to originate loans with high interest rates.[94] Although, theoretically, such payments could help cash-strapped borrowers spread the up-front costs of loan origination over the life of the loan, empirical data show that mortgage brokers typically retain 75% of yield-spread premiums as compensation.[95] Moreover, brokers have no obligation to disclose yields-spread premiums to borrowers,[96] and evidence suggests that racial minorities pay significantly more in yield-spread premiums than do white borrowers.[97]

Legislative Deregulation of the Mortgage Lending Industry

The decades-long trend of bank deregulation[98] culminated with the passage of the Gramm-Leach-Bliley Act[99] in 1999, permitting financial service providers to merge with insurers.[100] The trend began in 1980 when Congress preempted state usury ceilings with the Depository Institutions Deregulation and Monetary Control Act of 1980 (DIDMCA).[101] Effectively a legislative concession to the Savings and Loan (S&L) industry, the law helped the industry stay competitive with nonfederally chartered banks where consumers received higher rates of return.[102] With this law, Congress enabled the S&Ls to recoup the higher interest rates they were paying by allowing them to preempt state usury laws for loans to consumers secured by a first lien on their homes.[103]

Deregulation continued with the Alternative Mortgage Transaction Parity Act of 1982 (AMTPA),[104] extending federal mortgage lending regulations to most residential loans. This extension paved the way for certain loan products that are commonly challenged as predatory.[105] The Tax Reform Act of 1986[106] made home mortgage interest the only form of tax-deductible interest, creating incentives for homeowners to tap their existing home equity for a stream of future payments.[107] Next, the Financial Institutions Reform, Recovery, and Enforcement Act of 1989 (FIRREA)[108] addressed the costly S&L failures of the 1980s and created incentives for S&Ls to operate as thinly capitalized[109] mortgage brokers relying on the secondary market for loan funds.[110] Thus, banking deregulation not only paved the way for subprime lenders to charge high interest rates and fees, but it also prompted lenders with skewed incentives to enter the market[111]

Unsurprisingly, the financial services industry has opposed further regulation or increased liability by arguing that both will increase lenders' costs, thereby limiting the number of loans offered to underserved borrowers.[112] Consistent with this free-market ideology, consumer protection laws like the Truth in Lending Act (TILA)[113] and the Real Estate Settlement Procedures Act of 1974 (RESPA)[114] mandate disclosure of loan price information so that, in theory, borrowers may "comparison shop" for loans with sufficient and accurate pricing information.[115] In practice, however, such mandatory disclosures are often too little, too late.[116]

The Home Ownership and Equity Protection Act (HOEPA),[117] a 1994 amendment to TILA aimed at the harmful effects of predatory lending, applies only to home equity or refinance loans, not open-ended extensions of credit or purchase money mortgages.[118] The act does not cap interest rates or origination fees, but it does mandate heightened disclosures and prohibit certain loan terms for "high-rate, high-fee" loans.[119] Lenders may easily evade HOEPA disclosure requirements, however, by styling their loans as open-ended lines of credit or pricing them just below HOEPA's interest rate triggers, which are so high that "most lenders, including predatory lenders, are able to price their loans below [them]."[120] In sum, existing consumer protection laws, which aim at ensuring fair competition through disclosure, have proved ineffective to combat the harmful effects of concentrated subprime lending.[121]

RISK-BASED PRICING AND SUBPRIME LOANS

The prime home mortgage is largely a binary product: either a borrower meets the lender's criteria and is granted a loan at the current interest rate or fails to meet the lender's criteria and is denied. The subprime market's use of differential pricing in the form of interest rates and origination fees tied to risk is a relatively new phenomenon facilitated by technological advances in automated underwriting and credit scoring.[122] In an efficient market the subprime loan's price compensates the lender for the precise increase in risk associated with extending credit to that subprime borrower.[123] However, strong empirical evidence suggests many subprime lenders exploit information asymmetries created by lack of price transparency and a highly segmented market to overcharge[124] subprime borrowers.[125] Empirical data support the conclusion that "the higher rates charged by subprime lenders cannot be fully explained solely as a function of the additional risks they bear."[126] A borrower's willingness to pay, rather than the forces of an efficient market, may drive much subprime pricing.

For decades economists have recognized that the unavailability of accurate market information (and unequal access to what little information exists) prevents credit markets from reaching efficient pricing. Stiglitz and Weiss famously posited that lenders' inability to accurately assess the credit risks posed by borrowers artificially shrinks the amount of available credit.[127] Engel and McCoy more recently argue that securitization has eliminated such "credit rationing."[128] Rather, they assert, market segmentation permits lenders to exploit borrowers who lack accurate market information by charging them above-market rates.[129] Such borrowers are typically those "disconnected from the credit market," many of whom "were historically excluded from the home-mortgage market because of credit rationing and discrimination."[130]

The secrecy of subprime mortgage rates at the retail level hinders efficiency in subprime mortgage markets.[131] Both prime borrowers and subprime mortgage brokers are able to shop for capital using published rate tables. Subprime borrowers, in contrast, do not have access to such rate tables, which are not published by subprime originators.[132] The prices offered subprime borrowers are effectively set by originators' chosen markup.[133] Moreover, subprime mortgage rates are typically so complex that even with perfect price transparency comparison shopping would be difficult.[134]

The segmentation of the subprime market from its prime counterpart frustrates comparison shopping between the two. Empirical evidence of a price discontinuity between the prime and subprime interest rates suggests that such segmentation exists and that subprime loans are overpriced.[135] In an efficient market, one would expect that "interest rates for a spectrum of consumers with the best- to the worst-quality credit would be continuous."[136] Instead, it is "an observable and enduring feature" of the mortgage market that the lowest subprime interest rate is generally two percentage points higher than the highest prime rate.[137] This gap in pricing *alone* reveals that there is a lack of crossover from subprime to prime markets and that some borrowers at the top of the subprime risk pool have been overcharged.[138] Segmentation of the prime from subprime markets limits the range of borrowers' perceived loan options, which facilitates exploitation.[139]

In the subprime market, risk may not be closely tied to price after all. Lenders lose money when a borrower defaults and either high foreclosure costs or insufficient revenues from foreclosure sale leave the lender with less than the full outstanding principal. But of all residential loan defaults, relatively few end in foreclosure,[140] and though subprime foreclosure rates are higher than those in the prime market, losses to lenders are "typically less than 1% of the outstanding dollar balances annually."[141] Lenders recover delinquency costs through late fees and other charges.[142] Foreclosure is expensive, but subprime lenders account for this by limiting the loan-to-value ratio to 65% to 75% (compared to a limit of 80% in the prime market) with the differential between the home's market price and the value of the loan covering the costs associated with foreclosure.[143] ... When a borrower's willingness to pay, rather than the forces of an efficient market,

dictates loan pricing, the stage is set for exploitation. Lenders need only identify borrowers willing to pay above-market rates.[144] When willingness to pay correlates with residence in a formerly redlined area, targeting overpriced loans to such borrowers constitutes housing discrimination.

CAUSES OF THE GEOGRAPHIC CONCENTRATION OF SUBPRIME LENDING

Capital Flows: Gentrification and Unequal Access to "Good" Credit Opportunities

In the 1990s, increased investment in real property laid the groundwork for the expansion of subprime lending. Political economists have linked booms in real property investment to periods in the business cycle when excesses of capital make profitable investment opportunities in the production sector hard to identify.[145] During the stock market boom of the 1990s, significant amounts of capital were available to flow into real-property-based investments. As securitization linked global capital and residential real estate, mortgage transactions became standardized and depersonalized. Housing value transitioned "from a dwelling use-value to a debt-encumbered portfolio asset."[146] This shift toward an increasingly investment-based function of mortgage lending caused money to flow into communities that, only decades earlier, had been explicitly redlined and then only reluctantly served by mainstream banks and mortgage insurers.[147] With houses defined as a "portfolio asset," dormant equity in so-called cash-poor, house-rich neighborhoods came to represent potentially lucrative profit streams. This effect was most pronounced in gentrifying areas where property values were rising dramatically.[148]

As capital flowed into gentrifying inner cities, simple geographic redlining became more difficult, and new forms of market segmentation became necessary for profit maximization.[149] After modeling loan and lender data, scholars have concluded that "[i]nner city reinvestment creates landscapes where deep-pocket prime banks are pursuing wealthy (and predominantly white) gentrifiers alongside firms marketing to low-and moderate-income borrowers (mostly black)."[150] Unsurprisingly, the lower-income segment of the market is dominated by subprime lenders. Thus, even as gentrification brought mainstream bank capital to formerly redlined neighborhoods, "good" credit opportunities were largely directed to wealthy white gentrifiers and denied to existing residents of lower-income and racial minority status.[151] Although Wall Street capital has found its way to the inner city, when sought by longtime residents of such areas, it is often delivered through middlemen at a considerable markup.

Creditworthiness: The Increasing Role of FICO Scores in Underwriting Subprime Loans

The concentration of subprime lending is in part caused by increasing reliance on Fair, Isaacs and Company (FICO) credit scores to assess a borrower's creditworthiness. Credit scoring, which has been described as constituting a "sort of economic opportunity rating,"[152] raises equality concerns because blacks are three times more likely than whites to have a high-risk credit score.[153] In addition, a correlation exists between the prevalence of low credit scores and the percentage of minorities in a given zip code.[154] [L]enders may use low credit scores as proxies for profitability, targeting high-cost loan products to neighborhoods where lower scores are concentrated.

FICO scores, originally designed for use by credit card issuers, have played an increasingly large role in the underwriting of subprime loans.[155] The scores are based on a model of the repayment behavior of a statistical set of borrowers with varying credit histories.[156] FICO enjoys a virtual monopoly on the credit-scoring market and does not release the proprietary formula used to calculate scores.[157]

Some credit history features that may justify a loan denial, such as the existence of open consumer finance accounts or an insufficient credit history, work against borrowers from neighborhoods where traditional financing is unavailable.[158] FICO scores appear to prefer track records of the *right kind* of consumer credit, disproportionately raising the scores of those who adhere to credit practices traditionally recognized as prudent[159] and depressing the scores of those who have lived nontraditional economic lives. The fundamental problem is that the FICO formula cannot assess its indicia of creditworthiness in context.[160] Subprime borrowers tend to "fall off the scale" of desirable credit scores.[161] In apparent recognition of this bias against historically underserved borrowers, FICO developed a new credit scoring system for "non-traditional" borrowers with thin or no credit history.[162] The mortgage industry seems to be more interested in that system than other credit providers.[163]

Furthermore, some subprime lenders may be preventing their primes-qualified customers from exiting the subprime market. Many subprime lenders have failed to report their borrowers' repayment habits to credit bureaus, making it more difficult for subprime borrowers to improve their credit scores and move into the prime market.[164] Peter McCorkell, general counsel for FICO, speculates that the subprime lenders' underreporting may be an attempt to prevent their lower-risk subprime borrowers from being "picked off" by prime lenders.[165]

Finally, credit scoring exhibits the same self-reinforcing effects observed in the real estate appraisal context. When lack of credit history initially forces a borrower or consumer to accept higher fees or interest rates, the more expensive financing may affect the borrower's subsequent ability to pay, "justifying" a low credit score or further depressing it. Alternatively, Peter Swire posits that black borrowers expecting to face lending discrimination will rationally choose to under-invest in their own creditworthiness.[166] Lenders respond by lowering the borrowers' credit ratings, beginning the cycle anew.[167] In sum, lenders' increasing reliance on credit scores exacerbates the concentration of subprime lending in racial minority and low-income neighborhoods because FICO scores penalize the credit practices of historically underserved borrowers, and reflect inconsistent credit-reporting practices of subprime lenders.

Separating Capital from the Site of the Deal: Depersonalization of the Lending Transaction

Increased standardization of the lending process reinforces the geographic concentration of subprime lending by replacing personal borrower-lender relationships with risk-based pricing formulas that perpetuate historical discrimination. Structural changes in mortgage markets—securitization, credit scoring, and automatic underwriting—have standardized lending procedures. However, increased use of automated underwriting and credit scoring may decrease borrowers' bargaining power regarding the specific terms of their home mortgages.[168] Automation may have the most significant impact on those who have lived "non-traditional" economic lives.[169] Also, "[s]ecuritization almost completely depersonalizes the lending process and deprives the borrower of the advantages of a personal relationship with her lender."[170] Not only does this depersonalization reduce the chances of a loan being restructured to prevent default, but it focuses the loan originator's attention on achieving secondary market profits, rather than on finding a loan well-suited to a borrower's needs.[171] Instead of serving borrowers, lenders must satisfy the "demands of distant investors and institutions" whose only interests are the profit stream represented by the securitized mortgage pool and the level of risk associated with it.[172] This disjunction between the borrower and the ultimate beneficiary of the mortgage (the security holder) obscures what was once the hallmark of the industry: that both borrower and lender profited from the transaction.

As capital becomes separated from the site of the deal and "[p]ersonal and local relationships are exchanged for impersonal and distant monetary contacts,"[173] opportunities for bigoted loan officers to discriminate against prospective borrowers decrease. But automation paves the way for the exploitation paradigm of housing discrimination.[174]

Lending approval and pricing are now determined by complex equations of credit scores and collateral value. If these indices of risk—the real numbers in the lending equation—reflect historic inequities from now-illegal discrimination, using an algebraic formula to determine loan prices and terms will simply perpetuate the embedded inequities. When indicia of historic inequities are purposefully employed to target unsophisticated and underserved lenders for overpriced loans, such conduct should be considered actionable housing discrimination.

Finding Profits: Intrafirm Segmentation and Targeted Loan Marketing

Market segmentation, both between competing firms and within a single firm, allows lenders to maximize profits by aggressively marketing subprime loans to low-income and minority neighborhoods. The market for residential mortgage loans remains highly segmented.[175] Interfirm market segmentation—the concentration of subprime lenders, finance companies, and pawn shops in low-income and minority neighborhoods and a corresponding concentration of elite federally-insured deposit banks in white neighborhoods—can trace its roots directly to the sordid history of bank redlining.[176] However, as banks have been permitted to consolidate into large financial holding companies straddling both prime and subprime markets, they have developed a profit incentive to maintain their *intrafirm* market segmentation.[177] Deregulation unleashed competitive forces that caused banks to fight for the most profitable borrowers,[178] and the segmentation of retail lending markets increases profits by facilitating price discrimination within the customer base of a single firm. As one study notes, in gentrifying inner cities "[n]ew lines of stratified reinvestment are laid atop prior rounds of redlining, discrimination, and disinvestment. Institutional segmentation is replacing exclusion and credit rationing."[179]

Technology has facilitated concerted intrafirm market segmentation by enabling lenders to compile lists of customers with the geodemographic or credit history profiles they deem most profitable.[180] Subprime loans are aggressively marketed to these populations,[181] which tend to have lower levels of education and reside in "underserved" neighborhoods.[182]

Sophisticated consumer-profiling technologies have an especially pronounced impact on the distribution of subprime loans because most subprime loans are sold *to*, not sought *by*, borrowers.[183] By exploiting disparities in borrowers' education, sophistication, financial desperation, or fear of discrimination at elite banking institutions,[184] lenders can locate and target borrowers who are willing to pay more for loans.[185] Subdividing the market and targeting potential customers by age, sex, income, education, occupation, ethnic origin, social class, and geography allows lenders to focus on proxies for profitability, directing more expensive loan products to those borrowers they believe will pay more.[186]

Moreover, if a subprime borrower qualifies for a prime loan, a subprime lender has no incentive to offer this borrower the prime rates that are available elsewhere in the lender's firm. Mortgage brokers lending a bank's money at a markup do not want to lose their customers and commissions to the bank's prime-market branches.[187] The aggregation of profits at the parent company level belies the firm's profit motives for maintaining the segmentation of its own retail lending business.

Prime-market banks may also have public image reasons for keeping their subprime affiliates distinct, further contributing to the segmentation of the lending market.[188] Such motivations are demonstrated by a district court's recent refusal to dismiss a fair lending case against subprime lender Equicredit or its parent, Bank of America.[189] In *Johnson v. Equicredit Corporation of America*, the plaintiff alleged that in the Chicago area, Equicredit made its subprime loans almost exclusively in minority areas, while its parent, Bank of America, made prime loans to similarly situated whites in predominantly white areas.[190] The *Johnson* plaintiffs did not argue that Bank of America should be held liable for the alleged discrimination of its subsidiary Equicredit. Rather, they claimed that Bank of America *itself* had violated the FHA, the Equal Credit Opportunity Act (ECOA),[191] and 42 U.S.C. § 1981 by providing "different types of loans depending on the racial demographics of the area in which the borrower resides."[192]

The court's acceptance of the plaintiffs' proffered comparison—Equicredit's subprime borrowers with Bank of America's prime borrowers—is significant. Often, the failure to identify appropriate, "similarly situated" parties of another race for comparison is a crucial obstacle to establishing discrimination under a disparate treatment theory.[193]

Intrafirm segmentation of credit markets may be a new manifestation of the older, simpler geographic redlining. Just as redlining can be explained as a method of profit-maximizing by facilitating price discrimination,[194] targeting market segments that display indices of profitability that correlate with protected categories of race, sex, or national origin can also allow for above-market pricing....

NOTES

1. Latimore v. Citibank Fed. Sav. Bank, 151 F.3d 712, 713 (7th Cir. 1998).
2. *Id.*
3. *Id.*
4. Brief for the United States as Amicus Curiae Supporting Plaintiffs, at 2, Hargraves v. Capital City Mortgage Corp., 140 F. Supp. 2d 7 (D.D.C. 2000) (No. 98–1021), available at http://www.usdoj.gov/crt/housing/documents/hargraves1.htm [hereinafter Brief for the United States].
5. *Id.* at 2–3.
6. *Id.* at 3.
7. *Id.*

8. *Id.* at 2.

9. Throughout this Comment, "redlining" refers to the practice of denying the extension of credit to a specific geographic area due to the income, race, or ethnicity of its residents. "Reverse redlining" refers to the targeting of persons for credit on unfair terms based on their income, race, or ethnicity. Reverse redlining typically occurs in communities that were once redlined. See United Cos. Lending Corp. v. Sargeant, 20 F. Supp. 2d 192, 203 n.5 (D. Mass. 1998).

10. See, e.g., DAN IMMERGLUCK, CREDIT TO THE COMMUNITY: COMMUNITY REINVESTMENT AND FAIR LENDING POLICY IN THE UNITED STATES 267 (2004) ("The problem of poor access to mortgage loans has been transformed into a problem of poor access to fairly priced credit and one of frequently unsustainable credit promoted by abusive lenders.").

11. Am. Fin. Servs. Ass'n v. City of Oakland, 104 P.3d 813, 824 (Cal. 2005).

12. It is generally accepted that not all subprime loans are predatory, but that nearly all predatory loans are subprime.

13. Christopher A. Richardson, Predatory Lending and Housing Disinvestment 19 (Feb. 2003) (unpublished manuscript, on file with the *California Law Review*), available at http://papers.ssrn.com/sol3/papers.cfm?abstract_id=338660.

14. In the Past four years, twenty-six states have enacted predatory lending legislation. Baher Azmy, *Squaring the Predatory Lending Circle: A Case for States as Laboratories of Experimentation*, 57 FLA. L. REV. 295, 295 (2005). The predatory lending debate, however, suffers from the difficulties of defining a "predatory" loan. Using lists of prohibited loan terms or interest-rate triggers to define predatory loans simply gives unscrupulous lenders a target to avoid. DEP'TS OF THE TREASURY AND HOUS. AND URBAN DEV., CURBING PREDATORY HOME MORTGAGE LENDING 17 (2000), available at http://www.huduser.org/Publications/pdf/treasrpt.pdf [hereinafter HUD-TREASURY REPORT]. In addition, any list of predatory practices is destined to be incomplete because "bad actors are constantly developing new abusive practices, sometimes to evade new government regulation" and "a list does not consider the context in which the alleged abuse has occurred." *Id.*

15. HUD-TREASURY REPORT AT 23. In this comment I have artificially simplified America's multi-ethnic population into black and white. Contemporary segregation of blacks from whites is directly rooted in historic, state-sponsored discrimination. Whereas today so-called "ethnic" neighborhoods may be the result of residents' volitional housing choices, the continued segregation of blacks from whites may not be divorced from its historical causes. My argument that racially concentrated subprime lending constitutes housing discrimination is thus limited to subprime lending targeted at black borrowers or predominantly black neighborhoods.

16. CALVIN BRADFORD, RISK OR RACE? RACIAL DISPARITIES AND THE SUBPRIME REFINANCE MARKET 3 (2002), available at http://www.knowledgeplex.org/kp/report/report/relfiles/ccc_0729_risk.pdf.

17. Governor Edward M. Gramlich, Subprime Mortage Lending: Benefits, Costs, and Challenges, Remarks at the Financial Services Roundtable Annual Housing Policy Meeting, Chicago, Illinois (May 21, 2004), available at http://www.federalreserve.gov/boarddocs/speeches/2004/20040521/default.htm. Preliminary estimates by Freddie Mac suggest that between 10% and 35% of subprime borrowers could have qualified for a prime loan. Freddie Mac, Automated Underwriting: Making Mortgage Lending Simpler and Fairer for America's Families Chap. 5 (Sept. 1996), available at http://www.freddiemac.com/corporate/reports/moseley/chap5.htm.

18. Discrimination based on an individual's geographic location does not violate the Fair Housing Act, which prohibits discrimination based on "race, color, religion, sex, familial status or national origin." 42 U.S.C. §§3604(a)-(b) (1968). More generally, fundamental guarantees of civil rights such as the Equal Protection Clause accrue to "people, not places." Reeder v. Kansas City Bd. Of Police Comm'rs, 796 F.2d 1050, 1053 (8th Cir. 1986) (citing McGowan v. Maryland, 366 U.S. 420, 427 (1961)).

19. Paul S. Calem et al., *Neighborhood Patterns of Subprime Lending: Evidence from Disparate Cities*, 15 HOUSING POL'Y DEBATE 603, 604 (2004), available at http://content.knowledgeplex.org/kp2/cache/documents/58732.pdf. In one study, researchers modeled loan data from seven cities in the years 1997 and 2002. *Id.* at 603. After controlling for demographic and economic variables, they concluded that "neighborhood minority share is consistently significant and positively related to subprime share in both years." *Id.* See also Elvin K. Wyly et al., *Has Mortgage Capital Found an Inner-City Spatial Fix?*, 15 HOUSING POL'Y DEBATE 623, 672 (2004), available at http://content.knowledgeplex.org/kp2/cache/documents/58733.pdf. According to the authors' data, both race and geography are tied to the likelihood of receiving a subprime loan, and "[a] black person requesting a loan in a core gentrified neighborhood is more than twice as likely to end up at a subprime lender than an otherwise similar black person elsewhere in the metropolitan area." *Id.*

20. The 2000 joint HUD-Treasury report found that in predominantly African American neighborhoods 51% of refinancing loans were subprime compared to a mere 9% of loans in predominantly white neighborhoods. HUD-TREASURY REPORT, *supra* note 14, at 23. A borrower from an African American neighborhood seeking a home refinance loan is thus five times more likely to receive a subprime loan than a borrower from a white neighborhood *Id.* Moreover, the higher concentration of subprime loans in minority areas persists when neighborhood income is taken into account: in upper-income African American neighborhoods nearly 40% of home refinance loans were subprime, compared to 5% in upper-income while neighborhoods and 20% in lower-income white neighborhoods. *Id.*

21. See, e.g., Sheryll D. Cashin, *Drifting Apart: How Wealth and Race Segregation are Reshaping the American Dream*, 47 VILL. L. REV. 595, 596 (2002); Nancy A. Denton, *The Role of Residential Segregation in Promoting and Maintaining Inequality in Wealth and Property*, 34 IND. L. REV. 1199, 1201 (2001).

22. DOUGLAS S. MASSEY & NANCY A. DENTON, AMERICAN APARTHEID: SEGREGATION AND THE MAKING OF THE UNDERCLASS 191 (1993).

23. David M. Cutler, Edward L. Glaeser & Jacob L. Vigdor, *The Rise and Decline of the American Ghetto*. 107 J. POLITICAL ECON. 455, 465–66 (1999) ("To a great extent, the modem spatial distribution of races in American cities was established by 1940.").

24. Cashin, *supro* note 27, at 596 ("Currently, with each passing decade, we as a nation are becoming increasingly segregated by income.").

25. MELVIN L. OLIVER & THOMAS M. SHAPIRO, BLACK WEALTH/WHITE WEALTH: A NEW PERSPECTIVE ON RACIAL INEQUALITY 67–90 (1995).

26. See, e.g., Press Release, Woodstock Institute, Report Finds Dual Market in Refinance Loans: Subprime Lenders Dominate Lending in Minority Neighborhoods (Nov. 15, 1999) (summarizing report analyzing home refinance lending in the Chicago area and documenting the extreme segmentation of mortgage markets by race and neighborhood) available at http://woodstockinst.org/document/2stepsback.html; Assocs. Home Equity Servs., Inc. v. Troup, 778 A.2d 529, 536 n.2 (N.J. Super. Ct. App. Div. 2001) (citing the findings of Elvin Wyly that

HMDA data support the existence of a "dual housing finance market... in New Jersey for the refinance and home repair loans" with "urban areas of heavy minority concentration [] being disproportionately serviced by subprime lenders").

27. Wyly et al., *supra* note 25, at 657.
28. This sort of "feedback loop" is common to many theories of discrimination. Daria Roithmayr tells a similar "market failure story" about persistent racial disparity in law school admissions rates. She uses the antitrust theories of market lock-in and path dependence to show how a racial group's early monopoly can become "self-reinforcing and ultimately locked in." See Daria Roithmayr, *Locked in Inequality: The Persistence of Discrimination*, 9 Mich. J. Race & L. 31, 33 (2003). Gunnar Myrdal described this phenomenon as the "vicious circle" or the "principle of cumulation" by which cause and effect mutually reinforce each other. Gunnar Myrdal, An American Dilemma: The Negro Problem and Modern Democracy 75 (1942). For example, Myrdal explains, "an increase in white prejudice has the effect of pressing down still further the Negro plane of living, which again will increase prejudice, and so on, by way of mutual interaction between the two variables, *ad infinitum*." *Id.* at 1066.
29. For a summary of the history of mortgage discrimination and redlining, see Immergluck, *supra* note 10, at 87–108.
30. United Cos. Lending Corp. v. Sargeant, 20 F. Supp. 2d 192, 203 n.5 (D. Mass. 1998).
31. Immergluck, *supra* note 10, at 87.
32. *Id.* at 88.
33. Massey & Denton, *supra* note 28, at 51.
34. *Id.*
35. *Id.* at 52.
36. *Id.*
37. Amy Hillier. *Who Received Home Loans? Home Owners Loan Corporation Lending and Discrimination in Philadelphia in the 1930s*, 2 J. Plan. Hist. 3,4 (2003) ("Recent research challenges this causal relationship between HOLC maps and disinvestments."
38. *Id.* ("[L]enders continued to make loans in areas colored red (although the interest rates were higher).").
39. Massey & Denton, *supra* note 28, at 51.
40. Stuart, *supra* note 58, at 45–47; *see also* Immergluck, *supra* note 10, at 91.
41. *See* Massey & Denton, *supra* note 28 at 51; *supra* notes 3–45 and accompanying text.
42. FHA Underwriting Manual, supra note 54, at Part I, 121.
43. Immergluck, *supra* note 10, at 95 ("[T]he major federal housing program made housing much more affordable primarily to those white buyers buying homes in racially pure and mostly suburban communities."); Stuart, *supra* note 58, at 54.
44. FHA Underwriting Manual, *supra* note 54 at Part I, ¶ 131.
45. Stuart, *supra* note 58, at 47.
46. FHA Underwriting Manual, *supra*.note 54, at Part II, ¶ 208.
47. *See* 114 Cong. Rec. 3421 (1968) ("Eighty percent of the nonwhite population of metropolitan areas in 1967 lived in central cities.").
48. FHA Underwriting Manual, *supra* note 54, at Part II, ¶ 204.
49. *Id.* at Part II, ¶ 233.
50. *Id.* at Part II, ¶ 229.
51. *Id.* at Part II, ¶ 227.

52. *Id.* at Part II, ¶ 228. The Federal Housing Administration encouraged the use of restrictive covenants to prevent properties from being sold to blacks, IMMERGLUCK, *supra* note 10, at 94, until the Supreme Court declared this type of covenant unconstitutional in 1948. See generally Shelley v. Kraemer, 334 U.S. 1 (1948) (holding that judicial enforcement of racially restrictive covenants violates the Fourteenth Amendment).

53. *Id.* at Part II, ¶ 229.

54. STUART, *supra* note 58, at 55.

55. IMMERGLUCK, *supra* note 10, at 95.

56. Stuart, *supra* note 58, at 35. The 1936 FHA Manual charges each Insuring Office to maintain a record of "Established Ratings of Location" and suggests a "combination of cards and maps" be used: "First the neighborhoods are outlined on maps. The better locations are rated by the use of the Rating of Location grid." FHA UNDERWRITING MANUAL, *supra* note 54, at Part II, ¶ 209. Then "descriptive materials should be placed on a card so that the basis of the rating may be recorded." *Id.* The records were maintained by the chief valuator and were available for use whenever a subsequent request for mortgage insurance on a property within that area was made. *Id.*

57. STUART, *supra* note 58, at 35.

58. *Id.* 30.

59. THE NAT'L ADVISORY COMM'N ON CIVIL DISORDERS, REPORT OF THE NATIONAL ADVISORY COMMISSION ON CIVIL DISORDERS 1 (1968); *see also* MASSEY & DENTON, *supra* note 28, at 3–4, 193–94.

60. Fair Housing Act, Pub. L. No. 90–284, Title VIII, 82 Stat. 81 (1968) (codified as amended at 42 U.S.C. §§ 3601 et seq. (2000)).

61. 42 U.S.C. § 3601.

62. 114 CONG. REC. 3422 (1968) (statement of Sen. Mondale).

63. See, e.g., Traffocante v. Metro Life Ins. Co., 409 U.S. 205, 209–11 (1972) holding that persons who lost the social benefits of living in an integrated community were "aggrieved" persons under the FHA).

64. Mayers v. Ridley, 465 F.2d 630, 652 (D.C. Cir. 1972).

65. Huntington Branch, NAACP v. Town of Huntington, 844 F.2d 926, 937 (2d Cir. 1988) (quoting Otero v. N.Y. Hous. Auth., 484 F.2d 1122, 1134 (2d Cir. 1973)).

66. Such affirmative duties are imposed on HUD by 42 U.S.C. § 3608(e)(5). See, e.g., NAACP v. Sec'y of HUD, 817 F.2d 149 (1st Cir. 1987) ("Title VIII imposes upon HUD an obligation to do more than simply refrain from discriminating (and from purposely aiding discrimination by others)."). Such affirmative duties do not extend to private actors.

67. 42 U.S.C. §§ 3604(a)-(b) (1968).

68. 42 U.S.C. § 3605.

69. *Id.*

70. *Id.*; see also Harper v. Union Sav. Ass'n, 429 F. Supp. 1254, 1257, 1259 (N.D. Ohio 1977) (commenting that the phrase "terms and conditions" should be given the "broadest possible construction").

71. See, e.g., Nat'l Fair Hous. Alliance v. Prudential Ins. Co. of Am., 208 F. Supp. 2d 46, 56 (D.D.C. 2002) ("Plaintiffs persuasively argue that … the broad, general language [of the FHA]—reflected in phrases such as 'otherwise make unavailable or deny'—was intended to be flexible enough to cover multiple types of housing-related transactions.").

72. From 1994 to 1999, total annual home-loan originations grew 60%, from $773 billion to $1.275 trillion. HUD-TREASURY REPORT, *supra* note 14, at 29. Even more pronounced was the

growth of lending to lower- and middle-income borrowers, which saw an 80% increase between 1993 and 1999. *Id.* at 24.

73. Subprime loans as a percentage of total originations grew from 4.5% to 12.5% from 1994 to 1999. *Id.* at 29. One source reported that the subprime share of the overall mortgage market tripled between 1994 and 1997—from under 5% to 15%. Howard Lax et al., *Subprime Lending: An Investigation of Economic Efficiency,* 15 Housing Pol'y Debate 533, 534 n.3 (2004).

74. Carrick Mollenkamp et al., *Banker Beware: As Economy Slows, 'Subprime' Lending Looks Even Riskier.* Wall St. J., Aug. 16, 2001, at Al.

75. Kenneth Temkin et al., U.S. Dep't of Hous. & Urban Dev., Subprime Markets, the Role of GSEs, and Risk-Based Pricing vii (2002), (available at http://www.huduser.org/publications/hsgfin/ subprime. html.

76. Securitization works as follows: A mortgage loan originator transfers a pool of loans to a "special purpose corporation, trust, or other legally separate entity" known as a special purpose vehicle (SPV). Steven L. Schwarcz. *The Alchemy of Asset Securitization,* 1 Stan. J. L. Bus. & Fin. 133, 135 (1994). For the securities to be acceptable on the market, the sale from the originator to the SPV must be a "true sale" so that the originator reduces the amount of liability attached to the loans when transferred. *Id.* (A "true sale" is a sale that, under bankruptcy law, removes the receivables from the seller's bankruptcy estate.) *Id.* The SPV then creates securities based on the income stream from the loans. *Id.* Securitization was made possible by technological advances allowing investment banks to assess and minimize risk associated with a pool of loans. *Id.* A vigorous debate is now underway as to whether securitization provides holders of mortgage-backed securities too much insulation from the predatory practices of the originators of the securitized loans.

77. City of Oakland v. Am. Fin. Servs. Ass'n, 104 P.3d 813, 833 (Cal. 2005) (George, C.J., dissenting) ("The bulk sale of mortgage loans on the secondary market is the primary profit incentive for subprime mortgage lenders."). Investors purchased more than $60 billion of subprime mortgage-backed securities in 1997, compared to a mere $10 billion in 1991. HUD-Treasury Report, *supra* note 14, at 41.

78. See, e.g., Stuart, *supra* note 58, at 25.

79. Kurt Eggert, *Held Up in Due Course: Predatory Lending, Securitization, and the Holder in Due Course Doctrine.* 35 Creighton L. Rev. 503, 537 (2002). With the federal government's full credit behind them, these securities were seen as virtually "risk free." *Id.* Furthermore, GSEs only purchase loans that meet strict underwriting requirements, minimizing the risk associated with the securitized pool of loans. *Id.*

80. *Id.*

81. *Id.* at 538.

82. See Kathleen W. Johnson, *Consumer Loan Securitization,* in The Impact Of Public Policy On Consumer Credit 301 (Thomas A. Durkin & Michael E. Staten, eds. 2002); Eggert, *supra* note 116, at 536.

83. Mollenkamp et al., *supra* note 111.

84. *Id.*

85. Wyly et al., *supra* note 25, at 623. Citibank promptly paid $215 million to settle predatory lending charges brought by the Federal Trade Commission. *Id.* at 625 n. 1.

86. *Id.* at 624; Kathleen C. Engel & Patricia A. McCoy, *A Tale of Three Markets: The Law and Economics of Predatory Lending,* 80 tex. L. Rev. 1255, 1296 (2002).

87. Eggert, *supra* note 116, at 553.

88. *Id.*

89. *Id.*

90. *Id.* Because a number of states require only minimal capitalization for brokers, many such brokers may be judgment-proof. *Id.* at 556.

91. Howell Jackson, Predatory Mortgage Lending Practices: Abusive Use of Yield Spread Premiums, Testimony at U.S. Senate Committee on Banking, Housing, and Urban Affairs, Washington, D.C., (Jan. 8, 2002), available at http://banking.senahe.gov/02_01hrg/010802/jackson.htm#N_7.

92. A subprime loan is "overpriced" if the interest rate and origination fees paid are incommensurate with the additional risk posed by the borrower.

93. Taiesha L Cantwell, *Yield-Spread Premiums: Who's Working for the Borrower? HUD's Erroneous Regulation and Its Bar on Plaintiffs*, 21 Law & Ineq. 367, 370–71 (2003); see also Engel & McCoy, *supra* note 123, at 1264; Hud-Treasury Report, *supra* note 14, at 80. "The term 'par rate' refers to the rate offered to the broker (through the lender's price sheets) at which the lender will fund 100% of the loan with no premium or discounts to the broker." Hud-Treasury Report, *supra* note 15 at 40.

94. Engel & McCoy, *supra* note 123, at 1264.

95. Jackson, *supra* note 128.

96. Engel & McCoy, *supra* note 123, at 1264.

97. Jackson, *supra* note 128.

98. Immergluck, *supra* note 10, at 266 ("In the last twenty-five years, there has been a deliberate and organized movement, aggressively promoted by the financial services sector, Congress, and many federal regulators, to reduce the public-sector oversight of the financial services sector."). Immergluck argues that the deregulationist stance ignores the fact that the federal government is largely responsible for today's "robust" financial services market and much of the most important "financial infrastructure" of U.S. mortgage markets. *Id.* at 266–67.

99. Pub. L. No. 106–102, 113 Stat. 1338 (1999) (codified as amended in scattered sections of 15 U.S.C. and 12 U.S.C.).

100. Matthew Lee, *Community Reinvestment in a Globalizing World: To Hold Banks Accountable, from The Bronx to Buenos Aires, Beijing, and Basel*, in Organizing Access to Capital 135, 144–45 (Gregory D, Squires ed., 2003). The Gramm-Leach-Bliley Act paved the way for Citibank and Travelers Group to merge to form CitiGroup in 2000. *Id.*

101. Pub. L. No. 96–221, 94 Stat. 132 (codified as amended in scattered sections of 12 U.S.C.).

102. Cathy Lesser Mansfield, *The Road to Subprime "HEL" was Paved with Good Congressional Intentions: Usury Deregulation and the Subprime Home Equity Market*, 51 S.C. L. Rev. 473, 520–32 (2000).

103. As Mansfield notes:

    It didn't take long after DIDMCA was adopted for some second mortgage lenders, and for other lenders who had been making high cost consumer loans, to notice that DIDMCA appeared to allow them to charge an unlimited amount of interest provided they took a first lien on the borrower's home.

    Id. at 511. Although the courts have consistently held that the DIDMCA provisions do apply to any first lien, Mansfield contends such an interpretation misreads Congress's goal of promoting home ownership. *Id.* at 517. After DIDMCA, interest on a used-car loan, for instance, may grossly exceed state usury laws so long as it is secured by a first lien on the borrower's home. *Id.* at 517.

104. Pub. L. No. 97-320, §§ 801-807, 96 Stat. 1469, 1545-48 (codified amended at 12 U.S.C. §§3801-3805 (2000)).

105. Engel & McCoy, *supra* note 123, at 1275. The loan products allowed by the AMTPA include adjustable-rate mortgages, mortgages with balloon payments, and non-amortizing mortgages where payments only cover interest but do not pay down the principal. *Id.*

106. Pub. L. No. 99-514, 100 Stat. 2085 (codified as amended at 26 U.S.C. § 1 et seq. (2000)).

107. TEMKIN ET AL., *supra* note 112, at viii.

108. Pub. L. No. 101-73, 103 Stat. 183 (codified as amended in scattered sections of 12 U.S.C.).

109. "Thinly capitalized" mortgage brokers maintain a relatively small volume of capital as they originate loans for wholesale lenders. Thinly capitalized brokers are more likely to be judgment-proof. Eggert, *supra* note 116, at 556.

110. JOHN C. WEICHER, THE HOME EQUITY LENDING INDUSTRY: REFINANCING MORTGAGES FOR BORROWERS WITH IMPAIRED CREDIT 43-44 (1997).

111. See *supra* Part II.A.2.

112. This argument assumes that the mortgage market functions efficiently—an assumption that both empirical and anecdotal evidence undermine and that courts have said must be relaxed, if not rejected altogether. See Honorable v. Easy Life Real Estate Sys., 100 F. Supp. 2d 885, 888 (N.D. Ill. 2000). The argument has met with varied success in court, as evidenced by the California Supreme Court's acceptance of it. City of Oakland v. Am. Fin. Servs. Ass'n. 104 P.3d 813, 824 (Cal. 2005) ("[I]ncreased regulation generally entails additional cost, decreasing further the availability of loan funds to subprime borrowers."). Other courts have flatly rejected it. See, e.g., *Honorable*, 100 F. Supp. 2d at 890 (describing the defendant's argument that imposing civil-rights liability on lenders harms the people the laws were designed to help as an "ancient and disreputable proposition").

113. Pub. L. No. 90-321, 82 Stat. 146 (1968) (codified as amended at 15 U.S.C. §§ 1601-1693(c) (2000)).

114. Pub. L. No. 93-533, 88 Stat. 1724 (codified as amended at 12 U.S.C. §§ 2601-2617 (2000)).

115. See Engel & McCoy, *supra* note 123, at 1268. This regulatory philosophy comports with U.S. law's preference for vigorously enforcing fair competition but treating the results of a bargained-for-exchange as presumptively valid.

116. *Id.* at 1307.

117. 15 U.S.C. §§ 1601, et. seq.

118. HUD-TREASURY REPORT, *supra* note 14, at 53. "Purchase money mortgages" are loans used to purchase property, as opposed to "home equity loans" by which a borrower borrows against the equity in a home she already owns.

119. *Id.* HOEPA applies to loans (1) with "an annual percentage rate (APR) of more than 10 percentage points above the yield on Treasury securities of comparable maturities"; or (2) which bear points and fees that exceed the greater of 8% of the loan amount or $400. *Id.* HOEPA subjects such "high-rate, high fee" loans to restrictions on the use of prepayment penalties, balloon payments, and negative amortization. *Id.* Negative amortization refers to a loan for which monthly payments are insufficient to cover the interest due, thereby causing the amount of principal to increase over the life of the loan. Engel & McCoy, *supra* note 123, at 1263.

120. Engel & McCoy, *supra* note 123, at 1307–08.

121. A full exposition of the shortcomings of existing consumer protection statutes is beyond the scope of this Comment. For a more complete discussion, see Engel & McCoy, *supra* note 123, at 1305–09.

122. Peter L. McCorkell, *The Impact of Credit Scoring and Automated Underwriting on Credit Availability*, in The Impact of Public Policy on Consumer Credit *supra* note 119, at 210, ("Until 1995, scoring was seldom—if ever—used in mortgage lending.").

123. Alan M. White, *Risk-Based Mortgage Pricing: Present and Future Research*, 15 Housing Pol'y Debate 503 (2004). In an efficient market, risk-based pricing makes credit available to economically disadvantaged borrowers who would otherwise be denied access to credit. This is accomplished by matching a borrower with a loan priced precisely to reflect the borrower's risk.

124. A subprime borrower is "overcharged" when her loan bears an interest rate and orgination fees that are incommensurate with the additional risk she poses as a borrower.

125. White, *supra* note 160, at 504.

126. Lax et al., *supra* note 110, at 535.

127. Joseph E. Stiglitz & Andrew Weiss, *Credit Rationing in Markets with Imperfect Information*, 71 Am. Econ. Rev. 393, 393 (1981). The credit rationing theory asserts that information asymmetries combine with adverse selection problems to cause lenders to artificially shrink the supply of available credit in order to identify good credit risks. The adverse-selection problem operates as follows: lenders want to lend to risk-averse borrowers because they are less likely to default, but risk-averse borrowers are more likely to be deterred by higher interest rates. *Id.* Risk-*taking* borrowers, in contrast, are more likely to default but less likely to be deterred by high interest rates. *Id.* According to Stiglitz and Weiss, because high rates will deter those borrowers to whom lenders wish to lend, lenders set artificially low loan prices. *Id.* at 394. At lower interest rates, demand exceeds supply and lenders have a pool of potential borrowers from which to choose, allowing them to screen and reject high-risk borrowers. *Id.*

128. Engel & McCoy, *supra* note 123, at 1278–79.

129. *Id.* at 1280.

130. *Id.* Such "disconnected" borrowers are analogous to the "antimarket" consumers identified by Troutt: immobile urban poor who seek "economic survival, rather than economic stability" in the ghetto. Troutt, *supra* note 55, at 428–30.

131. White, *supra* note 160, at 509. ("The rate tables used by wholesale subprime lenders are available only to brokers and are sometimes regarded as trade secrets.").

132. *Id.*

133. *Id.* at 512.

134. Engel & McCoy, *supra* note 123, at 1284 (comparing prime mortgage with "payment terms that are relatively easy to analyze" with predatory loans with terms "that require borrowers to make difficult probabilistic computations about the likelihood and magnitude of future market events").

135. *Id.* at 513.

136. *Id.*

137. *Id.*

138. Engel & McCoy, *supra* note 123, at 1280–81.

139. See, e.g., Honorable v. Easy Life Real Estate Sys., 100 F. Supp. 2d 885, 888 (2000) (noting defendants were able to charge "above-market prices [for rehabbed homes] by, in effect,

taking the unsophisticated, first-time buyers … out of the competitive market by … controlling their access to potential properties, loans, down payments, attorneys and all other information"). The *Honorable* court went on to quote Hanson and Kysar's argument "that 'market outcomes frequently will be heavily influenced, if not determined, by the ability of one actor to control the format of information, the presentation of choices, and, in general, the setting within which market transactions occur.'" *Id.* (quoting Jon G. Hanson & Douglas Kysar, *Taking Behavioralism Seriously: The Problem of Market Manipulation*, 74 N.Y.U. L. Rev. 630,655 (1999)).

140. Elizabeth Renuart, Commentary, *Toward One Competitive and Fair Mortgage Market: Suggested Reforms in* A Tale of Three Markets *Point in the Right Direction*, 82 Tex. L. Rev. 421,427–28(2003).

141. White, *supra* note 160, at 507–08.

142. Renuart, *supra* note 177, at428.

143. *Id.*

144. Lenders' strategies for doing so are addressed *infra* in Part II.C.4.

145. Wyly et al., *supra* note 25, at 629 ("[P]roperty booms are a leading indicator of recession and crisis, appearing as a 'kind of last-ditch hope for finding productive uses for rapidly overaccumulating capital.'" (citing David Harvey, The Urbanization of Capital (1985)).

146. *Id.* at 631 n.5 ("There is considerable evidence, drawn from a variety of sources, of a structural expansion in residential mortgage lending over the past 15 or so years; indeed, some measures of growth suggest that we may be seeing a partial disengagement of residential capital flows from the traditional sources of mortgage demand.").

147. *Id.* at 663 (finding strong empirical support for the hypothesis that "[t]he restructuring of financial services that culminated in the late 1990s created new linkages between the reinvested inner city and national and international capital markets. Lenders restructured their operations and found new ways of reaching profit opportunities in parts of the city that were once seen as unacceptable risks.").

148. *Id.*

149. *Id.* at 632.

150. *Id.* at 672.

151. In fact, Wyly et al. found that "[a] black person requesting a loan in a core gentrified neighborhood is more than twice as likely to end up at a subprime lender than an otherwise similar black person elsewhere in the metropolitan area." *Id.*

152. Immergluck, *supra* note 10, at 265.

153. Fed. Trade Comm'n, Public Forum: The Consumer and Credit Scoring 122 (1999), available at http://www.ftc.gov/bcp/creditscoring/creditscorexscript.pdf [hereinafter FTC Report].

154. Robert B. Avery et al., *Credit Scoring: Statistical Issues and Evidence from Credit-Bureau Files*, 28 Real Est. Econ. 523, 537(2000).

155. McCorkell, *supra* note 159, at 210.

156. Stuart, *supra* note 58, at 97.

157. FTC Report, *supra* note 190, at 307.

158. In his defense of credit scoring, Peter McCorkell, vice president and general counsel of FICO, contends that "the data simply do not support the often-heard contention that giving negative weight to finance company usage necessarily disadvantages minority and low-income borrowers." McCorkell, *supra* note 159, at 217.

159. FTC Report, *supra* note 190, at 30–32. For example, if a borrower's age, time at present address, time at current job, and homeownership status are all credit score factors, a borrower close to retirement who owns her own home and has held the same job for the bulk of her career is likely to receive high scores in *each* category. Her score will be boosted even if the predictive value of such redundant information is limited. FICO claims to accurately discount those factors that overlap in order to avoid artificially inflating scores. *Id.* Of course, without ability to peer into FICO's "black box," those on the outside will never know whether the company's procedures to mitigate redundancies are effective.

160. As Anthony Taibi notes, frequent changes of residence or employment lower the FICO score. Anthony D. Taibi, *Banking. Finance, and Community Economic Empowerment: Structural Economic Theory. Procedural Civil Rights, and Substantive Racial Justice*, 107 Harv. L. Rev. 1463, 1469 (1994). Yet frequent changes of residence or employment may indicate that the borrower is committed to improving her family's quality of life and thus is actually a good credit risk. Moreover, the factors may penalize borrowers for circumstances beyond their control that do not affect an ability to repay. For instance, borrowers may have consumer finance accounts because they experienced discrimination by traditional credit providers. Finally, credit scores do not reflect participation in informal local economies that may amount to responsible economic behavior. *Id.*

161. Weicher, *supra* note 147, at 36–37. Weicher's contention that FICO scores are thus not used in underwriting home loans appears to be outdated.

162. Brad Finkelstein, *FICO Introduces 'Alternative' Credit Score*, Nat'l Mortgage News, Sept. 1, 2004, at 44.

163. *Id.*

164. FTC Report, *supra* note 190, at 205.

165. *Id.* at 225. The joint HUD-Treasury report agreed that subprime lenders may not be reporting some of their borrowers' good credit history information in order to "capture" those borrowers and prevent them from graduating to the prime loans to which their history of subprime payments might entitle them. HUD-Treasury Report, *supra* note 14, at 6.

166. Peter P. Swire, *Equality of Opportunity and Investment in Creditworthiness*, 143 U. Pa. L. Rev. 1533, 1541 (1995).

167. *Id.* at 1535. Swire bases his theory on a nationwide survey by the Federal Reserve that found that only 44% of black households maintain checking accounts as compared to nearly 80% of all other households. *Id.* at 1536. Swire's theory appears to fit into patterns of self-reinforcing disinvestment that have been identified by several authors.

168. *Id.*

169. See *supra* note 195

170. Eggert, *supra* note 116, at 565.

171. See *supra* Part II.A.2.

172. Robin Paul Malloy, Law And Market Economy: Reinterpreting The Values Of Law And Economics 52 (2000).

173. *Id.* at 54.

174. *Id.* at 53 ("[C]oncerns for efficiency and profit maximization may actually increase the incidence of racial discrimination in the market for home mortgages.").

175. See, e.g., Engel & McCoy, *supra* note 123, at 1270.

176. See *supra* Part I.A.

177. Intrafirm segmentation is the division of the retail lending market into segments served by distinct affiliates or subsidiaries of the same parent financial institution. Intrafirm market segmentation is well-documented. See, e.g., Cal. Reinv. Comm., Stolen Wealth: Inequities in California's Subprime Mortgage Market 46, 48 (2001) (finding that in Los Angeles, CitiGroup's subprime affiliate, CitiFinancial, was nearly four times as likely to loan to a lower-income borrower than its prime lending branch, Citibank; in Oakland, subprime lender CitiFinancial was nearly three times as likely to lend to black borrowers as it was to lend to whites).

178. Timothy C. Lambert, Note, *Fair Marketing: Challenging Pre-Application Lending Practices*, 87 Geo. L.J. 2181, 2185 (1999) ("In this context, 'risk' is no longer defined in terms of default, but as the failure to be significantly profitable."). Lambert asserts a novel and compelling argument that fair lending laws should reach the pre-application practices of banks who fail to market to potential minority borrowers, thus systematically denying them access to credit. *Id.* A related argument may be built from Lambert's analysis: that lenders do market to minority communities, but that they offer credit on inferior terms, thus discriminating not in access to credit but in the terms and conditions on which it is offered.

179. Wyly et. al., *supra* note 25, at 677.

180. Lambert, *supra* note 215, at 2185; Wyly et. al., *supra* note 25, at 635 (noting that "automation in credit scoring and underwriting had the effect of reducing processing costs, offering new ways for lenders to find profitable borrowers in the inner cities").

181. See, e.g., Hargraves v. Capital City Mortgage Corp., 140 F. Supp. 2d 7, 21 (D.D.C. 2000) (noting that lender defendant made a "disproportionately large number of loans in neighborhoods that are over 90 percent black"); Brief for the United States, *supra* note 4, at 2 ("Since its inception in 1979, [defendants] have intentionally directed their marketing and loan solicitation efforts almost exclusively toward borrowers and properties in African American neighborhood").

182. Hud-Treasury Report, *supra* note 14, at 37; Wyly et al., *supra* note 25, at 672. Lower credit scores also correlate with lower education levels and location in underserved neighborhoods, suggesting that low credit scores are proxies for profitability and an easy way to market high-priced loan products see *supra* Part II.C.2; Avery et al., *supra* note 191, at 537.

183. Bradford, *supra* note 16, at 77.

184. See Immergluck, *supra* note 10, at 124; Engel & McCoy, *supra* note 123, at 1280; Swire, *supra* note 203, at 1541.

185. Engel & McCoy, *supra* note 123, at 1280–81. To exploit information asymmetries, lenders must "identify people who are disconnected from the credit economy and therefore unlikely or unable to engage in comparison shopping." *Id.* at 1281. Engel and McCoy assert that lower-income persons of color are most likely to meet these criteria and that such potential borrowers may be easily identified by use of HMDA or census data. *Id.*

186. Lambert, *supra* note 215, at 2190–91.

187. As the general counsel for FICO recognizes, "Economically-disadvantaged neighborhoods are less likely to attract multiple mainstream lenders, so residents of those neighborhoods may have a hard time finding low-cost lenders even when they, individually, would qualify for prime rates." McCorkell, *supra* note 159, at 214.

188. Engel & McCoy, *supra* note 123, at 1289–90.

189. Johnson v. Equicredit Corp. of Am., No. 01 C 5197, 2002 WL 448991 (N.D. Ill. Mar. 22, 2002)
190. *Id.* at *l.
191. Pub. L. No. 90–321, 88 Stat. 1521 (1974) (codified as amended at 15 U.S.C. § 1691 (2000)).
192. *Johnson*, 2002 WL 448991, at *5.
193. See *infra* notes 235–246 and accompanying text.
194. See *supra* notes 46–50 and accompanying text.

JOURNALING QUESTION

Why do you think people agreed to mortgages that they could not afford?

22.
BLACK MIDDLE-CLASS NEIGHBORHOODS

MARY PATTILLO

The dominant image American media show of black neighborhoods is "the ghetto," an inner-city space wracked by poverty and crime. Contrast that with the million-dollar apartments in newly gentrified Harlem and with black suburban communities. Middle-class black families, or just non-poor black families, can afford to leave the ghettos. Yet racial segregation, at all income levels, continues to exist. As Mary Pattillo shows, when blacks move into white middle-income neighborhoods, whites move out. Thus, blacks who choose integrated living may well find that an elusive goal. But not all blacks prefer living in majority-white neighborhoods. What are some of the many reasons why a black family, whatever the income, would choose to raise children in a black neighborhood?

CLARIFYING TERMS AND METHODS

For sociologists, none of the words in the phrase "black middle-class neighborhood" is self-evident, each requiring some statement of the author's intent and meaning. In the literature cited here, the terms black or African American most often include black immigrants from the Caribbean, Africa, and elsewhere, but not black Hispanics. The sustained discussion of the differences between American-born and foreign-born blacks is more common in studies of immigration and ethnicity (Foner 2001, Waters 1999), although there is increased attention in urban sociology to black ethnic variation (Adelman et al. 2001, Denton & Massey 1989, Freeman 2002, Logan & Deane 2003).

Whereas defining "black" is challenging, defining "middle class" will never produce full consensus. In the studies reviewed here, this concept is variously operationalized as two to four times the poverty line by family size; the upper ranges of categorical income groupings; the sign and significance of the coefficient on a continuous measure of income; those people who live in a middle-class neighborhood; white-collar workers; and so on. Perhaps most precise would be to title this review "black *nonpoor* neighborhoods" because the income, occupation, and educational range of the middle class is so broad as to include terminal high school graduates as well as those with incomes over $75,000 per year.

"Neighborhood" is perhaps the most straightforward concept, if the least organic. With few exceptions, quantitative studies define the neighborhood as the census tract. This geographic area of 2,500 to 8,000 residents is widely accepted as approximating a neighborhood when using census data. Qualitative and ethnographic studies of neighborhoods and communities (larger areas that are collections of neighborhoods) derive their objects of study more from indigenous experiences of the social and geographic landscapes.

The social scientific methods of studying black middle-class neighborhoods are as diverse as the answers to who is black, who is middle class,

Excerpted from Mary Pattillo, "Black Middle-Class Neighborhoods," *Annual Review of Sociology* 31 (2005), 305–29. References have been edited.

and what is a neighborhood. The two primary approaches are (a) to investigate middle-class black individuals as they hold preferences for certain kinds of neighborhoods, make choices about if and/or where to move, and ultimately reside in places that can be compared with the places of other individuals; and (b) to study black middle-class neighborhoods as whole contexts that can be compared with other contexts (white neighborhoods, Hispanic neighborhoods), or that can be richly described for the nature of interaction and identity formation therein.

NEIGHBORHOOD PEFERENCES

Orlando Patterson (1997) chastises scholars in the social sciences for always seeing the glass half empty. He reads the evidence presented thus far about the lower levels of residential segregation for middle-class blacks compared with poor blacks, and the commensurate upgrading of their residential environs, as proof that conditions have improved dramatically for the black middle class in the post–Civil Rights era. For Patterson, the elusiveness of full parity is still troublesome, but not to the erasure of the clear signs of progress. When reflecting on the factors that underlie observed racial segregation and neighborhood quality disparities, Patterson writes:

> Euro-American attitudes now make possible the complete integration of the metropolis *if only Afro-Americans were willing to live in neighborhoods in which they were a quarter of the population.* This is not an unreasonable bargain. Euro-Americans are, after all, over 80% of the population, so there is some give on their part in their willingness to live in neighborhoods with less than their proportion of the population. At the same time, this attitudinal change permits Afro-Americans to live in mixed neighborhoods where the proportion of Afro-Americans is almost twice that found in the general population.
>
> (Patterson 1997, p. 46, emphasis in original; for similar statements, see Clark 1986, 1991; Clark & Dieleman 1996; Thernstrom & Thernstrom 1997).

The analysis of white and black preferences for varying neighborhood racial compositions is perhaps the most contentious subfield in the study of race and place. The irony of this debate is that both sides are reading the same evidence. It is well established that blacks on the whole prefer neighborhoods that are 50% black and 50% white, and that whites on the whole prefer neighborhoods that are roughly 80% white and 20% black (assuming a bi-racial world). To be sure, both of these scenarios represent some level of racial integration. It is equally clear that these desires cannot be met simultaneously because by the time blacks' compositional preferences are met, the black population has exceeded the tolerance levels (or attraction levels) of most whites, and the neighborhood "tips" (Schelling 1971, 1972). Given these facts, one side must alter their preferences to achieve residential integration. Who should?

This question is obviously a normative, not a scientific, one. Moreover, as many students of segregation and preferences note, the notion that residential segregation is now primarily the result of the individual preferences of whites and blacks overlooks the evidence on the role of institutional discrimination by real estate agents, mortgage lenders, insurers, and appraisers in constraining the choices of African Americans (Galster 1988, Ross & Yinger 2002, Squires & O'Connor 2001, Turner et al. 2002). The debate also assumes that racial residential integration is a goal that trumps (or should trump) other residential desires among blacks and whites, and that if blacks and/or whites just knew that a little more tolerance on their parts could move us to a more residentially integrated country, they would acquiesce. I discuss these considerations of "values" further in the conclusion, returning here to the empirical findings regarding preferences.

Farley et al. (1978) published the first major article on preferences of blacks and whites for neighborhoods of varying racial compositions using data from the Detroit Area Study. They pioneered the "show card" method, in which respondents are shown drawings of a group of houses representing a hypothetical neighborhood. The houses are shaded either black or white to indicate the home of a black or white family, and the cards vary with respect to what proportion of houses are occupied by blacks or whites. Respondents are then asked a series of questions about their preference for, level of comfort in, desire to move into, or likelihood of moving out of such neighborhoods. This method was refined and replicated in the Multi-City Study of Urban Inequality on which a significant amount of this research is based (Adelman 2005, Bobo & Zubrinsky 1996, Charles 2000, Farley et al. 1997, Freeman 2000, Krysan 2002, Krysan & Farley 2002, Timberlake 2000, Zubrinsky & Bobo 1996).

Krysan & Farley (2002, table 1) offer the most straightforward description of the residential preferences of African Americans. Exactly half of the blacks surveyed in Atlanta, Boston, Detroit, and Los Angeles ranked the picture for the hypothetical half black–half white neighborhood as the most attractive, and another 22% ranked this kind of neighborhood the second most attractive (out of five neighborhood choices). Very few blacks (only 2%) found being the only black person in an otherwise all-white neighborhood the most attractive option, while opinions on all-black neighborhoods were split: 27% ranked it the first or second and 48% ranked it the fourth or fifth most attractive alternative. White respondents are often asked a different set of questions and shown different cards, but to provide some perspective on their preferences, roughly 60% of whites across the four metropolitan areas would be uncomfortable in a neighborhood that contained 8 blacks and 6 whites (just over half black) (Farley et al. 1997, figure 4), and only 31% of whites would move into such a neighborhood (Krysan & Farley 2002, p. 960). This degree of willingness of whites to move into majority black neighborhoods shows a significant improvement over time (see Farley et al. 1994). This is the glass-half-full trend that Patterson beseeches scholars to celebrate. Still, the empty

half of the glass exposes the point that in some metropolitan areas with especially large black populations (metropolitan New Orleans is 38% black, metropolitan Washington, DC, is 27% black, and many other metropolitan areas are about 20% African American) and in central cities with even higher black concentrations, the aversion of whites to blacks in their neighborhoods makes residential integration very unstable, always bumping up against racial tipping points (see Ellen 2000 for a discussion of stable racial integration).

Beyond describing the neighborhood racial preferences of whites and blacks, this literature goes on to explore why blacks (and whites) hold these preferences. Here, the diversity of indexes and methodological approaches makes comparison difficult, but I present some of the main findings for black preferences here. Krysan & Farley (2002; also see Zubrinsky & Bobo 1996) emphasize the fear that blacks have of white hostility as driving blacks' preferences for half-and-half or slightly majority black neighborhoods, although cases could also be made from their data for the strength of an ideological commitment to integration among blacks who choose the half-and-half neighborhoods, and racial solidarity/affinity among blacks who prefer the all-black neighborhoods. Fear of white hostility is also the major reason behind blacks' unwillingness to move into an all-white neighborhood. (A clear majority of blacks, 89%, are willing to move into a neighborhood that is 75% white).

To understand the particular preferences of middle-class blacks, the authors find that blacks with more education are less likely to want to live in majority black neighborhoods than those with less education, but the effect of income is relatively weak, with only one of the four income categories reaching significance. None of the socioeconomic variables predicted blacks' preferences for a majority white neighborhood over an integrated neighborhood, and neither did they significantly predict blacks' willingness to move into all-white or all-black neighborhoods. Zubrinsky & Bobo (1996) and

Freeman (2000) similarly report limited support for a class-based model of residential preferences for blacks. So, again, with the exception of education, middle-class blacks do not seem to hold preferences that are distinct from other blacks with regard to neighborhood racial composition. Timberlake (2000), using the same data but with different constructs and focusing on Atlanta, stresses in-group affinity among blacks as the major predictor of their preferences and again finds only sparse evidence that class affects blacks' preferences. Bobo & Zubrinsky (1996) find that the "warmer" blacks feel about whites, the more open they are to integration (a different dependent variable). They find no effect of in-group affinity in determining blacks' attitudes toward integration, and they did not study differences by class.

The two studies that investigate how blacks' neighborhood preferences translate into their actual residential environs (Adelman 2005, Freeman 2000) find that blacks who prefer more whites in their neighborhoods are significantly more likely to have more whites in their neighborhoods—indicating that preferences are not completely unattainable—but that the magnitude of the effect is relatively small. For example, Adelman (2005, figure 1) reports that the neighborhoods of blacks who desire to live with proportionally more blacks are 25% white, compared with the neighborhoods of blacks who desire to live with proportionally more whites, which are on average 30% white. This is not a very sizeable return to blacks' preferences for living with whites.

Perhaps the most interesting twist about social class in all these studies is the following: Black homeowners are consistently more likely to prefer integrated neighborhoods over all-black neighborhoods, they prefer fewer black neighbors in general, and they are more willing to move into all-white neighborhoods than renters, yet, despite these preferences, black homeowners consistently live in blacker neighborhoods than renters (Adelman 2005, Alba et al. 2000, Alba & Logan 1993, Freeman 2000, Logan et al. 1996, South & Crowder 1998). That black homeowners' preferences do not match their realities is suggestive evidence that they face discrimination in the housing market, and that entry into predominately home-owning white neighborhoods is more difficult than entry into white neighborhoods with considerable rental housing.

A correlative question regarding the neighborhood racial preferences of blacks and whites is the following: Are the stated preferences actually about race or about some other neighborhood characteristics that may be associated with racial composition? The fact that at least 20% of African Americans express an aversion to all-black neighborhoods (they rate them as least attractive or would not move into them) suggests either a nontrivial amount of self-hate among blacks, or that racial composition is a marker of other neighborhood characteristics that blacks and whites want to avoid. Harris (1999, 2001) has shown, using data from Chicago, that the dissatisfaction of both whites and blacks (a different outcome measure from preferences) in neighborhoods with greater black representation disappears completely for blacks when crime, physical deterioration, schools, and poverty rates are controlled. For whites, those same controls almost erase whites' stated dissatisfaction with black neighborhoods as well. Harris (2001, p. 12) concludes that "Blacks and Whites are not averse to Black neighbors per se, but rather that both prefer high-socioeconomic-status neighborhoods and that these neighborhoods tend to have small Black populations." Leaving aside the possibility that subjective assessments of neighborhood conditions such as crime cannot be disentangled from a neighborhood's racial composition (see Quillian & Pager 2001), Emerson et al. (2001) find evidence contrary to Harris's using data from a national telephone survey. They find a persistent negative association between the percentage of blacks in a hypothetical neighborhood and whites' willingness to buy a house in that neighborhood, controlling for the quality of schools, the crime rate, and housing values. This is an area in which more research is needed to determine if race is simply a proxy for other neighborhood characteristics.

Investigators disagree over the importance of racial neighborhood preferences for creating or perpetuating racial segregation, the roots of these preferences, their relationship to social class for blacks, and their validity in actually measuring racial sensitivities. Nonetheless, there are three important areas of consensus in this subfield. First, as Clark (1991) writes, "the dynamics of change that come from preferences are determined more by whites' decisions than by blacks' or Hispanics' decisions" (p. 17). That is, all students of this issue recognize the greater ability of whites to actualize their preferences through moving into and out of neighborhoods. Second, whites are less tolerant of integration than are other racial/ethnic groups. Zubrinsky & Bobo (1996, p. 367) describe the pathetic irony that "blacks are at once the most open to integration and yet most often seen as the least desirable neighbors." Finally, the actual moving behavior of whites and blacks makes the gulf in tolerance even more clear. Hwang & Murdock (1998) show that 28% of the growth in suburban black populations between 1980 and 1990 happened in suburbs that were 90% or more white, and another 40% of the growth was in suburbs that were 75%–90% white (author's tabulations from Hwang & Murdock 1998, table 1; also see Glaeser & Vigdor 2001, p. 5). These data illustrate that blacks act on their willingness to move into predominately white areas. Studying the actual moving behavior of whites, however, Quillian (2002, p. 212) writes, "Whites move to destinations that are Whiter than their origin [tracts] and are by far most likely to move to the Whitest possible destinations."

CONCLUSION

"After I leave the skyscraper jungle of midtown Manhattan, I head back to my home in (do or die) Bed-Stuy, Brooklyn," writes African American

journalist Cora Daniels, corroborating the trend she finds among her black professional interviewees to choose predominately black neighborhoods. She continues, "Sure, I could afford to live in more integrated areas, but I don't want to. I like to come home to a place and be surrounded by folks who would not think of asking me, why?" (Daniels 2004, pp. 178–79). Patterson (1997) would be disappointed with Daniels's choice of neighborhood, as he would with similar declarations made by journalist Sam Fulwood (1996), by Karyn Lacy's (2002, 2005) black suburbanites, by the many black professionals interviewed in Feagin & Sikes's (1995) *Living with Racism*, and by the upper- and middle-class blacks who have moved back to Harlem and Chicago's South Side to inaugurate an exclusive black cultural renaissance in those areas (Boyd 2000, Pattillo 2003, Prince 2004, Taylor 2002). Despite the survey data that reveal blacks' clear preference for integration with whites, these are the kinds of statements that instead support arguments that racial segregation results from "neutral ethnocentrism" (Clark 1991) on the part of both whites and blacks, and that the particular segregation of middle-class blacks results from their inability to slough off their racial identities for ones based on class. And who said, after all, that residential integration with whites is still the preeminent goal to which blacks (and whites) should aspire? Legal scholarship on "nonsegregation," as opposed to desegregation or integration (Bell 2001, Calmore 1993, Forman 1971), which emphasizes choice and access and allows for voluntary self-segregation, calls into question the unilateral and in some spheres largely unsuccessful focus on racial integration (of neighborhoods, schools, workforces, etc.). In the housing arena these authors argue that the emphasis on desegregation over the allocation of resources to improve the quality of existing predominately black neighborhoods has retarded any progress in addressing the affordable housing needs of poor African Americans.

Notwithstanding these and other scholarly and political debates about racial segregation and the black neighborhoods it creates, blacks are surely and steadily acting on their stated preferences for integration, and to a much greater extent than are whites. An inspection of contemporary neighborhood-level racial demographics proves that blacks are already being more flexible than their preferences would predict. As already stated, most of the preferences research finds that blacks prefer neighborhoods that are half black and half white; short of this possibility, they prefer slightly more blacks as opposed to slightly more whites. But in 2000, only 20% of African Americans lived in neighborhoods that were 50%–80% black (Glaeser & Vigdor 2001, Table 2). A greater proportion (35.6%) lived in neighborhoods that were 10%–50% black. When informally surveying the racial composition of their metropolitan areas, perhaps blacks do recognize that they are being a bit selfish in wanting to move to half-and-half or slightly blacker neighborhoods, and they prioritize instead the lofty goal of integrated living. Whites, on the other hand, stick to their guns. They say they do not want to live with blacks (they are more willing to live with Hispanics and Asians), and they mean it. They will move out if/when blacks move in (Crowder 2000), and they will almost always choose a white neighborhood over an integrated one (South & Crowder 1998, Quillian 2002). In so doing, they have been able to preserve 56% of all metropolitan neighborhoods as less than 5% black (Glaeser & Vigdor 2001, table 2).

The research to date on black middle-class neighborhoods and their middle-class residents underscores the complexities of this experience. Judging from the weak association between socioeconomic status and racial residential preferences—with the possible exception of education—middle-class blacks are diverse in their feelings about integration, no more or less likely to look for it than their less-well-off racial peers. They profess a taste for integration but a longing for the comfort of segregation. They exhibit simultaneous attraction and aversion to black neighborhoods stemming from their association of black neighborhoods with bad behaviors, but tempered by their belief that blacks are easier to get along with than whites. Among the middle class, there is a growing cadre of romantics who are determined to take back some of the most notoriously disinvested enclaves of black America: Harlem; southeast Washington, DC; Oakland; Chicago's Black Belt. Black preferences overall are no doubt shaped by the daily experience of disadvantage in their current neighborhoods. Although more advantaged than poor blacks, middle-class blacks live with more crime, more poverty, more unemployment, fewer college graduates, more vacant housing, and more single-parent families than similar whites, and indeed than much poorer whites. Moving to the suburbs makes residential life a little more comfortable, but it does not erase the racial disadvantage. These disparities alone underscore the continuing need for race-based affirmative action, for ignoring the importance of race would have college admissions officers, for example, assume that a middle-class black student has it better than a working-class white student.

Finally, middle-class black neighborhoods do not exist in vacuums. They are linked to the preferences and behaviors of whites as individuals and as institutional actors. Whites' growing liberalism on issues of racial integration has contributed to the decrease in racial segregation, the increase in the number of integrated neighborhoods, and the particular neighborhood privileges that middle-class blacks enjoy over poor blacks. But if residential integration is to remain the optimal remedy to the unequal circumstances and outcomes of middle-class blacks, more progress must be made in changing whites' preferences and, particularly, their behaviors. In that vein, perhaps a more fruitful endeavor might be to study the ideologies, practices, and cultures of white neighborhoods, rather than black ones (Kefalas 2003).

NOTE

I thank Brian Stults for analysis of the 1990 and 2000 censuses to produce the statistics on the distribution of the black population across neighborhood types. Thanks also to John Logan and Douglas Massey for their comments on this paper.

REFERENCES

Adelman RM. 2005. The roles of race, class, and residential preferences in the neighborhood racial compositions of middle-class blacks and whites. *Soc. Sci. Q.* 86:209–28.

Adelman RM, Hui-shien T, Tolnay S, Crowder KD. 2001. Neighborhood disadvantage among racial and ethnic groups: residential location in 1970 and 1980. *Sociol. Q.* 42:603–32.

Alba RD, Logan JR. 1993. Minority proximity to whites in suburbs: an individual-level analysis of segregation. Am. J. Sociol. 98:1388–427.

Alba RD, Logan J, Stults B. 2000. How segregated are middle-class African Americans? *Soc. Probl.* 47:543–58.

Bell D. 2001. Bell, J., dissenting. In *What Brown versus Board of Education Should Have Said: The Nation's Top Legal Experts Rewrite America's Landmark Civil Rights Decision*, ed. JM Balkin, pp. 185–200. New York: NY Univ. Press.

Bobo L, Zubrinsky CL. 1996. Attitudes on residential integration: perceived status differences, mere in-group preference, or racial prejudice? *Soc. Forces* 74:883–909.

Boyd M. 2000, Reconstructing Bronzeville: racial nostalgia and neighborhood redevelopment. *J. Urban Aff.* 22:107–22.

Calmore JO. 1993. Spatial equality and the *Kerner Commission Report*; A back-to-the future essay. N. C. Law Rev. 71:1487–518.

Charles CZ. 2000. Neighborhood racial-composition preferences: evidence from a multiethnic metropolis. *Soc. Probl.* 47:379–407.

Clark WAV. 1986. Residential segregation in American cities: a reviw and interpretation. *Popul. Res. Policy Rev.* 5:95–127.

Clark WAV. 1991. Residential preferences and neighborhood racial segregation: a test of the Schelling segregation model. *Demography* 28:1–19.

Clark WAV, Dieleman FM. 1996. *Households and Housing: Choice and Outcomes in the Housing Market.* Rutgers, NJ: Rutgers Univ. Cent. Urban Policy Res.

Crowder K. 2000. The racial context of white mobility: an individual-level assessment of the white flight hypothesis. *Soc. Sci. Res.* 29:223–57.

Daniels C. 2004. *Black Power, Inc.: The New Voice of Success.* Hoboken, NJ: Wiley.

Denton NA, Massey D. 1989. Racial identity among Caribbean Hispanics: the effect of double minority status on residential segregation. *Am. Sociol. Rev.* 54:790–808.

Ellen IG. 2000. *Sharing America's Neighborhoods: The Prospects for Stable Racial Integration.* Cambridge, MA: Harvard Univ. Press.

Farley R, Fielding E, Krysan M. 1997. The residential preferences of blacks and whites: a four-metropolos analysis. *Hous. Policy Debate* 8:763–800.

Farley R, Schuman H, Bianchi S, Colasanto D, Hatchett S. 1978. Chocolate city, vanilla suburbs: Will the trend toward racially separate communities continue? *Soc. Sci. Res.* 7:319–44.

Farley R, Steeh C, Krysan M, Jackson T, Reeves K. 1994. Stereotypes and segregation: neighborhoods in the Detroit area. *Am J. Sociol.*100:750–80.

Feagin J, Sikes M. 1995. *Living with Racism: The Black Middle-Class Experience.* Boston: Beacon.

Foner N, ed. 2001. *Islands in the City: West Indian Migration to New York.* Berkeley: Univ. Calif. Press.

Forman RE. 1971. *Black Ghettos, White Ghettos, and Slums.* Englewood Cliffs, NJ: Prentice Hall.

Freeman L. 2000. Minority housing segregation: a test of three perspectives. *J. Urban Aff.* 22:15–35.

Freeman L. 2002. Does spatial assimilation work for black immigrants in the US? *Urban Stud*: 39:1983–2003.

Fulwood S. 1996. *Waking from the Dream: My Life in the Black Middle Class.* New York: Anchor Books.

Galster GC. 1988. Residential segregation in American cities: a contrary review. *Popul. Res. Policy Rev.* 7:93–112.

Glaeser E, Vigdor J. 2001. Racial segregation in the 2000 census: promising news. *Cent. Urban. Metrop. Policy Rep.* Washington, DC: Brookings Inst. http://www.brookings.edu/es/urban/census/glaeser.pdf. Accessed Aug. 30, 2004.

Harris DR. 1999. Property values drop when blacks move in, because...: racial and socioeconomic determinants of neighborhood stability. *Am. Sociol. Rev.* 64:461–79.

Harris DR. 2001. Why are whites and blacks averse to black neighbors? *Soc. Sci. Res.* 30:100–16.

Hwang SS, Murdock SH. 1998. Racial attraction or racial avoidance in American suburbs? *Soc. Forces* 77:541–65.

Kefalas M. 2003. *Working-Class Heroes: Protecting Home, Community, and Nation in a Chicago Neighborhood.* Berkeley: Univ. Calif. Press.

Krysan M. 2002. Community undersirability in black and white: examining racial residential preferences through community perceptions. *Soc. Probl.* 49:521–43.

Krysan M, Farley R. 2002. The residential preferences of blacks: Do they explain persistent segregation? *Soc. Forces* 80:937–80.

Lacy KR. 2005. Black spaces, black places: strategic assimilation and identity construction in middle-class suburbis. *Ethn. Racial Stud.* In press.

Lacy KR. 2002. "A part of the neighborhood?": Negotiating race in American suburbs. *Int. J. Sociol. Soc. Policy* 22:39–74.

Logan JR, Alba RD, Leung SY. 1996. Minority access to white suburbs: a multiregional comparison. *Soc. Forces* 74:851–81.

Logan JR, Deane G. 2003. *Black Diversity in America.* Albany, NY: Lewis Mumford Cen. Comp. Urban Reg. Res. http://browns4.dyndns.org/cen2000_s4/BlackWhite/BlackDiversityReport/black-diversity01.htm. Accessed Jan. 7, 2005.

Patterson O. 1997. *The Ordeal of Integration: Progress and Resentment in America's 'Racial' Crisis.* New York: Basic Civitas.

Pattillo M. 2003. Negotiating blackness, for richer or for poorer. *Ethnography* 4:61–93.

Prince S. 2004. *Constructing Belonging: Class, Race, and Harlem's Professional Workers.* New York: Routledge.

Quillian L. 2002. Why is black-white residential segregation so persistent? Evidence on three theories from migration data. *Soc. Sci. Res.* 31:197–29.

Ross SL, Yinger J. 2002. *The Color of Credit: Mortgage Discrimination, Research Methodology, and Fair-Lending Enforcement*. Boston: MIT Press.

Schelling TC. 1971. Dynamic models of segregation. *J. Math. Sociol.* 1:143–86.

Schelling TC. 1972. A process of residential segregation: neighborhood tipping. In *Racial Discrimination in Economic Life*, ed. AH Pascal, pp. 157–84. Lexington, MA: Lexington Books.

South SJ, Crowder KD. 1998. Leaving the 'hood: residential mobility between black, white, and integrated neighborhoods. *Am. Sociol. Rev.* 63:17–26.

Squires GD, O'Connor S. 2001. *Color and Money: Politics and Prospects for Community Reinvestment in Urban America*. Albany: SUNY Press.

Taylor MM. 2002. *Harlem Between Heaven and Hell*. Minneapolis: Univ. Minn. Press.

Thernstrom S, Thernstrom A. 1997. *America in Black and White: One Nation, Indivisible*. New York: Simon & Schuster.

Timberlake JM. 2000. Still life in black and white: effects of racial and class attitudes on prospects for residential integration in Atlanta. *Sociol. Inq.* 70:420–45.

Turner MA, Ross S, Galster G, Yinger J. 2002. Discrimination in metropolitan housing markets: national results from Phase 1 HDS 2000. *Rep. 410821*. Washington, DC: Urban Inst. http://www.urban.org/url.cfm?ID=410821. Accessed Aug. 30, 2004.

Waters M. 1999. *Black Identities: West Indian Immigrant Dreams and American Realities*. New York: Russell Sage Found.

Zubrinsky CL, Bobo L. 1996. Prismatic metropolis: race and residential segregation in the city of the angels. *Soc. Sci. Res.* 25:335–74.

JOURNALING QUESTION

If you decide to start a family, what kind of neighborhood would you like to raise your children in? What would the ethnic distribution be like? Or, if you already have children, why have you chosen your current neighborhood?

23.
DENIED ACCESS TO TRADITIONAL FOODS

Including the Material Dimension to Institutional and Environmental Racism

KARI MARIE NORGAARD

Most Americans get food from stores. They do not grow, fish, hunt, or gather a significant portion of their diet. But that is not true of all Americans: some communities retain a closer relationship with the production of their food. Until recently, as Kari Marie Norgaard shows us, the Karuk Tribe of California was able to fish for salmon as a very significant part of their diet. By denying them fishing rights and doing damage to the land and water that supported them, the Karuk are being deprived of the right to feed themselves. This has direct health consequences, as store-bought, prepared foods replace the healthier choices of former time, and the longstanding American idea that people live longer nowadays is challenged. What other things are lost when food moves from a communal activity to a grocery-store expedition?

Last year we caught an all-time low, less than a hundred fish at Ishi Pishi Falls with extended effort, meaning that we was down there fishing hard and we had a lot of people fishing hard down there, and that's not all right. What about the lamprey? What about the sturgeon? What about the spring salmon? What about the fall run? We're talking about a total collapse in our fishery.

Ron Reed, Traditional Karuk Fisherman

Members of the Karuk Tribe of California are intimately dependent upon salmon both physically and culturally. Salmon has been both the primary food and the basis of the prosperous subsistence economy of the Karuk people since time immemorial. The recent and ongoing elimination of traditional foods including multiple runs of salmon, Pacific lamprey, sturgeon, and other aquatic species from the Klamath River system is producing extreme adverse healthy, social, economic and spiritual effects on Karuk people. The estimated rates of diabetes and heart conditions are three and four times the U.S. average. Despite their epidemic levels, diabetes has recently appeared in the Karuk population. Furthermore, the destruction of the Klamath River fishery has led to both poverty and hunger. Prior to contact with Europeans and the destruction of the fisheries, the Karuk, Hupa and Yurok tribes were the wealthiest people in what is now known as California. Today they are amongst the poorest.

Environmental racism is understood to be a product of institutional racism (Bullard 1993, Pellow and Brulle 2005). Yet most scholars discuss institutional racism in terms of spatial segregation or lack of access to social resources such as education and social or economic capital (e.g., Stretesky and Hogan 1998). Analyses of poverty fail to consider the material basis of wealth in nature, or the importance of maintaining relationships with land as a means of cultural or spiritual sovereignty. For

Excerpted from Kari Marie Norgaard, "Denied Access to Traditional Foods: Including the Material Dimension to Institutional and Environmental Racism," Presented, American Sociological Association Annual Meeting, Montreal, 2006. References have been edited.

Native people in particular, primary mechanism of institutionalized environmental racism and genocide has been the disruption of relationships with the land that forms the basis of culture, livelihood, spirituality and identity. The intentional destruction of the bison, food source for tribes of the Great Plains, is a case in point. Yet despite forced relocation, reservation systems and regulations such as the Dawes Act, which reduced access to land, disrupted subsistence use activities and forced capitalist modes of behavior onto Native community structure, many Native people retain relationships with the land, plants and animals with whom their cultures, religious systems and economies have evolved. These relationships continue to form the spiritual, cultural and economic basis for tribal sovereignty.

INSTITUTIONAL AND ENVIRONMENTAL RACISM

The present situation in which Karuk people face hunger and serious health problems resulting from denied access to their traditional food fits within the framework of what is known as "environmental justice." For the past several decades it has been recognized that poor people and people of color are most likely to pay the price of various forms of environmental degradation (e.g., Bullard 1993). Environmental justice literature identifies environmental racism as a product of institutional racism. "Many of the differences in environmental quality between black and white communities result from institutional racism. Institutional racism influences local land use, enforcement of environmental regulations, industrial facility siting, and where people of color live, work, and play" (Bullard 1993).

Yet most discussions of institutional racism and environmental decline have focused on dynamics of housing segregation and the enforcement of health and safety violations, but failed to take into account institutional racism in the production of wealth and poverty through disruption of relationships with land, or the importance of maintaining relationships with land as a means of carrying out culture. These latter features of institutional racism are central to understanding the impoverishment and genocide of Native people. Similarly, most discussion of environmental racism as faced by Native Americans has focused on exposure to pollution on Native lands through waste trading, landfills and waste incinerators (Geddicks 1994). These circumstances are more similar to the conditions faced by African Americans fighting toxic exposure, which led to the emergence of an environmental justice framing. Institutionalized racism with respect to Native people is most often discussed as the absence of economic infrastructure, unemployment, inadequate education and health care, forms of institutional racism that parallel the political circumstances and history of other urban based racial minorities.

Institutionalized racism manifests not only as a disproportionate burden of exposure to environmental hazards, but also as denied access to decision making and control over resources, which in the case of tribal peoples may form the basis of material, cultural and spiritual survival. In the case of the Karuk and many other tribes, poverty has been systematically produced alongside environmental decline as outside user groups destroy resources upon which Native people have subsisted. Before the impacts of dams, mining and overfishing, the Karuk people subsisted off salmon year-round for tens of thousands of years. Now poverty and hunger rates for the Karuk Tribe are amongst the highest in the state and nation. The devastation of the resource base, especially the fisheries, is also directly linked to the disproportionate unemployment and low socioeconomic status of Karuk people today.

Little or no discussion has focused on the relationship of resource destruction by non-Indians (destruction of the material basis of wealth through environmental decline) and present day poverty, or the importance of maintaining relationships with land as a means of carrying out culture. Within a capitalist framework we might speak in terms of access to means of production rather than exposure due to spacial segregation. Yet because disrupted cultures were not capitalist but subsistence based, and because impacts are not only economic but cultural and physical. I therefore use the term "denied access to relationships with land."

METHODS

This research was conducted on site in the Karuk ancestral territory along the Klamath River over a nine-month period in the spring and summer of 2005. The information presented is complied from four main sources: archival material, in-depth interviews with Karuk tribal members, Karuk medical records and the 2005 Karuk Health and Fish Consumption Survey. In-depth interviews were used to gather detailed information from tribal members regarding the above issues of concern. Socioeconomic questions focused on perceptions of employment, the local economy, food gathering and emigration. Information was also gathered on family history and health conditions over time. In-depth interviews were conducted with a total of 18 individuals. These individuals served as "key informants" regarding a range of cultural and fisheries topic. Data on income, employment, unemployment and poverty rates are from the U.S. Census, the Bureau of Indian Affairs and the Karuk Tribal Census.

The 2005 Karuk Health and Fish Consumption Survey was distributed to adult tribal members within the ancestral territory. The survey had a response rate of 40 percent, a total of 90 individuals. The survey contained 61 questions designed to evaluate the range of economic, health and cultural impacts for Tribal members of the decline in quality of the Klamath River system. The survey allowed for the collection of quantitative data regarding economic patterns, health conditions and fish consumption that has been long absent in the broader discussion of tribal impacts of riverine health.

HEALTH AND ECONOMIC CONDITIONS

The Karuk Tribe resides in northern California along the Klamath River. Approximately one third of their population continue to live in their ancestral territory. The Karuk are the second largest tribe in California. Since 1979, when they gained federal recognition, the Karuk have experienced a political, economic and ethnic renewal (Bell 1991, Nagel 1996). Members are actively recovering cultural traditions, including language use, ceremonial practices and traditional basketweaving. The Karuk Tribe has a Department of Natural Resources and is involved in land management, although the U.S. Forest Service is the dominant land manager in the region (99 percent of the land area is managed by the Forest Service).

Salmon has been both the primary food and the basis of the prosperous subsistence economy of the Karuk people since time immemorial. Although they are very modern people, members of the Karuk Tribe remain intimately dependent upon salmon both culturally and physically as a source of subsistence food in a remote region with extreme unemployment and poverty. With the loss of the most important food source, Spring Chinook salmon in the 1970s, the Karuk people hold the dubious honor of experiencing one of the most recent and dramatic diet shifts of any Native tribe in the United States. Self-report data indicate that the percentage of adult tribal members eating traditional foods once a week or more has dropped from 65 percent when they were teenagers to less than 25 percent in 2004. Many Karuk frame their situation as a case of *denied access to traditional foods*. Over 80 percent of households surveyed in 2005 indicated that they were unable to gather adequate amounts of eel, salmon or sturgeon to fulfill their family needs. Most households that caught salmon, steelhead, eels and sturgon report catching 10 or fewer, and no households report catching more than 50 eels or Fall or Spring Chinook Salmon. Furthermore, 40 percent of tribal members report that there are species of fish their family once gathered that they no longer harvest. For most of these species the decline in harvest is quite recent.

DEPLETION OF RESOURCES BY OTHER NON-INDIAN CULTURAL GROUPS

Karuk people are denied access to traditional foods due to direct competition of resource use by non-Indians. Whereas long-standing cultural traditions existed for regulating and sharing fish and other resources both within the Karuk Tribe and between neighboring tribes, the entry of non-Indian groups into the region led to conflict and dramatic resource depletion (McEvoy 1986). The arrival of miners, the military and settlers into Karuk territory was accompanied by direct genocide in which many people and much knowledge of traditional foods was lost (Norton 1979). Extensive overfishing at the river mouth, overfishing of ocean stocks, hydraulic mining and the construction of dams that now block access to spawning upstream habitat of Spring Chinook salmon are also among the chief causes of resource depletions. For example, over half of those surveyed report that Spring Chinook became an insignificant source of food during the 1960s and 1970s, within a decade of the completion of Iron Gate dam. More recently conflicts over in-stream water flows may be understood as examples of depletion of resource by non-Indians.

REGULATION BY OUTSIDE AGENCIES

A second factor denying Karuk people access to traditional foods is denied access to land management techniques due to regulation of the resource by outside or non-Indian agencies. The disruption of traditional land management techniques, especially practices of burning, is significant for both forest and aquatic species. White settlers and miners did not understand the role of fire in the forest ecosystem. Since the gold rush period, Karuk people have been forcibly prevented from setting fires needed to manage the forest, prolong spring run-off and create proper growing conditions for acorns and other foods. More recently, the rights of Karuk people to fish have been contested as well. During the 1970s the federal government denied Karuk people the right to continue their traditional fishing practices (Norton 1979) by arresting them and even incarcerating them. Karuk fishing rights have yet to be acknowledged by the U.S. government.

Other regulations are a response to resource depletion by non-Indians. These regulations have often failed to take into account the Karuk as original inhabitants. As a result they have attempted to balance the subsistence needs of Karuk people with recreational desires of non-Indians from outside the area. Vera Davis notes the imbalance and injustice of this view, "Now I don't think that no one has a right to tell us when we can do it when you have people who pay hundreds of dollars to come in, kill the venison and get the horns. I don't think that is fair because this is our livelihood" (Vera Davis quoted in Salter 2003, p. 32). In the Health and Fish Consumption Survey, individuals were asked whether members of their household had been questioned or harassed by game wardens while fishing for a number of aquatic food species. Thirty-two percent reported that they had experienced harassment. To be fined or have a family member imprisoned imposes a significant economic burden on families. This is a risk that many are unwilling or unable to take. Of those reporting harassment, 36 percent reported that they had decreased their subsistence or ceremonial activities as a result of such contacts.

Regulations affect not only fishing but also hunting, mushroom gathering and gathering of basketry materials. Tribal Vice-chairman and Ceremonial Leader Leaf Hillman describes this situation: "The act of harvesting a deer or elk to be consumed by those in attendance at a tribal ceremony was once considered an honorable, almost heroic act. Great admiration, respect and celebration accompanied these acts and those who performed them. Now these acts (if they are to be done at all) must be done in great secrecy, and often in violation of Karuk custom, in order to avoid serious consequences." As Hillman further explains it, government regulations force assimilation to the point of criminal indictment:

> In order to maintain a traditional Karuk lifestyle today, you need to be an outlaw, a criminal, and you had better be a good one or you'll likely end up spending a great portion of your life in prison. The fact of the matter is that it is a criminal act to practice a traditional lifestyle and to maintain traditional cultural practices necessary to manage important food resources or even to practice our religion. If we as Karuk people obey the "laws of nature" and the mandates of our Creator, we are necessarily in violation of the white man's laws. It is a criminal act to be a Karuk Indian in the 21st century.
>
> Leaf Hillman, 2004

IMPACTS OF DENIED ACCESS TO TRADITIONAL FOODS AS INSTITUTIONAL AND ENVIRONMENTAL RACISM

HEALTH EFFECTS

The loss of traditional food sources is now recognized as being directly responsible for a host of diet-related illnesses among Native Americans, including diabetes, obesity, heart disease, tuberculosis, hypertension, kidney troubles and strokes (Joe and Young 1993). Indeed, diabetes is one of the most significant health problems facing Native peoples today (Olson 2001). The estimated diabetes rate for the Karuk Tribe is 21 percent, nearly four times the U.S. average. The estimated rate of heart disease for the Karuk Tribe is 39.6 percent, three times the U.S. average. Despite their epidemic levels, diabetes has recently appeared in the Karuk population. Most families report the first appearance of diabetes in the 1970s. Data from the 2005 Karuk Health and Fish Consumption Survey show that the loss of the most important food source, the Spring Chinook salmon run, is directly linked to the appearance of epidemic rates of diabetes in Karuk families.

One of the most significant consequences of diabetes is a decrease in life span. Although there are many stories of Karuk ancestors living to very old ages, even 100 years or more, numerous tribal members reported that, as Judy Grant put it, "They seem to be dyin' younger."

> I've been to way too many funerals the last couple of years and that's not all right.
> That seems to me that they're just getting younger and younger.
>
> Ron Reed, traditional Karuk fisherman

> I think people are dying younger too. I think it's the food. Because my husband's father was 91 when he died. Diabetes is what killed him....[W]hen we were doin' research on the family a lot of the death certificates are from the diabetes. Most of them, almost all of them.
>
> Selma George, wife of Karuk tribal member

For virtually all Karuk tribal members the traditional diet has been replaced by store-bought and/or commodity food. Unfortunately, as Professor Harriet Kuhnlein, Founding Director of the Centre for Indigenous Peoples' Nutrition and Environment, and others note, "the market foods derived from plants that are available and used by families of indigenous peoples do not contain high nutrient density, but provide carbohydrates, energy, and nutrients through fortification" (Kuhnlein and Chan 2000, 617; see also Kuhnlein et al. 1994; Receveur et al. 1997; Morrison et al. 1995).

According to the survey, about 20 percent of Karuk people depend on food rations through government commodity programs. Significant concern has been expressed about commodity foods distributed to Indian people as a cause of obesity (USDA Food and Nutrition Service 1991) since the use of this program is high among Indian populations. Other studies have discussed the poor availability of high-fiber, low-fat foods in commodity food programs and called for change in these programs (Burhansstipanov and Dresser 1994).

Dietary recommendations for diabetic patients generally include the reduction of total and saturated fats and an increase in complex carbohydrates (Howard et al. 1991), conditions present in the traditional diet of the Karuk. Thus, the Karuk traditional diet was not only useful as a *preventative* of diabetes, it is also an important *treatment* for this disease. One significant element of the high-salmon content of the traditional Karuk diet is the presence of omega-3 fatty acid. Omega-3 fatty acids have been linked with a number of significant health benefits including reduced risk of heart attacks, strokes and Alzheimer, prevention of osteoporosis, a diabetic treatment, improved mental health and improved brain development in infant. Furthermore, elders within the tribe have successfully curbed diet-related diseases by increasing fish consumption. Karuk elder Marge Houston experienced multiple heart attacks. But since dramatically increasing her consumption of salmon, her heart condition and cholesterol levels have improved significantly:

> You talk to a good many of the Karuk elders and they all have cholesterol, heart problems. I've had a six-way bi-pass. Two aneurisms and an arterial-femural bi-pass graft. I've been cut from stem to here. From here to here, in six different surgeries. I had my first heart problem in '95. My diet was basically Top Ramen, easy boxed, mixes. You know…chips, sodas, you know….Very, very poor. But now I eat good and my cholesterol has been under 200 for going on my third year. I ate salmon on a regular basis in the beginning when I found out how dangerous my cholesterol was. That's where I think the wild food is good. It makes a difference when I can have salmon or venison as opposed to a fatty beef or pork. Now my doctor says I have the numbers of a young person.
>
> Marge Houston, Karuk tribal member

ECONOMIC EFFECTS

Lack of traditional food impacts the Karuk Tribe not only through decreased nutritional content of specific foods, but also by an overall absence of food, leaving Karuk people with basic issues of food security. Salmon was a critical food and the basis of a prosperous traditional economy for the Karuk people. Therefore, it should come as no surprise that the destruction of the fishery has resulted in both poverty and hunger. One of the more difficult aspects of the Karuk situation for non-Indians to grasp is the fact that Karuk people have experienced relatively high rates of subsistence living until quite recently. With the destruction of the once-abundant salmon population it is no longer possible for people to subsist on these foods. Ron Reed, traditional fisherman and cultural biologist for the Karuk Tribe, notes the impossibility of feeding the current tribal population from the one remaining fishing site at Ishi Pishi falls: "We had over 100 villages up and down the Klamath River, with fishing sites associated with each village. Now we are trying to feed our people off one fishery. It's not possible." Although salmon was not bought and sold as part of a cash economy, the presence of this food meant that people didn't need to spend money buying other foods at the grocery store or be forced to rely on government commodities, as is now the case. In a recent report on the nutritional analysis of traditional and present-day foods, Karuk tribal member and registered dietician Jennifer Jackson notes the high cost of purchasing food at the local store:

> In addition to commodity foods, Karuk people must rely on foods available in grocery stores….The yearly median Karuk tribal income is $13,000 or [approximately] $270/week. Yet the average cost for a two-person family to eat healthy foods, based on the prices of foods available at the local grocery store in Orleans, is estimated at approximately $150/week. Note that this represents 55% of the income of an average family for the week! A high percentage of Karuk families are therefore dependent on other forms of income or food assistance, such as the commodity food programs. And thus the cycle of poor nutrition continues.
>
> (Jackson 2005, 11)

Cost replacement analysis conducted in the spring of 2005 puts the cost of purchasing salmon at over $4,000 per tribal member per year (Stercho 2005). For the entire Karuk Tribe the annual total would be approximately $13 million per year (Stercho 2005). In the communities within the ancestral territory this amount would represent over half of the average per capita annual income.

TRADITIONAL FOODS AND CULTURAL SURVIVAL

For Indigenous Peoples, the collective right to food and food sovereignty are indispensable for the continuation of their cultures and Indigenous identity. The freedom for self determination of Indigenous Peoples involves not only access to but also control and management of their territories and natural resources.

> Statement of the Indigenous Peoples at the
> Third Regional Consultation for
> Latin American and the Caribbean FAO and
> NDO/CSO Guatemala, April 2004

Back in the 1900s when the spring run was effectively cut off from the Upper Basin also began a dramatic decline in traditional values within the Karuk tribe.

> Ron Reed, traditional Karuk fisherman

Beyond its importance as direct subsistence and its specific health benefits, traditional food and food-gathering activities are at the very heart of Karuk culture. The activities of managing, gathering, preparing and consuming traditional foods serves the functions of passing on traditional ecological knowledge, stories within the community and from one generation to the next. Food-related activities serve as social glue that binds the community together, they outline social roles that provide a sense of identity and serve as the vehicle for the transmission of values. Traditional fisherman Ron Reed describes "being Indian" as an activity. One's identity, worldview, values and knowledge base emerge from lived experience, from participating in activities that Karuk people have carried out for generations, from going through the world in relationship with specific places.

> You can give me all the acorns in the world, you can get me all the fish in the world, you can get me everything for me to be an Indian, but it will not be the same unless I'm going out and processing, going out and harvesting, gathering myself. I think that really needs to be put out in mainstream society that it's not just a matter of what you eat. It's about the intricate values that are involved in harvesting these resources, how we manage them for these resources and when. This knowledge is incorporated under our ceremonies.
>
> Ron Reed, traditional Karuk fisherman

The act of living in a traditional way, of harvesting and preparing and distributing traditional foods, leads to knowledge and imparts Karuk values of responsibility and relationship. Ron Reed describes how the activity of fishing is a forum for passing on both physical qualities, such as balance, and cultural tradition to his sons: "Fishing down at Ishi Pishi Falls you learn how to gain your balance. You learn the traditional values down there, the taboos and things like that, because it is a sacred fishery and there are certain rules that you abide by."

Traditional food is not only important as culture, sustenance and spirituality, it can also serve the *social* function of bringing families and the community together. Anthropologist Robin Peterson (2005) describes the social importance of eels:

> Eeling is an important time for families to get together. Eel roasts used to be common during the springtime, bringing many families together for socializing. Today there are not enough eel to have these gatherings anymore. Many eelers commented on how eeling gives young people something to do. However, when there are not enough eel to make it worthwhile for them to go then they look for other activities to fill their time. In a rural area, these "alternative" activities often include alcohol and drugs, as well as "getting into trouble." As more young people

are placed in rehab or jail, the family structure begins to break down. Impacts also occur on an inter-tribal level, including the trading of resources, inter-tribal marriage, and participation in ceremonies.

(Peterson, 2005)

Frank Lake describes the centrality of food at social gatherings, describing food as "the glue or an adhesive that holds all the other social or cultural or spiritual activities together":

> And with the ceremonies, when people come together, someone will bring a deer, someone will bring acorns, someone will bring huckleberries, whoever happened to have some abundance to share or even gathered in mind to have for the ceremony. And certain get to be known for what they can bring. That, too, then becomes the reliance. So, again, the food becomes the glue or an adhesive, in many ways, that holds all the other social or cultural or spiritual activities together.

Frank Lake, Karuk descendant

Stories about the land are also important for the way they bring people together:

> If you don't have people out gathering, then stories about the land aren't being shared. Stories that share information and bring people together. It's like the difference between, "Where did you get the huckleberries." "Well, I was out with this and blah blah blah... This is how it was. I know this." So a story goes along with the food. Whereas if someone just went down and bought blueberries at Cotsco, like, "How was that Costco trip?" "Oh, town traffic was bad." Or it's like, "We don't have acorns, so thank goodness, we have this commodity flour." It's a conversation stopper.

Frank Lake, Karuk descendant

One remaining fishing site, Ishi Pishi Falls, is a place of sustenance, but also a place of stories and socializing. Carrie Davis describes the excitement of spending time with friends at the Falls when she was a child:

> It's a real social spot. You see people you might not see very often here. You know during salmon time, whenever you were fishing, you'd see them. I remember being excited because I may be seeing my friends every now and then, I would know that I'd get to spend the day with all those kids. I didn't get that chance all the time.

Carrie Davis, Karuk tribal member

As these multi-generational family and social food gathering activities disappear, the food disappears but also an entire field of social relations is lost.

DENIED ACCESS TO TRADITIONAL FOODS AND RELATIONSHIPS WITH LAND: A MATERIAL BASE FOR INSTITUTIONAL AND ENVIRONMENTAL RACISM

As the quality of Klamath River system and salmon populations has declined, Karuk people are denied access to their traditional foods. Economic, health and cultural impacts are devastating. Damage to the environment by non-Indians leads further racism and genocide as illustrated by interviews and statistics. But it is also the case that racism can lead to environmental decline. Karuk and non-Indian relations in the Klamath region over the past 150 years since contact can be understood as a cycle whereby historical cultural genocide and ongoing racism against the Karuk tribe manifests as environmental decline today, and this environmental degradation in turn manifests as institutionalized racism and cultural genocide in the present day. Yet overlooked within environmental sociology is the extent to which racism and cultural genocide may in turn produce further environmental decline. The Karuk people evolved sophisticated land management practices including the regulation of the fisheries and the management of the forest through fire (Salter 2003, McEvoy 1986). Ceremonial practices including the First Salmon Ceremony regulated the timing of fishing to allow for escapement and thus continued prosperous runs. Forests were burned to increase production of food species, especially acorns and bulbs. Burning also influenced the local hydraulic cycles, increasing seasonal runoff into creeks.

Western scientists and social scientists alike follow in the tradition that prior to European contact our continent was an untouched wilderness. Yet in fact salmon, acorns and hundreds of food and cultural-use species were actively managed by Native peoples. The abundance of these species reported at the time of Lewis and Clarke and early settlers was a product of this management in which high-quality seeds were selected, the production of bulbs was enhanced through harvest, oak populations reinforced through fire and fish populations carefully managed. The disruption of these practices has contributed to the decline of the Klamath River ecosystem. To ignore the role of Native land management practices in ecosystem health—and their disruption in environmental decline—is yet another extension of the faulty assumption that prior to European contact the land was an untouched wilderness.

I have argued for the necessity of including the material basis of wealth in understandings of institutionalized racism, and for increased understanding of the role of racism and genocide as contributing factors to environmental degradation within the field of environmental sociology. Although the significance of denied access to relationships with land is particularly salient for Native peoples, parallel processes apply to the production of poverty and environmental inequity for other racial minorities systematically displaced from the land, such as Chinese and African Americans. Black farmers and Chinese miners have been systematically deprived of the ability to accumulate capital and/or maintain control over food production systems (see, e.g., Gilbert, Wood and Sharp 2002; Gilbert, Sharp and Felin 2002; Wood and Gilbert 2000).

BIBLIOGRAPHY

Bell, Maureen *Karuk: The Upriver People* Happy Camp, CA: Naturgraph Publishers, 1991.

Bullard, RD. 1993 "Race and environmental justice in the United State" *Yale Journal of International Law* 18(1): 319–335.

Burhansstipanov, Linda, and Connie Dresser. 1994. *Documentation of the Cancer Research Needs of American Indians and Alaska Natives.* Bethesda, Md.: Cancer Control Science Program, Division of Cancer Prevention and Control, National Cancer Institute.

Geddicks, A. "The new resource wars: native and environmental struggles against multinational corporations" South End Press, 1994.

Gilbert, J., G. Sharp and S. Felin 2002 "The loss and persistence of black-owned farms and farmland: a review of the research literature and implications." *Southern Rural Sociology* 18(2): 1–30.

Gilbert, J., S. W. Wood, and G. Sharp 2002."Who owns the land? Agricultural land ownership by race/ethnicity" *Rural America* 17(4), December: 55–62.

Howard, B. V., Abbott, W. G., & Swinburn, B. A. (1991) Evaluation of metabolic effects of substitution of complex carbohydrates for saturated fat in individuals with obesity and NIDDM. *Diabetes Care*, 14, 786–795.

Joe, Jennie and Robert Young *Diabetes as a disease of civilization: the impact of cultural change on indigenous people* Berlin: Walter de Gruyter and Co., 1993.

Kuhnlein, Harriet V and H. M. Chan 2000. "Environment and Contaminants in Traditional Food Systems of Northern Indigenous Peoples" *Annual Review of Nutrition* 20: 595–626.

Kuhnlein Harriet, Appavoo DM, Morrison N Soueid R and P. Pierrot 1994. "Use and Nutrient Composition of Traditional Sahtu (Hareskin) Dene/Metis food" *Journal of Food Composition Anals* 7: 144–157.

McEvoy, Arthur E. *The fisherman's problem: ecology and law in the California fisheries 1850–1980.* Cambridge University Press, 1986.

Morrison N. E., Receveur O., Kuhnlein H. V., Appavoo D. M., Soueida R., Pierrot P. Contemporary Sahtú Dene/Métis use of traditional and market food. *Ecol. Food Nutr.* 1995; 34:197–210

Norton, Jack *Genocide in northwestern California: when our worlds cried* San Francisco: Indian Historian Press, 1979.

Olson, Brooke 2001. "Meeting the Challenges of American Indian Diabetes: anthropological perspectives on treatment and prevention" in Trfzer and Weiner (eds). *Medicine Ways: Disease, Health and Survival among Native Americans* Walnut Creek, CA: Alta Mira, 2001.

Pellow, David Naguib and Robert J. Brulle *Power, Justice, and the Environment A Critical Appraisal of the Environmental Justice Movement* MIT Press: Cambridge, 2005.

Receveur O, M Boulay and H Kuhnlein 1997. "Decreasing traditional food use affects diet quality for adult Dene/Metis in 16 Communities of the Canadian Northwest Territories" *Journal of Nutrition.* 127: 2179–2186.

Salter, John F. "White Paper on behalf of the Karuk Tribe of California: a context statement concerning the effect of Iron Gate Dam on traditional resource uses and cultural patterns of the Karuk people within the Klamath River Corridor, 2003" available online at http://elibrary. ferc. gov/idmws/docket_sheet.asp.

Stercho, Amy 2005 "The importance of place-Based fisheries to the Karuk Tribe of California: a socio-economic study" Master's thesis, Humboldt State University, Arcata, California.

Stretesky, Paul and Michael Hogan 1998 "Environmental justice: an analysis of Superfund sites in Florida" *Social Problems* 45(2): 268–287.

USDA Food and Nutrition Service. 1991. "The Food Distribution Program on Indian Reservations (FDPIR)." *Food Program Facts.* Alexandria, Va.: Food and Nutrition Service.

Wood, Spencer and Jess Gilbert 2000 "Returning African-American farmers to the land: recent trends and a policy rationale." *Review of Black Political Economy* 27(4), Spring: 43–64.

JOURNALING QUESTION

In many inner cities, it is very hard to get fresh and wholesome ingredients to do home cooking, and people have to rely on fast food and prepared foods. What are the health and social consequences of that?

Education

24.

RACE, INEQUALITY, AND EDUCATIONAL ACCOUNTABILITY

The Irony of "No Child Left Behind"

LINDA DARLING-HAMMOND

One could claim that the No Child Left Behind Act was an attempt to address the inequalities of American public education. Yet by measuring end results—"achievement scores" of one sort and another—the act had the ultimate effect of exacerbating many of the problems it should have been solving. Linda Darling-Hammond suggests that some of the problem might be solved by paying attention to teacher training and interstate reciprocity for teachers. But given local funding for education and, thus, the United States' enormously disparate levels of money spent on pupils, can any federally mandated act bring equality to education?

In 2002, many Civil Rights advocates initially hailed the Bush Administration's major Education Bill, optimistically entitled "No Child Left Behind" (NCLB), as a step forward in the long battle to improve education for those children traditionally left behind in American schools—in particular, students of color and those living in poverty, new English learners and students with disabilities. The broad goals of NCLB are to raise the achievement levels of all students and to close the achievement gap that parallels race and class distinctions. On its face, the Act intends to accomplish this by focusing schools' attention on improving test scores for all groups of students, providing parents more educational choices and ensuring better-qualified teachers.

The agenda is laudable, but this complex 1,000-page law has affected states, districts, schools and students in a variety of unintended ways. The nicknames proliferating as this intrusive legislation plays out across the country give a sense of some of the anger and confusion left in its wake: "No Child Left Untested," "No School Board Left Standing" and "'No Child's Behind Left" are just a few of them. More than 20 states and dozens of school districts have officially protested the Act, voting to withdraw from participation, withhold local funding for implementation or resist specific provisions. One state and a national teachers association have brought lawsuits against the federal government based on the unfunded costs and

Excerpted from Linda Darling-Hammond, "Race, Inequality and Educational Accountability: The Irony of 'No Child Left Behind,'" *Race Ethnicity and Education* 10 (2007): 245–60. References have been edited.

dysfunctional side-effects of the law. Members of the Congressional Black Caucus, among other federal legislators, have introduced bills to place a moratorium on high-stakes standardized testing, a key element of NCLB; withhold school sanctions until the bill is fully funded and require progress toward adequate and equitable educational opportunities for students in public schools. And the Harvard Civil Rights Project, along with other advocacy groups, has warned that the law threatens to increase the growing dropout and push-out rates for students of color, ultimately reducing access to education for these students (Sunderman & Kim, 2004).

As evidence of its unintended consequences emerges, it seems increasingly clear that NCLB as currently implemented is more likely to harm most of the students who are the targets of its aspirations than to help them, and it is more likely to undermine—some would even say destroy—the nation's public education system than to improve it. These outcomes are likely because the underfunded Act layers onto a grossly unequal school system a set of unmeetable test score targets that disproportionately penalize schools serving the neediest students, while creating strong incentives for schools to keep out or push out those students who are low achieving in order to raise school average test scores.

Furthermore, the Act's regulations have caused a number of states to abandon their thoughtful diagnostic assessment and accountability systems—replacing instructionally rich, improvement-oriented systems with more rote-oriented, punishment-driven approaches—and it has thrown many high-performing and steadily improving schools into chaos rather than helping them remain focused and deliberate in their ongoing efforts to serve students well.

While well intentioned, it has become clear that the Act will, in the next few years, label most of the nation's public schools "failing," even when they are high performing and improving in achievement. Already more than one-third of public schools have been targeted as having failed to make "Adequate Yearly Progress" (AYP), and studies suggest that at least 80% of schools in most states will have failed to achieve AYP by 2014 (see, for example, Wiley et al., 2005). Because of the multiple subgroup targets that must be achieved for different racial/ethnic and income groups on multiple tests—representing more than 30 different targets in diverse schools—and the law's "catch 22" for English language learners, 99% of California schools are expected to "fail" by this date (Packer, 2004).

A California study found that:

> [failing] schools were designated not because tests had shown their overall achievement levels to be faltering, but because a single student group—disabled learners or Asian students, for example—had fallen short of a target. As a result, the chances that a school would be designated as failing increased in proportion to the number of demographic groups served by the school. (Novak & Fuller, 2003)

This "diversity penalty" sets up the prospect that the schools serving the neediest students will be first to lose funds under the law. And in some high-achieving states that have set very high standards for themselves, large numbers of schools are dubbed "failing" because they fall below these standards, even though they score well above most other schools in the nation and the world.

Some believe this is a prelude to voucher proposals aimed at privatizing the education system, since the public will have been besieged with annual reports about failing public schools which the law's unmeetable requirements guarantee cannot be remedied. In addition to the perverse consequences for school systems, the law will lead to reductions in federal funding to already under-resourced schools and it will sidetrack funds needed for improvement to underwrite transfers for students to other schools (which, if they are available, may offer no higher-quality education). If left unchanged, the Act will deflect needed resources for teaching and learning to ever more intensive testing of students, ranking of schools, bussing of students and Lawyers' fees for litigating the many unintended consequences of the legislation.

Most unhappily, some of the Act's most important and potentially productive components—such as the effort to ensure all students have highly qualified teachers and successful educational options and supports—are in danger of being extinguished by the shortcomings of a shortsighted, one-way accountability system that holds children and educators to test-based standards they cannot meet while it does *not* hold federal or state governments to standards that would ensure equal and adequate educational opportunity.

INEQUALITY IN EDUCATION: WHAT NCLB DOES NOT CHANGE

The first problem—one that NCLB does not acknowledge or address—is the enormous inequality in the provision of education in the United States. Unlike most countries that fund schools centrally and equally, the wealthiest U.S. public schools spend at least 10 times more than the poorest schools—ranging from over $30,000 per pupil to only $3,000; and these disparities contribute to a wider achievement gap than in virtually any other industrialized country. Within states, the spending ratio between high and low spending schools is typically at least 2 or 3 to 1.

The school disparities documented in Jonathan Kozol's (1991) *Savage Inequalities* have not lessened in recent years. As documented in federal statistics and a large number of current lawsuits, schools serving large numbers of low-income students and students of color have larger class sizes, fewer teachers and counselors, fewer and lower-quality academic courses, extracurricular activities, books, materials, supplies and computers, libraries and special services (Darling-Hammond, 2004a). Resources are so severely inadequate in the growing number of "apartheid" schools serving more than 90% "minority" students that legal action to challenge school funding systems is underway in more than half the states. These conditions are vividly illustrated in this description of Luther Burbank Middle School, which serves low-income students of color in San Francisco who are plaintiffs in a school funding lawsuit:

At Luther Burbank School, students cannot take textbooks home for homework in any core subject because their teachers have enough textbooks for use in class only.... Some math, science, and other core classes do not have even enough textbooks for all the students in a single class to use during the school day, so some students must share the same one book during class time...For homework, students must take home photocopied pages, with no accompanying text for guidance or reference, when and if their teachers have enough paper to use to make homework copies.... The social studies textbook Luther Burbank students use is so old that it does not reflect the breakup of the former Soviet Union. Luther Burbank is infested with vermin and roaches and students routinely see mice in their classrooms. One dead rodent has remained, decomposing, in a corner in the gymnasium since the beginning of the school year. The school library is rarely open, has no librarian, and has not recently been updated. Luther Burbank classrooms do not have computers. Computer instruction and research skills are not, therefore, part of Luther Burbank students' regular instruction in their core courses. The school no longer offers any art classes for budgetary reasons. Two of the three bathrooms at Luther Burbank are locked all day, every day. The third bathroom is locked during lunch and other periods during the school day, so there are times during school when no bathroom at all is available for students to use. Students have urinated or defecated on themselves at school because they could not get into an unlocked bathroom.... When the bathrooms are not locked, they often lack toilet paper, soap, and paper towels, and the toilets frequently are clogged and overflowing.... Ceiling tiles are missing and cracked in the school gym, and school children are afraid to play basketball and other games in the gym because they worry that more ceiling tiles will fall on them during their games.... The school heating system does not work well. In winter, children often wear coats, hats, and gloves during class to keep warm. Eleven of the 35 teachers at Luther Burbank have not yet obtained regular, non-emergency credentials, and 17 of the 35 teachers only began teaching at Luther Burbank this school year.

(*Williams v. State of California, Superior Court of the State of CA for the County of San Francisco*, 2001, Complaint, 58–56)

Under No Child Left Behind, these dreadful school conditions are left largely untouched. Although, the Act orders schools to ensure that 100% of students test at levels identified as "proficient" by the year 2014—and to make mandated progress toward this goal each year—the small per-pupil dollar allocation the law makes to schools serving low-income students is well under 10% of schools' total spending, far too little to correct these conditions. While the law focuses on test scores as indicators of school quality, it largely ignores the resources that *enable* school quality. It does not provide substantial investments in the under-resourced schools where many students are currently struggling to learn, nor does it require that states demonstrate progress toward equitable and adequate funding or greater opportunities to learn. Although the law includes another set of requirements to ensure that all students receive "highly qualified teachers," as discussed in a later section, the lack of adequate federal support for actually making this possible currently makes this promise a hollow one in many communities.

TEST OR INVEST? HOW NCLB TREATS SCHOOLS SERVING THE NATION'S NEEDIEST STUDENTS

The biggest problem with die Act is that it mistakes measuring schools for fixing them. It sets annual test score goals for every school—and for subgroups of students within schools—that are said to constitute "Adequate Yearly Progress." Schools that do not meet these targets for each subgroup each year are declared in need of improvement and, later, failing. This triggers interventions

(notification to parents of the school's label and a three-month period to write a school improvement plan). Students must be allowed to transfer out of "failing" schools at the school's expense; schools stand to be reconstituted or closed, and states and districts stand to lose funds based on these designations. Unfortunately, the targets—based on the notion that 100% of students will score at the "proficient" level on state tests by the year 2014—were set without an understanding of what this goal would really mean.

First, of course, there is the fundamental problem that it is impossible to attain 100% proficiency levels for students on norm-referenced tests (when 50% of students by definition must score below the norm and some proportion must by definition score below any cut point selected)—the kind of tests that have been adopted by an increasing number of states due to the specific annual testing requirements of NCLB. Criterion-referenced tests also typically use an underlying norm-referenced logic in selecting items and setting cut scores, although in theory, the target could at least remain fixed on these tests. Even if tests were not constructed in this way, the steepness of the standard is unrealistic. Using a definition of proficiency benchmarked to the National Assessment of Educational Progress, one analyst has calculated that it would take schools more than 160 years to reach such a target in high school mathematics if they continued the fairly brisk rate of progress they were making during the 1990s (Linn, 2003).

Even more problematic is that the Act requires that schools be declared "failing" if they fail to meet these targets for each subgroup of designated students annually. It requires the largest gains from lower-performing schools, ignoring the fact that these schools serve needier students and are generally less well funded than those serving wealthier and higher-scoring students. To complicate things more, those that serve large numbers of new English language learners (what the law calls "Limited English Proficient" [LEP] students) and some kinds of special needs students (what the law calls "students with disabilities" are further penalized by the fact that students are assigned to these subgroups *because* they cannot meet the standard, and they are typically removed from the subgroup when they do meet the standard. Thus these schools will not ever be able to meet the proficiency benchmark the law has set... [o]ne could argue, quite legitimately, that at least some of the schools identified as "needing improvement" (a designation that changes to "failing" if targets are not met after three years) indeed are dismal places where little learning occurs, or are complacent schools that have not attended to the needs of all their less advantaged students—schools that need to be jolted to change. And, it is fair to suggest that underserved students in such schools deserve other choices if they cannot change.

These important arguments are part of the law's theory of action: that low-quality schools will be motivated to change if they are identified and shamed, and that their students will be better served if given other educational options. These outcomes may in fact occur in some cases. The problem is that the law actually works in many other cases to label schools as failing even when they are succeeding with the very students the law wants to help, and it creates incentives that can reduce the quality of education such schools can provide, while providing few real options for their students to go to better schools.

How might the goal of improving schools actually, paradoxically, undermine them? First, there is evidence from states that have used similar accountability provisions—applying labels of failure to low-scoring schools that serve low-income students reduces the schools' ability to attract and keep qualified teachers. For example, in North Carolina, analysts found that the state labeling system made it more difficult for the neediest schools to attract or retain high-quality teachers (Clotfelter et al., 2003). Similarly, Florida's use of aggregate test scores, unadjusted for student characteristics, in allocating school rewards and sanctions led to reports that

qualified teachers were leaving the schools rated "D" or "F" in droves, to be replaced by teachers without experience or training (DeVise, 1999). As one principal queried, "Is anybody going to want to dedicate their lives to a school that has already been labeled a failure?"

Second, schools that have been identified as not meeting AYP standards stand to lose federal funding, thus having even fewer resources to spend on the students they are serving. Rather than seeking to ensure that students attend adequately funded and well-managed schools that would enable them to learn to higher levels, NCLB seeks to expand students' opportunities by offering them the chance to transfer out to other "non-failing" public schools if their school is declared "failing." This option is to be funded through the resources of the "failing" school, as are funds for supplemental services for such things as tutoring or after-school programs.

While the choice option may be a useful idea in theory, such alternatives are providing little overall improvement in the opportunities of most students in poor rural or inner-city schools, because—addition to the fact that this option for some comes at the expense of school funding for their peers—there are frequently not "non-failing" public schools with open seats available to transfer to nearby. The best schools are already quite full, and they have no incentive to admit low-income students with low test scores, poor attendance records or substantial educational needs who will "bring down" their average and place the school at risk of receiving sanctions. Furthermore, the best-resourced schools are typically not close to the inner city or poor rural neighborhoods where struggling schools are concentrated. Thus, rather than expanding educational opportunities for low-income students and students of color, the law is more likely in many communities to reduce still further the quality of education available in the schools they must attend. A better approach would be to invest in the needed improvements in such schools in the first place, and to measure their progress on a variety of indicators in ways that give them credit for improvements they produce for the students they serve.

ALICE IN WONDERLAND ACCOUNTABILITY

Although the stated goals of No Child Left Behind are to improve achievement and enhance equity, its complex regulations for showing "Adequate Yearly Progress" toward test score targets aimed at "100%-proficiency" have created a bizarre situation in which schools that are improving and closing the achievement gap are often declared failing. For example, in San Diego, California, Marston Middle School, a well-regarded school that serves a diverse student population with a large number of low-income, minority and English language learning students, greatly improved achievement for all groups over several years as its faculty worked intensely on literacy development (Darling-Hammond et al., 2003). In 2003, the first year of NCLB, Marston far exceeded its state and federal school growth targets, showing gains for Latino students and low-income students of more than four times the targeted increases. However, the school failed to meet AYP because its white students, who already scored near the top on the state tests, did not improve "sufficiently"—largely because they had nearly hit the testing ceiling. While Marston Middle School did what NCLB presumably encourages—increase achievement and reduce the achievement gap—it was punished under the law.

Meanwhile, in Minnesota, where eighth-graders score first in the nation in mathematics and near the top in other subjects as well, more than 80% of public schools will soon be declared in "need of improvement" and not long after, as "failing" and in need of reconstitution. This is because, in the baffling world that federal policy has invented, schools in states with the highest standards will have the most schools found wanting, even if their students achieve at levels substantially above those of schools in other states. Consequently, many states formally lowered their standards in order to avoid having

most of their schools declared failing. And states that worked hard to create forward-looking performance assessment systems during the 1990s have begun to abandon them for antiquated multiple-choice tests, since the more progressive approaches do not fit the federal mandate for annual testing that allows students and schools to be ranked and compared.

This not only reduces the chances that schools will be able to focus on helping students acquire critical thinking, research, writing and production abilities; it also reduces the chances that students who learn in different ways and have different talents will have opportunities to show what they have learned. Analysts have raised concerns about how the law's requirements are leading to a narrower curriculum; to test-based instruction that ignores critical real-world skills, especially for lower-income and lower-performing students; and to less useful and engaging education (Neill, 2003). Equally important is the growing evidence that the law's punitive approach may actually reduce access to education for the most vulnerable students, rather than increasing it.

HIGHER SCORES, FEWER STUDENTS

Perhaps the most adverse, unintended consequence of NCLB's accountability strategy is that it undermines safety nets for struggling students rather than expanding them. The accountability provisions of the Act actually create large incentives for schools that can to keep such students out and to hold back or push out students who are not doing well. A number of studies have found that systems that reward or sanction schools based on average student scores create incentives for pushing low-scorers into special education so that their scores won't count in school reports (Allington & McGill-Franzen, 1992; Figlio & Getzler, 2002), retaining students in grade so that their grade-level scores will look better (Haney, 2000; Jacob, 2002), excluding low-scoring students from admissions (Smith, 1986; Darling-Hammond, 1991) and encouraging such students to leave schools or drop out (Smith, 1986; Orfield & Ashkinaze, 1991; Haney, 2000).

Researchers have found higher rates of grade retention and dropping out in states and cities that have instituted test requirements for promotion or graduation (Orfield & Ashkinaze, 1991; Heubert & Hauser, 1999; Roderick et al., 1999; Clarke et al., 2000; Jacob, 2001; Lilliard & DeCicca, 2001; Wheelock, 2003), as well as a widening gap in graduation rates between white and minority students (Orfield et al., 2004). Schools' responses to the incentives created by high-stakes tests can cause gaming that produces higher scores at the expense of vulnerable students' education. Studies in New York, Texas and Massachusetts have showed how schools have raised their test scores while "losing" large numbers of low-scoring students.

For example, recent studies have found that the "Texas Miracle," which was the model for the federal No Child Left Behind Act, boosted test scores in part by keeping many students out of the testing count and making tens of thousands disappear from school altogether (Dobbs, 2003). The "disappeared" are mostly students of color. A longitudinal student-level study in one large Texas city found that the introduction of high-stakes graduation tests with school sanctions in the tenth grade was associated with sharp increases in ninth-grade student retention and high levels of student dropout and disappearance. Of the large share of students held back in the ninth grade, most of them African American and Latino, only 12% ever made it to the tenth-grade test that drove school rewards. Grade retention was associated with increases in school tenth-grade test scores and related accountability ratings, and with higher rates of dropouts for students. Other gaming strategies included exempting students from testing via special education placement and LEP status, skipping students past key testing grades and transferring students to non-traditional settings (Heilig, 2006).

Overall, fewer than 70% of white students who enter ninth grade in Texas graduate from high school four years later, and the proportions for African American and Latino students are only 50% (Haney, 2000). Unhappily, the celebrated score gains for African American and Latino students appear in substantial part to be a function of high dropout and push-out rates for these students. Paradoxically, NCLB's requirement for disaggregating data and tracking progress for each subgroup of students increases the incentives for eliminating those at the bottom of each subgroup who struggle to learn, especially where schools have little capacity to improve the quality of services such students receive.

In Texas, New York, Massachusetts and many other states where tests alone are supposed to drive improvement, large numbers of students of color are taught by under-prepared and inexperienced teachers—which, research shows, significantly affects passing rates on the state tests (Ferguson, 1991; Fetler, 1999; Fuller, 1998, 2000; Darling-Hammond, 2004a, b). Where states have replaced investing with testing, students in many communities are forced to attend under-resourced schools where they lack the texts, materials and qualified teachers needed for learning. Indeed, studies show that these schools—which lack a stable cadre of skilled teachers to develop stronger teaching strategies—have the least capacity to improve under accountability plans, and therefore are most likely to respond by excluding high-need students or gaming the system (Mintrop, 2003; Diamond & Spillane, 2002; Rustique-Forrester, 2005).

The current conditions of schooling for many students of color and low-income students in the United States strongly resemble those that existed before *Brown* v. *Board of Education* (1954) sought to end separate and unequal education. Unfortunately, NCLB, while rhetorically appearing to address these problems, actually threatens to leave more children behind. The incentives created by an approach that substitutes high-stakes testing for highly effective teaching are pushing more and more of the most educationally vulnerable students out of school earlier and earlier. In a growing number of states, high school completion rates for African American and Latino students have returned to pre-1954 levels. In these states, two-way accountability does not exist: The child is accountable to the state for test performance, but the state is not held accountable to the child for providing adequate educational resources.

The consequences for individual students who are caught in this no-win situation can be tragic, as most cannot go on to further education or even military service if they fail these tests, drop out or are pushed out to help their schools' scores look better. The consequences for society are also tragic, as more and more students are leaving school earlier and earlier—some with only a seventh or eighth grade education—without the skills to be able to join the economy. These students join what is increasingly known as a "school-to-prison pipeline" (Wald & Losen, 2003), carrying an increasing number of undereducated youth almost directly into the criminal justice system. Indeed, prison enrollments have tripled since the 1980s and the cost of the criminal justice system has increased by more than 600% (while public education spending grew by only 25% in real dollars). More than half of inmates are functionally illiterate and 40% of adjudicated juveniles have learning disabilities that were not addressed in school (Darling-Hammond, 2004b).

States end up paying $30,000 per inmate to keep young men behind bars when they were unwilling to provide even a quarter of this cost to give them good schools. Increasingly, this growing strain on the economy is deflecting resources away from the services that could make people productive. California and Massachusetts had the dubious distinction this past year of being the first states to pay as much for prisons as for higher education.

WHAT IT WOULD TAKE TO REALLY LEAVE NO CHILD BEHIND

There are many ways in which No Child Left Behind would need to be amended if it were to do less harm and more good, including supporting states to use more thoughtful assessments, and to use them for improving curriculum rather than for punishing students or schools. School progress should be evaluated on multiple measures—including such factors as attendance, student progress and continuation, course passage and classroom performance on tasks beyond multiple-choice tests—and gains should be evaluated with measures showing how individual students improve over time, rather than school averages that are influenced by changes in who is assessed. Determinations of school progress should reflect a better grounded analysis of schools' actual performance and progress rather than a statistical gauntlet that penalizes schools serving the most diverse populations. Targets should be based on sensible goals for student learning that also ensure appropriate assessment for special education students and English language learners and credit for the gains these students make over time. And "opportunity-to-learn standards," specifying the provision of adequate materials, facilities and teachers, should accompany assessments of student learning.

Most important, investments should be made in the ability of schools to hire and support highly effective teachers and leaders, providing them with adequate resources and intensive opportunities to learn to teach struggling students. While recent studies have found that teacher quality is one of the most important school variables influencing student achievement (Darling-Hammond, 2000), teachers are the most inequitably distributed school resource (National Commission on Teaching and America's Future, 1996, 2003).

One of the great ironies of the federal education programs designed to support the education of students who are low income and who have greater educational needs is that schools have often served these students with unqualified teachers and untrained aides, rather than the highly skilled teachers envisioned by federal laws. The very purpose of decades of federal legislation—to ensure greater opportunities for learning for these students—has been undermined by local inability to provide them with teachers who know how to meet their needs.

In states that have lowered standards rather than increasing incentives to teaching, it is not uncommon to find urban and poor rural schools where one-third or more of the teachers are working without preparation, certification or mentoring (see e.g. Darling-Hammond, 2004b). In schools with the highest minority enrollments, students have less than a 50% chance of getting a mathematics or science teacher with a license and a degree in the field that they teach (Oakes, 1990). As a result, students who are the least likely to have learning supports at home are also least likely to have teachers who understand how children learn and develop, who know how to teach them to read and problem solve, and who know what to do if they are having difficulty.

Thus, one of the most important aspects of No Child Left Behind is that it requires all schools to provide "highly qualified teachers" to all students. This requirement—that all teachers be fully certified and show competence in the subject areas they teach—is intended to correct this longstanding problem. However, the federal government has allowed states to call teachers "highly qualified" before they have become prepared and met standards, and it has invested little in creating stronger preparation and incentives to teach.

This problem must be understood if it is to be solved. There are actually at least three or four times as many credentialed teachers in the USA as there are jobs, and many states and districts have surpluses. What often looks like a teacher shortage is actually mostly a problem of getting teachers from where they are trained to where they are needed and keeping teachers in the profession, especially in central cities and poor rural areas. More than 30%

of beginners leave teaching within five years, and low-income schools suffer from even higher turnover rates (Darling-Hammond & Sykes, 2003). In this context, producing more teachers—especially through fast-track routes which tend to have high attrition—is like struggling to fill a leaky bucket rather than fixing it.

Not surprisingly, teachers are less likely to enter and stay in teaching where salaries are lower and working conditions are poorer. They are also more than twice as likely to leave if they have not had preparation for teaching and if they do not receive mentoring in their early years on the job (Henke et al., 2000; National Commission on Teaching and America's Future, 2003). These are problems that can be successfully addressed through policy. States and districts that have increased and equalized salaries to attract qualified teachers, created strong preparation programs so that teachers are effective with the students they will teach and provided mentoring to beginners, have eliminated shortages, developed a strong teaching force and improved student achievement (for examples, see Darling-Hammond & Sykes, 2003).

But solving this problem everywhere requires national action. The distributional inequities that lead to the hiring of unqualified teachers are caused not only by disparities in pay and working conditions, but also by interstate barriers to teacher mobility, inadequate recruitment incentives to distribute teachers appropriately and fiscal conditions that often produce incentives for hiring the least expensive rather than the most qualified teachers, And while the nation actually produces far more new teachers than it needs, some specific teaching fields experience real shortages. These include teachers for children with disabilities and those with limited English proficiency as well as teachers of science and mathematics. Boosting supply in the fields where there are real shortfalls requires targeted recruitment and investment in the capacity of preparation institutions to expand their programs to meet national needs in key areas.

While No Child Left Behind sets an expectation for hiring qualified teachers, it does not include the policy support to make this possible. The federal government should play a leadership role in providing an adequate supply of well-qualified teachers just as it does in many other countries (see, for example, Darling-Hammond, 2005), and as it has in providing an adequate supply of well-qualified physicians in the USA. When shortages of physicians were a major problem more than 40 years ago, Congress passed the 1963 Health Professions Education Assistance Act to support and improve the caliber of medical training, create and strengthen teaching hospitals, provide scholarships to medical students and create incentives for physicians to train in shortage specialties and to locate in underserved areas. Similar federal initiatives in education were effective during the 1960s and 70s but were eliminated in the 1980s.

If the USA is to address one of the most important sources of inequality in its schools, it will need a federal teacher policy that will: (1) *recruit new teachers* who prepare to teach in high-need fields and locations, through service scholarships and forgivable loans that allow them to receive high-quality teacher education; (2) *strengthen teachers' preparation* through incentive grants to schools of education to create professional development schools, like teaching hospitals, to train prospective teachers in urban areas and to expand and improve programs to prepare special education teachers, teachers of English language learners and teachers in other areas where our needs exceed our current capacity; and (3) *improve teacher retention and effectiveness* by ensuring

they have mentoring support during the beginning teaching stage when 30% of them drop out (for a discussion, see Darling-Hammond & Sykes, 2003).

For an annual cost equivalent to 1% of the Bush Administration's $300 billion tax cut in 2003 or the equivalent of one week's combat costs during the War in Iraq, the nation could fully subsidize, with service scholarships, the high-quality preparation of 40,000 teachers annually to teach in high-need fields and high-need schools—enough to fill every new vacancy filled by an unprepared teacher each year; seed 100 top quality urban teacher education programs; ensure mentors for all of the new teachers who are hired each year; and provide incentives to bring expert teachers into high need schools. With focus, it would be possible to ensure that all students are taught by well-qualified teachers within the next five years.

Obviously, students will not learn to higher levels unless they experience good teaching, a strong curriculum and adequate resources. Merely adopting tests and punishments will not create an accountability system that increases the likelihood of good practice and reduces the likelihood of harmful practices. In fact, as we have seen, adopting punitive sanctions without investments increases the likelihood that the most vulnerable students will be more severely victimized by a system not organized to support their learning. A policy agenda that leverages equitable resources and invests strategically in high-quality teaching would support *real* accountability—that is, accountability to children and parents for providing the conditions under which students can be expected to learn.

NOTE

A version of this article was published in Deborah Meier and George Wood (Eds) (2004) *Many children left behind* (New York, Beacon Press).

REFERENCES

Advocates for Children (2002) *Pushing out at-risk students: an analysis of high school discharge figures—a joint report by AFC and the Public Advocate.* Available online at: www.advocatesforchildren.org/pubs/pushout-11-20-02.html (accessed 30 December 2002).

Clarke, M., Madaus, G., Pedulla, J. & Shore, A. (2000, January) *Statements: an agenda for research on educational testing* (Boston, MA, National Board on Educational Testing and Public Policy).

Clotfelter, C., Ladd, H., Vigdor, J. & Diaz, R. (2003) Do school accountability systems make it more difficult for low performing schools to attract and retain high quality teachers?, paper prepared for the *Annual Meeting of the American Economic Association*, Washington, DC, February.

Darling-Hammond, L. (1991) The implications of testing policy for quality and equality, *Phi Delta Kappan*, November, 220–225.

Darling-Hammond, L. (2000) Teacher quality and student achievement, *Educational Policy Analysis Archives*, 8(1). Available online at: http://epaa.asu.edu/epaa/v8nl (accessed 1 August 2007).

Darling-Hammond, L. (2004a) The color line in American education; race, resources, and student achievement, *W.E.B. DuBois Review: Social Science Research on Race*, 1(2), 213–246.

Darling-Hammond, L. (2004b) What happens to a dream deferred? The continuing quest for equal educational opportunity, in: J. A. Banks (Ed.) *Handbook of research on multicultural education* (2nd edn) (San Francisco, CA, Jossey-Bass), 607–630.

Darling-Hammond, L. (2005) Teaching as a profession: lessons in teacher preparation and professional development, *Phi Delta Kappan*, 87(3), 237–240.

Darling-Hammond, L., Hightower, A. M., Husbands, J., LaFors, J. R., Young, V. M. & Christopher, C. (2003) *Building instructional quality: 'inside-out' and 'outside-in' perspectives on San Diego's school reform* (Seattle, WA, Center for the Study of Teaching and Policy, University of Washington).

Darling-Hammond, L. & Sykes, G. (2003) Wanted: a national teacher supply policy for education: the right way to meet the "highly qualified teacher" challenge, *Educational Policy Analysis Archives*, 11(33). Available online at: http://epaa.asu.edu/epaa/v11n33/ (accessed 1 August 2007).

DeVise, D. (1999, November 5) A+ plan prompts teacher exodus in Broward County, *Miami Herald*.

Diamond, J. & Spillane, J. (2002) *High stakes accountability in urban elementary schools: challenging or reproducing inequality?* Institute for Policy Research Working Paper (Evanston, IL, Northwestern University Institute for Policy Research).

Dobbs, M. (2003, November 9) Education "miracle" has a math problem, *The Washington Post*.

Ferguson, R. F. (1991) Paying for public education: new evidence on how and why money matters, *Harvard Journal on Legislation*, 28(2), 465–498.

Fetler, M. (1999) High school staff characteristics and mathematics test results, *Education Policy Analysis Archives*, 7(9). Available online at: http://epaa.asu.edu/epaa/v7n9 (accessed 1 August 2007).

Figlio, D. N. & Getzler, L. S. (2002) *Accountability, ability, and disability: gaming the system?* (New York, National Bureau of Economic Research).

Fuller, E. (1998) *Do properly certified teachers matter? A comparison of elementary school performance on the TAAS in 1997 between schools with high and low percentages of properly certified regular education teachers* (Austin, TX, The Charles A. Dana Center, University of Texas at Austin).

Fuller, E. (2000) Do properly certified teachers matter? Properly certified algebra teachers and Algebra I achievement in Texas, paper presented at the *Annual Meeting of the American Educational Research Association*, New Orleans, LA, April.

Haney, W. (2000) The myth of the Texas miracle in education, *Education Policy Analysis Archives*, 8(41). Available online at: http://epaa.asu.edu/epaa/v8n41/ (accessed 1 August 2007).

Heilig, J. V. (2006) *Progress and learning of urban minority students in an environment of accountability.* Ph.D. thesis, Stanford University.

Henke, R. R., Chen, X., Geis, S. & Knepper, P. (2000) *Progress through the teacher pipeline: 1992–93 college graduates and elementary/secondary school teaching as of 1997.* NCES 2000–152 (Washington, DC, National Center for Education Statistics).

Heubert, J. & Hauser, R. (Eds) (1999) *High stakes: testing for tracking, promotion, and graduation.* A report of the National Research Council (Washington, DC, National Academy Press).

Jacob, B. A. (2001) Getting tough? The impact of high school graduation exams, *Education and Evaluation and Policy Analysis,* 23(2), 99–122.

Jacob, B. A. (2002) *The impact of high-stakes testing on student achievement: evidence from Chicago.* Working Paper (Cambridge, MA, Harvard University).

Kozol, J. (1991) *Savage inequalities* (New York, Crown Publishing).

Lilliard, D. & DeCicca, P. (2001) Higher standards, more dropouts? Evidence within and across time, *Economics of Education Review,* 20(5), 459–473.

Linn, R. L. (2003) Accountability: responsibility and reasonable expectations, *Educational Researcher,* 32(7), 3–13.

Mintrop, H. (2003) The limits of sanctions in low-performing schools: a study of Maryland and Kentucky schools on probation, *Education Policy Analysis Archives,* 11(3). Available online at: http://epaa.asu.edu/epaa/v11n3.html (accessed 15 November 2004).

National Commission on Teaching and America's Future (1996) *What matters most: teaching for America's future* (New York, NCTAF).

National Commission on Teaching and America's Future (2003) *No dream denied: a pledge to America's children* (Washington, DC, NCTAF).

Neill, M. (2003) Leaving children behind: how No Child Left Behind will fail our children, *Phi Delta Kappan,* 85(3), 225–228.

Novak, J. & Fuller, B. (2003) *Penalizing diverse schools? Similar test scores but different students bring federal sanctions* (Berkeley, CA, Policy Analysis for California Education).

Oakes, J. (1990) *Multiplying inequalities: the effects of race, social class, and tracking on opportunities to learn mathematics and science* (Santa Monica, CA, The RAND Corporation).

Orfield, G. & Ashkinaze C. (1991) *The closing door: conservative policy and black opportunity* (Chicago, IL, University of Chicago Press).

Packer, J. (2004) No Child Left Behind and adequate yearly progress fundamental flaws: a forecast for failure, paper presented at the *Center for Education Policy Forum on Ideas to Improve the Accountability Provisions,* Washington, DC, 28 July.

Roderick, M., Bryk, A. S., Jacob, B. A., Easton, J. Q. & Allensworth, E. (1999) *Ending social promotion: results from the first two years* (Chicago, IL, Consortium on Chicago School Research).

Rustique-Forrester, E. (2005) Accountability and the pressures to exclude: a cautionary tale from England, *Education Policy Analysis Archives,* 13(26). Available online at: http://epaa.edu/epaa/v13n26/ (accessed 1 August 2007).

Smith, F. (1986) *High school admission and the improvement of schooling* (New York, New York City Board of Education).

Sunderman, G. & Kim, J. (2004) *Inspiring vision, disappointing results: four studies on implementing the No Child Left Behind Act* (Cambridge, MA, Harvard Civil Rights Project).

Wald, M. & Losen, D. (2003) *Deconstructing the school to prison pipeline* (San Francisco, CA, Jossey-Bass).

Wiley, E. W., Mathis, W. J. & Garcia, D. R. (2005) The impact of the adequate yearly progress requirement of the federal "No Child Left Behind" Act on schools in the Great Lakes region (Tempe, AZ, Educational Policy Studies Laboratory, Arizona State University).

JOURNALING QUESTION

When you were in grade school, did you have to take standardized tests? What do you remember about that experience, and how well do you think those tests reflected what you were getting out of your education?

25.
THE IMPACT OF "COLORBLIND" IDEOLOGIES ON STUDENTS OF COLOR

Intergroup Relations at a Predominantly White University

AMANDA E. LEWIS, MARK CHESLER, AND TYRONE A. FORMAN

Bonillo-Silva and colleagues introduced the concept of "color-blind racism." Amanda Lewis, Mark Chesler, and Tyrone Forman look at how that is experienced by students of color on a largely white university.

The "ivory tower" may be more aptly named than we often realize, the expression denoting its whiteness more than its isolation from the rest of American society. The National Guard didn't have to walk the students in this article onto campus, as happened in some places in Jim Crow days, but that doesn't mean that racism is over. As the language of racism moves from name-calling and symbolic cross-burning to the more subtle expressions of "colorblind" racism, the responses demanded from students of color are necessarily more complicated and nuanced. If telling a person that he or she is "racist" is itself at best rude and more likely seen as horrible name-calling, how can students of color draw attention to the racism they experience during interactions with white students?

How students of color feel about their personal encounters with racism—about having racially coded characteristics ascribed to them, of being excluded from mainstream activities and struggling with having self-perceptions that do not match the expectations of the majority group and others, and so forth—provides critical insights to this discussion. The perspectives of Black, Latino/a, Asian, and Native American students, in their own voices, reveal a great deal about the behaviors of White students—behaviors that often are unintended, invisible to, or not understood by White students themselves. This article focuses on the ways in which various groups of students of color at a large predominantly White public university experience and interpret their relationships with their White peers in the classroom and on campus. It reports findings from focus group research with students of color that identifies the particular challenges these students face on such campuses and explores the meanings for students of color of White students' actions and reactions in interracial situations. Students of color themselves highlighted the impact of White students' purported "colorblindness" with regard to race and ethnicity. This article attempts to explain how this colorblind ideology often blinds White students to their own color-conscious behavior and its subsequent stereotyping effects. It also places collegiate racial peer relations within both their appropriate institutional context and the wider societal context, specifically examining how these macro-level factors set the stage for micro-level interactions.

Excerpted from Amanda E. Lewis, Mark Chesler, and Tyrone A. Forman, "The Impact of 'Colorblind' Ideologies on Students of Color: Intergroup Relations at a Predominantly White University," Journal of Negro Education 69 (2000): 74–91. References have been edited.

METHOD

The data for this study were drawn from transcripts of 15 group interviews, or small structured discussions, conducted with 75 undergraduate students of color (Black, Latino/a, Asian, and Native Americans) who were enrolled at a large, research-oriented university in the midwestern United States. All of the discussion groups were homogeneous by race/ethnicity and mixed by gender. The discussion leaders were students who were specially trained in focus group interviewing techniques; in every case they were of the same race/ethnicity as the group being interviewed.

MAJOR THEMES IN THE CAMPUS EXPERIENCES OF STUDENTS OF COLOR

Though some of the six themes discussed in this article address the direct or indirect insults targeted at students of color, others capture requests from, pressures upon, or sometimes even demands (i.e., for conformity, assimilation, and/ or information) presented to these students by their White peers. All of the themes reflect a response triggered either internally (i.e., emotional pain, anger, and/or questioning of one's identity and sense of place) if not externally. (i.e., defensiveness, withdrawal, debate, explanation). First, however, a caveat: Although most of the students who participated in our study spoke negatively about their interactions with their White peers, some exceptions were evident. When probed about whether a White student had ever personally offended them with a racist comment or behavior, several students of color replied simply, "No." Other student of color mentioned Whites whom they knew behaved differently from most White students:

> Since I've been here, one of my closest friends, she's White, and she's very aware of how…what it means for her to be a White woman, what it means to me, how she fits into the broad framework. You know, she's not necessarily knowledgeable about everything about Asian American culture, but I tell her.
>
> (an Asian American Female student)

When it comes to White people, you can really tell who grew up in an all-White neighborhood and who didn't. I know this friend of mine, he lived in an all-Black neighborhood and he was just totally comfortable around any color of people at any time. He could speak to anyone. He was totally natural about it, not tip-toeing, making sure he didn't step on anybody's toes.

> (a Black Male Student)

Students of color perceived these "exceptional" White students to have some understanding of "what it means to be a White," and believed this to make a huge difference in their relationships.

RACIAL STEREOTYPING

We identified two different strains of racial stereotyping: academic and behavioral. Though these two types are closely related, it is also important to distinguish between them, as described in the following discussion.

Academic Stereotyping ("Oh, my God, this Black person said something that was intelligent!")

Several study participants maintained that they were stereotyped by their fellow White students or viewed as less competent by virtue of their racial membership. Many felt that Whites often targeted them as "affirmative action attendees" or tokens:

> They know that I'm there and, in a sense, expect lower scores for me because I am Black. We had taken an exam and people were looking at the scores and a White student was shocked that I did extremely well on the exam.
>
> (a Black Female Student)

> I've noticed that in my science classes people just assume that since I'm Asian American that I'm supposed to be good at this. I struggle through classes just as they do, but there's still that stereotype that if you're Asian American and you're in the sciences you know your stuff, you don't have to study all the time.
>
> (an Asian American Male Student)

[In a Spanish class], because I was Mexican, people assumed I would know Spanish, and I didn't. When they found out I didn't really know it they said, "You're just Latina on the outside, not on the inside."

(a Latina Student)

Across the board, the students of color noted that, by their stereotyping, their White peers seemed to convey that they "knew something" about them or could ascertain something about their academic abilities and/or proclivities based on their apparent or signaled racial affiliation (i.e., that a particular student would be smart, slow, scientific-minded, etc.).

Though the racial stereotypes about the academic ability and potential of students of color varied for different groups, the impact of the assumptions were similar in their negative effect, a finding that has been confirmed in the literature. For example, Chan (1991) and Chan and Hune (1995) noted that although stereotypes of Asian Americans as the model minority seem relatively benevolent, they mask the current and prevalent discrimination that Asian Americans experience in social and economic realms. Such stereotypes further place extraordinary pressures on Asian American students to perform academically and ignore both the great variety in experience of different individuals and members of different Asian American ethnic groups. As Essed (1997) has pointed out, those who are the targets of racist stereotypes typically face a range of experiences where they are constructed as "Other," excluded, and made to feel inferior. Similarly, Feagin, Vera, and Imani (1996) noted the following in their study of the experiences of African American students at a predominantly White university: "A white gesture that might be seen as complimentary if it were solely based on achievement criteria is (here) taken as offensive because of the racial stereotype implied in the white action" (p. 66). The application of group stereotypes to individuals created distress among the students of color in our study and

led to personal struggles about their identity and competence. It also forced them to choose whether or not they wanted to conform to the stereotypical notions.

Behavioral Stereotyping ("Show us the 'M. C. Hammer'")

The students of color in our study contended that they did not experience stereotypes merely in relation to academic issues but also relative to expectations of their interpersonal behavior and cultural styles. As a Latino student noted, "The other class members would look to the Latinos for good stories about life in the barrio." Other students of color shared similar perceptions:

I think most of them think you are from the ghetto, and if you are here you are on financial aid. You can tell this from the conversation in class. This one girl made it seem that Blacks are all lower class and don't know anything but the ghetto.

(a Black Female Student)

Every day, little things happen, like, one time when I was living on my hall someone was playing loud music, like M. C. Hammer was rapping. So they said to me, "Show us the 'M. C. Hammer'! How you do the M. C. Hammer?"—like I'm *supposed* to know! I was the only Black person on my floor, and It was like I was supposed to know how to do it. I said, "I don't even dance that well." I mean, 1 can dance, but I can't do the M. C. Hammer and the Running Man and this other stuff.

(a Black Male Student)

Behavioral stereotypes, though also sometimes seemingly benevolent, are similar to academic stereotypes in that they originate both from vestiges of older, genetically based racist notions and from nouveau, culturally based explanations. They are based on the expectation by Whites that all students of color are experientially expert in their groups' minority experience, which is often equated with poverty. Thus, all Blacks and Latinos/as are expected to know about poverty and urban life, and they are simultaneously expected to be or behave in certain ways (i.e., be meek, rhythmic, spiritual).

PRESSURES OR EXPECTATIONS TO ASSIMILATE: "YOU'RE AMERICAN! SPEAK ENGLISH, DAMN IT!"

Ironically, the students of color in our study noted that while they were experiencing pressures from Whites to be "representatives" of their racial/ethnic groups, they were also experiencing pressures to assimilate into the mainstream, or dominant White, culture. For example,

> People tell me, "You're American! Speak English, damn it!" when I am struggling to learn Spanish. I have no patience for that whatsoever. When I'm in my dorm room and my next door neighbors are Puerto Rican, they're from New York, and we're speaking Spanish, others come in and they're like, "What are you doing that for? We don't understand you when you speak Spanish. That's rude."
>
> (a Latina Student)

> To be an Afro-American student here means you have to learn how to adapt and deal with the pressures, not only school, but from the white majority. You have to build a tolerance to certain things, like the white majority structure. You really have to be within yourself and know who you are. If not you could be caught in the system and lose your identity as an Afro-American person.
>
> (a Black Male Student)

As noted by Feagin et al. (1996) and other researchers, such pressure to assimilate is a salient theme throughout the literature on students of color at predominantly White colleges and universities. According to Duster (1991): "Those [Asian American students] more integrated into the mainstream white culture noted that white acquaintances would frequently make a distinction between them and other Asian-Americans, usually through remarks intended as compliments, such as, 'You're not like other Asians'" (p. 23). Indeed, the emerging literature points out that Whites often see themselves as the norm and

as being without racial or cultural specificity (e.g., as neutral, nonracial persons); they thus view their own sociocultural norms of interaction as universal rather than particular (Doane, 1997; Fine, Powell, Weis, & Wong, 1997; Frankenberg, 1994; Lewis, 1998). As a result, White students may often be unaware that their assumptions about normal or appropriate views, styles, or behaviors are quite culturally specific and read others' differences as deviance or divergence from their assumedly universal norms.

A number of students in our study also reported that many of their White peers attempted to ignore or erase these differences by treating the race or culture of students of color as trivial, meaningless or invisible. As these students related:

> It really bothers me when a White person says, "Well, why can't we see each other as individuals instead of race being always an issue?" I always come out and say, "I can't understand why you would think we can separate race and see each other as individuals, when my ethnicity is part of who I am and something I can't ignore."
>
> (a Latina Student)

> When I met my roommate, who's White, she said, "Well, I'm not going to think of you as Black. I'll just think of you as my friend who has a natural suntan."
>
> (a Black Female Student)

> People are constantly saying, "Oh, I thought you were white." And I say, "No, I'm Native American." And they say, "Well you look White." I tell them my mom is White. People expect this Indian with a feather in her hair. I think people make a lot of assumptions about your ethnicity. I don't mind if people ask, but it really upsets me when people make assumptions about who you are.
>
> (a Native American Female Student)

These themes also are repeated in much of the literature on the racial climate of U.S. college campuses (Duster, 1991; Feagin & Vera, 1995; Thomas, 1991). That literature reveals that students of color feel they are required to "blend in" on predominantly White campuses while at the same time the application of academic and behavioral stereotypes emphasizes their group characteristics and difference. This dilemma was captured precisely in one student-interviewee's comment that she was either "totally marginalized" or stereotyped as "*the Asian American woman.*" Her comments reflect two halves of the same coin in which students of color feel they are expected to be different from Whites in certain ways but, at the same time, to be or at least pursue sameness with Whites. Naturally, this conflict causes a great deal of confusion, frustration, and pain for those who experience it. Taking the form of direct or implicit insults and demands (e.g., to assimilate, to act out cultural stereotypes, to explain), this push-and-pull generates daily quandaries about whether to resist or conform both internally, with regard to identity, and externally, with regard to behavior and challenge.

EXCLUSION AND MARGINALITY: "THIS SCHOOL IS FOR EUROPEANS!"

The students of color we interviewed reported experiences in and out of the classroom in which they felt they were excluded from peer interactions with or by White students, either through deliberate actions or through the "normal" course of intergroup relationships. The following comments are illustrative:

> I've always felt left out of study groups. It's almost like they [White students] have these cliques already. They're going to do much better because of the groups they have. They have their friends who took the class before and have all these resources that we don't have.
>
> (a Latino Student)

Since I'm a science major, I've had to take a lot of labs. It seems like the last person who doesn't have a partner is *me*. I generally expect to be paired up with a student by the teacher.

(a Black Male Student)

There was a Black woman who had written a paper and a White woman who had written a paper about the same topic. The class could ask either of them questions. The Black woman would start talking about the topic and everyone would start to direct their questions toward the White woman. The Black woman was obviously upset but no one noticed, and she got up and left the class early. And no one noticed, and no one said anything.

(a Latina Student)

White students look over you if they have a question. One time this guy sitting next to me didn't know anyone and went around me to ask the other guy about a question on the homework and I'm sitting right there. He made a point to go around me.

(a Black Male Student)

The students of color in our study perceived that many of the networks available to White students were closed off to them and difficult to access or even that they were not wanted in their academic settings. McBay (1986) reported a similar phenomenon in her study of racial climate at another predominantly White university, where over 40% of Black alumni indicated that they experienced "a sense of racial isolation" and of not fitting in or belonging to the larger community during their student days (p. 10). As one student in our sample stated, "It's good for me to converse with people of my own race, but some days I can go the whole day and not see another Black person on this campus."

One byproduct of being the target of stereotypic expectations is a sense of distance from and discomfort with others. When this is combined with the behavioral exclusion practiced by some White students, whether consciously and deliberately or not, and certainly experienced by many students of color, it leads to and supports the actual separation of racial/ethnic groups in campus daily life, as evidenced by these comments:

> The first day I walked in there I sat in the front. All these white people sat in the back, and they avoided sitting next to the people of color. Every time we had a project to do in groups, our group always was the

group of people of color. When our teaching assistant noticed that and started separating us into groups, these other people wouldn't even listen to what we had to say. So from then on we're like, "No, we're not going to be with them."

(a Black Female Student)

You sit next to them, and they look at each other like, "Oh, my God, she's sitting next to me! Get away! A person of color!" When you walk in and they're, like, all eyes on you to see what you're wearing, how you wear it, the way you speak, whether you have a Spanish accent.

(a Latina Student)

There is some tension, I think, among the White students about things like the minority lounges that we have, and some of the parties and things we go to, or when a group of Afro-Americans gets together. I think White people somewhat fear that, or it seems that they fear it.

(a Black Male Student)

Some students of color respond to these perceived exclusions by further separating themselves from Whites. According to McBay (1986), "separation, meaning the movement of Blacks together to form a more positive and affirmative environment than that provided by the larger White community," is a common adaptation to the challenges students of color faced on predominantly White campuses (p. 14). However, such adaptations carry their own dilemmas. As related by the Task Force on Racial and Cultural Concerns (1990), "[M]any students, both minority and non-minority, feel isolated from students of different backgrounds from their own" (p. 1). That report further maintained that both minority and majority students felt "slighted" by the lack of attention other groups paid them in social interactions and activities: "Minority students deplore white students' hesitance about approaching students of color. They ask, 'Why would you consider Black students sitting together as hostile. All the white students sit together. Is that

hostile'?" (p. 6). Thus, as noted by the students in our sample, when students of color retreat to "their side," they are chastised for separating themselves when they are actually trying to find and create supportive spaces within campus environments that they often experience as racially hostile or exclusive.

WHITE IGNORANCE AND INTERPERSONAL AWKWARDNESS: "WHY ISN'T THE PALM OF YOUR HAND THE SAME COLOR AS THE BACK?"

Racial/ethnic separation—in neighborhoods, in elementary and secondary schools, and on college campuses—both creates and reinforces cultural ignorance and interpersonal awkwardness. Whereas students of color must learn about Whites and White culture in order to survive, let alone advance, in U.S. society, White students are under little pressure to learn about minority cultures or traditions. Indeed, the students of color in our sample reported that their White peers often knew little if anything about their group's histories or cultures. They further reported that White students often were uncomfortable in their presence or awkward and fearful about how to relate to them.

They [White students] ask stupid things, like, "Why is your hair straight?" "Why do you fling your hair around all day?" We have to know about their culture, and they don't have to take the time to find out about what we're about, what our culture is about, why we react to things, how we feel about certain things.

(a Black Female Student)

When I was in an English class, one of the White men in the class said, "Well, I don't know what everyone's all worked up about. I've never seen any act of racism on campus."

(a Latino Student)

I remember once the day after Columbus Day, I said that what happened to Native Americans was comparable to what happened to the Jews during World War II. I said that it wasn't the same, but there were parallels. And someone in the class said that I was wrong and went into all these details about the Holocaust. I was thinking that the details weren't my point.

(a Native American Male Student)

I don't know about tension, but there's just an awkwardness. Like, many White people don't know whether to say, "Hi," or not....Sometimes they don't speak, and sometimes they do speak.

(a Black Female Student)

These students' experiences with their peers' ignorance—or innocence—are not unique. Feagin et al. (1996) reported similar phenomena based upon their interviews with African American college students. They noted that although White students sometimes act appropriately in interactions with Black peers out of overt bigotry; at other times Students of color also often experience this "not knowing" about others—or rather, what they perceive as White students' feeling that they do not need to know about others—as arrogance. Instead of providing opportunities for opening discourse, White students' expressions of socially structured as well as personal ignorance often reinforce racial boundaries by reinforcing a sense of difference and distance. As the students of color we interviewed repeatedly reported, they end up having both to know about Whites and to teach Whites about themselves, or to suffer misconceptions and the attribution of aloofness or resistance.

A related aspect of White ignorance and interpersonal awkwardness is the repeated mention by these students of color that their White peers were very careful not to say the "wrong thing" about a topic addressing race or ethnicity in their presence. Several members of our sample noted that White students, in their interactions with students of color, frequently sought to create the illusion of peace and harmony and withdrew from or even denied uncomfortable racial/ethnic realities. They maintained that this was due either to White students'

concerns about political correctness or their fear of challenge and confrontation.

In a political science class, when the teaching assistant asked us how we all felt about affirmative action, the Whites looked at the Blacks, waiting for an answer from us. They want to hear what we're going to say before they say anything. They don't usually open their mouth after you say something. They are afraid if they say something they might offend us, and we'll go off on them.

(a Black Male Student)

One thing that I always run into with White students is that you can say things and they're, like, "That's not really me. What did I do?" You know, "Why are you attacking me?" And they don't listen to what you are saying. They don't listen to the content.

(an Asian American Female Student)

I find a lot of times, when talking about issues of race. White students want to feel good and hold your hand, and don't want to see color and want to be unified. They want us to be White and not have to deal with us being Black.

(a Black Female Student)

I remember this one White [female student] saying, "I'm really a nice person, and I get along with Latinos." Like, "I want you to approve of me." I didn't say anything. I just let it go by.

(a Latina Student)

White students' confusion, or reticence and defensiveness, often feels to students of color like an unwillingness to engage. White students' personalization of racial phenomena, and their attempts to reduce intergroup relations to the individual level, appears to many students of color as denial of structural racism and a lack of recognition of differences and/or group-level discrimination. Moreover, some students of color indicate that they see such silence or withdrawal as a lack of caring about these issues or about their potential offense or pain. This leads to a lack of on-going student dialogue across racial/

ethnic difference (Task Force on Racial and Cultural Concerns, 1990).

WHITE RESENTMENT AND HOSTILITY ABOUT AFFIRMATIVE ACTION

Though the specific legal and administrative issues surrounding affirmative action have changed shape throughout the years, the widespread perception that minority student admissions and advancement are due primarily to unearned preference and only minimally, if at all, to talent persists. Indeed, that perception has probably escalated in the midst of current debates on and off campus, as reflected in the following comments from our student participants:

[White] students directly asked me about affirmative action and was I a "token" student. Its like, yeah, you must of gotten here because you're a token student anyway. You must be stupid.

(a Black Male Student)

I came from out of state, and I was very intimidated by the university. I was appalled when a White got up and pointed his finger at me and said, "I don't think it's right that you go to school here when my best friend doesn't!" I thought that was kind of outrageous, so I said, "You know nothing about me! You should get over your ignorance and find out something about people you don't know anything about. You're just making generalizations." But then I felt bad because I started to try to justify myself for being here, and in my opinion I don't have anything to prove to him. I only have to prove things to myself. From then on, I knew it was going to be a hard road.

(a Black Female Student)

These kinds of interactions inevitably lead students of color to feel less than full citizenship on campus. Duster (1991) documented similar responses in his study, in which students of color made statements such as: "I feel like I have Affirmative Action stamped on my forehead," "We're guilty until proven innocent," and "There's no way to convince whites we belong here" (p. 19).

In such settings, group-level struggles over resources clearly are played out in interpersonal interactions (Blumer, 1958). Some of the resources being struggled over are as simple as funds, time, and space for curricular and cocurricular student activities. However, in a society in which higher education is a central element of one's cultural capital, attendance and graduation from a "good college" is an important resource. Group-level struggles for access to such institutions, both numerically and symbolically, are captured and illuminated in the issue of racial/ethnic representation on the college campus. Under far too many circumstances, students of color on predominantly White campuses are seen as filling a role—that is, as providing something that the university needs, namely, diversity—rather than as individual students seeking to receive an education (Woo, 1994).

The nature of the current debate about affirmative action is replete with rhetoric about the lowering of academic standards and the generally lesser credentials or competence of students of color. In interviews with White students on four majority-White college campuses, Bonilla–Silva and Forman (2000) found that White students' views of the social world often lead them to believe that racism is a problem of the past, solved either by the Emancipation Proclamation or the civil rights movement. They reported White students' general belief that discrimination no longer exists and that if Blacks are not doing well in society currently it is because of personal or cultural deficiencies. This rhetoric, and its associated affirmation of White racial disadvantage and victimization in the face of what is perceived as unmerited Black privilege, serves only to drive students of color into even more vulnerable and protective stances and to perpetuate stereotyped, awkward, separated, and hostile climates for all students, but especially students of color.

THE FOCUS ON BLACK AND WHITE

The dominant focus on Black–White relations in most discussions about campus racial/ethnic climate was sometimes found to create problems for the Latino/a, Asian American, and Native American students of color in our study. Two students offered the following comments:

> If you're in class and they start talking about people of color issues, I guess many of us are offended when it's always just the Black issues that are discussed. It's not even Latinos.
>
> (a Latina Student)

> I remember a lot of times in class discussion when we talked, it was like they would say something about an issue and I would bring up the Asian American perspective or what I felt about it, and they would be like, "Yeah, that's nice, but here's the real issue."
>
> (an Asian American Male Student)

As these comments reveal, racial/ethnic relations are not only an issue between students of color and their White peers but between students of color from different groups. Duster's (1991) research yielded a statement from a Chicano student confirming this view:

> ...they [African American students] talk about racism and then a Chicano/Latino will go, "Oh yeah, I know what you mean," and they'll just look at you or if you're not dark enough they don't think you've experienced it and I've come out and say, "Well, Chicano/Latinos face racism, too."
>
> (p. 35)

In such exchanges, Latino/a, Asian American, and Native American students report feeling additionally excluded and marginalized.

THE BROADER SOCIAL CONTEXT OF CAMPUS INTERGROUP RELATIONS

How can the co-existence of rhetorical colorblindness and behavioral color consciousness in the collegiate context be explained? What is it about the ideologies and experiences of White college students that lead to these dynamics? What is it about the institutional context and operations of higher education in the United States that permits, supports, and reproduces them?

U.S. college campuses, though unique in many ways, are not exempt from the larger social trends that take place beyond their ivy-covered walls. Over the last several years, new literature has emerged on the changing nature of racial/ethnic attitudes, racism, and discrimination in our society. This literature challenges a re-thinking of the trends in racial/ethnic relations witnessed on college campuses in the light of the wider social context. Some scholars have argued that the change in the collegiate racial/ethnic climate is primarily one of degree—that is, there is less racism and ethnic discrimination, or these phenomena are milder than they used to be. Others have argued that the two are just as pervasive as in the past, yet they manifest themselves in different ways and therefore "look" different (Bobo, Kluegel, & Smith, 1997; Bonilla–Silva, 1997; Bonilla–Silva & Lewis, 1999; Kinder & Sanders, 1996). According to Bonilla–Silva (1997):

> In sum, whites today exhibit a very different racial ideology than during the apartheid period of race relations. The new ideology of whites, characteristic of the distal and antagonistic post-civil rights race relations, avoids direct hostility toward minority groups, affirms the principles of equal opportunity and egalitarianism, but at the same time rejects programs that attempt to ameliorate racial inequality in reality rather than in theory. Generally speaking, contemporary white ideology denies the fact that race imposes a number of constraints upon minorities and proclaims that we are all individual actors with similar opportunities in the market.
>
> (p. 22)

Such trends and transformations explain why the students we interviewed did not report high levels of traditional racial/ethnic prejudice or explicit exclusion, but they did report numerous, more subtle, but still potent negative interactions.

As the nation debates the question of whether racism and ethnic discrimination are history, numbers of White Americans are concluding that individual effort and merit should be the only criteria used to allocate positions or resources in society. This logic seems to lie behind much of the White student behavior reported by the students of color in our study. Whites' "new racism" asserts a kind of free market individualism in which they can imagine a colorblind world, where all should (and can) compete freely and equally (Bobo et al., 1997). In the collegiate context, for instance, and in much of the popular media, the typically higher scores of White students on standardized aptitude tests and their greater status and privilege in society are thus interpreted as meritorious achievement, instead of as the outcome of what Feagin et al. (1996) attribute to their "accumulated social, economic, and political privileges" (pp. 152–153). Additionally, arguments interpreting the disproportionate success of Whites as due to merit and ability reciprocally locate all responsibility for their lack of success and negative social outcomes on the disadvantaged themselves. These perspectives set the stage for viewing affirmative action as an assault on fair play and White students' meritorious achievement or earned status, rather than as a strategic effort to redress inequality and create a more diverse and creative learning environment for all students. They further fuel the kind of resentment, hostility, and sense of victimhood among White students that students of color in our focus groups reported witnessing.

Both White students and students of color enter college with assumptions and expectations formed through earlier experiences both in and outside the educational system. Students who have grown up in a context of widespread racial segregation often have their first real contact with people of other racial groups when they come to college (Massey & Denton, 1993). In recent research conducted at four universities around the country, many White students reported having had very little to no contact with people of color before arriving on campus (Bonilla–Silva & Forman, 2000).

Long histories of racism—both covert and overt, institutionalized and interpersonal—which have created and enforced the segregated living spaces and privileged life chances of Whites, are treated by many White college students as coincidence rather than as the product of deeply embedded patterns of social dominance. White students typically utilize their personal experience of an homogeneous upbringing, combined with what they glean from media reports and from school and other sources of information, to make assumptions about what racial and ethnic minority identities are or are not about and what it *should* mean to be Black, Asian or Native American, Latino/a, and White. Indeed, the notion of Whiteness as normative is integral to the operation of the new racial paradigm in that it creates an assumed center to which others are expected to conform (Feagin & Vera, 1995; Fine et al., 1997; Frankenberg, 1994; Lewis, 1998). Many students of color, in turn, bring with them to the predominantly White college campus experiences of exclusion, oppression, and unequal educational and social opportunity. These students must negotiate their own sense of what it means to be a person of color in the face of racial/ethnic stereotypes and calls for colorblindness about issues addressing race/ethnicity and minority status.

It is not only precollegiate experiences that dispose White students to view, expect to view, and behave toward students of color in stereotypical ways. The contemporary collegiate environment sets the stage for White students to actualize these attitudes and behaviors—indeed, that environment reinforces and reproduces them. Several authors have drawn attention to the powerful effects of the organizational climate of higher education on all students' experiences. Hurtado (1992), for example, has pointed to institutional issues such as selectivity and campus size, "responsiveness to the entrance of Black students, program responses, and the attitudinal or perceptual climate" (p. 542) as contributing factors. Chesler and Crowfoot (1997) have drawn attention to issues such as organizational mission and culture, pedagogy, operational styles of dominant elites or power-holders, and the nature and distribution of key resources. Others contend that institutional factors can lead to a sort of "academic colonialism" that shapes both the patterns of interaction as well as the attitudes and behaviors of individuals within institutions (Arce, 1978), including those reported in previous sections of this article. Thus, powerful institutional norms have been shown to influence all participants in the academy.

CONCLUSION

College represents the first opportunity many young people have to engage in sustained interaction with peers and elders of different races, ethnicities, and economic classes. Collegiate social environments such as the classroom and dormitory represent unique opportunities for students to learn whether and how to work together with others who are different from themselves and to decide how to think and behave in the inevitably racially and ethnically mixed settings of their future. Some of this learning, accomplished or avoided by White students and students of color in college when they are on the verge of adulthood, has long-term implications. At college age, and in higher education settings, young people may be more willing and able to take risks, to unlearn old patterns of social interaction and to discover new intellectual and social evidence about their own and others' race/ethnicity than at any prior or subsequent time in their lives. Yet too often, by design or omission, colleges miss the opportunity to teach positive forms of interracial/ethnic interaction, and therefore fail to help lay the groundwork for real changes in group relations and the distribution of power on campus and in

the society. The findings of even this limited study make it clear that for many students of color, life within on the college campus offers increasingly daunting challenges that White students and many White faculty do not understand and with which they do not have to contend.

Ironically, many collegiate Whites increasingly imagine students of color to be recipients of an unfair system—affirmative action—in which students of color have the upper hand. Rather than seeing the working of organizational norms and expectations regarding interpersonal behavior as evidence of institutionalized "White power," today's White college students are behaving more and more as if students of color are actual or potential deviants from consensually accepted norms. Many White students are confused about the resultant dynamics, and some resentfully contend that the overt discrimination of the past is now being used as an excuse to give students of color an undeserved advantage over them. They further maintain that affirmative action policies run counter to the principles of meritocracy, equality, and colorblindness. Though in the abstract these are important ideals, at this stage in our nation's history, we believe them to be merely ideals to be worked toward. Any policy, practice, or behavior that takes these ideals as fact and assumes that they currently govern collegiate or public life, ignores enduring realities of vast inequality and persistent discrimination based on race and ethnicity. The attempt to dispel these myths, to uncover disturbing patterns in interracial/interethnic peer relations on the college campus, and to create more just patterns in collegiate relations, is not merely a matter of fairness or of enriching the educational experiences of all. It is a matter of constructing a more realistic, just, and livable future for our society.

REFERENCES

Arce, C. (1978). Chicano participation in academe: A case of academic colonialism. *Grito de Sol: A Chicano Quarterly, 3,* 75–104.

Blumer, H. (1958). Race prejudice as a sense of group position. *Pacific Sociological Review*, 1, 3–7.

Bobo, L., Kluegel, J., & Smith, R. (1997). Laissez-faire racism: The crystallization of a kinder, gentler, antiblack ideology. In S. A. Tuch & J. K. Martin (Eds.), *Racial attitudes in the 1990s: Continuity and change* (pp. 15–42). Westport, CT: Praeger.

Bonilla–Silva, E. (1997). Rethinking racism: Toward a structural interpretation. *American Sociological Review*, 62, 465–480.

Bonilla–Silva, E., & Forman, T. (2000). '"I am not a racist, but…": Mapping White college students' racial ideology in the USA. *Discourse and Society*, 11, 50–85.

Bonilla–Silva, E., & Lewis, A. (1999). The "new racism": Toward an analysis of the U.S. racial structure, 1960s–1990s. In P. Wong (Ed.), *Race, nation and citizenship* (pp. 55–101). Boulder, CO: Westview Press.

Chan, S. (1991). *Asian Americans: An interpretive history*. Boston: Twayne.

Chan, K., & Hune, S. (1995). Racialization and panethnicity: From Asians in America to Asian Americans. In W. Hawley & A. Jackson (Eds.), *Toward a common destiny* (pp. 205–233). San Francisco: Jossey–Bass.

Chesler, M., & Crowfoot, J. (1991). Racism on campus. In W. May (Ed.), *Ethical issues in higher education* (pp. 195–230). New York: Macmillan.

Doane, A. J. (1997). White identity and race relations in the 1990s. In G. L. Carter (Ed.), *Perspectives on current social problems* (pp. 151–159). Boston: Allyn & Bacon.

Duster, T. (1991). *The diversity project*. Berkeley, CA: Institute for the Study of Social Change.

Essed, P. (1997). Racial intimidation: Sociopolitical implications of the usage of racist slurs. In S. H. Riggins (Ed.), *The language and politics of exclusion: Others in discourse* (pp. 131–152). Thousand Oaks, CA: Sage.

Feagin, J., & Vera, H. (1995). *White racism*. New York: Routledge.

Feagin, J., Vera, H., & Imani, N. (1996). *The agony of education: Black students at White colleges and universities*. New York: Routledge.

Fine, M., Powell, L., Weis, L., & Wong, L. M. (1997). *Off White: Readings on race, power and society*. New York: Routledge.

Frankenberg, R. (1994). *The social construction of Whiteness: White women, race matters*. Minneapolis: University of Minnesota Press.

Hurtado, S. (1992). The campus racial climate: Contexts of conflict. *Journal of Higher Education*, 63, 539–569.

Kinder, D. R., & Sanders, L. (1996). *Divided by color*. Chicago: The University of Chicago Press.

Lewis, A. (1998). *Theorizing Whiteness: Interrogating uninterrogated racial privilege* (Working Paper No. 568). Ann Arbor: University of Michigan, Center for Research on Social Organization.

Massey, D., & Denton, N. (1993). *American apartheid: Segregation and the making of the underclass*. Cambridge, MA: Harvard University Press.

McBay, S. (1986). *The racial climate on the MIT campus*. Cambridge, MA: Massachusetts Institute of Technology.

Task Force on Racial and Cultural Concerns. (1990). *A report of student concerns about issues of race and racism in the School of Public Health*. Ann Arbor: University of Michigan School of Public Health.

Thomas, G. (1991). *Black students in higher education: Conditions and experiences in the 1970s*. Westport, CT: Greenwood Press.

Woo, D. (1994). The "overrepresentation" of Asian Americans: Red herrings and yellow perils. In F. Pincus & H. Ehrlich (Eds.), *Race and ethnic conflict* (pp. 314–325). Boulder, CO: Westview Press.

JOURNALING QUESTION

What are the racial groups on your campus, and what are the most racist words, experiences, or activities you have seen at your college? How did you respond?

Policing and Prison

26.

DEADLY SYMBIOSIS

Rethinking Race and Imprisonment in Twenty-First-Century America

LOÏC WACQUANT

Public schools in American cities have had two main tasks: Americanizing immigrant children and preparing them for jobs. In the past, the work available for those children was primarily factory jobs, hence the long-standing focus on attendance, punctuality, neatness, and orderliness, and the desks lined in neat rows like assembly line stations. Today, however, those factory jobs have left American cities, if not the nation entirely, along with small, locally owned stores and businesses. In neighborhoods segregated by race, local middle-class working possibilities have been foreclosed. And now inner city, black "ghetto" schools—like the public housing in the ghettos—resemble prisons more than factories, with guards and metal detectors and little focus on job skills or learning. Meanwhile, prisons, once hoped to be sites of rehabilitation and education, have become places of ongoing "detention," long-term holding pens. Loïc Wacquant sees these "brute facts"—the extraordinary "blackening" of American prisons and the shockingly high imprisonment rate of black men—as "the dark side" of the American dream. Can there be an American ideal—hard-working families in suburban communities—without an imagined other side in opposition?

Consider three brute facts about racial inequality and imprisonment in contemporary America:

(i) Since 1989 and for the first time in national history, African Americans make up a majority of those entering prison each year. Indeed, in four short decades, the ethnic composition of the U.S. inmate population has reversed, turning over from 70 percent white at mid-century to nearly 70 percent black and Latino today, although ethnic patterns of criminal activity have not fundamentally changed during that period.

(ii) The rate of incarceration for African Americans has soared to levels unknown in any other society and is higher now than the total incarceration rate in the Soviet Union at the zenith of

Excerpted from Loïc Wacquant, "Deadly Symbiosis: Rethinking Race and Imprisonment in Twenty-First-Century," Boston Review Vol 27, No. 2 (2002): p. 23–31. Notes have been renumbered and edited.

the Gulag and in South Africa at the height of the anti-apartheid struggle. As of mid-1999, close to 800,000 black men were in custody in federal penitentiaries, state prisons, and county jails—one male out of every twenty-one, and one out of every nine between twenty and thirty-four.[1] On any given day, upwards of one third of African-American men in their twenties find themselves behind bars, on probation, or on parole. And, at the core of the formerly industrial cities of the North, this proportion often exceeds two thirds.

(iii) The ratio of black to white imprisonment rates has steadily grown over the past two decades, climbing from about five to one to eight and a half to one. This rising "racial disproportionality" can be traced directly to the War on Drugs launched by Ronald Reagan and expanded under George Bush, Sr., and Bill Clinton. In ten states, African Americans are imprisoned at more than ten times the rate of European Americans. And in the District of Columbia, blacks were thirty-five times more likely than whites to be put behind bars in 1994.[2]

Students of crime and justice know these grim facts but disagree about their explanation. Most analysts account for the sudden "blackening" of the *carceral system*—comprising jails, state prisons, federal prisons, and private detention facilities—in terms of trends in crime and its judicial treatment (arrest, prosecution, sentencing); a few have considered such non-judicial variables as the size of the black population, economic factors (the poverty rate, unemployment, income), the value of welfare payments, support for religious fundamentalism, and the dominant political party. But these factors, taken separately and in conjunction, simply cannot account for the magnitude, rapidity, and timing of the recent racialization of U.S. imprisonment, especially as crime rates have been flat and later declining over the past quarter-century.[3]

BLACK HYPERINCARCERATION

To understand these phenomena, we first need to break out of the narrow "crime and punishment" paradigm and examine the broader role of the penal system as an *instrument for managing dispossessed and dishonored groups*.[4] And second, we need to take a longer historical view on the shifting forms of ethno-racial domination in the United States. This double move suggests that the astounding upsurge in black incarceration in the past three decades results from the obsolescence of the ghetto as a device for caste control and the correlative need for a substitute apparatus for keeping (unskilled) African Americans in a subordinate and confined position—physically, socially, and symbolically.

In the post–civil Rights era, the remnants of the dark ghetto and an expanding carceral system have become linked in a single system that entraps large numbers of younger black men, who simply move back and forth between the two institutions. This carceral mesh has emerged from two sets of convergent changes: sweeping economic and political forces have reshaped the mid-century "Black Belt" to *make the ghetto more like a prison*; and the "inmate society" has broken down in ways that *make the prison more like a ghetto*. The resulting symbiosis between ghetto and prison enforces the socioeconomic marginality and symbolic taint of an urban black sub-proletariat. Moreover, by producing a racialized public culture that vilifies criminals, it plays a pivotal role in remaking "race" and redefining the citizenry.

A fuller analysis would reveal that this increasing use of imprisonment to shore up caste division in American society is part of a broader "upsizing" of the state's penal sector, which, together with the drastic "downsizing" of its social welfare sector, aims at enforcing a regime of flexible and casual wage labor as a norm of citizenship for unskilled segments of the postindustrial working class.[5] This emerging *government of poverty* weds the "invisible hand" of a deregulated labor market to the "iron fist" of an omnipresent punitive apparatus. It is anchored not by a "prison industrial complex," as political opponents of the policy of mass incarceration maintain,[6] but by a system of gendered institutions that monitor, train, and neutralize populations recalcitrant or superfluous to the new economic and racial regime: men are handled by its penal wing while (their) women and children are managed by a revamped welfare-workfare system designed to buttress casual employment.

So the hypertrophic growth of imprisonment is one component of a more comprehensive restructuring of the American state to suit the requirements of neoliberalism. But race plays a special role in this emerging system. The United States far outstrips all advanced nations in the international trend towards the penalization of social insecurity. And just as the dismantling of welfare programs was accelerated by a cultural and political conflation of blackness and undeservingness,[7] so, too, the "great confinement" of the rejects of market society—the poor, mentally ill, homeless, jobless, and useless—can be painted as a welcome "crackdown" on *them*, those dark-skinned criminals from a pariah group still considered alien to the national body. The handling of the "underclass" question by the prison system at once reflects, reworks, and reinforces the racial division of American society and plays a key role in the fashioning of a post-Keynesian American state.

"PRISONIZATION" OF THE GHETTO

The hyperghetto [the more prison-like ghetto of today] presents four main characteristics that differentiate it sharply from the communal ghetto of mid-century and converge to make its social structure and cultural climate akin to those of the prison. I will consider each in turn by drawing a schematic contrast between the mid-century "Bronzeville" depicted by St. Clair Drake and Horace Cayton in *Black Metropolis* and the South Side of Chicago as I observed it some forty years later through fieldwork, statistical analysis, and survey data.

CLASS SEGREGATION OVER RACIAL SEGREGATION

Mid-century American ghettos contained a full complement of classes, for the simple reasons that the black bourgeoisie was barred from escaping while a majority of adults were gainfully employed in a gamut of occupations. True, from the 1920s onward, Chicago's South Side featured clearly demarcated subdivisions stratified by class, with the small elite of black doctors, lawyers, teachers, and businessmen residing in the more stable and desirable neighborhoods adjacent to white districts at the southern end, while the families of laborers and domestic workers massed themselves in areas of blight, crime, and dissolution towards the northern end.[8] But the social distance between the classes was limited by physical proximity and extensive family ties; the black bourgeoisie's economic power rested on supplying goods and services to its lower-class brethren.

Moreover, "brown" residents of the city were united in their rejection of caste subordination and an abiding concern to "advance the race," despite internecine divisions and the mutual panning of "big Negroes" and "riff-raff."[9] As a result, the postwar ghetto was integrated *both socially and structurally.*

Today's black bourgeoisie still lives under strict segregation and its life chances continue to be curtailed by its geographic and symbolic contiguity with the African-American sub-proletariat. Nonetheless, it has gained considerable physical distance from the heart of the ghetto by establishing satellite black neighborhoods at the Urban periphery and in the suburbs. Its economic basis has shifted from the black community to the state; employment in public bureaucracies accounts for most of the growth in the number of professional, managerial, and technical positions held by African Americans over the past thirty years. The genealogical ties of the black bourgeoisie to the black poor have also grown more remote and diffuse. Moreover, the historic center of the Black Belt has experienced massive depopulation and deproletarianization, such that a large majority of its residents are no longer employed: two thirds of the adults in Bronzeville did not hold a job in 1980, compared to fewer than half thirty years earlier, and three out of every four households were headed by women, while the official poverty rate hovered near 50 percent.

These shifts in the social composition of the ghetto make it socially akin to the prison, dominated as the latter is by the most precarious fractions of the urban proletariat: the unemployed, the casually employed, and the uneducated. In 1991, fully 36 percent of the half-million people housed by U.S. jails were jobless at the time of their arrest and another 15 percent worked only part-time or irregularly. One half had not finished high school and two thirds earned less than a thousand dollars a month; in addition, half the inmates were raised in homes receiving welfare and only 16 percent were married.[10] Residents of the hyperghetto and clients of the prison system thus present similar profiles in economic marginality and social disintegration.

LOSS OF A POSITIVE ECONOMIC FUNCTION

The transformed class structure of the hyperghetto is a direct product of its evolving position in the transformed urban political economy of the past three decades. From the Great Migration of the interwar years to the 1960s, the ghetto served a positive economic function as reservoir of cheap and pliable labor for the city's factories. By the 1970s, the engine of the metropolitan economy had passed from manufacturing to business and knowledge-based services and to factories relocated in suburbs and exurbs, in anti-union states in the South, and in foreign countries.

Between 1954 and 1982, the number of manufacturing establishments in Chicago plunged from 10,288 to 5,203, while the number of production workers sank from nearly half a million to 172,000. The demand for black labor plummeted accordingly, rocking the entire black class structure (in

1945, half of all employed African Americans in Chicago were blue-collar wage earners).

As Jeremy Rifkin points out, just as mechanization had enabled Southern agriculture to dispense with black labor a generation earlier, "automation and suburban relocation created a crisis of tragic dimension for unskilled black workers" in the North, as "for the first time in American history, the African American was no longer needed in the economic system" of the metropolis.[11] The effects of technological upgrading and postindustrialization were intensified by sustained residential segregation, the breakdown of public schools, and the renewal of working-class immigration from Latin America and Asia—all of which helped consign the vast majority of uneducated blacks to economic redundancy. Instead of providing a reservoir of cheap labor, the hyperghetto now stores a *surplus population* devoid of market utility, in which respect it also increasingly resembles the prison system.

FROM COMMUNAL TO STATE INSTITUTIONS

The organizations that formed the framework of everyday life for urban blacks were created and run by African Americans. The black press, churches, lodges and fraternal orders, social clubs and political machine knit together a dense fabric of resources and sociability that supported African American ethnic pride and group uplift. For their 200,000 members, the five hundred religious congregations that dotted the South Side were not only places of worship and entertainment but also a potent vehicle for individual and collective mobility. In the economic realm, too, African Americans could seek or sustain the illusion of autonomy and advancement. To be sure, Negro enterprise was small-scale and commercially weak: the three most numerous types of black-owned firms were beauty parlors, grocery stores, and barber shops. But the popular "doctrine of the 'Double-Duty Dollar'" according to which buying from black concerns would "advance the race," promised a path to economic independence from whites. And the "numbers game," with some 500 stations employing 5,000 and paying yearly wages in excess of a million dollars for three daily drawings, seemed to prove that one could indeed erect a self-sustaining economy within Black Metropolis.[12]

By the 1980s, this organizational landscape had shifted radically, as a result of the generalized devolution of public institutions and commercial establishments in the urban core as well as by the cumulative demise of black associations.[13] The physical infrastructure and business base of the South Side had been decimated, with thousands of boarded-up stores and abandoned buildings rotting away along deserted boulevards strewn with debris and garbage. Arguably the most potent component of the communal ghetto, the church, lost its capacity to energize and organize social life on the South Side. Storefront operations closed in the hundreds and the congregations that endured struggled for survival against the indifference or hostility of local residents. Similarly, the black press grew outside of the ghetto but virtually disappeared within it. In 1941, there were five black weeklies in Bronzeville; forty years later, the *Chicago Defender* alone remained in existence and then, only as a pale shadow of its former glorious self.

The vacuum created by the crumbling of the ghetto's indigenous organizations has been filled by *state bureaucracies of social control*, themselves largely staffed by the new black middle class whose expansion hinges, not on its capacity to serve its community, but on its willingness to serve as *custodian* of the black urban sub-proletariat on behalf of white society. By the 1980s, the basic institutions on Chicago's South Side were (i) astringent and humiliating welfare programs, bolstered and replaced by "workfare" after 1996, which restricted access to the public aid rolls and pushed recipients into the low-wage labor market; (ii) decrepit public housing that subjected its tenants and the surrounding population to extraordinary levels of criminal insecurity, infrastructural blight, and official scorn; (iii) failing institutions of public health and education operating with resources, standards, and results typical of

Third World countries; and (iv) not least, the police, the courts, probation officers, parole agents, and "snitches" recruited by the thousands to extend the mesh of state surveillance and capture deep into the hyperghetto.[14]

LOSS OF THE "BUFFERING" FUNCTION

As it deteriorated economically and organizationally, the ghetto also lost its capacity to buffer its residents from external forces. No longer Janus-faced, offering a sheltered space for collective sustenance and self-affirmation in the face of hostility and exclusion, it has devolved into a one-dimensional machinery for brutal relegation, a human warehouse for the segments of urban society deemed disreputable, derelict, and dangerous. And, with the conjoint contraction of the wage-labor market and the welfare state in the context of continued segregation, it has become saturated with economic, social, and physical insecurity. Social relations in the hyperghetto now have a distinctly carceral cast: fear and danger pervade public space; interpersonal relations are riven with suspicion and distrust, feeding mutual avoidance and retraction into one's private defended space; violence is the prevalent means for upholding respect, regulating encounters, and controlling territory; and relations with official authorities are suffused with animosity and diffidence—patterns familiar to students of social order in the contemporary U.S. prison.[15]

Consider the state of public housing, as well as retirement homes, single-room occupancy hostels, homeless shelters, and other establishments for collective living, which now look and feel much like houses of detention. "Projects" have been fenced in, their perimeters placed under beefed-up security patrols and authoritarian controls, including identification-card checks, signing in, electronic monitoring, police infiltration, random searches, curfews, segregation, and head counts—techniques which, Jerome Miller points out, are "all familiar procedures of efficient prison management."[16] Over the past decade, the Chicago Housing Authority has deployed its own police force and even sought to institute its own "misdemeanor court" to try misbehaving tenants on the premises. As one elderly resident of a District of Columbia project under such quasi-penal supervision observed: "It's as though the children in here are being prepared for incarceration, so when they put them in a real lock-down situation, they'll be used to being hemmed in."[17]

Public schools in the hyperghetto have similarly deteriorated to the point where they operate in the manner of *institutions of confinement* whose primary mission is not to educate but to ensure "custody and control"—to borrow the motto of many departments of corrections. Like the prison system, their recruitment is severely skewed along class and ethno-racial lines: 75 percent of the pupils in Chicago's public schools come from families living under the official poverty line and nine of every ten are black or Latino. Like inmates, these children are herded into decaying and overcrowded facilities that resemble fortresses, complete with razor wire on outside fences, bricked up windows, heavy locks on iron doors, metal detectors at the gates, and hallways patrolled by armed guards.

Indeed, it appears that the main purpose of these schools is simply to "neutralize" youth by holding them under lock and key for the day. Certainly, it is hard to maintain that educating them is a priority when half of the city's high schools place in the bottom one percent on the American College Test, two thirds of the city's ghetto students fail to graduate, and those who do graduate read, on average, at an eighth-grade level.[18] At any rate, the carceral atmosphere of schools and the constant presence of armed guards in uniform habituates the children of the hyperghetto to the demeanor, tactics, and interactive style of the correctional officers many of them are bound to encounter shortly after their school days are over.

"GHETTOIZATION" OF THE PRISON

In the two decades following the climax of the Civil Rights movement, the racial and class backlash that reconfigured the city also ushered in a sweeping transformation in the purpose and social organization of the carceral system. In the past few decades, the explosive growth of the incarcerated population has led to rampant prison overcrowding; the rapid rise in the proportion of inmates serving long sentences, the spread of ethnically-based gangs, and a flood of young convicts and drug offenders deeply rooted in the informal economy and oppositional culture of the street, have combined to undermine the older "inmate society" depicted in the classic prison research of the postwar decades.[19] The "Big House" with its correctional ideal of melioristic treatment and community reintegration of inmates—gave way to a race-divided and violence-ridden "warehouse" geared solely to the physical sequestering of social rejects.

It is difficult to characterize the changes that have remade the American prison in the image of the ghetto over the past three decades, not only because American prisons are so diverse, but also because we have remarkably little on-the-ground data on social and cultural life inside the contemporary penitentiary. Nonetheless, one can provisionally single out five tendencies that fortify the convergence of ghetto and prison in the large (post) industrial states that have put the United States on the path to mass imprisonment.

THE RACIAL DIVISION OF EVERYTHING

The world of inmates used to be organized around a relatively stable set of positions and expectations defined primarily in terms of criminal status and prison conduct. In Gresham Sykes's classic account, we have "rats" and "center men" who betray the core value of solidarity among inmates by violating the ban on communication with custodians; "merchants" who peddle goods in the illicit economy of the establishment; "gorillas" who prey on weak inmates to acquire cigarettes, food, clothing, and deference; and "wolfs," "punks," and "fags," who play out sexual scripts adopted behind bars.[20] This older order has now been replaced by a chaotic and conflictual setting wherein "racial division has primacy over all particular identities and influences all aspects of life."[21]

The ethnic provenance or affiliation of the inmates determines their ward, tier, cell, and bunk-bed assignments; their access to food, telephone, television, visitation, and in-house programs; their associations and protections, which in turn determine the probability of being the victim or perpetrator of violence. Elective loyalty to inmates as a generic class, with the possibility of remaining non-aligned, has been superseded by forced and exclusive loyalty to one's "race" defined in rigid, caste-like manner, with no in-between and no position of neutrality—just as it is in the urban ghetto. And the central axis of stratification inside the "pen" has shifted from the vertical cleavage *between prisoners and guards* (marked by prohibitions against "ratting on a con," "talking to a screw," or exploiting other inmates), to horizontal cleavages between black, Latino, and white prisoners (with Asians most often assimilated to whites and Middle Easterners given a choice of voluntary affiliation).

FROM "CONVICT CODE" TO "STREET CODE"

Along with racial division, the predatory culture of the street, centered on hypermasculine notions of honor, toughness, and coolness has transformed the social structure and culture of jails and prisons. The "convict code," rooted in solidarity among inmates and antagonism towards guards has been swamped by the "code of the street," with its ardent imperative of individual "respect" secured through the militant display and demonstrated readiness to mete out physical violence.[22] According to John Irwin, "the old 'hero' of the prison world—the 'right guy'—has been replaced by outlaws and gang members," who have "raised toughness and mercilessness to the top of prisoners' value systems."[23] Ethnically-based street gangs and "supergangs," such as the Disciples, El Rukn, Vice Lords, and Latin Kings in Illinois, the Mexican Mafia, Black Guerrilla Family, and Aryan Brotherhood in California, and the

Netas in New York City, have taken over the illicit prison economy and destabilized the entire social system of inmates, forcing a shift from "doing your own time" to "doing gang time." They have even precipitated a thorough restructuring of the administration of large-scale prison systems, from Illinois to California to Texas.[24]

These changes, together with the rising tide of drugs, have disrupted the old inmate structure of power and produced increased levels of interpersonal and group brutality. As Johnson writes, "what was once a repressive but comparatively safe 'Big House' is now often an unstable and violent social jungle" in which social intercourse is infected with the same disruption, aggression, and unpredictability as in the hyperghetto.[25]

PURGING THE UNDESIRABLES

The Big House of the postwar decades was animated by the idea that punishment should ultimately help resocialize inmates and thus reduce the probability of further offenses once they returned to society. This philosophy of rehabilitation was repudiated in the 1970s, and today's prison aims solely to *neutralize* offenders—and individuals thought to be likely to violate the law, such as parolees—both *materially*, by removing them physically into an institutional enclave, and *symbolically*, by drawing a hard and fast line between criminals and law-abiding citizens. The now-dominant "law and order" paradigm jettisons ideas of prevention and proportionality in favor of direct appeals to popular resentment through measures that dramatize the fear and loathing of crime, which is presented as the abhorrent conduct of defective individuals. The mission of today's prison is thus identical to that of the classical ghetto, whose *raison d'être* was precisely to quarantine a polluting group from the urban body.

THE RACIALIZATION OF JUDICIAL STIGMA

The contemporary prison can be further likened to the ghetto in that the stigma of penal conviction has been prolonged, diffused, and re-framed in ways that assimilate it to an ethno-racial stigma—something permanently attached to the body of its bearer. In other liberal-democratic societies, the status dishonor and civic disabilities of being a prisoner are temporary and limited: they affect offenders while they are being processed by the criminal justice system and typically wear off shortly after the prisoner's release; to ensure this, laws and administrative rules set strict conditions and limits on the use and diffusion of criminal justice information.

The resurgence and popularity of genetic pseudo-explanations of crime is indicator of the bent towards the compulsive racialization of criminals. Thus, a recent authoritative compendium on crime edited by James Q. Wilson and Joan Petersilia opens with two long chapters that review "Criminogenic Traits" and "Biomedical Factors in Crime" For Harvard psychologist Richard Herrnstein, serious crimes are not culturally or historically defined but "crimes that are wrong in themselves."[26] "it would be an overstatement to say 'once a criminal always a criminal it would be closer to the truth than to deny the evidence of a unifying and long-enduring pattern of encounters with the law for most serious offenders." This pattern cannot be explained by "accidents, situations, and social forces," as these only "modulate the criminogenic factors" of low intelligence, antisocial personality, and male chromosomes. Herrnstein does not discuss ethno-racial differences in criminality, but it requires little effort to infer from his argument that the disproportionate incarceration of blacks must be caused in part by innate criminal propensities, given what he calls "a scientific consensus that criminal and antisocial behavior can have genetic roots."[27]

CARCERAL RECRUITMENT AND AUTHORITY

Today's prison further resembles the ghetto for the simple reason that an overwhelming majority of its occupants originate from the racialized core of the country's major cities, and return there upon releases-only to be soon caught again in police dragnets and sent away for ever-longer sojourns behind bars, in a self-perpetuating cycle of escalating socioeconomic marginality and legal incapacitation. Thus, in the late 1980s, three of every four inmates serving sentences in the entire state of New York came from *seven black and Latino neighborhoods* of New York City, which also happened to be the poorest areas of the city. Every year these segregated and dispossessed districts furnished a fresh contingent of 25,000-odd inmates, while 23,000 ex-convicts were discharged, most of them on parole, right back into these devastated areas. A conservative estimate, given a statewide felony recidivism rate of 47 percent, is that within a year, some 15,000 of them found their way back "upstate" and behind bars.[28] The fact that 46 percent of the inmates of New York state prisons issue from neighborhoods served by the sixteen worst public schools of the city ensures that their clientele will be duly replenished for years to come.

The contemporary prison system and the ghetto not only display a similarly skewed recruitment and composition in terms of class and caste. The prison also duplicates the authority structure characteristic of the ghetto in that it places a population of poor blacks under the direct supervision of whites—in this case, lower-class whites. In the communal ghetto of the postwar era, black residents chaffed under the rule of white landlords, white employers, white unions, white social workers, and white policemen.[29] Likewise, at century's end, the convicts of New York City, Philadelphia, Baltimore, Cleveland, Detroit, and Chicago, who are overwhelmingly African-American, serve their sentences in establishments staffed by officers who are overwhelmingly white. In Illinois, for instance, two thirds of the state's 41,000 inmates are blacks who live under the watch of an 8,400-member uniformed force that is 84 percent white. In Michigan and Pennsylvania, 55 percent of prisoners are black but only 13 and 8 percent of guards, respectively, come from the Afro-American community. In Maryland, the correctional staff is 90 percent white and monitors an inmate population that is 80 percent black. With the proliferation of detention facilities in rural areas, the economic stability and social welfare of lower-class whites from the declining hinterland has come to hinge, perversely, on the continued socioeconomic marginality and penal restraint of ever-larger numbers of lower-class blacks from the urban core.

The convergent changes that have "prisonized" the ghetto and "ghettoized" the prison in the aftermath of the civil rights revolution suggest that the stupendous increasing over representation of blacks behind bars does not stem simply from the discriminatory targeting of specific penal policies such as the War on Drugs (as Michael Tonry suggests) or from the sheer destabilizing effects of the increased penetration of ghetto neighborhoods by the penal state (as Jerome Miller argues).[30] These two factors are clearly at work but they fail to capture the precise nature and full magnitude of the transformations that have interlocked the prison and the (hyper)ghetto into a *single institutional mesh* suited to fulfill anew the mission historically imparted to America's "peculiar institutions."

Thus, consider the *timing of racial transition*: with a lag of about a dozen years, the "blackening" of the carceral population has closely followed the demise of the Black Belt as a viable instrument of caste containment in the urban-industrial setting. A century earlier, David Oshinsky points out, the sudden penal repression of African Americans had helped to shore up "the walls of white supremacy as the South moved from an era of racial bondage to one of racial caste."[31] The thesis of a structural and functional linkage between ghetto and prison is also verified by the *geographic patterning* of racial disproportionality: outside of the South—which for obvious historical reasons requires a separate analysis—the black-white gap in incarceration is more pronounced and has increased faster in those states of the Midwest and Northeast that are the historic cradle of the Northern ghetto.[32] The intertwining of the urban Black Belt and the carceral system is

further evidenced, and in turn abetted, by the *fusion of ghetto and prison culture*, as vividly expressed in the lyrics of "gangsta rap" singers and hip hop artists, in graffiti and tattooing, and in the dissemination, to the urban core and beyond, of language, dress, and interaction patterns innovated inside of jails and penitentiaries.

MAKING "RACE," SHAPING CITIZENS

By assuming a central role in the contemporary government of race and poverty—at the crossroads of the deregulated low-wage labor market, a revamped "welfare-workfare" apparatus designed to support casual employment, and the vestiges of the ghetto—the overgrown American carceral system has become a major engine of symbolic production in its own right. Just as bondage imposed "social death" on imported African captives and their descendants,[33] mass incarceration induces civic death for those it ensnares. Today's inmates are the targets of three forms of exclusion:

(i) Prisoners are denied access to valued cultural capital: At a time when university credentials are becoming a prerequisite for employment in the (semi-)protected sector of the labor market, inmates have been made ineligible for higher-education Pell Grants. The exclusion started with drug offenders in 1988, continued with convicts sentenced to death or lifelong imprisonment without the possibility of parole in 1992, and ended with all remaining state and federal prisoners in 1994. This expulsion was passed by Congress for the sole purpose of accentuating the symbolic divide between criminals and "law-abiding citizens" in spite of overwhelming evidence that prison educational programs drastically cut recidivism as well as help to maintain carceral order.

(ii) Prisoners are systematically excluded from social redistribution and public aid in an age when work insecurity makes access to such programs more vital than ever for those dwelling in the lower regions of the socio-economic hierarchy. Laws deny welfare payments, veterans benefits, and food stamps to anyone in detention for more than sixty days. The Work Opportunity and Personal Responsibility Act of 1996 farther banishes most ex-convicts from Medicaid, public housing, Section 8 vouchers, and related forms of assistance.

(iii) Convicts are banned from political participation via "criminal disenfranchisement" practiced on a scale and with a vigor unimaginable in any other country. All but four states deny the vote to mentally competent adults held in detention facilities; thirty-nine states forbid convicts placed on probation from exercising this political right; and thirty-two states also disenfranchise parolees. In fourteen states, ex-felons are barred from voting even when they are no longer under criminal justice supervision—for life in ten of these states. The result is that nearly 4 million Americans have temporarily or permanently lost the ability to cast a ballot, including 1.47 million who are not behind bars and another 1.39 million who served their sentences in full.[34] A mere quarter century after acceding to full voting rights, one

black man in seven nationwide is banned from the electoral booth through penal disenfranchisement and seven states permanently deny the vote to more than one fourth of their black male residents.

Through this triple exclusion, the prison and the criminal justice system contribute to, the ongoing reconstruction of the "imagined community" of Americans around a polar opposition. On the one handstand praiseworthy "working families," implicitly white, suburban, and deserving; on the other hand, a despicable "underclass" of criminals, loafers, and leeches—by definition dark-skinned, undeserving, and personified by the dissolute teenage "welfare mother" and the dangerous street "gang banger." The former are exalted as the living incarnation of genuine American values self-control, deferred gratification, subservience of life to labor. The latter is condemned as the loathsome embodiment of their abject desecration, the "dark side" of the "American dream" of affluence and opportunity for all, believed to flow from morality anchored in conjugality and work. And the line that divides them is increasingly being drawn, materially and symbolically, by the prison.

NOTES

This article is adapted from a book being completed, entitled *Deadly Symbiosis*.

1. An additional 68,000 black women were locked up, a number higher than the *total* carceral population of any one major western European country. Because males compose over 93 percent of the U.S. state and federal prison population and 89 percent of jail inmates, and because the disciplining of women from the lower class and caste continues to operate primarily through welfare and workfare, this article focuses solely on men. But a full-fledged analysis of the distinct causes and consequences of the astonishing growth in the imprisonment of black (and Hispanic) women is urgently needed, in part because the penal confinement of women has immensely deleterious effects on their children.

2. Steven R. Donziger, *The Real War on Crime: The Report of the National Criminal Justice Commission* (New York: Harper Perinnial, 1996), 104–5; Marc Mauer, "Racial Disparities in Prison Getting Worse in the 1990s," *Overcrowded Times* 8 (1997): 8–13.

3. For a more detailed examination, see Loïc Wacquant, "Crime et châtiment en Amérique de Nixon à Clinton," *Archives de politique criminelle* 20 (Spring 1998): 123–38, and Alfred Blumstein,

"U.S. Criminal Justice Conundrum: Rising Prison Populations and Stable Crime Rates," *Crime and Delinquency* 44 (1998): 127–35.

4. In this, I follow George Rusche: "Punishment must be understood as a social phenomenon freed from both its juristic concept and its social ends—that is, its official mission of crime control, so that it may be replaced in the complete system of strategies, including social policies, aimed at regulating the poor. But I do *not* follow Rusche in (i) postulating a *direct* link between brute economic forces and penal policy; (ii) reducing economic forces to the sole state of the *labor market,* and still less the supply of labor; (iii) limiting the control function of the prison to lower *classes,* as distinct from other subordinate categories (ethnic or national, for instance); (iv) omitting the ramifying *symbolic* effects that the penal system exercises by drawing, dramatizing, and enforcing group boundaries. Indeed, in the case of black Americans, the symbolic function of the carceral system is paramount. See George Rusche, "Labor Market and Penal Sanction: Thoughts on the Sociology of Punishment," in *Punishment and Penal Discipline,* eds. Tony Platt and Paul Takagi (Berkeley, Calif.: Crime and Social Justice Associates, 1980), 11.

5. See Loïc Wacquant, *Les Prisons de la misère* (Paris: Editions Raisons d'sgir, 1999). Translated as *Prisons of Poverty* (Minneapolis: University of Minnesota Press, 2009).

6. See Avery F. Gordon, "Globalism and the Prison Industrial Complex: An Interview with Angela Davis," *Race and Class* 40 (1999): 145–57.

7. Martin Gilens, *Why Americans Hate Welfare: Race, Media, and the Politics of Anti-Poverty Policy* (Chicago: The University of Chicago Press, 2000).

8. E. Franklin Frazier, *The Negro Family in the United States* (Chicago: The University of Chicago Press, 1932).

9. St. Clair Drake and Horace R. Cayton, *Black Metropolis: A Study of Negro Life in a Northern City* (New York: Harper and Row, 1962), 716–28.

10. Caroline Wolf Harlow, *Profile of Jail Inmates 1996* (Washington, D.C.: Bureau of Justice Statistics, 1998).

11. Jeremy Rifkin, *The End of Work: The Decline of the Global Labor Force and the Dawn of the Post-Market Era* (New York: JP Tarcher and Putnam, 1995), 79. Also see Thomas J. Sugrue, *The Origins of the Urban Crisis: Race and Inequality in Postwar Detroit* (Princeton, N.J.: Princeton University Press, 1996), 125–52.

12. Drake and Cayton, *Black Metropolis,* 710–11, 650, 430–1, and 438–9, respectively.

13. See Loïc Wacquant, "Negative Social Capital: State Breakdown and Social Destitution in America's Urban Core, "*The Netherlands Journal of the Built Environment* 13 (1998): 25–40.

14. Jerome G. Miller, *Search and Destroy: African-American Males in the Criminal Justice System* (Cambridge: Cambridge University Press, 1997), 102–3.

15. On crime, see Dougalus S. Massey and Nancy A. Denton, *American Apartheid: Segregation and the Making of the Underclass* (Cambridge, Mass.: Harvard University Press, 1993); Lauren J. Krivo and Ruth D. Peterson, "Extremely Disadvantaged Neighborhoods and Urban Crime," *Social Forces* (December 1996); on the distorting effects of physical violence on social relations and everyday life, see Alex Kotlowitz, *There Are No Children Here: The Story of Two Boys Growing Up in the Other America* (New York: Anchor Books, 1991), p. 619–650; LeAlan Jones and Lloyd Newman, *Our America: Life and Death on the South Side of Chicago* (New York: Washington Square Press, 1997); Loïc Wacquant, "Inside the Zone: The Social Art of the Hustler in the Black American Ghetto, "*Theory, Culture, and Society* 15 (1998), 1–36; on prison

culture, see Leo Carroll, *Hacks, Blacks, and Cons: Race Relations in a Maximum Security Prison* (Lexington, Mass.: Lexington Books, 1974); James B. Jacobs, *Stateville: The Penitentiary in Mass Society* (Chicago: The University of Chicago Press, 1977); John Irwin, *Prisons in Turmoil* (Boston: Little, Brown, 1980).

16. Miller, *Search and Destroy*, 101.

17. Cited in Ibid., 101.

18. Chicago Tribune (Staff of the) *The Worst in America* (Chicago: Contemporary Press, 1992), 12–3.

19. The essential works on this point are Irwin, *Prisons in Turmoil*; and John Irwin, *The Felon*, new edition (Berkeley, Calif.: University of California Press, 1990).

20. Gresham M. Sykes, *The Society of Captives: A Study of a Maximum Security Prison* (Princeton, N.J.: Princeton University Press, 1958).

21. Irwin, *The Felon*, v; see also Leo Carroll, "Race, Ethnicity, and the Social Order of the Prison," in *The Pains of Imprisonment*, eds. Robert Johnson and Hans Toch (Beverly Hills, Calif.: Sage, 1982), 181–201; Robert Johnson, *Hard Time: Understanding and Reforming the Prison*, 2d ed. (Belmont, Calif.: Wadsworth Publishing, 1996); Victor Hassine, *Life Without Parole: Living in Prison Today*, 2d ed. (Boston: Roxbury Publications, 1999), 71–8.

22. On the "inmate code," see Gresham Sykes and Sheldon Messinger, "The Inmate Social System," in *Theoretical Studies in Social Organization of the Prison*, eds. Richard Cloward et al. (New York: Social Science Research Council, 1960), 6–10; on the "street code," see Elijah Anderson, *Code of the Street: Decency, Violence, and the Moral Life of the Inner City* (New York: W.W. Norton &Company, 1998).

23. Irwin, *The Felon*, vii.

24. Jacobs, *Stateville*, 137–74; Irwin, *Prisons in Turmoil*, 186–92; Steve J. Martin and Sheldon Ekland-Olson, *Texas Prisons: The Walls Came Tumbling Down* (Austin, Tex.: Texas Monthly Press, 1987).

25. Johnson, *HardTime*, 133.

26. Joan Petersilia, "Parole and Prisoner Reentry in the United States," in *Prisons: Crime and Justice*, eds. Michael Tonry and Joan Petersilia (Chicago: The University of Chicago Press, 1999).

26. Richard J. Herrnstein, "Criminogenic Traits," in *Crime: Public Policies for Crime Control*, eds. James Q. Wilson and Joan Petersilia (San Francisco: ICS Press, 1995), 40, 41, 62, 56–7, 58.

27. Herrnstein, "Criminogenic Traits," 55, 62, 58.

28. Edwin Ellis, *The Non-Traditional Approach to Criminal Justice and Social Justice* (New York: Community Justice Center, 1993).

29. Kenneth B. Clark, *Dark Ghetto: Dilemmas of Social Power* (Middletown, Conn.: Wesleyan University Press, 1965).

30. Michael Tonry, *Malign Neglect: Race, Crime, and Punishment in America* (New York: Oxford University Press, 1995); Miller, *Search, and Destroy*.

31. David M. Oshinsky, *"Worse Than Slavery": Parchman Farm and the Ordeal of Jim Crow Justice* (New York: Free Press, 1996), 57.

32. Mauer, "Racial Disparities."

33. Orlando Patterson, Slavery and Social Death (Cambridge, Mass.: Harvard University Press, 1982).

34. Jamie Fellner and Marc Mauer, *Losing the Vote: The Impact of Felony Disenfranchisement in the United States* (Washington, D.C.: Human Rights Watch and The Sentencing Project, 1998).

JOURNALING QUESTION

Do you find the media image of prisons to accurately represent the racial distribution of inmates? How do you think producers decide how to present prison populations in movies and television?

27.

U.S. EXPERIENCES WITH RACIAL AND ETHNIC PROFILING

History, Current Issues, and the Future

DAVID A. HARRIS

Most of the discussion about "racial profiling" in police work—that is, using race or, particularly after September 11, 2001, "ethnic markers" in deciding who to stop and search on the highway or in the airport—has focused on whether or not it works. If you pull young, Middle Eastern-looking men out of line in the airport, are you more likely to find terrorists than if you pull elderly white women out of line? If you stop young black men on the highway, are you more likely to find drug dealers than if you stop old white folks? David Harris moves us past this question, because racial profiling has other consequences that may well stand in the way of catching criminals: It alienates entire communities of people who might be in a better position than police officers to turn in terrorists and drug dealers alike; and it turns the eyes of police officers away from genuinely "suspicious behavior." Yet police—black as well as white—continue to use racial profiling. If the behavior these officers are engaging in is "racist," does this mean that individual policemen and policewomen are themselves racist, or is this a measure of the racism built into the police system itself? Is a police officer, acting as a police officer, to be judged as an individual or as a police officer?

INTRODUCTION

Since the middle of 1998, racial or ethnic profilings—police use of racial or ethnic appearance as one factor, among others, to determine who to stop, question and search—has remained part of the public dialogue in the U.S. on the issues of crime control and racial justice. But on September 11, 2001, the context of the discussion changed. The singular events of that day served not to push the debate over racial profiling off of the national agenda, but instead to re-focus the debate. Many Americans had been against the use of race or ethnic appearance in police profiling before September 11, 2001; in one notable poll, more than 80% of all Americans surveyed—not just 80% of all African Americans

or Latinos, but 80% of all Americans—wanted the practice stopped (Newport 1999). After the attacks, nearly 60% of all Americans—including African Americans and Latinos, many of whom had felt the sting of profiling themselves—thought that using profiles to focus intensive scrutiny on Arabs and Muslims in airports made perfect sense (Jones 2001).

Thus this seems a particularly apt point at which to consider the lessons we have learned about racial and ethnic profiling in the U.S., and to see how this dovetails with the work of researchers and the experiences of police departments in other nations, since the U.S. is hardly alone in having encountered issues related to racial and ethnic biases in the

Excerpted from David A. Harris, "U.S. Experiences with Racial and Ethnic Profiling: History, Current Issues, and the Future," *Critical Criminology* 14 (2006): 213–39 and references have been edited.

context of policing. (FitzGerald and Sibbit, 1997; Fitz-Gerald 1999; Macpherson of Cluny et al. 1999; MVA and Miller, 2000; Waddington et al. 2004; Wortley and Tanner 2004) Just as important, this gives us a chance to look to the future.

HISTORY: THE MODERN BACKGROUND

The law enforcement tactic that has become known in the U.S. as racial profiling emerged in the early 1980s as part of the effort of the U.S. government to attack drug trafficking. The U.S. Drug Enforcement Administration (DEA) had, for some years, used lists of the common characteristics of drug courier arrestees to construct what they called "drug courier profiles" (Harris 2002, at 20). DEA agents used these drug courier profiles to attempt to identify passengers on commercial airliners who might be transporting narcotics in quantity. The DEA claimed that its efforts utilizing these profiles succeeded; DEA agents made regular arrests of passengers carrying illegal drugs. The rate of success or effectiveness of the use of these profiles—that is, a comparison of the number of stops and searches yielding drugs to the number of persons stopped, questioned, and searched who did not have drugs or any other contraband—never seemed to enter into the discussion (Harris 2002, at 19–21). Many questioned the rigor of these drug courier profiles, given that judicial opinions containing the testimony of DEA agents showed startling inconsistencies on the use of the profiles (Cole 2000, at 48–49). For example, Case A might say that agents considered the person observed suspicious because he got off the plane first; Case B might find the person was suspicious because he got off last; Case C would say agents considered it suspicious that the person got off in the middle of all of the passengers. Such inconsistencies seemed to show that the DEA based its profiles not on the full universe of relevant data, thoroughly analyzed, but on the use of selective, anecdotal thinking dressed up as something vaguely scientific.

Nevertheless, by the mid 1980s, the DEA had become fully convinced of the effectiveness of drug courier profiling in airports. At the same time, concerns arose that drug traffickers had begun to use America's vast system of interstate highways to move large quantities of their narcotics. Therefore, the DEA sought to meld the profiling tactic with the enforcement of highway traffic safety laws (Harris 2002, at 20–23). Traffic laws in the U.S. have always regulated both driving and the condition of vehicles in incredible detail (Harris 1997, at 558–559). As a result, any American police officer can easily observe a traffic offense by almost any driver by following the driver's vehicle for just a few blocks (Id. at 557–558). This meant that officers could make traffic stops without the slightest interest in driving safety, merely using traffic regulation as a mere pretext for drug enforcement investigation, without any actual suspicion that the driver had engaged in any drug crime; the U.S. Supreme Court declared such stops perfectly legal (Whren v U.S. 1996). Thus the DEA thought that, with training in the use of profiling, police officers across the country could become soldiers in America's so-called "war on drugs," fighting the battle on the country's highways.

The DEA thus became the main engine of the effort that took profiling from airports, where it had affected relatively few people, onto streets and highways all over the U.S., exposing far greater numbers of Americans to stops, searches, and treatment reserved for suspected criminals (Harris 2002, at 22). The DEA did this not stealthily but openly and deliberately, through a program with the catchy name "Operation Pipeline." Operation Pipeline used millions of U.S. taxpayer dollars to teach police officers from around the nation how to use profiles to catch drug couriers on the roads. Operation Pipeline aimed to train as many officers as possible in the nuances of highway drug interdiction; these officers would then return to their own police departments, where they would train other officers and put together drug interdiction units within their own police agencies. The DEA trained tens of thousands of officers in the course of the Pipeline program, particularly among members of state police forces (Harris 2002, at 23).[1]

As late as 2000, the DEA still insisted that it did not use, and never had used, racial or ethnic appearance in its profiles, and did not train police officers under its tutelage to do so (Kocieniewski 2000, at A1). So how did race become part of the profiles that these police officers used to make these drug interdiction stops? There are, at the very least, substantial reasons to doubt the DEA's denials. For example, a typical videotape produced for training purposes by the DEA in cooperation with a state police department lists the telltale signs that drug interdiction officers should watch for—that is, the factors in the profile—when observing cars and drivers on the highway ([U.S. DEA and New Mexico State Police] 1986). It also demonstrates the proper use of these clues and the correct way to make a drug interdiction traffic stop by showing a number of scripted stops, acted out to appear completely realistic. The training tape explicitly discusses many factors in the profile, i.e., the indicators to watch for; at no point does the videotape say that police officers should look more carefully at persons who appear to have particular racial or ethnic characteristics. But all of the scripted demonstration stops—not one, not some, but all of them—involve drivers with Spanish surnames. The message comes through clearly—"Hispanics are more likely to carry drugs than other drivers" even if the video communicates it only implicitly.

Beyond the DEA's actions, U.S. government intelligence bulletins for state and local police also encouraged officers involved in drug interdiction to harbor increased suspicion about particular racial and ethnic groups. At the same time that the DEA trained police officers in drug interdiction and profiling tactics, the U.S. government constantly disseminated intelligence to police agencies on drug trafficking organizations and activities. This intelligence often included information pointing, in very general ways, to particular ethnic groups

(Harris 2002, at 49). For example, the intelligence might indicate that police officers in a particular state should watch for Jamaican marijuana traffickers transporting the drug on the state's highways, many of whom would be wearing their hair in the traditional long braids of Rastafarians (as for any African American person not engaged in narcotics transportation who might wear those same braids, too bad). Or government intelligence sent to police might indicate that Hispanic gangs were moving quantities of cocaine by vehicle across particular states. Few police officers could miss the implication: they could, and should, sharpen their drug interdiction efforts by using visible physical characteristics of particular minority groups as profile indicators.

Beyond the formal DEA training and U.S. government intelligence, one cannot underestimate the belief among at least some American police officers that African Americans and Latinos were simply more crime prone, and therefore anyone with these racial or ethnic characteristics should be regarded as more suspicious than a comparably situated white person. In other words, it was not just profiling itself that caused racial bias to infect police work in the U.S. on highways in the 1980s and 1990s; it was also the attitudes, beliefs, and stereotypes that at least some police officers brought with them to the tactic. Many believed that paying extra attention to African Americans and Latinos constituted a rational approach to police work, and that they could come to no other reasonable conclusion. They believed that the evidence simply proved that African Americans and Hispanics in the U.S. were disproportionately involved in crime. For example, Marshall Frank, who served in the Miami-Dade (Florida) police force for 30 years before retiring as a captain, put these sentiments into words in an article he published in the *Miami Herald* newspaper (Frank 1999, at B 7.). What should police do, he asked, when they see a car driven through a white neighborhood with a young African American man at the wheel, and another in the passenger seat?

Assuming that the police witness no crime, should the officers use some kind of traffic enforcement pretext to stop the car and investigate its occupants to ascertain what they are doing in a white neighborhood? Yes, Frank answers unequivocally; the police should stop them, no matter that some will call this racial profiling. Frank says that readers can "label me a racist if you wish, but the cold fact is that African Americans comprise [sic] 12% of the nation's population, but occupy nearly half the state and federal prison cells. African Americans account for 2,165 inmates per 100,000 population, versus 307 for non-Hispanic whites and 823 for Hispanics." This means, Frank says, that since African Americans commit disproportionate amounts of crime, police should use their discretion to do disproportionate numbers of stops and searches of them. Frank's statement captured the sentiment of many in law enforcement neatly: we know whom we arrest and whom we incarcerate; a disproportionate number are African American or Latino. Therefore it simply makes sense to focus our attention on them, and to stop and search and question more of them. We will catch more criminals that way.

Frank's comments—and the beliefs of many police officers who agree with him—cast the discussion of the issue into an unfortunate false dilemma: are white police officers racist bigots, or clear-eyed realists? The misleading nature of the question conceals a sad reality: all types of American police officers seem to share Frank's views, not just white officers. In 1999, as part of its periodic large-scale national surveys into the experiences of Americans with crime and criminal justice, the Bureau of Justice Statistics, a unit of the U.S. Department of Justice, conducted an additional survey called Contacts Between the Police and the Public (U.S. Department of Justice 2001). This survey asked approximately 90,000 Americans about their own experiences with police over the previous six months; perhaps not surprisingly, young African American males were the most likely of any demographic group to have experienced traffic stops by police, to have experienced multiple stops, and to believe that these stops were motivated by their race. But the survey also revealed something that many considered startling. The stops of young African Americans were as likely to come at the hands of African American or Hispanic police officers as white officers. In other words, the race of the individual police officer seemed to make no difference in police officer behavior; rather, this was a matter of the institution of the police department and its values.

Just as important, Frank and those who agree with him seem unaware that researchers and scholars of police behavior have discredited the most basic assumption of Frank's argument not just relatively recently (Elliot 1995), but long ago (Kitsuse and Cicourel 1963). Statistics concerning who gets arrested and incarcerated do not measure who commits crime, as Frank seems to believe. Rather, statistics on arrests measure something quite different—patterns in the use of the police power to arrest. Likewise, statistics on incarceration measure the "incarceration activity" of other actors: judges pronouncing sentence, prosecutors, defense counsel, and defendants crafting plea bargains, and legislatures setting criminal penalties, among others. These constitute important phenomena, and measurement and study of them can reveal significant truths. But they do not measure what Frank and others think: the rate of engagement in crime by various racial and ethnic groups. This point is not only that members of law enforcement are incorrect when they believe themselves justified in using racial or ethnic appearance as a marker of higher than normal potential criminality. Rather, it is that this inaccurate belief becomes the basis for a self-filling prophecy. Officers concentrate their observation and enforcement activity on drivers and pedestrians who are African American or Hispanic because these people are arrested and incarcerated more often. Since officers focus on these particular citizens, they inevitably arrest more of them than they would otherwise. This means that disproportionate numbers of them enter the criminal justice system as defendants, and are incarcerated. This, of course, becomes justification for the next round of intensive observation and arrest.

In the mid 1990s, attorneys filed the first two legal actions explicitly challenging racial profiling—one each against the New Jersey State Police and the Maryland State Police. Both police forces vigorously denied that they used race or ethnic appearance as a targeting factor. But when, several years on, statistics on the practices of both police departments became public in the course of these cases, the reality of racial profiling became difficult to deny. In Maryland, on Interstate Highway 95 (the main north—south highway serving the heavily populated East Coast of the U.S.), African Americans constituted approximately 17% of the population of drivers; nevertheless, they were more than 70% of all drivers the state police stopped (Lamberth 1996a). In New Jersey, though African Americans were only 13.5% of the drivers on the New Jersey Turnpike, they were 35% of all the drivers that the state police stopped, and over 70% of all those that the state police arrested (Lamberth 1996b). Data from both states confirmed what many African Americans and Latino Americans had said for years: they experienced police stops and searches, and on-the-roadway investigation as possible drug traffickers, much more frequently than their presence on the highway or their driving behavior would lead one to predict.

THE CENTRAL EMPIRICAL QUESTION: DOES IT WORK?

The emergence of the data from the states of New Jersey and Maryland, which demonstrated for the first time that at least those police forces did indeed use racial or ethnic characteristics as indicators of criminal suspicion, marked the first important turn in the debate in the U.S. From that point forward, fewer law enforcement officials and their supporters argued that racial profiling simply did not exist. Instead, they made a different argument: we're not interested in race, except as it indicates a greater propensity to engage in criminal offenses. If sometimes use race to focus our enforcement efforts, this is because it helps us target those more likely to be criminals. This became the central justification for racial profiling: by using race as a targeting factor, police would apprehend more offenders.

A key point in the public discussion of the issue—overlooked by nearly everyone involved in the debate over racial and ethnic profiling in the U.S.—was that the justification of profiling as an effective tactic was not a proven fact, but an assumption. No empirical evidence existed proving that police got a better return on enforcement efforts when they targeted African Americans and Latinos than when they simply went after those who behaved suspiciously, regardless of race or ethnic appearance. Nevertheless, the assumption that racial and ethnic profiling helped police do a better job was accepted as "just common sense," as something no well-informed person would question, regardless of the fact that this had never been empirically established.

As a way to challenge and test the assumption that racial profiling made law enforcement efforts more effective, a new concept developed: hit rates (Harris 1999, at 295–296). At what rate did police "hit"—apprehend criminals—when using racial targeting, as opposed to when police did not use race this way (i.e., when they stopped and searched whites)? Calculating hit rates required finding the answers to two questions. First, a researcher would ask if the data indicated that the jurisdiction under observation appeared to be using racial and ethnic characteristics to "target" police enforcement efforts. If the answer to this first question was "yes" then one would then seek to measure the rate of hits—the rate at which police officers succeeded in finding drugs, guns, or other contraband, or made other arrests—when they stopped, questioned, and searched people, and then to separate and compare the hit rates for African Americans and Latinos to the hit rates for whites. This would yield an answer to a question that had, thus far, not been asked, since it had always been assumed that racial or ethnic profiling worked well: did the use of the tactic actually help police catch more criminals, as so many people—both police officers and civilians—seemed to believe?

Evidence related to the first question—whether racial or ethnic profiling was being used—had already been assembled for some police departments, such as the Maryland State Police and the New Jersey State Police. The availability of new data meant that the question could be answered in other departments, too. For example, in New York City, a study compared the frequency of stops and "frisks" of whites, African Americans, and Latinos (Spitzer 1999).[2] Latinos made up about 23% of the city's population, but they were 33% of all of those stopped and frisked. African Americans were about 26% of New York's population, but they made up about 52% of all of those stopped and frisked. Whites, who made up 40% of the population, were only 10% of all of those stopped and frisked. Explanations other than the use of race or ethnicity were carefully considered. For example, officials said that the disproportional use of stops and frisk against minority populations resulted from witness reports to police indicating that an outsized number of suspected criminals were African American or Latino. The data did not support this assertion; reports of crime accompanied by suspect descriptions resulted in only a very small percentage of all stops and frisks, and they could not explain the large disproportion. Other officials said that the disproportional use of stops and frisks against minorities were due to areas with higher minority populations having higher crime rates, resulting in larger deployments of police officers, increasing the likelihood that police would encounter and stop minority citizens. The data did not support this position, either; stops and frisks of minority persons actually occurred most frequently in areas with lower crime rates and mostly white populations. In fact, none of the alternative explanations could explain the

patterns in the data. Only one thing did: police in New York were using race and ethnic appearance, among other factors, to decide whom to stop and frisk.

As to the second question, if proponents of racial and ethnic profiling were right, using profiles that included racial and ethnic appearance should succeed more often than (or at very least as often as) enforcement based on other, less sophisticated techniques. In any event, it should not succeed less often than traditional policing. In other words, hit rates for African Americans and Latinos should be higher than for whites. But in fact, in departments that focused on African Americans, Latinos, and other minorities, the rates of searches that succeeded in finding contraband like drugs or guns were actually lower for minorities than were the hit rates for whites (who of course were not apprehended by using a racial or ethnic profile, but instead through police observation of suspicious behavior). In other words, when police agencies used race or ethnic appearance as a factor—not as the only factor but one factor among many—they did not get the higher returns from their enforcement efforts that they were expecting. Instead, they got lower returns than when they did not use race or ethnicity. To return to the example of New York City, when police stopped and frisked persons on the street using race or ethnic appearance as one factor in deciding whom to stop, hit rates were 10.5% and 11.5% for African Americans and Latinos, respectively. When New York City police stopped and frisked whites in encounters in which race or ethnic appearance were not, of course, factors, the hit rate was 12.6% (Spitzer 1999). With a sample size of over 170,000 stops and frisks, these statistically significant differences surprised many people, because they directly contradicted the long-held assumption that using race or ethnic appearance would help police; instead, it hindered them. The New York data are consistent with data from across the country on this same point (Harris 2002, Ch. 4).

This underlying reason for these results is subtle but important: race and ethnic appearance are very poor predictors of behavior. And it is behavior—criminal behavior, that is—that should actually interest police involved in crime fighting, not appearance. Race and ethnicity describe people well, and there is absolutely nothing wrong with police using skin color or other features to describe known suspects (meaning that police suspect a person whom a witness has physically described). Police act appropriately when they use race this way. Race serves well as one way to describe physical appearance, because of its easy visibility and its salience to the human brain. Further, the immutability of race, unlike a suspect's clothing or hairstyle, makes it all the more valuable as part of a witness's description. But in a situation in which both the crime and the perpetrator are unknown—prototypically, trafficking in or carrying illegal narcotics on highways or roads, the crimes that police have used racial profiling to combat in the U.S.—there is no description of any particular suspect in play. More important, because the perpetrators of these crimes are unknown, what police are actually interested in is the criminal behavior itself, not what someone looks like; racial or ethnic appearance is used only as a proxy indicator of the (possible) existence of the criminal behavior. Focusing on those who "look like" drug couriers distracts police from the real task at hand. Instead of paying the most careful possible attention to how people behave, police using racial or ethnic profiling are distracted by something almost entirely irrelevant: personal appearance, and whether it fits the preconception the officer has of a "criminal" or "drug dealer." The results in a measurable drop in accuracy.

If using racial and ethnic profiling harms the accuracy of police efforts to catch criminals, these practices also cause harm in other ways. Because using profiling based on race causes police to turn their attention to a higher percentage of innocent African Americans and Latinos than they would if they only focused on criminal behavior, police end up spreading their enforcement activities far too widely and indiscriminately. The results of this misguided effort have been disastrous for law enforcement: constant stopping, questioning, and searching of people who "look like" suspects, most of which constitutes wasted effort because the vast majority of those they stop are hard working, tax paying citizens. But the damage actually goes far deeper, and has a negative impact on how police perform their core function of crime fighting.

SPECIFIC ISSUES AND PROBLEMS THAT HAVE ARISEN IN THE U.S. CONCENING RACIAL AND ETHINIC PROFILING

Many police officers consider raising the issue of racial or ethnic profiling to be nothing less than a direct accusation of police racism—both generally and personally. They feel that those who discuss the subject do so in order to imply that all police officers are racists and perform their duties in a racist fashion. Officers feel the sting of this accusation keenly. They have often told the author that they have a job that puts them in daily contact with many more people belonging to minority groups than most Americans ever do, that they work with people of other races regularly, and that calling them racists is not just inaccurate but unfair. They feel as if others judge them far too harshly in this regard and are without any real standing to do so, because so few other "white" Americans in other professions have any but the most casual encounters with African American or Latino people. One can readily see that this attitude would stymie any real discussion of the issue, and keep any progress from being made.

The most effective response to this type of thinking has been to take the focus off the behavior of individual officers, and instead to take aim at racial profiling as an institutional problem. That is, the primary problem raised by profiling does not come from bigoted individuals within police departments—some small number of white officers who do not like African Americans or Latinos. Of course, those officers are a problem, and must be rooted out. But the real problem is the institutional assumptions that have allowed profiling to take root and even flourish in some places. These assumptions all come down to the idea that using racial or ethnic characteristics as ways of selecting suspects is an effective and successful way to do the job; academy training, field training, and even the policies of some police departments have sometimes reflected these assumptions. By stressing that the problem with profiling is the faulty assumptions in policing generally about its efficacy, officers can be brought around to seeing that the issue of racial profiling should not be read as an indictment of them personally. Rather, it is an institutional problem, for which we must seek institutional solutions.

The view of the problem as institutional, and especially that the issue is not an accusation of racism of white officers, receives powerful support from the aforementioned Contacts Between the Police and the Public survey, the large-scale study of the experiences of Americans with police conducted in 1999 by the Bureau of Justice Statistics of the U.S. Department of Justice and published in 2001 (U.S. Department of Justice 2001). Recall that African American respondents who reported being stopped were asked the race of the officer. According to the report, when black citizens found themselves subject to police stops, they "generally had a worse outcome"—that is, they experienced more stops, more searches, and were issued more citations than whites—"whether they were stopped by a white officer or a black officer" (U.S. Department of Justice 2001, at 17). In other words, the race of the officer was not important in the use of profiling; it was as likely to happen at the hands of African American officers as it was at the hands of a white officer. The problem was not the racism of white officers generally, or even just a few bad white officers. Rather, the problem permeates the institution of policing.

The emphasis on *institutional* behavior, habits, and practices has an additional benefit. It gives one a way to deal with (and often to head off entirely) the almost inevitable argument that racial profiling is just "a few bad apples," not the entire profession.

The question becomes not how we might get rid of the few bad cops (which we surely must), but instead how we can change the institution of policing or the police department so that the best instincts of the many good officers can thrive and predominate. In Britain, similar debates about "institutional racism" in policing came to a head as a result of an enquiry into the police's handling of the racist murder of Afro-Caribbean British teenager Stephen Lawrence (Macpherson 1999). The enquiry found that a culture of "institutional racism" the police force had served to damage the successful investigation of this murder case.

THE FUTURE

At present, even years after the public discourse over racial profiling began in the U.S. in earnest, the issue retains its vitality. The media continues to cover the issue, though usually at the level of local stories. And state and local governments around the country continue to take legislative and administrative action to address the problem. A particularly good recent example comes from the state of Kansas (Kansas Legislature 2005). Kansas is, by any measure, a very conservative state with a right-leaning electorate (Frank 2004). Yet in 2005, the Kansas legislature passed, and the governor of the state signed into law, a comprehensive anti-racial profiling law.

Police departments around the country continue to show interest in how to cope with the problem of racial and ethnic profiling. Hundreds of police departments have taken steps (such as the initiation of data collection) to meet this challenge on their own initiative, without any legal requirement that they do so (Grogger 2005). Many hundreds of others have done so because laws in their states have required them to act (e.g., Attorney General of Missouri 2005).

Since the events of September 11, 2001, the public discussion of racial and ethnic profiling in the U.S. changed and intensified, with the focus shifting to Arabs and Muslims. They quickly became the new subjects of profiling in the U.S. This development garnered both applause and public support, regardless of the fact that it surely had a severe negative impact on Arabs and Muslims living law-abiding lives in the U.S. For example, the African American social critic, writer, and commentator Stanley Crouch, winner of a prestigious MacArthur Foundation Fellowship, used his nationally syndicated newspaper column to proclaim that profiling was absolutely required to win the war against radical Islam, the cost to law abiding Arabs and Muslims be damned. "So if pressure has to be kept on innocent Arabs until those Arabs who are intent on committing mass murder are flushed out, that is the unfortunate cost they must pay to reside in this nation." (Crouch 2002, at 41). The Bush Administration took a similar (if more rhetorically measured) stand. Even as they issued guidelines to federal law enforcement prohibiting the use of race or ethnic appearance as a factor in deciding who to stop and search, they included an explicit exception for purposes of meeting threats posed in the area of national security and immigration—precisely the area in which racial or ethnic profiling was most likely to occur (U.S. Department of Justice 2003). Thus the U.S.'s global war on terror—including the invasions of both Afghanistan and Iraq and detentions of persons outside the U.S. for alleged connections to terrorism—also became an issue of security within the U.S. The impact on Muslims, Arabs, and people from the Middle East and South Asia who reside within the U.S. has been huge, and one of its chief manifestations has been the use of racial and ethnic profiling of these populations (Welch 2003). Thus racial and ethnic profiling of these populations can be seen as one of the ways in which the war on terror has shown up on U.S. soil.

With the stakes as great as they are with mass murder through to suicide terrorism, it is not surprising that people take the attitude that the government should try any countermeasure that might make us safer from our deadly and determined enemies. But it is an illusion—and a dangerous one—to assume that profiling using racial or ethnic characteristics

will make us safer. Take just one aspect of counter-terrorism work that will be all important in the future: the gathering of intelligence on possible al Qaeda sleeper cells consisting of Muslims from the Middle East. This is obviously the most vital of tasks. There are basically two ways that this might be done. First, government agents might attempt to infiltrate these cells. But given their secret and isolated nature, the language and cultural barriers, and the lack of appropriately qualified agents for such a task, this seems unlikely to succeed as a central strategy. The other possibility is to solicit and gather pieces of information from others—in other words, to work actively to obtain information from non-Qaeda members who happen to have it. Logic and common sense dictate that the likeliest—and perhaps the only—possible source for this information will be the Muslim and Middle Eastern communities themselves. The members of these communities are the people most likely to have encounters, knowing or unknowing, casual or otherwise, with potential terrorists from the Middle East or with citizens—so-called "homegrown terrorists"—who are intent on committing terrorist acts. They will know the languages used, and understand the cultural customs and subtle behavioral cues in a way that outsiders to the community could not (Harris 2005). The members of these communities must become the trusted partners of law enforcement tasked with counter-terrorism duties. And in fact there is some evidence that, at least as far as street-level agents are concerned, the F.B.I.—the American law enforcement organization that has been given the job of counter-terrorism—understands the importance of building these kinds of relationships with Muslim and Arab communities (Harris 2005). They know that with partnership comes communication; well-cultivated avenues of communication produce opportunities for information to flow. And that is what will bring intelligence dividends. When communities have relationships with law enforcement agencies, when they consider themselves to be allies of these agencies, and when a sufficient

degree of trust develops between them and their partners in law enforcement, valuable intelligence will result. This returns us, of course, to the observations of Lea and Young (1993): without strong, positive relationships of respect with the communities law enforcement serves, the police—whether involved in investigations of garden-variety crime or of terrorism—cannot expect a steady flow of crucial information from the community.

If anyone doubts this, take the example of Lackawanna, a small community outside of the city of Buffalo, New York. Lackawanna is where the U.S. government claims to have won one of its most substantial victories on American soil against al Qaeda terrorists (U.S. Department of Justice 2005). Six men from Lackawanna, all Muslims of Arab descent, were investigated, charged, and are now imprisoned on terrorism-related charges. All have been convicted of supporting and advancing the goals of al Qaeda, as part of their duties as members of a sleeper cell in Lackawanna. The interesting point, however, is how the case was broken—how the terrorist cell was uncovered. It was not wiretaps or fancy technology in use by the FBI or the CIA; it was not intercepted emails, or encryption schemes broken by massive, sophisticated computers at the U.S. National Security Agency. Rather, the Lackawanna cell was broken because members of the Arab and Muslim community in Lackawanna—the community there is made up largely of people who immigrated from Yemen—brought information to law enforcement that indicated possible involvement of the young men with al Qaeda (Harris 2005). Without this important information, the U.S. government might never have known about the cell. Worse, its terrorist masters might have activated it, resulting in the

same kind of damage witnessed in the U.S. in 2001, in Madrid in 2003, or in London in 2005.

The lesson is perhaps subtle, but important. If law enforcement uses racial or ethnic profiling against Middle Eastern, South Asian, and Muslim communities now, this sends a clear message that we regard everyone in those communities as suspects just by virtue of their Middle Eastern, South Asian, and Muslim identities. This might, of course, offend some of the people in these communities, but worries about giving offense or political correctness should not distract us from the real issue. Rather, the important thing is that if we treat the community in its entirety as suspects, they will respond just as any other community would: they will begin to fear law enforcement, to regard police as enemies instead of as partners. This reaction aligns perfectly with what any observer of human nature would expect. But the result could be catastrophic: if people in the Middle Eastern and Muslim communities fear law enforcement, they will simply be that much less likely to pass on important information that might be key to our counter-terrorism efforts. If they fear that contact with law enforcement will cause problems for them, or for their family members or friends, they will minimize that contact. To put it in concrete terms, if Yemenis in Lackawanna felt that the FBI or the local police regarded them as potential terrorism suspects just because of their demographic characteristics, the information on the sleeper cell in the town might never have come to the fore. Thus the use of racial or ethnic profiling now, in the struggle against our terrorist enemies, is not just potentially unpleasant for those subjected to it. It is unwise in the extreme—a strategy profoundly against our own self-interest.

NOTES

1. The U.S. has tens of thousands of independent police forces with different, sometimes overlapping, jurisdictions. Each state will typically have its own state police forces, and counties and cities within the states almost always have their own totally separate police forces, as do numerous smaller and specialized jurisdictions—townships, universities, transit systems, municipal

public housing authorities, and the like. The state police departments were the key component in the DEA's Operation Pipeline strategy, because state police have the primary responsibility for regulating traffic on the U.S. interstate highway system.

2. Frisk is the term that American police and courts use to describe a brief on-the-street search.

REFERENCES

Cole, D. (2000). *No Equal Justice: Race and Class in the American Criminal Justice System.* New York: The New Press.

Crouch, Stanley (March 14, 2002). U.S. Must Stay Tough About Sealing Borders, New York Daily News.

Elliot, Delbert (Nov. 1995). *Lies, Damn Lies, and Arrest Statistics,* Southerland Award presentation to the American Society of Criminology, Boston, Mass.

FitzGerald, Marian, *Final Report Into Stop and Search,* December 1999, accessed at http://www.met.police.uk/publications/stop_search/report.htm.

FitzGerald, Marian, and Sibbit, Rae, *Ethnic monitoring in Police Forces: A Beginning.* Home Office Research Study 173 (1997).

Frank, Marshall (19 Oct. 1999). *Racial Profiling: Better Safe than Sorry.* Miami Herald.

Frank, Thomas (2004). What's the Matter with Kansas? How Conservatives Won the Heart of America. New York: Metropolitan Books.

Grogger, Jeffrey, *Using the Veil of Darkness Approach to Test for Racial Profiling in Oakland Traffic Stops,* presentation to Northwestern University 2005 National Symposium on Racial Profiling, April 26, 2005, Rosemont, Illinois, available at http://server.traffic.northwestcrn.edu/ppp/Grogger.pps.

Harris, D.A. (2002). *Profiles in Injustice: Why Racial Profiling Cannot Work.* The New Press: New York.

Harris, D.A. (2005). *Good C ops: The Case for Preventive Policing.* New York: The New Press.

Harris, David A. (1997). Driving While Black and All Other Traffic Offenses: The Supreme Court and Pretextual Traffic Stops, *87 Journal of Criminal Law and Criminology* 544.

Harris, David A. (1999). The Stories, the Statistics, and the Law: Why Driving While Black Matters, *84 Minnesota Law Review* 265.

Jones, Jeffrey M. *Americans Felt Uneasy Toward Arabs Even Before September* 11, Gallup Poll, Sept. 28, 2001.

Kansas Legislature (2005) Regular Session, *An Act Concerning Racial and Other Profiling,* 2005 Kan. S.B. 77, enacted April 18, 2005.

Kitsuse, John, and Cicourel, Aaron (Fall 1963). *A Note on the Use of Official Statistics,* Social Problems.

Kocieniewski, David (29 Nov. 2000). *U.S. Wrote Outline for Race Profiling, New Jersey Argues.* New York Times.

Lamberth, John (1996a). Report of Dr. John Lamberth, plaintiff's expert, in Wilkins v. Maryland State Police, Civil No MJG-93-468 (D. Md. 1996).

Lamberth, John (1996b). Report of Dr. John Lamberth, defendant's expert, Revised Statistical. Analysis of the Incidence of Police Stops and Arrests of Black Drivers/Travelers on the New Jersey Turnpike Between Interchanges 1 and 3 from the Years 1988 Through 1991 (1996), in State v. Pedro Soto, 734 A. 2d 350 (N.J. Super. Ct. Law. Div. 1996).

Lea, John, and Young, Jock, *What Is To Be Done About Law and Order? Crisis in the Nineties* (Pluto Press, 1993), originally published as *What Is To Be Done About Law and Order? Crisis in the Eighties* (Penguin Books Ltd., 1984).

Macpherson of Cluny, Sir William (advised by Cook, T., Sentamu, The Right Reverend Dr. John, and Stone, R.), The Steven Lawrence Inquiry (1999).

Missouri Attorney General's Office, 2004 Annual Report, Missouri Vehicle Stops, background information accessed at http://www.ago.state.mo.us/racialprofiling/racialprofiling. htm#background, June 15, 2005.

MVA and Miller, Joel (2000). Profiling Populations Available for Stops and Searches, Police Research Series Paper 131, Policing and Reducing Crime Unit, Research, Development, and Statistics Directorate, Home Office.

Newport, Frank, *Racial Profiling is Seen as Widespread. Particularly Among Young Black Men*, Gallup Poll, Dec. 9, 1999.

Spitzer, Eliot, The New York City Police Departments "Stop and Frisk" Practices: A Report to the People of the State of New York. 1 December 1999. The full report is available at http://www. oag.state.ny.us/press/reports/stop_frisk/stop_frisk.html.

U.S. Department of Justice, *Policy Guidance and Fact Sheet on Racial Profiling*, June 2003.

U.S. Department of Justice, *Preserving Life and Liberty: Waging the War on Terror*, available at http:// www.lifeandliberty.gov/subs/a_terr.htm, 15 June, 2005.

U.S. Department of Justice, Bureau of Justice Statistics, *Contacts Between Police and the Public* (2001).

U.S. Drug Enforcement Administration and New Mexico State Police, *Operation Pipeline*, videocassette, 1986.

Waddington, P.A.J., Stenson, Kevin, and Don, David (Nov. 2004). In Proportion, Race, and Police Stop and Search. 44 *British Journal of Criminology* 889.

Welch, Michael (2003). Trampling Human Rights in the War on Terror: Implications to the Sociology of Denial. *12 Critical Criminology* 1.

Whren v. U.S., 517 U.S. 806 (1996).

Wortley, Scot, and Tanner, Julian (2004). Data, Denials and Confusion: The Racial Profiling Debate in Toronto. *45 Canadian Journal of Criminology and Crime and Justice* 367.

JOURNALING QUESTION

Have you ever said, or heard someone say, when they are falsely accused, "Do I look like a thief/terrorist/shoplifter?" How does that relate to racial profiling?

Media

28.

THE NORMATIVE MULATTOES

The Press, Latinos, and the Racial Climate on the Moving Immigration Frontier

JOSÉ ANTONIO PADÍN

As immigrant groups have moved to the United States, many have undergone a "whitening" process. Jews, Irish, and Italian immigrants were all labeled as "nonwhite" and only slowly became seen as white Americans. More recent immigrants include large numbers of people from Latin America, and more of them are now moving into states that had no previous Latino presence. By looking at the newspaper treatment of the new Latin American immigration into Oregon, José Padín shows how the racial identity of this group is currently and actively being formed by local media. Neither simply "whitened" nor "blackened," a more complicated story of who these new immigrants are, and of what America is and is (in danger of) becoming, emerges. Is "conditional whitening" unique to Latin Americans? Or is something like that also to be found in the stories of earlier immigrant groups?

Studies of new immigration to the United States have deployed the concept of a *context of reception* to great advantage (Portes and Rumbaut 2001). A context of reception is shaped by the policies and institutions that affect immigrants and by the presence or absence of coethnic networks. This concept is especially helpful in the comparative study of new immigrant adaptation: immigrant groups in the *same region* can face very different contexts of reception, and the same national-origin group can face substantially different contexts of reception *across regions*. There is one dimension of the context of reception that has been neglected to date, although it figures to gain increasing prominence. Latin America accounts for more than half of all new immigrants to the United States, and during the past decade Latin American immigrant streams swelled in many states where the Latino population was very small or barely existed before 1990. As a result of these new immigration patterns, Latino population enclaves are forming in parts of the United States where "race relations" have traditionally been defined in black and white. The newcomers are bound to strain, perhaps even precipitate a

Excerpted from José Antonio Padín, "The Normative Mulattues: The Press, Latinos, and the Racial Climate on the Moving Immigration Frontier," Sociological Perspectives 48 (2005): 49–75. Notes and references have been renumbered and edited.

redefinition, of the dominant black-white axis of racial distinction. The context of immigrant reception along the moving frontier of Latino immigration will be shaped by processes that define the place of these newcomers *in relation to* whites and blacks.

People of Latin American ancestry have historically presented a dilemma for U.S. conceptions of race. The basic axis of race distinction in the United States is dichotomous, and Latin Americans do not always fit neatly within a racial dichotomy. Ambivalence and ambiguity have always characterized the racial status of Latinos. Mexicans, for example, experienced de jure and de facto segregation, either alongside African Americans or singled out as a distinct "race" (Almaguer 1994; De León 1983; Leiker 2002; Lippard 1847; Montejano 1987; Pitti 2003). In spite of this experience, even during the Jim Crow era, the racial status of Mexicans was not fixed or uniform: in some settings they were legally treated as whites (Montejano 1987); in other settings some early-twentieth-century advocacy organizations fought to have white status recognized under the law (Foley 2002). There is no indication that this racial ambivalence is disappearing. The racial identity of Latinos is remarkably variegated and fluid—across *and within* national-origin Latino groups (Goode 1998; Portes and Rumbaut 2001; Ramos-Zayas 2003). The experience of racial discrimination shaping these identities is quite varied as well (Hughes 2003; Lopez 2002; Portes and Rumbaut 2001; Urciuoli 1996). Few generalizations hold across Latino groups, but one that does confirms their status ambiguity: majorities of the U.S.-born Latinos define themselves, *racially*, as something other than white, black, Asian, or Indian (Portes and Rumbaut 2001).

This article is a study of how Latinos, or Hispanics, are being incorporated into the symbolic cultural grid of racial distinction in the United States. The analytic focus is the media, specifically, the daily press...I have performed content analysis of fourteen years of reporting on Latinos in the principal newspaper of Oregon, one of the states that makes up what might be thought of as the new Latino immigration frontier...

To avoid unnecessary confusion, a clarification regarding the paper's scope is in order. Latinos, or Hispanics, are a diverse pan-ethnic population—racially, ethnically, and linguistically. This internal diversity of the Latino/Hispanic population is not the focus of this article. Instead, this is a study of how Latinos/Hispanics as a pan-ethnic construct start to take shape in the cumulative pattern of newspaper reporting. Ethnicity and race often become a salient issue as a result of perceptions of competition (Cox 1959; Freeman and Rodgers 1999; van den Berghe 1967), and the sheer size of a population tends to make perceptions of competition and ethnic fears more acute (Blalock 1956). As the new "largest minority" an otherwise diverse Latin American–ancestry population is attracting growing attention in the United States—as "Hispanics" or "Latinos." Marketing and publicity industries are keen on the "Latino/Hispanic" demographic (Dávila 2001). Optimistic cultural critics see "Hispanics" as the leavening for a new, self-consciously hybrid American identity (Stavans 2001). The growing "Hispanic" population has struck a ghastly end-of-American-civilization chord with conservative talk radio celebrities (Savage 2003) and their higher-brow counterparts among public intellectuals (Huntington 2004). In all of these instances, imputations are made about Latinos/Hispanics as a collectivity. This imaginary collectivity, as it takes shape in the daily press chronicle, is the focus of my analysis.[1]

THEORY CONTEXT: THE "NEW" RACISM AND THE MEDIA

Racial attitudes research generally agrees that contemporary U.S. racism is less overt than it used to be, it tends to be garbed in nonracial rhetoric, and it is often unconscious or marginally conscious. Some of this research supports the idea that modern racism is largely symbolic, which is to say that it rests on cognitive maps that gain their force, not because they are empirically correct, but by virtue of their consonance with certain forms of symbolism structuring affect or cognition (Kinder and Sears 1981; Sears 1988; Sears et al. 1997). Self-interested behavior, a seemingly straightforward and pure type of "normative orientation" (Parsons 1949), is not immune from the effects of "subtle" contemporary racism: employers and individuals in other gatekeeper roles routinely rely on racist generalizations to compensate for imperfect information (Lundberg and Startz 2000; Massey and Lundy 2001; Pager 2003; Wilson 1996). "Blacks," "whites," and so on, are not mere attitudinal objects; these are terms that demarcate normatively charged boundaries and, by extension, cultural symbols to mark and separate different types of persons.

Contemporary racism also tends to be "cultural" rather than "biological" (Bobo 2001), which is to say that stereotypes about "racial" groups now rest on perceptions about the quality of *cultural inheritance* within those populations, not the quality of genetic inheritance. Beliefs about black *culture* underlie the widespread impression among whites in the United States that blacks transgress the norms of autonomy and hard work (Gilens 1999), flaunt universalistic egalitarian norms in the pursuit of particularistic group gain (Bobo and Kluegel 1993; Sniderman and Carmines 1997), and are criminally inclined (Krysan 2002; Peffley and Hurwitz 1997).

Racism has become widely discredited in the United States (Schumann et al. 1997), and yet it survives as a significant stratifying force (Brown et al. 2003). In part, and paradoxically, racism survives tinder layers of seemingly nonracial rationalizations made necessary by the very strength of antiracist values (Feagin and Vera 1995). Racism also survives because the symbolic worldview that undergirds it is continually propagated by the media in general and the news in particular. The news in the United States continues to taint the public reputations of nonwhite populations, not by explicitly expounding outdated racist doctrine, but through a brisk traffic in unwarranted associations between "racial" groups and a variety of objectionable behaviors. In the news, and the media more broadly, the unsympathetic poor, "welfare abuse," indolence, and crime decidedly have a "color" (Dixon and Linz 2000a, 2000b; Eschholz, Chiricos, and Gertz 2003; Gilens 1999; Iyengar 1991; Iyengar and Kinder 1987; Oliver and Fonash 2002). In spite of changing attitudes, the content of the news is libelous to nonwhites, especially blacks. Because of changing attitudes, the process that spoils identities (Goffman 1963) and reproduces a poisoned culture unfolds silently in U.S. newsrooms.

Journalists and their editors are normatively bound by professional ethics that call for objectivity in reporting, but they are not immune from cognitive modes that permeate the wider culture. In spite of sincere efforts to report the news free of bias, racial bias can and does persist in news reporting—as a result of culturally grounded stereotypes that pervade decision making in newsrooms (Gilens 1999; Stocking and Gross 1989); because successful editors and news professionals must have a keen sense for the "newsworthy," which puts a premium on skillfully crafting stories that resonate with audience prejudice, moral or otherwise (Glasser and Ettema 1991; McManus 1994); and because news organizations uncritically adopt views of major institutional suppliers of raw news material for their industry (Fishman 1980; Gans 1979; Herman and Chomsky 1988; Tuchman 1978). Some of the key institutional suppliers of news information—police departments, the criminal justice system, and political parties—are key to the reproduction of spoiled racial identities (Brown et al. 2003). While news professionals are subject to the influence of factors that contribute to the manufacture and traffic in racial stereotypes, like other gatekeepers, they act in a normative climate that creates pressures to imagine the contrary (Feagin and Vera 1995). Although each act of discrimination by an individual employer, property manager, real estate agent, or police officer contributes in a small way to the perpetuation of racial stereotypes, by virtue of the commercial media's concentration and reach (McChesney 1999), there is no parallel to the role of media and news professionals as gatekeepers in the dissemination of the symbolism on which racial status distinctions are founded. In sum, the media are a key nexus in the manufacture and dissemination of social difference codes (Ridgeway 2000)—dichotomous discourses that define boundaries between bona fide members of a national community and internal and external threats to a morally functioning society (Alexander 1992)—and the news is the most authoritative source of media information. If contemporary U.S. racism is more subtle than it used to be, the contribution of mass media to the "racialization" of a group is bound to occur through patterns of image association that are tacit and cumulative (Entman 1990).

Before addressing the empirical question at hand—whether, and if so, how the local press contributes to a climate of new Latino immigrant reception that racializes this population—we need a conceptual framework, some guiding hypotheses, and methods able to grapple with tacit patterns of racialization. I turn to these now.

FOUR MODES OF SYMBOLIC ASSIMILATION

An analysis to determine whether and, if so, how the news racializes any population needs to be grounded in a theoretical awareness of the contingent nature of racial status (cf. Waters 1999 on black status; Hartigan 1999 and Sugrue 1996 on white status). The scope for status contingency is likely to be greater yet for groups of Latin American ancestry whose racial status has been historically ambiguous; they are bound to be seen in a variety of lights, depending on the circumstances, and hence occupy an ambivalent place in relation to the racial symbolism of dualistic normative grids. A need arises to conceptualize a variety of *modes of symbolic incorporation* into race-coded normative worldviews. Four hypothetical modes of Latino symbolic incorporation (or racialization) can be inferred from a variety of literatures.

One mode of symbolic incorporation involves the juxtaposition of normative antipathies between Americans (read, whites) and Latinos, and by extension, normative affinities between the latter and blacks. This mode of racialization is defined around a white/nonwhite axis of distinction. Latinos, like blacks, are symbolically on the wrong side of the tracks. Historically, there has been such a tendency to incorporate Latinos as nonwhites, partly as a result of the way U.S. relations with Latin America have shaped conceptions of U.S. national identity (Pike 1992) and partly as a result of domestic, often very local, political and economic interest configurations (Almaguer 1994; De León 1983; Montejano 1987). Contemporary patterns of segregation still bear the burden of this history, especially in labor markets (Catanzarite 2000; Valle and Torres 2000), neighborhoods (Denton and Massey 1989; Massey and Bitterman 1985), and schools (Matute-Bianchi 1986). Recent work shows that awareness of this racialization among young Latinos shapes what some are calling a *reactive ethnicity* (Hughes 2003; Portes and Rumbaut 2001; Ramos-Zayas 2003). Studies of the images of Latinos in cinema (Noriega 1997), in television (Greenberg et al. 1980; Lichter and Amundson 1996; National Council of La Raza 1997), and in broadcast news (Dixon and Linz 2000a, 2000b; Mendez-Mendez and Alverio 2001; National Council of La Raza 1997) show that the various media are accessories to this process of Latino racial stigmatization. Is this true of newspapers? Research specifically on newspapers is scant (National Council of La Raza 1997), but studies of the press spanning several decades and regions (Fishman and Casiano 1969; Simon and Alexander 1993; Turk et al. 1989; Vargas 2000) show that newspaper coverage of Latinos tends to be stigmatizing.[2] The first working hypothesis follows.

Hypothesis 1: "Blackening," or Unequivocal Racialization
News reporting on Latinos will associate the group with morally threatening cultural orientations and behavior patterns, the most typical of which are

associated in white public opinion and the media with African Americans: a deficient work ethic, dependence, "welfare abuse," crime, and family dysfunction.

A second mode of symbolic incorporation is the reverse of the first. Racialization occurs through a juxtaposition of normative affinities between Latinos and "Americans" (read, whites) and invidious tacit contrasts between Latinos and blacks. "Whitening" might be used to describe location and predicament of Latinos in this instance. There is some historical and contemporary evidence of such "whitening." As Montejano (1987) has shown, even during the Jim Crow era, the status of Mexican Americans in Texas often varied considerably from county to county: they experienced segregation as nonwhites in some counties, yet were treated as whites in others. The precise status of Mexicans was dependent on the context-specific configurations of class interests that divided the white population and on the shifting interests of actors in the political arena. Contemporary research on neighborhood preferences in the United States also suggests a subtle process of social whitening at work: Latinos, like Asian and white survey respondents, exhibit a significant preference for black-avoidance (Bobo and Zubrinsky 1996; Massey 2001; Welch and Sigelman 2000; Zubrinsky and Bobo 1996).

Historically, the room for Latino social whitening may have been limited, but Herbert Gans (2001) has suggested provocatively that in the post–Civil Rights era the scope for social whitening has widened considerably for nonblacks. Civil rights gains and attitudinal changes, coupled with marked growth of nonblack, nonwhite immigration from Asia and Latin America (and, surely, a host of other unspecified conditions), have brought about a shift in the primary axis of racial distinction. A white/nonwhite divide, Gans has argued, is being replaced by a black/nonblack divide. Consequently, with far greater ease than their ancestors, Asian and Latino immigrants discover elbow room to redeem tainted identities (see also Wu 2002). The plausibility of

this whitening scenario is certainly enhanced by the fact that Latin American immigrants—the largest stream of contemporary immigrations—are no strangers to the practice of "social whitening" (Andrews 1991; Twine 1998; Wade 1993; Wright 1990). The second working hypothesis is consistent with this route of assimilation.

Hypothesis 2: "Whitening"
Newspaper reporting on Latinos will not associate the group with cultural and behavioral inclinations that discredit African Americans in U.S. culture. Instead, the news will portray a group that shares core "American" values: enterprise, autonomy, family values, and respect for the law.

On careful examination social whitening turns out not to be a simple path but a mine field. It implies a third possible mode of symbolic Latino incorporation. "Whitening" presupposes racial impurity (biological or, today, cultural); hence, social redemption is *conditional* on successfully disproving racist assumptions and stereotypes. Thus, conditionality defines a unique, intermediate, racial status predicament. *Conditional social whitening* creates an intermediate tier in what was previously a two-tier, dichotomized, racial status order. Although it is probably too soon to know whether conditional social whitening will generate a clear three-tier racial status hierarchy (see Bonilla-Silva 2002) or whether it is a transitional status in a two-tier hierarchy, conceivably it could turn out to be both, particularly if the precise racial status of individual Latinos comes to depend on socioeconomic status. Class advantages, in addition to physical appearance and speech, would put whitening within the reach of some, but persistent class disadvantages among sizable pockets of Latinos or Asians would put it beyond reach. The third working hypothesis follows.

Hypothesis 3: Conditional Whitening
News about Latinos will tend to portray them as a contradictory population: possessing some cultural and behavioral orientations that are consistent with

core "American" values but also harboring other cultural and behavioral orientations that pose a threat to the nation. Or, put bluntly, "like whites" in some respects and "like blacks" in others.

Finally, a fourth mode of Latino symbolic incorporation is conceivable. Rather than racialization, it would involve assimilation into an American culture that is simultaneously changed in the process in such a way that conventional racial distinctions lose their salience. Inclusive, nonracial conceptions of U.S. national identity always have existed, although they have never been dominant: some were incubated by antiracist movements that are unfortunately underappreciated in the study of U.S. history (Aptheker 1992; Skotnes 1996), and some even drew on Latin America as a symbolic source of national renewal (Pike 1992). Stavans (2001) has put forward the provocative thesis that, under the influence of mass Latin American immigration, we might witness the emergence of a new dominant and hybrid conception of U.S. national identity—a U.S. *mestizo* national identity, that is, a conception of nation in which pride of place is equally shared by African, Indian, Asian, and European heritage. Stavans is a cultural and literary critic, not a social scientist, but the thesis of Latin Americanization leading to a mestizo U.S. national construct is nonetheless a plausible long-term scenario. Specific mechanisms opening the way for this scenario still need to be worked out, but the growth of the Latino population is clearly one of the enabling conditions: a growing, racially ambiguous, buffer stratum reduces political status conflict along the black-white boundary and facilitates racial depolarization. Latin American creolized/mestizo identities could become a second enabling condition, the cultural yeast to activate homegrown antiracist currents. Valle and Torres (2000) have argued, and present some evidence from California supporting the claim, that the growth of the Latino populations in a region can diffuse racial polarization in the political arena and facilitate the rise of multiracial political movements. The fourth working hypothesis may now be formulated.

Hypothesis 4: Latino Incorporation = U.S. Racial Depolarization
Newspaper reporting will recognize in Latinos a unique cultural influence that contributes to the redefinition of U.S. national identity and the healing of racial division.

With a conceptual model and hypotheses now set, let me turn to the empirical analysis of fourteen years of newspaper reporting on Latinos in Oregon. I would like to suggest that strong support for any of the four working hypotheses just presented would constitute prima facie evidence of newspaper influence on the racial climate of new Latino immigrant reception.

METHODS AND DATA

Daily newspapers, it has been noted, continue to be a primary source of news in the United States. This is particularly true in Portland, the principal metropolitan market in Oregon, which, like a growing number of cities, has only one daily newspaper. The Portland *Oregonian* is, in addition, the newspaper of widest circulation in the U.S. Pacific Northwest (Audit Bureau of Circulations 2003).

Earlier research on Latinos in the press has been based on samples with a relatively short time frame, making it susceptible to short-term or random fluctuations in the news. To avoid this problem, my analysis is based on sample data from a much longer period. The sample consists of articles that appeared in the *Oregonian* between January 1, 1988, and December 31, 2001. This fourteen-year span coincides with a period of high Latino immigration and population growth and brackets the 1990 and 2000 decennial censuses, which offered ample occasion to report, and reflect, on significant demographic changes under way in Oregon and the nation.

The sample was obtained using the full *Oregonian* electronic archives. Two hundred articles were randomly selected from all stories published by the *Oregonian* between January 1, 1988, and December 31, 2001, containing the terms "Latino" or "Hispanic" in the headline or lead paragraph. As I explained in the introduction, the paper's focus is the news on the pan-ethnic construct Latino/Hispanic; hence, specific national-origin designators were not used to define the sampling frame.

DISCUSSION

Each of my four hypotheses spells out a pattern of press coverage that corresponds to four distinct modes of Latino assimilation. Three of the them specify a distinct path of racialization: (1) as non-whites into a dichotomous racial order, (2) whitening, and (3) conditional whitening. Given the nature of modern racism, the expectation is for racialization not to be explicit. Rather, if the news racializes Latinos, it ought to occur through a cumulative pattern of reporting that tacitly locates this growing population in Oregon in a race-coded normative grid that separates bona fide Americans from internal or external groups that pose a moral and cultural threat to the nation. The fourth hypothesis expected no pattern of racialization but news narratives that somehow imagine the immigrants to be representatives of a new mestizo United States. It is now possible to pass judgment on the level of support for each hypothesis in light of the findings.

LIKE BLACKS?

The first hypothesis predicted that newspaper coverage of Latinos in areas of recent and high immigration would associate the group fairly consistently with forms of cultural and behavioral deviance commonly associated with black cultural threats to American values. The analysis of fourteen years of news coverage in the *Oregonian* yields weak support for this first hypothesis. Although there was no shortage of news associating Latinos with a host of social problems and normative threats, sympathetic news was even more frequent (44 percent to 52 percent of the sample, respectively). Sympathetic newspaper articles as a whole portray Latinos as a group that not only enriches the American cultural landscape but also a strong work ethic that

values autonomy and self-reliance. This contrasts sharply with the portrayal of blacks in the news. Even though there was certainly no shortage of news highlighting Latinos as a social problem, both the abundance and the type of redeeming news on Latinos runs against the grain of the first hypothesis.

HISPANIC WHITENING?

The second hypothesis entertained the possibility that, whatever the misgivings about immigrants qua immigrants, in the post–Civil Rights era new Latino immigrants will find a form of mainstream acceptance that eluded earlier generations and that continues to elude black Americans. This *whitening hypothesis* implies a pattern of news reporting on Latinos that is sympathetic, that clearly locates the population within the symbolism of core national values, and that clearly if tacitly sets the group apart from the normative and social dysfunction associated with blacks. My analysis of the 1988–2001 *Oregonian* data finds some support for this hypothesis, but it needs to be qualified.

A number of the key findings are consistent with the *whitening* (or Gans) hypothesis. First, the proportion of stories representing the growing Latino population sympathetically was anything but trivial: slightly over half of the articles in the sample were sympathetic, either outright sympathetic or mixed, but with an emphasis on Latinos as a social asset. News often becomes meaningful by presenting stories that fit, explicitly or implicitly, within a larger normative drama. When all the Latinos-as-social-asset news stories were aggregated into a smaller number of thematic clusters, the overwhelming majority fell under one dominant rubric: *autonomy and self-reliance*. The news under this rubric symbolically places the growing Latino population of Oregon on the in-side of a very charged normative border—a stark contrast with the news representation of African Americans. Family dysfunction, another "pathology" strongly associated with African Americans, was an *absolutely* insignificant theme (not a single article in the sample, $N = 200$). As the whitening hypothesis would predict, *some* of the strongest sympathetic images of Latinos are at the same time images that make them *unlike* what is commonly believed about black Americans.

Other findings in the analysis, however, do not support the whitening hypothesis. Nearly half the sample consisted of unsympathetic stories. Out of nine themes explored that could portray Latinos as a burden or threat to host communities, the welfare theme was by far die most salient.... Moreover, when the salient liability themes were combined into broader thematic rubrics, the two most common (accounting for over 80 percent of unsympathetic stories) were *cultural/behavioral deviance* and *tax burden*. Welfare, tax burden, problematic cultural differences, and crime—the major themes falling under these two rubrics—establish a tacit normative kinship between Latinos and blacks. This runs against the grain of the whitening hypothesis. What is puzzling here is that it would seem impossible for the same group to earn a public reputation for entirely contrary attributes: the virtue of autonomy, enterprise, and self-reliance; the vice of "welfare."

CONDITIONAL WHITENING

The strikingly ambivalent picture of Latinos that emerges from the press does not quite fit the whitening hypothesis but is entirely consistent with the third hypothesis, *conditional whitening*. Conditional whitening is a mode of incorporation available to populations that are at once racially suspect and in a position to redeem their suspect status. This is a contradictory, and intermediate, racial status, which is consistent with the ambivalent mix of sympathetic and unsympathetic associations found in the analysis. The rapidly growing Latino population seemingly straddles the dichotomies defining boundaries circumscribing the "sphere of fellow feeling" in civil society (Alexander 1992). The social difference codes implicit in the news turn up a mixed reading on Latinos: *"like us"* in some ways—enterprising,

industrious, autonomous, immigrant stock of myth, stuff of the nation—*"unlike us"* (but like blacks) in other ways—bound by particularistic ethnic attachments, wont to abuse the public trust (welfare), and alien to conventional norms of public morality (crime). Salient news frames show a certain inclination to extend Latinos a reputation credit that eludes African Americans, yet it comes with a rich admixture of tacit attributions that raise doubts about the group's cultural lineage.

DOES LATINO ASSIMILATION LEAD TO A MESTIZO U.S. IDENTITY AND RACIAL DEPOLARIZATION?

The fourth hypothesis was the most speculative, based on a plausible future rather than historical or contemporary evidence. A growing Latin American population, the reasoning goes, holds the potential to bring about a cultural watershed in the United States: a new, hybrid, multiethnic, multiracial, conception of U.S. national identity that blurs traditional racial distinctions. In short, new generations of Latino immigrants precipitate in part, and are incorporated into, a mestizo United States. This is a theoretical scenario involving longer-term (and still vaguely specified) processes. Because of the longer time horizon, it is more difficult to make a fair conclusive evaluation, even with a fourteen-year data set. With this caveat in mind, the findings show little indication of press awareness of a connection between growing Latino populations and the emergence of an ethnically and "racially" hybrid American identity. It could well be that cultural changes that are consistent with the Latino population growth → mestizo United States hypothesis are in fact occurring but that they fail to attract the attention of newsmakers because they do not fit conventional frames defining what is newsworthy about "race," ethnicity, and immigration. Future research on how the media shape the climate of new immigrant incorporation should find ways to continue to explore this hypothesis.

CONCLUSION

This article has sought to make a contribution to two intersecting research agendas: work on immigration that has brought attention to the importance of variable contexts of reception on the status of new immigrants and their children and debates about the possible impact of "Latin Americanization" on U.S. race relations. Research on immigrant contexts of reception has examined a variety of institutions that shape those contexts but not the effects of the media in general or the news in particular. This article broadens the analytic scope of its core concept—*context of reception*—to include the role of a neglected institution—the daily press—in shaping *climates of reception.*

Sociological research on racial stratification in the United States has started to break out from the rigid habit of considering only black-white relations (Bobo et al. 2000; Bonilla-Silva 2002; Massey 2001). Although the research effort is still in an embryonic stage, some of the most interesting work has started to look at the impact of growing Latin American, Asian, and other populations on racial stratification in the United States (Bonilla-Silva and Glover 2004; Foner and Fredrickson 2004; Gans 2001). The contribution of this article to that area of research is threefold. First, it develops a clear conceptual model of *modes of symbolic incorporation* that captures the variety of ways in which nonwhite, nonblack populations might be assimilated into the dominant race-coded moral worldview of the United States. Second, it presents four hypotheses corresponding to these four modes of symbolic incorporation that define a transparent and empirically testable criterion of racialization. These hypotheses should serve as a set of coordinates for the study of key questions regarding the future of racial stratification in the United States: (1) How does the assimilation of new immigrant populations redefine the normative system of racial distinctions? (2) Does the mode of racialization of new immigrant populations vary regionally, or is there a consistent national pattern? Third, this paper advances the study of racial stratification in the United States by providing an empirical test of some arguments about "Latin Americanization" that have to date been largely a matter of speculation.

Oregon was selected as a case study because, like most of the states that experienced the highest rates of Latino population growth over the past decade, a sizable Latino presence is a fairly recent phenomenon. More than anywhere else, the suddenness of demographic change in these "new frontier states" raises poignant questions about the implications of a Latino presence for a racial status order cast primarily in black and white.

My objective has been to identify whether the daily press is contributing to a particular *mode* of Latino incorporation into the symbolic grid of race-coded normative distinctions. I found strongest support for the conditional whitening hypothesis: news reporting that extends Latinos a line of *normative reputation credit* but simultaneously portrays the group as a social burden and a moral threat.

Latinos were portrayed as a population strongly motivated to achieve, with an inclination for autonomy and self-reliance, and strong family values. All of these images are in stark contrast to the usual news fare on African Americans. To this extent, the daily press has created a favorable climate of reception for Latino immigrants in Oregon over the past decade and a half. At the same time, the frequency of unsympathetic news portraits and the salience of some key themes—welfare, crime, cultural incompatibility—cast doubt on the normative orientation of the Latino newcomers. What emerges from the cumulative pattern of press reporting on Latinos is a racial construct of mixed black and white normative lineage: like whites in some ways, like blacks in others—"normative mulattoes."

Three broad implications follow. First, *conditional whitening* suggests a departure from a bipartite system of U.S. symbolic racial classification. Second, it suggests the continuity of black stigma: whiteness and blackness remain fixed as symbolic points of reference for racial judgment. Third, if conditional whitening is contingent not only on symbolic distance from blackness but also on socioeconomic attainment, an accumulation of class disadvantages among a segment of immigrant and second-generation Latinos and growing demands for access to public remedies stand a good chance of activating the "racial suspicions" that make up the unsympathetic half of the mulatto symbolic predicament of Hispanics.

The usual caveats are in order. Key findings were quite robust, and it may be that the racial climate of reception in the Oregon press is representative of patterns in others states on the new Latino immigration frontier. Yet such a possibility can only be entertained as a working hypothesis and needs to be evaluated by comparable research examining other regions. This article is intended also to motivate interest in the comparative study of the regional media, their role in shaping distinct contexts of new immigrant reception, and their contribution to changes in the symbolic map of race. Only comparative research will be able to show if there is a consistent pattern across regions warranting general claims about a new emerging form of U.S. racial-ethnic stratification or if, as in the past, the racial climate of new Latino immigrant incorporation varies significantly across contexts.

I would like to conclude by offering a reflection that, strictly speaking, reaches beyond the data but places the findings against a larger canvas. Racial matters have always been intertwined in complicated ways with the exercise of classic-based economic and political power. As we are well aware, racial slander can be used to lend populist appeal to political agendas that in fact seek to redistribute resources upward (Katz 1993; Kelley 1997; Reed 1999; Steinberg 1995). I would like to suggest that the ambivalent portrait of Latinos in the news follows this age-old pattern. Ambivalent news reporting on Latinos—the judgments implied in "conditional whitening"—may be more than just lazy or stereotyped reporting; it is perhaps a novel permutation of a type of moralizing that gives powerful societal interests mean-spirited mass appeal and punishes the disenfranchised. The tale has a moral that fits nicely with neoliberal ideological broadsides against the welfare state: If Hispanic immigrants are willing to sweat, and then some, welcome them. Beware, however, that they may just entertain the foolish notion (as "the blacks" do?) that mere hard work brings with it any social entitlement or harbor expectations that every common man be extended the status of a gentleman.[3] The irony of this twist on the old race-coded story should be clear: in the measure that it acquires currency it contributes to a political climate that ultimately places working people in general in the United States at risk of becoming aliens in their land—citizens stripped of what T. H. Marshall once called the social rights of citizenship.

NOTES

The author wishes to thank Leonard Cain, Eduardo Bonilla-Silva, the *Sociological Perspectives* editors, and three anonymous reviewers for the journal for valuable critical comments. Thanks also go to Meghan Mahoney and James Bachmeier for meticulous and dedicated research assistance. The research for this article was supported in part by a Provost Faculty Enhancement Grant at Portland State University.

1. I use the terms "Latino" and "Hispanic" interchangeably throughout this article. Although they are increasingly used interchangeably in most contexts, they still carry ideological baggage. No meaning should be attached to my tendency to use one of these pan-ethnic designators with greater frequency.

2. Greenberg et al. 1983, which reports no overrepresentation of Latinos in crime reporting in six southwestern dailies, is a puzzling exception, but arguably the results of that study reflected a

much narrower operationalization of "negative reporting." We learn from studies of network news that the "crime" most strongly associated with Latinos—one that casts a long shadow over the entire population regardless of nativity—is illegal immigration (Méndez-Méndez and Alverio 2001). Articles stressing the litany of (real or imagined) burdens that "illegals" impose on host communities escaped the narrower operationalization of Greenberg et al. 1983. For evidence on the role of the press historically in shaping perceptions of Latinos, see Acuña 1981; Montejano 1987; Romo 1983; Valdés 1991; Valdés 2000.

3. Readers will recognize the reference to T. H. Marshall's view that the modern welfare state transformed the contours of capitalism by conferring on every man the status of a gentleman. The sexist language is clearly dated but is probably not entirely out of place in what is, after all, a morality tale.

REFERENCES

Acuña, Rodolfo. 1981. *Occupied America: The Chicano's Struggle toward Liberation*. New York: Harper & Row.

Alexander, Jeffrey. 1992. "Citizen and Enemy as Symbolic Classification." Pp. 289–308 in *Cultivating Differences*, edited by M. Lamont and M. Fournier. Chicago: University of Chicago Press.

Almaguer, Tomás. 1994. *Racial Fault Lines: The Historical Origins of White Supremacy in California*. Berkeley: University of California Press.

Andrews, George Reid. 1991. *Blacks and Whites in São Paulo Brazil, 1888–1988*. Madison: University of Wisconsin Press.

Aptheker, Herbert. 1992. *Anti-racism in U.S. History: The First Two Hundred Years*. New York: Greenwood Press.

Audit Bureau of Circulations. 2003. "ABC: eCirc for Newspapers." http://abcas3.accessabc.com/ ecirc/index.html. Retrieved November 2003.

Ball-Rokeach, Sandra J., Multon Rokeach, and Joel W. Grube. 1984. *The Great American Values Test: Influencing Behavior and Belief through Television*. New York: Free Press.

Blalock, Hubert M. 1956. "Economic Discrimination and Negro Increase." *American Sociological Review* 21:584–88.

Bobo, Lawrence. 2001. "Racial Attitudes and Relations at the Close of the Twentieth Century." Pp. 264–301 in *America Becoming: Racial Trends and Their Consequences*, edited by N. J. Smelser, W. J. Wilson, and F. Mitchell. Washington, DC: National Academy Press.

Bobo, Lawrence and James R. Kluegel. 1993. "Opposition to Race-targeting: Self-Interest, Stratification Ideology, or Racial Attitudes." *American Sociological Review* 58(4):443–64.

Bobo, Lawrence D., Melvin L. Oliver, James H. Johnson Jr., and Abel Valenzuela Jr., eds. 2000. *Prismatic Metropolis: Inequality in Los Angeles*. New York: Russell Sage Foundation.

Bobo, Lawrence and Camile L. Zubrinsky. 1996. "Attitudes toward Residential Integration: Perceived Status Differences, Mere In-Group Preference, or Racial Prejudice?" *Social Forces* 74:883–909.

Bonilla-Silva, Eduardo. 2002. "We Are All Americans!: The Latin Americanization of Racial Stratification in the USA." *Race and Society* 5(1):3–16.

Bonilla-Silva, Eduardo and Karen S. Glover. 2004. "'We are All Americans': The Latin Ameicanization of Race Relations in the U.S." Pp. 149–83 in *Changing Terrain of Race and Ethnicity*, edited by Maria Keysan and Amanda Lewis. New York: Russell Sage.

Brown, Michael K, Martin Carnoy, Elliot Currie, Troy Duster, and David B. Oppenheimer. 2003. *Whitewashing Race: The Myth of a Color-Blind Society.* Berkeley: University of California Press.

Catanzarite, Lisa. 2000. "Brown Collar Jobs: Occupational Segregation and Earnings of Recent-Immigrant Latinos." *Sociological Perspectives* 43:45–76.

Cox, Oliver Cromwell. 1959. *Caste, Class, and Race: A Study in Social Dynamics.* New York: Monthly Review Press.

Dávila, Arlene. 2001. *Latinos Inc.: The Marketing and Making of a People.* Berkeley: University of California Press.

De León, Arnoldo. 1983. *They Called them Greasers: Anglo Attitudes towards Mexicans in Texas, 1821–1900.* Austin: University of Texas Press.

Denton, Nancy A. and Douglas S. Massey. 1989. "Racial Identity among Caribbean Hispanics: The Effect of Double Minority Status on Residential Segregation." *American Sociological Review* 54:790–806.

Dixon, Travis L. and Daniel Linz. 2000a. "Overrepresentation and Underrepresentation of African Americans and Latinos as Lawbreakers on Television News." *Journal of Communication* 50:131–54.

———. 2000b. "Race and the Misrepresentation of Victimization on Local Television News." *Communication Research* 27:547–63.

Domke, David. 2000. "Strategic Elites, the Press, and Race Relations." *Journal of Communication* 50:115–40.

Entman, Robert M. 1990. "Modern Racism and the Images of Blacks in Local Television News." *Critical Studies in Mass Communication* 7(4):332–45.

Eschholz, Sara, Ted Chericos, and Marc Gertz. 2003. "Television and Fear of Crime; Program Types, Audience Traits, and the Mediating Effects of Perceived Neighborhood Racial Composition." *Social Problems* 50(3):395–405.

Feagin, Joe R. and Hernan Vera. 1995. *White Racism: The Basics.* New York: Routledge.

Fishman, Joshua A. and Heriberto Casiano. 1969. "Puerto Ricans in Our Press." *Modern Languages Journal* 53:15–62.

Fishman, Mark. 1980. *Manufacturing the News.* Austin: University of Texas Press.

Foley, Neil. 2002. "Becoming Hispanic: Mexican Americans and Whiteness." Pp. 49–57 in *White Privilege*, edited by P. S. Rothenberg. New York: Worth.

Freeman, Richard B. and William M. Rodgers III. 1999. *Area Economic Conditions and the Labor Market Outcomes of Young Men in the 1990s Expansion.* NBER Working Paper No. 7073. Cambridge, MA: National Bureau of Economic Research.

Foner, Nancy and George Fredrickson. 2004. *Not Just Black and White: Historical and Contemporary Perspectives on Immigration, Race, and Ethnicity in the United States.* New York: Russell Sage Foundation.

Gans, Herbert. 1979. *Deciding What's News.* New York: Pantheon.

———. 2001. "The Possibility of a New Racial Hierarchy in the Twenty-first-Century United States." Pp. 642–50 in *Social Stratification*, edited by D. B. Grusky. Boulder, CO: Westview Press.

Gilens, Martin. 1999. *Why Americans Hate Welfare: Race, Media, and the Politics of Antipoverty Policy.* Chicago: University of Chicago Press.

Glasser, Theodore L. and James S. Ettema. 1991. "Investigative Journalism and the Moral Order." Pp. 203–25 in *Critical Perspectives on Media and Society*, edited by R. K. Avery and D. Eason. New York: Guilford Press.

Goffman, Erving. 1963. *Stigma: Notes on the Management of Spoiled Identity.* Englewood Cliffs, NJ: Prentice Hall.

Goode, Judith. 1998. "The Contingent Construction of Local Identities." *Identities* 5(1):33–64.

Greenberg, Bradley S., Carrie Heeter, Judee K. Burgoon, Michael Burgoon, and Felipe Korzenny. 1980. *Life on Television: Content Analyses of U.S. TV Drama.* Norwood, NJ: Ablex Publishing.

———. 1983. "Local Newspaper Coverage of Mexican Americans." *Journalism Quarterly* 60:671–76.

Hartigan, John, Jr. 1999. *Racial Situations: Class Predicaments of Whiteness in Detroit.* Princeton, NJ: Princeton University Press.

Herman, Edward S. and Noam Chomsky. 1988. *Manufacturing Consent: The Political Economy of the Mass Media.* New York: Pantheon Books.

Hughes, Diane. 2003. "Correlates of African American and Latino Parents' Messages to Children about Ethnicity and Race: A Comparative Study of Racial Socialization." *American Journal of Community Psychology* 31(1–2):15–33.

Huntington, Samuel P. 2004. "The Hispanic Challenge." *Foreign Policy* 141 (March–April). http://www.foreignpolicy.com. Retrieved May 2004.

Iyengar, Shanto. 1991. *Is Anyone Responsible? How Television Frames Political Issues.* Chicago: University of Chicago Press.

Iyengar, Shanto and Donald R. Kinder. 1987. *News That Matters: Television and American Public Opinion.* Chicago: University of Chicago Press.

Katz, Michael B. 1993. "The Urban 'Underclass' as a Metaphor of Social Transformation." Pp. 3–23 in *The "Underclass" Debate: Views from History,* edited by M. B. Katz. Princeton, NJ: Princeton University Press.

Kelley, Robin D. G. 1997. *Yo' Mama's Disfunktional! Fighting the Culture Wars in Urban America.* Boston: Beacon Press.

Kinder, Donald R. and David O. Sears. 1981. "Prejudice and Politics: Symbolic Racism versus Racial Threats to the Good Life." *Journal of Personality and Social Psychology* 40:414–31.

Krysan, Maria. 2002. "Community Undesirability in Black and White: Examining Racial Residential Preferences through Community Perceptions." *Social Problems* 49(4):521–43.

Leiker, James N. 2002. "Race Relations in the Sunflower State." *Kansas History* 25(3):214–36.

Lichter, S. Robert and Daniel R. Amundson. 1996. "Don't Blink: Hispanics in Television Entertainment." National Council of La Raza, Washington, D.C.

Lippard, George. 1847. *Legends of Mexico.* Philadelphia: T. B. Peterson.

Lopez, Nancy. 2002. "Race-Gender Experiences and Schooling: Second-Generation Dominican, West Indian, and Haitian Youth in New York City." *Race, Ethnicity, and Education* 5(1):67–89.

Lundberg, Shelly J. and Richard Startz. 2000. "Inequality and Race: Models and Policy." Pp. 269–95 in *Meritocracy and Economic Inequality,* edited by K. Arrow, S. Bowles, and S. Durlauf. Princeton, NJ: Princeton University Press.

Massey, Douglas S. 2001. "Residential Segregation and Neighborhood Conditions in U.S. Metropolitan Areas." Pp. 391–434 in *America Becoming: Racial Trends and Their Consequences,* vol. 1, edited by N. J. Smelser, W. J. Wilson, and F. Mitchell. Washington, DC: National Academy Press.

Massey, Douglas S. and Brooks Bitterman. 1985. "Explaining the Paradox of Puerto Rican Segregation." *Social Forces* 64:306–27.

Massey, Douglas S. and Garvey Lundy. 2001. "Use of Black English and Racial Discrimination in Urban Housing Markets." *Urban Affairs Review* 36(4):452.

Matute-Bianchi, María Eugenia. 1986. "Ethnic Identities and Patterns of School Success and Failure among Mexican-descent and Japanese American Students in a California High School: An Ethnographic Analysis." *American Journal of Education* 95:233–55.

McChesney, Robert W. 1999. *Rich Media, Poor Democracy: Communication Politics in Dubious Times.* New York: New Press.

McManus, John M. 1994. *Market-driven Journalism: Let the Citizen Beware?* Thousand Oaks, CA: Sage.

Méndez-Méndez, Serafín and Dianne Alverio. 2001. "Network Brownout 2001: The Portrayal of Latinos in Network Television News, 2000." Report prepared for the National Association of Hispanic Journalists.

Montejano, David. 1987. *Anglos and Mexicans in the Making of Texas, 1836–l986.* Austin: University of Texas Press.

National Council of La Raza. 1997. "Out of the Picture: Hispanics in the Media." Pp. 21–35 in *Latin Looks: Images of Latinas and Latinos in the United States,* edited by C. E. Rodriguez. Boulder, CO: Westview Press.

Noriega, Chon. 1997. "Citizen Chicano: The Trials and Titillations of Ethnicity in the American Cinema, 1935–62." Pp. 85–103 in *Latin Looks: Images of Latinas and Latinos in the United States,* edited by C. E. Rodriguez. Boulder, CO: Westview Press.

Oliver, Mary Beth and Dana Fonash. 2002. "Race and Crime in the News: Whites' Identification and Misidentification of Violent and Nonviolent Criminal Suspects." *Media Psychology* 4(4):137–56.

Pager, Devah. 2003. "The Mark of a Criminal Record." *American Journal of Sociology* 108(5):937–75.

Parsons, Talcott. 1949. *The Structure of Social Action.* Glencoe, IL: Free Press.

Peffley, Mark and John Hurwitz. 1997. "Racial Stereotypes and Whites' Political Views of Blacks in the Context of Welfare and Crime." *American Journal of Political Science* 41(1):30–60.

Pike, Fredrick P. 1992. *The United States and Latin America: Myths and Stereotypes of Civilization and Nature.* Austin: University of Texas Press.

Pitti, Stephen J. 2003. *The Devil in Silicon Valley: Northern California, Race, and Mexican Americans.* Princeton, NJ: Princeton University Press.

Portes, Alejandro and Ruben G. Rumbaut. 2001. *Legacies: The Story of the Immigrant Second Generation.* Berkeley: University of California Press.

Ramos-Zayas, Ana Yolanda. 2003. *National Performance: The Politics of Class, Race, and Space in Puerto Rican Chicago.* Chicago: University of Chicago Press.

Reed, Adolph, Jr., ed. 1999. *Without Justice for All: The New Liberalism and Our Retreat from Equality.* Boulder, CO: Westview Press.

Ridgeway, Cecilia L. 2000. "Social Difference Codes and Social Connections." *Sociological Perspectives* 43:1–12."

Romo, Ricardo. 1983. *East Los Angeles: History of a Barrio.* Austin: University of Texas Press.

Savage, Michael. 2003. *Savage Nation: Saving America from the Liberal Assault on Our Borders, Language and Culture.* Nashville, TN: Thomas Nelson.

Schuman, Howard, Charlotte Steeh, Lawrence Bobo, and Maria Krysan. 1997. *Racial Attitudes in America: Trends and Interpretations.* Cambridge, MA: Harvard University Press.

Sears, David O. 1988. "Symbolic Racism." Pp. 53–84 in *Eliminating Racism: Profiles in Controversy,* edited by P. A. Katz and D. A. Taylor. New York: Plenum.

Sears, David O., Colette Van Laar, Mary Carrillo, and Rick Kosterman. 1997. "Is It Really Racism? The Origins of White Americans' Opposition to Race-targeted Policies." *Public Opinion Quarterly* 61:16–53.

Simon, Rita J. and Susan H. Alexander. 1993. *The Ambivalent Welcome: Print Media, Public Opinion and Immigration.* Westport, CT: Praeger.

Sniderman, Paul M. and Edward G. Carmines. 1997. *Reaching Beyond Race.* Cambridge, MA: Harvard University Press.

Skotnes, Andor. 1996. "The Communist Party, Anti-Racism, and the Freedom Movement: Baltimore, 1930–34." *Science and Society* 60(2):164–94.

Stavans, Ilan. 2001. *The Hispanic Condition: The Power of a People.* New York: Rayo/ HarperCollins.

Steinberg, Stephen. 1995. *Turning Back: The Retreat from Racial Justice in American Thought and Policy.* Boston: Beacon Press.

Stocking, S. Holly and Paget Gross. 1989. *How Do Journalists Think? A Proposal for the Study of Cognitive Bias in the Newsroom.* Bloomington: Eric Clearinghouse, Indiana University.

Sugrue, Thomas J. 1996. *The Origins of the Urban Crisis: Race and Inequality in Postwar Detroit.* Princeton, NJ: Princeton University Press.

Tuchman, Gaye. 1978. *Making News: A Study in the Construction of Reality.* New York: Free Press.

Turk, J. V., J. Richard, R. L. Bryson Jr., and S. M. Johnson. 1989. "Hispanic Americans in the News in Two Southwestern Cities." *Journalism Quarterly* 66:107–13.

Twine, France Winddance. 1998. *Racism in a Racial Democracy: The Maintenance of White Supremacy in Brazil.* New Brunswick, NJ: Rutgers University Press.

Urciuoli, Bonnie. 1996. *Exposing Prejudice: Puerto Rican Experiences of Language, Race, and Class.* Boulder, CO: Westview Press.

Valdés, Dennis Nodín. 1991. *Al Norte: Agricultural Workers in the Great Lakes Region, 1917–1970.* Austin: University of Texas Press.

Valdés, Dionicio Nodín. 2000. *Barrios Norteños: St. Paul and Midwestern Mexican Communities in the Twentieth Century.* Austin: University of Texas Press.

Valle, Victor M. and Rodolfo D. Torres. 2000. *Latino Metropolis.* Minneapolis: University of Minnesota Press.

van den Berghe, Pierre L. 1967. *Race and Racism: A Comparative Perspective.* New York: Wiley.

Vargas, Lucila. 2000. "Genderizing Latino News: An Analysis of a Local Newspaper's Coverage of Latino Current Affairs." *Critical Studies in Media Communication* 17:261–92.

Wade, Peter. 1993. *Blackness and Race Mixture: The Dynamics of Racial Identity in Colombia.* Baltimore: Johns Hopkins University Press.

Waters, Mary. 1999. *Black Identities: West Indian Immigrant Dreams and American Realities.* New York and Cambridge, MA: Russell Sage Foundation and Harvard University Press.

Welch, Susan and Lee Sigelman. 2000. "Getting to Know You? Latino-Anglo Social Contact." *Social Science Quarterly* 81:67–83.

Wilson, William J. 1996. *When Work Disappears: The World of the New Urban Poor.* New York: Knopf.

Wright, Winthrop R. 1990. *Cafe con Leche: Race, Class, and National Image in Venezuela.* Austin: University of Texas Press.

Wu, Frank H. 2002. *Yellow: Race in America beyond Black and White.* New York: Basic Books.

Zubrinsky, Camile and Lawrence Bobo. 1996. "Prismatic Metropolis: Race and Residential Segregation in the City of Los Angeles." *Social Science Research* 25:335–74.

JOURNALING QUESTION

Which groups in the United States do you think are most likely to benefit from "conditional whitening" during the next ten years, and why?

29.

ANATOMY OF A SPECTACLE

Race, Gender, and Memory in the Kobe Bryant Rape Case

JONATHAN MARKOVITZ

A black man accused of raping a white woman is perhaps the quintessential American tale: it is a classic theme, reworked again and again as American ideas about black men, white women, and rape each change with the times.

The story used to be all about the black man—how dangerous, how fearful, and how bestial a being it was that slavery kept in chains. Later, the accusation itself became the story: this accusation, above all else, could be seen as the excuse for lynching and torturing black men (even boys).

But women (even girls) do get raped, though most often by men of the same race, by neighbors and family members, by boyfriends and husbands. Women who made the accusation of rape learned quickly that if a woman did not "behave herself," rape would be seen as deserved punishment for dressing sexily, being out late, or other gender violations. So rape became an important story to tell in America—that it happened, happened a lot, and like lynching for blacks, was a way to keep women "in their place."

With all of these stories so deeply and actively a part of American culture, small wonder that a young white woman's accusation of rape by a black male athlete—Kobe Bryant—became a "spectacle," a big news item. Jonathan Markovitz asks us to consider how collective memories explain the many angry reactions to that story. Are there ways that the media could have drawn on those memories to defuse, rather than to incite, public anger?

On June 30, 2003, Los Angeles Lakers star Kobe Bryant flew to Eagle, Colorado, to undergo arthroscopic surgery. The next afternoon a 19-year-old White woman who had been working at Bryant's hotel filed criminal charges against Bryant, reporting that he had sexually assaulted her the previous night. After initially denying that he had either raped or had sex with the woman, Bryant eventually admitted to having had consensual sex with her, but he continued to deny the rape charges.[1] These charges and the consequent legal proceedings became the subject of intense media scrutiny over the next year, subsiding only when the criminal case was dropped and a civil suit settled in the fall of 2004. This was the most closely followed case involving a professional athlete and the criminal justice system since the O.J. Simpson murder trial, and it was one of the most closely watched cases involving interracial sexuality and allegations of violence in the post-civil rights era. Because there were nearly 200,000 victims of rape, attempted rape, or sexual assault in the United States in 2003 (U.S. Department of Justice, 2004), and because there were press reports of an average of nearly

Excerpted form Jonathan Markovitz, "Anatomy of a Spectacle: Race, Gender, and Memory in the Kobe Bryant Rape Case," *Sociology of Sport Journal* 23(2006); 396–418. Notes and references have been numbered and edited.

100 cases a year of professional or college basketball and football players accused of battering or sexually assaulting a woman in the 5 years preceding the charges against Bryant (Lapchick, 2004), it is worth asking why this particular case was singled out.

I argue that the answer has to do with the ways in which the case worked to illuminate bitter divisions in American society, as the allegations against Bryant brought forth tensions involving conceptions of Black masculinity, White femininity (and mainstream feminism), and the role of sport and celebrity in public life. The questions that concern much of the media (Did he do it? Was she just out for fame? Was his "nice guy" image a façade, hiding true brutality?) are, therefore, not nearly as interesting as the more fundamental issues the case raises about the ideological forces that work to bind the culture of the United States together and that threaten to pull it apart. To begin to shed light on those forces, I present a preliminary analysis of the polities of racialized and gendered mass-media spectacles, and I suggest that the divisions revealed by the Bryant case involve long histories of struggles by social movements and state actors over the meanings of categories of race and gender.

These struggles have influenced the ways in which various segments of the American public understand history. People's understandings of the past help shape their understandings of the present, and social actors can tap into historical understandings for strategic purposes. Contemporary understandings of race, gender, and crime are very much indebted to rhetorical battles fought long ago, and invocations of collective memory can help to determine how various audiences make sense of public dramas unfolding in the mass media. Audiences who are aware of long histories of racial injustice may understand events like the Bryant case, and may be appealed to, differently than would audiences without this kind of historical knowledge. Similarly, people who are aware of the ways in which sexist stereotypes have shaped mass media and legal discourse surrounding rape are likely to respond to a highly publicized rape case quite differently than would people who lack such awareness. I argue, therefore, that public responses to the Bryant case cannot be understood without considering the ways in which historical sensibilities have been shaped by feminist interventions into public discourse surrounding rape and antiracist critiques of stereotypes of Black masculinity. Ultimately, the two parties at the center of the criminal trial and civil suit should not be seen merely as individuals but as figures who represent a variety of discourses of race, gender, and sexuality that have been constructed and refined over centuries. I suggest that one way to understand the public reaction to this case is to examine the ways these discourses have been pitted against each other.

THEORY AND METHODS

One important starting point for many studies of collective memory is the mass media. Kitch (2006) points out that "popular media are a primary source of what most people know about history" (p. 95). Much work has been done on collective memory in film and television, but, in some ways, the most important arena for the construction of collective memory may well be journalism. Journalism has been said to be "the first draft of history," but it might make sense to see it as the first draft of collective memory as well. Edy (1999) writes, "Journalists' depictions of the past have repercussions for the ways in which a community relates to its past. It may be that journalists' work impacts whether we remember our past at all" (p. 73).

While every part of the mass media has a role to play in the construction of collective memory, journalism may be particularly powerful since, as Edy (1999), points out,

> The documentary style of journalists' work gives them a unique authority in telling the story of the past. That authority may make for more powerful emotional connections on the part of the audience. The viewer who sits through action and horror films without difficulty may find the image of

Robert Kennedy as he lay dying on the floor of a hotel kitchen far more troubling because it is "real." (p. 73)

The emotional investment that people make in the news and the fact that journalistic accounts often form the raw material for later accounts of events that can be dramatized in film, television, or literature or commented on in music or other forms of art suggest that the news is a uniquely important site for investigations of the dynamics of collective memory. For that reason, an analysis of press coverage served as the first step in my investigation of the role of collective memory in the Kobe Bryant case.

To gain a sense of how collective memory might play into public understandings of the Kobe Bryant case, I searched the LexisNexis and Ethnic NewsWatch newspaper and magazine databases using the key words *Kobe Bryant* and *rape*.[2] I eliminated all articles with fewer than 250 words because they did not address the case in depth. Still, I was left with more than 800 articles from the sports sections, editorial and op-ed pages, entertainment sections, and straight news sections of local, regional, and national papers and magazines. I conducted a qualitative content analysis coding for recurrent themes and paying special attention to the ways in which the coverage invoked collective memory. (Collective memory was invoked, for example, when the African American press contextualized the case by referring to histories of lynching, or when the mainstream press explained the privacy issues in rape cases by referencing legislative battles surrounding rape in the 1970s.)

My intent is to provide a theoretical investigation into the dynamics of collective memory and to touch on some of the ways in which various segments of the American public might use their understandings of the past when trying to make sense of the politics of race, gender, and justice in the present. To begin to assess the ways in which various audiences rely on collective memory in order to make sense of contemporary circumstances, it is necessary to look beyond coverage of those contemporary circumstances and to begin to consider audiences' preexisting understandings of the past.

The first part of my analysis of the case discusses the kinds of historical context that various audiences might have brought to bear when trying to come to terms with the case. To provide a sense of the kinds of collective memories that coverage of the case was likely to evoke, I build on existing scholarship about the racial dynamics of the NBA and about media representations of rape and of allegations of interracial sexual violence. I provide a brief history of racial spectacles that have been at the center of a tremendous number of "memory projects," or "concerted efforts to secure presence for certain elements of the past" (Irvin-Zarecka, 1994, p. 8). These are events that were covered in hundreds, or thousands, of articles that have been the subject of documentary films or that have provided the occasion for national debates regarding the state of contemporary race relations. They are events that were often referred to explicitly in coverage of the Bryant case. I suggest that it is reasonable to think that even when they are not invoked explicitly, they are the kinds of events that some segments of the population had at their disposal when looking for context to help think about the case.

Finally, I look to one other kind of "memory project" that 1 argue is relevant for understandings of the case. Because so much of the coverage of the case centered on privacy issues, and because one of the most frequent types of explicit invocations of the past in the coverage of the case involved references to rape jurisprudence in the 1970s, I investigate the ways in which rape-reform legislation acts as the institutional embodiment of collective memory of a sexist legal system and of 1970s-era feminist activism. Legal scholars of critical race theory have investigated the ways in which the law has worked to construct categories of race and gender (Crenshaw, 1995; Roberts 1995). My discussion of the rape-shield statutes builds on this body of scholarship, arguing that rape-reform legislation has helped to shape understandings of sexualized stereotypes and privacy. Rape-reform legislation emerged as a direct response to the antirape movement, and contemporary media discussions of this legislation invoke memories of rape victims' being tried for their sexuality and blamed for their own rapes.

This article suggests that an analysis of collective memory is crucial for any investigation into the dynamics of racial spectacles. I argue that the Bryant case cannot be understood without grappling with ways in which collective memories of racist violence and sexist injustice were constructed and deployed in the mass media. More generally, this article highlights the ways in which social struggles of the past continue to reverberate and work to shape understandings of race and gender in the present.

PART I: RAPE ALLEGATIONS AND MEMORIES OF RACIAL SPECTACLES

The spectacle surrounding the Bryant rape case is, of course, inseparable from Bryant's fame as a superstar player in the NBA. Bryant was a key member of the Los Angeles Lakers team that won national championships in 3 consecutive years, from 2000 to 2002. Kellner (2004) describes NBA basketball as "sexy, showing glistening and well-honed male bodies in a state of semi-undress, clad in skimpy jerseys and shorts. Compared to the male gladiator body armor of football players and the nineteenth-century full body attire of baseball, basketball present[s] a mode of male beefcake, especially with TV close-ups capturing the hard and agile bodies of NBA hunks"(p. 307). Boyd and Shropshire (2000) also remark on the relative vulnerability and intimacy of basketball players, writing that, as opposed to "baseball and especially football, in basketball the player's faces are easy to see and thus easy to use in advertisements. Because of this intimacy, there is a clear identification between fans and individual players, or at least with players as we perceive them to be" (p. 3). The physical vulnerability and intimacy of basketball and the heightened possibilities

for fan identification with NBA players are particularly notable given the racial dynamics of a sport in which a disproportionate number of payers are Black, while the majority of fans are White[3].

Alexander (1994) notes that Black bodies displayed "for public consumption have been an American spectacle for centuries. This history moves from public rapes, beatings, and lynchings to the gladiatorial arenas of basketball and boxing" (p. 92). The bodies of African American athletes from a variety of sports have been at the center of a number of mass media spectacles in recent years, most notably involving Mike Tyson and O.J. Simpson, but NBA players have been particularly likely to occupy center stage in American racial discourse. When Latrell Sprewell allegedly choked and threatened to kill his coach, the media regularly "represented the incident in ways that vilified Sprewell through the use of derogatory images of Black men" (Tucker, 2003, p. 315), failing to consider Sprewell's claims about the coach's abusive behavior and regularly referring to Sprewell in animalistic terms, variously characterizing him as a "garbage-picking raccoon," a "tamed lion," or other "subordinated jungle beasts." Chris Webber, Allen Iverson, and most recently Ron Artest have all received substantial media attention for violent actions, and it would be impossible to begin to quantify the amount of ink spilled documenting the sexual behavior of Dennis Rodman, Wilt Chamberlain, and Magic Johnson. Even Michael Jordan, whose dominant media representation is a perfectly tamed and commodified image of Black masculinity, has been packaged as a sex object in his ads for Hanes underwear (Tucker). More broadly, Banet-Weiser (1999) argues that media construction of the NBA has been shaped by racist discourse, claiming that the "NBA exploits and makes exotic the racist stereotypes of the Black menace, even as it domesticates this cultural figure" (p. 406).

Tucker (2003) sums up many of the points discussed previously by noting that "in ways absent from other sports, then, the Blackness, sexuality, and the physical and emotional vulnerability of the majority of players are stamped on the face of the game of basketball" (p. 313). Because NBA players are always already at the center of an eroticized and racialized mass-media spectacle, it is not surprising that allegations of sexual misconduct on the part of an NBA superstar should be immediately seized on and scrutinized for larger lessons about celebrity, gender, and racial conflict in American society. When the allegations involve charges of interracial sexual assault, as in the Bryant case, the resulting media attention can powerfully, and uncomfortably, resonate with age-old narratives of Black sexuality.

RACE MATTERS

There has been notable frustration on the part of various commentators who have been unable to come to terms with people who "insist" on seeing the case in racialized terms and who argue instead that the only issues of import in the case have to do with gender, celebrity, and wealth[4]. Yet opinion polls suggest that there arc racialized differences in public reactions to the case. A *USA Today*/CNN/ Gallup poll conducted in August 2003 showed that White respondents were nearly twice as likely as Black respondents to see the charges against Bryant as "probably true," while Blacks were nearly five times more likely than Whites to be "very sympathetic" toward Bryant (USA [Today]/CNN/Gallup, 2003). When attempting to explain this apparently racial division in reactions to the case, it seems reasonable to suggest that understandings of history may play a role in determining how people evaluate evidence and think of media coverage. Histories of racializcd spectacles might be particularly noteworthy in this regard.

Leonard (2004) writes that "the discursive field surrounding rape allegations represents a continuation of long-standing fears, myths, and hatred of Black male bodies, all of which are wrapped up in the histories of lynchings, injustice, and state violence" (p. 294). Lynchings, in particular, played a major role in fostering a set of symbolic connections

between Black masculinity and sexualized criminality. While there are many parallel histories of lynching, involving victims of different races and ethnicities, the majority of lynchings occurred in the Southern United States after Reconstruction, and the primary victims were African American men (Brundage, 1993; Carrigan & Webb, 2003). Public apologists for these killings including senators and congressmen fighting against federal anti-lynching legislation, and Southern editorial writers inevitably claimed that lynching was a method of punishing Black men who raped White women. Yet members of the mobs themselves cited rape as the reason for only a minority of lynchings. Furthermore, the extra-legal character of lynchings meant that there was generally not even a semblance of due process or, usually, any reliable evidence to support the rape charges (Markovitz, 2004). But the fictional nature of the links between lynching and rape did nothing to diminish the power that public defenses of lynching had to shape understandings of race and gender. By the early years of the 20th century, these defenses took the form of increasingly standardized narratives featuring pure White women, chivalrous and heroic White male defenders, and monstrous Black rapists. Narratives of lynching help account for the numerous "spectacle lynchings" that could draw hundreds and even thousands of participants or spectators to lynchings that were often announced in local newspapers (Brundage, 1993; Carrigan, 2004). Reports of such lynchings, disseminated to national audiences by an approving White press, reinforced such narratives, while the mythical Black rapist became a popular figure in virtually every arena of popular culture. The character of Gus in D.W. Griffith's *The Birth of a Nation* (1915) is only the most famous embodiment of this figure.

MORE THAN MEMORY: CONTEMPORARY RACIAL SPECTACLES

It would be a mistake to suggest that the racist stereotypes that were so central to the dynamics of lynching have remained static or that their strength is undiminished. Instead, these stereotypes were challenged, almost from the moment of their inception, as an antilynching movement spanning the final decades of the 19th century and the early decades of the 20th devoted the bulk of its resources to eliminating (or "exploding" in the movement's parlance) the myth of the Black rapist (Markovitz, 2004). Dramatic evidence of the success of the antilynching movement's battles over lynching rhetoric can be found in the reception of Clarence Thomas' outraged declaration that he was the victim of a "high-tech lynching" as he faced Anita Hill's allegations of sexual harassment during his nomination process to become associate justice on the United States Supreme Court.... The antilynching movement's claim that the rape charges in lynching narratives were myths had become, by 1991, part of a racialized common sense.[5]

Acknowledging that stereotypes of Black male sexuality have changed over time does not, however, mean that they are irrelevant for understanding more recent racialixed media spectacles. Indeed, there is no shortage of examples in which the circulation of such stereotypes has had dramatic consequences. Thus, for example, political advertisements in the 1988 presidential election, featuring the convicted rapist Willaim ("Willie") Horton, associated Massachusetts governor Michael Dukakis with the looming specter of Black rape and played a key role in costing Dukakis the election.[6]...Perhaps the most dramatic case involving stereotypes of Black male sexuality in recent memory involved Trisha Meili, a White investment banker who was raped, beaten, and left for dead in New York's Central Park in 1989.

Trisha Meili (who had been identified only as the "Central Park Jogger" until revealing her identity in 2003 as part of a promotional campaign for her upcoming book tour) remembers nothing about the attack and has never claimed to be able to identify her assailants (Heller, 2004). But five teenagers from Harlem (four were Black, one was Latino) were soon arrested for the crime, and they were tried and convicted the next year. There was never any forensic evidence or witness testimony tying the defendants to the attack, so they were convicted solely on the basis of confessions they later tried to retract, claiming that they had been coerced. In January of 2002, a man named Matias Reyes, who had been convicted of a series of rapes and murders and who was serving a sentence of 33-1/3 years to life, confessed to having raped Meili and said that he had acted alone (Schanberg, 2002). DNA tests quickly confirmed that the semen that had been found at the crime scene matched Reyes'. In December 2002, shortly after the final defendant had completed his term and been released from prison, the Stale Supreme Court set aside the guilty verdicts.

The case has been widely compared to the Scottsboro case of the 1930s, in which nine Black boys and young men were falsely accused of raping two White women (Goodman, 1995).... From the beginning, the media frenzy surrounding the crimes in Central Park that night relied heavily on racially coded language and stereotyping. The group of teens was consistently referred to in animalistic terms, most frequently as a "wolf pack," and a new term was coined to describe their actions that night: *wilding*. The mainstream press accepted the validity of the confessions without any serious scrutiny, even when crucial elements of the confessions contradicted each other, and even when DNA evidence revealed the overall weakness of the prosecution's case.

The tone of the news coverage was echoed by public figures, as then Mayor Ed Koch regularly referred to the defendants as "monsters," while Donald Trump paid for full-page ads in every daily paper in New York calling for the death penalty in the case, saying that the defendants "should be forced to suffer" (quoted in Hancock, 2003, p. 4). The hysteria generated in the case paved the way for the reinstatement of the death penalty in New York, and contributed to "rage against juvenile crime" at the national level, and to a sentiment that led, by the mid-1990s, to the passage of laws in most states providing for children to be tried as adults (Hancock, 2003, p. 5).

RACE, MEMORY, AND SKEPTICISM

This is an admittedly skeletal history of American racialized spectacles, but it should be sufficient to provide a sense of the kinds of context that are available to various audiences when they try to make sense of the Bryant case. Audiences who are aware that there is a longstanding media fascination with, and history of inflating, allegations of Black male sexual deviance and violence might be more likely to approach with caution new media spectacles involving Black masculinity. And people who are familiar with the history of criminal penalties and extralegal violence meted out to Black men on the basis of evidence that was subsequently revealed to be fabricated or unreliable seem quite likely to be skeptical of new charges of interracial sexual violence that lack compelling evidence. Indeed, Bryant's defense team tapped into this history at one point in the pretrial maneuvering by noting that "there is lots of history of Black men being falsely accused of this crime by White women" (NBCSports.com, 2004), while the Black press regularly sought to contextualize the Bryant case by referencing the kinds of history that I've outlined previously....

Collective memory works here as a lens: It encourages readers to focus on the case in ways that require evaluating evidence quite differently than do the mass media.[7] For readers who follow the logic of such accounts, it is impossible to see the Bryant case in isolation since the mass media representations of the case become understood as links in long chains of images of Black men as sexually monstrous. Bryant himself cannot be seen as an individual superstar with immense wealth and privilege; instead he is connected to what Gooding-Williams (1993) would sec as a vast "storehouse" of racial imagery (p. 163). A substantial portion of any racial divide in reactions to the Bryant case may well have to do with the fact that African Americans are more likely to have been exposed to versions of collective memory that include knowledge of spectacularized forms of racist injustice.

But if racialized differences in collective memory account for some of the hesitancy on the part of African Americans (and, it should be said, of people from other racial groups who are also familiar with the kinds of history discussed previously) to accept the validity of the rape allegations in the Bryant case, memories of the past were not the only basis for a belief that the case against Bryant was tainted by racism. Instead, aspects of the racial politics directly surrounding the Bryant case itself should have been cause for serious concern. David Leonard (2003) notes that Eagle County, where the trial was to take place, is "almost 90% white, and less than .02% Black" (p. B4). More important, the Eagle County Sheriff's department had a well-documented history of racial profiling and had settled a lawsuit after it was revealed that deputies had stopped hundreds of Black and Latino drivers, telling them that "they fit a profile of drug smugglers because each had California license plates and 'because of the color of their skin.'" Leonard (2004) argues that this "history and the fact that the lead investigator in the Bryant case was named in the racial profiling case is a testament to the ways in which race will continue to filter interpretations and understandings of the Kobe Bryant trial" (p. 305), although his broader point is that the bulk of commentators in the mass media were intent on *ignoring* this history or declaring it irrelevant. Compelling evidence that the racism of the Eagle County legal establishment was not confined to the past came with the disclosure that members of the district attorney's and sheriff's offices "had ordered T-shirts depicting a stick figure being hanged" and including "derogatory statements" about Bryant (Pankratz & Lipsher, 2003, p. B-04). District Attorney Mark Hurlbert initially denied that anyone on his staff had ordered any of the shirts, but he then issued a statement apologizing for having been unintentionally misleading and said that he had disposed of his own shirt immediately (Fox News, 2003). For anyone who was already wary of the possibility that Bryant might, as a Black man charged with raping a White woman, be a metaphorical lynch victim facing trumped-up charges, the fact that such T-shirts were owned by key members of the legal establishment that was seeking to try him could hardly have been reassuring. Thus, it is likely that, for many observers, a collective memory of lynching and other racist spectacles was bolstered by the contemporary state of racial affairs in Eagle County on the eve of Bryant's trial.

PART II: THE INSTITUTIONALIZATION OF MEMORY: FEMINIST STRUGGLE AND RAPE-REFORM LEGISLATION

If there was good reason for skepticism about the charges against Bryant on the part of people whose sensibilities and beliefs were shaped by a knowledge and collective memory of racism, there were also ways in which collective memory may have prepared other audiences to see Bryant as likely to have committed the crime. Most important to consider here are people whose understanding of rape is informed by feminism and by the antirape movement of the 1970s. Such people would know that false allegations of rape are rare, since women who charge rape are often subjected to brutal treatment by the legal system and generally would have very little to gain from false charges. Moreover, because a key part of the legal maneuvering in the lead-up to the trial centered on the accuser's sexual and medical history, the case resonated quite strongly with decades-long feminist concerns about violations of rape victims' privacy.

WHITE FEMALE SEXUALITY ON TRIAL

The sexual history of Bryant's accuser became an issue almost immediately after charges were filed, since Bryant's defense team wanted to argue that injuries to Bryant's accuser were a result of having had sex with someone other than Bryant. Rowe, McKay, & Miller (2000) have argued that in racial

sport spectacles of the 1990s involving Magic Johnson and Mike Tyson, discourses that had figured Black male athletes as powerful and invincible were transformed into discourses of Black male vulnerability by refocusing the discussion and invoking stereotypes of "active" female sexuality. They argued, "In this way, the body of the Black male elite athlete is protected from racist discourses that seek to reduce it to no more than blind sexual urges—only by projecting such identity upon the bodies of women" (p. 258).

The notion of linking representations of Black male monstrosity with images of White women's sexual excess can also be traced back to lynching narratives and the discourse of chivalry, Black men may have been the most direct targets of the racist discourse surrounding lynching, but because lynchings were defended in the name of White women, lynching narratives also worked to place limits on While women's sexual freedom. As Hall (1993) has argued, "The right of the southern lady to protection presupposed her obligation to obey" (p. 151). While lynching has been widely understood as a method of terrorizing African American communities and enforcing racialized hierarchies, stereotypes of Black sexual monstrosity worked to create a "legacy of terror" (Hall, 1993, p. 153) that reinforced White women's dependency on White men. White women who failed to live up to the standards of behavior suggested by the stereotype of the "pure white woman" that was so central to lynching narratives were demonized as "fallen women" (Apel, 2004, p. 28). This stereotype was fully in play during the Kobe Bryant criminal proceedings but was not uncontested. Instead, use of this stereotype provided the opportunity for the prosecution and the press to discuss the importance of rape reform legislation and, in the process, to invoke collective memories of a sexist legal system and of feminist activism.

The strategy of representing Bryant's accuser as excessively sexually active was on display in the preliminary hearing, at which point the lead defense attorney asked the detective who had interviewed Bryant's accuser if the accuser's injuries might be consistent with having had "sex with three men in three days" (Brennan, 2003, p. A4). This question set the tone for the defense strategy throughout the case. The prosecution argued that this defense strategy conflicted with Colorado's rape-shield law, which was intended to provide victims of sexual assault with "greater protection from humiliating and embarrassing 'fishing expeditions' into their past sexual conduct, without a preliminary showing that evidence thus elicited will be relevant to some issue in the pending case."[8] The defense argued that there was no conflict, since the evidence they were looking for was directly relevant to the question of whether the victim's injuries were sustained through the violent act that Bryant was accused of. The judge in the case agreed with the defense, allowing limited evidence about the sexual activity of the alleged victim, but this decision came only after a series of blunders on the part of the court that catapulted the issues of rape victims' privacy and rape-shield laws to a national stage.

The court twice released Bryant's accuser's name on its Web site, citing "clerical errors" and mistakenly e-mailed copies of the transcripts from a closed-door session, regarding the admissibility of evidence about the accuser's sexual history, to members of a variety of news organizations. The trial judge apologized to the accuser and ordered the news organizations not to publish any information contained in the transcripts,[9] but the apologies did little to reassure the accuser or her family, who decided to stop cooperating with the prosecution, thus effectively ending the criminal case. Advocates for rape victims saw the decision to allow evidence about the accuser's sexual experiences into trial, along with the court's errors, as potentially chilling. A spokesperson for the Colorado Coalition Against Sexual Assault reacted to the court's actions by saying, "No wonder women are so afraid to go to police when they are raped.... Not only do you have to relive the rape, but the defense lawyers try

to broadcast every other aspect of your private life" (quoted in Reid, 2004, p. A2). But while rape-victim advocates were critical of the court's actions, they tended to argue that the most serious breaches of the alleged victim's privacy were beyond the ability of the court to prevent. As the media searched relentlessly for every detail of the alleged victim's personal life, not only exposing her name but also speculating about her mental health and providing information about her sexual past, the case exposed the limits to the protection that rape-shield laws could provide.[10]

Rape-shield laws were a direct response to arguments made by the antirape movement of the 1970s that the practice of allowing testimony about a rape victim's sexual history into evidence was a key factor in the underreporting of rape, because it ensured that legal proceedings surrounding rape worked to place the victim, and her sexuality, on trial. The ordeal faced by rape victims in the courtroom, often referred to as "a second rape," could be a powerful deterrent when considering filing charges. In addition, the antirape movement argued that allowing irrelevant information about a victim's sexuality into legal proceedings worked to seriously taint the legal notion of "consent," which is central in determining whether a rape has been committed. For example, in her analysis of rape reforms, Ireland (1976) notes that "'consent' in a rape case has been found in the manner of the victim's dress, in her presence at a bar, or in her previous sexual conduct" (p. 189). The rape-reform movement achieved some of the most notable legislative victories of 1970s-era feminism, and by 1980, 45 states had rewritten their rape laws to limit the admissibility of evidence about an alleged rape victim's sexual history (Tanford & Bocchino, 1980). I would suggest that the rape-shield statutes can be seen as the institutionalized embodiment of collective memories of sexist treatment of rape victims and of feminist efforts to challenge such treatment, since these laws point to the problems of the past that account for their origin: Presumably, no one would have bothered to write such laws if the treatment of rape victims in the criminal justice system hadn't been seen as a serious problem.

PRIVACY AND THE LIMITS OF THE LAW

The media's obsession with every detail of the life of the alleged victim in the Bryant case demonstrated that, at least in high-profile cases, rape-shield statutes were incapable of fully protecting privacy rights, since the kinds of abuse that state legislatures were concerned with could happen outside of the courtroom. A good deal of the potentially embarrassing information in the Bryant case was, however, gathered by the defense team and contained in the documents that the court mistakenly released to the press. So, when the judge attempted to prevent publication of the leaked information, the goal was to prevent the court's actions from contributing unnecessarily to a climate outside the courtroom that could become even more emotionally abusive (Henson & Weinstein, 2004, p. D1). Still, the media organizations that were told not to publish the leaked transcripts immediately appealed the order. The Colorado Supreme Court heard the case and decided that while there is generally a "heavy presumption" against the constitutional validity of any form of prior restraint (any effort on the part of the state to prevent publication of any statement), Colorado's rape-shield statute addressed a state interest of the "highest order," and prior restraint could be justified as a method of securing this interest. The Court allowed the decision to ban disclosure of the contents of the transcripts.

The media organizations appealed the Colorado Supreme Court's ruling, asking the United States Supreme Court to rule that the ban on publication was unconstitutional. Justice Stephen Breyer (2004) weighed in, refusing to overturn the ban, but saying that the news organizations could refile their petition after waiting two days, since "a brief delay will permit the state courts to clarify, perhaps avoid, the controversy at issue here." The trial judge ordered the prosecution and defense to produce an edited version of the transcripts that could be released to the media. Rather than risk an unfavorable ruling from the Supreme Court that might be a major setback for first amendment principles, the news organizations appear to have made a tactical decision to end the appeals process.

The prior restraint issues were of major concern to the media and provided the occasion for dozens of articles weighing the need to protect rape victims' privacy with the public need to be informed. The bulk of articles that I examined that discussed the legal strategies in the case focused on the rape-shield statutes. The need for and history behind such statutes were addressed frequently. Analysis of the rape-shield laws often entailed discussions of whether particular pieces of information about the victim's sexuality or mental health were relevant in determining her credibility and whether the rape-shield laws might exclude information that was necessary for Bryant's legal team to mount an appropriate defense. Press accounts often misinterpreted the Colorado rape-shield law by suggesting that it ruled out *any* evidence about an alleged victim's sexual past.[11] In fact, while it was true that the law created a legal presumption that such evidence was irrelevant, a number of exceptions to that presumption were provided for by the statute. Bryant's defense team was thus regularly mischaracterized as challenging the rape-shield statute.[12] Instead, the strategy that proved most successful for the defense was to argue that evidence of the alleged victim's sexual activity in the time period surrounding the alleged assault should be seen as falling within the exceptions carved out by the law. This mischaracterization was not inconsequential. Because the media regularly focused on the rape-shield laws, representing them, appropriately, as the legislative embodiment of the 1970s antirape movement,[13] the notion that Bryant's defense was in conflict with these laws made it possible to see the prosecution as a surrogate for feminism, and to see Bryant's defense as having to overcome not the claims of one woman but the institutionalized force of an entire social movement.[14]

PART III: A CLASH OF DISCOURSES AND CONTESTS OVER MEMORY

For some commentators whose skepticism about the charges against Bryant was rooted in collective memories of lynching and knowledge of past racist spectacles, the specter of a feminist movement pitted against a Black man was all too familiar. For antiracist activists, allegations of White women's victimization at the hands of Black men have long required a great deal of care and scrutiny because such allegations were central to the dynamics of lynching and the maintenance of White supremacy. Hutchinson (2004) writes that "there's a reason many blacks buy Bryant's racial victim claim. For decades, the Klan used white fears of black men raping white women to terrorize blacks. Older blacks still have vivid and painful memories of the lynch murders of fourteen year old Emmett Till for allegedly whistling at a white woman in 1955 in Mississippi, and Mack Charles Parker for the alleged rape of a white woman in 1959 in Louisiana." The antirape movement of the 1970s was largely a White women's movement, and it has been long criticized for reliance on racist stereotypes. Angela Davis' (1981) well-known analysis of the antirape movement's rhetoric concludes that the foundational texts of the movement, including Susan Brown miller's *Against Our Will* (1975), "have facilitated the resurrection of the timeworn myth of the Black rapist" (p. 182).[15]

The often-unacknowledged racist legacies of the antirape movement leave contemporary feminist rhetoric particularly vulnerable to claims of racism. For example, one way to explain the ease with which supporters of Clarence Thomas were able to dismiss Anita Hill's allegations of sexual harassment is that the legal strategies animating her charges were a product of the same 1970s-era activism indicted by Davis and were thus possible to represent as tainted by "White women's feminism." Feminist supporters

of Bryant's accuser found themselves dealing with a similar dynamic. For example, Reed (2004) writes about the Bryant case as part of an ongoing "war against Black men," and sees what he refers to as the "Ku Klux Feminists" of CNN, including Naomi Wolf and Wendy Murphy, as important soldiers in this war.[16] Reed argues that Susan Brownmiller "and other well-known feminists have an irrational hatred of Black men" (p. 45), The comparison to the Klan is a clear indication that Reed's rhetoric is exceptionally inflammatory, but he is not alone in his assessment of the Bryant case as being marked by feminist complicity in the metaphorical lynching of a Black man.

CONCLUSION

In the fall of 2004, after the dismissal of the criminal charges in the Bryant case, *The Los Angeles Times* ran an article titled "Kobe's Second Act: It All Worked Out for Him: No Shaq, No Phil, No Prison. But Have We Worked Out Our Feelings About Him?" (Kaye, 2004). The article rehearses some of the details of Bryant's career and asks, "Knowing what we now know, should we root for him?" A similar article focuses on Los Angeles Lakers fans and parents, who were said to be "torn over Kobe," "disillusioned by the sexual assault charges," and wrestling with "rooting for one of their favorites" (Braxton, 2004, p. E1). The kinds of explanations that are offered in these articles for the conflicted feelings that people have when considering the Bryant case are fairly superficial, revolving around notions of celebrity, the costs of fame, and the inability to know the person beneath the image of the sports hero. But the question of whether to sympathize with Kobe Bryant is a vexing one for anyone concerned with the dynamics of race, gender, and violence as represented in popular culture and the mass media. No doubt there are many reasons that people might be "torn over Kobe," but one set of tensions is never addressed in the media coverage. For audiences who are concerned with a variety of oppressive forces, and whose sensibilities and collective memories are shaped by recognition of the value of struggles for social justice, coming to terms with the Bryant case is no simple matter. As commonsense belief systems shaped by antiracist struggle conflict sharply with commonsense belief systems shaped by feminist politics and the antirape movement of the 1970s, the question of what, exactly, it means to root for Kobe Bryant remains. Is this possible without trivializing not only the suffering of his alleged victim but also rape itself? Alternatively, what does it mean to withdraw support from a Black man charged with the rape of a White woman, especially once the criminal charges have been dropped? Can this be done without falling prey to some of the most corrosive and enduring racist stereotypes in American society? Rowe, McKay, and Miller (2000) argue that the "difficulty of disentangling assumptions of guilt or innocence of an appalling sexual crime from preexisting racist and sexist discourses—not to mention the knowing exploitation of those discourses by both prosecution and defense—reveals the extent to which ideologies of power are ever-present in the practice of everyday life and in the conduct of cultural politics" (p. 259). In the end it is not just difficult, but it is impossible to separate thoughts about guilt and innocence from ages-old narratives of race and gender in cases like these, and the question of whether or not to root for Kobe Bryant is implicated in, and inseparable from, a clash of discourses. An antisexist discourse that would highlight the privacy rights of rape victims clashes with an antiracist discourse that seeks to link Bryant to victims of a racist legal system and to victims of extralegal violence.

In her discussion of racial discourse surrounding the O.J. Simpson case, Crenshaw (1997) argues that inadequate attention to the ways in which categories of gender and race intersect led to a dominant framing of the case that pitted feminists against antiracist activists and suggested that "race and gender were locked in a zero-sum game in which a win for Blacks was a loss for women,

and vice versa" (p. 145). Crenshaw's point about the perils of failing to account for the complexities of intersecting forms or oppression provides an important note of caution for anyone trying to come to terms with the Bryant case. As long as the case is seen in "he said/she said" terms, or as long as the framing suggests that there are two clearly distinct sides, and that one must be worthy of support and the other of condemnation, it is impossible to more fully assess the complexities of the racial and gendered dynamics in play. More specifically, the "zero-sum" game that Crenshaw refers to obscures the need for critical assessment of the ways in which the case resonates with ages-old stereotypes of race *and* gender.

Crenshaw (1997) argues that the Simpson case and other cases "involving such vexed categories as race, gender, and class" call for "an intersectional politics that merges feminist and antiracist critiques of institutional racism and sexism" (p. 158). Of course, figuring out how to develop and mobilize such an intersectional politics is far from clear. McDonald (1999) credits antiracist activists and feminists for their critiques of the ways in which media coverage can work to determine dominant understandings of sexualized violence, yet she notes that antiracist and feminist arguments have gained little traction within the mass media and that media attention to "violent actions does not necessarily translate into critical understanding" (p. 128). Crenshaw (1997) is similarly concerned with the inability of activists to intervene in unfolding sports spectacles in politically useful ways. She notes that the kinds of issues surrounding sexual violence and racial injustice that played out in the Simpson case have been usefully analyzed by feminists and antiracist activists, but she argues that, as the case unfolded, "there was no readily accessible framework that allowed the critiques to be aligned in a complementary rather than implicitly oppositional fashion" (p. 159). As the Kobe Bryant case unfolded more than a decade later, very little appears to have changed. Collective memories of racist spectacles and of sexist treatment of rape victims at the hands of the legal system were mobilized in order to garner support for particular parties involved in the case, but there were few signs of an organized "feminist antiracist" (p. 157) response that was simultaneously attentive to the sexist and racist dimensions of the case.

Irwin-Zarecka (1994) writes that collective memory "is best located not in the minds of individuals, but in the resources they share" (p. 4). At one level, this is just a definition of collective memory. But it is also a methodological claim. The point here is that the way to assess the nature of collective memory is not necessarily to conduct interviews or to accumulate survey data to determine how people are thinking about the past. Instead, Irwin-Zarecka's claim suggests that the task for the analyst of collective memory is to look to shared resources, or to the cultural production of widely disseminated versions of the past. Clearly, I have taken this suggestion to heart, looking not to "the minds of individuals" but to the media and the legal system as sites where collective memory is constructed and deployed. Still, an analysis of cultural production can ultimately only provide clues as to how people might make use of their understandings of the past in making sense of the present. Irvin-Zarecka (1994) cautions that

> an abundance of resources docs not guarantee that people actually use them....As we look at a collective memory, at what it offers and at how its offerings change, we ought to remain modest in our claims. Individuals arc perfectly capable of ignoring even the best told stories, of injecting their own, subversive meanings into even the most rhetorically accomplished "texts"—and of attending to only those ways of making sense of the past that fit their own. (p. 4)

To determine how, and whether, "people actually use" the cultural resources and kinds of collective memory that I have discussed in this article when following racialized and gendered spectacles, it would be necessary to conduct research into "the minds of individuals." Empirical research along these lines might involve interviews or surveys that seek to measure what people knew about histories of racial injustice before the allegations against Bryant surfaced, or whether and how people thought about history and memory as the case unfolded. The theoretical investigation into the dynamics of collective memory that I have conducted in this article is ultimately speculative and only one step in a larger process of assessing the ways in which collective memory can influence public responses to contemporary events.

The question of whether or not Bryant is guilty of rape is beyond the scope of this article, but I do hope to have provided some of the conceptual tools necessary to make sense of the ways in which memories of racialized spectacles and memories of sexist practices surrounding treatment of rape victims were pitted against each other in what became a clash of antiracist and antisexist discourses. As members of various constituencies approach unfolding racialized and gendered spectacles, the understandings that they come to are not generated whole cloth on the spot but are instead informed by collective memories that have been constructed as products of long histories of political struggle. In an attempt to understand the social nature of individual consciousness, Antonio Gramsci argued that it was necessary to take on the task of "'knowing thyself' a product of the historical process to date, which has deposited in you an infinity of traces, without leaving an inventory." To achieve this kind of self-knowledge, "it is imperative at the outset to compile such an inventory" (Said, 1978, p. 25). This essay highlights the value of such a compilation project—only by reckoning with the traces or collective memories of struggles over race and gender is it possible to begin to come to terms with the nature of the disparate reactions to the Kobe Bryant rape case.

NOTES

I would like to thank Annelies Knoppers and the anonymous reviewers for their extremely generous and helpful comments.

1. *Sexual assault* is Colorado's legal term for rape.
2. The Ethnic News Watch database provides full-text access to hundreds of newspapers and magazines of the ethnic press, including access to most of the nation's African American newspapers.
3. In February 2004, 77% of NBA players were African American, while only 21% were White (Lelinwaller 2004).
4. See K. Johnson (August 26, 2004), J. Johnson (2004), and Shipp (2003).
5. I am following Gramsci's notion of "common sense" here, in that I see common sense as socially constructed and as the product of discursive battles over hegemony. See Markovitz (2004, p. 15) for more on this idea. For much more detailed discussions of the Hill/Thomas hearings, see Morrison (1992) and Markovitz (2004).
6. On the impact of the Willie Horton ad, see Feagin and Vera (1995).
7. There are numerous examples of stories seeking to explain support for Bryant by referencing histories of racism. See Deggans (2006).
8. Justice Bender, joined by Justices Martinze and Rice: dissenting opinion in *The People of the State of Colorado v. Defendant: Kobe Bean Bryant*, Case No. 04SA200, Supreme Court of Colorado, July 19, 2004.
9. "Bryant's Accuser's Ordeal Shows Limits of Rape Shield Laws," Editorial. *Chicago Sun Times*, August 16, 2004.
10. See "Bryant's Accuser's Ordeal Shows Limits of Rape Shield Law." Editorial, *Chicago Sun-Times*, August 16, 2004, for an assessment of the ways in which the Bryant case is likely to deter rape victims from coming forward.
11. See, for example, Young (2003).
12. Luzadder and Siemaszko (2004), Lipsher (2004).
13. For an example of the press addressing the links between the antirape movement and the rape-shield laws, see Markets & Marek (2003). See also Young (2003).
14. The stakes of the case, and the idea that Bryant's defense team was in conflict not only with the accuser in the case but also with a broader antirape movement, are also highlighted in a series of articles that quote rape-victim advocates and antirape organizations expressing concern about the repercussions of the case. See Harden (2004).
15. Critiques of the racism of the antirape movement, or of the movement's lack of attention to the concerns of women of color, have been important for challenges to the essentialism in much of mainstream feminism. See Crenshaw (1995) and Harris (1990) for overviews of these challenges.
16. Reed (2004). See also Maddox (2004), Hilliard (2003), Hobbs (2004), and Reed (2003).

REFERENCES

Alexander, E. (1994). "Can you be black and look at tills?" Reading the Rodney King video(s). InT. Golden (Ed.), *Black male: Representations of masculinity in contemporary American art* (pp. 91–115). New York: Whitney Museum of American Art.

Apel, D. (2004). *Imagery of lynching: Black men, white women, and, the mob.* New Brunswick, NJ: Rutgers University Press.

Banet-Weiser, S. (1999). Hoop dreams: Professional basketball and the politics of race and gender. *Journal of Sport & Social Issues, 23*(4), 403–420.

Boyd, T., & Shopshire, K.L. (2000). Introduction: Basketball Jones: A new world order? In T. Boyd & K.L. Shopshire (Eds.), *Basketball Jones: America above the rim* (pp. 1–12). New York: New York University Press.

Braxton, G. (2004, June 12). Tom over Kobe. *Los Angeles Times*, p. El.

Brennan, C. (2003, October 11). Bryant lawyer kicks up ruckus: Attorneys attack, defend Mackey's tactics in hearing. *Rocky Mountain News*, p. 4A.

Breyer, S. (2004, July 26). Supreme Court of the United States, No. 04A73 Associated Press, et al. *v.* District Court for the Fifth Judicial District of Colorado, On application for stay. Retrieved August 30, 2004, from https://web.lexis-nexis.com/universe.

Brownmiller, S. (1975). *Against our will: Men, women and rape.* New York: Bantam Books.

Brundage, W.F. (1993). *Lynching in the new south: Georgia and Virginia*, 1880–930. Chicago: University of Illinois Press.

Carrigan, W.D. (2004). *The making of a Lynching culture: Violence and vigilantism in central Texas 1836–1916.* Urbana, IL: University of Illinois Press.

Carrigan, W.D., & Webb, C. (2003). The lynching of persons of Mexican origin or descent in the United States, 1848 to 1928. *Journal of Social History, 37*(2), 411–438.

Crenshaw, K. (1995). Mapping the margins: Intersectionality, identity politics, and violence against women of color. In K. Crenshaw, et al. (Eds.), *Critical race theory: The key writings that formed the movement* (pp. 357–383). New York: New Press.

Crenshaw, K. (1997). Color-blind dramas and racial nightmares: Reconfiguring racism in the post-civil rights era. In T. Morrison &C.B. Lacour (Eds.), *Birth of a nation 'hood: Gaze, script, and spectacle in the O.J. Simpson case* (pp. 97–168). New York: Pantheon.

Davis, A. (1981). *Women, race, and class.* New York: Vintage.

Deggans, E. (2006, May 7). Why the rush to protect 'our own'? *St. Petersburg Times.* Retrieved November 15, 2003, from https:/web.lexis-nexis.com/universe.

Edy, J. (1999). Journalistic uses of collective memory. *Journal of Communication.* Spring, 71–85.

Feagin, J. & Vera, H. (1995). *White racism: The basics.* New York: Routledge.

Fox News. (2003, December 19). Kobe T-shirts dog Eagle County prosecutors. Retrieved November 15, 2003, from www.foxnews.com/story/0,2933,106247,00.html.

Gooding-Williams, R. (1993). "Look: A Negro!" In R. Gooding-Williams (Ed.), *Reading Rodney King, reading urban uprising.* New York: Routledge. 157–177.

Goodman, J. (1995). *Stories of Scottsboro.* New York: Vintage.

Griffith, D.W. (1915) *The Birth of a Nation.* (Film). Epoch Producing Corporation: USA.

Hall, J.D. (1993). Revolt against chivalry: Jesse Daniel Ames and the women's campaign against lynching. New York: Columbia University Press.

Hancock, L. (2003, Jan/Feb). Wolf pack: The press and the central park jogger. *Columbia Journalism Review.* Retrieved November 15, 2003, from https://web.lexis-nexis.com/universe.

Harden, B. (2004, September 3). Bryant case is called a setback; recent rape victims cite confidentiality breach, advocates say. *The Washington Post*, p. A08.

Harris, A. (1990). Race and essentialism in feminist legal theory. *Stanford Law Review, 42*(3), 581–616.

Heller, D. (2004). Anatomies of rape. *American Literary History, 16*(2), 329–349.

Henson, S., & Weinstein, H. (2004. July 20). Courts bar disclosure by media; Colorado justices rule, 4–3, that documents accidentally released in the Bryant case cannot be published. *Los Angeles Times*, p. D1.

Hilliard, L. (2003, December 4). The naked truth: High profile black stars undergoing high tech lynching. *The Mississippi Link*. P. 1.

Hobbs, C. (2004, September 9). What Kobe Bryant's rape charge dismissal means. *Capital Outlook*. Retrieved November 15, 2003, from https://web.lexis-nexis.com/universe.

Hutchinson, E.O. (2004). Race was inevitable in Bryant's case. *Alternet*. Retrieved July 20, 2006, from www.alternet.org/story/17723.

Ireland, M.J. (1976, Winter). Reform rape legislation: A new standard of sexual responsibility. *University of Colorado Law Review, 49*(2), 185–204.

Irwin-Zarecka, I. (1994). Frames of remembrance: The dynamics of collective memory. New Brunswick: Transaction.

Johnson, J. (2004, January 28). Bryant's defense team taking big risk if it relies on race card being an ace. *The Columbus Dispatch*, p. 11A.

Johnson, K. (2004, Aug 26). In Kobe Bryant case, issues of power, not of race. *The New York Times*, p. 12.

Kaye, E. (2004, October 31). Kobe's second act: It all worked out for him: No Shaq, no Phil, no prison. But have we worked out our feelings about him? *The Los Angeles Times*. Retrieved November 15, 2004, from https://web.lexis-nexis.com/universe.

Kellner, D. (2004). The sports spectacle, Michael Jordan, and Nike. In P.B. Miller & D.K. Wiggins (Eds.), *Sport and the color line: Black athletes and race relations in twentieth-century America*. New York: Routledge.

Kitch, C. (2006). "Useful memory" in Time Inc. magazines: Summary journalism and the popular construction of history. *Journalism Studies, 7*(1), 94–110.

Lapchick, R.E. (2004). The Kobe Bryant case: Athletes, Violence, stereotypes and the games we play. *Center for the study of sport in society*. Retrieved May 15, 2006, from www.sportinsociety.org/rel-article34.html.

Lelinwaller, M. (2004, July 13). Basketball is flip side of baseball. *Philadelphia Inquirer*. Retrieved November 15, 2004, from https://web.lexis-nexis.com/universe.

Leonard, D.J. (2003). Racing sports. *Popmatters*, 9.11. Retrieved November 15, 2004, from www.popmatters.com/sports/features/030911-kobe.shtml.

Leonard, D.J. (2004, August). The next M.J. or the next O.J.? Kobe Bryant, race, and the absurdity of colorblind rhetoric. *Journal of Sport & Social Issues, 28*(3) 284–313.

Lipsher, S. (2004, January 14). NBA defease tests rape-shield law. *The Denver Post*. p. D-4.

Luzadder, D., & Siemaszko, C. (2004, January 22). Team Kobe can fight privacy law. *New York Daily News*, p. 20.

Maddox, A. (2004, August 26–September 1). Critical thinking takes a hike in the Bryant case. Editorial. *New York Amsterdam News*. p. 12.

Markels, A., & Marek, A.C. (2003, October 13). A seismic shift in sex-case law. *U.S. News and World Report*, p. 45.

Markovitz, J. (2004). *Legacies of lynching: Racial violence and memory*. Minneapolis: University of Minnesota Press.

McDonald, M.G. (1999). Unnecessary roughness: Gender and racial politics in domestic violence media events. *Sociology of Sport Journal, 16*, 111–133.

Morrison, T. (Ed.). (1992). Race-ing justice, en-gendering power: Essays on Anita Hill, Clarence Thomas, and the construction of social reality. New York: Pantheon.

NBCSports.com. (2004, January 26). Attorney: Race possible motive in Kobe accusation: Suggestion made amid dispute over notes by rape crisis center. Retrieved November 15, 2004, from http://msnbc.com/id/4031624.

Pankratz, H., & Lipsher, S. (2003, December 12). Lawyers battle over t-shirts, media leaks judge wants names of seekers of anti-Kobe items. *The Denver Post*, p. B-04.

Reed, I. (2003). CNN's Ku Klux feminists unleashed on Kobe. *Konch Magazine*, 7/2. Retrieved November 15, 2004, from www.ishmaelreedpub.com.

Reed, I. (2004, Spring). MJ, Kobe, and Ola Benga: continuing the US war against black men. *Black Renaissance/Renaissance Noire, 15*(3), 43–59.

Reid, T.R. (2004, July 24). Some sexual details on accuser allowed; judge's ruling marks victory for Bryant. *Washington Post*, p. A2.

Roberts, D. (1995). Punishing drug addicts who have babies: Women of color, equality, and the right of privacy. In K. Crenshaw, et al. (Eds.), *Critical race theory: The key writings that formed the movement* (pp. 384–425). New York: New Press.

Rowe, D., McKay, J., & Miller, T. (2000). Panic sport and the racialized masculine body. In J. McCay, M.A. Messner, & D. Sabo (Eds.), *Masculinities, gender relations, and sport* (pp. 245–262). Thousand Oaks, CA: Sage.

Said, E. (1978). *Orientalism*. New York: Vintage.

Schanberg, S. (2002, November 20–26). A journey through the tangled case of the central park jogger: When justice is a game. *The Village Voice*. Retrieved November 15, 2003, from www.villagevoice.com/news/0247,schanberg,39999,l.html.

Shipp, E.R. (2003, October 2). Don't play race card in Kobe Bryant case. *The San Diego Union-Tribune*, p. B11.

Tanford, J.A., & Bocchino, A.J. (1980). Rape victim shield laws and the sixth amendment. *University of Pennslyvania Law Review, 128*, 544–602.

Tucker, L. (2003, November). Blackballed: Basketball and representations of the black male athlete. *American Behavioral Scientist, 47*(3), 306–328.

USA Today/CNN/Gallup poll results. (2003, August 7). Retrieved November 15, 2004, from www.usatoday.com/sports/basketball/nba/lakers/2003-08-07-kobe-usat-gallup.htm.

U.S. Department of Justice, Office of Justicc Programs. (2004, September). National crime victimization survey. Retrieved November 15, 2004, from www.rainn.org/docs/statistics/ncvs2004.pdf.

Young, C. (2003, October 27). Those accused of rape have rights, too. *The Boston Globe*. p. A13.

JOURNALING QUESTION

What were the first rape cases you remember hearing about? Was race a part of the story?

Family

30.
FROM *SHATTERED BONDS: THE COLOR OF CHILD WELFARE*

DOROTHY ROBERTS

The word "innocent" is routinely linked with the word "child." Whatever the responsibilities of adults for their own circumstances, surely children cannot be held accountable. Yet, as anyone who's seen photos of children in war-torn countries, in famines, or at the scene of natural disasters can attest to, children are made victims. Dorothy Roberts shows that children are also the victims of racism in America. It is nothing less than shocking to read that, as she tells us, the racial disparity of the child welfare system is like that of the prisons.

People do want to "rescue" children, to help children even if we do not have the political will to make more fundamental changes. So the root causes of famines may remain untouched, but food aid goes to children. In what ways has that very approach, rescuing the children without fixing the problem, created the problems in the child welfare system that Roberts describes?

THE COLOR OF AMERICA'S CHILD WELFARE SYSTEM

The child welfare system has always discriminated against Blacks, but its racism looked very different a century ago. Black families were virtually excluded from openly segregated child welfare services until the end of World War II.[1] Wealthy do-gooders began a charitable mission in the late nineteenth century to save poor children from parental cruelty and indigence. The orphanages they established to rescue destitute immigrant children refused to accept Blacks. The few "colored orphan asylums" were woefully inferior and overcrowded. By the time of the 1923 census, thirty-one northern states reported a total of 1,070 child-caring agencies. Of these agencies, 35 were for Black children only, 264 accepted all races, 60 took nonwhite children except Blacks, and 711 were reserved for white children.[2] Needy Black children were more likely to be labeled delinquent: "the major child caring institution for Black and other nonwhite children was the prison."[3] In the early part of the century, Black people relied primarily on extended family networks and community resources such as churches, women's clubs, and benevolent societies to take care of children whose parents were unable to meet their needs.

The child welfare system began to recognize Black children in the 1930s when services shifted from

Excerpted from Dorothy Roberts, *Shattered Bonds*: The Color of Child Welfare (New York: Basic Books, 2002), 6–10, 13–25. Notes have been renumbered and edited.

institutions to foster care and from private to public agencies.[4] Religious charities, which dominated child placements in large cities after World War II, continued to practice blatant racial discrimination. In New York City, for example, Jewish and Catholic agencies used religious preferences to close their doors to the city's predominantly Protestant Black children.[5] In 1973, the New York Civil Liberties Union filed a lawsuit challenging the city's participation in the agencies' racial discrimination. Although *Wilder* v. *Sugarman* was finally settled in 1988, the fight continued into the 1990s over the city's violations of the settlement agreement. In place of the segregated services, the city permitted an informal system that distributed children to foster care agencies based on gradations of skin shade and hair texture.[6]

The proportion of Black children in the public child welfare caseloads steadily increased in the years after World War II. The segment composed of nonwhite children almost doubled between 1945 and 1961, from 14 percent to 27 percent.[7] Twenty-four percent of the children served by public agencies in 1961 were Black. The child welfare rolls steadily filled with Black children over the next two decades. Then in the late 1980s two things happened to cement the child welfare systems current relationship to Black Americans: both the total size of the foster care population and the share of Black children exploded. The number of children in foster care has doubled in the last two decades, from 262,000 in 1982 to 568,000 in 1999.[8] The enormous growth in foster care caseloads in the late 1980s was concentrated primarily in cities, where there are sizable Black communities.[9] In 1986, Black children, who were only 15 percent of the population under age eighteen, made up about one-quarter of children entering foster care and 35 percent of children in foster care at the end of that year.[10] Today, *42 percent of all children in foster care nationwide are Black*, even though Black children constitute only 17 percent of the nations youth.[11]

Black families are the most likely of any group to be disrupted by child protection authorities.

Black children even stand out from other minorities. Latino and Asian American children are *underrepresented* in the national foster care population. Latino children make up only 15 percent of children in foster care although Latino children now outnumber Blacks in the general population. (Under U.S. Bureau of Census standards, children of "Hispanic origin" may be of any race.) Take, for instance, California, a state with a large Latino population. In 1995, 5 percent of all Black children in California were in foster care, compared to less than 1 percent of Latino children.[12] Only 1 percent of children in foster care nationwide are from Asian/Pacific Islander families.

The proportion of Black children in out-of-home care in large states such as California, Illinois, New York, and Texas ranges from three times to more than ten times as high as the proportion of white children.[13] Although only 19 percent of the child population in Illinois is Black, Black children make up more than 75 percent of the foster care population. Black children in Illinois were reported for maltreatment at a rate of 33 per 1000, compared to a rate of less than 10 per 1000 for white and Latino children.[14]

In big cities, the foster care population is almost exclusively Black, with a smaller percentage of Latino children, and only a tiny fraction of white children. More than 70 percent of foster children in San Francisco in 1994 were Black, although Blacks made up only 10 percent of the city's population.[15] Researchers found that Black children in San Diego are "markedly overrepresented" in the foster care system—at a rate of six times their proportion of the general population.[16]

The racial imbalance in New York City's foster care population is truly mind-boggling: out of 42,000 children in the system at the end of 1997, only 1,300 were white.[17] About 30 percent of the children who live in New York City are white. Yet white children make up only 3 percent of its foster care caseload. Less than 24 percent in foster care are Latino and the vast majority—73 percent—are

African American. Clearly, child welfare authorities consider foster care a last resort when it comes to white families.

Black children, on the other hand, are separated from their parents with relative ease. One out of every twenty-two Black children in New York City is in foster care. The systems grasp is even tighter on poor Black neighborhoods, such as Central Harlem, where one out of ten children has been placed in foster care. This means that in every apartment building in Central Harlem, we could expect to find at least one family whose children are in state custody. This is a far cry from the more reasonable odds for white children—only one out of 385.[18] Black children are ten times more likely to be placed in foster care in New York City than white children.

Although there are larger numbers of Black children in systems like Chicago and New York, the overrepresentation of these children is even greater in cities where Blacks are more of a minority. Researchers have proposed a "visibility hypothesis" to account for this disparity. The visibility hypothesis suggests that "there is a higher probability for minority children to be placed in foster care when living in a geographic area where they are relatively less represented (i.e., more 'visible')."[19] The chances of a Black child being placed in foster care are high in cities where Blacks make up a third to half of the population, but the chances are even higher where Blacks are a tiny minority. A comparison of foster care and census data in southern California revealed that where Blacks constitute 15 percent of the census, they are placed at a rate three times greater than their census proportion. Where they constitute less than 2 percent of the census, their placement rate soars to fifteen times their proportion of the population.[20] Researchers hypothesize that visibility increases the chances of minority placement because agencies are more likely to investigate underrepresented groups or because these groups lack social supports that could ward off investigation.

In summary, the foster care system in the nation's cities operates as an apartheid institution. It is a system designed to deal with the problems of minority families—primarily Black families—whereas the problems of white families are handled by separate and less disruptive mechanisms. That so many caseworkers, judges, and lawyers work every day in the belly of this system without speaking out shows just how accustomed we have become to racial separation in America. They routinely see nothing but Black parents and children in child welfare agencies and courts. But it seems normal to many Americans that Black families are more often split apart and supervised by the state.

THE SYSTEM'S INFERIOR TREATMENT OF BLACK CHILDREN

The first time I met Devon at her apartment in a stable Chicago neighborhood, she was anxious to show me around. The seven-room apartment was neat and well maintained. "You see, there's plenty of space for my nieces and nephews," she pointed out as we walked down the long corridor. We passed two bedrooms—one occupied by her sixteen-year-old daughter, Ebony–on our way to the dining room, where we sat down at the table to talk. Along one wall were stacked a number of plastic bins, which Devon said held the children's clothes. On the other wall was a chest of drawers filled with papers concerning het case–DCFS reports, psychological evaluations, medical records, court documents, her diplomas from child development classes. Devon pulled out a stack of photos of four smiling children celebrating birthdays and dressed in Halloween costumes. "These are my kids," she told me proudly.

Devon calls her nieces and nephews her kids because she has cared for them since they were toddlers. She took in her brother, the father of the children, and their mother, who had a serious drug addiction. Two of the children were born while the family was staying with her. In 1994, shortly after she had given birth to her sixth child, the mother told Devon that she was going to the hairdresser—and never came back. The oldest boy, who had a different father, went to live with a stepmother. The newborn was adopted by a white family. DCFS allowed Devon to keep the remaining four children, with ages spread between one and four.

Devon devoted her life to the children. All the children have asthma and developmental problems, and Devon had to master a complicated schedule involving dispensing numerous medications, transporting the children to school, family therapy sessions, and medical appointments, and keeping up with daily loads of laundry. She took classes so that she could receive a special license for relative foster care for medically complex children. When the mother's rights were terminated in April 1999, Devon made plans to adopt the children.

"I can't remember a time when I wasn't taking care of somebody's kids," Devon told me. She grew up with ten brothers and sisters on Chicago's west side. Her abusive mother kicked her out of the house in 1976 when she was nineteen, a college student with a baby girl named Portia. The frightened young mother found herself alone in the streets clutching her seven-month-old daughter and a garbage bag filled with her belongings. Devon went to live with an older sister for the next year and a half. She juggled courses in pediatrics and nutrition at Malcolm X College while caring for Portia and earned an associate degree in 1980. Devon soon started living with Ebony's father, an older man who was nothing but trouble. "He was a loser, a gambler, and a womanizer," Devon told me. "He never beat me, but he slept around." She kicked him out when their daughter Ebony was three years old. 'I was taking care of him and my daughters," Devon says. "I got tired of doing bad with a grown man. I can do bad all by myself."

Hoping to eventually get a job helping children, Devon took classes in child development, psychology, and pediatrics at local colleges as often as she could. She also volunteered for the Chicago Public Schools and worked as a counselor for a local social services agency, giving parents information about health, nutrition, and parenting skills. "I used to

ride to work on the city bus dressed up like a block of cheese or a carton of milk," Devon chuckled.

But family crises kept interrupting Devon's plans for a career. She raised three children of a sister who was strung out on drugs and alcohol. Three of her brothers, all drug addicts, were sent to prison. Devon regularly visited one who was incarcerated in Illinois. Then Devon suffered a personal setback. She was diagnosed in 1991 with cervical cancer, which she blames on a sexually transmitted disease she got from Ebony's father. The cancer spread to her breast. She underwent a lumpectomy, followed by radiation and chemotherapy. She had barely recovered when another brother who had contracted AIDS arrived in Chicago from Los Angeles where he had worked as a fashion designer. While he lay dying at a respite home, Devon and another sister took turns attending to him. When her sister had a stoke, "everything fell to me," Devon says. She finally received her B.A. from Loyola University in 1994, a year after her brother's death. "He made me promise on his death bed that I would continue taking care of my nieces and nephews," Devon told me. By then, the four children Devon now hoped to adopt were already living with her.

Everything went smoothly until the private agency that supervised her case assigned a new caseworker. The caseworker told Devon her apartment wasn't large enough for the children and that she would have to move. She noted that a hospital reported to DCFS that Devon had been treated for a mouse bite. She told Devon that she would have to prove she had a source of income other than the payments she received from DCFS to care for the children. Devon made sure her landlord repaired the baseboards where the mouse had apparently entered. She began looking for a bigger apartment that she could afford. In June 1999, the caseworker and one of the children's doctors got into an argument during an appointment, and Devon reported the caseworker's unprofessional conduct to DCFS. Devon believes the caseworker then decided to retaliate. Later that month, Devon and the children were enjoying a picnic celebrating her niece's graduation from kindergarten. In the middle of the festivities, security guards surrounded the family. The caseworker grabbed the terrified children and put them in a car, handing Devon a notice that DCFS was removing them from her custody.

The children were placed in foster care with a family in a distant suburb. Devon was allowed two supervised visits with the children in the first month after they were taken. Then the caseworker informed her that she couldn't see them again because they were being transitioned to adoption by their new foster mother. The caseworker thwarted Devon's attempts to contact the children.

Devon showed me a large stuffed dog holding a heart with the inscription "I love you." "She wouldn't let me give this to the children because it's inappropriate for me to show them any affection," Devon said. "She told me it would confuse them."...

Devon pursued every legal avenue she could find to regain custody of the children. At the removal hearing in juvenile court, she attempted to put on several witnesses to testify on her behalf, including a psychologist from University of Illinois at Chicago. But the judge refused to hear them. She filed an appeal of the judge's decision upholding the removal, scraping together the money to pay a private attorney to represent her. Her papers argue that DCFS failed to consider that she had successfully taken care of the children for more than seven years and that the children wanted to live with her. Devon showed me letters from her pastor, the children's teachers, a school principal, and the family's doctors praising her care for her nieces and nephews. "When I found out my rights, it became grounds for the agency to call me aggressive and confrontational," Devon says.

What seemed to trouble Devon most was that she was never given a chance to explain to the children why she disappeared. "Until my last dying breath, I'll continue to fight for my children," she told me. "All I can do is fight to let the kids know I didn't give up on them."

Not only are Black children the most likely to enter the child welfare system, but they also fare the worst under the state's supervision. Black children have the greatest odds of being removed from their homes and the smallest chance of being either reunited with their patents or adopted. They spend the most time in foster care and receive the least helpful services. The inferior treatment of Black children seems to be orchestrated at the policy level. As the child welfare caseloads have became increasingly Black, the number of out-of-home placements has risen dramatically as has the portion of funds spent on foster care as opposed to intact-family services.[21]

THE SYSTEM'S CHANGING RACIAL COMPOSITION AND APPROACH TO CHILD WELFARE

The child welfare crusade was conceived by early-twentieth-century progressives as a social reform movement that addressed a wide range of children's problems. Rescuing children from maltreatment by removing them from their homes was part of a broader campaign to remedy the social ills, including poverty, that harmed children. The movement also created the juvenile courts, opposed child labor, and lobbied for mandatory school attendance laws.[22] The crusaders established pensions for widows and single mothers to reduce the need for child removal. To be sure, the early reformers judged poor families by elitist standards and excluded Black children altogether. But they advocated a view of child maltreatment as an urgent *social* problem that should be addressed through various forms of *social* welfare and not just taking children from their parents. They understood that children's welfare was tied to social conditions that could only be improved by societywide reforms.

Efforts to develop a system rooted in a social vision of child welfare were squelched by the 1970s. In an attempt to secure bipartisan support for government spending on poor children, liberals such as Senator Walter Mondale abandoned their focus on poverty's harms to children. "This was part of a conscious strategy to dissociate efforts against abuse from unpopular poverty programs," writes public affairs professor Barbara Nelson in *Making an Issue of Child Abuse.* "The purpose was to describe abuse as an all-American affliction, not one found solely among low-income people.[23] Instead, Congress launched a campaign against the national problem of child abuse with the passage of the Child Abuse Prevention and Treatment Act in 1974. The government promoted, and the public came to accept, a medical model of child abuse—"a distinguishable pathological agent attacking the individual or family that could be treated in a prescribed manner and would disappear."[24] What was understood by some advocates as a social problem rooted in poverty and other societal inequities became widely interpreted as a symptom of individual parents' mental depravity.

This conception of children's problems came at great cost to poor families. For one thing, it is not at all clear that the focus on child protection has actually made children any safer. Child welfare researcher Duncan Lindsey makes a compelling case that there is no evidence that the enormous increase in child abuse reporting since the 1970s has reduced child abuse fatalities.[25]

What the new approach slashed was not child maltreatment but child welfare services. In the past several decades, the number of children receiving child welfare services has declined dramatically, while the foster care population has skyrocketed. These seemingly conflicting numbers reflect the transformation of the child welfare system from a social service system that tried to help needy families to a child protection system that investigates allegations of abuse and neglect. The number of children served by the child welfare system dropped from nearly 2 million in 1977 to 1 million in 1994.[26] The decrease reflects the dwindling number of children who received services while living at home.

At the same time, the number of white children in the system fell precipitously. The child welfare system served more than 1 million white children in 1977 but less than half that number (456,000) by 1994. As the child welfare rolls became increasingly Black, state and federal governments spent more money on out-of-home care and less on in-home services. Between 1977 and 1994, there was a 60 percent decline nationwide in the number of children receiving services in their homes.[27] For example, the percentage of children in the California system receiving family maintenance services fell from 31 percent in 1988 to 26 percent in 1995, while the foster care caseloads doubled.[28] One explanation for the shift in services is that children have more serious problems today, forcing agencies to direct a greater portion of their limited resources to crisis situations that require out-of-home care. But I don't think it's a coincidence that family services declined as the child welfare system began to serve fewer white and more Black children.

The same sort of metamorphosis occurred when the civil rights movement made the welfare system available to Black citizens.[29] Just as Blacks were once ignored by the child welfare system, Blacks were largely excluded from the New Deal welfare programs by restrictive state eligibility requirements. Aid to Dependent Children, enacted in 1935 to prevent removal of children from their homes for financial reasons, went primarily to white mothers. In the 1960s, the welfare rights movement secured entitlements to welfare benefits. Welfare caseloads that were once almost exclusively white quickly became half nonwhite. Expanding welfare entitlements fit within President Lyndon Johnson's War on Poverty, whose federal housing and economic programs attempted to integrate more Blacks into the national political economy. But as welfare became increasingly associated with Black mothers, it became increasingly burdened with behavior modification rules, work requirements, and reduced effective benefits levels. Black welfare recipients were stigmatized as lazy, dependent, and depraved.

The image of the welfare mother changed from the worthy white widow to the immoral Black welfare queen. By the mid-1990s, the American public equated welfare with Black social degeneracy and successfully demanded that the federal safety net for poor children be dismantled and that welfare recipients be put to work.

The abrogation of child welfare's social service function in the 1970s occurred as a white backlash decimated the War on Poverty programs. In *The Color of Welfare*, sociologist Jill Quadagno demonstrates that whites opposed the War on Poverty precisely because of its link to Black civil rights.[30] For example, federal housing subsidies plummeted after 1968, when white homeowners, backed by the powerful real estate lobby, resisted residential integration. White Americans rejected a social welfare solution to poverty at the same time that they rejected a social welfare solution to child maltreatment. As the welfare and child welfare systems oversaw an increasingly Black clientele, they both reduced their services to families while intensifying their punitive functions.

BLACK CHILDREN ARE MORE LIKELY TO BE SEPARATED FROM THEIR PARENTS

The child protection philosophy that has reigned for the past three decades has served Black families poorly. The worst part of this punitive approach is that it unnecessarily separates Black children from their parents. Child protective agencies are far more likely to place Black children in foster care rather than offering their families less traumatic assistance. As I pointed out, the systems orientation changed along with the racial composition of its caseloads. Black children have suffered the most from this shift: agencies put Black children in out-of-home custody at dramatically higher rates than other children. According to federal statistics, 56 percent of Black children in the child welfare system have been placed in foster care—twice the percentage for white children.[31] A national study of child protective services by the U.S. Department of Health and Human Services reported that "minority children, and in particular African American children, are more likely to be in foster care placement than receive in-home services, *even when they have the same problems and characteristics as white children.*"[32]

White children who are abused or neglected are twice as likely as Black children to receive services in their own homes, avoiding the emotional damage and physical risks of foster care placement. Put another way, most white children who enter the system are permitted to stay with their families, whereas most Black children are taken away from theirs. Foster care is the main "service" that state agencies provide to Black children brought to their attention. Government authorities appear to believe that maltreatment of Black children results from pathologies intrinsic to their homes and that helping them requires dislocating them from their families. Child welfare for Black children usually means shattering the bonds with their parents.

It bears pausing a moment to visualize the consequences of the system's racially divided treatment of children. Once caseworkers determine that a report of child abuse or neglect is "indicated," or substantiated by evidence, they must next decide how to protect the child. The most critical choice they make is whether to remove the child from the home or to provide services to the family while keeping it intact. The repercussions of this decision are monumental.

Think for a moment what it means to rip children from their parents and their brothers and sisters and to place them in the care of strangers. Removing children from their homes is perhaps the most severe government intrusion into the lives of citizens. It is also one of the most terrifying experiences a child can have. Because parents involved with child protective services are so often portrayed as brutal monsters, the public usually ignores the trauma experienced by the children. But most children in foster care, who typically have been removed because of neglect, have close and loving relationships with their parents, and it is indescribably painful to be separated from them. "Children do not oblige us by hating their parents the way we may think they should," says Richard Wexler, director of the National Coalition for Child Protection Reform. "Often, neglected children love their parents just as much as our children love us. Tearing children from their parents almost always leaves emotional scars."[33]

When children are seized from helpless parents by more powerful government agents, it creates a sense of vulnerability and betrayal in children, who rely on their parents to keep them safe. It is doubly traumatic to then be dropped unexpectedly into the care of a strange adult. This is true even in the best of foster homes, never mind what befalls children in the hands of uncaring or abusive foster parents. The emotional damage increases with the length of time children spend separated from their families and with the number of moves they are required to make.

Of course, these harms of removal may be outweighed by the harm of leaving children with violent or extremely neglectful parents. In some extreme cases, it would be ludicrous to worry about harming children by rescuing them from life-threatening situations. But just as we should pay attention to the risks of child maltreatment, we should not minimize the very real pain caused by separating children from their families. The damage caused by disrupting these ties may be far greater than the harm agencies are trying to avoid.

The judge commended Devon for her extraordinary devotion to her four nieces and nephews, whom she showered with affection, tirelessly shuttled to specialists, and advocated for in social service offices. But that didn't stop him from breaking up her family because her apartment was too small. Whatever risks Devon's home posed for those children could not possibly have outweighed the certain emotional damage the caseworker caused when she abruptly sent them away from their aunt. According to psychologist Seth Farber, "only

a small minority of these children have been separated from parents who are dangerous to them. The overwhelming majority have been separated from loving and responsible parents. One does not need to be a child psychologist to realize the devastating effect of removing a child from parents with whom he or she is deeply bonded.[34] And there is no justification for dismissing the pain of family breakup because of race.

There are other devastating consequences of removal, as well. When children are taken from the home, the chances for long-term state interference in the family are intensified. It becomes likely that children will spend months or years in foster care and may never make it back to their families. The racial split in in-home services versus out-of-home placements, then, has a tremendously adverse impact on Black families.

BLACK CHILDREN SPEND MORE TIME IN FOSTER CARE

The racial disparity in child removal is enough to indict the system. But taking children from their homes is only the beginning of the state's inferior treatment of Black families. Once Black children enter the foster care system, they remain there longer, are moved more often, and receive less desirable placements than white children. White children tend to return home quickly, whereas Black children tend to languish in foster care. Nearly half of white children who are placed in foster care return home within three months; very few Black children do.[35] This timing is especially significant because the probability of children being reunited with their parents is high immediately after placement. But the chances of reunification begin to dwindle rapidly after the first five months of placement.[36]

BLACK CHILDREN RECEIVE INFERIOR SERVICES

Not only do Black children enter the system in disproportionate numbers and for longer periods of time, but they also receive lower-quality services once they get there. Studies show that Black children involved in the child welfare system receive inferior treatment according to every measure, including provision of both in-home and adoption services, recommended versus actual length of placement, and worker contact with the child and caregivers.[37]

Inadequate housing is often part of the reason Black children are placed in substitute care or are not reunited with their parents. A national study of Black children in foster care conducted by the National Black Child Development Institute in 1989 found that more than 10 percent of children entered foster care from shelters and that inadequate housing was a factor in nearly one-third of placements.[38] U.S. Department of Health and Human Services study found that Black children in the system are more likely to come from families with housing problems than white children.[39] Yet the study also discovered that among families with housing problems, white families are offered housing services at almost twice the rate as Black families (43 percent compared to 25 percent).

Caseworkers put the least effort into keeping Black foster children in contact with their parents and into returning them home.[40] Black parents often get lousy visitation arrangements, at times and places that make it hard for them to see their children. One study discovered that Black children had fewer visits with their parents, fewer services overall, and less contact with caseworkers. The findings suggested that their parents were viewed as "less likely to profit from services designed to enhance their ability to maintain or assume responsibility for caring for their children at home."[41] A grand jury that reviewed foster care files in Contra Costa County, California, in 1995 criticized caseworkers for "ethnic insensitivity" in handling minority children in the system.[42] Records for white children were "consistently more detailed, better prepared, and oriented toward family reunification, adoption, or guardianship" than records for minority children, the grand jury said. The jurors discovered that whereas white children's files contained

"well-documented" permanency plans, "records reviewed did not exhibit reasonable and consistent efforts on the part of social workers to research and document, in detail, the backgrounds of the minority child." The result was "considerable delay" in minority children's progress through the system.

The provision of mental health treatment further illustrates the racial gap in services....The research showed that white children benefited both from stronger legal advocacy for mental health services and from judicial preferences in favor of ordering these services for whites. In other words, Black children removed from their homes were less likely than white children to receive mental health counseling because judges and caseworkers fail to recommend it for them and because the services aren't available in their neighborhoods.

The alternative to receiving counseling for many Black children in foster care is being labeled a problem child or juvenile delinquent, with far more punitive consequences. Although Black foster children receive less mental health counseling, they are more likely to be sent to institutions.[43] A 1998 study of out-of-home care in California discovered that caseworkers more frequently placed African American children in "treatment" foster care, such as a psychiatric facility, as opposed to foster family or kinship home placement.[44] Caseworkers were likely to place children they thought had behavioral disturbances in these specialized settings as a way of addressing the perceived problem. The study's author noted that the decision to place a child in treatment foster care has a number of negative implications: it often requires moving the child a long distance from his or her family; it implies that the child is "different" from children who are placed with families; and it costs much more than foster family and kinship care.

BLACK CHILDREN ARE MORE LIKELY TO GET STUCK IN FOSTER CARE

Partly as a result of this inferior treatment, Black children are less likely than white children to be either returned home or adopted. A study of more than 8,000 children in the California foster care system from 1989 to 1992 found that race played a role in both outcomes: "Being African American was associated with a significant decrease relative to other groups in the probability of both discharge to family or guardian and adoption.[45] The researchers concluded, "The lower [chances] of favorable discharge for African American children indicate that, once in care, many of these children are likely to remain indefinitely."

Another analysis of the California data found that Black children were twice as likely to remain in foster care as to be adopted, whereas white children were twice as likely to be adopted as to remain in care. Black children's odds of being adopted are five times less than those of white children.[46] Latino children were about equally likely to experience either outcome. A similar finding was reported in a study of family reunification in Maricopa County, Arizona: Black children in this sample were half as likely as white children to return home.[47]

When children in foster care have neither biological nor adoptive homes to go to, they often become legal orphans. Courts may terminate the rights of their parents but have no new parents to give them, so the children remain in foster care, with no legal ties to any parent. Black children are the most likely to acquire this unenviable status because their odds of being reunited with their parents and of adoption are both so miserable. As a result, most of the 118,000 children nationwide whose family ties have been severed and who are waiting to be adopted are Black.[48]

A recent trend in the placement of Black children is affecting the quality of services they get. More and more Black children are placed with relatives, an arrangement known as kinship care. Between 1986 and 1990, the proportion of foster children living with relatives grew from 18 percent to 31 percent in twenty-five states.[49] In Illinois, for example, placements with relatives increased 232

percent in a five-year period.[50] By 1997, there were at least as many relative care givers as traditional foster parents in California, Illinois, and New York.[51] An exploding foster care population combined with a shortage of licensed nonrelative foster homes made relatives an attractive placement option.[52] The passage of federal law that encouraged family preservation and court decisions guaranteeing relatives the opportunity to serve as foster care providers also facilitated this development.[53] In the landmark 1979 decision *Miller v. Youakim*, for example, the United States Supreme Court held that otherwise eligible relatives could not be denied foster parent certification and the same financial support as non-kin providers."[54]

Kinship care has many advantages for Black children. It usually preserves family, community, and cultural ties. But it also has a downside. Kinship care follows a familiar pattern of discriminatory services. Black children in kinship care receive fewer services than do children in nonrelative foster care and fewer services than white children in kinship care. Agencies tend to devote fewer resources to reunification of children in kinship foster care with their parents.[55] Caseworkers have less contact with relatives and the children in their care and are less likely to offer them services.[56] In a Baltimore study, for example, twice as many foster care families received two or more services as families involved in kinship care.[57] A lawsuit filed in 1986 by the Legal Aid Society on behalf of children in kinship foster care in New York City charged that the child welfare agency delayed paying relatives their stipends and issuing children their Medicaid cards and failed to provide families with necessities such as beds, clothes, and school supplies.[58]

Of particular concern is the inferior health care received by children in kinship foster care. According to a 1995 federal report, children placed with relatives were less likely to receive health-related services than children in traditional foster care; in fact, they were three times as likely to get no routine health care at all.[59] In a study of premature, low-birth-weight infants in kinship care, only 13 percent received appropriate health care.[60] Most of the children did not receive adequate well-baby visits or immunizations, and many used emergency rooms for primary care.

It seems that some agencies view the placement of children with relatives as a way of cutting costs. Perhaps they believe that children need fewer services if they are being cared for by a grandmother or an aunt. But many kinship care givers come from poor or low-income families like the grandchildren, nieces, and nephews placed in their homes. They are more likely to be single females and to have less income, more health problems, and more children to take care of than nonrelative foster parents.[61] A study of foster parents in Ohio found that although African American foster parents reported more satisfaction with fostering than whites, they experienced more economic barriers to providing foster care.[62] They are therefore in *greater* need of state assistance. Because Black children are the most likely to be placed with relatives, these policies systematically provide inferior financial support and services for Black children in state custody.

Why would Americans prefer a punitive system that needlessly separate thousands of children from their parents and consigns millions more to social exclusion and economic deprivation? Racism is at the heart of this tragic choice. Only by coming to terms with child welfare's racial injustice can we turn from the costly path of family destruction.

NOTES

1. Andrew Billingsley and Jeanne M. Giovannoni, *Children of the Storm: Black Children and American Child Welfare* (New York: Harcourt Brace Jovanovich, 1972), pp. 34–38; David Rosner and Gerald Markowitz, "Race, Foster Care, and the Politics of Abandonment in New York City," *American journal of Public Health* 87 (1997); 1844.
2. Billingsley and Giovannoni, *Children of the Storm*, p. 76.
3. Ibid., p. 80.
4. Ibid., pp. 77–79.
5. Rosner and Markowitz, "Race, Foster Care, and the Politics of Abandonment in New York City"; Nina Bernstein, *The Lost Children of Wilder: The Epic Struggle to Change Foster Care* (New York: Pantheon, 2001); Richard Wexler, *Wounded Innocents: The Real Victims of the War Against Child Abuse* (Buffalo, N.Y.: Prometheus Books, 1990, 1995), pp. 221–224.
6. Bernstein, *The Lost Children of* Wilder; "Foster Placement by Skin Shade Is Charged," *New York Times*, January 18, 1990, p. B1.
7. Billingsley and Giovannoni, *Children of the Storm*, p. 93.
8. U.S. Dept. of Health and Human Services, Administration for Children and Families, "The AFCARS Report: Current Estimates as of October 2000," p. 1, available at www.acf.dhhs.gov/programs/cb; Office of the Assistant Secretary for Planning Evaluation, U.S. Department of Health and Human Services, *Trends in the Well-Being of Children and Youth*: 1996 (Washington, D.C.: U.S. Department of Health and Human Services, 1996), p. 2.
9. Robert Goerge, Fred Wulczyn, and Allen Harden, "New Comparative Insights into States and Their Foster Children," *Public Welfare* 54 (1996): 12, 15.
10. Select Committee on Children, Youth, and Families, *U.S. Children and Their Families: Current Conditions and Recent Trends* (Washington, D.C.: U.S. House of Representatives, 1989).
11. Administration for Children and Families, U.S. Department of Health and Human Services, "The AFCARS Report: Current Estimates as of October 2000," p. 2 (reporting that 42 Percent of children in foster care are Black).

12. California, Legislative Analyst's Office, *Child Abuse and Neglect in California: A Review of the Child Welfare Services Program* (Sacramento: Legislative Analyst's Office, 1996).
13. Robert M. Goerge, Fred S. Wulczyn, and Allen Harden, *Foster Care Dynamics, 1983–1992: California, Illinois, Michigan, New York, and Texas—A First-Year Report from the Multi-State Foster Care Data Archive* (Chicago: Chapin Hall Center for Children, 1994).
14. Bong Joo Lee and Robert Goerge, "Poverty, Early Child bearing, and Child Maltreatment: A Multinomial Analysis," *Children and Youth Services Review* 21 (1999): 755.
15. Teresa Moore, "Social Worker's Hard Choices, Soft Heart," *San Francisco Chronicle* March 8, 1995, p. Al.
16. Ann F, Garland et al., "Minority Populations in the Child Welfare System: The Visibility Hypothesis Reexamined," *American Journal of Orthopsychiatry* 68 (1998): 142.
17. Martin Guggenheim, "Somebody's Children: Sustaining the Family's Place in Child Welfare Policy," *Harvard Law Review* 113 (2000): 1716, 1718. n. 11, citing New York City Administration for Children's Services, *Selected Child Welfare Trends* 81 (1998).
18. Ibid.; Center for an Urban Future, "Race, Bias, and Power in Child Welfare," *Child Welfare Watch* (Spring/Summer 1998): 1.
19. Ann F. Garland et al., "Minority Populations in the Child Welfare System: The Visibility Hypothesis Reexamined," *American Journal of Orthopsychiatry* 68 (1998): 142, 143 Shirley Jenkins and Beverly Diamond, "Ethnicity and Foster Care: Census Data as Predictors of Placement Variables," *American Journal of Orthopsychiatry* 55 (1985): 267.
20. Garland et al., "Minority Populations in the Child Welfare System," p. 145.
21. Leroy H. Pelton, *For Reasons of Poverty: A Critical Analysis of the Public Child Welfare System in the United States* (New York: Praeger, 1989), p. 20.
22. William I. Trattner, *From Poor Law to Welfare State; A History of Social Welfare in America* (New York: Free Press, 1989), pp. 110–139.
23. Barbara J. Nelson, *Making an Issue of Child Abuse: Political Agenda Setting for Social Problems* (Chicago: University of Chicago Press, 1984).
24. Alvin Schorr, "The Bleak Prospect for Public Child Welfare," *Social Service Review* 74 (2000): 124.
25. Duncan Lindsey, *The Welfare of Children* (New York: Oxford University Press, 1994), pp. 89–126.
26. U.S. Department of Health and Human Services, Children's Bureau, *National Study of Protective, Preventive, and Reunification Services Delivered to Children and Their Families* (Washington, D.C.: U.S. Government Printing Office, 1997).
27. Ibid.
28. Legislative Analyst's Office, *Child Abuse and Neglect in California*.
29. Dorothy Roberts, *Killing the Black Body: Race, Reproduction, and the Meaning of Liberty* (New York: Pantheon, 1997), pp. 203–209.
30. Jill Quadagno, *The Color of Welfare: How Racism Undermined the War on Poverty* (New York: Oxford University Press, 1994).
31. U.S. Department of Health and Human Services, *National Study*.
32. U.S. Department of Health and Human Services, *National Study*, Executive Summary, Finding 4, p. 3 (emphasis added).
33. Richard Wexler, "Geisinger Case Badly Mishandled; Early Intervention Leads to Much Better Solutions in Child Endangerment Cases," *Portland Press Herald*, May 4, 2000, p. 11.

34. Seth Faber, "The Real Abuse," *National Review,* April 12, 1993, p. 47.

35. U.S. Department of Health and Human Services, *National Study.*

36. Mark E. Courtney and Vin-Ling Irene Wong, "Comparing the Timing of Exists from Substitute Care," *Children and Youth Services Review* 18 (1996): 307, 320.

37. Ibid.; Mary M. Close, "Child Welfare and People of Color: Denial of Equal Access," *Social Work Research and Abstracts* (1983): 13; and Ketayun H. Gould, "Limiting Damage Is Not Enough: A Minority Perspective on Child Welfare Issues," in *Child Welfare: An Africentric Perspective,* ed, Joyce E. Everett, Sandra S. Chipungu, and Bogart R. Leashore (New Brunswick, N.J.: Rutgers University Press, 1991), pp. 58, 59.

38. Loring P. Jones, "Social Class, Ethnicity, and Child Welfare," *Journal of Multicultural Social Work* 6 (1997): 123, 128, citing National Black Child Development Institute, *The Black Child in Foster Care* (Washington, D.C.: National Black Child Development Institute, 1989).

39. U.S. Department of Health and Human Services, *National Study.*

40. Close, "Child Welfare and People of Color"; Sandra M. Stehno, "The Elusive Continuum of Child Welfare Services: Implications for Minority Children and Youth," *Child Welfare* 69 (1990): 551.

41. Close, "Child Welfare and People of Color," p. 19.

42. Erin Hallissy, "Foster Care Criticized by Grand Jury; System Assailed as Unfair to Minority Children," *San Francisco Chronicle,* June 1, 1995, p. A13.

43. Mary Davidson and Gary Anderson, "Child Welfare and Title VI," *Social Work* (March 1982): 147, 150 n. 10.

44. Mark E. Courtney, "Correlates of Social Worker Decisions to Seek Treatment-Oriented Out-of-Home Care," *Children and Youth Services Review* 20 (1998): 281.

45. Courtney and Wong, "Comparing the Timing of Exits from Substitute Care," p. 328.

46. Richard P. Barth, "Effects of Age and Race on the Odds of Adoption versus Remaining in Long-Term Out-of-Home Care," *Child Welfare* 76 (1997): 285.

47. S. McMurtry and G. Lie, "Differential Exit Rates of Minority Children in Foster Care," *Social Work Research and Abstracts* 28 (1992): 42.

48. Administration for Children and Families, U.S. Department of Health and Human Services, "The AFCARS Report: Current Estimates as of October 2000," p. 3.

49. Annie Woodley Brown and Barbara Bailey-Etta, "An Out-of-Home Care System in Crisis: Implications for African American Children in the Child Welfare System," *Child Welfare* 76 (1997): 76.

50. James Gleeson, "Kinship Care as a Child Welfare Service: The Policy Debate in an Era of Welfare Reform," *Child Welfare* 75 (1996): 419, 429.

51. James P Gleeson et al., "Understanding the Complexity of Practice in Kinship Foster Care," *Child Welfare* 76 (1997): 801, 802.

52. Rob Geen, "In the Interest of Children: Rethinking Federal and State Policies Affecting Kinship Care," *Policy and Practice* (March 2000): 19, 21; Jill Duerr Berrick, "When Children Cannot Remain Home: Foster Family Care and Kinship Care," *Future of Children* (1998): 72, 74.

53. Madeleine L. Kurtz, "The Purchase of Families into Foster Care: Two Case Studies and the Lessons They leach," *Connecticut Law Review* 26 (1994): 1453, 1454; Geen, "In the Interest of Children," pp. 21–22; Gleeson, "Kinship Care as a Child Welfare Service," p. 425.

54. 440 U.S. 125 (1979).

55. Kurtz, "The Purchase of Families into Foster Care," p. 1472.

56. Timothy Gebel, "Kinship Care and Nonrelative Family Foster Care: A Comparison of Caregiver Attributes and Attitudes," *Child Welfare* 75 (1996): 5; Jill D. Berrick et al., "A Comparison of Kinship Foster Homes and Foster Family Homes: Implications for Kinship Foster Care as Family Preservation," *Children and Youth Services Review* 16 (1994): 33; Gleeson et al., "Understanding the Complexity of Practice in Kinship Foster Care," p. 803.

57. Maria Scannapieco et al., "Kinship Care and Foster Care: A Comparison of Characteristics and Outcomes," *Families in Society* 78 (1997): 480, 487.

58. Maria Gottlieb Zwas, "Kinship Foster Care: A Relatively Permanent Solution," *Fordham Urban Law Journal* 20 (1993): 343, 355–356.

59. "Foster Care: Health Needs of Many Young Children Are Unknown and Unmet Letter Report Number HEHS–95–114 (Washington, D.C.: Government Accounting Office) March 26, 1995.

60. S. Gennaro, "Vulnerable Infants: Kinship Care and Health," *Pediatric Nursing* (1998): 119.

61. Gleeson, "Kinship Care as a Child Welfare Scrvice" p. 442; Gleeson et al., "Understanding the Complexity of Practice in Kinship Foster Care," p. 803; Berrick et al., "A Comparison of Kinship Foster Homes and Foster Family Homes," pp. 36, 57.

62. Ramona Denby and Nolan Rindfleisch, "African Americans' Foster Parenting Experiences: Research Findings and Implications for Policy and Practice," *Children and Youth Service Review* 18 (1996): 544, 547.

JOURNALING QUESTION

If you were a caseworker, what would you have done to help Devon and the children?

31.

BECOMING AN AMERICAN PARENT

Overcoming Challenges and Finding Strength in a New Immigrant Latino Community

KRISTA M. PERREIRA, MIMI V. CHAPMAN, AND GABRIELA L. STEIN

Adolescence is hard enough for anyone. The transition from child to adult is notoriously difficult for both adolescents and their parents. For immigrant families, this transition is all the harder: as children grow up and out of their parents' homes, they are also growing up and into a culture different from that of their parents. As Krista Perreira, Mimi Chapman, and Gabriela Stein show, parents chose to come to the United States specifically to help their children. But that move also had a cost for their children, as they lost the companionship and support of their extended families and communities. These authors show that to ease this transition, Latino parents draw upon community supports, open up communication, and respect and empathize with their adolescents. Do you think that the strategies they use would be helpful for nonimmigrant families as well?

At the turn of the 21st century, Latinos became the largest minority group living in the United States, and Latino youth became the fastest growing segment of the U.S. population under 18 years of age (Ramirez & de la Cruz, 2003; U.S. Census Bureau, 2001). The majority of these Latino youth are the first-generation or second-generation children of immigrants (Hernandez, 1997; Suárez-Orozco & Suárez-Orozco, 2001). Given these demographic trends, practitioners and researchers in several fields (e.g., education, health, psychology, public policy, and social work) have become increasingly interested in understanding the normative behaviors and adaptive strategies of Latino parents and the developmental outcomes of their children.

Using qualitative methods, this analysis explores the ways in which Latinos describe their migration and acculturation experiences in relation to their role as parents in one of the fastest growing new immigrant–receiving communities in the United States—North Carolina. Through our research, we develop a model of risk and resiliency that incorporates the culture and diversity of Latino immigrant families. Our model describes factors that influence acculturative stress and intergenerational conflict in Latino immigrant families and parents' cultural adaptations to life in the United States. Based on our analysis, we identify a wide array of intervention points that may enhance clinicians' abilities to work constructively with Latino parents and youth. As a result, this analysis provides new insights that researchers can use in developing community programs and therapeutic interventions that support the transitions of Latino immigrant youth and their families to the United States.

Excerpted from Krista M. Perreira, Mimi V. Chapman, and Gabriela L. Stein, "Becoming an American Parents: Overcoming Challenges and Finding Strength in a New Immigrant Latino Community, "*Journal of Family Issues*, 27 (2006): 1383–1414. References have been edited.

METHOD

INFORMANTS

An extremely heterogeneous group, Latinos include persons of various racial and socioeconomic backgrounds from more than 20 countries of origin (Harwood et al., 2002). They differ substantially in terms of the historical and personal circumstances of their arrivals to the United States, their levels of acculturation to the United States, and their experiences with the local communities in which they settle (Garcia, 2001; Massey, Durand, & Malone, 2002; Portes & Rumbaut, 2001; Vega, 1990). Our data consist of 18 interviews with first-generation Latino immigrant parents living in North Carolina. North Carolina's Latino population grew 394% from 77,000 in 1990 to 379,000 in 2000 (U.S. Census Bureau, 2001). In 2000, it was the fastest growing Latino immigrant community in the United States and reflected a new trend in the demography of immigration—settlement in the South, Midwest, and mountainous regions of the United States (Johnson, Johnson-Webb, & Farrell, 1999).

Although Latinos in North Carolina are more likely to be recent immigrants, on average, their demographic characteristics are similar to Latinos living in other parts of the United States (see Ramirez & de la Cruz, 2003, and Suro & Passel, 2003, for comprehensive reviews). The majority of North Carolina's Latino population is foreign born (61%), male (60%), under age 25 (53%), and of Mexican heritage (65%). They speak only Spanish (82%) and have not completed high school by age 25 (55%). Given these labor market disadvantages, it is not surprising to find a high unemployment rate (8%), high poverty rate (25%), and low rate of health insurance (46%) within North Carolina's Latino immigrant population (U.S. Census Bureau, 2001).

The characteristics of the Latino parents we interviewed were quite similar to those of the average Latino family in North Carolina. The majority of the parents interviewed were mothers (83%) who were married or living with a partner (80%). Most

(61%) of our parents and children had moved to the United States from Mexico within the past 5 years.... Four were from Colombia; two were from Argentina; and one was from El Salvador. Despite their limited time in the United States, 28% of the children and 17% of their parents identified as bicultural on the 10-item Psychological Acculturation Scale (Tropp, Coll, Alarcon, & Vazquez Garcia, 1999). Several had lived in traditional receiving communities in California, New York, New Jersey, Texas, or Florida prior to moving to North Carolina. The ages of our parental respondents varied from 30 to 51 years, with a mean age of 39 years. Their adolescent children varied in age from 12 to 17 years with a mean age of 14 years. Although many (57%) had not completed high school and spoke little or no English, most of the mothers interviewed worked in the service sector as housekeepers, child care providers, and nurse's aides. Their partners and the fathers interviewed also tended to work in the service sector but as manual laborers (e.g., gardeners, painters, carpenters). They reported earning an average of $1,855 per month but indicated that their earnings varied significantly throughout the year. As a result, their annual incomes were typically below $20,000. Given that the families were supporting at least 4 persons with this income, nearly all of them lived at or near the federal poverty level ($18,392 for a family of 4) in 2002.

PROCEDURES

Our 18 in-depth interviews with Latino parents were conducted as part of a larger study that included in-depth interviews with one adolescent child of each parent and the completion of a survey that included questions on socioeconomic background, acculturation, and mental health. Informants completed the survey component after the completion of the in-depth interview...

By listening to our informants tell their stories, we gained insight into the process of becoming a Latino immigrant parent in the United States. The qualitative research process allowed our informants to teach us, from their perspective, about the issues and concerns of greatest relevance to their lives. They contextualized their immigration experiences for us and informed us about what systems were most helpful to them, what struggles were the most difficult or the most easily overcome, and how parents and youth saw their relationships with one another.

IMMIGRATION AS A PARENTING DECISION

Theories of migration focus on immigration as an economic decision aimed at improving individual or household wealth and supported by social and structural forces that reduce the challenges of migration and increase the expected gains from migration (Massey et al., 2002). Our interviews demonstrated that at least for Latino immigrants with children, the decision to immigrate could also be understood as a parenting decision. Nearly three quarters (N = 13) of our informants spontaneously mentioned at least one aspect of parenting when asked "What motivated your family to move to this country?" The major parenting themes that initially resonated with respondents as they discussed their motivations to immigrate to the United States included helping their children to obtain a better education, to secure a better economic future, to grow up in a safer environment, and to reconnect with family...

Exemplifying migration as a parenting decision aimed at securing a better education and economic future for her children, a Mexican mother explained,

In our country, it would be difficult for them to be able to study in the university. So the motivation for our move was my kids. So that they could study.

Exemplifying the quest for physical security for children, a Colombian woman stated with nervous laughter,

I have a niece, and oh my God, I don't want her to grow up over there. If it were for me, I'd bring my entire family here! Oh my God! The adolescents, my God, are very dangerous! It's a war of complete

distrust of everyone. We just count on ourselves. It's not that adolescents are bad, but it's the internal condition of living: no work, no opportunities, poor education, expensive education, no respect for private space, and saddest of all, no compassion for people.

Several of the immigrant parents interviewed for our study had been separated from their children for months or years. In some cases, children were left in their home countries while the parents initiated the migration process. In other cases, children moved to the United States and stayed with extended family or a father before the mother and other children followed. Thus, as parents and their children are adjusting to life in the United States, they are also adjusting to each other (Suárez-Orozco & Suárez-Orozco, 2001).

Emphasizing family reunification as a primary motivation for their move to the United States, one 42-year-old mother explained her decision to come despite her husband's discouragement. She said,

He told us that we would have a lot of problems here because of the language. The children would have to adapt. I would have to find a job.... And I still said, "No. I want to come," because it had been such a long time since we had seen him.

A statement by a younger mother reflected this same sentiment:

When my husband would come visit us every 3 or 4 months and he would leave, [my daughters] would cry. They would tell him, "I will go with you Daddy. I will go with you." And so when my family would make comments that I could not come here, that I would never have a complete home like my father's other daughters, that is what drove me to say, "I am going." And I decided to come.

As the interviews progressed, all of our respondents eventually discussed one or more aspects of their migration and acculturation experiences in relation to their roles as parents. Following inspection, these could be categorized as aspects of immigrant parenting that required overcoming new challenges or finding new strengths.

OVERCOMING CHALLENGES

Although the journey to the United States began with hope for their economic futures and the futures of their children, the realities of immigration took root quickly. Nearly all of our respondents reported facing tremendous challenges as they began to help their children navigate their new environments and cope with significant personal losses and unexpected changes in family roles and responsibilities....Many (67%) of our informants also discussed facing these challenges while struggling through generalized anxiety regarding their new living environment and its effects on their children. For more than half (56%) of our informants, one particularly salient aspect of the new environment was race and ethnicity. For the first time, our informants were interacting with African Americans and confronting negative U.S. social stereotypes of Latinos.

NAVIGATING NEW SOCIAL CONTEXTS

As parents discussed their migration and acculturation experiences, they focused on the challenges of learning a new language and building community with Americans. The difficulty of learning a new language and culture were coupled with the challenges associated with navigating the U.S. school and health care systems and balancing work and family.

Language

In helping their children navigate a new world, parents must first overcome the language barrier. Without the ability to communicate, parents felt helpless, alienated, and unable to advocate on behalf of their children. A well-educated Argentinean mother commenting on her first memory of the United States said, "I didn't understand anything completely—nothing. That put me in a type of jail, you know. I couldn't communicate for the first time in my life. It was like I wasn't a part of this society."

The language barrier became increasingly palpable, as parents sought to help their children do their homework and navigate the school system. As one Mexican mother commented, "Well, basically, when she started elementary school. It was a little hard because P's first language was Spanish. In that time, I did not speak English to help her." As children learn English in school, they sometimes come to resent their parents' Spanish monolingualism or become embarrassed by their parents. One mother explained to us,

> Oh, yes, when [my daughter] started going to school, that was when she started learning English.... Her problem was that she would come home and she would start to talking to me in English, and I would say, "Speak Spanish." And she would say, "Why, if I don't need it?" She started rebelling, like saying, "Oh no. I don't want to speak Spanish."... And she would say, "Mommy, why can't Daddy go to the [school] conferences? It is that I don't want you to go." And so for me, it was not hard. It was extremely hard. Because I would feel really badly, really badly.... And I would say, "Daughter, I am your mother."... There was a time, when she was already about 8 years old...that she wanted to run away from home to live with her friend because her friend had an American mom, and I was a Hispanic mom.

Community

As they continued their struggle with the language, parents explained that they began to struggle with the culture as well. Without a sense of community and without knowing the parents of their children's friends, they did not feel safe allowing their children to attend friends' parties, to attend sleepovers, or to go to the movies with their peers. One mother expressed the sentiments of many of our informants, saying,

> In Mexico, I knew all the families of my son's friends. I knew the mothers, the fathers, and even some of the grandparents. I had visited their homes and they, ours. Here, it's different. I don't know the families of his friends.

The dispersed nature of communities in the United States and the challenges of using public transportation in the United States contributed to our parents' sense of the lack of community. Most of our parents were accustomed to communities where walking around town was the norm. Without owning a car or having the ability to drive, parents felt trapped and unable to help their children take advantage of community-based resources.

School

For most immigrant parents and children, the school is their first institutional contact in the United States. Within schools, youth become exposed to the native culture for the first time, interact with immigrant and native children of their same ethnicity, and form beliefs about what society and persons outside of their family expect from them. Those beliefs and expectations are communicated to immigrant parents and become a part of parents' acculturation experiences as well.

Parents had positive impressions of their children's schools when teachers had high expectations for their children, called to discuss a child's progress, and had access to interpreters. A Mexican mother captured this type of positive experience, saying,

> For me, [the schooling experience] is very good, because when the children are late with assignments or miss school, they call immediately. If school starts at 8 am, by 8:30 a.m. they have called, "Your child—why didn't he come to school?" Or they talk to you about assignments, "Why is your child afraid? Why doesn't your child participate?" All of this— they are very interested. They get very involved with the family…. When I have had problems with the children at school, they look for an interpreter for me. I have had a lot of help with people translating for me about what my children's problems were at school…. I have had luck that there have been people there who have helped me.

Parents had negative experiences when Spanish–English interpreters were not available, when school administrators or teachers did not explain requirements for successful completion of a grade, and when their children's peers communicated negative stereotypes about Latino immigrants. Explaining his frustration with poor communication between his family and school administrators, a father related his experience:

> This is a long story. She was advised by someone in the main office (I have the person's name) to register for ESL classes. "Take all ESL classes your first year," that's what she was told. That made sense. You must first learn English so that you can continue your studies in English. What we didn't know is that she would repeat her 9th year. She lost the entire year. The ESL classes replaced her requirements for that year. The problem we have is that no one explained this to us at the beginning. We found out when the report card arrived at the end of the school year…. We weren't informed. [My wife] who speaks English, called the school a few times about something else, but nothing was said to us. They must have known this at the beginning, when they advised her. Being immigrants is hard this way. We are here for our children's future, but the school doesn't explain to us the important decision they made. Not even [our daughter] knew she wasn't going to pass the grade.

Describing her child's experiences with discrimination in the schools, a mother said,

> For both [of my children] there was discrimination. From the Americans, the Blacks…. Above all, they had a lot of problems on the bus, because [the Blacks] would bother them or say things to them. They would even talk among themselves, "Look at those poor Hispanics."

Health

Although not as significant as the school environment for most parents, contact with the health care system also shapes their acculturation experiences. In our very first interview, one mother expressed a sentiment that was repeated throughout the rest of the study.

> Thank God we have not had sickness…. I pray to God that my children don't get sick because here,

getting sick would be terrible. In my country, no, because she was covered by health insurance for everything. Not here. This frightens me.

Although immigrant parents recognized that high-quality medical care was available for children in the United States, they felt that cost made this care inaccessible to their children and worried about their children getting seriously ill. Even when affordable care was available to children, parents reported difficulties scheduling appointments. Appointments were canceled frequently, and a visit to the doctor's office sometimes required taking a full day off of work or school to wait to be seen.

Work

Finally, a few immigrant parents expressed a concern with finding the appropriate balance between work and family. Although parents recognized that time spent working was not spent with their children, the economic necessities of then lives prevented them from finding more of a balance. Parents expressing this sentiment sometimes blamed themselves for conflicts with their adolescent children and the delinquent behaviors of other adolescents. For example, a mother working as a housekeeper said,

If [parents] are going to bring [their kids] over here, [I'd advise the parents] to pay attention to them, spend more time with them.... Sometimes [teenage pregnancy and drug use] is your fault for not paying attention to them. Sometimes you only put effort into your work, work, work. And you forget that you are a mother, that you are a father.... You displace your family because you have so much work. Sometimes parents even have two jobs, and they don't spend any time with their kids. And when you turn around, your home has been destroyed, your kids are destroyed.

COPING WITH LOSS AND FAMILY CHANGE

Parents' comments regarding the challenges of balancing work and family in the United States begin to suggest that the loss of extended family connections and changes in the family dynamic may be among the most significant aspects of an immigrant parent's migration and acculturation experience. When asked what she liked least about living in the United States, one mother cried with tremendous grief,

Missing my family. That is very difficult. My sons, my grandchildren, my aunts, uncles, their children. I've also left my fiancé. He promises me that he will come here, but it's been very difficult for him to legally enter this country. My son is probably going to marry soon. He has a serious girlfriend. They're all over there. It's very difficult.

As they coped with their grief and their loss of family connections, our informants also coped with changes in their living arrangements, changes in socioeconomic status, changes in their roles and responsibilities within the family, and changes in the traditions and values being adopted by their children. These changes magnified their sense of loss and sacrifice. Thinking of changes in her living arrangements and social status as she moved to the United States, a mother working in child care remarked,

In Colombia, we had a very high social status. My husband worked at the university. I, too, worked at the university. We had very good jobs. We had an apartment.... We had our own cars. We had servants in our home. We had children in private schools. It was high status.... We use to have a beautiful, modern house. My children had their own rooms. Here, the three of us live in one bedroom of someone else's house. We sleep in one bed. We use to have separate beds.... Adjusting to what we don't have anymore is still difficult. But, it was traumatic when we first moved here.

Several other parents echoed these sentiments as they discussed the challenges of living with extended family members and the lack of privacy in their current living situations. In the words of a mother from Mexico, "We want to live alone. That would be best. But right now, we can't."

Living in close quarters and with limited economic resources may accentuate the stresses experienced by parents and children as they contend with changing family roles and responsibilities. In some cases, fathers began taking more responsibility for some aspects of parenting because they had lived in the United States longer and spoke more English. As one mother explained to us,

> The one who goes to meetings here, who takes care of everything, is my husband. In Colombia, it was me. In Colombia, it was me who went to the meetings and got involved in everything at the children's schools and everything. But here, it is my husband.

In other cases, informants focused on changes in the relationships between themselves and their children and changes in the expectations that they had for their children. They identified a level of assertiveness and independence in their children that was attributed to both the resourcefulness of their children in acculturating to the United States and their children's greater level of acculturation to U.S. norms for teenagers.

As exemplified by one father's comment, these changes were sometimes viewed with pride:

> When we came from New York, I would ask her, "Daughter, come and help me call this store." And she did not have the courage. And now, yes. Whatever I don't know, she knows. She can get by [on her own] now.... She has matured a lot in the past 2 years. I think the changes in this country have pushed her to more maturity.

In other cases, this newfound assertiveness and independence in their children was characterized negatively, as rebelliousness that goes beyond what would have been expected in their home countries. Concerns about the growing independence or rebelliousness of their children were sometimes linked to parents' concerns about children losing their cultural heritage and adopting American values and behaviors. Thinking about a recent argument with her daughter about going to a sleepover, one mother explained,

> She and I have very different beliefs, in terms of outings, in terms of school.... I get nervous because these types of things don't happen in Mexico.

Similarly another mother talked to us about changes she had noted in her daughters attitude.

> She doesn't want to eat tortillas. She just wants to eat bread. She wants to think like people here do, like Americans.... Like, she tells me that I shouldn't let my husband tell me, "Do this for me. Bring me that." Or "Bring everything close to me." She says, "No Mom. You shouldn't do it. So that he also has to do things too." I say, "No. That's impossible, because that is the way things are there. That is the way it is in Mexico."

FEARING A NEW ENVIRONMENT

At times, concerns about their children losing their cultural heritages or adopting American values and behaviors were expressed as generalized anxiety or specific fears about life in the United States. Expressions of generalized anxiety included comments about the potential dangers of allowing children in the United States to stay out late at night; attend parties with U.S.-born friends; and become exposed to the types of violence that parents had seen on television, read about in the paper, or heard about from others. Despite seeing the United States as a land of better opportunities and futures for their children, many parents also viewed the United States as a potentially toxic environment (Garbarino, 1995). They felt that constant vigilance was necessary to ensure that their children were not exposed to possible dangers. Emblematic of the general anxiety felt by immigrant parents, one mother said,

> I don't feel safe even leaving my kids at a day care, because I have seen so much injustice. So much.... That is why I have always preferred to work at night. So that during the day I can care for my kids and at night my husband watches them. That is what we all do, the majority of Hispanics.

Specific fears focused on how their children's bad friends might encourage their child to take up illicit drugs, skip school, take part in gang activities, or become pregnant. One mother confided,

> I'm most concerned about his American friends. I don't even know their families. I've seen some of the boys, some of them. I worry that my son will pick up the customs of the Americans here. You know, using drugs, becoming too independent. That is what most worries me.

ENCOUNTERING AND CONFRONTING RACISM

To some extent, the concerns and fears expressed by Latino immigrant parents may result from their first encounters with other races and their first experiences as a minority in the United States. Explicitly commenting on the socioeconomic and ethnic heterogeneity of the United States, one mother said,

> [In Colombian schools], the groups were very homogenous. And here, the groups are different. The kids from different cultures and different socioeconomic classes are suffering.

For other immigrant parents, comments were more explicitly focused on racism and discrimination. When asked what they liked least about the United States and when asked about their experiences with school and health systems, more than half of our informants mentioned at least one aspect of racism and discrimination. They had personally experienced racism or discrimination; internalized racist remarks; or expressed racist sentiments toward other Latino immigrants and other ethnic groups, especially African Americans.

Children typically experienced racism or discrimination at school and communicated this to their parents. One parent discussed how an African American boy had teased her son on the bus until they had a fistfight. Another described how her daughter had witnessed a group of African American boys beating up a Latina girl. Other parents explained how both White and African American peers ostracized their Latino children at school.

After both experiencing racism for themselves and observing racist interactions between others, parents and children began internalizing racist attitudes toward other Latinos. As an example of this, one parent explained how her boys had become selective in choosing Latino friends:

> [My boys] don't want to hang out with Hispanics, especially those who only waste their time, or those that dress badly.... I notice that they are prejudiced against even Hispanics who dress like this [really loose pants worn down under the bottom]. And so I have said to them, it's one thing to dress like that, but what [the Hispanics] feel and think is something else. But they say that they see how [the Hispanics] behave in school and they prefer not to socialize with them. So they do have Hispanic friends, but they are very highly selected. Those who do well in school and behave...or those that speak English really well or those born here.

Parents and children also began adopting racist viewpoints, especially toward African Americans. As one father described his initial living experience in North Carolina, he said,

> [The apartment] was really small, and well, here we had plenty of problems.... Over there [in Argentina], we are used to treating everyone the same, in a friendly manner. So we let [the Black kids] in. But they knew no limits.... One day they broke the door, and they came in. They hit my daughter. And we realized that we needed to interact differently. That it was different [in the United States]. And that is how we became aware of these cultural issues personally.

In other studies, immigrant parents have recounted similar experiences navigating new social contexts (Bender et al., 2001; Clark, 2002; Olmedo, 2003), coping with loss and family change (Williams et al., 2002), fearing a new environment (Cooper, 2005; Reese, 2002), and encountering and confronting racism (Conchas, 2001; Ochoa, 2000; Williams et al., 2002). When children express embarrassment about their parents' English-language skills and cultural heritage, parents feel disrespected. When teachers, school administrators, or health care providers fail to communicate with them, parents feel marginalized and disenfranchised. When the demands of work combine with the absence of strong kinship networks in their new homes, parents feel overwhelmed. Coupled with the perceived dangers of the U.S. environment and negative influences of U.S. peers, immigrant parents adapt by limiting their children's activities and controlling their friendships more than they might have in their home countries (Reese, 2002). As described below, immigrant parents also adapt by empowering themselves and their children (Ceballo, 2004; Ochoa, 2000; Olmedo, 2003; Reese, Kroesen, & Gallimore, 2000).

FINDING STRENGTH

The new immigrant parents we interviewed found strength in overcoming these challenges. They actively sought to transform adversity and foster resilience in their children.... First, Latino immigrant parents directly expressed empathy with their children for the challenges they faced and showed tremendous respect for the capacity of their children to adapt. Second, they expressed a strong interest in learning about resources to help their children and, if these resources were not available, they worked to foster support for their children. Third, they worked with their children to develop bicultural coping skills. Finally, they sought to increase communication with their children and advised future immigrants to do the same.

EMPATHIZING WITH AND RESPECTING ADOLESCENT CHILDREN

All of our informants empathized with the suffering and loss that their children had experienced during their family's transition to the United States. As a result, many parents had come to admire the resilience of their children. One mother's empathy and admiration exemplifies best what we heard from many:

> I think that she is a girl that is adaptable, sensible, calm.... In her country, everything was different.

She had her father. She had her nanny that loved her. She [the nanny] would have her favorite foods ready for her. She'd set out her clothes to wear each day. Thank God she has adapted to all this.... She has overcome, because she is a very special girl.... My gratitude for this child reaches to the sky.... This child is very, very good. She is exceptional.

Parents also identified their children as a source of strength and support. As a second mother discussed traveling in the trunk of a car to migrate to the United States, she stated,

> [My daughter] gave me strength during the trip. I would say to her, "Oh my god, daughter. We are at a point where we can still not go on. Why don't we go back? We are going to suffocate where they are going to put us." And she said, "No, Mami. Let's go," because she really wanted to come here. And she gave me strength. I said, "look at where they are going to put us, no let's not go on." And she said, "yes," and gave me strength to go on. That is how we made it.

SEEKING HELP AND FOSTERING SUPPORTS

To help support their adolescent children's transition to life in the United States, many of the interviewed parents were engaged in supportive activities and programs offered through local Latino community centers and school groups. Despite its historical importance in the adaptation of many immigrants to the United States (Menjivar, 2003), the church was noticeably absent as a source of support for immigrant parents who participated in this study. In the new receiving community from which our respondents were recruited, local Catholic, Protestant, and evangelical churches provide financial support to Latino community centers rather than directly providing services.

One parent explained how she helped her son deal with the transition to school in the United States by finding him a tutor through a local Latino community center. After explaining how her daughter had gotten into a fight with a White American student who had been teasing her about her Latino heritage, another parent told how she was working with the school to find a school counselor for her daughter. As one mother explained, these services were very supportive:

> Of course, at first when she started going to school, she did not speak English, and neither did I. And we suffered a lot. I think it was what motivated me to go to look for [a Latino community center]. For me, the [Latino Community Center] is like a second home. There are times when there are problems in my own house, like with health, like my husband's recent accident. And there are times that I feel more comfortable, more relaxed at the [Latino Community Center] than in my own home because I know I am going to arrive home to find stress—that sometimes there is not enough money, that there are problems, that I have a pain here, my husband, the appointments. I have three children who go to three different schools, and my life is very hard.

In addition, parents eagerly probed interviewers for information about additional resources in their communities available to help Latino immigrants. They expressed a desire for psychological counseling for themselves and their children. They expressed a desire for more involvement in children's schools, One parent even expressed an interest in building community through neighborhood work groups similar to those in her home country.

DEVELOPING BICULTURAL COPING SKILLS

Through these established community groups and on their own, parents worked to develop bicultural coping skills in their children (Delgado-Gaitan, 1993). For some parents, the development of bicultural coping skills began with recognition of the differences between the United States and their home countries. With this recognition came an understanding that migration involved an adaptation process. As two parents explained,

> [It is] a difficult adaptation for her during this adolescent time. What I tell her is ... we have to try to adapt ourselves to what is happening and to try to

give of ourselves to others, to give to those who are different from us so that we can be at peace. During this time, we can feel things. We can feel sad, lonely. But we must remember that we are going through an adaptation that is physical, spiritual, and emotional.
> She has to acculturate because of school and because of her friends.... Here she has to be mixed. [But], she has to preserve her identity. She is a Hispanic, and she has a rich culture.

Given that many of our parents were encountering ethnic diversity and racism for the first time, parents also focused on helping their children understand racial differences and cope with racism and discrimination. Parents reported talking with their children about how best to assert their rights when they felt discriminated against and how to interpret negative or stereotypical images about Latinos. They also sought to overcome negative stereotypes by helping their children to develop a positive image of themselves and their heritages. The following excerpt demonstrates this best:

> [Our kids] hear really bad comments [about Mexicans]. So I started thinking, "What can I do so that my daughter grows to love her state, where she is from, her land." ... And so, I started telling her about my mom, that she was very nice. And I would start... cooking for them things so that they could start tasting, start enjoying [Mexican things].... And I started bringing her typical dresses that I would get at the Mexican stores.... And that is how they started changing their minds.... Even now, sometimes her friends come to play over here, and she asks me to tell them what Mexico is like.... And I tell them, "We dance like this or like that over there." Or I will play Mexican music for them.... I tell them nice things. And now they have gotten it. They're Mexican.

In addition to speaking with their children directly about the acculturation process and about race and ethnicity, our informants also demonstrated bicultural coping skills by speaking with their children about how best to achieve academic and economic success in the United States. They emphasized educational attainment and encouraged their children to study. One mother reported advising her daughter as follows:

> And you're going to study and study and study.... You have to demand more so that they demand more of you. We have to take advantage of being in this country—in the United States. We have to go to high school. And probably we can even go to the university and beyond.

A second mother shared with us what she says to her sons:

> You will be more than him, if you put in a good effort. You will be more than he is.... If you study, if you put in a good effort, perhaps he will end up working for you.... That's why you should study. So that you don't go into construction like your Dad, So that you don't have to go and clean bathrooms or houses.

INCREASING PARENT–CHILD COMMUNICATION

The fact that many parents reported talking with their children about the process of adaptation to the United States, race and discrimination, and pathways to economic success in the United States suggests that increased parent–child communication is a tool used by immigrant parents to help promote resiliency. When asked what type of advice one would give a parent who was moving to the United States from your home country, nearly half of our informants recommended improving parent–child communication. They recommended that new immigrant parents be attentive to their children'sneeds, make time to talk with their children, and speak openly and honestly about issues their children would face as adolescents and as immigrants in the United States, In the words of a Mexican mother,

> I would give the advice to speak openly about everything, about everything in terms of that possibility to be exposed to: that they are vulnerable to drugs, that they are vulnerable to temptations, that their sexuality starts to wake up. [I would advise new immigrant parents] that they have to teach [their children and] that they have to protect them.

Our interviews with Latino immigrant parents identified four strategies that immigrant parents use to empower themselves and their children—empathizing with and respecting adolescent children, seeking help and fostering social support for their children, developing bicultural coping skills in their children, and improving their communication with their children. Our findings add to the growing body of knowledge about how Latino immigrant parents help to support their children despite having limited socioeconomic resources and English-language skills (Ceballo, 2004; Ochoa, 2000; Olmedo, 2003; Reese et al., 2000). Parents clearly communicate the importance of education to their children and encourage them to do well, they convey a high degree of respect and trust in their teenage children, and they insulate their children against negative U.S. social stereotypes of Latino immigrants by providing them with more positive cultural images.

REFERENCES

Bender, D. E., Harbour, C., Thorp, J., & Morris, P. (2001). Tell me what you mean by "si": Perceptions of quality of prenatal care among immigrant Latina women. *Qualitative Health Research*, 11(6). 780–794.

Ceballo, R. (2004). From barrios to Yale: The role of parenting strategies in Latino families. *Hispanic Journal of Behavioral Sciences*, 26(2), 171–186.

Clark, L. (2002). Mexican-origin mothers' experiences using children's health care services. *Western Journal of Nursing Research*, 24(2), 159–179.

Conchas, G.Q. (2001). Structuring failure and success: Understanding the variability in Latino school engagement. *Harvard Educational Review, 71*(3), 475–504.

Cooper, C. (2005). Including Latino immigrant families, schools, and community programs as research partners on the good path of life. In T. Weisner (Ed.), *Discovering successful pathways in children's development: Mixed methods in the study of childhood and family life* (pp. 329–358). Chicago: University of Chicago Press.

Delgaldo-Gaitan, C. (1993). Parenting in two generations of Mexican American families. *International Journal of Behavioral Development, 16,* 409–427.

Garbarino, J. (1995). *Raising children in a socially toxic environment.* San Francisco: Jossey-Bass.

Garcia, E. C. (2001). Parenting in Mexican American families. In N. B. Webb (Ed.), *Culturally diverse parent-child and family relationships: A guide for social workers and other practitioners* (pp. 157–180). New York: Columbia University Press.

Harwood, R., Leyendecker, B., Carlson, V., Asencio, M., & Miller, A. (2002). Parenting among Latino families in the U.S. In M. H. Bornstein (Ed.), *Handbook of parenting: Social conditions and applied parenting* (2nd ed., pp. 21–46). Mahwah, NJ: Lawrence Erlbaum.

Hernandez, D. (1997). Child development and the social demography of childhood. *Child Development, 68*(1), 149–169.

Johnson, J. H., Johnson-Webb, K. D., & Farrell, W. C. (1999). Newly emerging Hispanic communities in the United States: A spatial analysis of settlement patterns, in-migration fields, and social receptivity. In F. D. Bean & S. Bell-Rose (Eds.), *Immigration and opportunity* (pp. 263–310). New York: Russell Sage.

Massey, D. S., Durand, J., & Malone, N. (2002). *Beyond smoke and mirrors: Mexican immigration in an era of economic integration.* New York: Russell Sage.

Menjivar, C. (2003). Religion and immigration in comparative perspective: Catholic and evangelical Salvadorans in San Francisco, Washington, D.C., and Phoenix. *Sociology of Religion. 64*(1), 21–45.

Ochoa, G. L. (2000). Mexican Americans' attitudes toward and interactions with Mexican immigrants: A qualitative analysis of conflict and cooperation. *Social Science Quarterly. 81*(1), 84–105.

Olmedo, I. M. (2003). Accommodation and resistance: Latinas struggle for their children's education. *Anthropology and Education Quarterly. 34*(4), 373–395.

Portes, A., & Rumbaut, R. G. (2001). *Legacies: The story of the immigrant second generation.* Berkeley: University of California Press.

Ramirez, R. R., & de la Cruz, G. P. (2003). The Hispanic population in the United States: March 2002. *Current Population Reports,* pp. 20–545.

Reese, L. (2002). Parental .strategies in contrasting cultural settings: Families in Mexico and "El Norte." *Anthropology and Education Quarterly, 33*(1), 30–59.

Reese, L., Kroesen, K., & Gallimore, R. (2000). Agency and school performance among urban Latino youth. In R. Taylor & M. Wang (Eds.), *Resilience across contexts: Family, work, culture and community* (pp. 295–232). Mahwah. NJ: Lawrence Erlbaum.

Suárez-Orozco, C., & Suárez-Orozco, M. M. (2001). *Children of immigration.* Cambridge, MA: Harvard University Press.

Suro, R. & Passel, J. S. (2003). *The rise of the second generation: Changing patterns in Hispanic population growth* (Pew Hispanic Center Reports). Retrieved June 1, 2006, from http://pewhispanic. org/files/reporis/22.pdf.

Tropp, L. R., Coll, C. G., Alarcon, 0., & Vazquez Garcia, H. A. (1999). Psychological accultura-tion: Development of a new measure for Puerto Ricans on the U.S. mainland. *Education and Psychological Measurement. 59*(2). 351–367.

U.S. Census Bureau. (2001). *Summary tape files. 1–4. census 1990–2000.* Retrieved July 31, 2003, from http://www.census.gov/main/www/cen2000.html.

Vega, W. (1990). Hispanic families in the 1980s: A decade of research. *Journal of Marriage and Family. 52*, 1015–1024.

Williams, L, S., Alvarez, S. D. & Hauck, K. (2002). My name is not Maria: Young Latinas seeking home in the Heartland. *Social Problems. 49*(4). 563–584.

JOURNALING QUESTION

What supports did your parents rely on to get you through your teenage years?

Health Care

32.
THE ROLE OF RACE IN THE CLINICAL PRESENTATION

MATTHEW R. ANDERSON, SUSAN MOSCOU, CELESTINE FULCHON, AND
DANIEL R. NEUSPIEL

"A 42-year-old white male presents with…," "An 82-year-old black male presents with…," "An 18-year-old black female presents with…," "A 37-year-old Asian male presents with …" So begins a standard clinical presentation—an almost ritual incantation of age, race, and gender before the presentation (the symptoms, signs, damage, or illness). But why, Matthew Anderson and his coauthors ask, is that relevant? In the case of race, they argue, this information is as likely to be misleading as it is to be helpful. This is partly because of the inherent confusions in trying to "identify" a patient's race. People in the "mixed race" movement, for example, have been engaging in a bone marrow donor drive, trying to find suitable bone marrow donors and, thus, acting as if "mixed race" were itself a race category. Also, race categories are inherently unstable: as Anderson et al. show, in one New York hospital, 6.5% patients who were admitted twice were assigned to a different race on their second admission. But even for the 93.5% whose race was consistently identified, what, exactly, is it that doctors learn from this identification? Why do you think that doctors have been reluctant to drop race as a patient identifier?

Traditionally, clinical presentations begin with a patient's age, race or ethnicity, and gender. This format implies that these variables are important, objective, and biologic facts that are requisite for clinical reasoning. It is argued that racial identifiers are necessary because they provide clues about disease probabilities, particularly genetic conditions,[1] predict drug response,[2] help clinicians form a mental picture, and provide information about the patient's diet, education, and culture.[3] However, race as a taxonomic category has been increasingly questioned over the past 100 years. Most, though not all, current scholars view racial categories as a reflection of social, not biological, divisions.

Caldwell, Popenoe,[4] and Witzig[5] challenged the use of race in case presentations. They noted ambiguities surrounding the meaning of race and its lack of validity as a scientific construct. Caldwell and Popenoe concluded that "The diagnostic and therapeutic utility of the terms black and white is limited." Witzig favored abandoning racial identifications but suggested that ethnicity may be useful if considered in concert with other variables such as class, culture, religion, and education.

Excerpted from Matthew R. Anderson, Susan Moscou, Celestine Fulchon, and Daniel R. Neuspiel, "The Role of Race in the Clinical Presentation," *Family Medicine* 33 (2001): 430–34. Notes have been renumbered and edited.

Additionally, Caldwell, Popenoe, and Witzig found that racial identifiers were potentially prejudicial to patients.

There are, however, arguments for not excluding information about race. Considerable epidemiological evidence demonstrates marked health disparities among racial groups.[6,7] Further, historic patterns of racial disparities have fueled a growing interest in racism and its role in maintaining these disparities[8-10] The growing interest in minority health[11] and culturally competent care[12] requires that clinicians address the role of race and its effect on patients. If clinicians omit race because it is not a biological variable, do they risk ignoring or, worse, concealing important social data about their patients? Recognizing this dilemma, the question becomes: "How and when should clinicians include information about a patient's race?"

RACIAL IDENTIFIERS

The use of racial identifiers in clinical medicine can be traced back to at least the mid-19th century,[13] but a recent survey found that the majority of medical schools still teach students to include race in patient written and oral presentations.[4] Some physical assessment texts,[14,15] but not all,[16,17] suggest that race be considered as part of the data identifying patients.

Despite the widespread use of racial identifiers in clinical medicine, racial classification poses conceptual and methodological difficulties.[18] There is no gold standard for racial classification, and definitions of race vary widely....

Health care settings, particularly those receiving federal funding, use racial and ethnic categories derived from the Office of Management and Budget's (OMB) Directive 15.[19] Directive 15 recognizes five races (American Indian or Alaska Native, Asian, black or African-American, Native Hawaiian or Other Pacific Islander, and white) and two ethnic groups (Hispanic or Latino and not Hispanic or Latino).

Notably, OMB considers its categories as "social-political constructs" that "should not be interpreted as being scientific or anthropological in nature." There is no reason to assume that OMB categories are well-suited for the purposes of genetic, clinical, or epidemiologic research. In fact, racial categories have increased and decreased over time and will undoubtedly change again. The recent census option to select multiple races will challenge the traditional clinical practice of assigning patients and research subjects a unique race.

DETERMINING A PATIENT'S RACE

Many states throughout the 20th century legislated definitions of race.[20] These definitions were often concerned with preserving the purity of the white race, so that individuals of mixed-white/non-white descent were assigned the non-white race. This practice was justified by what was known as the "one drop of black blood" theory.

What race would be assigned to the child of a white mother and a black father? Is the child white, black, mixed, or some other term? The National Center for Health Statistics publishes algorithms for determining the race of newborns. Prior to 1989, this child would be given the race of the non-white parent. After 1989, this newborn was assigned the race of the mother.[21] Therefore, this infant would have been considered black in 1988 and white in 1990. Clearly, neither of these definitions are biologically based; rather, they reflect the social nature of racial identity.

Clinicians are not given formal instruction in discerning a patient's race. Sapira suggests questioning the patient when the clinician is "in doubt about the proper term,"[15] and DeGowin and DeGowin[14] state that the "patient may not be able to give a satisfactory answer." Many practitioners decide racial or ethnic designations based on the patient's skin color, hair texture, spoken language, last names, and behaviors.[3]

In clinical practice, patients may be assigned different races at different times. In an observational study of patients admitted to New York hospitals, Blustein found that admission clerks assigned patients to racial categories without formal rules. The clerks had been instructed to avoid direct questioning of the patient.[22] In this study, 6.5% of the 767 patients were found to have been assigned a different race on their second admission. Similar inconsistencies in racial classification have been noted when birth and death certificates of infants have been examined.[23,24]

Many people seen in U.S. clinical practice consider themselves biracial or multiracial. Assigning a single race to these patients is inaccurate; it may be misleading and potentially offensive. Given the problems with racial identifications a Centers for Disease Control working group proposed that "Race and ethnicity status should be self-identified using a multiple-choice option," and that "Observer-derived measures of race and ethnicity should be eliminated."[25]

RACE AS A PROXY FOR GENETIC VARIATION

The racial categories commonly used in clinical practice describe population groupings containing billions of people. Most human variation, however, occurs within these large racial groups and not between them.[26] Any classification of genetic variation is arbitrary because clear boundaries do not divide humanity. The utility of racial categories is further limited by the intermingling of human populations.[27] Clinically important mutations, such as hemoglobin S, may arise independently in different populations and thus straddle racial categories.

Clinicians often cite sickle-cell disease as a condition justifying the use of racial identifiers, but the sickle-cell mutation is found in a number of populations outside of Africa (including Sicily, Saudi Arabia, and India). We, as well as others,[5] have witnessed delay in the diagnosis of sickle-cell crisis in a Puerto Rican patient labeled as a Hispanic and, therefore, assumed not to be at risk for sickle-cell disease.

A better way to obtain useful information about genetic risk is to ask patients detailed questions concerning their family history, perceived ethnicity, and geographic background. A patient whom the clinician perceives as white may be self-identified as a Russian Jew, a Guatemalan of Basque origin, a Sicilian, or an African-American.

RACE AND SOCIAL CLASS

The complex relationship between race and social class has important implications for clinical medicine. Class indicators, such as income, education, and occupation, are significant predictors of health status.[28] Vital statistics in the United States generally do not include class as a category even when economic data may be available. Racial categories are often interpreted as proxy markers for class.[29] Medical researchers and clinicians may substitute race in place of a thorough social history.

These practices lead to a racialization of social problems, i.e. the attribution of social differences to problems of race. Much of the reported health differential between racial groups disappears when researchers control for measures of social class such as educational level or income.[30,31] To conceptualize these differentials as racial often leads to speculation about biological factors, when the real problems may be economic. Further, the use of race as a proxy for social status relies on stereotypes concerning the social status of different racial groups. Perhaps the 50-year-old black alcoholic male is an IBM executive, or the 50-year-old white executive has a cocaine problem. Racial categories describe broad social groups within which there is much variation with respect to social status and health risk.

What are some alternatives to using race as a proxy for social class? More clinical value may come from explicit measurement of factors like education, income, occupation, total wealth, housing, marital status, immigration status, and type of health insurance. Kiefer suggests a contextual approach to the social history involving the information on class/culture, service area, gender, and person.[32]

Race is not a substitute for a good social history. A patient's skin color does not provide information about birthplace, education, occupation, income, place of residence, language, or cultural beliefs or preferences.

DO RACIAL IDENTIFIERS STIGMATIZE?

Research continues to demonstrate that patients receive different care based on their race or ethnicity in ways that do not appear medically justified.[33,34] It has been argued that the use of racial identifiers reinforces existing patterns of unequal care by evoking stereotypes (positive or negative) in the minds of clinicians.

Consider a case presentation we observed in which a clinically well postpartum patient was described as a "34-year-old, black, cocaine-using mom who just delivered her 11th child prematurely." When the patient presentation pairs a behavior (cocaine use) with a race (black), this may elicit expectations about the patient's lifestyle, suitability for certain medical interventions, and even her value as a human being. Murrell[35] noted that negative stereotypes about pregnant Africans-American women persist regardless of their income, education, and insurance status. Not surprisingly, Murrell found that African-American women perceived their prenatal care as inaccessible, and many saw their providers as indifferent or not respectful.

There is a body of research examining how racial identifiers may influence clinical decisions. Some of this research has been descriptive (behavior observed at hospital rounds and chart reviews).[36,37] Other investigators have had clinicians respond to mock case presentations in which the patient's race is varied.[38-40] As a group, these studies support the hypothesis that race does influence clinical decisions in ways often unfavorable to minority patients.

On the other hand, excluding racial identifiers from the clinical database poses a different set of problems. Race influences patients' lives (positively or negatively) and influences the care they receive. Prohibiting the mention of race in the clinical presentation does not make these concerns disappear.

If clinicians wish to include race, then the information might be better placed in the social history and not in the opening sentence of the presentation. Discussing race with patients may be useful as a way to facilitate a less-biased relationship.

THE BOTTOM LINE

What, then, should be the role of race in the clinical presentation? The following guidelines have been helpful to us as clinicians and educators. These guidelines are not offered as a set of hard and fast rules. They are offered in the hope that they will stimulate dialogue and facilitate a reconceptualization of race and its role in medicine.

GUIDELINES

1. *Race should be ascertained by self-identification.* The most valid way to determine a patient's race is to ask the patient. Patients can have no race, one race, or more than one race.

2. *Race should be record in the social history.* Clinicians may wish to include racial identifiers to elicit sources of stress, strengths, and supports available to patients and families. Race belongs on the social history, not in the first sentence of the clinical presentation.

3. *Race should not be used as a proxy for genetic variation.* When a patient's specific genetic varient is known (e.g. sickle-cell disease), this should be mentioned. When the differetial diagnosis includes diseases with a genetic basis, clinicians should seek specific information about the patient's family, ethnic, and geographic backround. This information should be recorded in the social or family history.

4. *Race should not be used as a proxy for social class.* The patient's social class can provide clinically

useful information and should be specifically described using variable such as education level, occupation, area of residence, etc.

5. *Racism and its effects on health and the patient-clinician relationship should be considered part of the clinical encounter.* Patients' reports of past, current, or anticipated experiences of racism provide information about stress and potential sources of psychological or physical harm. Racism influences health, access to health care, treatment regimens, and patient-clinician encounters. Self-identified racial or ethnic identifiers need to be included in the medical facility's administrative database so the effects of racism can be studied at an institutional level.

6. *Medical researchers need to adopt a more critical attitude toward their own use of racial identifiers.* If medical researchers continue to use broad-based racial categories as proxies for genetic variation or social class, clinicians are unlikely to change their own practices.

NOTES

1. Waldenstrom J. Disease, race, geography, and genes. J Gen Intern Med 1990;228:419–24.
2. Hall WD. A rational approach to the treatment of hypertention in special populations. Am Fam Physician 1999;60:156–62.
3. Moscou S. Racial and ethnic identifications. Nurse Pract 1996;21:8, 11–2.
4. Caldwell SH, Popenoe R. Perceptions and misperceptions of skin color. Ann Intern Med 1995;122:614–7.
5. Witzig R. The medicalization of race: scientific legitimization of a flawed social construct. Ann Intern Med 1996;125:675–9.
6. US Department of Health and Human Services. Report of the Secretary's Task Force on Black and Minority Health. Washington, DC: US Government Printing Office, 1985.
7. Smith DB. Health care divided: race and healing a nation. Ann Arbor, Mich: University of Michigan Press, 1999.
8. Bhopal R. Spectre of racism in health and health care: lessons from history and the United States. BMJ 1998;316:1970–3.
9. Geiger HJ. Annotation: racism resurgent—building a bridge to the 19th century. Am J Public Health 1997;87:1076–86.
10. Jones CP. Levels of racism: a theoretic framework and gardener's tale. Am J Public Health 2000;90:1212–5.
11. Dedicated issue on minority health. Fam Med 1998;30(3):158–235.
12. Like RC, Steiner RP, Rubel AJ. Recommended core curriculum guidelines on culturally sensitive and competent health care. Fam Med 1996;28(4):291–7.
13. Warner JH. The therapeutic perspective: medical practice, knowledge, and identity in America, 1820–1885. Cambridge, Mass: Harvard University Press, 1986.
14. Degowin RL. DeGowin and DeGowin's diagnostic examination, sixth edition. New York: McGraw-Hill, Inc, 1994.
15. Sapira JD. The art science of bedside diagnosis. Baltimore: Willams & Wilkins, 1990.
16. Bickley LS, Hoekelman RA. Bate's guide to physical examination and history taking seventh edition. Philadelphia: Lippincott, Willams & Willkins, 1999.
17. Seidell HM, Ball JW, Dains JE, Benedict GW. Mosby's guide to physical examination, forth edition. St Louis: Mosby, Inc, 1999.

18. Hahn RA, Stroup DF. Race and ethnicity in public health surveillance: criteria for the scientific use of social categories. Public Health Rep 1994;109:7–15.

19. Office of Management and the Budget. Revisions to the standard for the classification of federal data on race and ethnicity. Federal Register 1997;62:58781–90.

20. Haney Lopez IF. White by law: the legal construction of race. New York: New York University Press, 1996.

21. Hahn RA. The state of federal health statistics on racial and ethnic groups. JAMA 1992;267:268–71.

22. Blustein J. The reliability of racial classifications in hospital discharge abstract data. Am J Public Health 1994;84: 1018–21.

23. Hahn RA, Mulinare J, Teutsch SM. Inconsistencies in coding of race and ethnicity birth and death in US infants: a new look at infant mortality, 1983 through 1985. JAMA 1992;267:259–63.

24. Frost F, Shy KK. Racial differences between linked birth and infant death records in Washington State. Am J Public Health 1980;70:974–6.

25. Centers for Disease Control and Prevention. Use of race and ethnicity in public health surveillance: summary of the CDC/ATSDR Workshop. MMWR Morb Mortal Wkly Rep 1993:42 (no. RR-10):1–17.

26. Barbujani G, Magagni A, Minch E, Cavalli-Sforza LL. An apportionment of human DNA diversity. Proc Natl Acad Sci USA 1997;94:4516–9.

27. Marks J. Human biodiversity: genes, race, and history. New York: Walter de Gruyter, Inc, 1995.

28. Navarro V. Class and race: life and death situations. Monthly Review 1991;43(4):1–13.

29. Williams DR. Race/ethnicity and socioeconomic status: measurement and methodological issues. Int J Health Serv 1996;26:483–505.

30. Lillie-Blanton M, Parsons PE, Gayle H, Dievler A. Racial differences in health: not just black and white, but shades of gray. Annu Rev public Health 1996;17:411–48.

31. Lilie-Blanton M, LaVeist T. Race/ethinicity, the social environment, and health. Soc Sci Med 1996;43:83–91.

32. Kiefer CW. Health work with the poor. New Brunswick, NJ: Rutgers, 2000.

33. Josefson D. Pain relief in the US emergency room is related to patients' race. BMJ 2000;320:139.

34. Canto JG, Allison JJ, Kiefe CI, et al. Relation of race and sex to the use of reperfusion therapy in Medicare beneficiaries with acute myocardial infarcion. N Engl J Med 2000;342:1094–100.

35. Murrell NL, Smith R, Gill G, Oxley G. Racism and health care access: a dialogue with child-bearing women. Health Care Woman Int 1996;17:149–59.

36. Flaherty JA, Meagher R. Measuring racial bias in inpatient treatment. Am J Psychiatry 1980;137:679–82.

37. Finucane RE, Carrese JA. Racial bias in presentation of cases. J Gen Intern Med 1990;5:120–1.

38. Loring M, Powell B. Gender, race and DSM-III: a study of the objectivity of psychiatric diagnostic behavior. J Health Soc Behav 1988;29:1–22.

39. Lewis G, Craft-Jeffreys C, David A. Are British psychiatrists racist? Br J Psychiatry 1990;157: 410–5.

40. Schulman KA, Berlin JA, Harless W, et al. The effect of race and sex on physicians' recommendations for cardiac catheterization. N Engl J Med 1999;340:618–26.

JOURNALING QUESTION

How do you think doctors identify you in their charts? Do you think that using race is helpful to them in treating you?

33.
RACE MATTERS
Health Care Stories from Black America

SUSAN STARR SERED AND RUSHIKA FERNANDOPULLE

The United States is unique in the developed world in not having a universal health care system. Health insurance in this country is made available to people through their jobs, which means that unemployed people, or part-time workers, are doubly burdened: they are poor, and they don't have access to medical services. More than 46 million Americans are estimated to be without medical insurance. Other countries have felt that they must take care of their own, that citizens must take care of each other when sickness falls upon them. One way of thinking says that the lack of universal health insurance in America disproportionately impacts black Americans because of racism, which makes them more likely to be un- or underemployed. But is it possible that the relationship is more complicated: is it the racism in America that permits us not to offer insurance to all? Because of racism, is there perhaps no communal sense of "us," of "our own citizens," and that is what allows us to privatize health care?

RACE AND CASTE

The links between employment and health care are key components of the political and economic policies that are creating a caste of the ill, infirm, and marginally employed. Issues of race are critical to this argument for two reasons: racial discrimination strengthens the pull of the death spiral; and race itself has always been the basis of a caste system in America.

Considering the experience of African Americans historically as well as today, Indian anthropologist Ursula Sharma convincingly argues for applying the notion of *caste*—as opposed to *ethnicity* or *class*—to the racial categorization of black people in the United States. First, she points out, use of the word *caste* distinguishes the situation of African Americans from ethnic groups such as Poles and Italians, who, though originally distinct as immigrants with well-defined cultures, over time became assimilated in America. Rigid racial boundaries are quite different from those facing white immigrant groups. Second, because of entrenched racism, African Americans experience few opportunities for class mobility. Even when they become affluent, they are still "black" and do not enjoy the same status and privileges as white Americans.[1]

Other scholars emphasize the biological, sexual, and marital ideologies that underpin racial categorization in America. John Dollard, writing in 1937, argues: "American caste is pinned not to cultural but to biological features—to color, features, hair form, and the like. This badge is categorical regardless of the social value of the individual." Moreover, Dollard clarifies, "class conflict centers around economic position and advantage, whereas the caste

Susan Starr Sered and Rushika Fernandopulle, "Race Matters: Health Care Stories from Black America," in *Uninsured in America: Life and Death in the Land of Opportunity* (Berkeley: University of California Press, 2005), 152–62. Notes, references, and figure have been renumbered and edited.

conflict centers around social, and ultimately sexual contact."

Picking up on these insights, this chapter draws attention to some of the ways in which our racialized health care system has contributed to the construction of physical markers that reinforce ideologies of immutable racial difference.

In their landmark study of race, medicine, and health care in the United States, Michael Byrd and Linda Clayton show that "legally sanctioned medical and environmental neglect of enslaved Africans and the institutionalization of an inconstant, often inferior, 'slave health subsystem'—processes that began in the seventeenth century—had future implications and dire consequences for Black people. A 'slave health deficit' transmitted from Africa by the Atlantic slave trade became institutionalized in English North America. Race in the embryonic health system became a marker almost as important as it was in the institution of slavery."

Writing about the historical processes that led to the creation of a "Black health and health care underclass,"[2] Byrd and Clayton write: "Caste, race, and class problems distorted the nation's hospital system from its beginnings. The nation's early hospitals discriminated against and sometimes medically abused Black patients.... The foundations of the American health delivery system were built on a class-stratified, racially segregated, and discriminatory basis." As is typical in caste systems, ideology was invoked to justify social hierarchies: "The professional assumption of poor health as 'normal' for Blacks remained ingrained in the minds of White American physicians—who went so far as to create a lexicon of 'Negro disease' and alternate physiological mechanisms based on race—well into the twentieth century."

Moreover, these racial hierarchies proved resistant to change, another trait common to caste systems. Along with Medicare and Medicaid legislation, the passage of the 1964 Civil Rights Act, which desegregated hospitals, helped to improve the health status of African Americans through the mid-1970s, as federal funding increased access to medical care. In 1975, however, Byrd and Clayton note, health progress for black Americans "virtually stopped ... as the commitment, political support, and funding for the special programs" waned. After 1980, these authors argue, the health status of African Americans actually deteriorated relative to that of whites.

Increasing residential segregation has been a key factor in this deterioration. Other factors include continuing discrimination in hiring practices, welfare reform policies that have led to large numbers of African American women losing their Medicaid enrollment, and a growing political inclination to incarcerate African American men.

TIMOTHY'S STORY: "NO BENEFITS, NO MEDICAL"

Denise's potent voice resonates through the small but crowded Pentecostal church in Decatur, Illinois, where she and her husband, Timothy, are part of the prayer team that stands in front of the pulpit, charged with the sweet duty of inviting the all-black congregation to feel the presence of the Holy Spirit. Timothy small of build and soft of voice compared to his statuesque wife, more than makes up for his slight stature by choosing an array of ultra-stylish clothes. Dressed in a spiffy white suit jacket cut well below his hips and adorned with shiny gold buttons, Timothy looks as if he shops at a boutique that caters to televangelists or soul music stars. They are, indeed, a striking couple on the Sunday that we meet them for the first time.

At our second meeting, we have to do a double-take in order to recognize them. Shepherded to our house after work by a local pastor, they seem to have none of the personal power that had beamed from their faces at church. Instead, their bearing proclaims nervousness, timidity—the psychic act of shrinking down in order to take up less space that so many African Americans learn to execute when they enter white neighborhoods.

Denise and Timothy were born in southern Illinois. Both have worked at a variety of blue-collar jobs since 1970, when they left high school. This is a second marriage for both of them. They wed after living together for a number of years. Looking at Denise with obvious affection, Timothy explains, "Couldn't find no one else to put up with me, and she couldn't find no one else either, so we stayed with each other. We figured we'd been together so long we might as well get married."

Timothy has never worked at a job that offered health insurance. At all his jobs, "even the job that I have now, the work is strenuous and the work is hard, but yet still, they don't have no health insurance."

Timothy's current job is at an animal feed plant in the countryside outside Decatur. The plant is exposed to the elements—no heat in the freezing Decatur winters and no air conditioning in the boiling Decatur summers.

The work involves stacking up bird seed and dog food, lifting sacks that weigh anywhere from twenty-five to sixty-five pounds, day in and day out. We ask Timothy how many sacks he lifts in a day.

"Whoa, I mean, there's no end to it. Putting them on pallets. Stacking up pallets with forklifts. Sometimes we're stacking them ten high, sometimes we're stacking them sixteen high. The feed comes down a machine into the sack, it goes on the conveyor belt, and the machine sews it. Then we stack it. When the stack is over our heads, we throw the sacks up. You get it up there the best you can."

Standing five foot nine (in platform shoes), Timothy finds this work physically demanding. Denise tells us that he is "wore out" from the work and that his health has deteriorated in the past year.

For this work, Timothy is paid $7 an hour, with no benefits. Much to our surprise, he tells us that there is not much turnover on the job, "because they know folks want a job. They hold on to people for a good while."

The air in the warehouse where the seed sacks are stored is almost always filled with dust from wheat, oats, and other grains. Although the workers wear face masks to protect their lungs from the dust, one of Timothy's co-workers was hospitalized because of lung damage. We ask whether the employer paid for the medical care and medication. "No, no, no, no, no, no, no." Then we ask whether the injured employee received workers' compensation payments. "No, no, no, no, no, no, no. They don't have it. No benefits, no medical." None of Timothy's jobs has ever paid well or provided health insurance, but he claims that some, such as construction jobs, have been more "lenient" regarding paying for workplace injuries—although…construction jobs in fact are not all that "lenient" either.

Timothy injured his knee, tearing cartilage, while on his current job. The knee became infected. The emergency room treated the infection but told him that he needed surgery to correct the torn cartilage, which required a down payment of $1,000. He also was told that without the surgery, he might not be able to use his knee later on. He does not have the $1,000 down payment and has not had the surgery.

We ask whether the hospital referred him to its charity care program.

"No, they just said they will not do nothing till we come up with the first thousand dollars." Timothy suspects that the hospital took this position because he has already incurred medical debt of about $30,000, accumulated over the years in the wake of other injuries and infections.

Both Timothy and Denise have worked their entire lives, yet they have no savings and do not own their house. Nonetheless, Timothy would take a lower-paying job if it provided health benefits. He has never received any sort of basic, ongoing health care, and, after years of hard work, his age has begun to catch up with him. He is experiencing several disturbing symptoms. Without dental care, he has lost quite a few teeth. He knows he needs glasses (he buys them without a prescription at Walgreens for a couple of dollars) but has not had his eyes checked in ten years. He also has been bothered by periodic numbness in his arms; it feels as if he is "losing circulation" in his arms.

Most distressing, Timothy has been experiencing rectal bleeding for a number of years. The bleeding is sporadic: sometimes "it comes out like a woman's period," and sometimes it will stop for a day or so. "So I know there's something that's not right." The bleeding seems to have worsened since he started his current job. He knows he needs to see a doctor. "If I can get a job with medical insurance or something where we'll pay fifty percent and they pay fifty percent, yeah, I'll go have it checked out." This rectal bleeding is particularly problematic, as it may be an early (or, at this point, not so early) sign of colon cancer or other serious illness that could be treated if caught in time but could prove fatal with delays.

RACE HEALTH, AND HEALTH CARE

Timothy's career path is not unusual for African American men in the United States. Almost one-third of African American workers are employed in low-wage jobs, in contrast to fewer than 20 percent of white workers who hold such jobs. African Americans are three times as likely as whites to have family incomes below the poverty line. Black workers are also more likely than whites to be employed in temporary jobs, which rarely include health care benefits. Moreover, even with comparable levels of education, nonwhites earn less than whites.

Partly because of discrimination in hiring, and partly because they are stuck in low-wage or temporary jobs, black Americans are less likely than white Americans to have health insurance. African Americans make up 12 percent of the workforce but represent 16 percent of the working uninsured. Overall, in 2003, 20.8 percent of black Americans and 35.7 percent of Hispanics were uninsured, compared to 14.5 percent of white Americans (see figure 1).

The gap in insurance rates is part of a larger picture of racial disparities in health outcomes in the United States. African Americans are much

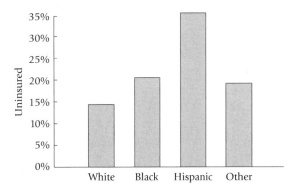

FIGURE 1. The uninsured, by race, under age 65 (first half of 2003). *Source*: Rhoades 2004.

more likely than whites to die of cancer, heart disease, and diabetes; and the maternal mortality rate for black women is three to four times that among whites. Infant mortality among black children is more than twice that for whites. Life expectancy overall is five years shorter for African Americans, and this disparity is even more marked in poorer areas of the country. African American women are more than twice as likely to die of cervical cancer as white women and are more likely to die of breast cancer than women of any other racial or ethnic group. Overall, 40 percent of black men die prematurely, often from strokes, as do 37 percent of Hispanic men, compared to 21 percent of white men.

Although many factors account for differences in health status, experts agree that good access to appropriate health services could reduce many of these disparities. In spite of their higher mortality and morbidity for cardiovascular disease, African Americans and Hispanics are less likely to receive treatment for these conditions and are especially less likely to receive high-tech cardiac procedures such as cardiac catheterization and coronary revascularization. African American women are diagnosed more frequency than white women with late-stage breast cancer—probably related to barriers that prevent them from accessing life-saving diagnostic services and treatment.

DENISE'S STORY: "THEY ARE SO PREJUDICED"

For Denise's part, the best job she ever had was at the Caterpillar plant, where she worked for eight years. During that time, she enjoyed excellent benefits, including good health insurance with dental care and full coverage for her three children.

When she became pregnant in 1991, she was working in the Caterpillar paint shop. The work involved cleaning out the inside of large iron vats. Leaning into a vat, she bumped her abdomen on a handle, causing a miscarriage. At the same time, the ongoing strain of the paint shop work injured her back.

She went to a doctor, who told her to stay off work until she felt fully recovered from both the miscarriage and the back injury. But before the doctor released her for work, Caterpillar insisted that she return to the plant. She was fired when she told Caterpillar that she was still unable to work. Denise explains, "I didn't understand these things at first, like people do now. I didn't know then about getting a lawyer or anything about that. So that was just it."

After the Caterpillar experience, Denise worked at a series of jobs as a nurse's assistant. But these jobs typically involved lifting patients, and she was unable to stay for very long at any one nursing home. None of these jobs offered health insurance.

In the mid-1990s, after her children were grown and out of the house, Denise became involved with drugs and alcohol. In 1999, as she puts it, the Lord helped her leave that behind. Since then, she has been an active member of her church community and has learned that she needs to take responsibility for her own life.

At the time of our meeting, she was enrolled in Medicare, receiving disability payments. But she told us that the Medicare would be cut off soon—she just didn't know when. Denise has a number of nagging medical problems with her eyes and her feet and knows she should take care of them before

the Medicare runs out, but she is not quite sure how to go about this.

Compounding her anxiety about her health is the fear that she will never again be able to find a good job. Over the past year, she has picked up some casual work at a beauty parlor, but nursing jobs seem to have dried up, and she believes that she has no hope of landing the kind of job that will provide long-term employment or health benefits. Denise's assessment of her job prospects is probably correct, for two somewhat different reasons.

First, when the large manufacturing plants in Decatur close or move abroad, the government and the unions provide job retraining programs for the workers who are laid off. One of the most popular programs offers certification as a hospital aide or a certified nurse's aide (CNA), work that had not previously required formal training or certification, at least in the Decatur area. Given the long history of racial and gender discrimination in the town's factories and labor unions, this kind of service-sector work had been an extremely important job niche for African American women, who were unlikely to land the higher-paying manufacturing jobs with union contracts.

But the new job training programs available to "displaced" manufacturing employees now are turning out large numbers of white men and women who have received free training and certification, giving them an advantage in the health service–sector job market. African American women we spoke to in Decatur told us, in puzzlement, that it had always been easy to find jobs as a nurse's aide but that all the jobs have now begun to demand certification. Like Denise, these women didn't know what this certification was or how to go about getting it. (They would not have been eligible for the job retraining programs, in any case, since they were not officially classified as "displaced workers.")

A second issue that affects Denise's chances of landing a good job is her felony history (drug related). This record will make it impossible for her to work at a nursing home or hospital.

With the three-strikes-you're-out policy and tougher drug laws...U.S. prisons increasingly are filled with minorities who have been arrested on minor drug charges. These charges are now classified as felonies, making it nearly impossible for people like Denise to find a job. As Marc Mauer notes, "Prisons in the United States are increasingly serving as institutions of the poor and minorities. Half of all prison inmates today are African American and 16% are Hispanic; their median annual income prior to incarceration was less than $10,000."

We ask Denise and Timothy what it is like for an African American family to try to arrange health care, without insurance, in the mostly white towns of southern Illinois. "Well, if they ain't got no money, black people ain't going to get nothing," Denise asserts. "With white people, they overlook [medical bills], but some, a lot of them here in Decatur, they're so prejudiced. They are so prejudiced."

Denise recalls an incident from a couple of years ago. "I called for a job that I saw advertised. And they told me that they need a person right then, right then, right then. I was talking on the phone. I guess I talk like I'm not a black person. And I was talking, and he said, 'Oh, come on. I need somebody right away. I'll guarantee that I'll hire you. Come on in.' Well, I went in, sit down, and talk to him, and he said, 'Oh, I'm sorry, I've already filled that position.' Now that really hurt me. He had told me to come on in, yes, because I had experience in that job. When he seen the color of my skin, that was it."

Denise's experience is not unique. A number of large-scale studies document that when well-matched pairs of black and white job applicants apply for the same advertised jobs, the black applicant is less likely to be offered the job.

Denise and Timothy are not interested in public aid. As Denise says, "I'd rather work and make my own money with the strength that God gave me." They also do not relish the paperwork and personal questions that people must answer in order to receive public aid. But they would like the government to make health care available to people like themselves who don't have a lot of money but are not (yet) "flat-out" broke.

NOTES

1. Other scholars, including Michael Byrd and Linda Clayton (2002) and Douglas Massey and Nancy Denton (1993), identify the persistent, pervasive, and castelike features of America's racial hierarchy.

2. This phrase, coined by Byrd and Clayton (2002), was inspired by the insights of Dr. M. Alfred Haynes.

REFERENCES

Byrd, Michael and Linda Clayton. 2002. An American Health Dilemma: Race, Medicine and Health care in the United States, 1900–2000. New York: Routledge.

Dollard, John. 1937. Caste and Class in a Southern Town. Garden City, N.Y: Doubleday.

Massey, Douglas and Nancy Denton. 1993. American Apartheid: Segregation and the Making of the Underclass. Cambridge, MA: Haward University Press.

Mauer, Marc. 2000. "The Racial Dynamics of Imprisonment," In Building Violence: How America's Rush to Incarcerate Creates More Violence, ed., John P. May pp 47–50. Thousand Oaks, CA: Sage Publications.

Rhoades Jeffrey. 2004. "The Uninsured in America." Statistical Brief #41. Medical Expenditure Panel Survey. Available online at www.meps.ahrq.gov/papers/st41/stat4.html. (Accessed October, 26, 2004.)

JOURNALING QUESTION

Have you, or anybody in your family or friendship network, ever had to forego needed medical care because you couldn't afford it? What was that (or what would that be) like for you?

GLOBALIZATION, IMMIGRATION, AND CITIZENSHIP

34.
FLYING THE MEXICAN FLAG IN LOS ANGELES

ANUPAM CHANDER

Flags are powerful symbols and lend themselves to dramatic display. One can literally wrap a flag around oneself, wear it on one's clothing, raise it in improbable places, tear it down and burn it, all making clear and powerful statements without actually hurting anyone. Flags are our best-recognized symbols of nation-states, so flying two flags, claiming two flags, might indeed be a statement about national identity. But people may also wear an American flag and a Jewish Star, Christian Cross, Gay Pride Flag, or other identifier without calling down the wrath that the Mexican flag caused, as described in this article. Could there be a symbolic presentation of "Mexican American" that would not have angered people? Or was the anger about immigration and Mexican Americans in the United States, and not really about fears of dual citizenship?

When Cardinal Roger Mahony took the podium to address a rally supporting immigrants on Olvera Street in Los Angeles in May 2006, he began by asking those waving Mexican flags to please "roll up flags from other countries."[1] On Spanish language radio, announcers implored their audience to leave the Mexican flag at home, and to wave the Star Spangled Banner instead. Indeed, the hoisting of the Mexican tricolor during the immigration marches of 2006 drew the ire of many. Some perceived it as a demonstration of disloyalty to the United States. Even more insidiously, according to some it offered a daring revelation of the marchers' true intent: "This is how America is going to be taken over without a shot being fired."[2]

This apprehension about the potential mixed loyalties of immigrants finds grounding (without the nativist animus) in two distinct and well-respected philosophical traditions. Civic republicans worry about the harm to the body politic from people who disperse their political allegiances.[3] Some compare dual nationality to bigamy, and declare it a similarly improbable balancing act.[4] For a civic republican, draping the Mexican flag around one's shoulders would signal a determination to maintain an allegiance to a foreign land, when one's political energies should be directed to the community in which one lives. Many cosmopolitans would have the opposite worry—that waving the Mexican flag might demonstrate a commitment to one people, rather than to humanity at large. For them, local attachment reflects atavistic loyalties to kinfolk and insufficient sympathy for the rest of the world. Kwame Anthony Appiah associates this form of cosmopolitanism with the Cynics, to whom the cosmo-politan formulation is credited, and distinguishes it from his own more "rooted" cosmopolitanism.[5] The rootless cosmopolitan would find fault with strident nationalism of any kind, whether reflecting an attachment to the immediate state or to a distant homeland. Others have critiqued both of these approaches.[6] My own arguments toward that end can be found in my paper entitled "Diaspora Bonds."[7]

In the present essay I do not wish to question Cardinal Mahony's intentions[8] or the political wisdom of his strategy.[9] Rather, I hope to show that the strategy bears a price. The strategy relies on

Anupam Chander, "Flying the Mexican Flag in Los Angeles," *Fordham Law Review* 75, no 5 (2007): 2469–2482.

one of two underlying logics: hide or change. The first logic dictates that, for political advantage, one should stash the Mexican flag in a closet in one's house and appear in public shorn of any partiality towards a foreign nation. The second logic suggests that, in order to be American, one should fly but one flag, and it should be red, white, and blue. Either logic, I will argue, diminishes us—as a country and as human beings. Hiding suggests that the United States is not prepared to accept the immigrant as he or she truly is. Changing embraces an assimilationist ethic, establishing one proper mode of being American.

Some will say that the price of conforming to a singular national identity is acceptable. My goal here is not to demonstrate that we should not pay this price; others have offered reasons to promote a world integrated through individual political affiliations.[10] I hope here simply to identify the costs of this political strategy and offer suggestions for their amelioration.

This essay proceeds as follows. Part I describes the vitriol heaped on the marchers who dared to fly the Mexican flag. Part II revisits the run-up to the Japanese internment, and its consequences for Japanese Americans in Post-War America; the lessons learned by Japanese Americans might give us pause today. Part III identifies the possible adverse consequences of the request not to fly the Mexican flag. Part IV considers the claim that the Mexican flag makes plain its bearer' hidden agenda: to restore all of California to Mexico.

I. "GO BACK HOME"

When the immigration marches first erupted across the country in 2006, commentators seized on the display of the Mexican flag in order to brand the marchers disloyal to the United States. Some called for those carrying the Mexican flag to "go back home" to Mexico.[11] Critics saw the Mexican flag as the impudent[12] demonstration of loyalty to a foreign country. "Call it racism, call it whatever you want, but the fact is that the waving of Mexico's flag

showed the rest of us, even this die-hard liberal, that a large portion of the illegal immigrant community are not Americans" said one spectator "if people want to be Americans, then they need to support Americans, and that means waving the American flag" [13] On television, a prominent columnist declared, "The student brandishing the Mexican flag signals divided loyalty or perhaps loyalty to a foreign powery."[14] The founder of California-based "Save Our State" complained, "This isn't Mexico...This is America...What [annoys me] most is the arrogance that they are going to fly a foreign flag on my soil."[15] Dan Stein, president of the nativist Federation for American Immigration Reform, complained that "Mexico apparently believes that they send people here, who become U.S. citizens and keep allegiance to Mexico."[16] Worse, some saw it as a declaration of war: "It reinforces what we keep hearing from the protesters, that this land used to be Mexico and they are going to take it back."[17] A Colorado state representative called it an "in-your-face rebellion."[18] Some found evidence of a "fifth column" and proclaimed the Chicano mayor of Los Angeles to be a general in this column.[19]

Perhaps heeding the call of a national radio talk show host,[20] a few even burned the Mexican flag. In Arizona, a vigilante border patrol group recited the Pledge of Allegiance before setting alight the Mexican flag.[21] While it burned they chanted, "Long live George Washington! God bless America!"[22] In Arizona, "when students raised a Mexican flag over Apache Junction High School...other students yanked it down and burned it."[23]

The organizers of the march had anticipated this backlash.[24] They warned pro-immigration rights supporters to put aside the Mexican flag and hoist the American flag instead: "Wary of confrontations, organizers of a giant pro-immigration rally this weekend have issued a directive: Keep your Mexican flags at home."[25] Organizers even handed out American flags to marchers.[26] The Mexican government cautioned against waving its flag: "The Mexican consul in San Diego, Luis Cabrera, appeared on Spanish-language television...to discourage students from waving Mexican flags."[27] The organizers of the Dallas march posted the following "rule" for the April 2006 march: "No Mexican flags. Only U.S. flags will be displayed. Wear white to signify peace. No negative messages. All banners must be positive."[28]

This strategy was not uncontested, even at the time. For some, "the Mexican flag is too meaningful a symbol to be set aside, particularly by recent immigrants."[29] And, of course, despite the organizer's imploring, many marchers still flew the Mexican flag, sometimes in conjunction with the American flag, and sometimes alone. Before we consider their own explanations in Part III below, I want to recall earlier episodes in American history that remind us that these battles have been fought before, just with different ethnic casts.

II. AMERICANS, BONA FIDE

A 1925 photograph shows 50,000 members of the Ku Klux Klan, marching down Pennsylvania Avenue in Washington D.C.; their hoods off, they carry American flags.[30] A year earlier another group had trodden that same path, but these were 100,000 men from the National Catholic Holy Name Society, "carrying papal banners and United States flags."[31]

Throughout American history, those who declared themselves bona fide Americans questioned the loyalty of various groups seeking full membership in the American polity. American Catholics, for example, found themselves the target of such attacks in the early twentieth century. For Catholics in the period between world wars, the hostility they faced led them ironically "to exert a greater degree of organized political power."[32] By carrying both flags at the 1924 march, the organizers sought "to show forth visibly among men the truth that loyalty to country and loyalty to Catholicity were not incompatible."[33] The accusation of dual loyalty has been leveled against many groups through American history (and the history of many other nations as well). It has been

leveled, for example, against Jewish Americans.[34] In the last century, it has been leveled with perhaps the most devastating effect against Japanese Americans.

American actions at home during World War II saw such distrust turned into tragedy. One hundred and twenty thousand people of Japanese descent in the United States were deported from their west coast homes to prison camps scattered through inland deserts and swamps.

The military report by General John L. DeWitt justifying their incarceration sought to demonstrate the threat that people of Japanese descent posed to the United States. General DeWitt cited their lack of assimilation, their tightly knit family and social networks, their ties to Japan by race, culture, and custom as evidence of their danger. The fact that some had remained steadfast Buddhists was also cited. In upholding a curfew against a Japanese American citizen, the U.S. Supreme Court in Gordon Hirabayashi's case pointed to similar factors—a failure to assimilate and the fact that children attended Japanese language schools in the United States or in Japan, which, the Court reasoned, might cultivate allegiance to Japan.[35]

The popular press meanwhile denounced the menace of this "fifth column." *Time* magazine, like the other leading periodicals and newspapers of the day, alerted Americans to the dangers of the Japanese Americans living among them. In an article titled "No. 1 Fifth Column" in January 1942, *Time* warned, "In the 157,905 Japanese in the Hawaiian Islands (more than one-third of the population), Tokyo had plenty of talent...[36] The irony of this claim, of course, is that Japanese Americans were not interned wholesale in Hawaii—they were too important to the military and economic operations in those islands. A further irony: After Pearl Harbor, many Japanese Americans wore "American-flag pins saying 'I am an American' on coat lapels."[37] Flying the American flag proved futile against an enraged public unwilling to accept the veracity of public displays of allegiance.

Mexican consulates today offer an extensive array of services for Mexican citizens in the United States, hoping thereby to strengthen the bonds with their diaspora. But in 1942, the "association of influential Japanese residents with Japanese Consulate" was held to be a marker of disloyalty.[38] Of course, the nativist ire against the Mexican flag bearers is a far cry from the rampant public racism that was prelude to internment. Yet, there are similarities today, and lessons we might do well to remember.

III. EMBRACING AMERICA BY ERASING ONE'S PAST

Challenged by the Klan and others as un-American, Catholic leaders in the 1920s sought to demonstrate their patriotism by promoting "Americanization."[39] They "encouraged immigrants to learn English and embrace "American 'principles.'"[40] Some Catholics dissented, fearing that such an approach might "homogenize American culture in the image of Anglo-Saxon Protestantism"[41] at the expense of their heritage:

> Reverend John O'Grady, who had represented the National Catholic War Council at an Interior Department Americanization conference, denounced the effort to deprive immigrants of all of their European ideas and culture. "The democratic ideals of the immigrant have helped to make America, in the beginning," he insisted," and they can aid in its further development today." O'Grady called for substituting the homogenizing "Americanization" program for one that promoted citizenship.[42]

Perhaps if the dissenters had prevailed, it might have been less possible for a prominent academic today to proclaim America's core national identity as "Anglo-Protestant."[43] These dissenters raised a principal difficulty with the response to the accusation of being un-American: the risk that the challenge will be met by denying central parts of one's own history.

The lesson learned by Japanese Americans from internment was to assimilate, to insist on their singular loyalty to the United States, even at the expense of their ties to their homeland. The children of internees reported on a national survey that they felt pressure within their families to "Americanize" and assimilate into mainstream society, and they attributed "the loss of Japanese language and culture to the internment's effect."[44] Even the internment itself was to be forgotten, a stigma not to be revealed to the next generation,[45] which could grow up hoping to be embraced as American. Discussions of the internment itself were "taboo," "a skeleton in the family closet."[46] Karen Korematsu, Fred Korematsu's daughter, learned of her father's challenge to internment from a high school presentation.

Consider one characterization of the immigrant march strategy. According to Jennifer Allen, executive director of the immigrant rights group Border Action Network, "immigrant families in southern Arizona are telling one another to carry the American flag in their hands, but hold the Mexican flag in their hearts."[47] Such a public-private bifurcation between hand and heart is all too common for many groups seeking acceptance within mainstream society. One scholar describes "women who straighten their noses or hair to achieve a 'Queen Elizabeth exterior' while retaining a 'Jewish heart.'"[48] Another classic formulation is, "Dress British, think Yiddish."[49] Holding an American flag but keeping the Mexican flag in one's heart might consist in either "passing" or "covering," to borrow Kenji Yoshino's helpful distinction.[50] Passing involves deception: trying to convince the mainstream world that you too belong to them. Covering, on the other hand, involves a mutual understanding: downplaying your difference to please a mainstream audience that understands your difference but is uncomfortable with it.[51] Both are strategies of assimilation.

The Mexican American who heeds the call not to wave the Mexican flag, though she might wish to do so, might be passing: hoping that viewers will not recognize the Mexican affiliation hidden in her heart, and take her for an American of Mexican origin. Mexico would then represent a past to forget, not a future to be embraced.

Yoshino describes four axes along which covering can occur: appearance ("how an individual physically presents herself to the world"); affiliation (an individual's "cultural identification"); activism ("how much she politicizes her identity"); and association ("her choice of fellow traveler").[52] The decision to wave (or not wave) the Mexican flag concerns all four axes: the physicality of the Mexican flag flying on an American street (appearance); the flag's representation of one's association with Mexico and Mexican Americans (affiliation); the confident message that a foreign flag sends (activism); and the flag's embrace of Mexican Americans (association).

The strategy of changing our public behavior for social comfort is a common one. We might change our accent, cut our hair, wear a suit—that is, perform—to accommodate the preferences of our observers. Indeed, this is a part of membership in society; we would not want everyone to behave exactly as they might wish. As Yoshino writes, "Assimilation is often a precondition of civilization—to speak a language, to curb violent urges, and to obey the law are all acts of assimilatiori."[53] Yoshino rejects only "coerced assimilation not supported by reasons."[54] As Yoshino immediately notes, whether a reason for a preferred behavior is good enough to justify social or legal coercion will prove controversial. But as Yoshino writes, there is a "dark side of assimilation."[55] This dark side can be found in the challenge assimilation poses to autonomy and "authenticity"—an individual's capacity to script her own life.

Even a seemingly benign strategy designed for immediate political advantage for a worthy cause should give us pause. This strategy exacts a price not only from Mexican Americans but also from other Americans. It suggests that, as a nation, we are hostile to foreigners who seek to maintain their ties to their homeland.[56] For some—but not by any means all—Mexican Americans, it poses a challenge to their desire to maintain an important link to their homeland.

Consider the marchers' own words. Antonio Rodriguez, "a construction worker born and raised in Fresno, said he participated in the protest to support...co-worker from Mexico."[57] Rodriguez, an American citizen by birth, said, "We don't stop being Americans. We don't stop being Mexicans. We are both."[58] The many Mexican American high school students who were interviewed by reporters often expressed similar views. Griselda Sapien, an immigrant high school senior from Mexico, declared, "I am proud of both countries."[59] Davis, California high school student Alex Cervantes carried both flags over the Yolo Causeway to join a rally at California's capital.[60] The son of Mexican immigrants, he saw the Mexican flag as "a symbol of their success as well as their struggle,"[61] and both flags together as "a symbol of unification."[62] Even some of those who carried only an American flag expressed their preference to have carried both: "I had an American flag," said high school junior Carolina Arredondo; "I wanted to take both flags, but I could only carry one."[63] As the columnist Clarence Page described, the marchers often displayed what W. E. B. Du Bois called "double consciousness."[64]

Some saw the foreign flag as a declaration of cultural solidarity rather than national identity. Some sought to embrace a Chicano identity and thereby demonstrate solidarity with other Mexican Americans. (This is the multiculturalist account, distinct from the diaspora account, of contemporary citizenship.)[65] Alvaro Huerta, director of community education and advocacy for the Coalition for Humane Immigrant Rights of Los Angeles, argued, "Carrying the flag of one's native land 'represents culture and heritage, not national identity.'"[66] One Phoenix high school senior offered a similar explanation, stating that the Mexican flag represents "our culture, our heritage, where we are from."[67] University of California Irvine professor Frank Bean saw the flag as a symbol of solidarity in the face of anti-immigrant action: "They are saying, 'We are together in fighting against these people who are trying to make felons out of us,'" he said.[68] Isidro D. Ortiz, a political scientist and professor of Chicano and Chicana studies at San Diego State University, sees the flag as "primarily a symbol of Mexican pride, "but" in the current climate of the United States, Latinos also wave it to express dissatisfaction with how they are treated."[69] Ortiz argued that Mexican immigrants "have been trying for some time to imagine themselves as a part of the United States…What they've experienced is refusal."[70] Given the construction of modern identity, requiring someone to yield connection with a homeland imposes for many an important loss.

A political strategy of hiding the Mexican flag is of course not the same as a legal requirement to yield foreign ties. Yet, my concern is that the practical effect of embracing such a strategy might well go beyond the superficial. Covering or passing might transform over time into conversion, as one adapts and internalizes the demands of society. Yoshino identifies conversion—"a spiritual transformation of our core"—as a third form of assimilation in addition to passing and covering.[71] Told that it is improper to hold two allegiances even in the depths of one's heart, one might find one's core commitments themselves shifting over time.

For homeland nations, this strategy might bear yet another price. It might lead to reluctance to maintain the diaspora bonds which link homeland to expatriate. This rupture comes precisely at the time that developing countries such as Mexico are making concerted efforts to nurture such diaspora ties.[72] Homeland governments have found that diaspora bonds must be nurtured, lest they wither over time and distance. The assimilationist strategy may lead people to contribute less to their homeland. It may help cement the brain drain aspect of migration.

We already see some evidence of the larger implications of the demand to demonstrate one's status as a bona fide American. One prominent columnist suggested this summer that the failure of Mexican citizens in the United States to exercise their right to vote absentee in Mexican elections demonstrated their singular loyalty to the United States.[73]

IV. FEAR OF A BROWN CALIFORNIA

The flags of many other nations have long been flown proudly in the United States without attracting the same furor as that drawn by the hoisting of the Mexican tricolor in 2006. On St. Patrick's Day, Republic of India Day, or Israel Day, the flags of various nations have flown in the United States largely without protest. Yet, perhaps there is something different about flying the Mexican flag in Los Angeles. After all, Los Angeles was once part of Mexico. Anna Deavere Smith's *Twilight Los Angeles* begins by narrating the words of a Mexican American Angeleno who recalls an ancestor who fought with Pancho Villa against the United States. Does his long memory reflect a hidden ambition? Are we seeing that war's bloodless reprise?

The geographic, demographic, and perhaps economic circumstances are also distinct. Mexico is a nation of 100 million, many of whom live within a day's drive of Los Angeles. The economic disparity between America and Mexico is stark. Average per capita income in Mexico is $7,310, while in the United States it is $43,740.[74]

What if households from East L.A. to Westwood freely flew the Mexican flag? Are we witnessing the reconquest of California as one prominent scholar, Samuel Huntington, labels it? Huntington writes, "Mexican immigration is leading toward the demographic reconquista of areas Americans took from Mexico by force in the 1830s and 1840s."[75] In his new book *State of Emergency*, Pat Buchanan sounds an even more alarmist note.[76] Buchanan claims to uncover an "Aztlan ploft" aimed "at reannexation of the Southwest, not militarily, but ethnically, linguistically, and culturally, through transfer of millions of Mexicans into the United States and a migration of "Anglos' out of the lands Mexico lost in 1848."[77] Buchanan sees the Mexican diaspora as an invasion force:

> The presence in the United States of a vast diaspora that retains its emotional and blood ties to Mexico provides Mexico City with immense leverage to

advance an agenda that entails the steady diminu-tion of U.S. sovereignty and economic and politi-cal merger of the United States with Mexico. The marches against Proposition 187 under a "sea of Mexican flags," the "Grand March" of half a million Hispanics in Los Angeles for amnesty on May Day 2006, that shocked U.S. politicians with its display of Hispanic power, show how potent is the machine Mexico is building inside the United States.[78]

Is this war by other means?

This appears quite unlikely. Mexican Americans do not wish to overthrow the U.S. government or to secede from the Union, but rather to become a part of it. Those who purport to identify a sinister intent rely on a handful of isolated statements from fringe groups to string together an alleged conspir-acy among millions. The claim smacks of the dis-loyalty grossly assumed of Japanese Americans in World War II.

In addition, while their presence may pressure U.S. foreign policy in favor of Mexico, Mexican Americans are far from capturing Mexican issues on the national stage. The immigration marches, for example, succeeded in routing the proposed punitive antiimmigrant legislationi,[79] but did not liberalize immigration. Mexican Americans even lack political power proportionate to their numbers in the state of California. Furthermore, rather than a third-world invasion, the opposite is more likely true. First, Americans are establishing beachheads in Mexico. Colonies of American retirees now dot the Mexican coastline from Baja to the Gulf of Mexico.[80] I suspect that few of these Americans have given up their allegiance to the United States, though many might have taken up a new loyalty to Mexico. Second, the Mexican diaspora in the United States exerts political power in Mexico.[81] Ernesto Zedillo, who served as President of Mexico from 1994 to 2000, received a Ph.D. at Yale, while his successor, Vicente Fox, had had a prior career as an executive at American multinational Coca-Cola.

On the legal side, the North American Free Trade Agreement, along with its side agreements, saw the export of U.S. laws, not the import of Mexican laws.

In sum, California will not be reclaimed by Mexico, but many Mexican Americans will likely demonstrate a commitment to their homeland. This will evince itself in a variety of ways, some cul-tural (for example, in music, dance, language, and art) and some political (for example, involvement in hometown associations, voting, and diaspora bonds).[82] But a commitment to Mexico is not incon-sistent with a commitment to the United States.

CONCLUSION

We do not simply integrate immigrants into an existing American landscape, but we also expect that landscape to change upon their immigration.[83] But it will not undermine a national commitment to the U.S. Constitution. Those Mexican Americans who continue to hold passionate attachment to their homeland are likely to only increase our national commitment to the cause of justice around the world. They will not undermine our values, but rather extend them further.

NOTES

1. Day to Day (National Public Radio broadcast Apr. 11, 2006).
2. Morning Edition (National Public Radio broadcast May 2, 2006) (transcript quoting Atlanta resident) (emphasis added); see also Michelle Malkin, Racism Gets a Whitewash, Wash. Times, Apr. 2, 2006, available at http://washingtontimes.com/commentary/20060401–090702-114r.htm ("Advocates believe the reclamation (or reconquista) of Aztlan will occur through sheer demographic force.").
3. See generally David A. Martin, The Civic Republican Ideal for Citizenship, and for Our Common Life, 35 Va. J. lnt'l L. 301 (1994); Stanley A. Renshon, Dual Citizenship and

American Democracy: Patriotism, National Attachment, and National Identity, 21 Soc. Phil. & Pol'y 100, 105 (2004) ("Advocates of dual citizenship consistently minimize the difficulties of being a fully engaged, knowledgeable, and effective citizen in one political system, much less two.").

4. See, e.g., Georgie Anne Geyer, Americans No More: The Death of Citizenship 68 (1996).

5. K. Anthony Appiah, Cosmopolitanism: Ethics in a World of Strangers (2006).

6. See, e.g., David A. Martin & T. Alexander Aleinikoff, Double Ties: Why Nations Should Lean to Love Dual Nationality, Foreign Pol'y, Nov.-Dec. 2002, at 80.

7. See generally Anupam Chander, Diaspora Bonds, 76 N.Y.U. L. Rev. 1005 (2001).

8. Last spring, Cardinal Roger Mahony courageously announced his intention to lead massive civil disobedience in the event Congress enacted a law barring the provision of aid to undocumented immigrants. See Editorial, The Gospel vs. H.R. 4437, N.Y. Times, Mar. 3, 2006, at A22.

9. Some claim that the "sea" of "llegal" immigrants waving Mexican flags doomed pro-immigrant legislation. See Teresa Watanabe, Latino Activists Put Faith in Ballots, L.A. Times, Sept. 10, 2006, at B1 ("'The mass sea of illegal aliens bearing foreign flags and hostile placards really produced a pronounced backlash [against pro-immigration activists], from which they've never recovered,' said John Keeley, spokesman for the Washington-based Center for Immigration Studies.").

10. Yossi Shain suggests that diasporas do not undermine the American creed, but help market it in their homelands. See generally Yossi Shain, Marketing the American Creed Abroad: Diasporas in the U.S. and Their Homelands (1999); see also Chander, *supra* note 7, at 1005; Anupam Chander, Homeward Bound, 81 N.Y.U. L. Rev. 60 (2006).

11. Dorothy Korber et al., Protests Sweep U.S.: Unity's Theme at Capitol as More U.S. Flags Flutter, Sacramento Bee, Apr. 11, 2006, at Al (quoting a protestor's statement on Fox News on March 29, 2006); Amanda Lee Myers, Mexican Flag a Lightning Bolt During Protests, Pitt. Post-Gazette, Apr. 9, 2006, at A6.

12. One commentator branded it "brazen and entitled." Mexican Flag, a Sign of Unity, May Also Divide, Wichita Eagle, Apr. 11, 2006, at 1B [hereinafter Mexican Flag].

13. Yvonne Wingett & Daniel Gonzalez, Mexican Flags at Immigrant Rallies Cause Flap, Chi. Sun Times, Apr. 6, 2006, at 10 (internal quotation marks omitted).

14. Korber et al., *supra* note 11 (quoting columnist Robert Novak's statement on Fox News on March 29, 2006).

15. Tempers Flare over Mexican Flags, Cincinnati Post, Mar. 29, 2006, at A8 (internal quotation marks omitted and second omission in original) [hereinafter Tempers Flare].

16. Myung Oak Kim, Foreign Flags Create Flap Mexican Banners at Recent Rallies Prompt Backlash, Rocky Mtn. News (Denver), Mar. 30, 2006, at A6.

17. Tempers Flare, *supra* note 15 (internal quotation marks omitted).

18. Kim, *supra* note 16 (quoting Corporal State Representative Dave Schultheis).

19. This is an accusation leveled by some bloggers against Los Angeles Mayor Antonio Villaraigosa. See Posting of Van Helsing to Fifth Column Takes Los Angeles, http://www.moonbattery. com/archives/2005/05/fifth column ta.html (May 19, 2005, 06:14).

20. See Joyce Howard Price, Protesters' Foreign Flags Alienate Conservatives, Wash. Times, Apr. 1, 2006, at A01 ("Syndicated radio talk-show host Michael Savage...urged listeners to burn the Mexican flag.").

21. Levi J. Long, Mexican-Flag Burners Plan More Protests, Ariz. Daily Star, Apr. 10, 2006, at B1.

22. Id.

23. Blake Herzog, Immigration Tensions Spark Flag-Burning in A. J., E. Valley Trib. (Ariz.), Mar. 31, 2006, available at http://www.eastvalleytribune.com/index.php?sty=62231.

24. Elliot Spagat, 50,000 Rally in Support of Illegal Immigrants, Contra Costa Times (Walnut Creek, Cal.), Apr. 10, 2006, at F4 ("'The more American flags, the better this is going to be,' said Ben Monterroso, an organizer with Service Employees International Union Local 1877").

25. Dianne Solis, Banner Moment Stirs Up Passions: Planners Want Old Glory Only at Local Immigrant Rally, Dallas Morning News, Apr. 4, 2006, at A1.

26. Id.

27. Spagat, *supra* note 24.

28. Solis, *supra* note 25.

29. Hiram Soto, Mexican Flag Kindles Passions Pro and Con, San Diego Union-Trib., Apr. 8, 2006, at B1.

30. See Lynn Dumenil, The Tribal Twenties: 'assimilated' Catholic' Response to Anti-Catholicism in the 1920s, 11 J. Am. Ethnic Hist. 21, 21 (1991).

31. Id.

32. Id. at 40.

33. Id. at 36 (internal quotation marks omitted).

34. See Abraham Foxman, We Are One, But Not the Same, Jerusalem Post, Aug. 31, 2006, at 14.

35. See Hirabayashi v. United States. 320 U.S. 81,96–97 (1943).

36. No. 1 Fifth Column, Time, Jan. 5, 1942, at 23–24, available at http://www.time.com/time/magazine/article/0,9171,795667,00.html.

37. Amy Iwasaki Mass, Psychological Effects of the Camps on Japanese Americans, in Japanese Americans: From Relocation to Redress 159, 159 (Roger Daniels et al. eds., rev. ed. 1991).

38. Hirabayashi, 320 U.S. at 98.

39. Dumenil, *supra* note 30, at 30.

40. Id.

41. See id.

42. Id.

43. Samuel P. Huntington, Who Are We: The Challenges to America's National Identity 30 (2004) ("The principal theme of this book is the continuing centrality of Anglo Protestant culture to American national identity.").

44. Donna K. Nagata & Yuzuru J. Takeshita, Coping and Resilience Across Generations: Japanese Americans and the World War 11 Internment, 85 Psychoanalytic Rev. 587, 604 (1998). The post-war decades saw dramatic shifts in religious identification and rates of intermarriage, both indicators of assimilation. See David J. O'Brien & Stephen S. Fugita, The Japanese American Experience 98 (Warren F. Kimball & David Edwin Harrell, Jr., eds., 1991) ("By the 1970s, intermarriage among the third generation Sansei had jumped to approximately 60 percent of all new marriages"); Eric Woodrum, An Assessment of Japanese American Assimilation, Pluralism, and Subordination, 87 Am. J. Soc. 157, 158–160 (1981) ("Upon arrival in the United States, 81% of Issei were affiliated with traditional Japanese religions," but by the time of interviews conducted in early 1960s, Western religious affiliation increased to include one-third of the Issei and slightly over one-half of the Nisei (52.6%) and Sansei (55.2%).

45. See Nagata & Takeshita, *supra* note 44, at 604 ("While virtually all Sansei wanted to know more about the internment, explicit family communication about the topic was rare."); see

also Chalsa M. Loo, An Integrative-Sequential Treatment Model for Posttraumatic Stress Disorder: A Case Study of the Japanese American Internment and Redress, 13 Clinical Psychol. Rev. 89, 102 (1993) ("For four decades, many Issei and Nisei did not discuss their camp experiences with anyone, even members of their own family.")

46. Nagata & Takeshita, *supra* note 44, at 604.

47. Myers, *supra* note 11 (emphasis added).

48. Kenji Yoshino, Covering: The Hidden Assault on Our Civil Rights 169 (2006).

49. Brendan Vaughan, Esquire: The Meaning of Life: Wit, Wisdom, and Wonder from 65 Extraordinary People 99 (2004) (attributing the remark, somewhat surprisingly, to Gene Simmons, lead singer of the rock band KISS).

50. Yoshino, *supra* note 48, at 18 (adopting the term "covering' from Erving Goffman).

51. Id.

52. Id. at 79.

53. Id. at 26.

54. Id.

55. Id. at xi.

56. One newspaper made this assimilationist demand quite clear: "In a larger sense, it also is an indicator of the kind of cultural awareness that immigrants may have to develop before American citizens will feel they can embrace the petitioners." Mexican Flag, *supra* note 12.

57. Bill McEwen, Immigrants Are Raising Their Flags—and Ours, Fresno Bee (Cal.), Apr. 11, 2006, at B1.

58. Id.

59. Ernesto Portillo, Jr., Mexican Flags Draw Defense by Marchers Waving Them, Ariz. Daily Star, Apr. 7, 2006, at Bl.

60. Korber et al., *supra* note 11.

61. Id.

62. Id.

63. Portillo, *supra* note 59.

64. Clarence Page, The Foreign Flag Rule, Bait. Sun, Apr. 14, 2006, at 11A; see also Chander, *supra* note 7, at 1023–27 (discussing the double consciousness of diasporas)

65. See Chander, *supra* note 7, at 1046–48 (discussing the inadequacies of multicultural account of citizenship).

66. Price, *supra* note 20.

67. Wingett & Gonzalez, supra note 13.

68. Anna Gorman, Flag's Meaning Is in the Eye of the Beholder, L.A. Times, Mar. 29, 2006, at A11.

69. Myers, *supra* note 11.

70. Id. Kevin Johnson chronicles the "ring of fire" that the United States seems to offer Mexican Americans seeking to become part of American life. See Kevin R. Johnson, "Melting Pot" or "Ring of Fire" Assimilation and the Mexican-American Experience, 85 Cal. L. Rev. 1259 (1997).

71. Yoshino, *supra* note 48, at 48.

72. Chander, *supra* note 10, at 1040–41.

73. Sergio Munoz, Putting the Dual-Loyalty Myth to Rest, L.A. Times, July 16, 2006, at M2 (describing the op-ed's author as "a former editorial writer for The Times…whose weekly syndicated column in Spanish appears in 20 newspapers in 12 countries").

74. World Bank, World Development Report 2007, at 289 (2006).

75. Huntington, *supra* note 43, at 221.

76. Patrick Buchanan, State of Emergency: The Third World Invasion and Conquest of America (2006).

77. Id. at 125.

78. Id.

79. Bill Ong Hing & Kevin R. Johnson, The Immigrant Rights Marches of 2006 and the Prospects for a New Civil Rights Movement, 42 Harv. C.R-C.L L. Rev. (vol 42, No 1, Winter 2007, p. 99–138), available at http://papers.ssrn.com/sol3/papers.cfm?abstractid=951268) (observing that the marches "influenced the national debate over immigration," such that "the most controversial parts of the Sensenbrenner bill appeared to have lost support").

80. According to one real estate promoter of American retirement in Mexico:

> The U.S. Department of State estimates that out of the approximately four million Americans living overseas, between 600,000 and one million are in Baja and elsewhere in Mexico—up from about 200,000 a decade ago. The population in Rosarito is estimated at 95,000 with perhaps as many as 35,000 North Americans.
>
> Many of the residential areas are gated communities much like the communities north of the border. Most of the American residential areas are beachfront properties at prices much lower than state side.

BajaRelocation.com, Retirement in Mexico, http://baja-relocation.com/retirement.htm (last visited Feb. 12, 2007).

81. See generally Kim Barry, Home and Away: The Construction of Citizenship in an Emigration Context, 81 N.Y.U. L. Rev. 11 (2006).

82. See generally Chander, *supra* note 10.

83. T. Alexander Aleinikoff, Speech at the Fordham Law Review Symposium: New Dimensions of Citizenship 21 (Sept. 30, 2006) (transcript on file with the Fordham Law Review) ("The world that immigrants integrate into is one that through their actions they help to make and to change.").

JOURNALING QUESTION

What symbols of ethnic or other identity do you wear or use to decorate your home? Can you imagine circumstances in which you would put them away so as not to make people think you were "un-American"?

35.
NEW COMMODITIES, NEW CONSUMERS

Selling Blackness in a Global Marketplace

PATRICIA HILL COLLINS

When people think about race in the context of the economy and work, they usually focus, as have the articles in this section, on production: how race affects the hiring and conditions of workers. Patricia Hill Collins asks us to broaden our thinking and to consider consumption as well as production. As Collins argues, blackness itself, and the bodies of young black men and women specifically, are commodities, and they are used to sell yet other commodities. Is blackness the only racialized identity that is commodified in America?

> It's just me against the world, baby, me against the world.
> I got nothin' to lose—it's just me against the world.
> (Tupac Shakur)

In the eyes of many Americans, African American youth such as hip hop legend Tupac Shakur constitute a threatening and unwanted population. No longer needed for cheap, unskilled labor in fields and factories, poor and working-class black youth find few job opportunities in the large, urban metropolitan areas where most now reside. Legal and undocumented immigrants now do the dirty work in the hotels, laundries, restaurants and construction sites of a growing service economy. Warehoused in inner city ghettos that now comprise the new unit of racial segregation, poor black youth face declining opportunities and an increasingly punitive social welfare state. Because African American youth possess citizenship rights, social welfare programs legally can no longer operate in racially discriminatory ways. Yet, rather than providing African American youth with educational opportunities, elites chose instead to attack the social welfare state that ensured benefits for everyone.

Fiscal conservatives have cut funding for public schools, public housing, public health clinics, and public transportation that would enable poor and working-class black youth to get to burgeoning jobs in the suburbs. Hiding behind a rhetoric of color-blindness, elites claim that these policies lack racial intentionality (Guinier and Torres, 2002; Bonilla-Silva, 2003). Yet when it comes to who is affected by these policies, African American youth constitute a sizable segment of the "truly disadvantaged" (Wilson, 1987). No wonder Tupac Shakur laments, "It's just me against the world, baby, me against the world. I got nothin' to lose—it's just me against the world."

Philosopher Cornel West posits that this attitude of "having nothing to lose" reflects a growing sense of nihilism among urban black American youth and argues that this form of hopelessness constitutes a greater danger to African Americans than that faced by any previous generation (West, 1993). But are African American youth as nihilistic as West suggests? In her study of pregnant, low-income black adolescent girls, sociologist Wendy Luttrell finds only optimism. Luttrell's subjects

Excerpted from Patricia Hill Collins," New Commodities, New Consumers: Selling Blackness in a Global Marketplace," *Ethnicities* 6(2006): 297–317. References have been edited.

were fully aware of how society looked down upon then and, in response, saw their unborn children as sources of hope. Historian Robin D.G. Kelley also presents a less fatalistic view. Tracing the history of how black male youth in postindustrial Los Angeles used gangsta rap to criticize police brutality, Kelley suggests that African American youth negotiated new strategies for grappling with the contradictions of a declining economy (Kelley, 1994: 183–227). Recognizing that black culture was a marketable commodity, they put it up for sale, selling an essentialized black culture that white youth could emulate yet never own. Their message was clear—"the world may be against us, but we are here and we intend to get paid."

With few exceptions, current literature on globalization fails to explain the experiences of contemporary African American youth with the new racialized social class formations of globalization.[1] Instead, African American youth are often conceptualized as a marginalized, powerless and passive population within macroeconomic policies of globalization. They serve as examples of an economic analysis that only rarely examines intersections of class and race. In contrast, I suggest that because African American youth are in the belly of the beast of the sole remaining world superpower, they present an important local location for examining new configurations of social class that is refracted through the lens of race, gender, age and sexuality. Stated differently, because they are centrally located within the United States, Black American youth constitute one important population of social actors who negotiate the contradictions of a racialized globalization as well as the new social class relations that characterize it.

This article asks, what might the placement of poor and working-class African American youth in the global political economy, both as recipients of social outcomes of globalization as well as social agents who respond to those outcomes, tell us about the new racialized class formations of globalization? Conversely, what light might the experiences of poor and working-class African American women and men shed on new global forms of racism? These are very large questions, and I briefly explore them by sketching out a two-part argument. First, I investigate how ideas of consumption, commodification and control situate black youth within a global political economy. I suggest that shifting the focus of class analysis from production to consumption provides a better understanding of black youth. Second, I develop a framework for understanding the commodification of black bodies that ties this process more closely to social class relations. In particular, I use the status of African American youth to explore how the literal and figurative commodification of blackness fosters new strategies of control. I examine the sex work industry, to illustrate the interconnections among consumption, commodification and control. I conclude the article with a brief discussion of the implications of my arguments.

NEW COMMODITIES: ADVANCED CAPITALISM AND BLACK BODY POLITICS

When it comes to grappling with the contradictions faced by poor and working-class African American youth, the persisting emphasis on production is necessary yet insufficient. Because work has disappeared, many African American urban neighborhoods provide few jobs for adults, let alone teenagers (Wilson, 1996). Moreover, because their neighborhood public schools do not prepare them for good jobs, African American youth cannot compete for them. This large and seemingly intractable population of inner city black youth who lack legitimate access to legal means of production constitute a political conundrum for American policy makers. Because non-incarcerated African American youth possess citizenship rights, employers can no longer compel them to work for no pay or for very low pay. Many poor and working-class black youth do work low-paid jobs in McDonald's, Burger King, Kentucky Fried Chicken and other fast food establishments, yet these are the jobs with no benefits and no future. At the same time, because many young black men in particular have prison records, employers will not hire them. Their income comes less through production, the steady albeit poorly paid jobs held by their parents and grandparents, and more through other means. Employment in the drug industry, continued dependence on people with income (parents, girlfriends, and/or the welfare state), as well as exploitation of one another (pimping) constitute important sources of income. When it comes to the status of poor and working-class black American youth, especially those who are unskilled and unemployed, highlighting jobs and studying social class relations primarily at the site of production misreads how black American youth participate in social class relations.

Complementing the traditional focus on production with greater attention to the growing significance of consumption within global capitalism provides new directions for understanding the experiences of African American youth. Black American youth are far from marginalized within a massive global black culture industry that uses their images to sell a wide array of products. Moreover, black American youth also constitute a consumer market of their own who will purchase music, alcohol, drugs, cell phones, gym shoes, their own images and other products that are created specifically for them. African American youth are not marginalized but rather remain essential to new consumer markets, both as suppliers of commodities that are bought and sold, and as reliable consumer markets.

African American youth are a hot commodity in the contemporary global marketplace and global media. Their images have catalyzed new consumer markets for products and services. The music of hip hop culture, for example, follows its rhythm and blues predecessor as a so-called crossover genre that is very popular with whites and other cultural groups across the globe. Circulated through film, television, and music, news and advertising, mass media constructs and sells a commodified black culture from ideas about class, gender and age. Through a wide array of genres ranging from talk

shows to feature length films, television situation comedies to CDs, video rentals to cable television, the images produced and circulated within this area all aim to entertain and amuse a highly segmented consumer market. This market is increasingly global and subject to the contradictions of global marketplace phenomena.[2]

One implication of the significance of consumption for understanding social class relations of black youth concerns the constant need to stimulate consumer markets. Contemporary capitalism relies not just on cutting the costs attached to production, but also on stimulating consumer demand. Just as sustaining relations of production requires a steady supply of people to do the work, sustaining relations of consumption needs ever-expanding consumer markets. Moreover, just as people do not naturally work and must be encouraged or compelled to do so, people do not engage in excess consumption without prompting. In this context, advertising constitutes an important site that creates demand for commodities of all sorts. Marketing and advertising often create demand for things that formerly were not seen as commodities, for example, the rapid growth of the bottled water industry, as well as for intangible entities that seem difficult to commodify. In this regard, the rapid growth of mass media and new informational technologies has catalyzed a demand for black culture as a commodity.

As the black culture industry recognizes, most market demand for products and services stems not from needs but rather from unmet desires that must be constantly stimulated. In this context, physical addictions create ideal consumers who are willing to assume debt to pay for their addictions. If consumers become addicted to tobacco, alcohol, drugs or similar products, despite health risks, they can be counted on to consume. As the repetitive behavior of shopping addicts suggests, the ideal consumer is one who is addicted to consumption itself, never mind the actual product or service consumed. In this context, the interconnections among the marketing of black culture, addictive behavior of consumers who buy its products, and any consumer debt that ensues are tightly linked.[3]

Under this ever-expanding impetus to create new consumer markets, nothing is exempt from commodification and sale, including the pain that African American youth experience with poverty and powerlessness. Nowhere is this more evident than in the contradictions of rap. As Cornel West points out, "[T]he irony in our present moment is that just as young black men are murdered, maimed and imprisoned in record numbers, their styles have become disproportionately influential in shaping popular culture" (West, 1993). In this context, rap becomes the only place where black youth have public voice, yet it is a public voice that is commodified and contained by what hip hop producers think will sell. Despite these marketplace limitations, rap remains a potential site of contestation, a place where African American youth can rebel against the police brutality, lack of jobs, and other social issues that confront them (Kelley, 1994). Thus, work on the black culture industry illustrates how images of black culture function to catalyze consumption.

The actual bodies of young African Americans may also be commodified as part of a new black body politics. Here, the literature on gender and globalization, especially the sex industry, is helpful in understanding how a new black body politics might operate within relations of consumption. Situating feminist analyses of body politics within relations of production and consumption that characterize contemporary globalization provides new avenues for understanding commodification and the emergence of a new black body politics.[4] For Marx, all workers under capitalism are alienated; they are objectified as they sell their labor power to employers for a wage in order to survive. For women, especially those in racial/ethnic groups as well as in industrializing and developing countries alike, good jobs are more difficult to find. Under these circumstances, some women do not sell their bodily labor to produce a commodity. Instead, their bodies become commodities. In a global context,

as newly industrializing countries struggle to find commodity niches in the global economy, they frequently find the best niches taken. Consequently, in some countries sex tourism becomes a significant market fostering national economic development and international capital accumulation (Wonders and Michalowski, 2001).

This new gender scholarship offers a new framework for analyzing a new black body politics that African American youth confront under conditions of globalization. In the United States, African Americans also find the good jobs taken and confront a similar issue of the pressures to commodify their bodies, especially if those bodies are young. More importantly, this impetus to commodify black bodies is not new. Chattel slavery in the American South prior to and during the formation of the American nation state clearly treated the bodies of people of African descent as commodities. Objectifying black bodies enabled slave traders and slave owners to turn black people's bodies into commodities. Slavers assigned monetary value to black people's bodies, and then traded black bodies as commodities on the open market.

Some scholars on race have taken a closer look at how the institution of chattel slavery accomplished this process of objectification, commodification and exploitation. Literary critic Hortense Spillers suggests that relations of slavery and colonialism transformed understandings of black people's bodies. Spillers identifies how "captive bodies," namely, the bodies of enslaved Africans, were severed from their agency, a use of violence that eliminated gender: "Their New World, Diasporic plight marked *a theft of the body*—a willful and violent ... severing of the captive body from its motive will, its active desire' (Spillers, 2000: 160). This theft of the body severed it from its own agency and thus formed the moment of objectification. Spillers suggests that this new objectified body became a canvas for racist discourse: "These indecipherable markings on the captive body render a kind of hieroglyphics of the flesh whose severe disjunctures come to be hidden to the cultural seeing by skin color" (Spillers, 2000: 61). Once objectified and marked in this fashion, slave owners and slave traders treated black bodies as commodities that can be traded, bought and sold on the open market.

The treatment of actual bodies as objects and subsequently as commodities within consumer markets as opposed to the appropriation of the labor power that bodies contain may be a more fundamental element of contemporary capitalist economies than is commonly recognized. French sociological theorist Colette Guillaumin lays the foundation for a different kind of historical materialist analysis that rests on body politics (Guillaumin, 1995). Like traditional social class analysis, Guillaumin focuses both on the economy (the exploitative dimension of appropriation for various social systems such as slavery and social institutions such as marriage), and on questions of power and domination. However, Guillaumin's materialist analysis differs from traditional functionalist and/or Marxist analyses of stratification/ class. In contrast to traditional social class analyses that begin with the sale of labor power within capitalist relations, Guillaumin's materialist framework originates in the appropriation of the body that contains the labor power itself. Because no form of measuring the value of labor in isolation from the body itself exists, Guillaumin contends that racism and sexism both draw upon this physical appropriation of bodies. Guillaumin identifies slavery as the fundamental historical relationship that fostered modern understandings of ideologies of race. Enslaving African bodies constituted the original theft—the stealing of labor came later. Racial ideologies explaining this process emerged after slavery was in effect. Guillaumin's theory of the sexual oppression of women (her analysis of *sexage*) follows a similar logic. For Guillaumin, the seizure of women's time, claiming the products of their bodies such as children, mandating that women use their bodies to fulfill a sexual obligation, requiring that women's bodies provide physical care for children,

the elderly, the sick as well as healthy men, all illustrate how men as a class feel that they can appropriate the bodies of women as a class. Guillaumin points out that people only publicly take that which they feel already belongs to them, as is the case of the public harassment of women in the workplace and on the street.

Guillaumin provides a provocative piece of the puzzle for constructing an argument concerning the commodification of the actual bodies as well as representations of the bodies of African American youth within contemporary global capitalist economies. New forms of commodification within the constant pressure to expand consumer markets catalyze a new black body politics where social class relations rest not solely on exploiting labor power and/or mystifying exploitation through images, but also on the appropriation of bodies themselves. Whereas young black bodies were formerly valued for their labor power, under advanced capitalism, their utility lies elsewhere.

NEW CONSUMERS: SEX WORK AND HIP HOP CAPITALISM

Here, I want to take a closer look at this process by exploring how sexuality has grown in importance in the commodification of the bodies and images of black American youth and how this sex work in turn articulates with black agency in responding to advanced capitalism. In essence, black youth are now caught up in a burgeoning sex work industry, one that is far broader than commercial sex work as depicted in the media. Young African Americans participate in the sex work industry, not primarily as commercial workers as is popularly imagined, but rather, as representations of commodified black sexuality as well as potential new consumer markets eager to consume their own images.

Racialized images of pimps and prostitutes may be the commercial sex workers who are most visible in the relations of production, yet the industry itself is much broader.[5] A broader definition of sex work suggests how the sex work industry has been a crucial part of the expansion of consumer markets.[6] The sex work industry encompasses a set of social practices, many of which may not immediately be recognizable as sex work, as well as a constellation of representations that create demand for sexual services, attach value to such services, identify sexual commodities with race, gender and age-specific individuals, and rules that regulate this increasingly important consumer market. Feminists argue that class, race, ethnicity, age and citizenship categories work to position women differently within the global sex work industry.[7] By far, international trafficking of women and girls for purposes of prostitution has received the lion's share of attention. Here, race, ethnicity and age shape the commodification of women's bodies to determine the value placed on categories of sex workers. The discussions of global prostitution and trafficking of women highlight the exploitation of large numbers of women, yet it is difficult to locate young African American women and the sex work of young black men within this literature. In particular, women who are not engaged in visible sex work or who do not show up on crime statistics on sex workers are often considered outside the realm of sex work.

Here, I want to pursue a different argument, namely, the case that sex work is permeating the very fabric of African American communities in ways that resemble how sex work has changed the societies of developing countries. In essence, poor and working-class African American youth increasingly encounter few opportunities for jobs in urban neighborhoods while the mass marketing of sexuality permeates consumer markets. In this sense, their situation resembles that of black youth globally who confront similar pressures in response to globalization. At the same time, the situation of African American youth is unique in that the sexualized images that they encounter are of themselves. In essence, their own bodies often serve as symbols of this sexualized culture, placing African American youth in the peculiar position claiming and rejecting themselves. How might this happen?

Offering a rare insight into adolescent sex work within an African society, Bamgbose describes how the domestic Nigerian sex work industry operates, one divided into a continuum of activities of the "Sugar Daddy Syndrome," "night brides," "floating prostitutes," "call girls," and finally, trafficking:

> Unlike the traditional prostitutes who are usually older women, adolescent prostitutes start their careers in prostitution in more comfortable hotel rooms or in a more sophisticated style. This is what gave rise to the form of prostitution termed the "Sugar Daddy Syndrome."
>
> (Bamgbose, 2002: 572)

Under the Sugar Daddy Syndrome, young girls patronize men, usually older in age, for sexual pleasure. Such older men, who are wealthy, are usually referred to as "sugar daddies" or "man friends." They are the favorites of adolescent girls who seek financial and material support in return for their services. The duration of this relationship lasts longer than a one-night stand, and the economic power wielded by such older and wealthy men, irrespective of educational status, puts the young girls involved in a particularly vulnerable position (Bamgbose, 2002: 572–3).

"Night brides" and "floating prostitutes" solicit their clients on the streets of major cities. They differ, however, in several ways. "Night brides" consist of young girls who search for customers on the street for a night of dating. They give preference to foreigners who are able to pay in foreign currency. One important aspect is that some are involved in sex work as a full-time activity, whereas others use it as part-time work. "Many of the part-timers are students in secondary schools and universities who combine prostitution with schooling. They need the money to pay fees or acquire material things, such as clothes and shoes" (Bamgbose, 2002: 573). In contrast to these girls who search for dates for one evening, "floating prostitutes" solicit business during the day and most closely resemble western notions of streetwalkers. Older men sexually abuse many of these girls in exchange for small amounts of money or gifts, which some hand over to their families. In contrast, college students in the sex work industry were more likely to work as, "call girls." In such cases, male or female pimps get in contact with already known and available girls whenever there is a demand for them.

The parallels between Nigerian responses to the IMF's structural adjustment policies and the reactions of poor and working-class African Americans to the social welfare policies of the Reagan/Bush administrations during this same period (1980–2005) are striking. With no jobs for its large youth population, poor Nigerian families learned to look the other way when traffickers commodified and exported its girls and women for the international sex industry and/ or when girls saw domestic sex work as their only option. They learned to accommodate a changing set of social norms that pushed young girls toward sex work, for some for reasons of basic survival, yet for others as part of the costs of upward social mobility. Poor and working-class African American girls seemingly confront a similar set of challenges in the context of a different set of circumstances. In this regard, the continuum of sex work from sugar daddies, night brides, floating prostitutes, call girls and trafficked women also applies, yet in a different constellation that reflects the political and economic situation of African Americans as well as cultural values of American society.

Two important features may shape young African American women's participation in the sex work industry. For one, because African American girls are American citizens, they cannot be as easily trafficked as other groups of poor women who lack U.S. citizenship. Girls are typically trafficked into the United States, not out of it. African American girls do enjoy some protections from these forms of exploitation, yet expanding the definition of sex work itself suggests that their patterns of participation have changed. For another, commercial sex work is not always a steady activity, but may occur simultaneously with other forms of income-generating

work. In the global context, women sex workers also engage in domestic service, informal commercial trading, market-vending, shining shoes, or office work (Kempadoo and Doezama, 1998: 3). In a similar fashion, African American girls may have multiple sources of income, one of which is sex work. The "night brides" and "call girls" of Nigeria may find a domestic counterpart among black American adolescent girls, yet this activity would not be labeled "sex work," nor would it be seen as prostitution. Restricting the concept of sex work and prostitute to the image of the streetwalker thus obscures the various ways that young black women's bodies and images are commodified and then circulated within the sex work industry.

"Sugar daddy" and "night bride" sex work may be taking on new life in the context of shrinking economic opportunities. Take, for example, the sexual histories of young, Southern, rural poor black women. Some women start having sex at very young ages, almost always with older men, and find that they have little ability to persuade their partners to use condoms (Sack, 2001). An informal sex-for-money situation exists, where nothing is negotiated up front. Rather, unstated assumptions, where women who engage in casual sex with men expect to be rewarded with a little financial help, perhaps in paying the rent, or in buying groceries, hold sway. From the outside, these behaviors may seem to be morally lax, yet the impoverished black women engaged in sex-for-money relationships desperately need the money, especially if they have elderly parents or dependent children (Sack, 2001). This informal sex-for-money situation is sex work. As Kempadoo points out, "[I]n most cases, sex work is not for individual wealth but for family well-being or survival" (Kempadoo and Doezama, 1998: 4).

The consequences of this sex-for-material-goods situation can be tragic. The pressures for young black women to engage in sex work have affected the rapid growth of HIV/AIDS among poor black women in the Mississippi Delta and across the rural South. Between 1990 and 2000, Southern states with large African American populations experienced a dramatic increase in HIV infections among African American women. For example, in Mississippi, 28.5 percent of those reporting new HIV infections in 2000 were black women, up from 13 percent in 1990. In Alabama, the number rose to 31 percent, from 13 percent, whereas in North Carolina, it rose to 27 percent, from 18 percent (Sack, 2001). Most of the women contracted HIV through heterosexual contact, and most found out that they were HIV positive when they became pregnant. The women took risks that may at first seem nonsensical. Yet in the context of their lives there was a sense that because they had so little control over other aspects of their lives, they felt that if God wanted them to get AIDS, then they resigned themselves to getting it.

These examples suggest that many young African American women resign themselves to commodifying their bodies as a necessary source of income. They may not be streetwalkers in the traditional sense, but they also view commodified black sexuality as the commodity of value that they can exchange. These relations also become difficult to disrupt in the context of a powerful mass media that defines and sells images of sexualized black women as one icon of seemingly authentic black culture. Young African American women encounter a set of representations that naturalizes and normalizes social relations of sex work. Whether she sleeps with men for pleasure, drugs, revenge, or money, the sexualized bitch constitutes a modern version of the Jezebel, repackaged for contemporary mass media. In discussing this updated Jezebel image, cultural critic Lisa Jones distinguishes between gold diggers/skeezers, namely, women who screw for status, and crack "hos," namely, women who screw for a fix (1994: 79). Some women are the "hos" who trade sexual favors for jobs, money, drugs and other material items. The female hustler, a materialist woman who is willing to sell, rent, or use her sexuality to get whatever she wants constitutes this sexualized variation of the bitch. This image appears

with increasing frequency, especially in conjunction with trying to catch an African American man with money. Athletes are targets, and having a baby with an athlete is a way to garner income. Black women who are sex workers, namely, those who engage in phone sex, lap dancing, and prostitution for compensation, also populate this universe of sexualized bitches. The prostitute who hustles without a pimp and who keeps the compensation is a bitch who works for herself.

Black male involvement in the sex work industry may not involve the direct exploitation of black men's bodies as much as the objectification and commodification of sexualized black male images within hip hop culture. The prevalence of representations of black men as pimps speaks to this image of black men as sexual hustlers who use their sexual prowess to exploit women, both black and white. Ushered in by a series of films in the "Blaxploitation" era, the ubiquitous black pimp seems here to stay. Kept alive through HBO produced quasi-documentaries such as *Pimps Up, Hos Down*, African American men feature prominently in mass media. Despite these media constructions, actual pimps see themselves more as businessman than as sexual predators. For example, the men interviewed in the documentary *American Pimp* all discuss the skills involved in being a successful pimp. One went so far as to claim that only African American men made really good pimps. Thus, the controlling image of the black pimp combines all of elements of the more generic hustler, namely, engaging in illegal activity, using women for economic gain, and refusing to work.

Representations of black women and men as prostitutes and pimps permeate music videos, film and television. In the context of a powerful global mass media, black men's bodies are increasingly objectified within popular culture in ways that resemble the treatment of all women. Violence and sexuality sell, and associating black men with both is virtually sure to please. Yet the real struggle is less about the content of black male and black female images and more about the treatment of black people's bodies as valuable commodities within advertising and entertainment. Because this new constellation of images participates in commodified global capitalism, in all cases, representations of black people's bodies are tied to structures of profitability. Athletes and criminals alike are profitable, not for the vast majority of African American men, but for the people who own the teams, control the media, provide food, clothing and telephone services to the prisons, and who consume seemingly endless images of pimps, hustlers, rapists, and felons. What is different, however, is how these images of authentic blackness generate additional consumer markets beyond the selling of these specific examples of cultural production.

Recognizing the value of commodified black culture, many African American rap stars have started their own record labels, clothing companies, and more recently, sports drink divisions. Their desire lies in sharing the profits of a huge global consumer market of youth who purchase the rap CDs, sports drinks, gym shoes, and clothing lines of hip hop culture. Take, for example, the 2003 release of Pimp Juice, a new sports beverage that was lauded by *Vibe* magazine as the best energy drink. Despite Pimp Juice's claims that it provides vitamins and that its 10 percent apple juice content makes it healthy, the yellow and white design of its can resembles beer cans. Initially, Pimp Juice was marketed within African American neighborhoods, yet by 2004 Pimp Juice was disseminated by 60 distributors in the United States, in 32 states and in 81 markets. According to its distributor, because Pimp Juice is flying off the shelves in the UK, the Caribbean Islands, and Mexico, the distributor aims to sell the product in Australia, Japan, China and Israel. The irony of this particular product is that Nelly, the rap star whose song titled "Pimp Juice" helped resurrect the popularity of the concept of the pimp, also owns the company that distributes Pimp Juice.

This one product illustrates the increasingly seamless relations among the commodification of

black images (pimp/prostitute), struggles between corporations and hip hop capitalists (rap star Nelly) in search of new consumer markets, the expansion of new consumer markets (how Pimp Juice is marketed to black consumers), and potentially new systems of control within African American civil society that grow from the same conditions that sparked changes within Nigerian society. Beverage makers claim that pimp juice is a benign sports drink—www.letitloose.com, Pimp Juice's official web site, describes it as a "healthy, non-carbonated energy drink possessing a tropical berry flavor"—yet when Black American youth buy pimp juice at their corner store, they most likely are singing the lyrics Nelly's song "Pimp Juice" while they pay $1.89 for one can of actual "Pimp Juice."

The lyrics of Nelly's song "Pimp Juice" make it clear what pimp juice really is and who it is for. Nelly opens his song by boasting that because his woman only wants him for his "Pimp juice." he needs to "cut her loose." He then moves on to describe the power seats, leather and sunroof of his pimp mobile. When "hoes see it," according to Nelly, they, "can't believe it." Nelly knows their game and puts them out, telling them to dust their shoes off so as not to touch his rug. For those who still don't get it, Nelly ends his song with a rousing definition of pimp juice: "your pimp juice is anything, attract the opposite sex, it could be money, fame, or straight intellect." Always an equal-opportunity kind of guy, Nelly proclaims, "[B]itches got the pimp juice too, come to think about it dirty, they got more than we do." By itself, the song "Pimp Juice" is just a song. Yet when coupled with the music video of Nelly representing a pimp and mass marketing campaigns that put cans of actual Pimp Juice in corner stores for young African Americans to see and buy, the circle is complete.

IMPLICATIONS

African American youths' encounters with Pimp Juice comprise the case examined here, yet the new commodities and new consumer markets in this example point to much larger issues. The hip hop capitalism of Nelly's brilliant marketing of "Pimp Juice" illustrates how sexualized understandings of black women's and men's bodies and culture become marketed and put up for sale in the global marketplace. It also focuses on new consumers of bodies and images, in particular, how black people become target audiences for their own degradation (e.g., the case of pimp juice) as well as Nelly's plans to go global with this popular product. When it comes to the commodification of black bodies, few African Americans celebrate the criminal justice system. At the same time, when it comes to the commodification of images associated with prison culture as well as an array of products that seemingly signal a seemingly authentic black culture, blacks are well represented among the consumers of these images.

This article points to the need to develop new frameworks for studying how non-immigrant or native populations fare under advanced capitalism. When it comes to race, globalization literature typically focuses on immigrant experiences catalyzed by transnational labor markets. The new racial/ethnic communities within the United States, Canada, the UK, France, the Netherlands and similar white societies garner the bulk of attention, with the core issue being the ability of such groups to assimilate into the host country. Whether voluntary immigrants or desperate refugees, the process of immigration signals leaving behind the unknown for the promise of an unknown and often hoped for better future. Yet how might we understand racial/ethnic populations with lengthy histories within the borders of advanced industrial societies? Poor and working-class African American youth, for example, are stuck in hyperghettos with nowhere to go. In this regard, African American youth share much with indigenous populations such as Native Americans, the Maori of New Zealand, and the Aboriginal peoples of Australia who faced conquest and genocide within their white settler societies and/or ethnic nation states. At the same time, because contemporary inner city African American youth are typically a third- and fourth-generation urban population, they share space with the very same new immigrant groups of color for whom America still represents new hope. In essence, this focus on African American youth and similar populations may shed light on what is in store for other groups who find themselves structurally irrelevant in their newly claimed societies. When Tupac Shakur and others of his generation say, "It's just me against the world, baby, me against the world. I got nothin' to lose— it's just me against the world" perhaps we should put down our cans of Pimp Juice and listen.

NOTES

1. For a discussion of general issues of globalization and race in the United States, see (Andrews, 1999; Barlow, 2003). For a comparative analysis of how African American, Caribbean and East African youth are situated in the global economy, see (Green, 2001). Green's study remains valuable, yet he implicitly upholds the nihilism thesis via his focus on powerlessness as an outcome of globalization.

2. This commodification of black culture and its use within advertising is nothing new. Take, for example, how images of blackness and black culture have long permeated American advertising campaigns. In her discussion of "contemptible collectibles," Patricia A. Turner examines how, since the early 1980s, interest in collecting "black Americana" has grown dramatically (Turner, 1994: 9–68). The vast amount of this "black" memorabilia is striking. From the Jolly Darkie Target Game (1890) marketed by Milton Bradley (whose goal was to score a bulls-eye by throwing a ball into the gaping mouth of a black male figure) (11), to *Darkie* toothpaste (renamed *Darlie* in the 1990s), people of African descent have figured prominently in commodity

capitalism and the growth of advertising designed to sell products. Through a comprehensive content analysis of the themes in these material objects, Turner demonstrates how closely tied black images actually were to the growth of marketplace relations in nineteenth century America. As Turner points out, "[E]ven after the institution of slavery was over, American consumers found acceptable ways of buying and selling the souls of black folk. Writers, dealers, and other authorities who persist in calling these toys, ephemeral objects, kitchenware, and related items *black* cultural artifacts are wrong. With few exceptions, these items were made by and for white people" (Turner, 1994: 11). Then and now, advertisers realize what is at stake in developing and packaging images of blackness that might help their projects sell to their target markets. In the past, images of Uncle Ben and Aunt Jemima seemed to be isolated symbols used to sell rice and pancake products.

3. It is important to remember that a material base underlies consumption. Consumers remain tethered to market economies not simply via psychology, but also through structures of debt. Increasingly sophisticated mechanisms of debt constitute the material base of consumption and thus are an essential albeit invisible part of the prompting that is needed for consumption. Credit encourages excess consumption, and businesses know it. Moreover, using credit encourages debt. The easy availability of credit cards for U.S. college students, for example, encourages excess consumption against the collateral of future earnings and/or the accumulated wealth of their families. In the United States, individuals are encouraged to see debt as a moral failing, the result of a series of poor choices of uncontrolled spending. Yet as a dimension of social class relations, the politics of credit and debt are far more complicated that the misguided actions of individual college students.

4. Feminist scholarship led the way in refocusing attention on the body itself as a site of objectification, commodification and exploitation. In the 1990s, post-structuralist analysis of the body examined how the objectification of women's bodies constituted a key pillar of gender oppression (Bordo, 1993). Rejecting biological notions of the body, such scholarship investigated how power relations of gender operate by writing cultural scripts onto women's bodies. This shift to conceptualizing the body as a canvas created space for new arguments about sexuality that challenged medical views of bodies solely as biological organisms that were ruled by allegedly natural instincts. Treating the body as a blank canvas also created space for arguments about multiple genders, not just the binary two of Western society. Thus, this basic shift in understandings of the body provided promising new avenues of investigation for scholars of gender and sexuality.

5. Feminist research has made important strides in moving beyond understandings of prostitution as inherently degrading. Liberal views imply that any participation in prostitution is evidence either of coercion (usually economic desperation) or immorality (Zatz, 1997). Building on Marxist theories of prostitution as alienated labor and of prostitutes as sex workers, radical feminists argue that because prostitution involves sex, it is linked as much to the organization of gender and sexuality as it is to the organization of wage labor. Collectively, feminist scholarship has shifted thinking away from seeing female prostitutes as passive victims of predatory systems of power and toward sex workers as agents or workers within a global sex work industry. This work extracts discussions of sex work from the psychological realm of the imagined relationship between worker and client, and back onto the significance of sex work in global capitalism. According to Kamala Kempadoo, the term *sex worker* suggests we "view prostitution not as an identity—a social or a psychological characteristic of women, often indicated

by 'whore'—but as an income-generating activity or form of labor for women and men. The definition stresses the social location of those engaged in sex industries as working people" (Kempadoo and Doezama, 1998: 3).

6. The global sex work industry has four main dimensions. First, through the increased movement of bodies associated with migration and the travel industry, sex tourism constitutes an increasing share of global sex work. "Global forces also shape the consumption of sexual services by fostering tourism as an industry aimed at those who have the resources to travel and purchase what they desire, thus, facilitating the commodification of both male desire and women's bodies within the global capitalist economy" (Wonders and Michalowski, 2001: 546). Second, sex workers who service clients constitute the foundation of the industry. Overwhelmingly female, sex workers come from all backgrounds, yet are most likely to be individuals whose position in society limits their structural power (race, ethnicity, poverty, citizenship status, etc.). Third, the global sex work industry generates income for groups that do not directly service clients but whose income depends on the profitability of sex for sale. Managers (pimps and madams), police, landlords, smugglers, and others who profit from sex work itself constitute a broad-based infrastructure of the global sex work industry. Finally, the sex work industry requires an advertising and marketing arm to create demand. Thus, mass media and the culture industry that stimulate male desire for sex workers constitute an essential part of the sex work industry. The vast pornographic empire in Los Angeles is part of this demand structure, as is the marketing of sexuality via forms as diverse as toothpaste advertisements and music videos.

7. Kempadoo takes issue with some versions of this depiction, viewing this approach as an example of cultural racism through international discourses on prostitution. According to Kempadoo, racial/ethnic women "seem to be trapped in underdeveloped states, Third World prostitutes continue to be positioned in this discourse as incapable of making decisions about their own lives, forced by overwhelming external powers completely beyond their control into submission and slavery. Western women's experience is thus made synonymous with assumptions about the inherent superiority of industrialized capitalist development and Third World women placed in categories of pre-technological 'backwardness,' inferiority, dependency and ignorance" (Kempadoo and Doezama, 1998: 12).

REFERENCES

Andrews, Marcellus (1999) *The Political Economy of Hope and Fear: Capitalism and the Black Condition in America.* New York: New York University Press.

Bamgbose, O. (2002) "Teenage Prostitution and the Future of the Female Adolescent in Nigeria," *International Journal of Offender Therapy and Comparative Criminology* 46(5): 569–85.

Barlow, Andrew L. (2003) *Between Fear and Hope: Globalization and Race in the United States.* Lanham, Maryland: Rowman & Littlefield.

Bonilla-Silva, E. (2003) *Racism without Racists: Color-blind Racism and the Persistence of Racial Inequality in the United States.* Lanham, MD: Rowman & Littlefield.

Bordo, S. (1993) *Unbearable Weight: Feminism, Western Culture and the Body.* Berkeley, CA: University of California Press.

Green, Charles (2001) *Manufacturing Powerlessness in the Black Diaspora: Inner City Youth and the New Global Frontier.* Walnut Creek, Calif.: AltaMira Press.

Guillaumin, C. (1995) *Racism, Sexism, Power and Ideology.* New York: Routledge.

Guinier, L. and G. Torres (2002) *The Miner's Canary: Enlisting Race, Resisting Power, Transforming Democracy.* Cambridge, MA: Harvard University Press.

Jones, Lisa (1994) *Bulletproof Diva: Tales of Race, Sex, and Hair.* New York: Doubleday.

Kelley, R.D.G. (1994) *Race Rebels: Culture, Politics, and the Black Working Class.* New York: Free Press.

Kamala Kempadoo and J. Doezema (1998) *Global Sex Workers: Rights, Resistance, and Redefinition.* New York: Routledge.

Sack, K. (2001) "AIDS Epidemic Takes Toll on Black Women," [http://www.nytimes. com/200l/07/03/health/03AIDS.html?pagewanted=print].

Spillers, H.J. (2000) "Mama's Baby, Papa's Maybe: An American Grammar Book," J. James and T.D. Sharpley-Whiting (eds) *The Black Feminist Reader*, pp. 57–87. Malden, MA: Blackwell.

Turner, P.A. (1994) *Ceramic Uncles and Celluloid Mammies: Black Images and Their Influence on Culture.* New York: Anchor

West, C. (1993) *Race Matters.* Boston, MA: Beacon Press.

Wilson, W.J. (1987) *The Truly Disadvantaged: The Inner City, the Underclass, and Public Policy.* Chicago: University of Chicago Press.

Wilson, W.J. (1996) *When Work Disappears: The World of the New Urban Poor.* New York: Knopf.

Wonders, N.A. and Michalowski, R.(2001) "Bodies, Borders, and Sex Tourism in a Globalized World: A Tale of Two Cities—Amsterdam and Havana", *Social Problems* 48(4): 545–71.

Zatz, N.D. (1997) "Sex Work/Sex Act: Law, Labor, and Desire in Constructions of Prostitution," *Signs* 22(2): 277–308.

JOURNALING QUESTION

Is there a commodified Asian identity? If so, how does that differ from the black identity?

36.
"AQUI ESTAMOS Y NO NOS VAMOS!"
Global Capital and Immigrant Rights

WILLIAM I. ROBINSON

William Robinson says that the immigration issue and related mobilizations, such as "A Day Without an Immigrant," have been called the new civil rights movement. One way of thinking about that is as if the "old" civil rights movement, the movement that addressed African American citizenship, is over. With the election of a black U.S. president, many are tempted to say that we are "past" that movement. Yet as Robinson shows, the position of Latino immigrant workers in the United States cannot be understood without the context of black–white race politics. How does globalization, the corporate control of goods and services and workers across national boundaries, reflect American race ideology?

A spectre is haunting global capitalism—the spectre of a transnational immigrant workers' uprising. An immigrant rights movement is spreading around the world, spearheaded by Latino immigrants in the U.S., who have launched an all-out fight-back against the repression, exploitation and racism they routinely face with a series of unparalleled strikes and demonstrations. The immediate message of immigrants and their allies in the United States is clear, with marchers shouting: *"aqui estamos y no nos vamos!"* (we're here and we're not leaving!). However, beyond immediate demands, the emerging movement challenges the very structural changes bound up with capitalist globalization that have generated an upsurge in global labor migration, thrown up a new global working class, and placed that working class in increasingly direct confrontation with transnational capital.

The U.S. mobilizations began when over half a million immigrants and their supporters took to the streets in Chicago on 10 March 2006. It was the largest single protest in that city's history. Following the Chicago action, rolling strikes and protests spread to other cities, large and small, organized through expanding networks of churches, immigrant clubs and rights groups, community associations, Spanish language and progressive media, trade unions and social justice organizations. Millions came out on 25 March for "national day of action." Between one and two million people demonstrated in Los Angeles—the single biggest public protest in the city's history—and millions more followed suit in Chicago, New York, Atlanta, Washington, D.C., Phoenix, Dallas, Houston, Tucson, Denver and dozens of other cities. Again, on 10 April, millions heeded the call for another day of protest. In addition, hundreds of thousands of high school students in Los Angeles and around the country staged walk-outs in support of their families and communities, braving police repression and legal sanctions.

Then on the first of May, International Workers' Day, trade unionists and social justice activists joined immigrants in "The Great American Boycott

Excerpted from William I. Robinson, "'Aqui estamos y no nos vamos!' Global capital and immigrant rights," *Race & Class* 48, 2 (2006): 77–91. Notes have been edited.

2006/A Day Without an Immigrant." Millions—perhaps tens of millions—in over 200 cities from across the country skipped work and school, commercial activity and daily routines in order to participate in a national boycott, general strike, rallies and symbolic actions. The May 1 action was a resounding success. Hundreds of local communities in the south, midwest, north-west and elsewhere, far away from the "gateway cities" where Latino populations are concentrated, experienced mass public mobilizations that placed them on the political map. Agribusiness in the California and Florida heartlands—nearly 100 percent dependent on immigrant labor—came to a standstill, leaving supermarket produce shelves empty for the next several days. In the landscaping industry, nine out of ten workers boycotted work, according to the American Nursery and Landscape Association. The construction industry suffered major disruptions. Latino truckers who move 70 percent of the goods in Los Angeles ports did not work. Care-giver referral agencies in major cities saw a sharp increase in calls from parents who needed last-minute nannies or baby-sitters. In order to avoid a total shutdown of the casino mecca in Las Vegas—highly dependent on immigrant labor—casino owners were forced to set up tables in employee lunch-rooms and hold meetings to allow their workers to circulate petitions in favor of immigrant demands. International commerce between Mexico and the United States ground to a temporary halt as protesters closed Tijuana, Juarez-El Paso and several other crossings along the 2,000-mile border.[1]

These protests have no precedent in the history of the U.S. The immediate trigger was the passage in mid-March by the House of Representatives of HR4437, a bill introduced by Republican representative James Sensenbrenner with broad support from the anti-immigrant lobby. This draconian bill would criminalize undocumented immigrants by making it a felony to be in the U.S. without documentation. It also stipulated the construction of the first 700 miles of a militarized wall between Mexico and the U.S. and would double the size of the U.S. border patrol. And it would apply criminal sanctions against anyone who provided assistance to undocumented immigrants, including churches, humanitarian groups and social service agencies.

However, the wave of protest goes well beyond HR4437. It represents the unleashing of pent-up anger and repudiation of what has been deepening exploitation and an escalation of anti-immigrant repression and racism. Immigrants have been subject to every imaginable abuse in recent years. Twice in the state of California they have been denied the right to acquire drivers' licences. This means that they must rely on inadequate or non-existent public transportation or risk driving illegally; more significantly, the drivers' licence is often the only form of legal documentation for such essential transactions as cashing checks or renting an apartment. The U.S. Mexico border has been increasingly militarized and thousands of immigrants have died crossing the frontier. Anti-immigrant hate groups are on the rise. The FBI has reported more than 2,500 hate crimes against Latinos in the U.S. since 2000. Blatantly racist public discourse that, only a few years ago, would have been considered extreme has become increasingly mainstreamed and aired in the mass media.

More ominously, the paramilitary organization Minutemen, a modern day Latino-hating version of the Ku Klux Klan, has spread from its place of origin along the U.S.-Mexican border in Arizona and California to other parts of the country. Minutemen claim they must "Secure the border" in the face of inadequate state-sponsored control. Their discourse, beyond racist, is neo-fascist. Some have even been filmed sporting T-shirts with the emblem "Kill a Mexican Today?" and others have organized for-profit "human safaris" in the desert. One video game discovered recently circulating on the Internet, "Border Patrol," lets players shoot at Mexican immigrants as they try to cross the border into the U.S. Players are told to target one of three immigrant groups, all portrayed in a negative, stereotypical way, as the figures rush past a sign that reads "Welcome to the United States." The immigrants are caricatured as bandolier-wearing "Mexican nationalists" tattooed "drug smugglers" and pregnant "breeders" who spring across with their children in tow.

Minutemen clubs have been sponsored by right-wing organisers, wealthy ranchers, business-men and politicians. But their social base is drawn from those formerly privileged sectors of the white working class that have been "flexibilized" and dis-placed by economic restructuring, the deregulation of labor and global capital flight. These sectors now scapegoat immigrants—with official encourage-ment—as the source of their insecurity and down-ward mobility.

Latino immigration to the U.S. is part of a world-wide upsurge in transnational migration generated by the forces of capitalist globalization. Immigrant labor worldwide is conservatively estimated at over 200 million, according to UN data.[2] Some 30 mil-lion are in the U.S. with at least 20 million of them from Latin America. Of these 20 million, some 11–12 million are undocumented (south and east Asia are also significant contributors to the undocu-mented population), although it must be stressed that these figures are low-end estimates.[3] The U.S. is by far the largest immigrant-importing country, but the phenomenon is global. Racist attacks, scape-goating and state-sponsored repressive controls over immigrants are rising in many countries around the world, as is the fightback among immigrant workers wherever they are found. Parallel to the U.S. events, for instance, the French government introduced a bill that would apply tough new controls over immigrants and roll back their rights. In response, some 30,000 immigrants and their supporters took to the streets in Paris on 13 May 2006 to demand the bill's repeal.

THE GLOBAL CIRCULATION OF IMMIGRANT LABOR

The age of globalization is also an age of unprec-edented transnational migration.[4] The corollary to an integrated global economy is the rise of a truly global—although highly segmented—labor mar-ket. It is a global labor market because, despite for-mal nation state restrictions on the free worldwide movement of labor, surplus labor in any part of the world is now recruited and redeployed through numerous mechanisms to where capital is in need of it and because workers themselves undertake worldwide migration, even in the face of the adverse migratory conditions.

Central to capitalism is securing a politically and economically suitable labor supply, and at the core of all class societies is the control over labor and disposal of the products of labor. But the link-age between the securing of labor and territoriality is changing under globalization. As labor becomes "free" in every corner of the globe, capital has vast new opportunities for mobilizing labor power where and when required. National labor pools are merging into a single global labor pool that services global capitalism. The transnational circulation of capital induces the transnational circulation of labor. This circulation of labor becomes incorpo-rated into the process of restructuring the world economy. It is a mechanism for the provision of labor to transnationalized circuits of accumulation and constitutes a structural feature of the global system.

While the need to mix labor with capital at diverse points along global production chains induces population movements, there are sub-processes that shape the character and direction of such migration. At the structural level, the uproot-ing of communities by the capitalist break-up of local economies creates surplus populations and is a powerful push factor in outmigration, while labor shortages in more economically advanced areas is a pull factor that attracts displaced peoples. At a behavioral level, migration and wage remittances become a family survival strategy made *possible* by the demand for labor abroad and made increasingly *viable* by the fluid conditions and integrated infra-structures of globalization.

The division of the global working class into "citizen" and "non-citizen" labor is a major new axis of inequality worldwide, further complicating the well-known gendered and racialized hierarchies among labor, and facilitating new forms of repressive and authoritarian social control over working classes. In an *apparent* contradiction, capital and goods move freely across national borders in the new global economy but labor cannot and its movement is subject to heightened state controls. The global labor supply is, in the main, no longer coerced (subject to extra-economic compulsion) due to the ability of the universalized market to exercise strictly economic discipline, but its movement is juridically controlled. This control is a central determinant in the worldwide correlation of forces between global capital and global labor.

The immigrant is a juridical creation inserted into real social relations. States create "immigrant labor" as distinct categories of labor in relation to capital. While the generalization of the labor market emerging from the consolidation of the global capitalist economy creates the conditions for global migrations as a world-level labor supply system, the maintenance and strengthening of state controls over transnational labor creates the conditions for immigrant labor as a distinct category of labor. The creation of these distinct categories ("immigrant labor") becomes central to the global capitalist economy, replacing earlier direct colonial and racial caste controls over labor worldwide.

But why is this juridical category of "immigrant labor" reproduced under globalization? Labor migration and geographic shifts in production are alterative forms for capitalists to achieve an optimal mix of their capital with labor. State controls are often intended *not to prevent* but to *control* the transnational movement of labor. A *free* flow of labor would exert an equalizing influence on wages across borders whereas state controls help reproduce such differentials. Eliminating the wage differential between regions would cancel the advantages that capital accrues from disposing of

labor pools worldwide subject to different wage levels and would strengthen labor worldwide in relation to capital. In addition, the use of immigrant labor allows receiving countries to separate reproduction and maintenance of labor, and therefore to "externalize" the costs of social reproduction. In other words, the new transnational migration helps capital to dispose of the need to pay for the reproduction of labor power. The inter-state system thus acts as a condition for the structural power of globally mobile transnational capital over labor that is transnational in actual content and character but subjected to different institutional arrangements under the direct control of national states.

The migrant labor phenomenon will continue to expand along with global capitalism. Just as capitalism has no control over its implacable expansion as a system, it cannot do away in its new globalist stage with transnational labor. But if global capital needs the labor power of transnational migrants, this labor power belongs to human beings who must be tightly controlled, given the special oppression and de-humanization involved in extracting their labor power as non-citizen immigrant labor. To return to the situation in the U.S. the immigrant issue presents a contradiction for political and economic elites: from the vantage points of dominant group interests, the dilemma is how to deal with the new "barbarians" at Rome's door.

Latino immigrants have massively swelled the lower rungs of the U.S. workforce. They provide almost all farm labor and much of the labor for hotels, restaurants, construction, janitorial and house cleaning, child care, gardening and landscaping, delivery, meat and poultry packing, retail, and so on. Yet dominant groups fear a rising tide of Latino immigrants will lead to a loss of cultural and political control, becoming a source of counter-hegemony and instability, as immigrant labor in Paris showed itself to be in the late 2005 uprising there against racism and marginality.

Employers do not want to do away with Latino immigration. To the contrary, they want to sustain a vast exploitable labor pool that exists under pre-carious conditions, that does not enjoy the civil, political and labor rights of citizens and that is disposable through deportation. It is the *condition of deportability* that they wish to create or preserve, since that condition assures the ability to super-exploit with impunity and to dispose of this labor without consequences should it become unruly or unnecessary. The Bush administration opposed HR4437 not because it was in favor of immigrant rights but because it had to play a balancing act by finding a formula for a stable supply of cheap labor to employers with, at the same time, greater state control over immigrants.

NEOLIBERALISM IN LATIN AMERICA

If capital's need for cheap, malleable and deport-able labor in the centers of the global economy is the main "pull factor" inducing Latino immigration to the U.S. the "push factor" the devastation left by two decades of neoliberalism in Latin America. Capitalist globalization—structural adjustment, free trade agreements, privatizations, the contrac-tion of public employment and credits, the break-up of communal lands and so forth, along with the political crises these measures have generated—has imploded thousands of communities in Latin America and unleashed a wave of migration, from rural to urban areas and to other countries, that can only be analogous to the mass uprooting and migra-tion that generally takes place in the wake of war.

Just as capital does not stay put in the place it accumulates, neither do wages stay put. The flip side of the intense upsurge in transnational migra-tion is the reverse flow of remittances by migrant workers in the global economy to their country and region of origin. Officially recorded international remittances increased astonishingly, from a mere $57 million in 1970 to $216 billion in 2005, accord-ing to World Bank data. This amount was higher than capital market flows and official development assistance combined, and nearly equalled the total amount of world FDI (foreign direct investment) in

2004. Close to one billion people, or one in every six on the planet, may receive some support from the global flow of remittances, according to senior World Bank economist Dilip Ratha.[5] Remittances have become an economic mainstay for an increas-ing number of countries. Most of the world's regions, including Africa, Asia, Latin America and southern and eastern Europe report major remit-tance inflows.

Remittances redistribute income worldwide in a literal or geographic sense but not in the actual sense of *redistribution*, meaning a transfer of some added portion of the surplus from capital to labor, since they constitute not additional earnings but the separation of the site where wages are earned from the site of wage-generated consumption. What is taking place is a historically unprecedented sepa-ration of the point of production from the point of social reproduction. The former can take place in one part of the world and generate the valued—then remitted—for social reproduction of labor in another part of the world. This is an emergent struc-tural feature of the global system, in which the site of labor power and of its reproduction have been transnationally dispersed.

Transnational Latino migration has led to an enormous increase in remittances from Latino ethnic labor abroad to extended kinship networks in Latin America. Latin American workers abroad sent home some $57 billion in 2005, according to the Inter-American Development Bank.[6] These remittances were the number one source of foreign exchange for the Dominican Republic, El Salvador, Guatemala, Guyana, Haiti, Honduras, Jamaica and Nicaragua, and the second most important source for Belize, Bolivia, Colombia, Ecuador, Paraguay and Surinam, according to the Bank. The $20 bil-lion sent back in 2005 by an estimated 10 million Mexicans in the U.S. was more than the country's tourism receipts and was surpassed only by oil and *maquiladora* exports.

These remittances allow millions of Latin American families to survive by purchasing goods either imported from the world market or produced locally or by transnational capital. They allow for family survival at a time of crisis and adjustment, especially for the poorest sectors—safety nets that replace governments and fixed employment in the provision of economic security. Emigration and remittances also serve the political objective of pacification. The dramatic expansion of Latin American emigration to the U.S. from the 1980s onwards helped to dissipate social tensions and undermine labor and political opposition to prevailing regimes and institutions. Remittances help to offset macroeconomic imbalances, in some cases averting economic collapse, thereby shoring up the political conditions for an environment congenial to transnational capital.

Therefore, bound up with the immigrant debate in the U.S. is the entire political economy of global capitalism in the western hemisphere—the same political economy that is now being sharply contested throughout Latin America with the surge in mass popular struggles and the turn to the Left. The struggle for immigrant rights in the U.S. is thus part and parcel of this resistance to neoliberalism, intimately connected to the larger Latin American—and worldwide—struggle for social justice.

No wonder protests and boycotts took place throughout Latin America on May 1 in solidarity with Latino immigrants in the US. But these actions were linked to local labor rights struggles and social movement demands. In Tijuana, Mexico, for example, *maquiladora* workers in that border city's in-bond industry marched on May 1 to demand higher wages, eight-hour shifts, an end to abuses and "despotism" in the *maquila* plants and an end to sexual harassment, the use of poison chemicals and company unions. The workers also called for solidarity with the "Great American Boycott of 2006 on the other side of the border" and participated in a protest at the U.S. consulate in the city and at the main crossing, which shut down cross-border traffic for most of the day.

THE NATURE OF IMMIGRANT STRUGGLES

Labor market transformations driven by capitalist globalization unleash what McMichael calls "the politics of global labor circulation"[7] and fuel, in labor-importing countries, new nativisms, waves of xenophobia and racism against immigrants. Shifting political coalitions scapegoat immigrants by promoting ethnic-based solidarities among middle classes, representatives of distinct fractions of capital and formerly privileged sectors among working classes (such as white ethnic workers in the U.S. and Europe) threatened by job loss, declining income and the other insecurities of economic restructuring. The long-term tendency seems to be towards a generalization of labor market conditions across borders, characterized by segmented structures under a regime of labor deregulation and racial, ethnic and gender hierarchies.

In this regard, a major challenge confronting the movement in the U.S. is relations between the Latino and the Black communities. Historically, African Americans have swelled the lower rungs in the U.S. caste system. But, as African Americans fought for their civil and human rights in the 1960s and 1970s, they became organized, politicized and radicalized. Black workers led trade union militancy. All this made them undesirable labor for capital—"undisciplined" and "noncompliant."

Starting in the 1980s, employers began to push out Black workers and massively recruit Latino immigrants, a move that coincided with deindustrialization and restructuring. Blacks moved from super-exploited to marginalized—subject to unemployment, cuts in social services, mass incarceration and heightened state repression—while Latino immigrant labor has become the new super-exploited sector. Employers and political elites in New Orleans, for instance, have apparently decided in the wake of Hurricane Katrina to replace that city's historically black working class with Latino immigrant labor. Whereas fifteen years ago no one saw a single Latino face in places such as Iowa or

Tennessee, now Mexican, Central American and other Latino workers are visible everywhere. If some African Americans have misdirected their anger over marginality at Latino immigrants, the Black community has a legitimate grievance over the anti-Black racism of many Latinos themselves, who often lack sensitivity to the historic plight and contemporary experience of Blacks with racism, and are reticent to see them as natural allies. (Latinos often bring with them particular sets of racialized relations from their home countries.)[8]

White labor that historically enjoyed caste privileges within racially segmented labor markets has experienced downward mobility and heightened insecurity. These sectors of the working class feel the pinch of capitalist globalization and the transnationalization of formerly insulated local labor markets. Studies in the early 1990s, for example, found that, in addition to concentrations in "traditional" areas such as Los Angeles, Miami, Washington, D.C., Virginia and Houston, Central American immigrants had formed clusters in the formal and informal service sectors in areas where, in the process of downward mobility, they had replaced "white ethnics" such as in suburban Long Island, the small towns of Iowa and North Carolina, in Silicon Valley and in the northern and eastern suburbs of the San Francisco Bay Area.[9]

The loss of caste privileges for white sectors of the working class is problematic for political elites and state managers in the U.S., since legitimation and domination have historically been constructed through a white racial hegemonic bloc. Can such a bloc be sustained or renewed through a scapegoating of immigrant communities? In attempting to shape public discourse, the anti-immigrant lobby argues that immigrants "are a drain on the U.S.economy." Yet, as the National Immigrant Solidarity Network points out, immigrants contribute $7 billion in Social Security a year. They earn $240 billion, report $90 billion, and are only reimbursed $5 billion in tax returns. They also contribute $25 billion more to the U.S. economy than they receive in health-care and social services.[10] But this is a limited line of argument, since the larger issue is the incalculable trillions of dollars that immigrant labor generates in profits and revenue for capital, only a tiny proportion of which goes back to them in the form of wages.

Moreover, it has been demonstrated that there is no correlation between the unemployment rate among U.S., citizens and the rate of immigration. In fact, the unemployment rate has moved in cycles over the past twenty-five years and exhibits a comparatively lower rate during the most recent (2000–2005) influx of undocumented workers. Similarly, wage stagnation in the United States appeared, starting with the economic crisis of 1973 and has continued its steady march ever since, with no correlation to increases or decreases in the inflow of undocumented workers. Instead, downward mobility for most workers is positively correlated with the decline in union participation, the decline in labor conditions and the polarization of income and wealth that began with the restructuring crisis of the 1970s and accelerated the following decade as Reaganomics launched the neo-liberal counterrevolution.[11]

Immigrant workers become the archetype of these new global class relations. They are a naked commodity, no longer embedded in relations of reciprocity rooted in social and political communities that have, historically, been institutionalized in nation states. Immigrant labor pools that can be super-exploited economically, marginalized and disenfranchised politically, driven into the shadows and deported when necessary are the very epitome of capital's naked domination in the age of global capitalism.

The immigrant rights movement in the U.S. is demanding full rights for all immigrants, including amnesty, worker protections, family reunification measures, a path to citizenship or permanent residency rather than a temporary "guest worker" program an end to all attacks against immigrants and to the criminalization of immigrant communities.

While some observers have billed the recent events as the birth of a new civil rights movement, clearly much more is at stake. In the larger picture, this goes beyond immediate demands; it challenges the class relations that are at the very core of global capitalism. The significance of the May 1 immigrant rights mobilization taking place on international workers' day—which has not been celebrated in the U.S. for nearly a century—was lost on no one.

In the age of globalization, the only hope of accumulating the social and political forces necessary to confront the global capitalist system is by transnationalizing popular, labor and democratic struggles. The immigrant rights movement is all of these—popular, pro-worker and democratic—and it is by definition transnational. In sum, the struggle for immigrant rights is at the cutting edge of the global working-class fight-back against capitalist globalization.

NOTES

1. For these details, and more, see, inter alia, summaries of press reports from around the U.S. compiled by *CIS-DC Info Digest* (Vol. 41, no. 17), "Tally of plant closings and demonstrations," available by request at http://www.mutualaid.org.
2. Manuel Orozco, "Worker remittances in an international scope," *Working Paper* (Washington, D.C., Inter-American Dialogue and Multilateral Investment Fund of the Inter-American Development Bank, March 2003), p. 1.
3. For this and more data and links to different academic and foundation reports and government census agencies, see the University of California at Santa Barbara website, http://aad.english.ucsb.edu.
4. On migration and globalization, and more generally on capitalism and migration, see, among others, Peter Stalker, *Workers Without Frontiers* (Boulder, CO, Lynne Riener, 2000); Robin Cohen. *The New Helots: migrants in the international division of labor* (Aldershot, Ashgate, 1987); Nigel Harris, *The New Untouchables: immigration and the new world worker* (London, I. B. Tauris, 1995); Stephen Castles and Mark J. Miller, *The Age of Migration: international population movements in the modern world* (New York, Palgrave Macmillan, 1993); Lydia Potts, *The World Labor Market: a history of migration* (London, Zed, 1990). For discussion of current topics and new directions in the sociology of migration, see Alejandro Portes, "Immigrant theory for a new century: some problems and opportunities, *International Migration Review* (Vol. 3, no. 4. 1997), p. 799–825. See also Alejandro Portes and Jozsef Borocz, "Contemporary immigration: theoretical perspectives on its determinants and modes of incorporation, *International Migration Review* (Vol. XXIII, no. 3, 1990), pp. 606–30.
5. For these details, see Richard Boudreaux, "The new foreign aid: the seeds of promise," *Los Angeles Times* (14 April 2006), p. 1A.
6. Inter-American Development Bank, *Remittances 2005: promoting financial democracy* (Washington, D.C., IDB, 2006).
7. Philip McMichael, *Development and Social Change: a global perspective* (Thousand Oaks, CA, Pine Forge Press, 1986), p. 189.
8. In a commentary observing that mainstream Black political leaders have been notably lukewarm to the immigrant rights movement. Keeanga-Yamahtta Taylor writes: "The displacement of Black workers is a real problem—but not a problem caused by displaced Mexican workers … if the state is allowed to criminalize the existence [of] immigrant workers this will only fan the flames of racism eventually consuming Blacks in a back draft of discrimination.

How exactly does one tell the difference between a citizen and a non-citizen? Through a massive campaign of racial profiling, that's how ... In fact, the entire working class has a stake in the success of the movement." She goes on to recall how California building owners and labor contractors replaced Black janitors with largely undocumented Latino immigrants in the 1980s. But after a successful Service Employees International Union drive in the "Justice for janitors" campaign of the late 1980s and 1990s, wages and benefits went up and the union's largely Latino members sought contractual language guaranteeing African Americans a percentage of work slots. See Taylor, "Life ain't been no crystal stair: Blacks, Latinos and the new civil rights movement, *Counterpunch* (9 May 2006), downloaded 18 May 2006, http://www.counterpunch.org/taylor05082006.html.

9. See the special issue of *NACLA Report on the Americas*, "On the line: Latinos on labor's cutting edge" (Vol. 30, no. 3, November/December 1996).

10. For this data, further information and links, see the Network's website at http://www.immigrantsolidarity.org.

11. For these details see http://aad.english.ucsb.edu/econimpacts.html.

JOURNALING QUESTION

If there were a "Day Without Immigrants" in your town right now, what would happen? What services are immigrants performing where you live?